Dynamic Asset Pricing Theory

THIRD EDITION

Darrell Duffie

Princeton University Press
Princeton and Oxford

Library of Congress Cataloging-in-Publication Data

Duffie, Darrell.
      Dynamic asset pricing theory / Darrell Duffie.—3rd ed.
        p. cm.
      Includes bibliographical references and index.
      ISBN 0-691-09022-X (alk. paper)
      1. Capital assets pricing model. 2. Portfolio management 3. Uncertainty.
      I. Title.
    HG4637.D84 2001
    332.6—dc21   2001021235

British Library Cataloging-in-Publication Data is available

For Colin

Contents

Preface   xiii

PART I   DISCRETE-TIME MODELS   1

1   Introduction to State Pricing   3
   A Arbitrage and State Prices   3
   B Risk-Neutral Probabilities   4
   C Optimality and Asset Pricing   5
   D Efficiency and Complete Markets   8
   E Optimality and Representative Agents   8
   F State-Price Beta Models   11
      Exercises   12
      Notes   17

2   The Basic Multiperiod Model   21
   A Uncertainty   21
   B Security Markets   22
   C Arbitrage, State Prices, and Martingales   22
   D Individual Agent Optimality   24
   E Equilibrium and Pareto Optimality   26
   F Equilibrium Asset Pricing   27
   G Arbitrage and Martingale Measures   28
   H Valuation of Redundant Securities   30
   I American Exercise Policies and Valuation   31
   J Is Early Exercise Optimal?   35
      Exercises   37
      Notes   45

3 The Dynamic Programming Approach **49**
   A The Bellman Approach 49
   B First-Order Bellman Conditions 50
   C Markov Uncertainty 51
   D Markov Asset Pricing 52
   E Security Pricing by Markov Control 52
   F Markov Arbitrage-Free Valuation 55
   G Early Exercise and Optimal Stopping 56
      Exercises 58
      Notes 63

4 The Infinite-Horizon Setting **65**
   A Markov Dynamic Programming 65
   B Dynamic Programming and Equilibrium 69
   C Arbitrage and State Prices 70
   D Optimality and State Prices 71
   E Method-of-Moments Estimation 73
      Exercises 76
      Notes 78

PART II   CONTINUOUS-TIME MODELS   **81**

5 The Black-Scholes Model **83**
   A Trading Gains for Brownian Prices 83
   B Martingale Trading Gains 85
   C Ito Prices and Gains 86
   D Ito's Formula 87
   E The Black-Scholes Option-Pricing Formula 88
   F Black-Scholes Formula: First Try 90
   G The PDE for Arbitrage-Free Prices 92
   H The Feynman-Kac Solution 93
   I The Multidimensional Case 94
      Exercises 97
      Notes 100

6 State Prices and Equivalent Martingale Measures **101**
   A Arbitrage 101
   B Numeraire Invariance 102
   C State Prices and Doubling Strategies 103
   D Expected Rates of Return 106

E Equivalent Martingale Measures 108
F State Prices and Martingale Measures 110
G Girsanov and Market Prices of Risk 111
H Black-Scholes Again 115
I Complete Markets 116
J Redundant Security Pricing 119
K Martingale Measures from No Arbitrage 120
L Arbitrage Pricing with Dividends 123
M Lumpy Dividends and Term Structures 125
N Martingale Measures, Infinite Horizon 127
   Exercises 128
   Notes 131

7 **Term-Structure Models** **135**
A The Term Structure 136
B One-Factor Term-Structure Models 137
C The Gaussian Single-Factor Models 139
D The Cox-Ingersoll-Ross Model 141
E The Affine Single-Factor Models 142
F Term-Structure Derivatives 144
G The Fundamental Solution 146
H Multifactor Models 148
I Affine Term-Structure Models 149
J The HJM Model of Forward Rates 151
K Markovian Yield Curves and SPDEs 154
   Exercises 155
   Notes 161

8 **Derivative Pricing** **167**
A Martingale Measures in a Black Box 167
B Forward Prices 169
C Futures and Continuous Resettlement 171
D Arbitrage-Free Futures Prices 172
E Stochastic Volatility 174
F Option Valuation by Transform Analysis 178
G American Security Valuation 182
H American Exercise Boundaries 186
I Lookback Options 189
   Exercises 191
   Notes 196

9 Portfolio and Consumption Choice **203**
    A Stochastic Control 203
    B Merton's Problem 206
    C Solution to Merton's Problem 209
    D The Infinite-Horizon Case 213
    E The Martingale Formulation 214
    F Martingale Solution 217
    G A Generalization 220
    H The Utility-Gradient Approach 221
        Exercises 224
        Notes 232

10 Equilibrium **235**
    A The Primitives 235
    B Security-Spot Market Equilibrium 236
    C Arrow-Debreu Equilibrium 237
    D Implementing Arrow-Debreu Equilibrium 238
    E Real Security Prices 240
    F Optimality with Additive Utility 241
    G Equilibrium with Additive Utility 243
    H The Consumption-Based CAPM 245
    I The CIR Term Structure 246
    J The CCAPM in Incomplete Markets 249
        Exercises 251
        Notes 255

11 Corporate Securities **259**
    A The Black-Scholes-Merton Model 259
    B Endogenous Default Timing 262
    C Example: Brownian Dividend Growth 264
    D Taxes and Bankruptcy Costs 268
    E Endogenous Capital Structure 269
    F Technology Choice 271
    G Other Market Imperfections 272
    H Intensity-Based Modeling of Default 274
    I Risk-Neutral Intensity Process 277
    J Zero-Recovery Bond Pricing 278
    K Pricing with Recovery at Default 280
    L Default-Adjusted Short Rate 281
        Exercises 282
        Notes 288

12 Numerical Methods **293**
   A Central Limit Theorems 293
   B Binomial to Black-Scholes 294
   C Binomial Convergence for Unbounded Derivative Payoffs . . 297
   D Discretization of Asset Price Processes 297
   E Monte Carlo Simulation 299
   F Efficient SDE Simulation 300
   G Applying Feynman-Kac 302
   H Finite-Difference Methods 302
   I Term-Structure Example 306
   J Finite-Difference Algorithms with Early Exercise Options . . . 309
   K The Numerical Solution of State Prices 310
   L Numerical Solution of the Pricing Semi-Group 313
   M Fitting the Initial Term Structure 314
      Exercises 316
      Notes 317

APPENDIXES   **321**

A Finite-State Probability **323**

B Separating Hyperplanes and Optimality **326**

C Probability **329**

D Stochastic Integration **334**

E SDE, PDE, and Feynman-Kac **340**

F Ito's Formula with Jumps **347**

G Utility Gradients **351**

H Ito's Formula for Complex Functions **355**

I Counting Processes **357**

J Finite-Difference Code **363**

Bibliography **373**

Symbol Glossary **445**

Author Index **447**

Subject Index **457**

Preface

THIS BOOK IS an introduction to the theory of portfolio choice and asset pricing in multiperiod settings under uncertainty. An alternate title might be *Arbitrage, Optimality, and Equilibrium,* because the book is built around the three basic constraints on asset prices: absence of arbitrage, single-agent optimality, and market equilibrium. The most important unifying principle is that any of these three conditions implies that there are "state prices," meaning positive discount factors, one for each state and date, such that the price of any security is merely the state-price weighted sum of its future payoffs. This idea can be traced to the invention by Arrow (1953) of the general equilibrium model of security markets. Identifying the state prices is the major task at hand. Technicalities are given relatively little emphasis so as to simplify these concepts and to make plain the similarities between discrete- and continuous-time models.ricing model.

To someone who came out of graduate school in the mid-eighties, the decade spanning roughly 1969–79 seems like a golden age of dynamic asset pricing theory. Robert Merton started continuous-time financial modeling with his explicit dynamic programming solution for optimal portfolio and consumption policies. This set the stage for his 1973 general equilibrium model of security prices, another milestone. His next major contribution was his arbitrage-based proof of the option pricing formula introduced by Fisher Black and Myron Scholes in 1973, and his continual development of that approach to derivative pricing. The Black-Scholes model now seems to be, by far, the most important single breakthrough of this "golden decade," and ranks alone with the Modigliani and Miller (1958) Theorem and the Capital Asset Pricing Model (CAPM) of Sharpe (1964) and Lintner (1965) in its overall importance for financial theory and practice. A tremendously influential simplification of the Black-Scholes model appeared in the "binomial" option pricing model of Cox, Ross, and Rubinstein (1979), who drew on an insight of Bill Sharpe.

Working with discrete-time models, LeRoy (1973), Rubinstein (1976), and Lucas (1978) developed multiperiod extensions of the CAPM. The "Lucas model" is the "vanilla flavor" of equilibrium asset pricing models. The simplest multiperiod representation of the CAPM finally appeared in Doug Breeden's continuous-time consumption-based CAPM, published in 1979. Although not published until 1985, the Cox-Ingersoll-Ross model of the term structure of interest rates appeared in the mid-seventies and is still the premier textbook example of a continuous-time general equilibrium asset pricing model with practical applications. It also ranks as one of the key breakthroughs of that decade. Finally, extending the ideas of Cox and Ross (1976) and Ross (1978), Harrison and Kreps (1979) gave an almost definitive conceptual structure to the whole theory of dynamic security prices.

Theoretical developments in the period since 1979, with relatively few exceptions, have been a mopping-up operation. Assumptions have been weakened, there have been noteworthy extensions and illustrative models, and the various problems have become much more unified under the umbrella of the Harrison-Kreps model of equivalent martingale measures. For example, the standard approach to optimal portfolio and consumption choice in continuous-time settings has become the martingale method of Cox and Huang (1989). An essentially final version of the relationship between the absence of arbitrage and the existence of equivalent martingale measures was finally obtained by Delbaen and Schachermayer (1999).

On the applied side, markets have experienced an explosion of new valuation techniques, hedging applications, and security innovation, much of this based on the Black-Scholes and related arbitrage models. No major investment bank, for example, lacks the experts or computer technology required to implement advanced mathematical models of the term structure. Because of the wealth of new applications, there has been a significant development of special models to treat stochastic volatility, jump behavior including default, and the term structure of interest rates, along with many econometric advances designed to take advantage of the resulting improvements in richness and tractability.

Although it is difficult to predict where the theory will go next, in order to promote faster progress by people coming into the field it seems wise to have some of the basics condensed into a textbook. This book is designed to be a streamlined course text, not a research monograph. Much generality is sacrificed for expositional reasons, and there is relatively little emphasis on mathematical rigor or on the existence of general equilibrium. As its title indicates, I am treating only the theoretical side of the story. Although it might be useful to tie the theory to the empirical side of asset pricing, we have excellent treatments of the econometric modeling of financial data, such as Campbell, Lo, and MacKinlay (1997) and Gourieroux and Jasiak (2000). I also leave out some important aspects of functioning security markets, such as asymmetric information and transactions costs. I have chosen to develop only some of the essential ideas of dynamic asset pricing, and even these are more than enough to put into one book or into a one-semester course.

Other books whose treatments overlap with some of the topics treated here include Avelleneda and Laurence (2000), Björk (1998), Dana and Jeanblanc (1998), Demange and Rochet (1992), Dewynne and Wilmott (1994), Dixit and Pindyck (1993), Dothan (1990), Duffie (1988b), Harris (1987), Huang and Litzenberger (1988), Ingersoll (1987), Jarrow (1988), Karatzas (1997), Karatzas and Shreve (1998), Lamberton and Lapeyre (1997), Magill and Quinzii (1994), Merton (1990), Musiela and Rutkowski (1997), Neftci (2000), Stokey and Lucas (1989), Willmott, Dewynne, and Howison (1993), and Wilmott, Howison, and Dewynne (1995). Each has its own aims and themes. I hope that readers will find some advantage in having yet another perspective.

A reasonable way to teach a shorter course on continuous-time asset pricing out of this book is to begin with Chapter 1 or 2 as an introduction to the basic notion of state prices and then to go directly to Chapters 5 through 11. Chapter 12, on numerical methods, could be skipped at some cost to the student's ability to implement the results. There is no direct dependence of any results in Chapters 5 through 12 on the first four chapters.

For mathematical preparation, little beyond undergraduate analysis, as in Bartle (1976), and linear algebra is assumed. Some familiarity with Royden (1968) or a similar text on functional analysis and measure theory, would also be useful. Some background in microeconomics would be useful, say Kreps (1990) or Luenberger (1995). Familiarity with probability theory at the level of Jacod and Protter (2000), for example, would also speed things along, although measure theory is not used heavily. In any case, a series of appendices supplies all of the required concepts and definitions from probability theory and stochastic calculus. Additional useful references in this regard are Brémaud (1981), Karatzas and Shreve (1988), Revuz and Yor (1991), and Protter (1990).

Students seem to learn best by doing problem exercises. Each chapter has exercises and notes to the literature. I have tried to be thorough in giving sources for results whenever possible and plead that any cases in which I have mistaken or missed sources be brought to my attention for correction. The notation and terminology throughout is fairly standard. I use $\mathbb{R}$ to denote the real line and $\overline{\mathbb{R}} = \mathbb{R} \cup \{-\infty, +\infty\}$ for the extended real line. For any set Z and positive integer n, I use Z^n for the set of n-tuples of the form $(z_1, \ldots, z_n)$ with z_i in Z for all i. An example is $\mathbb{R}^n$. The conventions used for inequalities in any context are

- $x \geq 0$ means that x is nonnegative. For x in $\mathbb{R}^n$, this is equivalent to $x \in \mathbb{R}^n_+$;
- $x > 0$ means that x is nonnegative and not zero, but not necessarily strictly positive in all coordinates;
- $x \gg 0$ means x is strictly positive in every possible sense. The phrase "x is strictly positive" means the same thing. For x in $\mathbb{R}^n$, this is equivalent to $x \in \mathbb{R}^n_{++} \equiv \mathrm{int}(\mathbb{R}^n_+)$.

Although warnings will be given at appropriate times, it should be kept in mind that $X = Y$ will be used to mean equality almost everywhere or almost surely, as the case may be. The same caveat applies to each of the above inequalities. A real-valued function F on an ordered set (such as $\mathbb{R}^n$) is *increasing* if $F(x) \geq F(y)$ whenever $x \geq y$ and *strictly increasing* if $F(x) > F(y)$ whenever $x > y$. When the domain and range of a function are implicitly obvious, the notation "$x \mapsto F(x)$" means the function that maps x to $F(x)$; for example, $x \mapsto x^2$ means the function $F : \mathbb{R} \to \mathbb{R}$ defined by $F(x) = x^2$. Also, while warnings appear at appropriate places, it is worth pointing out again here that, for ease of exposition, a continuous-time "process" will be defined throughout as a jointly (product) measurable function on $\Omega \times [0, T]$, where $[0, T]$ is the given time interval and $(\Omega, \mathcal{F}, P)$ is the given underlying probability space.

The first four chapters are in a discrete-time setting with a discrete set of states. This should ease the development of intuition for the models to be found in Chapters 5 through 12. The three pillars of the theory, *arbitrage*, *optimality*, and *equilibrium*, are developed repeatedly in different settings. Chapter 1 is the basic single-period model. Chapter 2 extends the results of Chapter 1 to many periods. Chapter 3 specializes Chapter 2 to a Markov setting and illustrates dynamic programming as an alternate solution technique. The Ho-and-Lee and Black-Derman-Toy term-structure models are included as exercises. Chapter 4 is an infinite-horizon counterpart to Chapter 3 that has become known as the *Lucas model*.

The focus of the theory is the notion of state prices, which specify the price of any security as the state-price weighted sum or expectation of the security's state-contingent dividends. In a finite-dimensional setting, there exist state prices if and only if there is no arbitrage. The same fact is true in infinite-dimensional settings under mild technical regularity conditions. Given an agent's optimal portfolio choice, a state-price vector is given by that agent's utility gradient. In an equilibrium with Pareto optimality, a state-price vector is likewise given by a representative agent's utility gradient at the economy's aggregate consumption process.

Chapters 5 through 11 develop a continuous-time version of the theory in which uncertainty is generated by Brownian motion. In Chapter 11, there is a transition to discontinuous information, that is, settings in which the conditional probability of some events does not adjust continuously with the passage of time. An example is Poisson arrival.

Chapter 5 introduces the continuous-trading model and develops the Black-Scholes partial differential equation (PDE) for arbitrage-free prices of derivative securities. The Harrison-Kreps model of equivalent martingale measures is presented in Chapter 6 in parallel with the theory of state prices in continuous time. Chapter 7 presents models of the term structure of interest rates, including the Black-Derman-Toy, Vasicek, Cox-Ingersoll-Ross, and Heath-Jarrow-Morton models, as well as extensions. Chapter 8 presents specific classes of derivative securities, such as futures, forwards, American options, and lookback options. Chapter 8 also introduces models of option pricing with stochastic volatility. The notion of an "affine" state process is used heavily in Chapters 7 and 8 for its analytical tractability. Chapter 9 is a summary of optimal continuous-time portfolio choice, using both dynamic programming and an approach involving equivalent martingale measures or state prices. Chapter 10 is a summary of security pricing in an equilibrium setting. Included are such well-known models as Breeden's consumption-based capital asset pricing model and the general equilibrium version of the Cox-Ingersoll-Ross model of the term structure of interest rates. Chapter 11 deals with the valuation of corporate securities, such as debt and equity. The chapter moves from models based on the capital structure of the corporation, in which default is defined in terms of the sufficiency of assets, to models based on an assumed process for the default arrival intensity. Chapter 12 outlines three numerical methods for calculating derivative security prices in a continuous-time setting: binomial approximation, Monte Carlo simulation of a discrete-time approximation of security prices, and finite-difference solution of the associated PDE for the asset price or the fundamental solution.

In preparing the first edition, I relied on help from many people, in addition to those mentioned above who developed this theory. In 1982,

Michael Harrison gave a class at Stanford that had a major effect on my understanding and research goals. Beside me in that class was Chi-fu Huang; we learned much of this material together, becoming close friends and collaborators. I owe him a lot. I am grateful to Niko and Vana Skiadas, who treated me with overwhelming warmth and hospitality at their home on Skiathos, where parts of the first draft were written.

I have benefited from research collaboration over the years with many co-authors, including George Constantinides, Qiang Dai, Peter DeMarzo, Larry Epstein, Nicolae Gârleanu, Mark Garman, John Geanakoplos, Pierre-Yves Geoffard, Peter Glynn, Mike Harrison, Chi-fu Huang, Ming Huang, Matt Jackson, Rui Kan, David Lando, Jun Liu, Pierre-Louis Lions, Jin Ma, Andreu Mas-Colell, Andy McLennan, Jun Pan, Lasse Pedersen, Philip Protter, Rohit Rahi, Tony Richardson, Mark Schroder, Wayne Shafer, Ken Singleton, Costis Skiadas, Richard Stanton, Jiongmin Yong, and Bill Zame. I owe a special debt to Costis Skiadas, whose generous supply of good ideas has had a big influence on the result.

I am lucky indeed to have had access to many fruitful research discussions here at Stanford, especially with my colleagues Anat Admati, Steve Boyd, Peter DeMarzo, Peter Glynn, Steve Grenadier, Joe Grundfest, Peter Hammond, Mike Harrison, Ayman Hindy, Harrison Hong, Ming Huang, Jack McDonald, George Parker, Paul Pfleiderer, Balaji Prabakar, Manju Puri, Tom Sargent, Bill Sharpe, Ken Singleton, Jim Van Horne, and Jeff Zwiebel, and elsewhere with too many others to name.

I am thankful to have had the chance to work on applied financial models with Mike Burger, Bill Colgin, Adam Duff, Stenson Gibner, Elizabeth Glaeser Craig Gustaffson, Corwin Joy, Vince Kaminsky, Ken Knowles, Sergio Kostek, Joe Langsam, Aloke Majumdar, Matt Page, Krishna Rao, Amir Sadr, Louis Scott, Wei Shi, John Uglum, and Mark Williams.

I thank Kingston Duffie, Ravi Myneni, Paul Bernstein, and Michael Boulware for coding and running some numerical examples, Linda Bethel for assistance with LaTeX and graphics, and, for production editing and typesetting, Laurie Pickert of Archetype and Tina Burke of Technical Typesetting. For assistance with bibliographic research, I am grateful to Yu-Hua Chen, Melissa Gonzalez, David Lee, and Analiza Quiroz. Jack Repcheck and Peter Dougherty have been friendly, helpful, and supportive editors.

Suggestions and comments have been gratefully received from many readers, including Fehmi Ashaboglu, Robert Ashcroft, Irena Asmundsen, Alexandre d'Aspremont, Flavio Auler, Chris Avery, Kerry Back, Yaroslav

Bazaliy, Ralf Becker, Antje Berndt, Michael Boulware, John Campbell, Andrew Caplin, Karen Chaltikian, Victor Chernozhukov, Hung-Ken Chien, Seongman Cho, Fai Tong Chung, Chin-Shan Chuan, Howie Corb, Qiang Dai, Eugene Demler, Shijie Deng, Michelle Dick, Phil Dolan, Rod Duncan, Wedad Elmaghraby, Kian Esteghamat, Mark Ferguson, Christian Riis Flor, Prashant Fuloria, John Fuqua, Nicolae Gârleanu, Mark Garmaise, Filippo Ginanni, Michel Grueneberg, Bing Han, Philippe Henrotte, Ayman Hindy, Yael Hochberg, Toshiki Honda, Taiichi Hoshino, Jiangping Hu, Ming Huang, Cristobal Huneeus, Don Iglehart, Michael Intriligator, Farshid Jamshidian, Ping Jiang, Shinsuke Kambe, Rui Kan, Ron Karidi, Don Kim, Felix Kubler, Allan Kulig, Yoichi Kuwana, Piero La Mura, Yingcong Lan, Joe Langsam, Jackie Lee, André Levy, Shujing Li, Wenzhi Li, Tiong Wee Lim, Jun Liu, Leonid Litvak, Hanno Lustig, Rob McMillan, Rajnish Mehra, Sergei Morozov, Christophe Mueller, Ravi Myneni, Lee Bath Nelson, Yigal Newman, Angela Ng, Kazuhiko Ōhashi, Hui Ou-Yang, John Overdeck, Hideo Owen, Caglar Ozden, Mikko Packalen, Jun Pan, Lasse Pedersen, Albert Perez, Monika Piazzesi, Jorge Picazo, Heracles Polemarchakis, Marius Rabus, Rohit Rahi, Shikhar Ranjan, Michael Rierson, Amir Sadr, Yuliy Sannikov, Marco Scarsini, Martin Schneider, Christine Shannon, Yong-Seok Shin, Mark Shivers, Hersir Sigurgeirsson, Marciano Siniscalchi, Ravi Singh, Ronnie Sircar, Viktor Spivakovsky, Lucie Tepla, Sergiy Terentyev, Rajat Tewari, Sverrir Thorvaldsson, Alex Tolstykh, Tunay Tunca, John Uglum, Len Umantsev, Stijn Van Nieuwerburgh, Laura Veldkamp, Mary Vyas, Muhamet Yildiz, Nese Yildiz, Ke Wang, Neng Wang, Chao Wei, Wei Wei, Pierre-Olivier Weill, Steven Weinberg, Seth Weingram, Guojun Wu, Pinghua Young, Assaf Zeevi, and Alexandre Ziegler, with apologies to those whose assistance was forgotten. I am especially grateful to the expert team of Japanese translators of the second edition, Toshiki Honda, Kazuhiko Ōhashi, Yoichi Kuwana, and Akira Yamazaki, all of whom are personal friends as well.

For the reader's convenience, the original preface has been revised for this third edition. Significant improvements have been made in most chapters. Chapter 11, "Corporate Securities," has been added for this edition. Errors are my own responsibility, and I hope to hear of them and any other comments from readers.

Darrell Duffie

I
Discrete-Time Models

This first part of the book takes place in a discrete-time setting with a discrete set of states. This should ease the development of intuition for the models to be found in Part II. The three pillars of the theory, *arbitrage*, *optimality*, and *equilibrium*, are developed repeatedly in different settings. Chapter 1 is the basic single-period model. Chapter 2 extends the results of Chapter 1 to many periods. Chapter 3 specializes Chapter 2 to a Markov setting and illustrates dynamic programming as an alternate solution technique. The Ho-and-Lee and Black-Derman-Toy term-structure models are included as exercises. Chapter 4 is an infinite-horizon counterpart to Chapter 3 that has become known as the *Lucas model*.

The focus of the theory is the notion of state prices, which specify the price of any security as the state-price weighted sum or expectation of the security's state-contingent dividends. In a finite-dimensional setting, there exist state prices if and only if there is no arbitrage. The same fact is true in infinite-dimensional settings under mild technical regularity conditions. Given an agent's optimal portfolio choice, a state-price vector is given by that agent's utility gradient. In an equilibrium with Pareto optimality, a state-price vector is likewise given by a representative agent's utility gradient at the economy's aggregate consumption process.

1
Introduction to State Pricing

THIS CHAPTER INTRODUCES the basic ideas in a finite-state one-period setting. In many basic senses, each subsequent chapter merely repeats this one from a new perspective. The objective is a characterization of security prices in terms of "state prices," one for each state of the world. The price of a given security is simply the state-price weighted sum of its payoffs in the different states. One can treat a state price as the "shadow price," or Lagrange multiplier, for wealth contingent on a given state of the world. We obtain a characterization of state prices, first based on the absence of arbitrage, then based on the first-order conditions for optimal portfolio choice of a given agent, and finally from the first-order conditions for Pareto optimality in an equilibrium with complete markets. State prices are connected with the "beta" model for excess expected returns, a special case of which is the Capital Asset Pricing Model (CAPM). Many readers will find this chapter to be a review of standard results. In most cases, here and throughout, technical conditions are imposed that give up much generality so as to simplify the exposition.

A. Arbitrage and State Prices

Uncertainty is represented here by a finite set $\{1, \ldots, S\}$ of states, one of which will be revealed as true. The N securities are given by an $N \times S$ matrix D, with D_{ij} denoting the number of units of account paid by security i in state j. The security prices are given by some q in $\mathbb{R}^N$. A *portfolio* $\theta \in \mathbb{R}^N$ has *market value* $q \cdot \theta$ and *payoff* $D^\top \theta$ in $\mathbb{R}^S$. An *arbitrage* is a portfolio θ in $\mathbb{R}^N$ with $q \cdot \theta \leq 0$ and $D^\top \theta > 0$, or $q \cdot \theta < 0$ and $D^\top \theta \geq 0$. An arbitrage is therefore, in effect, a portfolio offering "something for nothing." Not surprisingly, it will later be shown that an arbitrage is naturally ruled out, and this gives a characterization of security prices as follows. A

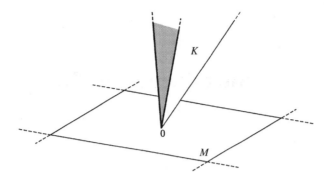

Figure 1.1.   *Separating a Cone from a Linear Subspace*

state-price vector is a vector ψ in $\mathbb{R}_{++}^S$ with $q = D\psi$. We can think of ψ_j as the marginal cost of obtaining an additional unit of account in state j.

Theorem. *There is no arbitrage if and only if there is a state-price vector.*

Proof: The proof is an application of the Separating Hyperplane Theorem. Let $L = \mathbb{R} \times \mathbb{R}^S$ and $M = \{(-q \cdot \theta, D^\top \theta) : \theta \in \mathbb{R}^N\}$, a linear subspace of L. Let $K = \mathbb{R}_+ \times \mathbb{R}_+^S$, which is a cone (meaning that if x is in K, then λx is in K for each strictly positive scalar λ). Both K and M are closed and convex subsets of L. There is no arbitrage if and only if K and M intersect precisely at 0, as pictured in Figure 1.1.

Suppose $K \cap M = \{0\}$. The Separating Hyperplane Theorem (in a version for closed cones that is found in Appendix B) implies the existence of a nonzero linear functional $F : L \to \mathbb{R}$ such that $F(z) < F(x)$ for all z in M and nonzero x in K. Since M is a linear space, this implies that $F(z) = 0$ for all z in M and that $F(x) > 0$ for all nonzero x in K. The latter fact implies that there is some $\alpha > 0$ in $\mathbb{R}$ and $\psi \gg 0$ in $\mathbb{R}^S$ such that $F(v, c) = \alpha v + \psi \cdot c$, for any $(v, c) \in L$. This in turn implies that $-\alpha q \cdot \theta + \psi \cdot (D^\top \theta) = 0$ for all θ in $\mathbb{R}^N$. The vector ψ/α is therefore a state-price vector.

Conversely, if a state-price vector ψ exists, then for any θ, we have $q \cdot \theta = \psi^\top D^\top \theta$. Thus, when $D^\top \theta \geq 0$, we have $q \cdot \theta \geq 0$, and when $D^\top \theta > 0$, we have $q \cdot \theta > 0$, so there is no arbitrage. ∎

B. Risk-Neutral Probabilities

We can view any p in $\mathbb{R}_+^S$ with $p_1 + \cdots + p_S = 1$ as a vector of probabilities of the corresponding states. Given a state-price vector ψ for the dividend-price pair (D, q), let $\psi_0 = \psi_1 + \cdots + \psi_S$ and, for any state j, let $\hat{\psi}_j = \psi_j/\psi_0$.

We now have a vector $(\hat{\psi}_1, \ldots, \hat{\psi}_S)$ of probabilities and can write, for an arbitrary security i,

$$\frac{q_i}{\psi_0} = \hat{E}(D_i) \equiv \sum_{j=1}^{S} \hat{\psi}_j D_{ij},$$

viewing the normalized price of the security as its expected payoff under specially chosen "risk-neutral" probabilities. If there exists a portfolio $\bar{\theta}$ with $D^\top \bar{\theta} = (1, 1, \ldots, 1)$, then $\psi_0 = \bar{\theta} \cdot q$ is the discount on riskless borrowing and, for any security i, $q_i = \psi_0 \hat{E}(D_i)$, showing any security's price to be its discounted expected payoff in this sense of artificially constructed probabilities.

C. Optimality and Asset Pricing

Suppose the dividend-price pair (D, q) is given. An *agent* is defined by a strictly increasing *utility function* $U : \mathbb{R}_+^S \to \mathbb{R}$ and an *endowment e* in $\mathbb{R}_+^S$. This leaves the *budget-feasible set*

$$X(q, e) = \{e + D^\top \theta \in \mathbb{R}_+^S : \theta \in \mathbb{R}^N, q \cdot \theta \leq 0\},$$

and the problem

$$\sup_{c \in X(q,e)} U(c). \tag{1}$$

We will suppose for this section that there is some portfolio θ^0 with payoff $D^\top \theta^0 > 0$. Because U is strictly increasing, the wealth constraint $q \cdot \theta \leq 0$ is then binding at an optimum. That is, if $c^* = e + D^\top \theta^*$ solves (1), then $q \cdot \theta^* = 0$.

Proposition. *If there is a solution to (1), then there is no arbitrage. If U is continuous and there is no arbitrage, then there is a solution to (1).*

Proof is left as an exercise.

Theorem. *Suppose that c^* is a strictly positive solution to (1), that U is continuously differentiable at c^*, and that the vector $\partial U(c^*)$ of partial derivatives of U at c^* is strictly positive. Then there is some scalar $\lambda > 0$ such that $\lambda \partial U(c^*)$ is a state-price vector.*

Proof: The first-order condition for optimality is that for any θ with $q \cdot \theta = 0$, the marginal utility for buying the portfolio θ is zero. This is expressed more precisely in the following way. The strict positivity of c^* implies that for any portfolio θ, there is some scalar $k > 0$ such that $c^* + \alpha D^\top \theta \geq 0$ for all α in $[-k, k]$. Let $g_\theta : [-k, k] \to \mathbb{R}$ be defined by

$$g_\theta(\alpha) = U(c^* + \alpha D^\top \theta).$$

Suppose $q \cdot \theta = 0$. The optimality of c^* implies that g_θ is maximized at $\alpha = 0$. The first-order condition for this is that $g'_\theta(0) = \partial U(c^*)^\top D^\top \theta = 0$. We can conclude that, for any θ in $\mathbb{R}^N$, if $q \cdot \theta = 0$, then $\partial U(c^*)^\top D^\top \theta = 0$. From this, there is some scalar μ such that $\partial U(c^*)^\top D^\top = \mu q$.

By assumption, there is some portfolio θ^0 with $D^\top \theta^0 > 0$. From the existence of a solution to (1), there is no arbitrage, implying that $q \cdot \theta^0 > 0$. We have

$$\mu q \cdot \theta^0 = \partial U(c^*)^\top D^\top \theta^0 > 0.$$

Thus $\mu > 0$. We let $\lambda = 1/\mu$, obtaining

$$q = \lambda D \partial U(c^*), \tag{2}$$

implying that $\lambda \partial U(c^*)$ is a state-price vector. ∎

Although we have assumed that U is strictly increasing, this does not necessarily mean that $\partial U(c^*) \gg 0$. If U is concave and strictly increasing, however, it is always true that $\partial U(c^*) \gg 0$.

Corollary. *Suppose U is concave and differentiable at some $c^* = e + D^\top \theta^* \gg 0$, with $q \cdot \theta^* = 0$. Then c^* is optimal if and only if $\lambda \partial U(c^*)$ is a state-price vector for some scalar $\lambda > 0$.*

This follows from the sufficiency of the first-order optimality conditions for concave objective functions. The idea is illustrated in Figure 1.2. In that figure, there are only two states, and a state-price vector is a suitably normalized nonzero positive vector orthogonal to the set $B = \{D^\top \theta : q \cdot \theta = 0\}$ of budget-neutral consumption adjustments. The first-order condition for optimality of c^* is that movement in any feasible direction away from c^* has negative or zero marginal utility, which is equivalent to the statement that the budget-neutral set is tangent at c^* to the preferred set $\{c : U(c) \geq U(c^*)\}$, as shown in the figure. This is equivalent to the statement that $\partial U(c^*)$ is orthogonal to B, consistent with the last corollary. Figure 1.3 illustrates a strictly suboptimal consumption choice c, at which the derivative vector $\partial U(c)$ is not co-linear with the state-price vector ψ.

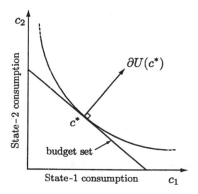

Figure 1.2. *First-Order Conditions for Optimal Consumption Choice*

We consider the special case of an *expected utility* function U, defined by a given vector p of probabilities and by some $u : \mathbb{R}_+ \to \mathbb{R}$ according to

$$U(c) = E[u(c)] \equiv \sum_{j=1}^{S} p_j u(c_j). \tag{3}$$

For $c \gg 0$, if u is differentiable, then $\partial U(c)_j = p_j u'(c_j)$. For this expected utility function, (2) therefore applies if and only if

$$q = \lambda E[Du'(c^*)], \tag{4}$$

with the obvious notational convention. As we saw in Section B, one can also write (2) or (4), with the "risk-neutral" probability $\hat{\psi}_j = u'(c_j^*)p_j / E[u'(c^*)]$, in the form

$$\frac{q_i}{\psi_0} = \hat{E}(D_i) \equiv \sum_{j=1}^{S} D_{ij}\hat{\psi}_j, \qquad 1 \le i \le N. \tag{5}$$

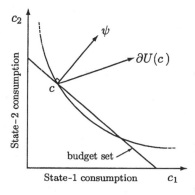

Figure 1.3. *A Strictly Suboptimal Consumption Choice*

D. Efficiency and Complete Markets

Suppose there are m agents, defined as in Section C by strictly increasing utility functions $U_1, \ldots, U_m$ and by endowments $e^1, \ldots, e^m$. An *equilibrium* for the *economy* $[(U_i, e^i), D]$ is a collection $(\theta^1, \ldots, \theta^m, q)$ such that, given the security-price vector q, for each agent i, θ^i solves $\sup_\theta U_i(e^i + D^\top \theta)$ subject to $q \cdot \theta \leq 0$, and such that $\sum_{i=1}^m \theta^i = 0$. The existence of equilibrium is treated in the exercises and in sources cited in the Notes.

With span$(D) \equiv \{D^\top \theta : \theta \in \mathbb{R}^N\}$ denoting the set of possible portfolio payoffs, markets are *complete* if span$(D) = \mathbb{R}^S$, and are otherwise *incomplete*.

Let $e = e^1 + \cdots + e^m$ denote the aggregate endowment. A consumption *allocation* $(c^1, \ldots, c^m)$ in $\left(\mathbb{R}_+^S\right)^m$ is *feasible* if $c^1 + \cdots + c^m \leq e$. A feasible allocation $(c^1, \ldots, c^m)$ is *Pareto optimal* if there is no feasible allocation $(\hat{c}^1, \ldots, \hat{c}^m)$ with $U_i(\hat{c}^i) \geq U_i(c^i)$ for all i and with $U_i(\hat{c}^i) > U_i(c^i)$ for some i. Complete markets and the Pareto optimality of equilibrium allocations are almost equivalent properties of any economy.

Proposition. *Suppose markets are complete and $(\theta^1, \ldots, \theta^m, q)$ is an equilibrium. Then the associated equilibrium allocation is Pareto optimal.*

This is sometimes known as *The First Welfare Theorem*. The proof, requiring only the strict monotonicity of utilities, is left as an exercise. We have established the sufficiency of complete markets for Pareto optimality. The necessity of complete markets for the Pareto optimality of equilibrium allocations does not always follow. For example, if the initial endowment allocation $(e^1, \ldots, e^m)$ happens by chance to be Pareto optimal, then any equilibrium allocation is also Pareto optimal, regardless of the span of securities. It would be unusual, however, for the initial endowment to be Pareto optimal. Although beyond the scope of this book, it can be shown that with incomplete markets and under natural assumptions on utility, for almost every endowment, the equilibrium allocation is not Pareto optimal.

E. Optimality and Representative Agents

Aside from its allocational implications, Pareto optimality is also a convenient property for the purpose of security pricing. In order to see this, consider, for each vector $\lambda \in \mathbb{R}_+^m$ of "agent weights," the utility function $U_\lambda : \mathbb{R}_+^S \to \mathbb{R}$ defined by

$$U_\lambda(x) = \sup_{(c^1, \ldots, c^m)} \sum_{i=1}^m \lambda_i U_i(c^i) \qquad \text{subject to } c^1 + \cdots + c^m \leq x. \qquad (6)$$

Lemma. *Suppose that, for all i, U_i is concave. An allocation $(c^1, \ldots, c^m)$ that is feasible is Pareto optimal if and only if there is some nonzero $\lambda \in \mathbb{R}^m_+$ such that $(c^1, \ldots, c^m)$ solves (6) at $x = e = c^1 + \cdots + c^m$.*

Proof: Suppose that $(c^1, \ldots, c^m)$ is Pareto optimal. For any allocation x, let $U(x) = (U_1(x^1), \ldots, U_m(x^m))$. Next, let

$$\mathcal{U} = \{U(x) - U(c) - z : x \in \mathcal{A}, z \in \mathbb{R}^m_+\} \subset \mathbb{R}^m,$$

where $\mathcal{A}$ is the set of feasible allocations. Let $J = \{y \in \mathbb{R}^m_+ : y \neq 0\}$. Since $\mathcal{U}$ is convex (by the concavity of utility functions) and $J \cap \mathcal{U}$ is empty (by Pareto optimality), the Separating Hyperplane Theorem (Appendix B) implies that there is a nonzero vector λ in $\mathbb{R}^m$ such that $\lambda \cdot y \leq \lambda \cdot z$ for each y in $\mathcal{U}$ and each z in J. Since $0 \in \mathcal{U}$, we know that $\lambda \geq 0$, proving the first part of the result. The second part is easy to show as an exercise. ∎

Proposition. *Suppose that for all i, U_i is concave. Suppose that markets are complete and that $(\theta^1, \ldots, \theta^m, q)$ is an equilibrium. Then there exists some nonzero $\lambda \in \mathbb{R}^m_+$ such that $(0, q)$ is a (no-trade) equilibrium for the single-agent economy $[(U_\lambda, e), D]$ defined by (6). Moreover, the equilibrium consumption allocation $(c^1, \ldots, c^m)$ solves the allocation problem (6) at the aggregate endowment. That is, $U_\lambda(e) = \sum_i \lambda_i U_i(c^i)$.*

Proof: Since there is an equilibrium, there is no arbitrage, and therefore there is a state-price vector ψ. Since markets are complete, this implies that the problem of any agent i can be reduced to

$$\sup_{c \in \mathbb{R}^S_+} U_i(c) \quad \text{subject to } \psi \cdot c \leq \psi \cdot e^i.$$

We can assume that e^i is not zero, for otherwise $c^i = 0$ and agent i can be eliminated from the problem without loss of generality. By the Saddle Point Theorem of Appendix B, there is a Lagrange multiplier $\alpha_i \geq 0$ such that c^i solves the problem

$$\sup_{c \in \mathbb{R}^S_+} U_i(c) - \alpha_i(\psi \cdot c - \psi \cdot e^i).$$

(The Slater condition is satisfied since e^i is not zero and $\psi \gg 0$.) Since U_i is strictly increasing, $\alpha_i > 0$. Let $\lambda_i = 1/\alpha_i$. For any feasible allocation $(x^1, \ldots, x^m)$, we have

$$\sum_{i=1}^m \lambda_i U_i(c^i) = \sum_{i=1}^m [\lambda_i U_i(c^i) - \lambda_i \alpha_i(\psi \cdot c^i - \psi \cdot e^i)]$$

$$\geq \sum_{i=1}^{m} \lambda_i [U_i(x^i) - \alpha_i(\psi \cdot x^i - \psi \cdot e^i)]$$

$$= \sum_{i=1}^{m} \lambda_i U_i(x^i) - \psi \cdot \sum_{i=1}^{m} (x^i - e^i)$$

$$\geq \sum_{i=1}^{m} \lambda_i U_i(x^i).$$

This shows that $(c^1, \ldots, c^m)$ solves the allocation problem (6). We must also show that no trade is optimal for the single agent with utility function U_λ and endowment e. If not, there is some x in $\mathbb{R}^S_+$ such that $U_\lambda(x) > U_\lambda(e)$ and $\psi \cdot x \leq \psi \cdot e$. By the definition of U_λ, this would imply the existence of an allocation $(x^1, \ldots, x^m)$, not necessarily feasible, such that $\sum_i \lambda_i U_i(x^i) > \sum_i \lambda_i U_i(c^i)$ and

$$\sum_i \lambda_i \alpha_i \psi \cdot x^i = \psi \cdot x \leq \psi \cdot e = \sum_i \lambda_i \alpha_i \psi \cdot c^i.$$

Putting these two inequalities together, we have

$$\sum_{i=1}^{m} \lambda_i [U_i(x^i) - \alpha_i \psi \cdot (x^i - e^i)] > \sum_{i=1}^{m} \lambda_i [U_i(c^i) - \alpha_i \psi \cdot (c^i - e^i)],$$

which contradicts the fact that, for each agent i, (c^i, α_i) is a saddle point for that agent's problem. ∎

Corollary 1. *If, moreover, $e \gg 0$ and U_λ is continuously differentiable at e, then λ can be chosen so that $\partial U_\lambda(e)$ is a state-price vector, meaning*

$$q = D\partial U_\lambda(e). \tag{7}$$

The differentiability of U_λ at e is implied by the differentiability, for some agent i, of U_i at c^i. (See Exercise 10(C).)

Corollary 2. *Suppose there is a fixed vector p of state probabilities such that, for all i, $U_i(c) = E[u_i(c)] \equiv \sum_{j=1}^{S} p_j u_i(c_j)$, for some $u_i(\cdot)$. Then $U_\lambda(c) = E[u_\lambda(c)]$, where, for each y in $\mathbb{R}_+$,*

$$u_\lambda(y) = \max_{x \in \mathbb{R}^m_+} \sum_{i=1}^{m} \lambda_i u_i(x_i) \quad \text{subject to } x_1 + \cdots + x_m \leq y.$$

In this case, (7) is equivalent to $q = E[Du'_\lambda(e)]$.

Extensions of this *representative-agent* asset pricing formula will crop up frequently in later chapters.

F. State-Price Beta Models

We fix a vector $p \gg 0$ in $\mathbb{R}^S$ of probabilities for this section, and for any x in $\mathbb{R}^S$ we write $E(x) = p_1 x_1 + \cdots + p_S x_S$. For any x and π in $\mathbb{R}^S$, we take $x\pi$ to be the vector $(x_1 \pi_1, \ldots, x_S \pi_S)$. The following version of the *Riesz Representation Theorem* can be shown as an exercise.

Lemma. *Suppose $F : \mathbb{R}^S \to \mathbb{R}$ is linear. Then there is a unique π in $\mathbb{R}^S$ such that, for all x in $\mathbb{R}^S$, we have $F(x) = E(\pi x)$. Moreover, F is strictly increasing if and only if $\pi \gg 0$.*

Corollary. *A dividend-price pair (D, q) admits no arbitrage if and only if there is some $\pi \gg 0$ in $\mathbb{R}^S$ such that $q = E(D\pi)$.*

Proof: Given a state-price vector ψ, let $\pi_s = \psi_s / p_s$. Conversely, if π has the assumed property, then $\psi_s = p_s \pi_s$ defines a state-price vector ψ. ∎

Given (D, q), we refer to any vector π given by this result as a *state-price deflator*. (The terms *state-price density* and *state-price kernel* are often used synonymously with state-price deflator.) For example, the representative-agent pricing model of Corollary 2 of Section E shows that we can take $\pi_s = u'_\lambda(e_s)$.

For any x and y in $\mathbb{R}^S$, the *covariance* $\text{cov}(x, y) \equiv E(xy) - E(x)E(y)$ is a measure of covariation between x and y that is useful in asset pricing applications. For any such x and y with $\text{var}(y) \equiv \text{cov}(y, y) \neq 0$, we can always represent x in the form $x = \alpha + \beta y + \epsilon$, where $\beta = \text{cov}(y, x)/\text{var}(y)$, where $\text{cov}(y, \epsilon) = E(\epsilon) = 0$, and where α is a scalar. This *linear regression* of x on y is uniquely defined. The coefficient β is called the associated *regression coefficient*.

Suppose (D, q) admits no arbitrage. For any portfolio θ with $q \cdot \theta \neq 0$, the *return* on θ is the vector R^θ in $\mathbb{R}^S$ defined by $R^\theta_s = (D^\top \theta)_s / q \cdot \theta$. Fixing a state-price deflator π, for any such portfolio θ, we have $E(\pi R^\theta) = 1$. Suppose there is a *riskless portfolio*, meaning some portfolio θ with constant return R^0. We then call R^0 the *riskless return*. A bit of algebra shows that for any portfolio θ with a return, we have

$$E(R^\theta) - R^0 = -\frac{\text{cov}(R^\theta, \pi)}{E(\pi)}.$$

Thus, covariation with π has a negative effect on expected return, as on might expect from the interpretation of state prices as shadow prices f wealth.

The *correlation* between any x and y in $\mathbb{R}^S$ is zero if either has zero variance, and is otherwise defined by

$$\text{corr}(x, y) = \frac{\text{cov}(x, y)}{\sqrt{\text{var}(x)\,\text{var}(y)}}.$$

There is always a portfolio θ^* solving the problem

$$\sup_\theta \text{corr}(D^\top \theta, \pi). \tag{8}$$

If there is such a portfolio θ^* with a return R^* having nonzero variance, then it can be shown as an exercise that, for any return R^θ,

$$E(R^\theta) - R^0 = \beta_\theta[E(R^*) - R^0], \tag{9}$$

where

$$\beta_\theta = \frac{\text{cov}(R^*, R^\theta)}{\text{var}(R^*)}.$$

If markets are complete, then R^* is of course perfectly correlated with the state-price deflator.

Formula (9) is a *state-price beta model*, showing excess expected returns on portfolios to be proportional to the excess return on a portfolio having maximal correlation with a state-price deflator, where the constant of proportionality is the associated regression coefficient. The formula can be extended to the case in which there is no riskless return. Another exercise carries this idea, under additional assumptions, to the *Capital Asset Pricing Model*, or *CAPM*.

Exercises

1.1 The dividend-price pair (D, q) of Section A is defined to be *weakly arbitrage-free* $q \cdot \theta \geq 0$ whenever $D^\top \theta \geq 0$. Show that (D, q) is weakly arbitrage-free if and only ¹ere exist ("weak" state prices) $\psi \in \mathbb{R}^S_+$ such that $q = D\psi$. This fact is known as 's *Lemma*.

ve the assertion in Section A that (D, q) is arbitrage-free if and only if
s some $\psi \in \mathbb{R}^S_{++}$ such that $q = D\psi$. Instead of following the proof
·ion A, use the following result, sometimes known as the *Theorem of the*

Suppose A is an $m \times n$ matrix. Then one and only one of the following

in $\mathbb{R}^n_{++}$ with $Ax = 0$.
$\mathbb{R}^m$ *with $y^\top A > 0$.*

1.3 Show, for $U(c) \equiv E[u(c)]$ as defined by (3), that (2) is equivalent to (4).

1.4 Prove the existence of an equilibrium as defined in Section D under these assumptions: There exists some portfolio θ with payoff $D^\top \theta > 0$ and, for all i, $e^i \gg 0$ and U_i is continuous, strictly concave, and strictly increasing. This is a demanding exercise, and calls for the following general result.

Kakutani's Fixed Point Theorem. *Suppose Z is a nonempty convex compact subset of $\mathbb{R}^n$, and for each x in Z, $\varphi(x)$ is a nonempty convex compact subset of Z. Suppose also that $\{(x, y) \in Z \times Z : x \in \varphi(y)\}$ is closed. Then there exists x^* in Z such that $x^* \in \varphi(x^*)$.*

1.5 Prove Proposition D. Hint: The maintained assumption of strict monotonicity of $U_i(\cdot)$ should be used.

1.6 Suppose that the endowment allocation $(e^1, \ldots, e^m)$ is Pareto optimal.

(A) Show, as claimed in Section D, that any equilibrium allocation is Pareto optimal.

(B) Suppose that there is some portfolio θ with $D^\top \theta > 0$ and, for all i, that U_i is concave and $e^i \gg 0$. Show that $(e^1, \ldots, e^m)$ is itself an equilibrium allocation.

1.7 Prove Proposition C. Hint: A continuous real-valued function on a compact set has a maximum.

1.8 Prove Corollary 1 of Proposition E.

1.9 Prove Corollary 2 of Proposition E.

1.10 Suppose, in addition to the assumptions of Proposition E, that

  (a) $e = e^1 + \cdots + e^m$ is in $\mathbb{R}^S_{++}$;
  (b) for all i, U_i is concave and twice continuously differentiable in $\mathbb{R}^S_{++}$;
  (c) for all i, c^i is in $\mathbb{R}^S_{++}$ and the Hessian matrix $\partial^2 U(c^i)$, which is negative semi-definite by concavity, is in fact negative definite.

Property (c) can be replaced with the assumption of *regular preferences*, as defined in a source cited in the Notes.

(A) Show that the assumption that U_λ is continuously differentiable at e is justified and, moreover, that for each i there is a scalar $\gamma_i > 0$ such that $\partial U_\lambda(e) = \gamma_i \partial U_i(c^i)$. (This co-linearity is known as "equal marginal rates of substitution," a property of any Pareto optimal allocation.) Hint: Use the following:

Implicit Function Theorem. *Suppose for given m and n that $f : \mathbb{R}^m \times \mathbb{R}^n \to \mathbb{R}^n$ is C^k (k times continuously differentiable) for some $k \geq 1$. Suppose also that the $n \times n$ matrix $\partial_y f(\bar{x}, \bar{y})$ of partial derivatives of f with respect to its second argument is nonsingular at some $(\bar{x}, \bar{y})$. If $f(\bar{x}, \bar{y}) = 0$, then there exist scalars $\epsilon > 0$ and $\delta > 0$ and a C^k function $Z : \mathbb{R}^m \to \mathbb{R}^n$ such that if $\|x - a\| < \epsilon$, then $f[x, Z(x)] = 0$ and $\|Z(x) - b\| < \delta$.*

(B) Show that the negative-definite part of condition (c) is satisfied if $e \gg 0$ and, for all i, U_i is an expected utility function of the form $U_i(c) = E[u_i(c)]$, where u_i is strictly concave with an unbounded derivative on $(0, \infty)$.

(C) Obtain the result of part (A) without assuming the existence of second derivatives of the utilities. (You would therefore not exploit the Hessian matrix or Implicit Function Theorem.) As the first (and main) step, show the following. Given a concave function $f : \mathbb{R}_+^S \to \mathbb{R}$, the *superdifferential* of f at some x in $\mathbb{R}_+^S$ is

$$\partial f(x) = \{ z \in \mathbb{R}^S : f(y) \le f(x) + z \cdot (y - x), \quad y \in \mathbb{R}_+^S \}.$$

For any feasible allocation $(c^1, \ldots, c^m)$ and $\lambda \in \mathbb{R}_+^m$ satisfying $U_\lambda(e) = \sum_i \lambda_i U_i(c^i)$,

$$\partial U_\lambda(e) = \bigcap_{i=1}^m \lambda_i \partial U_i(c_i).$$

1.11 (Binomial Option Pricing). As an application of the results in Section A, consider the following two-state ($S = 2$) option-pricing problem. There are $N = 3$ securities:

- (a) a stock, with initial price $q_1 > 0$ and dividend $D_{11} = Gq_1$ in state 1 and dividend $D_{12} = Bq_1$ in state 2, where $G > B > 0$ are the "good" and "bad" gross returns, respectively;
- (b) a riskless bond, with initial price $q_2 > 0$ and dividend $D_{21} = D_{22} = Rq_2$ in both states (that is, R is the riskless return and R^{-1} is the discount);
- (c) a *call option* on the stock, with initial price $q_3 = C$ and dividend $D_{3j} = (D_{1j} - K)^+ \equiv \max(D_{1j} - K, 0)$ for both states $j = 1$ and $j = 2$, where $K \ge 0$ is the *exercise price* of the option. (The call option gives its holder the right, but not the obligation, to pay K for the stock, with dividend, after the state is revealed.)

(A) Show necessary and sufficient conditions on G, B, and R for the absence of arbitrage involving only the stock and bond.

(B) Assuming no arbitrage for the three securities, calculate the call-option price C explicitly in terms of q_1, G, R, B, and K. Find the state-price probabilities $\hat{\psi}_1$ and $\hat{\psi}_2$ referred to in Section B in terms of G, B, and R, and show that $C = R^{-1}\hat{E}(D_3)$, where $\hat{E}$ denotes expectation with respect to $(\hat{\psi}_1, \hat{\psi}_2)$.

1.12 (CAPM). In the setting of Section D, suppose $(c^1, \ldots, c^m)$ is a strictly positive equilibrium consumption allocation. For any agent i, suppose utility is of the expected-utility form $U_i(c) = E[u_i(c)]$. For any agent i, suppose there are fixed positive constants $\bar{c}$ and b_i such that, for any state j, we have $c_j^i < \bar{c}$ and $u_i(x) = x - b_i x^2$ for all $x \le \bar{c}$.

(A) In the context of Corollary 2 of Section E, show that $u_\lambda'(e) = k - Ke$ for some positive constants k and K. From this, derive the CAPM

$$q = AE(D) - B \operatorname{cov}(D, e), \tag{10}$$

for positive constants A and B, where $\mathrm{cov}(D, e) \in \mathbb{R}^N$ is the vector of covariances between the security dividends and the aggregate endowment.

Suppose for a given portfolio θ that each of the following is well defined:

- the return $R^\theta \equiv D^\top \theta / q \cdot \theta$;
- the return R^M on a portfolio M with payoff $D^\top M = e$;
- the return R^0 on a portfolio θ^0 with $\mathrm{cov}(D^\top \theta^0, e) = 0$;
- $\beta_\theta = \mathrm{cov}(R^\theta, R^M) / \mathrm{var}(R^M)$.

The return R^M is sometimes called the *market return*. The return R^0 is called the *zero-beta return* and is the return on a riskless bond if one exists. Prove the "beta" form of the CAPM

$$E(R^\theta - R^0) = \beta_\theta E(R^M - R^0). \tag{11}$$

(B) Part (A) relies on the completeness of markets. Without any such assumption, but assuming that the equilibrium allocation $(c^1, \ldots, c^m)$ is strictly positive, show that the same beta form (11) applies, provided we extend the definition of the market return R^M to be the return on any portfolio solving

$$\sup_{\theta \in \mathbb{R}^N} \ \mathrm{corr}(R^\theta, e). \tag{12}$$

For complete markets, $\mathrm{corr}(R^M, e) = 1$, so the result of part (A) is a special case.

(C) The CAPM applies essentially as stated without the quadratic expected-utility assumption provided that each agent i is *strictly variance-averse*, in that $U_i(x) > U_i(y)$ whenever $E(x) = E(y)$ and $\mathrm{var}(x) < \mathrm{var}(y)$. Formalize this statement by providing a reasonable set of supporting technical conditions.

We remark that a common alternative formulation of the CAPM allows security portfolios in initial endowments $\hat{\theta}^1, \ldots, \hat{\theta}^m$ with $\sum_{i=1}^m \hat{\theta}^i_j = 1$ for all j. In this case, with the total endowment e redefined by $e = \sum_{i=1}^m (e^i + D^\top \hat{\theta}^i)$, the same CAPM (11) applies. If $e^i = 0$ for all i, then even in incomplete markets, $\mathrm{corr}(R^M, e) = 1$, since (12) is solved by $\theta = (1, 1, \ldots, 1)$. The Notes provide references.

1.13 An *Arrow-Debreu equilibrium* for $[(U_i, e^i), D]$ is a nonzero vector ψ in $\mathbb{R}^S_+$ and a feasible consumption allocation $(c^1, \ldots, c^m)$ such that for each i, c^i solves $\sup_c U_i(c)$ subject to $\psi \cdot c^i \leq \psi \cdot e^i$. Suppose that markets are complete, in that $\mathrm{span}(D) = \mathbb{R}^S$. Show that $(c^1, \ldots, c^m)$ is an Arrow-Debreu consumption allocation if and only if it is an equilibrium consumption allocation in the sense of Section D.

1.14 Suppose (D, q) admits no arbitrage. Show that there is a unique state-price vector if and only if markets are complete.

1.15 (Aggregation). For the "representative-agent" problem (6), suppose for all i that $U_i(c) = E[u(c)]$, where $u(c) = c^\gamma / \gamma$ for some nonzero scalar $\gamma < 1$.

(A) Show, for any nonzero agent weight vector $\lambda \in \mathbb{R}^m_+$, that $U_\lambda(c) = E[kc^\gamma / \gamma]$ for some scalar $k > 0$ and that (6) is solved by $c^i = k_i x$ for some scalar $k_i \geq 0$ that is nonzero if and only if λ_i is nonzero.

(B) With this special utility assumption, show that there exists an equilibrium with a Pareto efficient allocation, without the assumption that markets are complete, but with the assumption that $e^i \in \mathrm{span}(D)$ for all i. Calculate the associated equilibrium allocation.

1.16 (State-Price Beta Model).   This exercise is to prove and extend the state-price beta model (9) of Section F.

(A) Show problem (8) is solved by any portfolio θ such that $\pi = D^\top \theta + \epsilon$, where $\mathrm{cov}(\epsilon, D^j) = 0$ for any security j, where $D^j \in \mathbb{R}^S$ is the payoff of security j.

(B) Given a solution θ to (8) such that R^θ is well defined with nonzero variance, prove (9).

(C) Reformulate (9) for the case in which there is no riskless return by redefining R^0 to be the expected return on any portfolio θ such that R^θ is well defined and $\mathrm{cov}(R^\theta, \pi) = 0$, assuming such a portfolio exists.

1.17   Prove the Riesz representation lemma of Section F. The following hint is perhaps unnecessary in this simple setting but allows the result to be extended to a broad variety of spaces called *Hilbert spaces*. Given a vector space L, a function $(\cdot \mid \cdot) : L \times L \to \mathbb{R}$ is called an *inner product* for L if, for any x, y, and z in L and any scalar α, we have the five properties:

   (a) $(x \mid y) = (y \mid x)$
   (b) $(x + y \mid z) = (x \mid z) + (y \mid z)$
   (c) $(\alpha x \mid y) = \alpha(x \mid y)$
   (d) $(x \mid x) \geq 0$
   (e) $(x \mid x) = 0$ if and only if $x = 0$.

Suppose a finite-dimensional vector space L has an inner product $(\cdot \mid \cdot)$. (This defines a special case of a Hilbert space.) Two vectors x and y are defined to be *orthogonal* if $(x \mid y) = 0$. For any linear subspace H of L and any x in L, it can be shown that there is a unique y in H such that $(x - y \mid z) = 0$ for all z in H. This vector y is the orthogonal projection in L of x onto H, and solves the problem $\min_{h \in H} \|x - h\|$. Let $L = \mathbb{R}^S$. For any x and y in L, let $(x \mid y) = E(xy)$. We must show that given a linear functional F, there is a unique π with $F(x) = (\pi \mid x)$ for all x. Let $J = \{x : F(x) = 0\}$. If $J = L$, then F is the zero functional, and the unique representation is $\pi = 0$. If not, there is some z such that $F(z) = 1$ and $(z \mid x) = 0$ for all x in J. Show this using the idea of orthogonal projection. Then show that $\pi = z/(z \mid z)$ represents F, using the fact that for any x, we have $x - F(x)z \in J$.

1.18   Suppose there are $m = 2$ consumers, A and B, with identical utilities for consumption c_1 and c_2 in states 1 and 2 given by $U(c_1, c_2) = 0.2\sqrt{c_1} + 0.5\log c_2$. There is a total endowment of $e_1 = 25$ units of consumption in state 1.

(A) Suppose that markets are complete and that, in a given equilibrium, consumer A's consumption is 9 units in state 1 and 10 units in state 2. What is the total endowment e_2 in state 2?

(B) Continuing under the assumptions of part (A), suppose there are two securities. The first is a riskless bond paying 10 units of consumption in each state. The second is a risky asset paying 5 units of consumption in state 1 and 10 units in state 2. In equilibrium, what is the ratio of the price of the bond to that of the risky asset?

1.19 There are two states of the world, labeled 1 and 2, two agents, and two securities, both paying units of the consumption numeraire good. The risky security pays a total of 1 unit in state 1 and pays 3 units in state 2. The riskless security pays 1 unit in each state. Each agent is initially endowed with half of the total supply of the risky security. There are no other endowments. (The riskless security is in zero net supply.) The two agents assign equal probabilities to the two states. One of the agents is risk-neutral, with utility function $E(c)$ for state-contingent consumption c, and can consume negatively or positively in both states. The other, risk-averse, agent has utility $E(\sqrt{c})$ for nonnegative state-contingent consumption. Solve for the equilibrium allocation of the two securities in a competitive equilibrium.

1.20 Consider a setting with two assets A and B, only, both paying off the same random variable X, whose value is nonnegative in every state and nonzero with strictly positive probability. Asset A has price p, while asset B has price q. An arbitrage is then a portfolio $(\alpha, \beta) \in \mathbb{R}^2$ of the two assets whose total payoff $\alpha X + \beta X$ is nonnegative and whose initial price $\alpha p + \beta q$ is strictly negative, or whose total payoff is nonzero with strictly positive probability and always nonnegative, and whose initial price is negative or zero.

(A) Assuming no restrictions on portfolios, and no transactions costs or frictions, state the set of arbitrage-free prices (p, q). (State precisely the appropriate subset of $\mathbb{R}^2$.)

(B) Assuming no short sales ($\alpha \geq 0$ and $\beta \geq 0$), state the set of arbitrage-free prices (p, q).

(C) Now suppose that A and B can be short sold, but that asset A can be short sold only by paying an extra fee of $\phi > 0$ per unit sold short. There are no other fees of any kind. Provide the obvious new definition of "no arbitrage" in precise mathematical terms, and state the set of arbitrage-free prices.

Notes

The basic approach of this chapter follows Arrow (1953), taking a general equilibrium perspective originating with Walras (1877). Black (1995) offers a perspective on the general equilibrium approach and a critique of other approaches.

(A) The state-pricing implications of no arbitrage found in Section A originate with Ross (1978).

(B) The idea of "risk-neutral probabilities" apparently originates with Arrow (1970), a revision of Arrow (1953), and appears as well in Drèze (1971).

(C) This material is standard.

(D) Proposition D is the First Welfare Theorem of Arrow (1951) and Debreu (1954). The generic inoptimality of incomplete-markets equilibrium allocations can be gleaned from sources cited by Geanakoplos (1990). Indeed, Geanakoplos and Polemarchakis (1986) show that even a reasonable notion of constrained optimality generically fails in certain incomplete-markets settings. See, however, Kajii (1994) and references cited in the Notes of Chapter 2 for mitigating results. Mas-Colell (1987) and Werner (1991) also treat constrained optimality.

(E) The "representative-agent" approach goes back, at least, to Negishi (1960). The existence of a representative agent is no more than an illustrative simplification in this setting, and should not be confused with the more demanding notion of aggregation of Gorman (1953) found in Exercise 15. In Chapter 10, the existence of a representative agent with smooth utility, based on Exercise 1.11, is important for technical reasons.

(F) The "beta model" for pricing goes back, in the case of mean-variance preferences, to the capital asset pricing model, or CAPM, of Sharpe (1964) and Lintner (1965). The version without a riskless asset is due to Black (1972). Allingham (1991), Berk (1992), Nielsen (1990a), and Nielsen (1990b) address the existence of equilibrium in the CAPM. Characterization of the mean-variance model and two-fund separation is provided by Bottazzi, Hens, and Löffler (1994), Nielsen (1993b), and Nielsen (1993a). Löffler (1996) provides sufficient conditions for variance aversion in terms of mean-variance preferences.

Additional Topics: Ross (1976) introduced the *arbitrage pricing theory*, a multifactor model of asset returns that, in terms of expected returns, can be thought of as an extension of the CAPM. In this regard, see also Bray (1994a), Bray (1994b), and Gilles and LeRoy (1991). Balasko and Cass (1986) and Balasko, Cass, and Siconolfi (1990) treat equilibrium with constrained participation in security trading. See also Hara (1994).

Debreu (1972) provides a notion of regular preferences that substitutes for the existence of a negative-definite Hessian matrix of each agent's utility function at the equilibrium allocation. For more on regular preferences and the differential approach to general equilibrium, see Mas-Colell (1985) and Balasko (1989). Kreps (1988) reviews the theory of choice and utility representations of preferences. For Farkas's and Stiemke's Lemmas, and other forms of the Theorem of the Alternative, see Gale (1960).

Arrow and Debreu (1954) and, in a slightly different model, McKenzie (1954) are responsible for a proof of the existence of complete-markets equilibria. Debreu (1982) surveys the existence problem. Standard introductory treatments of general equilibrium theory are given by Debreu (1959) and Hildenbrand and Kirman (1989). In this setting, with incomplete markets, Polemarchakis and Siconolfi (1993) address the failure of existence unless one has a portfolio θ with payoff $D^\top \theta > 0$. Geanakoplos (1990) surveys other literature on the existence of equilibria in incomplete markets, some of which takes the alternative of defining security payoffs in nominal units of account, while allowing consumption of multiple commodities. Most of the literature allows for an initial period of consumption before the realization of the uncertain state. For a survey, see Magill and Shafer (1991). Additional results on incomplete-markets equilibrium include those of Araujo and Monteiro (1989), Berk (1997), Boyle and Wang (1999), and Weil (1992).

For related results in multiperiod settings, references are cited in the Notes of Chapter 2.

The superdifferentiability result of Exercise 10(C) is due to Skiadas (1995).

Hellwig (1996), Mas-Colell and Monteiro (1996), and Monteiro (1996) have recently shown existence of equilibrium with a continuum of states. Geanakoplos and Polemarchakis (1986) and Chae (1988) show existence in a model closely related to that studied in this chapter. Grodal and Vind (1988) and Yamazaki (1991) show existence with alternative formulations. With multiple commodities or multiple periods, existence is not guaranteed under any natural conditions, as shown by Hart (1975), who gives a counterexample. For these more delicate cases, the literature on generic existence is cited in the Notes of Chapter 2.

The binomial option-pricing formula of Exercise 1.11 is from an early edition of Sharpe (1985), and is extended in Chapter 2 to a multiperiod setting. The hint given for the demonstration of the Riesz representation exercise is condensed from the proof given by Luenberger (1969) of the *Riesz-Frechet Theorem*: For any Hilbert space H with inner product $(\cdot \mid \cdot)$, any continuous linear functional $F : H \to \mathbb{R}$ has a unique π in H such that $F(x) = (\pi \mid x)$, $x \in H$. The Fixed Point Theorem of Exercise 1.4 is from Kakutani (1941).

On the role of default and collateralization, see Geanakoplos and Zame (1999) and Sabarwal (1999). Gottardi and Kajii (1999) study the role and existence of sunspot equilibria. Pietra (1992) treats indeterminacy. Lobo, Fazel, Boyd (1999) address portfolio choice with fixed transactions costs.

2

The Basic Multiperiod Model

THIS CHAPTER EXTENDS the results of Chapter 1 on arbitrage, optimality, and equilibrium to a multiperiod setting. A connection is drawn between state prices and martingales for the purpose of representing security prices. The exercises include the consumption-based capital asset pricing model and the multiperiod "binomial" option pricing model.

A. Uncertainty

As in Chapter 1, there is some finite set, say Ω, of states. In order to handle multiperiod issues, however, we will treat uncertainty a bit more formally as a *probability space* $(\Omega, \mathcal{F}, P)$, with $\mathcal{F}$ denoting the *tribe* of subsets of Ω that are *events* (and can therefore be assigned a probability), and with P a *probability measure* assigning to any event B in $\mathcal{F}$ its probability $P(B)$. Those not familiar with the definition of a probability space can consult Appendix A. The terms "σ-algebra" and "σ-field," among others, are often used in place of the word "tribe."

There are $T + 1$ dates: $0, 1, \ldots, T$. At each of these, a tribe $\mathcal{F}_t \subset \mathcal{F}$ denotes the set of events corresponding to the information available at time t. In effect, an event B in $\mathcal{F}_t$ is known at time t to be true or false. (A definition of tribes in terms of "partitions" of Ω is given in Exercise 2.11.) We adopt the usual convention that $\mathcal{F}_t \subset \mathcal{F}_s$ whenever $t \leq s$, meaning that events are never "forgotten." For simplicity, we also take it that every event in $\mathcal{F}_0$ has probability 0 or 1, meaning roughly that there is no information at time $t = 0$. Taken altogether, the *filtration* $\mathbb{F} = \{\mathcal{F}_0, \ldots, \mathcal{F}_T\}$ represents how information is revealed through time. For any random variable Y, we let $E_t(Y) = E(Y \mid \mathcal{F}_t)$ denote the conditional expectation of Y given $\mathcal{F}_t$. (Appendix A provides definitions of random variables and of conditional expectation.) An *adapted process* is a sequence $X = \{X_0, \ldots, X_T\}$ such that for each t, X_t is a random variable with respect to $(\Omega, \mathcal{F}_t)$. Informally, this means that X_t is observable at time t. An adapted process X is a *martingale* if, for any times t and $s > t$, we have $E_t(X_s) = X_t$. As we shall see, martingales are useful in the characterization of security prices. In order to simplify things, for any two random variables Y and Z, we always write "$Y = Z$" if the probability that $Y \neq Z$ is zero.

B. Security Markets

A security is a claim to an adapted *dividend process*, say δ, with δ_t denoting the dividend paid by the security at time t. Each security has an adapted *security-price process* S, so that S_t is the price of the security, *ex dividend*, at time t. That is, at each time t, the security pays its dividend δ_t and is then available for trade at the price S_t. This convention implies that δ_0 plays no role in determining ex-dividend prices. The *cum-dividend* security price at time t is $S_t + \delta_t$.

Suppose there are N securities defined by the $\mathbb{R}^N$-valued adapted dividend process $\delta = (\delta^{(1)}, \ldots, \delta^{(N)})$. These securities have some adapted price process $S = (S^{(1)}, \ldots, S^{(N)})$. A *trading strategy* is an adapted process θ in $\mathbb{R}^N$. Here, $\theta_t = (\theta_t^{(1)}, \ldots, \theta_t^{(N)})$ represents the portfolio held after trading at time t. The dividend process δ^θ *generated* by a trading strategy θ is defined by

$$\delta_t^\theta = \theta_{t-1} \cdot (S_t + \delta_t) - \theta_t \cdot S_t, \tag{1}$$

with "θ_{-1}" taken to be zero by convention.

C. Arbitrage, State Prices, and Martingales

Given a dividend-price pair (δ, S) for N securities, a trading strategy θ is an *arbitrage* if $\delta^\theta > 0$. (The reader should become convinced that this is the same notion of arbitrage defined in Chapter 1.) Let Θ denote the space of trading strategies. For any θ and φ in Θ and scalars a and b, we have $a\delta^\theta + b\delta^\varphi = \delta^{a\theta+b\varphi}$. Thus the *marketed subspace* $M = \{\delta^\theta : \theta \in \Theta\}$ of dividend processes generated by trading strategies is a linear subspace of the space L of adapted processes.

Proposition. *There is no arbitrage if and only if there is a strictly increasing linear function $F : L \to \mathbb{R}$ such that $F(\delta^\theta) = 0$ for any trading strategy θ.*

Proof: The proof is almost identical to that of Theorem 1A. Let $L_+ = \{c \in L : c \geq 0\}$. There is no arbitrage if and only if the cone L_+ and the marketed subspace M intersect precisely at zero. Suppose there is no arbitrage. The Separating Hyperplane Theorem, in a form given in Appendix B for cones, implies the existence of a nonzero linear functional F such that $F(x) < F(y)$ for each x in M and each nonzero y in L_+. Since M is a linear subspace, this implies that $F(x) = 0$ for each x in M, and thus that $F(y) > 0$ for each nonzero y in L_+. This implies that F is strictly increasing. The converse is immediate. ∎

The following result gives a convenient *Riesz representation* of a linear function on the space of adapted processes. Proof is left as an exercise, extending the single-period Riesz representation lemma of Section 1F.

Lemma. *For each linear function $F : L \to \mathbb{R}$, there is a unique π in L, called the Riesz representation of F, such that*

$$F(x) = E\left(\sum_{t=0}^{T} \pi_t x_t \right), \qquad x \in L.$$

If F is strictly increasing, then π is strictly positive.

For convenience, we call any strictly positive adapted process a *deflator*. A deflator π is a *state-price deflator* if, for all t,

$$S_t = \frac{1}{\pi_t} E_t\left(\sum_{j=t+1}^{T} \pi_j \delta_j \right). \qquad (2)$$

A state-price deflator is variously known in the literature as a *state-price density*, a *pricing kernel*, and a *marginal-rate-of-substitution process*.

For $t = T$, the right-hand side of (2) is zero, so $S_T = 0$ whenever there is a state-price deflator. The notion here of a state-price deflator is a natural extension of that of Chapter 1. It can be shown as an exercise that a deflator π is a state-price deflator if and only if, for any trading strategy θ,

$$\theta_t \cdot S_t = \frac{1}{\pi_t} E_t\left(\sum_{j=t+1}^{T} \pi_j \delta_j^\theta \right), \qquad t < T, \qquad (3)$$

meaning roughly that the market value of a trading strategy is, at any time, the state-price discounted expected future dividends generated by the strategy. The *cum-dividend* value process V^θ of a trading strategy θ is defined by $V_t^\theta = \theta_{t-1} \cdot (S_t + \delta_t)$. If π is a state-price deflator, we have

$$V_t^\theta = \frac{1}{\pi_t} E_t\left(\sum_{j=t}^{T} \pi_j \delta_j^\theta \right).$$

The *gain process* G for (δ, S) is defined by $G_t = S_t + \sum_{j=1}^{t} \delta_j$, the price plus accumulated dividend. Given a deflator γ, the *deflated gain process* G^γ is defined by $G_t^\gamma = \gamma_t S_t + \sum_{j=1}^{t} \gamma_j \delta_j$. We can think of deflation as a change of numeraire.

Theorem. *The dividend-price pair (δ, S) admits no arbitrage if and only if there is a state-price deflator. A deflator π is a state-price deflator if and only if $S_T = 0$ and the state-price-deflated gain process G^π is a martingale.*

Proof: It can be shown as an easy exercise that a deflator π is a state-price deflator if and only if $S_T = 0$ and the state-price-deflated gain process G^π is a martingale.

Suppose there is no arbitrage. Then $S_T = 0$, for otherwise the strategy θ is an arbitrage when defined by $\theta_t = 0$, $t < T$, $\theta_T = -S_T$. The previous proposition implies that there is some strictly increasing linear function $F : L \to \mathbb{R}$ such that $F(\delta^\theta) = 0$ for any strategy θ. By the previous lemma, there is some deflator π such that $F(x) = E(\sum_{t=0}^{T} x_t \pi_t)$ for all x in L. This implies that $E(\sum_{t=0}^{T} \delta_t^\theta \pi_t) = 0$ for any strategy θ.

We must prove (2), or equivalently, that G^π is a martingale. From Appendix A, an adapted process X is a martingale if and only if $E(X_\tau) = X_0$ for any stopping time $\tau \leq T$. Consider, for an arbitrary security n and an arbitrary stopping time $\tau \leq T$, the trading strategy θ defined by $\theta^{(k)} = 0$ for $k \neq n$ and $\theta_t^{(n)} = 1$, $t < \tau$, with $\theta_t^{(n)} = 0$, $t \geq \tau$. Since $E(\sum_{t=0}^{T} \pi_t \delta_t^\theta) = 0$, we have

$$E\left(-S_0^{(n)} \pi_0 + \sum_{t=1}^{\tau} \pi_t \delta_t^{(n)} + \pi_\tau S_\tau^{(n)} \right) = 0,$$

implying that the deflated gain process $G^{n\pi}$ of security n satisfies $G_0^{n,\pi} = E(G_\tau^{n,\pi})$. Since τ is arbitrary, $G^{n,\pi}$ is a martingale, and since n is arbitrary, G^π is a martingale.

This shows that absence of arbitrage implies the existence of a state-price deflator. The converse is easy. ∎

D. Individual Agent Optimality

We introduce an agent, defined by a strictly increasing utility function U on the set L_+ of nonnegative adapted "consumption" processes, and by an *endowment process* e in L_+. Given a dividend-price process (δ, S), a trading strategy θ leaves the agent with the total consumption process $e + \delta^\theta$. Thus the agent has the *budget-feasible consumption set*

$$X = \{e + \delta^\theta \in L_+ : \theta \in \Theta\},$$

and the problem

$$\sup_{c \in X} U(c). \tag{4}$$

The existence of a solution to (4) implies the absence of arbitrage. Conversely, it can be shown as an exercise that if U is continuous, then the absence of arbitrage implies that there exists a solution to (4). For purposes of checking continuity or the closedness of sets in L, we will say that c_n converges to c if $E[\sum_{t=0}^T |c_n(t) - c(t)|] \to 0$. Then U is continuous if $U(c_n) \to U(c)$ whenever $c_n \to c$.

Suppose that (4) has a strictly positive solution c^* and that U is continuously differentiable at c^*. We can use the first-order conditions for optimality (which can be reviewed in Appendix B) to characterize security prices in terms of the derivatives of the utility function U at c^*. Specifically, for any c in L, the derivative of U at c^* in the direction c is the derivative $g'(0)$, where $g(\alpha) = U(c^* + \alpha c)$ for any scalar α sufficiently small in absolute value. That is, $g'(0)$ is the marginal rate of improvement of utility as one moves in the direction c away from c^*. This derivative is denoted $\nabla U(c^*; c)$. Because U is continuously differentiable at c^*, the function $c \mapsto \nabla U(c^*; c)$, on L into $\mathbb{R}$, is linear. Since δ^θ is a budget-feasible direction of change for any trading strategy θ, the first-order conditions for optimality of c^* imply that

$$\nabla U(c^*; \delta^\theta) = 0, \qquad \theta \in \Theta.$$

We now have a characterization of a state-price deflator.

Proposition. *Suppose that* (4) *has a strictly positive solution* c^* *and that* U *has a strictly positive continuous derivative at* c^*. *Then there is no arbitrage and a state-price deflator is given by the Riesz representation* π *of* $\nabla U(c^*)$:

$$\nabla U(c^*; x) = E\left(\sum_{t=0}^T \pi_t x_t \right), \qquad x \in L.$$

Despite our standing assumption that U is strictly increasing, $\nabla U(c^*; \cdot)$ need not in general be strictly increasing, but is so if U is concave.

As an example, suppose U has the *additive* form

$$U(c) = E\left[\sum_{t=0}^T u_t(c_t) \right], \qquad c \in L_+, \tag{5}$$

for some $u_t : \mathbb{R}_+ \to \mathbb{R}$, $t \geq 0$. It is an exercise to show that if $\nabla U(c)$ exists, then

$$\nabla U(c; x) = E\left[\sum_{t=0}^{T} u_t'(c_t) x_t \right]. \tag{6}$$

If, for all t, u_t is concave with an unbounded derivative and e is strictly positive, then any solution c^* to (4) is strictly positive.

Corollary. *Suppose U is defined by (5). Under the conditions of the proposition, for any times t and $\tau \geq t$,*

$$S_t = \frac{1}{u_t'(c_t^*)} E_t\left[S_\tau u_\tau'(c_\tau^*) + \sum_{j=t+1}^{\tau} \delta_j u_j'(c_j^*) \right].$$

For the case $\tau = t + 1$, this result is often called the *stochastic Euler equation*. Extending this classical result for additive utility, the exercises include other utility examples such as *habit-formation* utility and *recursive* utility. As in Chapter 1, we now turn to the multi-agent case.

E. Equilibrium and Pareto Optimality

Suppose there are m agents. Agent i is defined as above by a strictly increasing utility function $U_i : L_+ \to \mathbb{R}$ and an endowment process $e^{(i)}$ in L_+. Given a dividend process δ for N securities, an *equilibrium* is a collection $(\theta^{(1)}, \dots, \theta^{(m)}, S)$, where S is a security-price process and, for each i, $\theta^{(i)}$ is a trading strategy solving

$$\sup_{\theta \in \Theta} U_i(c) \text{ subject to } c = e^{(i)} + \delta^\theta \in L_+, \tag{7}$$

with $\sum_{i=1}^{m} \theta^{(i)} = 0$.

We define markets to be *complete* if, for each process x in L, there is some trading strategy θ with $\delta_t^\theta = x_t$, $t \geq 1$. Complete markets thus means that any consumption process x can be obtained by investing some amount at time 0 in a trading strategy that generates the dividend x_t in each future period t. With the same definition of Pareto optimality, Proposition 1D carries over to this multiperiod setting. Any equilibrium $(\theta^{(1)}, \dots, \theta^{(m)}, S)$ has an associated feasible consumption allocation $(c^{(1)}, \dots, c^{(m)})$ defined by letting $c^{(i)} - e^{(i)}$ be the dividend process generated by $\theta^{(i)}$.

Proposition. *Suppose $(\theta^{(1)}, \dots, \theta^{(m)}, S)$ is an equilibrium and markets are complete. Then the associated consumption allocation is Pareto optimal.*

The completeness of markets depends on the security-price process S itself. Indeed, the dependence of the marketed subspace on S makes the existence of an equilibrium a nontrivial issue. We ignore existence here and refer to the Notes for some relevant sources.

F. Equilibrium Asset Pricing

Again following the ideas in Chapter 1, we define for each λ in $\mathbb{R}^m_+$ the utility function $U_\lambda : L_+ \to \mathbb{R}$ by

$$U_\lambda(x) = \sup_{(c^{(1)}, \ldots, c^{(m)})} \sum_{i=1}^m \lambda_i U_i(c^i) \qquad \text{subject to } c^{(1)} + \cdots + c^{(m)} \le x. \qquad (8)$$

Proposition. *Suppose for all i that U_i is concave and strictly increasing. Suppose that $(\theta^{(1)}, \ldots, \theta^{(m)}, S)$ is an equilibrium and that markets are complete. Then there exists some nonzero $\lambda \in \mathbb{R}^m_+$ such that $(0, S)$ is a (no-trade) equilibrium for the one-agent economy $[(U_\lambda, e), \delta]$, where $e = e^{(1)} + \cdots + e^{(m)}$. With this λ and with $x = e = e^{(1)} + \cdots + e^{(m)}$, problem (8) is solved by the equilibrium consumption allocation.*

Proof is assigned as an exercise. The result is essentially the same as Proposition 1E. A method of proof, as well as the intuition for this proposition, is that with complete markets, a state-price deflator π represents Lagrange multipliers for consumption in the various periods and states for all of the agents simultaneously, as well as for the *representative agent* (U_λ, e).

Corollary 1. *If, moreover, U_λ is differentiable at e, then λ can be chosen so that for any times t and $\tau \ge t$, there is a state-price deflator π equal to the Riesz representation of $\nabla U_\lambda(e)$.*

Differentiability of U_λ at e can be shown by the arguments used in Exercise 1.10.

Corollary 2. *Suppose for each i that U_i is of the additive form*

$$U_i(c) = E\left[\sum_{t=0}^T u_{it}(c_t) \right].$$

Then U_λ is also additive, with

$$U_\lambda(c) = E\left[\sum_{t=0}^T u_{\lambda t}(c_t) \right],$$

where

$$u_{\lambda t}(y) = \sup_{x \in \mathbb{R}_+^m} \sum_{i=1}^{m} \lambda_i u_{it}(x_i) \qquad subject\ to\ x_1 + \cdots + x_m \leq y.$$

In this case, the differentiability of U_λ at e implies that for any times t and $\tau \geq t$,

$$S_t = \frac{1}{u'_{\lambda t}(e_t)} E_t \left[u'_{\lambda \tau}(e_\tau) S_\tau + \sum_{j=t+1}^{\tau} u'_{\lambda j}(e_j) \delta_j \right]. \qquad (9)$$

G. Arbitrage and Martingale Measures

This section shows the equivalence between the absence of arbitrage and the existence of a probability measure Q with the property, roughly speaking, that the price of a security is the sum of Q-expected discounted dividends.

There is *short-term riskless borrowing* if, for each given time $t < T$, there is a security trading strategy θ with $\delta_{t+1}^\theta = 1$ and with $\delta_s^\theta = 0$ for $s < t$ and $s > t+1$. The associated *discount* is $d_t = \theta_t \cdot S_t$. If there is no arbitrage, the discount d_t is uniquely defined and strictly positive, and we may define the associated *short rate* r_t by $1 + r_t = 1/d_t$. This means that at any time $t < T$, one may invest one unit of account in order to receive $1 + r_t$ units of account at time $t + 1$. We refer to $\{r_0, r_1, \ldots, r_{T-1}\}$ as the associated "short-rate process," even though r_T is not defined.

We suppose throughout this section that there is short-term riskless borrowing at some uniquely defined short-rate process r. We can define, for any times t and $\tau \leq T$,

$$R_{t,\tau} = (1 + r_t)(1 + r_{t+1}) \cdots (1 + r_{\tau-1}),$$

the payback at time τ of one unit of account borrowed risklessly at time t and "rolled over" in short-term borrowing repeatedly until date τ.

It would be a simple situation, both computationally and conceptually, if any security's price were merely the expected discounted dividends of the security. Of course, this is unlikely to be the case in a market with risk-averse investors. We can nevertheless come close to this sort of characterization of security prices by adjusting the original probability measure P. For this, we define a new probability measure Q to be *equivalent* to P if Q and P assign zero probabilities to the same events. An equivalent probability measure Q is an *equivalent martingale measure* if

$$S_t = E_t^Q \left(\sum_{j=t+1}^{T} \frac{\delta_j}{R_{t,j}} \right), \qquad t < T,$$

where E^Q denotes expectation under Q, and likewise $E_t^Q(x) = E^Q(x|\mathcal{F}_t)$ for any random variable x. An equivalent martingale measure is often called a *risk-neutral measure.*

It is easy to show that Q is an equivalent martingale measure if and only if, for any trading strategy θ,

$$\theta_t \cdot S_t = E_t^Q\left(\sum_{j=t+1}^{T} \frac{\delta_j^\theta}{R_{t,j}} \right), \qquad t < T. \tag{10}$$

If interest rates are deterministic, (10) is merely the total discounted expected dividends, after substituting Q for the original measure P. We will show that the absence of arbitrage is equivalent to the existence of an equivalent martingale measure.

The deflator γ defined by $\gamma_t = R_{0,t}^{-1}$ defines the *discounted gain process* G^γ. The word "martingale" in the term "equivalent martingale measure" comes from the following equivalence.

Lemma. *A probability measure Q equivalent to P is an equivalent martingale measure for (δ, S) if and only if $S_T = 0$ and the discounted gain process G^γ is a martingale with respect to Q.*

We already know from Theorem C that the absence of arbitrage is equivalent to the existence of a state-price deflator π. As explained in Appendix A, a probability measure Q equivalent to P can be defined in terms of a Radon-Nikodym derivative, a strictly positive random variable $\frac{dQ}{dP}$ with $E(\frac{dQ}{dP}) = 1$, via the definition of expectation with respect to Q given by $E^Q(Z) = E(\frac{dQ}{dP}Z)$, for any random variable Z. We will choose a particular equivalent probability measure Q by the Radon-Nikodym derivative $\frac{dQ}{dP} = \xi_T$, where

$$\xi_T = \frac{\pi_T R_{0,T}}{\pi_0}.$$

(Indeed, one can check that ξ_T is strictly positive and of expectation 1.) The *density process* ξ for Q is defined by $\xi_t = E_t(\xi_T)$. Relation (A.2) of Appendix A implies that for any times t and $j > t$, and any $\mathcal{F}_j$-measurable random variable Z_j,

$$E_t^Q(Z_j) = \frac{1}{\xi_t} E_t(\xi_j Z_j). \tag{11}$$

Fixing some time $t < T$, consider a trading strategy θ that invests one unit of account at time t and repeatedly rolls the value over in short-term riskless borrowing until time T, with final value $R_{t,T}$. That is, $\theta_t \cdot S_t = 1$ and $\delta_T^\theta = R_{t,T}$. Relation (3) then implies that

$$\pi_t = E_t(\pi_T R_{t,T}) = \frac{E_t(\pi_T R_{0,T})}{R_{0,t}} = \frac{E_t(\xi_T \pi_0)}{R_{0,t}} = \frac{\xi_t \pi_0}{R_{0,t}}. \tag{12}$$

From (11), (12), and the definition of a state-price deflator, (10) is satisfied, so Q is indeed an equivalent martingale measure. We have shown the following result.

Theorem. *There is no arbitrage if and only if there exists an equivalent martingale measure. Moreover, π is a state-price deflator if and only if an equivalent martingale measure Q has the density process ξ defined by $\xi_t = R_{0,t} \pi_t / \pi_0$.*

Proposition. *Suppose that $\mathcal{F}_T = \mathcal{F}$ and there is no arbitrage. Then markets are complete if and only if there is a unique equivalent martingale measure.*

Proof: Suppose that markets are complete and let Q_1 and Q_2 be two equivalent martingale measures. We must show that $Q_1 = Q_2$. Let A be any event. Since markets are complete, there is a trading strategy θ with dividend process δ^θ such that $\delta_T^\theta = R_{0,T} 1_A$ and $\delta_t^\theta = 0$, $0 < t < T$. By (10), we have $\theta_0 \cdot S_0 = Q_1(A) = Q_2(A)$. Since A is arbitrary, $Q_1 = Q_2$.

Exercise 2.18 outlines a proof of the converse part of the result. ∎

This martingale approach simplifies many asset pricing problems that might otherwise appear to be quite complex. This approach also applies much more generally than indicated here. For example, the assumption of short-term borrowing is merely a convenience. More generally, as elaborated in Chapter 6, one can typically obtain an equivalent martingale measure after normalizing prices and dividends by the price of some particular security (or trading strategy).

H. Valuation of Redundant Securities

Suppose that the given dividend-price pair (δ, S) is arbitrage-free, with an associated state-price deflator π. Now consider the introduction of a new security with dividend process $\hat{\delta}$ and price process $\hat{S}$. We say that $\hat{\delta}$ is *redundant* given (δ, S) if there exists a trading strategy θ, with respect to only the original security dividend-price process (δ, S), that *replicates* $\hat{\delta}$, in the sense that $\delta_t^\theta = \hat{\delta}_t$, $t \geq 1$. In this case, the absence of arbitrage for the "augmented" dividend-price process $[(\delta, \hat{\delta}), (S, \hat{S})]$ implies that $\hat{S}_t = Y_t$, where

$$Y_t = \frac{1}{\pi_t} E_t \left(\sum_{j=t+1}^{T} \pi_j \hat{\delta}_j \right), \qquad t < T.$$

If this were not the case, there would be an arbitrage, as follows. For example, suppose that for some stopping time τ, we have $\hat{S}_\tau > Y_\tau$, and that $\tau \leq T$ with strictly positive probability. We can then define the strategy:

(a) Sell the redundant security $\hat{\delta}$ at time τ for $\hat{S}_\tau$, and hold this position until T.

(b) Invest $\theta_\tau \cdot S_\tau$ at time τ in the replicating strategy θ, and follow this strategy until T.

Since the dividends generated by this combined strategy (a)–(b) after τ are zero, the only dividend is at τ for the amount $\hat{S}_\tau - Y_\tau > 0$, which means that this is an arbitrage. Likewise, if $\hat{S}_\tau < Y_\tau$ for some nontrivial stopping time τ, the opposite strategy is an arbitrage. We have shown the following.

Proposition. *Suppose (δ, S) is arbitrage-free with state-price deflator π. Let $\hat{\delta}$ be a redundant dividend process with price process $\hat{S}$. Then the augmented dividend-price pair $[(\delta, \hat{\delta}), (S, \hat{S})]$ is arbitrage-free if and only if it has π as a state-price deflator.*

In applications, it is often assumed that (δ, S) generates complete markets, in which case any additional security is redundant. Exercise 2.1 gives a classical example in which the redundant security is an option on one of the original securities.

I. American Exercise Policies and Valuation

We now extend our pricing framework to include a family of securities, called "American," for which there is discretion regarding the timing of cash flows.

Given an adapted process X, each finite-valued stopping time τ generates a dividend process $\delta^{X,\tau}$ defined by $\delta_t^{X,\tau} = 0, t \neq \tau$, and $\delta_\tau^{X,\tau} = X_\tau$. In this context, a finite-valued stopping time is an *exercise policy*, determining the time at which to accept payment. Any exercise policy τ is constrained by $\tau \leq \bar{\tau}$, for some *expiration time* $\bar{\tau} \leq T$. (In what follows, we might take $\bar{\tau}$ to be a stopping time, which is useful for the case of certain *knockout options*, as shown for example in Exercise 2.1.) We say that $(X, \bar{\tau})$ defines an *American security*. The exercise policy is selected by the holder of the security. Once exercised, the security has no remaining cash flows. A standard example is an American put option on a security with price process p. The American put gives the holder of the option the right, but not the obligation, to sell the underlying security for a fixed exercise price at any time before a given expiration time $\bar{\tau}$. If the option has an exercise price K and expiration time $\bar{\tau} < T$, then $X_t = (K - p_t)^+$, $t \le \bar{\tau}$, and $X_t = 0$, $t > \bar{\tau}$.

We will suppose that, in addition to an American security $(X, \bar{\tau})$, there are securities with an arbitrage-free dividend-price process (δ, S) that generates complete markets. The assumption of complete markets will dramatically simplify our analysis since it implies, for any exercise policy τ, that the dividend process $\delta^{X,\tau}$ is redundant given (δ, S). For notational convenience, we assume that $0 < \bar{\tau} < T$.

Let π be a state-price deflator associated with (δ, S). From Proposition H, given any exercise policy τ, the American security's dividend process $\delta^{X,\tau}$ has an associated cum-dividend price process, say V^τ, which, in the absence of arbitrage, satisfies

$$V_t^\tau = \frac{1}{\pi_t} E_t(\pi_\tau X_\tau), \qquad t \le \tau.$$

This value does not depend on which state-price deflator is chosen because, with complete markets, state-price deflators are all equal up to a positive rescaling, as one can see from the theorem and proposition of Section G.

We consider the optimal stopping problem

$$V_0^* \equiv \max_{\tau \in \mathcal{T}(0)} V_0^\tau, \tag{13}$$

where, for any time $t \le \bar{\tau}$, we let $\mathcal{T}(t)$ denote the set of stopping times bounded below by t and above by $\bar{\tau}$. A solution to (13) is called a *rational exercise policy* for the American security X, in the sense that it maximizes the initial arbitrage-free value of the resulting claim.

We claim that in the absence of arbitrage, the actual initial price V_0 for the American security must be the "rational value" V_0^*. In order to see this, suppose first that $V_0^* > V_0$. Then one could buy the American security, adopt for it a rational exercise policy τ, and also undertake a trading strategy replicating $-\delta^{X,\tau}$. Since $V_0^* = E(\pi_\tau X_\tau)/\pi_0$, this replication involves an initial payoff of V_0^*, and the net effect is a total initial dividend of $V_0^* - V_0 > 0$ and zero dividends after time 0, which defines an arbitrage.

Thus the absence of arbitrage easily leads to the conclusion that $V_0 \geq V_0^*$. It remains to show that the absence of arbitrage also implies the opposite inequality $V_0 \leq V_0^*$.

Suppose that $V_0 > V_0^*$. One could sell the American security at time 0 for V_0. We will show that for an initial investment of V_0^*, one can "super-replicate" the payoff at exercise demanded by the holder of the American security, *regardless of the exercise policy used*. Specifically, a *super-replicating trading strategy* for $(X, \bar{\tau}, \delta, S)$ is a trading strategy θ involving only the securities with dividend-price process (δ, S) that has the properties:

(a) $\delta_t^\theta = 0$ for $0 < t < \bar{\tau}$, and
(b) $V_t^\theta \geq X_t$ for all $t \leq \bar{\tau}$,

where, we recall, V_t^θ is the cum-dividend value of θ at time t. Regardless of the exercise policy τ used by the holder of the security, the payment of X_τ demanded at time τ is dominated by the market value V_t^θ of a super-replicating strategy θ. (In effect, one modifies θ by liquidating the portfolio θ_τ at time τ, so that the actual trading strategy φ associated with the arbitrage is defined by $\varphi_t = \theta_t$ for $t < \tau$ and $\varphi_t = 0$ for $t \geq \tau$.) Now, suppose θ is super-replicating, with $V_0^\theta = V_0^*$. If, indeed, $V_0 > V_0^*$, then the strategy of selling the American security and adopting a super-replicating strategy, liquidating at exercise, effectively defines an arbitrage.

This notion of arbitrage for American securities, an extension of the notion of arbitrage used earlier in the chapter, is reasonable because a super-replicating strategy does not depend on the exercise policy adopted by the holder (or sequence of holders over time) of the American security. It would be unreasonable to call a strategy involving a short position in the American security an "arbitrage" if, in carrying it out, one requires knowledge of the exercise policy for the American security that will be adopted by other agents that hold the security over time, who may after all act "irrationally."

Proposition. *Given $(X, \bar{\tau}, \delta, S)$, suppose (δ, S) is arbitrage-free and generates complete markets. Then there is a super-replicating trading strategy θ for $(X, \bar{\tau}, \delta, S)$ with the initial value $V_0^\theta = V_0^*$.*

In order to construct a super-replicating strategy, we will make a short excursion into the theory of optimal stopping. For any process Y in L, the *Snell envelope* W of Y is defined by

$$W_t = \max_{\tau \in \mathcal{T}(t)} E_t(Y_\tau), \qquad 0 \leq t \leq \bar{\tau}.$$

It can be shown as an exercise that for any $t < \bar{\tau}$, $W_t = \max[Y_t,$ $E_t(W_{t+1})]$. Thus $W_t \geq E_t(W_{t+1})$, implying that W is a supermartingale. As explained in Appendix A, this implies that we can decompose W in the form $W = Z - A$, for some martingale Z and some increasing adapted process A with $A_0 = 0$. This decomposition is illustrated in Figure 2.1 for the case in which Y is a deterministic process, which implies that W, Z, and A are also deterministic.

In order to prove Proposition I, we define Y by $Y_t = X_t \pi_t$, and let W, Z, and A be defined as above. By the definition of complete markets, there is a trading strategy θ with the property that

- $\delta_t^\theta = 0$ for $0 < t < \bar{\tau}$;
- $\delta_{\bar{\tau}}^\theta = Z_{\bar{\tau}} / \pi_{\bar{\tau}}$;
- $\delta_t^\theta = 0$ for $t > \bar{\tau}$.

Property (a) of a super-replicating strategy is satisfied by this strategy θ. From the fact that Z is a martingale and the definition of a state-price deflator, the cum-dividend value V^θ of the trading strategy θ satisfies

$$\pi_t V_t^\theta = E_t(\pi_{\bar{\tau}} \delta_{\bar{\tau}}^\theta) = E_t(Z_{\bar{\tau}}) = Z_t, \qquad t \leq \bar{\tau}. \tag{14}$$

From (14) and the fact that $A_0 = 0$, we know that $V_0^\theta = V_0^*$ because $Z_0 = W_0 = \pi_0 V_0^*$. Since $Z_t - A_t = W_t \geq Y_t$ for all t, from (14) we also know that

$$V_t^\theta = \frac{Z_t}{\pi_t} \geq \frac{1}{\pi_t}(Y_t + A_t) = X_t + \frac{A_t}{\pi_t} \geq X_t, \qquad t \leq \bar{\tau},$$

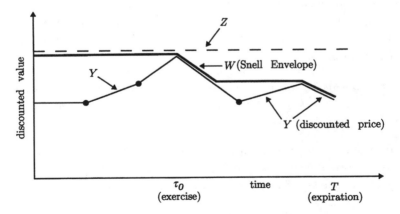

Figure 2.1. *Snell Envelope and Optimal Stopping Rule: Deterministic Case*

the last inequality following from the fact that $A_t \geq 0$ for all t. Thus the dominance property (b) is also satisfied, and θ is indeed a super-replicating strategy with $V_0^\theta = V_0^*$. This proves the proposition and implies that unless there is an arbitrage, the initial price V_0 of the American security is equal to the market value V_0^* associated with a rational exercise policy.

The Snell envelope W is also the key to finding a rational exercise policy. As for the deterministic case illustrated in Figure 2.1, a rational exercise policy is given by $\tau^0 = \min\{t : W_t = Y_t\}$. We now show the optimality of τ^0. First, we know that if τ is a rational exercise policy, then $W_\tau = Y_\tau$. (This can be seen from the fact that $W_\tau \geq Y_\tau$, and if $W_\tau > Y_\tau$, then τ cannot be rational.) From this fact, any rational exercise policy τ has the property that $\tau \geq \tau^0$. For any such τ, we have

$$E_{\tau^0}[Y(\tau)] \leq W(\tau^0) = Y(\tau^0),$$

and the law of iterated expectations implies that $E[Y(\tau)] \leq E[Y(\tau^0)]$, so τ^0 is rational.

We have shown the following.

Theorem. *Given $(X, \bar{\tau}, \delta, S)$, suppose (δ, S) generates complete markets. Suppose there is a state-price deflator π for (δ, S), and let W be the Snell envelope of $X\pi$ up to the expiration time $\bar{\tau}$. Then a rational exercise policy for $(X, \bar{\tau}, \delta, S)$ is given by $\tau^0 = \min\{t : W_t = \pi_t X_t\}$. The unique initial cum-dividend arbitrage-free price of the American security is*

$$V_0^* = \frac{1}{\pi_0} E[X(\tau^0)\pi(\tau^0)].$$

J. Is Early Exercise Optimal?

With the equivalent martingale measure Q defined in Section G, we can also write the optimal stopping problem (13) in the form

$$V_0^* = \max_{\tau \in \mathcal{T}(0)} E^Q\left(\frac{X_\tau}{R_{0,\tau}}\right). \tag{15}$$

This representation of the rational exercise problem is sometimes convenient. For example, let us consider the case of an American call option on a security with price process p. We have $X_t = (p_t - K)^+$ for some exercise price K. Suppose the underlying security has no dividends before or at the expiration time $\bar{\tau}$. We suppose positive interest rates, meaning that $R_{t,s} \geq 1$ for all t and $s \geq t$. With these assumptions, we will show that it is never optimal to exercise the call option before its expiration date $\bar{\tau}$.

This property is sometimes called "no early exercise," or "better alive than dead."

We define the "discounted price process" p^* by $p_t^* = p_t / R_{0,t}$. The fact that the underlying security pays dividends only after the expiration time $\bar{\tau}$ implies, by Lemma G, that p^* is a Q-martingale at least up to the expiration time $\bar{\tau}$. That is, for $t \leq s \leq \bar{\tau}$, we have $E_t^Q(p_s^*) = p_t^*$.

Jensen's Inequality can be used to show the following fact about convex functions of martingales, which we will use to obtain conditions for the no-early-exercise result.

Lemma. *Suppose $f : \mathbb{R} \times \mathbb{R} \to \mathbb{R}$ is convex with respect to its first argument, Y is a martingale, $\tau(1)$ and $\tau(2)$ are two stopping times with $\tau(2) \geq \tau(1)$, and Z is an adapted process. Then $f(Y_{\tau(1)}, Z_{\tau(1)}) \leq E_{\tau(1)}[f(Y_{\tau(2)}, Z_{\tau(1)})]$. Moreover, the law of iterated expectations implies that $E[f(Y_{\tau(1)}, Z_{\tau(1)})] \leq E[f(Y_{\tau(2)}, Z_{\tau(1)})]$.*

With the benefit of this lemma and positive interest rates, we have, for any stopping time $\tau \leq \bar{\tau}$,

$$E^Q \left[\frac{1}{R_{0,\tau}} (p_\tau - K)^+ \right] = E^Q \left[\left(p_\tau^* - \frac{K}{R_{0,\tau}} \right)^+ \right]$$

$$\leq E^Q \left[\left(p_{\bar{\tau}}^* - \frac{K}{R_{0,\tau}} \right)^+ \right]$$

$$\leq E^Q \left[\left(p_{\bar{\tau}}^* - \frac{K}{R_{0,\bar{\tau}}} \right)^+ \right]$$

$$= E^Q \left[\frac{1}{R_{0,\bar{\tau}}} (p_{\bar{\tau}} - K)^+ \right].$$

It follows that $\bar{\tau}$ is a rational exercise policy. In typical cases, $\bar{\tau}$ is the unique rational exercise policy.

If the underlying security pays dividends before expiration, then early exercise of the American call is, in certain cases, optimal. From the fact that the put payoff is increasing in the strike price (as opposed to decreasing for the call option), the second inequality above is reversed for the case of a put option, and one can guess that early exercise of the American put is sometimes optimal.

Exercise 2.1 gives a simple example of American security valuation in a complete-markets setting. Chapter 3 presents the idea in a Markovian setting, which offers computational advantages in solving for the rational exercise policy and market value of American securities. In Chapter 3 we also consider the case of American securities that offer dividends before expiration.

The real difficulties with analyzing American securities begin with incomplete markets. In that case, the choice of exercise policy may play a role in determining the marketed subspace, and therefore a role in pricing securities. If the state-price deflator depends on the exercise policy, it could even turn out that the notion of a rational exercise policy is not well defined.

Exercises

2.1 Suppose in the setting of Section B that S is the price process of a security with zero dividends before T. We assume that

$$S_{t+1} = S_t H_{t+1}; \qquad t \geq 0; \qquad S_0 > 0,$$

where H is an adapted process such that for all $t \geq 1$, H_t has only two possible outcomes $U > 0$ and $D > 0$, each with positive conditional probability given $\mathcal{F}_{t-1}$. Suppose β is the price process of a security, also with no dividends before T, such that

$$\beta_{t+1} = \beta_t R; \qquad t \geq 0; \qquad \beta_0 > 0,$$

where $R > 1$ is a constant. We can think of β as the price process of a riskless bond. Consider a third security, a *European call option* on S with *expiration* at some fixed date $\tau < T$ and exercise price $K \geq 0$. This means that the price process C^τ of the third security has expiration value

$$C_\tau^\tau = (S_\tau - K)^+ \equiv \max(S_\tau - K, 0),$$

with $C_t^\tau = 0$, $t > \tau$. That is, the option gives its holder the right, but not the obligation, to purchase the stock at time τ at price K.

The absence of arbitrage implies that $U = R = D$, or that $U > R > D$. We will assume the latter (nondegeneracy of returns) for the remainder of the exercise.

(A) Assuming no arbitrage, show that for $0 \leq t < \tau$,

$$C_t^\tau = \frac{1}{R^{\tau-t}} \sum_{i=0}^{\tau-t} b(i; \tau - t, p)(U^i D^{\tau-t-i} S_t - K)^+, \qquad (16)$$

where $p = (R - D)/(U - D)$ and where

$$b(i; n, p) = \frac{n!}{i!(n - i)!} p^i (1 - p)^{n-i} \qquad (17)$$

is the probability of i successes, each with probability p, out of n Bernoulli (independent binomial) trials. One can thus view (16) as the discounted expected exercise value of the option, with expectation under some probability measure constructed from the stock and bond returns. In order to model this viewpoint, let $\hat{S}$ be the process defined by

$$\hat{S}_{t+1} = \hat{S}_t \hat{H}_{t+1}; \qquad t \geq 0; \qquad \hat{S}_0 = S_0, \tag{18}$$

where $\{\hat{H}_0, \hat{H}_1, \ldots\}$ are Bernoulli trials with outcomes U and D of probability p and $1 - p$, respectively. Then (18) implies that

$$C_0^\tau = E\left[\frac{(\hat{S}_\tau - K)^+}{R^\tau}\right]. \tag{19}$$

(B) We take it that $\mathbb{F}$ is the filtration generated by the return process H, meaning that for all $t \geq 1$, $\mathcal{F}_t$ is the tribe generated by $\{H_1, \ldots, H_t\}$. We extend the definition of the option described in part (A) by allowing the expiry date τ to be a stopping time. Show that (19) is still implied by the absence of arbitrage.

(C) Show that markets are complete.

(D) The *moneyness* of a call option with expiration at a deterministic time $\tau < T$ and with strike price K is $(S_0 R^\tau - K)/K$. If the moneyness is positive, the option is said to be *in the money*. If the moneyness is negative, the option is said to be *out of the money*. If the moneyness is zero, the option is said to be *at the money*. For a put option with same strike K and expiration time τ, the moneyness is $(K - S_0 R^\tau)/K$ (minus the call moneyness), and the same terms apply. Let $S_0 = 100$, $U = 1.028$, $R = 1.001$, and $D = 0.978$. Plot (or tabulate) the price of European call and American call and put options, with expiration at $\tau = 100$, against moneyness.

(E) For the parameters in Part (D), suppose that up and down returns for the stock are equally likely in each period, and that one time period represents 0.01 years. Compute the annualized continuously compounding interest rate r, and the mean and standard deviation of the annual return $\rho = (\log S_{100} - \log S_0)/100$. Plot the likelihood of ρ as a frequency diagram, that is, showing the probability of each outcome of ρ above that outcome.

(F) A *barrier option* is one that can be exercised or not depending on whether or not the underlying price has crossed a given level before expiration. For example, a *down-and-out call*, at barrier $\underline{S}$, exercise time τ (possibly a stopping time), and exercise price $K \geq \underline{S}$, is a security that pays $1_A (S_\tau - K)^+$ at τ, where A is the event $\{\omega : \min\{S_0(\omega), S_1(\omega), \ldots, S_{\tau(\omega)}(\omega)\} > \underline{S}\}$. That is, A is the event that the minimum price achieved through τ is larger than the barrier $\underline{S}$. Show that an American down-and-out call, exercisable at any time $\tau \leq \bar{\tau}$, is rationally exercised (if at all) only at $\bar{\tau}$.

(G) For the parameters in Part (D), and $\bar{\tau} = 100$, price a down-and-out call with barrier $\underline{S} = 80$, for strikes K from 80 to 120. Plot (or, if you cannot, tabulate) the prices for integer K in this range.

(H) For the parameters in Part (D), price European and American up-and-out put options, with knockout barrier $\bar{S} = 120$. Again, obtain the prices for strikes ranging from 80 to 120. Plot (or, if you cannot, tabulate) the prices for integer K

in this range. For the special case of $K = 100$, plot the optimal exercise region for the American up-and-out put. That is, for each $t \leq 100$, show the set of outcomes for S_t at which it is optimal to exercise at time t.

2.2 Suppose in the context of problem (4) that (δ, S) admits no arbitrage and that U is continuous. Show the existence of a solution. Hint: A continuous function on a compact set has a maximum. In this setting, a set is compact if closed and bounded.

2.3 Suppose in the context of problem (4) that $e \gg 0$ and that U has the additive form (5), where for each t, u_t is concave with an unbounded derivative. Show that any solution c^* is strictly positive. Show that the same conclusion follows if the assumption that $e \gg 0$ is replaced with the assumption that markets are complete and that e is not zero.

2.4 Prove Lemma C. Hint: For any x and y in L, let

$$(x \mid y) = E\left(\sum_{t=0}^{T} x_t y_t\right).$$

Then follow the hint given for Exercise 1.17, remembering that we write "$x = y$" whenever $x_t = y_t$ for all t almost surely.

2.5 For U of the additive form (5), show that the gradient $\nabla U(c)$, if it exists, is represented as in (6).

2.6 (Consumption-based CAPM) Suppose $(c^{(1)}, \ldots, c^{(m)})$ is a strictly positive equilibrium consumption allocation and that for all i, U_i is of the additive form: $U_i(c) = E[\sum_{t=0}^{T} u_{it}(c_t)]$. Assume there is a constant $\bar{c}$ larger than c_t^i for all i and t such that, for all i and t, $u_{it}(x) = A_{it}x - B_{it}x^2$, $x \leq \bar{c}$, for some positive constants A_{it} and B_{it}. That is, utility is quadratic in the relevant range.

(A) In the context of Corollary 2 of Section F, show that for each t, there are some constants k_t and K_t such that $u'_{\lambda t}(e_t) = k_t + K_t e_t$. Suppose for a given trading strategy θ and time t that the following are well defined:

- $R_t^\theta = \theta_{t-1} \cdot (S_t + \delta_t)/\theta_{t-1} \cdot S_{t-1}$, the return on θ at time t;
- R_t^M, the return at time t on a strategy φ maximizing $\mathrm{corr}_{t-1}(R_t^\varphi, e_t)$, where $\mathrm{corr}_t(\cdot)$ denotes $\mathscr{F}_t$-conditional correlation;
- $\beta_{t-1}^\theta = \mathrm{cov}_{t-1}(R_t^\theta, R_t^M)/\mathrm{var}_{t-1}(R_t^M)$, the conditional beta of the trading strategy θ with respect to the market return, where $\mathrm{cov}_t(\cdot)$ denotes $\mathscr{F}_t$-conditional covariance and $\mathrm{var}_t(\cdot)$ denotes $\mathscr{F}_t$-conditional variance;
- R_t^0, the return at time t on a strategy η with $\mathrm{corr}_{t-1}(R_t^\eta, e_t) = 0$.

Derive the following beta-form of the *consumption-based CAPM*:

$$E_{t-1}(R_t^\theta - R_t^0) = \beta_{t-1}^\theta E_{t-1}(R_t^M - R_t^0). \tag{20}$$

(B) Prove the same beta-form (20) of the CAPM holds in equilibrium even without assuming complete markets.

(C) Extend the state-price beta model of Section 1F to this setting, as follows, without using the assumptions of the CAPM. Let π be a state-price deflator. For each t, suppose R_t^* is the return on a trading strategy solving

$$\sup_{\theta} \text{corr}_{t-1}(R_t^\theta, \pi_t).$$

Assume that $\text{var}_{t-1}(R_t^*)$ is nonzero almost surely. Show that for any return R_t^θ,

$$E_{t-1}(R_t^\theta - R_t^0) = \beta_{t-1}^\theta E_{t-1}(R_t^* - R_t^0),$$

where $\beta_{t-1}^\theta = \text{cov}_{t-1}(R_t^\theta, R_t^*)/\text{var}_{t-1}(R_t^*)$ and $\text{corr}_{t-1}(R_t^0, \pi_t) = 0$.

2.7   Prove Proposition E.

2.8   In the context of Section D, suppose that U is the *habit-formation* utility function defined by $U(c) = E[\sum_{t=0}^{T} u(c_t, h_t)]$, where $u : \mathbb{R}_+ \times \mathbb{R} \to \mathbb{R}$ is continuously differentiable on the interior of its domain and, for any t, the "habit" level of consumption is defined by $h_t = \sum_{j=0}^{t} \alpha_j c_{t-j}$ for some $\alpha \in \mathbb{R}^T$. For example, we could take $\alpha_j = \gamma^j$ for $\gamma \in (0, 1)$, which gives geometrically declining weights on past consumption. Calculate the Riesz representation of the gradient of U at a strictly positive consumption process c.

2.9   Consider a utility function U defined by $U(c) = V_0$, where the *utility process V* is defined recursively, backward from T in time, by $V_T = J(c_T, h(0))$ and, for $t < T$, by $V_t = J(c_t, E_t[h(V_{t+1})])$, where $J : \mathbb{R}_+ \times \mathbb{R} \to \mathbb{R}$ is increasing and continuously differentiable on the interior of its domain and $h : \mathbb{R} \to \mathbb{R}$ is increasing and continuously differentiable. This is a special case of what is known as *recursive utility*, and also a special case of what is known as *Kreps-Porteus* utility. Note that the utility function can depend nontrivially on the filtration $\mathbb{F}$, which is not true for additive or habit-formation utility functions. This utility model is reconsidered in an exercise in Chapter 3.

(A) Compute the Riesz representation π of the gradient of U at a strictly positive consumption process c.

(B) Suppose that h and J are concave and increasing functions. Show that U is concave and increasing.

2.10   In the setting of Section E, an Arrow-Debreu equilibrium is a feasible consumption allocation $(c^{(1)}, \ldots, c^{(m)})$ and a nonzero linear function $\Psi : L \to \mathbb{R}$ such that for all i, c^i solves $\max_{c \in L_+} U_i(c)$ subject to $\Psi(c^i) \leq \Psi(e^i)$. Suppose that $(c^{(1)}, \ldots, c^{(m)})$ and Ψ form an Arrow-Debreu equilibrium and that π is the Riesz representation of Ψ. Let S be defined by $S_T = 0$ and by taking π to be a state-price deflator. Suppose, given (δ, S), that markets are complete. Show the existence of trading strategies $\theta^{(1)}, \ldots, \theta^{(m)}$ such that $(\theta^{(1)}, \ldots, \theta^{(m)}, S)$ is an equilibrium with the same consumption allocation $(c^{(1)}, \ldots, c^{(m)})$.

2.11 Given a finite set Ω of states, a *partition* of Ω is a collection of disjoint nonempty subsets of Ω whose union is Ω. For example, a partition of $\{1, 2, 3\}$ is given by $\{\{1\}, \{2, 3\}\}$. The tribe on a finite set Ω generated by a given partition p of Ω, denoted $\sigma(p)$, is the smallest tribe $\mathscr{F}$ on Ω such that $p \subset \mathscr{F}$. Conversely, for any tribe $\mathscr{F}$ on Ω, the partition $\mathscr{P}(\mathscr{F})$ generated by $\mathscr{F}$ is the smallest partition p of Ω such that $\mathscr{F} = \sigma(p)$. For instance, the tribe $\{\varnothing, \Omega, \{1\}, \{2, 3\}\}$ is generated by the partition in the above example. Since partitions and tribes on a given finite set Ω are in one-to-one correspondence, we could have developed the results of Chapter 2 in terms of an increasing sequence $p_0, p_1, \ldots, p_T$ of partitions of Ω rather than a filtration of tribes, $\mathscr{F}_0, \mathscr{F}_1, \ldots, \mathscr{F}_T$. (In infinite-state models, however, it is more convenient to use tribes than partitions.)

We suppose for simplicity that $P(B) > 0$ for any nonempty event B. Given a subset B of Ω and a partition p of Ω, let $n(B, p)$ denote the minimum number of elements of p whose union contains B. In a sense, this is the number of distinct nonempty events that might occur if B is to occur. For $t < T$, let

$$n_t = \max_{B \in p_t} n(B, p_{t+1}).$$

Finally, the *spanning number* of the filtration $\mathbb{F}$ generated by $p_0, \ldots, p_T$ is $n(\mathbb{F}) \equiv \max_{t<T} n_t$. In a sense, $n(\mathbb{F})$ is the maximum number of distinct events that could be revealed between two periods.

Show that complete markets requires at least $n(\mathbb{F})$ securities, and that given the filtration $\mathbb{F}$, there exists a set of $n(\mathbb{F})$ dividend processes and associated arbitrage-free security-price processes such that markets are complete. This issue is further investigated in sources indicated in the Notes.

2.12 Given securities with a dividend-price pair (δ, S), extend Theorem G to show, in the presence of riskless borrowing at a strictly positive discount at each date, the equivalence of these statements:

(a) There exists a state-price deflator.
(b) There exists a deflator π such that (3) holds for any trading strategy θ.
(c) $S_T = 0$ and there exists a deflator π such that the deflated gain process G^π is a martingale.
(d) There is no arbitrage.
(e) There is an equivalent martingale measure.

2.13 Show, from (11) and (12), that (10) is indeed satisfied, confirming that Q is an equivalent martingale measure.

2.14 Show, as claimed in Section I, that if τ^* is a rational exercise policy for the American security X and if V^* is the cum-dividend price process for the American security with this rational exercise policy, then $V_\tau^* \geq X_\tau$ for any stopping time $\tau \leq \tau^*$.

2.15 (Aggregation Revisited). Suppose, in the context of the supremum (8), that $x \gg 0$ and, for all i, $U_i(c) = E[\sum_{t=0}^{T} u_t(c_t)]$, where, for all t, $u_t(x) = k_t x^{\gamma(t)}/\gamma(t)$, where k_t and $\gamma(t) < 1$, $\gamma(t) \neq 0$, are constants (depending on t).

(A) Show that U_λ is of the same utility form as U_i.

(B) Suppose that $\gamma(t)$ is a constant independent of t. Replace the assumption of complete markets in Proposition F with the assumption that $e \gg 0$ and that, for all i, there is a security whose dividend process is e^i. (This can easily be weakened.) Demonstrate the existence of an equilibrium with the same properties described in Proposition F, including a consumption allocation that is Pareto optimal.

2.16 (Put-Call Parity). In the general setting explained in Section B, suppose there exist the following securities:

    (a) a "stock," with price process X;
    (b) a European call option on the stock with strike price K and expiration τ;
    (c) a European put option on the stock with strike price K and expiration τ;
    (d) a τ-period zero-coupon riskless bond.

Let X_0, C_0, P_0, and B_0 denote the initial respective prices of the securities. Suppose there is no arbitrage, and that the stock pays no dividends before time τ. Solve for C_0 explicitly in terms of X_0, P_0, and B_0.

2.17 (Futures-Forward Price Equivalence). This exercise defines (in ideal terms) a *forward contract* and a *futures contract*, and gives simple conditions under which the *futures price* and the *forward price* coincide. We adopt the setting of Section B, in the absence of arbitrage. Fixed throughout are a *delivery date* τ and a settlement amount W_τ (an $\mathscr{F}_\tau$-measurable random variable).

Informally speaking, the associated forward contract made at time t is a commitment to pay an amount F_t (the forward price), which is agreed upon at time t and paid at time τ, in return for the amount W_τ at time τ. Formally speaking, the forward contract made at time t for delivery of W_τ at time τ for a forward price of F_t is a security whose price at time t is zero and whose dividend process δ is defined by $\delta_t = 0$, $t \neq \tau$, and $\delta_\tau = W_\tau - F_t$.

(A) Suppose that Q is an equivalent martingale measure and that there is riskless short-term borrowing at any date t at a discount d_t that is deterministic. Show that $\{F_0, F_1, \ldots, F_\tau\}$ is a Q-martingale, in that $F_t = E_t^Q(F_\tau)$ for all $t \leq \tau$.

A futures contract differs from a forward contract in several practical ways that depend on institutional details. One of the details that is particularly important for pricing purposes is *resettlement*. For theoretical modeling purposes, we can describe resettlement as follows: A futures-price process $\Phi = \{\Phi_0, \ldots, \Phi_\tau\}$ for delivery of W_τ at time τ is taken as given. At any time t, an investor can adopt a position of θ futures contracts by agreeing to accept the resettlement payment $\theta(\Phi_{t+1} - \Phi_t)$ at time $t + 1$, $\theta(\Phi_{t+2} - \Phi_{t+1})$ at time $t + 2$, and so on, until the position is changed (or eliminated). This process of paying or collecting any changes in the futures price, period by period, is called *marking to market*, and serves in practice to reduce the likelihood or magnitude of potential defaults. Formally, all of this means simply that the dividend process δ of the futures contract is defined by $\delta_t = \Phi_t - \Phi_{t-1}$, $1 \leq t \leq \tau$.

For our purposes, it is natural to assume that the delivery value Φ_τ is contractually equated with W_τ. (In a more detailed model, we could equate Φ_τ and W_τ by the absence of *delivery arbitrage*.)

(B) Suppose Q is an equivalent martingale measure and show that for all $t \leq \tau$, $\Phi_t = E_t^Q(W_\tau)$. It follows from parts (A) and (B) that with deterministic interest rates and the absence of arbitrage, futures and forward prices coincide.

(C) We now suppose that W_τ is the market value S_τ of a security with dividend process δ. Suppose that δ and the discount process $d = \{d_1, \ldots, d_T\}$ on riskless borrowing are both deterministic. Calculate the futures and forward prices, Φ_t and F_t, explicitly in terms of S_t, d, and δ.

2.18   Provide details fleshing out the following outline of a proof of the converse part of Proposition G.

Let $J = \{(x_1, \ldots, x_T) : x \in L\}$ and $H = \{(\delta_1^\theta, \ldots, \delta_T^\theta) : \theta \in \Theta\}$. Markets are complete if and only if $J = H$. By Theorem G, there is a unique equivalent martingale measure if and only if there is a unique state-price deflator π such that $\pi_0 = 1$. Suppose $H \neq J$. Since H is a linear subspace of J, there is some nonzero y in J "orthogonal" to H, in the sense that $E(\sum_{t=1}^T y_t h_t) = 0$ for all h in H. Let $\hat{\pi} \in L$ be defined by $\hat{\pi}_0 = 1$ and $\hat{\pi}_t = \pi_t + \alpha y_t$, $t \geq 1$, where $\alpha > 0$ is a scalar small enough that $\hat{\pi} \gg 0$. Then $\hat{\pi}$ is a distinct state-price deflator with $\hat{\pi}_0 = 1$. This shows that if there is a unique state-price deflator π with $\pi_0 = 1$, then markets must be complete. Hint: Let

$$(y \mid h) \equiv E\left(\sum_{t=1}^T y_t h_t\right), \qquad h \in H,$$

define an inner product $(\cdot \mid \cdot)$ for H in the sense of Exercise 1.17.

2.19   It is asserted in Section I that if W is the Snell envelope of Y, then $W_t = \max[Y_t, E_t(W_{t+1})]$. Prove this natural property.

2.20   Prove Lemma J.

2.21   Consider the "tree" of prices for securities A and B shown in Figure 2.2. At each node in the tree, a pair (p_A, p_B) of prices is shown, the first of which is the price of A at that node, the second of which is the price of B.

(A) Construct a probability space $(\Omega, \mathcal{F}, P)$, a filtration of tribes, $\{\mathcal{F}_0, \mathcal{F}_1, \mathcal{F}_2\}$, and a vector security price process V, that formally encode the information in the figure. Please be explicit. Take the security price process to be *cum dividend*, so that V_2 is both the price and the dividend payoff vector of the securities at time 2. There are no dividend payments in periods 0 and 1.

(B) Suppose there is no arbitrage. Find the price at time 0 of an American put option on asset B, with an exercise price of 95 and expiring at time 2. (Remember, this is an option to sell B for 95 at any of times 0, 1, or 2.)

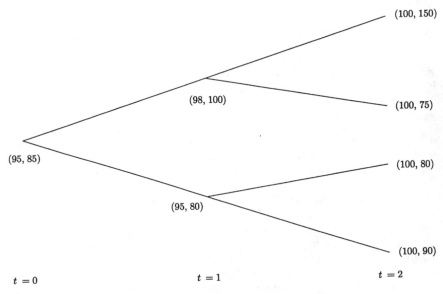

$t = 0$ $t = 1$ $t = 2$

Figure 2.2. *An Event Tree With Prices*

(C) Suppose the price at time 0 in the market of this put option is in fact 10 percent lower than the arbitrage-free price you arrived at in part B. Show explicitly how to create a riskless profit of 1 million dollars at time 0, with no cash flow after time 0.

(D) Suppose the price in the market of this put option is in fact 10 percent higher than the arbitrage-free price you arrived at in part B. Show explicitly how to create a riskless profit of 1 million dollars at time 0, with nonnegative cash flow after time 0. Hint: If you decide to sell the option, you should not assume that the person to whom you sold it will exercise it in any particular fashion.

2.22 Let $T = 1$, and suppose there are three equally likely states of world, ω_1, ω_2, and ω_3, one of which is revealed as true at time 1. A particular agent has utility function U and has equilibrium consumption choices $c_0 = 25$ and

$$c_1(\omega_1) = 9, \qquad c_1(\omega_2) = 16, \qquad c_1(\omega_3) = 4.$$

In each case below, compute the price of a security that pays 3 in state ω_1, 6 in state ω_2, and 5 in state ω_3. Show your work.

(A) Expected, but not time-additive, utility $U(c_0, c_1) = E[u(c_0, c_1)]$, with $u(x, y) = \sqrt{xy}$.

(B) Nonexpected utility $U(c_0, c_1) = \sqrt{c_0 \, c_1(\omega_1) \, c_1(\omega_2) \, c_1(\omega_3)}$.

2.23 For concreteness, the length of one period is one year. There are two basic types of investments. The first is riskless borrowing or lending. The equilibrium one-year short rate is 25 percent (simple interest per year), each year. (So one can invest 1 at time zero and collect 1.25 at the end of the first year, or invest 1 at the end of the first year and collect 1.25 at the end of the second year.) At the end of each year, a fair coin is flipped. A risky security has zero initial market value. Its market value goes up by one unit at the end of each year if the outcome of the coin flip for that year is heads. Its market value goes down by one unit at the end of each year if the outcome of the coin flip for that year is tails. For example, the price of the risky security at the end of the second year is -2, 0, or $+2$, with respective probabilities 0.25, 0.50, and 0.25.

There is also a European option to purchase the risky security above at the end of the second year (only) at an exercise price of 1 unit of account.

(A) Suppose there is no arbitrage. State the initial market price q of the option. (Show your reasoning.)

(B) Now suppose the option is actually selling for $q/2$. Construct a trading strategy that generates a net initial positive cash flow of 1000 units of account and no subsequent cash flows. (State a precise recipe for the quantities of each security to buy or sell, at each time, in each contingency.)

2.24 Prove Corollary F.

2.25 (Numeraire Invariance). Consider a dividend-price pair $(\delta, S) \in L^N \times L^N$, and a deflator γ. Let $\hat{S} = S\gamma$ and $\hat{\delta} = \delta\gamma$ denote the deflated price and dividend processes. Let θ be any given trading strategy. Show that the dividend process $\hat{\delta}^\theta$ generated by θ given $(\hat{\delta}, \hat{S})$ and the dividend process δ^θ generated by θ under (δ, S) are related by $\hat{\delta}^\theta = \gamma\delta^\theta$. Show that θ is an arbitrage with respect to (δ, S) if and only if θ is an arbitrage with respect to $(\hat{\delta}, \hat{S})$. If π is a state-price deflator for (δ, S), compute a state-price deflator $\hat{\pi}$ for $(\hat{\delta}, \hat{S})$ in terms of π and γ.

Notes

Radner (1967, 1972) originated the sort of dynamic equilibrium model treated in this chapter. The monograph by Magill and Quinzii (1996b) is a comprehensive survey of the theory of general equilibrium in incomplete markets.

(B) The model of uncertainty and information is standard. The model of uncertainty is equivalent to that originated in the general equilibrium model of Debreu (1953), which appears in Chapter 7 of Debreu (1959). For more details in a finance setting, see Dothan (1990).

(C–D) and G The connection between arbitrage and martingales given in Sections C and G, from the more general model of Harrison and Kreps (1979). Girotto and Ortu (1996) present general results, in this finite-dimensional setting, on the measure. The theorem no arbitrage and the existence of an equivalent martingale Harrison and Kreps of the results on optimality and state prices is also from Harrison and Kreps (1979). Girotto and Ortu (1994, 1997a, 1997b) fully explore this equivalence in dimensional multiperiod economies.

(E) The spirit of this section is from Kreps (1982) and Duffie and Huang (1985).

(F) The representative-agent state-pricing model for this setting was shown by Constantinides (1982). An extension of this notion to incomplete markets, where one cannot generally exploit Pareto optimality, is given by Cuoco and He (1992a).

(G–H) These sections are based on the ideas of Harrison and Kreps (1979).

(I) The modeling of American security valuation given here is similar to the continuous-time treatments of Bensoussan (1984) and Karatzas (1988), who do not formally connect the valuation of American securities with the absence of arbitrage, but rather deal with the similar notion of "fair price." Merton (1973b) was the first to attack American option valuation systematically using arbitrage-based methods and to point out the inoptimality of early exercise of certain American options in a Black-Scholes style setting. American option valuation is reconsidered in Chapters 3 and 8, whose literature notes cite many additional references.

(J) These results were developed in a continuous-time setting by Merton (1973b).

Additional Topics: The habit-formation utility model was developed by Dunn and Singleton (1986) and in continuous time by Ryder and Heal (1973). An application of habit formation to state-pricing in this setting appears in Chapman (1998b). The recursive-utility model, in various forms, is due to Selden (1978), Kreps and Porteus (1978), and Epstein and Zin (1989), and is surveyed by Epstein (1992). Koopmans (1960) presented an early precursor. The recursive-utility model allows for preference for earlier or later resolution of uncertainty (which have no impact on additive utility). This is relevant, for example, in the context of the remarks by Ross (1989), as shown by Skiadas (1998), and Duffie, Schroder, and Skiadas (1997). See Grant, Kajii, and Polak (2000) for more on preference for resolution of information. For a more general form of recursive utility than that appearing in Exercise 2.9, the von Neumann-Morgenstern function h can be replaced with a function of the conditional distribution of next-period utility. Examples are the local-expected-utility model of Machina (1982) and the *betweenness certainty equivalent* model of Chew (1983, 1989), Dekel (1989), and Gul and Lantto (1990). The equilibrium state-price associated with recursive utility is computed in a Markovian version of this setting by Kan (1995). For further justification and properties of recursive utility, see Chew and Epstein (1991), Skiadas (1998), and Skiadas (1997). For further implications for asset pricing, see Epstein (1988), Epstein (1992), Epstein and Zin (1999), and Giovannini and Weil (1989). Kan (1993) explored the utility gradient representation of recursive utility in his setting.

    The basic approach to existence given in Exercise 2.11 is suggested by Kreps (1982), and is shown to work for "generic" dividends and endowments, under technical regularity conditions, in McManus (1984), Repullo (1986), Magill and Shafer (1990), provided the number of securities is at least the literature spanning number of the filtration $\mathbb{F}$ (as suggested in Exercise 2.11(1985)). This literature is reviewed in depth by Geanakoplos (1990). See Duffie and the definition of spanning number in more general settings and for a continuous-time version of a similar result. Duffie and Shafer (1985, 1986b) show generic existence of equilibrium in incomplete markets; Hart (1975) gives a counterexample. Bottazzi (1995) has a somewhat more advanced version of this result in its single-period multiple-commodity version. See also Won (1996a, 1996b). Related existence topics are studied by Bottazzi and Hens (1996), Hens (1991), and Zhou (1997b). Dispersed expectations, in a temporary-equilibrium variant of the model, is shown to lead to existence by Henrotte (1994) and by Honda (1992). Alternative proofs of existence of equilibrium are given in the two-period version of the model by Geanakoplos and Shafer (1990), Hirsch, Magill, and Mas-Colell (1990), and Husseini, Lasry, and Magill (1990); and in a *T*-period version by Florenzano and Gourdel (1994). If one defines security dividends in nominal terms, rather than in units of consumption, then equilibria always exist under standard technical conditions on preferences and endowments, as shown by Cass (1984), Werner (1985), Duffie (1987), and Gottardi and Hens (1996), although equilibrium may be indeterminate, as shown by Cass (1989) and Geanakoplos and Mas-Colell (1989). On this point, see also Kydland and Prescott (1991), Mas-Colell (1991), and Cass (1991). Likewise, one obtains existence in a one-period version of the model provided securities have payoffs in a single commodity (the framework of most of this book), as shown by Chae (1988) and Geanakoplos and Polemarchakis (1986). Surveys of general-equilibrium models in an incomplete-markets setting are given by Cass (1991), Duffie (1992), Geanakoplos (1990), Magill and Quinzii (1996b), and Magill and Shafer (1991). In the presence of price-dependent options, existence can be more problematic, as shown by Polemarchakis and Ku (1990), but variants of the formulation will suffice for existence in many cases, as shown by Huang and Wu (1994) and Krasa and Werner (1991). Detemple and Selden (1991) examine the implications of options for asset pricing in a general equilibrium model with incomplete markets. Bajeux-Besnainou and Rochet (1996) explore the dynamic spanning implications of options. The importance of the timing of information in this setting is described by Berk and Uhlig (1993). Hindy and Huang (1993b) show the implications of linear collateral constraints on security valuation. Hara (1993) treats the role of "redundant" securities in the presence of transactions costs.

Hahn (1994, 1999) raises some philosophical issues regarding the possibility of complete markets and efficiency. The Pareto inefficiency of incomplete-markets equilibrium consumption allocations, and notions of constrained efficiency, are discussed by Hart (1975), Kreps (1979) (and references therein), Citanna, Kajii, and Villanacci (1994), Citanna and Villanacci (1993), and Pan (1993, 1995).

The optimality of individual portfolio and consumption choices in incomplete markets in this setting is given a dual interpretation by He and Pagès (1993). (Girotto and Ortu (1994) offer related remarks.) Methods for computation of equilibrium with incomplete markets are developed by Brown, DeMarzo, and Eaves (1996a), Brown, DeMarzo, and Eaves (1996b), and DeMarzo and Eaves (1996). See also the notes of Chapter 12.

Kraus and Litzenberger (1975) and Stapleton and Subrahmanyam (1978) present parametric examples of equilibrium. Hansen and Richard (1987) explore the state-price beta model in a much more general multiperiod setting.

Ross (1987) and Prisman (1985) show the impact of taxes and transactions costs on the state-pricing model. Hara (1993) discusses the role of redundant securities in the presence of transactions costs. The consumption-based CAPM of Exercise 2.6 is found, in a different form, in Rubinstein (1976). The aggregation result of Exercise 2.15 is based on Rubinstein (1974a). Rubinstein (1974b) has a detailed treatment of asset pricing results in the setting of this chapter. Rubinstein (1987) is a useful expository treatment of derivative asset pricing in this setting.

Cox, Ross, and Rubinstein (1979) developed the multiperiod binomial option pricing model analyzed in Exercise 2.1, and further analyzed in terms of convergence to the Black-Scholes formula in Chapter 12.

The role of production is considered by Duffie and Shafer (1986a) and Naik (1994). The Modigliani-Miller Theorems are reconsidered in this setting by DeMarzo (1988), Duffie and Shafer (1986a), and Gottardi (1995).

3

The Dynamic Programming Approach

THIS CHAPTER PRESENTS portfolio choice and asset pricing in the framework of dynamic programming, a technique for solving dynamic optimization problems with a recursive structure. The asset pricing implications go little beyond those of the previous chapter, but there are computational advantages. After introducing the idea of dynamic programming in a deterministic setting, we review the basics of a finite-state Markov chain. The Bellman equation is shown to characterize optimality in a Markov setting. The first-order condition for the Bellman equation, often called the "stochastic Euler equation," is then shown to characterize equilibrium security prices. This is done with additive utility in the main body of the chapter, and extended to more general recursive forms of utility in the exercises. The last sections of the chapter show the computation of arbitrage-free derivative security values in a Markov setting, including an application of Bellman's equation for optimal stopping to the valuation of American securities such as the American put option. An exercise presents algorithms for the numerical solution of term-structure derivative securities in a simple "binomial" setting.

A. The Bellman Approach

To get the basic idea, we start in the T-period setting of the previous chapter, with no securities except those permitting short-term riskless borrowing at any time t at the discount $d_t > 0$. The endowment process of a given agent is e. Given a consumption process c, it is convenient to define the agent's *wealth process* W^c by $W_0^c = 0$ and

$$
W_t^c = \frac{W_{t-1}^c + e_{t-1} - c_{t-1}}{d_{t-1}}, \qquad t \geq 1. \tag{1}
$$

49

Given a utility function $U : L_+ \to \mathbb{R}$ on the set L of nonnegative adapted processes, the agent's problem can be rewritten as

$$\sup_{c \in L_+} U(c) \qquad \text{subject to (1) and } c_T \leq W_T^c + e_T. \tag{2}$$

Dynamic programming is only convenient with special types of utility functions. One example is an additive utility function U, defined by

$$U(c) = E\left[\sum_{t=0}^{T} u_t(c_t)\right], \tag{3}$$

with $u_t : \mathbb{R}_+ \to \mathbb{R}$ strictly increasing and continuous for each t. Given this utility function, it is natural to consider the problem at any time t of maximizing the "remaining utility," given current wealth $W_t^c = w$. In order to keep things simple at first, we take the case in which there is no uncertainty, meaning that $\mathcal{F}_t = \{\Omega, \varnothing\}$ for all t. The maximum remaining utility at time t is then written, for each w in $\mathbb{R}$, as

$$V_t(w) = \sup_{c \in L_+} \sum_{s=t}^{T} u_s(c_s),$$

subject to $W_t^c = w$, the wealth dynamic (1), and $c_T \leq W_T^c + e_T$. If there is no budget-feasible consumption choice (because w is excessively negative), we write $V_t(w) = -\infty$.

Clearly $V_T(w) = u_T(w + e_T)$ for $w \geq -e_T$, and it is shown as an exercise that for $t < T$,

$$V_t(w) = \sup_{\bar{c} \in \mathbb{R}_+} u_t(\bar{c}) + V_{t+1}\left(\frac{w + e_t - \bar{c}}{d_t}\right), \tag{4}$$

the *Bellman equation*. For each $t < T$ and each w for which there is a solution to (4), let $C_t(w)$ denote a solution, and let $C_T(w) = w + e_T$. It is also left as an exercise to show that an optimal consumption policy c is defined inductively by $c_t = C_t(W_t^c)$. From (4), the *value function* V_{t+1} thus summarizes all information regarding the "future" of the problem that is required for choice at time t.

B. First-Order Bellman Conditions

Throughout this section, we take the additive model (3) and assume in addition that for each t, u_t is strictly concave and is differentiable on $(0, \infty)$. From Exercise 2.2, there exists an optimal consumption policy c^*. We assume that c^* is strictly positive. Let W^* denote the wealth process associated with c^* by (1).

Lemma. *For any* t, V_t *is strictly concave and continuously differentiable at* W_t^*, *with* $V_t'(W_t^*) = u_t'(c_t^*)$.

Proof is left as Exercise 3.4, which gives a broad hint. The first-order conditions for the Bellman equation (4) then imply, for any $t < T$, that the one-period discount is

$$d_t = \frac{u_{t+1}'(c_{t+1}^*)}{u_t'(c_t^*)}. \tag{5}$$

The same equation is easily derived from the general characterization of equilibrium security prices given by equation (2.9). More generally, the price $\Lambda_{t,\tau}$ at time t of a unit riskless bond maturing at any time $\tau > t$ is

$$\Lambda_{t,\tau} \equiv d_t \, d_{t+1} \cdots d_{\tau-1} = \frac{u_\tau'(c_\tau^*)}{u_t'(c_t^*)}, \tag{6}$$

which, naturally, is the marginal rate of substitution of consumption between the two dates.

The price of any security, in this deterministic setting, can be calculated in terms of the prices $\{\Lambda_{t,\tau}\}$ of zero-coupon bonds.

C. Markov Uncertainty

We take the easiest kind of Markov uncertainty, a *time-homogeneous Markov chain*. Let the elements of a fixed set $Z = \{1, \ldots, k\}$ be known as *shocks*. For any shocks i and j, let $q_{ij} \in [0, 1]$ be thought of as the probability, for any t, that shock j occurs in period $t + 1$ given that shock i occurs in period t. Of course, for each i, $q_{i1} + \cdots + q_{ik} = 1$. The $k \times k$ *transition matrix* q is thus a complete characterization of transition probabilities. This idea is formalized with the following construction of a probability space and filtration of tribes. It is enough to consider a state of the world as some particular sequence $(z_0, \ldots, z_T)$ of shocks that might occur. We therefore let $\Omega = Z^{T+1}$ and let $\mathscr{F}$ be the set of all subsets of Ω. For each t, let $X_t : \Omega \to Z$ (the random shock at time t) be the random variable defined by $X_t(z_0, \ldots, z_T) = z_t$. Finally, for each possible initial state i in Z, let P_i be the probability measure on $(\Omega, \mathscr{F})$ uniquely defined by the two conditions:

$$P_i(X_0 = i) = 1 \tag{7}$$

and, for all $t < T$,

$$P_i[X(t+1) = j \mid X(0), X(1), X(2), \ldots, X(t)] = q_{X(t),j}. \tag{8}$$

Relations (7) and (8) mean that under probability measure P_i, X starts at i with probability 1 and has the transition probabilities previously described informally. In particular, (8) means that $X = \{X_0, \dots, X_T\}$ is a *Markov process*: the conditional distribution of X_{t+1} given $X_0, \dots, X_t$ depends only on X_t. To complete the formal picture, for each t, we let $\mathscr{F}_t$ be the tribe generated by $\{X_0, \dots, X_t\}$, meaning that the information available at time t is that obtained by observing the shock process X until time t. The following lemma gives the complete flavor of the Markov property.

Lemma. *For any time t, let $f : Z^{T-t+1} \to \mathbb{R}$ be arbitrary. Then there exists a fixed function $g : Z \to \mathbb{R}$ such that for any i in Z,*

$$E^i\left[f(X_t, \dots, X_T) \mid \mathscr{F}_t\right] = E^i[f(X_t, \dots, X_T) \mid X_t] = g(X_t),$$

where E^i denotes expectation under P_i.

D. Markov Asset Pricing

Taking the particular Markov source of uncertainty described in Section C, we now consider the prices of securities in a single- or representative-agent setting with additive utility of the form (3), where, for all t, u_t has a strictly positive continuous derivative on $(0, \infty)$. Suppose, moreover, that for each t, there are functions $f_t : Z \to \mathbb{R}^N$ and $g_t : Z \to \mathbb{R}$ such that the dividend is $\delta_t = f_t(X_t)$ and the endowment is $e_t = g_t(X_t)$. Then Lemma 3C and the general gradient solution (2.9) for equilibrium security prices imply the following characterization of the equilibrium security price process S. For each t, there is a function $\mathscr{S}_t : Z \to \mathbb{R}^N$ such that $S_t = \mathscr{S}_t(X_t)$. In particular, for any initial shock i and any time $t < T$,

$$\mathscr{S}_t(X_t) = \frac{1}{\pi_t} E^i\left(\pi_{t+1}\left[f_{t+1}(X_{t+1}) + \mathscr{S}_{t+1}(X_{t+1})\right] \mid X_t\right), \tag{9}$$

where π is the state-price deflator given by $\pi_t = u_t'[g_t(X_t)]$. This has been called the *stochastic Euler equation* for security prices.

E. Security Pricing by Markov Control

We will demonstrate (9) once again, under stronger conditions, using instead Markov dynamic programming methods. Suppose that X is the shock process already described. For notational simplicity, in this section we suppose that the transition matrix q is strictly positive and that, for all t,

- u_t is continuous, strictly concave, increasing, and differentiable on $(0, \infty)$;
- $e_t = g_t(X_t)$ for some $g_t : Z \to \mathbb{R}_{++}$; and
- $\delta_t = f_t(X_t)$ for some $f_t : Z \to \mathbb{R}_{++}^N$.

We assume, naturally, that $\mathscr{S}_t : Z \to \mathbb{R}_{++}^N$, $t < T$, and that there is no arbitrage. We let Θ denote the space of trading strategies and L_+ the space of nonnegative adapted processes (for consumption). For each $t \leq T$, consider the value function $V_t : Z \times \mathbb{R} \to \overline{\mathbb{R}}$ defined by

$$V_t(i, w) = \sup_{(c, \theta) \in L_+ \times \Theta} E\left[\sum_{j=t}^{T} u_j(c_j) \,\Big|\, X_t = i\right], \qquad (10)$$

subject to

$$W_j^\theta = \theta_{j-1} \cdot \left[\mathscr{S}_j(X_j) + f_j(X_j)\right], \qquad j > t; \qquad W_t^\theta = w, \qquad (11)$$

and

$$c_j + \theta_j \cdot \mathscr{S}_j(X_j) \leq W_j^\theta + g_j(X_j), \qquad t \leq j \leq T.$$

One may think of $V_t(X_t, \cdot)$ as an indirect utility function for wealth at time t, given the current state X_t. The conditional expectation in (10) does not depend on the initial state X_0 according to Lemma 3C, so we abuse the notation by simply ignoring the initial state in this sort of expression. For sufficiently negative w, there is no (θ, c) that is feasible for (10), in which case we take $V_t(i, w) = -\infty$. For initial wealth $w = 0$ and time $t = 0$, (10) is equivalent to problem (2.4) with $S_j = \mathscr{S}_j(X_j)$ for any time j.

We now define a sequence $F_0, \ldots, F_T$ of functions on $Z \times \mathbb{R}$ into $\overline{\mathbb{R}}$ that will eventually be shown to coincide with the value functions $V_0, \ldots, V_T$. We first define $F_{T+1} \equiv 0$. For $t \leq T$, we recursively define F_t by the Bellman equation

$$F_t(i, w) = \sup_{(\bar{\theta}, \bar{c}) \in \mathbb{R}^N \times \mathbb{R}_+} G_{it}(\bar{\theta}, \bar{c}) \quad \text{subject to } \bar{c} + \bar{\theta} \cdot \mathscr{S}_t(i) \leq w + g_t(i), \quad (12)$$

where

$$G_{it}(\bar{\theta}, \bar{c}) = u_t(\bar{c}) + E\left[F_{t+1}\left(X_{t+1}, \bar{\theta} \cdot \left[\mathscr{S}_{t+1}(X_{t+1}) + f_{t+1}(X_{t+1})\right]\right) \,\Big|\, X_t = i\right].$$

The following technical conditions extend those of Lemma 3B, and have essentially the same proof.

Proposition. *For any i in Z and $t \leq T$, the function $F_t(i, \cdot) : \mathbb{R} \to \overline{\mathbb{R}}$, restricted to its domain of finiteness $\{w : F_t(i, w) > -\infty\}$, is strictly concave and increasing. If $(\bar{c}, \bar{\theta})$ solves (12) and $\bar{c} > 0$, then $F_t(i, \cdot)$ is continuously differentiable at w with derivative $F_{tw}(i, w) = u'_t(\bar{c})$.*

It can be shown as an exercise that unless the constraint of (12) is infeasible, a solution to (12) always exists. In this case, for any i, t, and w, let $[\Phi_t(i, w), C_t(i, w)]$ denote a solution. We can then define the associated wealth process W^* recursively, for any initial condition w, by $W_0^* = w$ and

$$W_t^* = \Phi_{t-1}(X_{t-1}, W_{t-1}^*) \cdot [\mathscr{S}_t(X_t) + f_t(X_t)], \qquad t \geq 1.$$

Let (c^*, θ^*) be defined, at each t, by $c_t^* = C_t(X_t, W_t^*)$ and $\theta_t^* = \Phi_t(X_t, W_t^*)$. The fact that (c^*, θ^*) solves (10) for $t = 0$ can be shown as follows: Let (c, θ) be an arbitrary feasible policy. For each t, from the Bellman equation (12),

$$F_t(X_t, W_t^\theta) \geq u_t(c_t) + E\big[F_{t+1}\big(X_{t+1}, \theta_t \cdot [\mathscr{S}_{t+1}(X_{t+1}) + f_{t+1}(X_{t+1})]\big)\big|X_t\big].$$

Rearranging this inequality and applying the law of iterated expectations,

$$E[F_t(X_t, W_t^\theta)] - E\big[F_{t+1}\big(X_{t+1}, W_{t+1}^\theta\big)\big] \geq E[u_t(c_t)]. \tag{13}$$

Adding (13) from $t = 0$ to $t = T$ shows that $F_0(X_0, W_0) \geq U(c)$. Repeating the same calculations for the special policy $(c, \theta) = (c^*, \theta^*)$ allows us to replace the inequality in (13) with an equality, leaving $F_0(X_0, W_0) = U(c^*)$. This shows that $U(c^*) \geq U(c)$ for any feasible (θ, c), meaning that (θ^*, c^*) indeed solves (10) for $t = 0$. An optimal policy can thus be captured in *feedback-policy* form in terms of the functions C_t and Φ_t, $t \leq T$. We also see that for all $t \leq T$, $F_t = V_t$, so V_t inherits the properties of F given by the last proposition.

We can now recover the stochastic Euler equation (9) directly from the first-order conditions to (12), rather than from the more general first-order conditions developed in chapter 2 based on the gradient of U.

Theorem. *Suppose c^* is a strictly positive consumption process and θ^* is a trading strategy such that $c_t^* = W_t^{\theta^*} + e_t - \theta_t^* \cdot S_t$. Then (c^*, θ^*) solves (10) for $t = 0$ if and only if, for all $t < T$,*

$$\mathscr{S}_t(X_t) = \frac{1}{u'_t(c_t^*)} E\big[u'_{t+1}(c_{t+1}^*)[\mathscr{S}_{t+1}(X_{t+1}) + f_{t+1}(X_{t+1})]\big|X_t\big].$$

The theorem follows from the necessity and sufficiency of the first-order conditions for (12), relying on the last proposition for the fact that

$$F_{t+1,w}(X_{t+1}, W^*_{t+1}) = u'_{t+1}(c^*_{t+1}). \tag{14}$$

In a single-agent model, we define a sequence $\{\mathcal{S}_0, \ldots, \mathcal{S}_T\}$ of security-price functions to be a *single-agent equilibrium* if $(e, 0)$ (no trade) solves (10) for $t = 0$, $w = 0$, and any initial shock i.

Corollary. $\{\mathcal{S}_0, \ldots, \mathcal{S}_T\}$ *is a single-agent equilibrium if and only if $\mathcal{S}_T = 0$ and, for all $t < T$, the stochastic Euler equation (9) is satisfied taking $c^* = e$.*

F. Markov Arbitrage-Free Valuation

Taking the setting of Markov uncertainty described in Section C, but assuming no particular optimality properties or equilibrium, suppose that security prices and dividends are given, at each t, by functions $\mathcal{S}_t$ and f_t on Z into $\mathbb{R}^N$. We also suppose that a state-price deflator π is given by $\pi_t = \psi_t(X_t)$ for some $\psi_t : Z \to (0, \infty)$. With this, we have, for $0 < t \le T$,

$$\mathcal{S}_{t-1}(X_{t-1}) = \frac{1}{\psi_{t-1}(X_{t-1})} E\left(\psi_t(X_t)\left[f_t(X_t) + \mathcal{S}_t(X_t)\right]\big|X_{t-1}\right). \tag{15}$$

In the special setting of Section E, for example, (9) tells us that we can take $\psi_t(i) = u'_t[g(i)]$.

Since $Z = \{1, \ldots, k\}$ for some integer k, we can abuse the notation by treating any function such as $\psi_t : Z \to \mathbb{R}$ interchangeably as a vector in $\mathbb{R}^k$ denoted ψ_t, with i-th element $\psi_t(i)$. Likewise, $\mathcal{S}_t$ can be treated as a $k \times N$ matrix, and so on. In this sense, (15) can also be written

$$\mathcal{S}_{t-1} = \Pi_{t-1}(f_t + \mathcal{S}_t), \tag{16}$$

where Π_{t-1} is the $k \times k$ matrix with (i, j)-element $q_{ij}\psi_t(j)/\psi_{t-1}(i)$. For each t and $s > t$, we let $\Pi_{t,s} = \Pi_t\Pi_{t+1}\cdots\Pi_{s-1}$. Then (16) is equivalent to, for any t and $\tau > t$,

$$\mathcal{S}_t = \Pi_{t,\tau}\mathcal{S}_\tau + \sum_{s=t+1}^{\tau} \Pi_{t,s}f_s. \tag{17}$$

As an example, consider the "binomial" model of Exercise 2.1. We can let $Z = \{0, 1, \ldots, T\}$, with shock i having the interpretation: "There have so far occurred i 'up' returns on the stock," as illustrated in Figure 3.1 for the case $T = 6$.

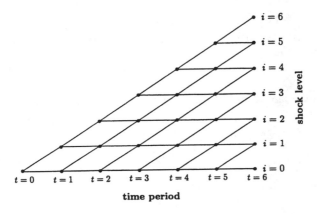

Figure 3.1. *A Binomial Tree*

From the calculations in Exercise 2.1, it is apparent that for any t, we may choose $\Pi_t = \Pi$, where

$$\Pi_{ij} = \frac{p}{R}, \qquad j = i + 1,$$

$$= \frac{1-p}{R}, \qquad j = i,$$

$$= 0, \qquad \text{otherwise,}$$

where $p = (R - D)/(U - D)$, for constant coefficients R, U, and D, with $0 < D < R < U$. For a given initial stock price x and any $i \in Z$, the stock-price process S of Exercise 2.1 can indeed be represented at each time t by $\mathscr{S}_t : Z \to \mathbb{R}$, where $\mathscr{S}_t(i) = xU^i D^{t-i}$.

We can recover the "binomial" option-pricing formula (2.16) by noting that the European call option with strike price K and expiration time τ may be treated as a security with dividends only at time τ given by the function $g : Z \to \mathbb{R}$, with $g(i) = [\mathscr{S}_\tau(i) - K]^+$. From (17), the arbitrage-free value of the option at time t is $C_t^\tau = \Pi^{\tau-t} g$, where Π^t denotes the t-th power of Π. This same valuation formula applies to an arbitrary security paying a dividend at time τ defined by some payoff function $g : Z \to \mathbb{R}$.

G. Early Exercise and Optimal Stopping

In the general Markov setting of Section F, consider an "American" security, defined by some payoff functions $g_t : Z \to \mathbb{R}_+$, $t \in \{0, \ldots, T\}$. As explained in Section 2I, the security is a claim to the dividend $g_\tau(X_\tau)$ at any stopping time τ selected by the owner. Expiration of the security at some time $\bar{\tau}$ is handled by defining g_t to be zero for $t > \bar{\tau}$. Given a state-price deflator π defined by $\pi_t = \psi_t(X_t)$, as outlined in the previous section, the rational exercise problem (2.13) for the American security, with initial shock i, is given by

$$J_0(i) \equiv \max_{\tau \in \mathcal{T}} \frac{1}{\psi_0(i)} E^i\left[\psi_\tau(X_\tau)g(X_\tau)\right], \tag{18}$$

where $\mathcal{T}$ is the set of stopping times bounded by T. As explained in Section 2I, if the American security is redundant and there is no arbitrage, then $J_0(i)$ is its cum-dividend value at time 0 with initial shock i. The Bellman equation for (18) is

$$J_t(X_t) \equiv \max\left(g_t(X_t), \frac{1}{\psi_t(X_t)} E\left[\psi_{t+1}(X_{t+1})J_{t+1}(X_{t+1}) \,\middle|\, X_t\right]\right). \tag{19}$$

It is left as an exercise to show that J_0 is indeed determined inductively, backward in time from T, by (19) and $J_T = g_T$. Moreover, as demonstrated in Section 2I, problem (18) is solved by the stopping time

$$\tau^* = \min\left\{t : J_t(X_t) = g_t(X_t)\right\}. \tag{20}$$

In our alternate notation that treats J_t as a vector in $\mathbb{R}^k$, we can rewrite the Bellman equation (19) in the form

$$J_t = \max\left(g_t, \Pi_t J_{t+1}\right), \tag{21}$$

where, for any x and y in $\mathbb{R}^k$, $\max(x, y)$ denotes the vector in $\mathbb{R}^k$ that has $\max(x_i, y_i)$ as its i-th element.

The Bellman equation (21) leads to a simple recursive solution algorithm for the American put valuation problem of Exercise 2.1. Given an expiration time $\bar{\tau} < T$ and exercise price K, we have $J_{\bar{\tau}+1} = 0$ and

$$J_t = \max\left[(K - \mathcal{S}_t)^+, \Pi J_{t+1}\right], \qquad t \leq \bar{\tau}. \tag{22}$$

More explicitly: For any t and $i \leq t$,

$$J_t(i) = \max\left([K - \mathcal{S}_t(i)]^+, \frac{p J_{t+1}(i+1) + (1-p)J_{t+1}(i)}{R}\right), \tag{23}$$

where $\mathcal{S}_t(i) = xU^i D^{t-i}$ and $p = (R - D)/(U - D)$, for constant coefficients R, U, and D, with $0 < D < R < U$.

More generally, consider an *American security* defined by dividend functions $h_0, \ldots, h_T$ and exercise payoff functions $g_0, \ldots, g_T$. For a given expiration time $\bar{\tau}$, we have $h_t = g_t = 0$, $t > \bar{\tau}$. The owner of the security chooses a stopping time τ at which to exercise, generating the dividend process δ^τ defined by

$$\delta_t^\tau = h_t(X_t), \qquad t < \tau,$$
$$= g_t(X_t), \qquad t = \tau,$$
$$= 0, \qquad\qquad t > \tau.$$

Assuming that δ^τ is redundant for any exercise policy τ, the security's arbitrage-free cum-dividend value is defined recursively by $J_{\tau+1} = 0$ and the extension of (21):

$$J_t = \max\left(g_t,\; h_t + \Pi_t J_{t+1}\right). \tag{24}$$

Exercises

3.1 Consider the classical "binomial" model of a price process S developed in Exercise 2.1. At each period t, the price $S(t)$ of the underlying security at time t is determined by $S(t) = S(t-1)H(t)$, where $H(t)$ is a random variable on $(\Omega, \mathcal{F}, P)$ whose possible outcomes are U and D, each occurring with strictly positive probability. The filtration $\{\mathcal{F}_0, \mathcal{F}_1, \ldots, \mathcal{F}_T\}$ is that generated by the "return process" H. The one-period interest rate is represented by the constant one-period return $R > 1$ on riskless investments. We suppose that $U > R > D > 0$, and that $S_0 > 0$. There are no dividends paid before T.

(A) Consider the following cancellable call option, a contract written between two parties A and B. At any even period, A has the right to purchase the asset from B at a fixed price K. At odd periods, B can cancel the contract by paying to A a fixed fee of F. The contract is initiated at time 0, and expires at time T, where T is even. The contract is initiated at time 0 with a payment of C units of account by A, paid to B. Counterparty A can also exercise the option at time 0, immediately after the initial payment of C to B. Both A and B have the right to transfer their contractual rights (or obligations) to a third party at any time, and the third parties that assume those rights or obligations may be paid, or pay, to do so. The assuming parties, moreover, have the right to further transfer the rights (or obligations) to other parties, and so on. Suppose there is no arbitrage in the market for this cancellable call, and that A and B have strictly increasing utilities for consumption processes (nonnegative adapted processes). Would the option be exercised by A before the last possible date T with strictly positive probability? If so, give a proof. If not, give a proof, for example in the form of a counterexample. Then provide an algorithm for the initial valuation of the cancellable option. That is, provide an easy computational algorithm for computing the initial price U_0 of the cancellable option. Prove that if the cancellable call option trades at time 0 at some price other than that determined by your algorithm, then there is an arbitrage. If an arbitrage calls for buying or selling the option, do not assume that the counterparty to the trade exercises its rights "rationally."

(B) Now consider an American put option to sell the underlying security with price process S at a fixed price K, at T or at any time before T, with the following exception. We will enforce the common stock-exchange rule of "no sale on a down tick," but only for the purposes of exercising the option. That is, at any time t, one may not exercise the option-provided right to sell the underlying security at time t for K if $S_t < S_{t-1}$. (The underlying security itself may be traded without constraints at any time, as usual.) In particular, this means that if the option has not been exercised before T, and if $S_T < S_{T-1}$, then the option expires worthless, even if the option is in the money at T. Provide an easy computational algorithm for calculating the arbitrage-free initial value U_0 of this special put option. You may assume that "$S_0 > S_{-1}$," so that exercise at time 0 is feasible. Prove that if the option trades at time 0 at some initial price other than that determined by your algorithm, there will exist an arbitrage. If an arbitrage calls for selling the option, do not assume that the option buyer exercises "rationally."

3.2 Prove the Bellman equation (4).

3.3 For each t and each w such that there exists a feasible policy, let $C_t(w)$ solve (4). Let W^* be determined by (1) with $c_{t-1} = C_{t-1}(W^*_{t-1})$ for $t > 0$. Show that an optimal policy c^* is given by $c^*_t = C_t(W^*_t)$, $t < T$, and $c^*_T = e_T + W^*_T$.

3.4 Prove Lemma 3B. Hint: If $f : \mathbb{R} \to \mathbb{R}$ is concave, then for each x, there is a number β such that $\beta(x - y) \le f(x) - f(y)$ for all y. If f is also differentiable at x, then $\beta = f'(x)$. If f is differentiable and strictly concave, then f is continuously differentiable. Let $w^* = W^*_t$. If $c^*_t > 0$, there is an interval $I = (\underline{w}, \bar{w}) \subset \mathbb{R}$ with $w^* \in I$ such that $v : I \to \mathbb{R}$ is well defined by

$$v(w) = u_t(c^*_t + w - w^*) + V_{t+1}(W^*_{t+1}).$$

Now use the differentiability of v, the definition of a derivative, and the fact that $v(w) \le V_t(w)$ for all $w \in I$.

3.5 Prove equation (9).

3.6 Prove Proposition 3E.

3.7 Prove Theorem 3E and its corollary.

3.8 Consider the case of securities in positive supply, which can be taken without loss of generality to be a supply of 1 each. Equilibrium in the context of Section E is thus redefined by the following: $\{\mathcal{S}_0, \dots, \mathcal{S}_T\}$ is an equilibrium if (c^*, θ^*) solves (10) at $t = 0$ and $w = \mathbf{1} \cdot [\mathcal{S}_0(X_0) + f_0(X_0)]$, where $\mathbf{1} = (1, \dots, 1)$ and, for all t, $\theta^*_t = \mathbf{1}$, and $c^*_t = g_t(X_t) + \mathbf{1} \cdot f_t(X_t)$. Demonstrate a new version of the stochastic Euler equation (9) that characterizes equilibrium in this case.

3.9 (Recursive Utility Revisited). The objective in this exercise is to extend the basic results of the chapter to the case of a recursive-utility function that generalizes additive utility. Rather than assuming a typical additive-utility function U of the form

$$U(c) = E\left[\sum_{t=0}^{T} \rho^t u(c_t)\right], \tag{25}$$

we adopt instead the more general recursive definition of utility given by $U(c) = Y_0$, where Y is a process defined by $Y_{T+1} = 0$ and, for any $t \le T$,

$$Y_t = J\left(c_t, E_t[h(Y_{t+1})]\right), \tag{26}$$

where $J : \mathbb{R}_+ \times \mathbb{R} \to \mathbb{R}$ and $h : \mathbb{R} \to \mathbb{R}$. This is the special case treated in Exercise 2.9 of what is known as recursive utility. (In an even more general recursive-utility model, the von Neumann-Morgenstern criterion $E[h(\cdot)]$ is replaced by a general functional on distributions, but we do not deal with this further generalization.) The special case $J(q, v) = u(q) + \rho v$ and $h(y) = y$ gives us the additively separable criterion (25). The conventional additive utility has the disadvantage that the elasticity of intertemporal substitution (as measured in a deterministic setting) and relative risk aversion are fixed in terms of one another. The recursive criterion, however, allows one to examine the effects of varying risk aversion while holding fixed the utility's elasticity of intertemporal substitution in a deterministic setting.

(A) (Dynamic Programming). Provide an extension of the Bellman equation (12) for optimal portfolio and consumption choice, substituting the recursive utility for the additive utility. That is, state a revised Bellman equation and regularity conditions on the utility primitives (J, h) under which a solution to the Bellman equation implies that the associated feedback policies solving the Bellman equation generate optimal consumption and portfolio choice. (State a theorem with proof.) Also, include conditions under which there exists a solution to the Bellman equation. For simplicity, among your conditions you may wish to impose the assumptions that J and h are continuous and strictly increasing.

(B) (Asset Pricing Theory). Suppose that J and h are differentiable, increasing, and concave, with h or J (or both) strictly concave. Provide any additional regularity conditions that you feel are called for in order to derive an analogue to the stochastic Euler equation (9) for security prices.

(C) (A Growth Problem). Let $G : Z \times \mathbb{R}_+ \to \mathbb{R}_+$ and consider the capital-stock investment problem defined by

$$\sup_{c \in L_+} U(c) \tag{27}$$

subject to $0 \le c_t \le K_t$ for all t, where $K_0, K_1, \ldots$, is a capital-stock process defined by $K_t = G(X_t, K_{t-1} - c_{t-1})$, and where $X_0, \ldots, X_T$ is the Markov process defined in

Section C. The utility function U is the recursive function defined above in terms of (J, h). Provide reasonable conditions on (J, h, G) under which there exists a solution. State the Bellman equation.

(D) (Parametric Example). For this part, in order to obtain closed-form solutions, we depart from the assumption that the shock takes only a finite number of possible values, and replace this with a normality assumption. Solve the problem of part (C) in the following case:

(a) X is the real-valued shock process defined by $X_{t+1} = A + BX_t + \epsilon_{t+1}$, where A and B are scalars and $\epsilon_1, \epsilon_2, \ldots$ is an *i.i.d.* sequence of normally distributed random variables with $E(\epsilon_t) = 0$ and $\mathrm{var}(\epsilon_t) = \sigma^2$.

(b) $G(x, a) = a^\gamma e^x$ for some $\gamma \in (0, 1)$.

(c) $J(q, w) = \log(q) + \rho \log(w^{1/\alpha})$ for some $\alpha \in (0, 1)$.

(d) $h(v) = e^{\alpha v}$ for $v \geq 0$.

Hint: You may wish to conjecture a solution to the value function of the form $V_t(x, k) = A_1(t) \log(k) + A_2(t)x + A_3(t)$, for time-dependent coefficients A_1, A_2, and A_3. This example is unlikely to satisfy the regularity conditions that you imposed in part (C).

(E) (Term Structure). For the consumption endowment process e defined by the solution to part (D), return to the setting of part (B), and calculate the price $\Lambda_{t,s}$ at time t of a pure discount bond paying one unit of consumption at time $s > t$. Note that α is a measure of risk tolerance that can be studied independently of the effects of intertemporal substitution in this model, since, for deterministic consumption processes, utility is independent of α, with $J[q, h(v)] = \log(q) + \rho \log(v)$.

3.10 Show equation (5) directly from equation (2.9).

3.11 (Binomial Term-Structure Algorithms). This exercise asks for a series of numerical solutions of term-structure valuation problems in a setting with binomial changes in short-term interest rates. In the setting of Section F, under the absence of arbitrage, suppose that short-term riskless borrowing is possible at any time t at the discount d_t. The one-period interest rate at time t is denoted r_t, and is given by its definition:

$$d_t = \frac{1}{1 + r_t}.$$

The underlying shock process X has the property that either $X_t = X_{t-1} + 1$ or $X_t = X_{t-1}$. That is, in each period, the new shock is the old shock plus a 0–1 binomial trial. An example is the binomial stock-option pricing model of Exercise 2.1, which is reconsidered in Section F. As opposed to that example, we do not necessarily assume here that interest rates are constant. Rather, we allow, at each time t, a function $\rho_t : Z \to \mathbb{R}$ such that $r_t = \rho_t(X_t)$. For simplicity, however, we take it that at any time t, the pricing matrix Π_t defined in Section F is of the form

$$(\Pi_t)_{ij} = \frac{p}{1 + \rho_t(i)}, \qquad j = i + 1,$$

$$= \frac{1 - p}{1 + \rho_t(i)}, \qquad j = i,$$

$$= 0, \qquad\qquad \text{otherwise,}$$

where $p \in (0, 1)$ is the "risk-neutral" probability that $X_{t+1} - X_t = 1$. Literally, we suppose that there is an equivalent martingale measure Q, in the sense of chapter 2, under which, for all t, we have

$$Q(X_{t+1} - X_t = 1 \mid X_0, \ldots, X_t) = p.$$

It may help to imagine the calculation of security prices at the nodes of the "tree" illustrated in Figure 3.1. The horizontal axis indicates the time periods; the vertical axis corresponds to the possible levels of the shock, assuming that $X_0 = 0$. At each time t and at each shock level i, the price of a given security at the (i, t)-node of the tree is given by a weighted sum of its value at the two successor nodes $(i + 1, t + 1)$ and $(i, t + 1)$. Specifically,

$$\mathscr{S}_t(i) = \frac{1}{1 + \rho_t(i)}[p(\mathscr{S}_{t+1}(i + 1) + f_{t+1}(i + 1)) + (1 - p)(\mathscr{S}_{t+1}(i) + f_{t+1}(i))].$$

Two typical models for the short rate are obtained by taking $p = 1/2$ and either

(a) the *Ho-Lee model*: For each $t < T$, $\rho_t(i) = a_t + b_t i$ for some constants a_t and b_t; or

(b) the *Black-Derman-Toy model*: For each t, $\rho_t(i) = a_t \exp(b_t i)$ for some constants a_t and b_t.

(A) For case (b), the Black-Derman-Toy model, prepare computer code to calculate the arbitrage-free price $\Lambda_{0,t}$ of a zero-coupon bond of any given maturity t, given the coefficients a_t and b_t for each t. Prepare an example taking $b_t = 0.01$ for all t and $a_0, a_1, \ldots, a_T$ such that $E^Q(r_t) = 0.01$ for all t. (These parameters are of a typical order of magnitude for monthly periods.) Solve for the price $\Lambda_{0,t}$ of a unit zero-coupon riskless bond maturing at time t, for all t in $\{1, \ldots, 50\}$.

(B) Consider, for any i and t, the price $\psi_t(i)$ at time 0 of a security that pays one unit of account at time t if and only if $X_t = i$.

Show that ψ can be calculated recursively by the "forward" difference equation

$$\psi_t(i) = \frac{\psi_t(i)}{2[1 + \rho_t(i)]} + \frac{\psi_t(i - 1)}{2[1 + \rho_t(i - 1)]}, \qquad 0 < i < t + 1,$$

$$= \frac{\psi_t(i - 1)}{2[1 + \rho_t(i - 1)]}, \qquad\qquad i = t + 1, \tag{28}$$

$$= \frac{\psi_t(i)}{2[1 + \rho_t(i)]}, \qquad\qquad i = 0.$$

The initial condition is $\psi_0(0) = 1$ and $\psi_0(i) = 0$ for $i > 0$. Knowledge of this "shock-price" function ψ is useful. For example, the arbitrage-free price at time 0 of a security that pays the dividend $f(X_t)$ at time t (and nothing otherwise) is given by $\sum_{i=0}^{t} \psi_t(i) f(i)$.

(C) In practice, the coefficients a_t and b_t are often fitted to match the initial term structure $\Lambda_{0,1}, \ldots, \Lambda_{0,T}$, given the "volatility" coefficients $b_0, \ldots, b_T$. The following algorithm has been suggested for this purpose, using the fact that $\Lambda_{0,t} = \sum_{i=0}^{t} \psi_t(i)$.

(a) Let $\psi_0(0) = 1$ and let $t = 1$.
(b) Fixing ψ_{t-1} and b_t, let $\lambda_t(a_{t-1}) = \sum_{i=0}^{t} \psi_t(i)$, where ψ_t is given by the forward difference equation (28). Only the dependence of the t-maturity zero-coupon bond price $\lambda_t(a_{t-1})$ on a_{t-1} is notationally explicit. Since $\lambda_t(a_{t-1})$ is strictly monotone in a_{t-1}, we can solve numerically for that coefficient a_{t-1} such that $\Lambda_{0,t} = \lambda_t(a_{t-1})$. (A Newton-Raphson search will suffice.)
(c) Let t be increased by 1. Return to step (b) if $t \le T$. Otherwise, stop.

Prepare computer code for this algorithm (a)–(b)–(c). Given $b_t = 0.01$ for all t, solve for a_t for all t, using the Black-Derman-Toy model, given an initial term structure that is given by $\Lambda_{0,t} = \alpha^t$, where $\alpha = 0.99$.

(D) Extend your code as necessary to give the price of American call options on coupon bonds of any given maturity. For the coefficients $a_0, \ldots, a_{T-1}$ that you determined from part (C), calculate the initial price of an American option on a bond that pays coupons of 0.013 each period until its maturity at time 20, at which time it pays 1 unit of account in addition to its coupon. The option has an exercise price of 1.00, ex dividend, and expiration at time 10. Do this for the Black-Derman-Toy model only.

Notes

(A–B) Bellman's principle of optimality is due to Bellman (1957). The proof for Lemma 3B that is sketched in Exercise 3.3, on the differentiability of the value function, is from Benveniste and Scheinkman (1979), and easily extends to general state spaces; see, for example, Duffie (1988c) and Stokey and Lucas (1989).

(C) Freedman (1983) covers the theory of Markov chains. For general treatments of dynamic programming in a discrete-time Markov setting, see Bertsekas (1976) and Bertsekas and Shreve (1978).

(D–F) This is a simple finite-horizon version of the Markov asset-pricing models of LeRoy (1973) and Lucas (1978) that are reviewed in Chapter 4. The semigroup pricing approach implicit in (17) is from Duffie and Garman (1991). The "binomial" option pricing model of Section F was developed by William Sharpe and by Cox, Ross, and Rubinstein (1979), and is further explored in Exercise 2.1 and in Chapter 12.

Additional Topics: Exercise 3.9, treating asset pricing with the recursive utility of Exercise 2.9, is extended to the infinite-horizon setting of Epstein and Zin (1989) in Exercise 4.12. See the Notes of Chapter 2 for additional references on recursive utility, and Streufert (1991a, 1991b, 1996) for more on dynamic programming with a recursive-utility function. For additional work on recursive utility and asset pricing in a discrete-time Markov setting, see Kan (1993, 1995) and Ma (1993b, 1994).

The extensive exercise on binomial term-structure models is based almost entirely on Jamshidian (1991c), who emphasizes the connection between the solution ψ of the difference equation (28) and state pricing of contingent claims. This connection is reconsidered in Chapters 7 and 12 for continuous-time applications. The two particular term-structure models appearing in this exercise are based, respectively, on Ho and Lee (1986) and Black, Derman, and Toy (1990). The parametric form shown here for the Ho-Lee model is slightly more general than the form actually appearing in Ho and Lee (1986). Most authors take the convention that X_{t+1} is $X_t + 1$ or $X_t - 1$, which generates a slightly different form for the same model. The two forms are equivalent after a change of the parameters. Pye (1966), whose work predates the notion of "risk-neutral valuation," provides a remarkably early precursor to these discrete-time Markovian models of the term structure. Continuous-time versions of these models are considered in Chapter 7. Chapter 12 also deals in more detail with algorithms designed to match the initial term structure. Exercise 12.5 demonstrates convergence, with a decreasing length of time period, of the discrete-time Black-Derman-Toy model to its continuous-time version. Jamshidian (1991c) considers a larger class of examples.

Derman and Kani (1994), Dupire (1994b), and Rubinstein(1994, 1995) provide various methods for calibrating a "binomial" Markov stock-price process, similar to that of Section F, to the available prices of options of various strike prices and, in some cases, of various maturities. This is part of a literature devoted to the *smile curve*, which refers to the shape often found for a plot of the "implied volatilities" of option prices derived from the Black-Scholes formula against the exercise prices of the respective options. If the assumptions underlying the Black-Scholes formula are correct, the implied volatility does not depend on the strike price. The smile curve is discussed once again in Chapter 8, under the topic of stochastic volatility. Related literature is cited in the Notes of Chapter 8.

Bossaerts, Ghysels, and Gourieroux (1996) analyze arbitrage-based pricing with stochastic volatility. Jouini, Koehl, and Touzi (1995) explore the effects of transactions costs and incomplete markets in this setting.

4

The Infinite-Horizon Setting

THIS CHAPTER PRESENTS infinite-period analogues of the results of Chapters 2 and 3. Although this setting requires additional technicalities and produces few new insights, it sometimes simplifies results and it serves the large-sample theory of econometrics, which calls for an unbounded number of observations. We start directly with a Markov dynamic programming extension of the finite-horizon results of Chapter 3, and only later consider the implications of no arbitrage or optimality for security prices without using the Markov assumption. Finally, we return to the stationary Markov setting to review briefly the large-sample approach to estimating asset pricing models. Only Sections A and B are essential; the remainder could be skipped on a first reading.

A. Markov Dynamic Programming

Suppose $X = \{X_0, X_1, X_2, \ldots\}$ is a time-homogeneous Markov chain of shocks valued in a finite set $Z = \{1, \ldots, k\}$, defined exactly as in Section C, with the exception that there is an infinite number of time periods. Given a $k \times k$ nonnegative matrix q whose rows sum to 1, sources given in the Notes explain the existence of a probability space $(\Omega, \mathcal{F}, P_i)$, for each initial shock i, satisfying the defining properties $P_i(X_0 = i) = 1$ and

$$P_i(X_{t+1} = j \mid X_0, \ldots, X_t) = q_{X(t), j}.$$

As in Chapter 3, $\mathcal{F}_t$ denotes the tribe generated by $\{X_0, \ldots, X_t\}$. That is, the source of information is the Markov chain $\{X_t\}$. This is the first appearance in the book of a set Ω of states that need not be finite, but because there is only a finite number of events in $\mathcal{F}_t$ for each t, most of this chapter can be easily understood without referring to Appendix C for a review of general probability spaces.

65

Let L denote the space of sequences of random variables of the form $c = \{c_0, c_1, c_2, \dots\}$ such that there is a constant $\bar{c}$ with the property that for all t, c_t is $\mathscr{F}_t$-measurable with $|c_t| \leq \bar{c}$. In other words, L is the space of bounded adapted processes. Agents choose a consumption process from the set L_+ of nonnegative processes in L. There are N securities; security n is defined by a dividend process $\delta^{(n)}$ in L and has a price process $S^{(n)}$ in L. A trading strategy is some $\theta = (\theta^{(1)}, \dots, \theta^{(N)}) \in \Theta \equiv L^N$. Each strategy θ in Θ generates a dividend process δ^θ in L defined, just as in Chapter 2, by

$$\delta_t^\theta = \theta_{t-1} \cdot (S_t + \delta_t) - \theta_t \cdot S_t, \qquad t \geq 0,$$

with "θ_{-1}" $= 0$ by convention. A given agent has an endowment process e in L_+ and, given a particular initial shock i, a utility function $U^i : L_+ \to \mathbb{R}$. The agent's problem is

$$\sup_{\theta \in \Theta(e)} U^i(e + \delta^\theta),$$

where $\Theta(e) = \{\theta \in \Theta : e + \delta^\theta \geq 0\}$.

In order to develop a time-homogeneous Markov model, we restrict ourselves initially to utility functions, endowments, and security dividends with special time-homogeneous properties. Given an initial shock i, consider the utility function $U^i : L_+ \to \mathbb{R}$ defined by a discount $\rho \in (0, 1)$ and a strictly increasing, bounded, concave, and continuous $u : \mathbb{R}_+ \to \mathbb{R}$ according to

$$U^i(c) = E^i \left[\sum_{t=0}^{\infty} \rho^t \, u(c_t) \right], \tag{1}$$

where E^i denotes expectation under the probability measure P_i associated with the initial shock $X_0 = i$. Suppose that $g : Z \to \mathbb{R}_{++}$ and $f : Z \to \mathbb{R}_{++}^N$ are such that for all t, the endowment is $e_t = g(X_t)$ and the dividend vector is $\delta_t = f(X_t)$. Finally, suppose that security prices are given by some fixed $\mathscr{S} : Z \to \mathbb{R}_{++}^N$ so that for all t, $S_t = \mathscr{S}(X_t)$.

We fix a portfolio b in $\mathbb{R}_{++}^N$ and think of $-b$ as a lower bound on short positions. This restriction will later be removed. For now, however, wealth is bounded below by

$$\underline{w} = \min_{i \in Z} -b \cdot [\mathscr{S}(i) + f(i)].$$

Let $D = Z \times [\underline{w}, \infty)$. A function $F : D \to \mathbb{R}$ is defined to be in the space denoted $B(D)$ if, for each i in Z, $F(i, \cdot) : [\underline{w}, \infty) \to \mathbb{R}$ is bounded, continuous, and concave. The *value* of the agent's control problem is some V in $B(D)$ with

$$V(i, w) = \sup_{(c, \theta) \in L_+ \times \Theta} U^i(c), \qquad (2)$$

subject to

$$W_0^\theta = w, \qquad (3)$$

$$W_t^\theta = \theta_{t-1} \cdot [\mathcal{S}(X_t) + f(X_t)], \qquad t \geq 1, \qquad (4)$$

$$c_t + \theta_t \cdot \mathcal{S}(X_t) \leq W_t^\theta + g(X_t), \qquad t \geq 0, \qquad (5)$$

$$\theta_t \geq -b, \qquad t \geq 0. \qquad (6)$$

We will solve for the value function V by taking an arbitrary F in $B(D)$ and, from this candidate, construct a new candidate, denoted $\mathcal{U}F$, that is described below. Our method will show that if $F = \mathcal{U}F$, then $F = V$. In fact, this approach also leads to an algorithm, called *value iteration*, for calculating V. This algorithm is laid out below. For any F in $B(D)$, let $\mathcal{U}F : D \to \mathbb{R}$ be defined by

$$\mathcal{U}F(i, w) = \sup_{(\bar{\theta}, \bar{c}) \in \mathbb{R}^N \times \mathbb{R}_+} u(\bar{c}) + \rho E^i [F(X_1, \bar{\theta} \cdot [\mathcal{S}(X_1) + f(X_1)])], \qquad (7)$$

subject to

$$\bar{c} + \bar{\theta} \cdot \mathcal{S}(i) \leq w + g(i), \qquad (8)$$

$$\bar{\theta} \geq -b. \qquad (9)$$

In other words, $\mathcal{U}F(i, w)$ is the supremum utility that can be achieved at (i, w), assuming that the value function in the next period is F.

Proofs of the next three results are left as exercises.

Fact. *If F is in $B(D)$, then $\mathcal{U}F$ is in $B(D)$.*

For any F and G in $B(D)$, let

$$d(F, G) = \sup\{|F(i, w) - G(i, w)| : (i, w) \in D\},$$

giving a notion of the distance between any two such functions. Clearly $F = G$ if and only if $d(F, G) = 0$.

Lemma. *For any F and G in $B(D)$, $d(\mathcal{U}F, \mathcal{U}G) \leq \rho d(F, G)$.*

Using this lemma, we can construct the unique solution F to the equation $\mathcal{U}F = F$, which is known as the *Bellman equation* for problem (2)–(6). The solution F is called the *fixed point* of $\mathcal{U}$ and, as shown by the following result, can be constructed as the limit of the finite-horizon versions of the value functions as the horizon goes to infinity.

Proposition. *Let $F_{-1}(i, w) = 0$ for all (i, w) in D, and let $F_t = \mathcal{U}F_{t-1}$, $t \geq 0$. Then $F(i, w) \equiv \lim_{t \to \infty} F_t(i, w)$ exists for all (i, w) in D and defines the unique function F in $B(D)$ satisfying $F = \mathcal{U}F$.*

We take F to be the unique fixed point of $\mathcal{U}$. We will show that F is the value function V of problem (2)–(6). Let $C : D \to \mathbb{R}_+$ and $\Phi : D \to \mathbb{R}^N$ be functions defined by letting $[C(i, w), \Phi(i, w)]$ solve (7)–(9). Given the initial conditions (i, w) of (2)–(6), let W^* be defined by $W_0^* = w$ and $W_t^* = \Phi(X_{t-1}, W_{t-1}^*) \cdot [\mathcal{S}(X_t) + f(X_t)]$, $t \geq 1$. Then let (c^*, θ^*) be defined by $c_t^* = C(X_t, W_t^*)$ and $\theta_t^* = \Phi(X_t, W_t^*)$, $t \geq 0$. We refer to any such (θ^*, c^*) as an *optimal feedback control*. The functions Φ and C are the associated feedback policy functions.

Theorem. *The value function V of (2)–(6) is the unique fixed point of $\mathcal{U}$. Any optimal feedback control (c^*, θ^*) solves (2)–(6).*

Proof: Let F be the unique solution of the Bellman equation $\mathcal{U}F = F$. Fix any initial shock i in Z and initial wealth w in $[\underline{w}, \infty)$. Let (θ, c) be an arbitrary feasible control. For any time t, by the Bellman equation (7)–(9),

$$F(X_t, W_t^\theta) \geq u(c_t) + \rho E^i\big[F(X_{t+1}, W_{t+1}^\theta) \mid X_t\big].$$

Multiplying through by ρ^t and rearranging,

$$\rho^t F(X_t, W_t^\theta) - \rho^{t+1} E^i\big[F(X_{t+1}, W_{t+1}^\theta) \mid X_t\big] \geq \rho^t u(c_t). \tag{10}$$

Taking expectations on each side, and using the law of iterated expectations,

$$E^i\big[\rho^t F(X_t, W_t^\theta)\big] - \rho^{t+1} E^i\big[F(X_{t+1}, W_{t+1}^\theta)\big] \geq E^i[\rho^t u(c_t)].$$

Calculating the sum of this expression from $t = 0$ to $t = T$, for any time $T \geq 1$, causes telescopic cancellation on the left-hand side, leaving only

$$E^i\big[F(X_0, W_0^\theta)\big] - \rho^{T+1} E^i\big[F(X_{T+1}, W_{T+1}^\theta)\big] \geq E^i\left[\sum_{t=0}^{T} \rho^t u(c_t)\right].$$

Since F is a bounded function and $\rho \in (0, 1)$, the limit of the left-hand side as $T \to \infty$ is $F(i, w)$. By the Dominated Convergence Theorem (Appendix C), the limit of the right-hand side is $U^i(c)$. Thus $F(i, w) \geq U^i(c)$. All of the above calculations apply for the given optimal feedback control (c^*, θ^*), for which we can replace the inequality in (10) with an equality, using the definition of C and Φ. This leaves $F(i, w) = U^i(c^*)$. It follows, since (i, w) is arbitrary, that F is indeed the value function and that (c^*, θ^*) is optimal, in that it solves (2)–(6), proving the result. ∎

B. Dynamic Programming and Equilibrium

Section A shows the existence of optimal control in feedback form, given by *policy functions* C and Φ that specify optimal consumption and portfolio choices in terms of the current shock-wealth pair (i, w). In order to characterize an equilibrium by the same approach, we adopt stronger utility conditions for this section. In addition to our standing assumption that u is strictly increasing, bounded, concave, and continuous, we add the following regularity condition.

Assumption A. *The function u is strictly concave and differentiable on $(0, \infty)$.*

We define $\mathscr{S}$ to be a single-agent *Markov equilibrium* if associated optimal feedback policy functions C and Φ can be chosen so that for any shock i, $C(i, 0) = g(i)$ and $\Phi(i, 0) = 0$. With this, the consumption and security markets always clear if the agent is originally endowed with no wealth beyond that of his or her private endowment. The short-sales restriction on portfolios is superfluous in equilibrium since this short-sales constraint is not binding at the solution $(e, 0)$, and since the equilibrium shown (which is the unique equilibrium) does not depend on the particular lower bound $-b$ chosen. (It is an exercise to verify this fact.) Our main objective is to demonstrate the following characterization of equilibrium.

Proposition. $\mathscr{S}$ *is a Markov equilibrium if and only if, for all i,*

$$\mathscr{S}(i) = \frac{1}{u'[g(i)]} E^i \left(\sum_{t=1}^{\infty} \rho^t u'[g(X_t)] f(X_t) \right). \tag{11}$$

The law of iterated expectations implies the following equivalent form of (11), sometimes called the stochastic Euler equation.

Corollary. *$\mathscr{S}$ is a Markov equilibrium if and only if, for any time t and any initial shock i,*

$$\mathscr{S}(X_t) = \frac{1}{u'[g(X_t)]} E^i(\rho u'[g(X_{t+1})][\mathscr{S}(X_{t+1}) + f(X_{t+1})] \mid X_t). \tag{12}$$

We will demonstrate these results by exploiting the following two properties of the value function V.

Fact 1. *For each i, $V(i, \cdot) : [\underline{w}, \infty) \to \mathbb{R}$ is increasing and strictly concave.*

Fact 2. *Fixing $\mathscr{S}$ arbitrarily, let (C, Φ) be optimal feedback policy functions, as above. Suppose, at a given i and $\hat{w} > \underline{w}$, that $\hat{c} = C(i, \hat{w}) > 0$. Then $V(i, \cdot)$ is continuously differentiable at $\hat{w}$ with derivative $V_w(i, \hat{w}) = u'(\hat{c})$.*

These two facts, proved in a manner similar to their analogues in Chapter 3, imply, from the first-order conditions of the Bellman equation (7) and the fact that V solves the Bellman equation, that C and Φ can be chosen with $C(i, 0) = g(i)$ and $\Phi(i, 0) = 0$ for all i if and only if

$$\mathscr{S}(i) = \frac{1}{u'[g(i)]} E^i(\rho u'[g(X_1)][\mathscr{S}(X_1) + f(X_1)]), \qquad i \in Z. \tag{13}$$

Then (13) is equivalent to (11) and (12), proving the proposition and corollary.

C. Arbitrage and State Prices

We turn away from the special case of Markov uncertainty in order to investigate the implications of lack of arbitrage and of optimality for security prices in an abstract infinite-horizon setting. Suppose Ω is a set, $\mathscr{F}$ is a tribe on Ω, and, for each nonnegative integer t, $\mathscr{F}_t$ is a finite subtribe with $\mathscr{F}_t \subset \mathscr{F}_s$ for $s \geq t$. We also fix a probability measure P on $(\Omega, \mathscr{F})$. As usual, we assume that $\mathscr{F}_0$ includes only events of probability 0 or 1. We again denote by L the space of bounded adapted processes. There are N securities; security n is defined by a dividend process $\delta^{(n)}$ in L and has a price process $S^{(n)}$ in L. A trading strategy is some $\theta = (\theta^{(1)}, \dots, \theta^{(N)}) \in \Theta \equiv L^{(N)}$.

An *arbitrage* is a trading strategy θ with $\delta^\theta > 0$. If there is no arbitrage, then for any T, there is no *T-period arbitrage*, meaning an arbitrage θ with $\theta_t = 0$, $t \geq T$. Fixing T momentarily, if there is no T-period arbitrage, then the results of Chapter 2 imply that there is a *T-period state-price deflator*, a strictly positive process π^T in L with $\pi_0^T = 1$ such that for any trading strategy θ with $\theta_t = 0$, $t \geq T$, we have $E(\sum_{t=0}^T \pi_t^T \delta_t^\theta) = 0$. Likewise, there is a $(T + 1)$-period state-price deflator π^{T+1}. It can be checked that the process $\hat{\pi}$ defined by $\hat{\pi}_t = \pi_t^T$, $t \leq T$, and $\hat{\pi}_t = \pi_t^{T+1}$, $t > T$, is also a $(T+1)$-period state-price deflator. By induction in T, this means that there is a strictly positive adapted process π such that, for any trading strategy θ with $\theta_t = 0$ for all t larger than some T, we have $E(\sum_{t=0}^{\infty} \pi_t \delta_t^{\theta}) = 0$. In particular, π has the property that for any times t and $\tau \geq t$, we have the now-familiar state-pricing relationship

$$S_t = \frac{1}{\pi_t} E_t \left(\pi_\tau S_\tau + \sum_{j=t+1}^{\tau} \pi_j \delta_j \right). \tag{14}$$

Equation (14) even holds when τ is a bounded stopping time. Unfortunately, there is no reason (yet) to believe that there is a state-price deflator, a strictly positive adapted process π such that (14) holds for τ an unbounded stopping time, or that for any t,

$$S_t = \frac{1}{\pi_t} E_t \left(\sum_{j=t+1}^{\infty} \pi_j \delta_j \right). \tag{15}$$

Indeed, the right-hand side of (15) may not even be well defined. We need some restriction on π!

We call an adapted process x *mean-summable* if $E(\sum_{t=0}^{\infty} |x_t|) < \infty$, and let L^* denote the space of mean-summable processes. If $\pi \in L^*$ and $c \in L$, then the Dominated Convergence Theorem (Appendix C) implies that $E(\sum_{t=0}^{\infty} \pi_t c_t)$ is well defined and finite, so L^* may be a natural space of candidate state-price deflators if (15) is to work.

D. Optimality and State Prices

An agent is defined by an endowment process e in the space L_+ of non-negative processes in L, and by a strictly increasing utility function $U : L_+ \to \mathbb{R}$. Given the dividend-price pair $(\delta, S) \in L^N \times L^N$, the agent faces the problem

$$\sup_{\theta} U(e + \delta^{\theta}). \tag{16}$$

We say that the utility function U is L^*-smooth at c if the gradient $\nabla U(c)$ exists and moreover has a unique Riesz representation π in L^* defined by

$$\nabla U(c; x) = E \left(\sum_{t=0}^{\infty} \pi_t x_t \right),$$

for any feasible direction x in L. (See Appendix B for the definition of the gradient and feasible directions.) For example, suppose that U is defined by $U(c) = E[\sum_{t=0}^{\infty} \rho^t u(c_t)]$, where $u : \mathbb{R}_+ \to \mathbb{R}$ is strictly increasing and continuously differentiable on $(0, \infty)$, and where $\rho \in (0, 1)$. Then, for any c in L_+ that is bounded away from zero, U is L^*-smooth at c, any x in L is a feasible direction at c, and

$$\nabla U(c; x) = E\left[\sum_{t=0}^{\infty} \rho^t u'(c_t) x_t\right], \quad x \in L, \tag{17}$$

implying that the Riesz representation of the utility gradient is in this case the process π defined by $\pi_t = \rho^t u'_t(c_t)$.

More generally, we have the following characterization of state-price deflators.

Proposition. *Suppose c^* solves (16), c^* is bounded away from zero, and U is L^*-smooth at c^*. Then the Riesz representation π of $\nabla U(c^*)$ is a state-price deflator.*

Corollary. *Suppose, moreover, that U is defined by*

$$U(c) = E\left[\sum_{t=0}^{\infty} \rho^t u(c_t)\right],$$

where $\rho \in (0, 1)$ and u has a strictly positive derivative on $(0, \infty)$. Then π, defined by $\pi_t = \rho^t u'(c_t^*)$, is a state-price deflator and, for any time t and stopping time $\tau > t$,

$$S_t = \frac{1}{u'(c_t^*)} E_t\left[\rho^{\tau-t} u'(c_\tau^*) S_\tau + \sum_{j=t+1}^{\tau} \rho^{j-t} u'(c_j^*) \delta_j\right].$$

This corollary gives a necessary condition for optimality that, when specialized to the case of equilibrium, recovers the stochastic Euler equation (12) as a necessary condition on equilibrium without relying on Markov uncertainty or dynamic programming. For sufficiency, we should give conditions under which the stochastic Euler equation implies that S is an equilibrium. For this, we define S to be a single-agent equilibrium if $\theta^* = 0$ solves (16) given S.

Theorem. *Suppose that U is strictly increasing, concave, and L^*-smooth at the endowment process e. Suppose that the endowment process e is bounded away from zero. Let $\pi \in L^*$ be the Riesz representation of $\nabla U(e)$. It is necessary and sufficient for S to be a single-agent equilibrium that π is a state-price deflator.*

The assumption that e is bounded away from zero is automatically satisfied in the Markovian example of Section A. Proof of the theorem is assigned as an exercise.

E. Method-of-Moments Estimation

Although it is not our main purpose to delve into econometrics, it seems worthwhile to illustrate here why the infinite-horizon setting is useful for empirical modeling.

Suppose, for some integer $m \geq 1$, that $B \subset \mathbb{R}^m$ is a set of parameters. Each b in B corresponds to a different Markov economy with the same state space Z. In particular, the transition matrix $q(b)$ of the Markov process X may vary with b. For instance, we could take a single agent with utility given by a discount factor $\rho \in (0, 1)$ and a reward function $u_\alpha(x) = x^\alpha/\alpha$ for $\alpha < 1$ (with $u_0(x) = \log x$). We could then take $m = 2$ and $b = (\rho, \alpha) \in B = (0, \infty) \times (-\infty, 1)$. In this example, the transition matrix $q(b)$ does not depend on b.

We fix some b_0 in B, to be thought of as the "true" parameter vector governing the economy. Our goal is to estimate the unknown parameter vector b_0.

For simplicity, we will assume that the transition matrix $q(b_0)$ of X is strictly positive. With this, a result known as the *Frobenius-Perron Theorem* implies that there is a unique vector $p \in \mathbb{R}^k_{++}$ whose elements sum to 1 with the property that $q(b_0)^\top p = p$. Letting $q(b_0)^t$ denote the t-fold product of $q(b_0)$, we see that $P_i(X_t = j) = q(b_0)^t_{ij}$, so that $q(b_0)^t$ is the t-period transition matrix. It can be shown that p is given by any row of $\lim_t q(b_0)^t$. Thus, regardless of the initial shock i, $\lim_t P_i(X_t = j) = p_j$. Indeed, the convergence to the "steady-state" probability vector p is exponentially fast, in the sense that there is a constant $\beta > 1$ such that for any i and j,

$$\beta^t[p_j - P_i(X_t = j)] \to 0. \tag{18}$$

From this, it follows immediately that for any $H : Z \to \mathbb{R}$ and any initial condition $j \in Z$, we have $E^j[H(X_t)] \to \sum_{i=1}^k p_i H(i)$, and again convergence is exponentially fast. The *empirical distribution vector* p_T of X at time T is defined by

$$p_{Ti} = \frac{1}{T}\#\{t < T : X_t = i\},$$

where $\#A$ denotes the number of elements in a finite set A. That is, p_{Ti} is the average fraction of time, up to T, spent in state i. From the law of large numbers for *i.i.d.* sequences of random variables, it is not hard to show that p_T converges almost surely to the steady-state distribution vector p. Proof of this fact is assigned as Exercise 4.14, which includes a broad hint. From this, we have the following form of the *law of large numbers for Markov chains*.

The Strong Law of Large Numbers for Markov Chains. For any $H : Z \to \mathbb{R}$, the empirical average $\sum_{t=0}^{T} H(X_t)/T$ converges almost surely to the steady-state mean $\sum_{i=1}^{k} p_i H(i)$.

Proof: Since $\sum_{t=0}^{T} H(X_t)/T = \sum_{i=1}^{k} p_{Ti} H(i)$, the result follows from the fact that $p_T \to p$ almost surely. ∎

Suppose that there is some integer $\ell \geq 0$ such that for each time t, the econometrician observes at time $t + \ell$ the data $h(Y_t)$, where $Y_t = (X_t, X_{t+1}, \dots, X_{t+\ell})$ and $h : Z^{\ell+1} \to \mathbb{R}^n$. For example, the data could be in the form of security prices, dividends, endowments, or functions of these. It is easy to check that the strong law of large numbers would apply even if $q(b_0)$ were not strictly positive, provided the t-period transition matrix $q(b_0)^t$ is strictly positive for some t. From this fact, Y also satisfies the strong law of large numbers, since Y can be treated as a Markov process whose $(\ell+1)$-period transition matrix is strictly positive. In particular, for any $G : Z^{\ell+1} \to \mathbb{R}$, the empirical average $\sum_{t=1}^{T} G(Y_t)/T$ converges almost surely to the corresponding steady-state mean, which is also equal to $\lim_t E^i[G(Y_t)]$, a quantity that is independent of the initial shock i.

We now specify some *test moment function* $K : \mathbb{R}^n \times B \to \mathbb{R}^M$, for some integer M, with the property that for all t, $E_t(K[h(Y_t), b_0]) = 0$. For a simple example, we could take the single-agent Markov equilibrium described by the stochastic Euler equation (13), where the utility function is specified as above by the unknown parameter vector $b_0 = (\rho_0, \alpha_0)$. For this example, we can let $Y_t = (X_t, X_{t+1})$ and let $h(Y_t) = (R_{t+1}, e_{t+1}, e_t)$, where $e_t = g(X_t)$ is the current endowment and R_t is the $\mathbb{R}^N$-valued return vector defined by

$$R_{it} = \frac{\mathscr{S}_i(X_t) + f_i(X_t)}{\mathscr{S}_i(X_{t-1})}, \quad i \in \{1, \dots, N\}.$$

With $M = N$ and $b = (\rho, \alpha)$, we can let

$$K_i[h(Y_t), b] = \frac{\rho e_{t+1}^{\alpha-1} R_{i, t+1}}{e_t^{\alpha-1}} - 1. \tag{19}$$

From (13), we confirm that $E_t[K(Y_t, b_0)] = 0$.

We know from the strong law of large numbers that, for each b in B, the empirical average $\bar{K}_T(b) \equiv \sum_{t=1}^{T} K(Y_t, b)/T$ converges almost surely to its stationary mean, denoted $\bar{K}_\infty(b)$. By the law of iterated expectations, for any initial state i,

$$E^i[K(Y_t, b_0)] = E^i(E_t[K(Y_t, b_0)]) = 0.$$

From this, we know that $\overline{K}_\infty(b_0) = 0$ almost surely. A natural estimator of b_0 at time t is then given by a solution $\hat{b}_t$ to the problem

$$\inf_{b \in B} \|\overline{K}_t(b)\|. \tag{20}$$

Any such sequence $\{\hat{b}_t\}$ of solutions to (20) is called a *generalized-method-of-moments*, or *GMM*, estimator of b_0. Under conditions, one can show that a GMM estimator is *consistent*, in the sense that $\hat{b}_t \rightarrow b_0$ almost surely. A sufficient set of technical conditions is as follows.

GMM Regularity Conditions. *The parameter set B is compact. For any b in B other than b_0, $\overline{K}_\infty(b) \neq 0$. The function K is Lipschitz with respect to b, in the sense that there is a constant k such that, for any y in $Z^{\ell+1}$ and any b_1 and b_2 in B, we have*

$$\| K(y, b_1) - K(y, b_2) \| \leq k \| b_1 - b_2 \| .$$

Theorem. *Under the GMM regularity conditions, a GMM estimator exists and any GMM estimator is consistent.*

The proof follows immediately from the following proposition.

Uniform Strong Law of Large Numbers. *Under the GMM regularity conditions,*

$$\sup_{b \in B} |\overline{K}_T(b) - \overline{K}_\infty(b)| \rightarrow 0 \quad \textit{almost surely.}$$

Proof: The following proof is adapted from a source indicated in the Notes. Without loss of generality for the following arguments, we can take $M = 1$. Since B is a compact set and K is Lipschitz with respect to b, for each $\epsilon \in (0, \infty)$ there is a finite set $B_\epsilon \subset B$ with the following property: For any b in B, there is some b_ϵ and b^ϵ in B_ϵ satisfying, for all y,

$$K(y, b_\epsilon) \leq K(y, b) \leq K(y, b^\epsilon), \qquad |K(y, b_\epsilon) - K(y, b^\epsilon)| \leq \epsilon. \tag{21}$$

As is customary, for any sequence $\{x_n\}$ of numbers, we let

$$\underline{\lim}_n x_n = \sup_n \inf_{k \geq n} x_k.$$

4.14   Prove the version of the strong law of large numbers shown in Section E. Hint: Prove the almost sure convergence of the empirical distribution vector p_T to p by using the strong law of large numbers for $i.i.d$ random variables with finite expectations. For this, given any $l \in Z$, let $\tau_n(l)$ be the n-th time $t \geq 0$ that $X_t = l$. Note that

$$Q_{nlj} \equiv \#\{t : X_t = j, \tau_n(l) \leq t < \tau_{n+1}\}$$

has a distribution that does not depend on n or the initial state i, and that for each l and j, the sequences $\{Q_{1lj}, Q_{2lj}, \dots\}$ and $\{t_n\}$, with $t_n = \tau_{n+1}(l) - \tau_n(l)$, are each $i.i.d.$ with distributions that do not depend on the initial state i. Complete the proof from this point, considering the properties, for each l and j in Z, of

$$\frac{N^{-1}\sum_{n=1}^{N} Q_{nlj}}{N^{-1}\sum_{n=1}^{N} t_n}.$$

Notes

(A–B) Freedman (1983) covers the theory of Markov chains. Revuz (1975) is a treatment of Markov processes on a general state space. Sections A and B are based on Lucas (1978), although the details here are different. LeRoy (1973) gives a precursor of this model. The probability space on which the Markov process X is defined is constructed in Bertsekas and Shreve (1978). The fixed-point approach of Section A is based on Blackwell (1965). Lemma 4A, in more general guises, is called Blackwell's Theorem. The results extend easily to a general compact metric space Z of shocks, as, for example, in Lucas (1978), Duffie (1988c), or Stokey and Lucas (1989). General treatments of dynamic programming are given by Bertsekas and Shreve (1978) and Dynkin and Yushkevich (1979). Smoothness of the policy function or the value function is addressed by Benveniste and Scheinkman (1979). Santos (1991, 1994) provides results on smoothness and references to the extensive related literature. Versions of some of the results for this chapter that include production are found in Brock (1979, 1982), Duffie (1988c), and Stokey and Lucas (1989). The recursive-utility model was introduced into this setting by Epstein and Zin (1989). See also Becker and Boyd (1993), Hong and Epstein (1989), Kan (1995), Ma (1993b, 1996), Streufert (1991a, 1991b, 1996). Wang (1993c, 1993d) show the generic ability to distinguish between additive and nonadditive recursive utility from security-price data.

(C–D) These sections are slightly unconventional, and are designed merely to bridge the gap from the finite-dimensional results of Chapter 2 to this infinite-dimensional setting. Strong assumptions are adopted here in order to guarantee the "transversality" conditions. Much weaker conditions suffice. See, for example, Kocherlakota (1990). Schachermayer (1994) and Santos and Woodford (1995) give conditions for the existence of a state-price deflator in this and more general settings. Glasserman and Jin (1999) provide new metrics for comparing candidate equivalent martingale measures. Yu (1999) treats arbitrage valuation with frictions in this setting.

Kandori (1988) gives a proof of Pareto optimality and a representative agent in a complete-markets general-equilibrium model. Examples are given by Abel (1988), Campbell (1986a), Donaldson, Johnson, and Mehra (1990), and Dumas and Luciano (1989). Further characterization of equilibrium is given by Prescott and Mehra (1980) and Donaldson and Mehra (1984).

For general results on equilibrium and asset pricing in this setting, see Araujo, Monteiro, and Páscoa (1996), Hernandez and Santos (1996), Levine (1989), Levine and Zame (1996, 1999), Lucas (1995), Magill and Quinzii (1994, 1996a), and Mehra (1988). Conditions for the existence of a stationary Markov equilibrium (with incomplete markets and heterogeneous agents) are given by Duffie, Geanakoplos, Mas-Colell, and McLennan (1994).

(E) This section gives a "baby version" of the estimation technique used in Hansen and Singleton (1982, 1983). Brown and Gibbons (1985) give an alternative exposition of this model. The generalized method of moments, in a much more general setting than that of Section E, is shown by Hansen (1982) to be consistent. We have used the exponential convergence of probabilities given by (18) to avoid the assumption that the shock process X is stationary. This extends to a more general Markov setting under regularity conditions. The proof given for the uniform strong law of large numbers is based on Pollard (1984). A general treatment of method-of-moments estimation can be found in Gallant and White (1988). Duffie and Singleton (1993), Lee and Ingram (1991), McFadden (1989), and Pakes and Pollard (1989) extend the GMM to a setting with simulated estimation of moments.

Additional Topics: Exercise 4.9 is based on Samuelson (1969) and Levhari and Srinivasan (1969), and is extended by Hakansson (1970), Blume, Easley, and O'Hara (1982), and others. For a related *turnpike* theorem, see Hakansson (1974), and for continuous-time turnpike results the Notes of Chapter 9. Many further results in the vein of Chapter 4 are summarized in Duffie (1988c) and, especially, Stokey and Lucas (1989).

The role of debt constraints in promoting existence of equilibria in this setting is developed by Florenzano and Gourdel (1993), Kehoe and Levine (1993), Levine and Zame (1996), and Magill and Quinzii (1994, 1996b).

The related issue of speculative bubbles is addressed by Gilles and LeRoy (1992a, 1992b, 1998), Magill and Quinzii (1996a), and Santos and Woodford (1995). Kurz (1993, 1997, 1998), Kurz and Beltratti (1996), and Kurz and Motolese (1999) develop the implications of stationarity and rationality in this setting, proposing a rational-beliefs model that allows individual probability assessments by agents to be restricted only by absence of conflict with long-run empirical behavior. Shannon (1996) gives conditions for determinacy. Hansen and Sargent (1990) have worked out extensive examples for equilibrium in this setting with quadratic utilities and linear dynamics.

A spate of literature has addressed the issue of asset pricing with heterogeneous agents and incomplete markets, partly spurred by the *equity-premium puzzle* pointed out by Mehra and Prescott (1985), showing the difference in expected returns between equity and riskless bonds to be far in excess of what one would find from a typical representative-agent model. Bewley (1982) and Mankiw (1986) have seminal examples of the effects of incomplete markets. The more recent literature includes Acharya and Madan (1993), Aiyagari and Gertler (1991), Calvet (1999), Constantinides and Duffie (1996), Duffie (1992), Haan (1996), Heaton and Lucas (1996), Judd (1997), Levine and Zame (1999), Lucas (1994), Marcet and Singleton (1999), Mehrling (1990, 1998), Sandroni (1995), Scheinkman (1989), Scheinkman and Weiss (1986), Svensson and Werner (1993), Telmer (1993), and Weil (1992). Others have attempted to resolve the perceived equity-premium puzzle by turning to more general utility functions, such as the habit-formation model (see, for example, Constantinides [1990] and Hansen and Jaganathan [1990]) or the recursive model (see Epstein and Zin [1989, 1991]). For the effect of first-order risk aversion or Knightian uncertainty, see Epstein and Wang (1994). Judd, Kubler, and Schmedders (1997) and Santos and Vigo (1998) treat the computation of equilibria in this setting. For more on computation of equilibria, see the Notes of Chapters 1, 2, and 12.

Dumas and Luciano (1989) treat optimal portfolio selection with transactions costs in this setting. Cover and Ordentlich (1996) is a recent example of the literature on optimal long-run returns, sometimes called log-optimal growth-rate models.

Barberis, Huang, and Santos (1999) proposed a limited-rationality asset pricing model that stressed the role of investors' aversion to negative asset returns.

II
Continuous-Time Models

Part II is a continuous-time counterpart to Part I. The results are somewhat richer and more delicate than those in Part I, with a greater dependence on mathematical technicalities. It is wiser to focus on the parallels than on these technicalities. Once again, the three basic forces behind the theory are arbitrage, optimality, and equilibrium.

Chapter 5 introduces the continuous-trading model and develops the Black-Scholes partial differential equation (PDE) for arbitrage-free prices of derivative securities. The Harrison-Kreps model of equivalent martingale measures is presented in Chapter 6 in parallel with the theory of state prices in continuous time. Chapter 7 presents models of the term structure of interest rates, including the Black-Derman-Toy, Vasicek, Cox-Ingersoll-Ross, and Heath-Jarrow-Morton models, as well as extensions. Chapter 8 presents specific classes of derivative securities, such as futures, forwards, American options, and lookback options. Chapter 8 also introduces models of option pricing with stochastic volatility. Chapter 9 is a summary of optimal continuous-time portfolio choice, using both dynamic programming and an approach involving equivalent martingale measures or state prices. Chapter 10 is a summary of security pricing in an equilibrium setting. Included are such well-known models as Breeden's consumption-based capital asset pricing model and the general equilibrium version of the Cox-Ingersoll-Ross model of the term structure of interest rates. Chapter 11 treats the valuation of equities and corporate bonds, beginning with "structural models," based on the capital structure of the firm and incentives of equity and debt holders, then turning to "reduced-form" models, based on an assumed stochastic arrival intensity of the stopping time defining default. Chapter 12 reviews numerical methods for calculating derivative security prices in a continuous-time setting, including Monte Carlo simulation of a discrete-time approximation of security prices, and finite-difference solution of the associated PDE.

5
The Black-Scholes Model

THIS CHAPTER PRESENTS the basic Black-Scholes model of arbitrage pricing in continuous time, as well as extensions to a nonparametric multivariate Markov setting. We first introduce the Brownian model of uncertainty and continuous security trading, and then derive partial differential equations for the arbitrage-free prices of derivative securities. The classic example is the Black-Scholes option-pricing formula. Chapter 6 extends to a non-Markovian setting using more general techniques.

A. Trading Gains for Brownian Prices

We fix a probability space $(\Omega, \mathscr{F}, P)$. A *process* is a measurable function on $\Omega \times [0, \infty)$ into $\mathbb{R}$. (For a definition of measurability with respect to a product space of this variety, see Appendix C.) The value of a process X at time t is the random variable variously written as X_t, $X(t)$, or $X(\cdot, t) : \Omega \to \mathbb{R}$. A *standard Brownian motion* is a process B defined by the properties:

   (a) $B_0 = 0$ almost surely;
   (b) for any times t and $s > t$, $B_s - B_t$ is normally distributed with mean zero and variance $s - t$;
   (c) for any times $t_0, \ldots, t_n$ such that $0 \leq t_0 < t_1 < \cdots < t_n < \infty$, the random variables $B(t_0), B(t_1) - B(t_0), \ldots, B(t_n) - B(t_{n-1})$ are independently distributed; and
   (d) for each ω in Ω, the *sample path* $t \mapsto B(\omega, t)$ is continuous.

It is a nontrivial fact, whose proof has a colorful history, that the probability space $(\Omega, \mathscr{F}, P)$ can be constructed so that there exist standard

Brownian motions. By 1900, in perhaps the first scientific work involving Brownian motion, Louis Bachelier proposed Brownian motion as a model of stock prices. We will follow his lead for the time being and suppose that a given standard Brownian motion B is the price process of a security. Later we consider more general classes of price processes.

The tribe $\mathcal{F}_t^B$ generated by $\{B_s : 0 \leq s \leq t\}$ is, on intuitive grounds, a reasonable model of the information available at time t for trading the security, since $\mathcal{F}_t^B$ includes every event based on the history of the price process B up to that time. For technical reasons, however, one must be able to assign probabilities to the *null sets* of Ω, the subsets of events of zero probability. For this reason, we will fix instead the *standard filtration* $\mathbb{F} = \{\mathcal{F}_t : t \geq 0\}$ of B, with $\mathcal{F}_t$ defined as the tribe generated by the union of $\mathcal{F}_t^B$ and the null sets. The probability measure P is also extended by letting $P(A) = 0$ for any null set A. This *completion* of the probability space is defined in more detail in Appendix C.

A *trading strategy* is an adapted process θ specifying at each state ω and time t the number $\theta_t(\omega)$ of units of the security to hold. If a strategy θ is a constant, say $\bar{\theta}$, between two dates t and $s > t$, then the total gain between those two dates is $\bar{\theta}(B_s - B_t)$, the quantity held multiplied by the price change. So long as the strategy is piecewise constant, we would have no difficulty in defining the total gain between any two times. In order to make for a general model of trading gains, a trading strategy θ is required to satisfy $\int_0^T \theta_t^2 dt < \infty$ almost surely for each T. Let $\mathcal{L}^2$ denote the space of adapted processes satisfying this integrability restriction. For each θ in $\mathcal{L}^2$, there is an adapted process with continuous sample paths, denoted $\int \theta dB$, that is called the *stochastic integral* of θ with respect to B. The definition of $\int \theta dB$ is outlined in Appendix D. The value of the process $\int \theta dB$ at time T is usually denoted $\int_0^T \theta_t dB_t$, and represents the total gain generated up to time T by trading the security with price process B according to the trading strategy θ.

An interpretation of $\int_0^T \theta_t dB_t$ can be drawn from the discrete-time analogue $\sum_{t=0}^T \theta_t \Delta^1 B_t$, where $\Delta^1 B_t \equiv B_{t+1} - B_t$, that is, the sum (over t) of the shares held at t multiplied by the change in price between t and $t + 1$. More generally, let $\Delta^n B_t = B_{(t+1)/n} - B_{t/n}$. In a sense that we shall not make precise, $\int_0^T \theta_t dB_t$ can be thought of as the limit of $\sum_{t=0}^{Tn} \theta_{t/n} \Delta^n B_t$, as the number n of trading intervals per unit of time goes to infinity. This statement is literally true, for example, if θ has continuous sample paths, taking "limit" to mean limit in probability. The definition of $\int_0^T \theta_t dB_t$ as a limit in probability of the discrete-time analogue extends to a larger class of θ, but not large enough to capture some of the applications in later chapters. The definition of $\int \theta_t \, dB$ given in Appendix D therefore admits any θ in $\mathscr{L}^2$.

The stochastic integral has some of the properties that one would expect from the fact that it is a good model of trading gains. For example, suppose a trading strategy θ is piecewise constant on $[0, T]$ in that, for some stopping times $T_0, \ldots, T_N$ with $0 = T_0 < T_1 < \cdots < T_N = T$, and for any n, we have $\theta(t) = \theta(T_{n-1})$ for all $t \in [T_{n-1}, T_n)$. Then

$$\int_0^T \theta_t \, dB_t = \sum_{n=1}^N \theta(T_{n-1})[B(T_n) - B(T_{n-1})].$$

A second natural property of stochastic integration as a model for trading gains is linearity: For any θ and φ in $\mathscr{L}^2$ and any scalars a and b, the process $a\theta + b\varphi$ is also in $\mathscr{L}^2$, and, for any time $T > 0$,

$$\int_0^T (a\theta_t + b\varphi_t) \, dB_t = a \int_0^T \theta_t \, dB_t + b \int_0^T \varphi_t \, dB_t.$$

B. Martingale Trading Gains

The properties of standard Brownian motion imply that B is a martingale. (This follows basically from the property that its increments are independent and of zero expectation.) A process θ is bounded if there is a fixed constant k such that $|\theta(\omega, t)| \leq k$ for all (ω, t). For any bounded θ in $\mathscr{L}^2$, the law of iterated expectations and the "martingality" of B imply, for any integer times t and $\tau > t$, that $E_t(\sum_{s=t}^{\tau} \theta_s \Delta^1 B_s) = 0$. This means that the discrete-time gain process X, defined by $X_0 = 0$ and $X_t = \sum_{s=0}^{t-1} \theta_s \Delta^1 B_s$, is itself a martingale with respect to the discrete-time filtration $\{\mathscr{F}_0, \mathscr{F}_1, \ldots\}$, an exercise for the reader. The same is also true in continuous time: For any bounded θ in $\mathscr{L}^2$, $\int \theta \, dB$ is a martingale. This is natural; it should be impossible to generate an expected profit by trading a security that never experiences an expected price change. If one places no bound or other restriction on θ, however, the expectation of $\int_0^T \theta_t \, dB_t$ may not even exist. Even if, for each T, $\int_0^T \theta_t \, dB_t$ and its expectation exist, $\int \theta \, dB$ need not be a martingale. Indeed, we may not have a reasonable model of trading gains without some restriction on θ, as shown by example in Chapter 6. The following proposition assists in determining whether the expectation or the variance of $\int_0^T \theta_t dB_t$ is finite, and whether $\int \theta dB$ is indeed a martingale. Consider the spaces

$$\mathcal{H}^1 = \left\{ \theta \in \mathcal{L}^2 : E\left[\left(\int_0^T \theta_t^2 dt \right)^{1/2} \right] < \infty, \qquad T > 0 \right\},$$

$$\mathcal{H}^2 = \left\{ \theta \in \mathcal{L}^2 : E\left(\int_0^T \theta_t^2 dt \right) < \infty, \qquad T > 0 \right\}.$$

Of course, $\mathcal{H}^2$ is contained by $\mathcal{H}^1$.

Proposition. *If θ is in $\mathcal{H}^1$, then $\int \theta dB$ is a martingale. If $\int \theta dB$ is a martingale, then*

$$\mathrm{var}\left(\int_0^T \theta_t dB_t \right) = E\left(\int_0^T \theta_t^2 dt \right). \tag{1}$$

A proof of the proposition is cited in the Notes.

C. Ito Prices and Gains

As a model of security-price processes, standard Brownian motion is too restrictive for most purposes. Consider, instead, a process of the form

$$S_t = x + \int_0^t \mu_s ds + \int_0^t \sigma_s dB_s, \qquad t \geq 0, \tag{2}$$

where x is a real number, σ is in $\mathcal{L}^2$, and μ is in $\mathcal{L}^1$, meaning that μ is an adapted process such that $\int_0^t |\mu_s| ds < \infty$ almost surely for all t. We call a process S of this form (2) an *Ito process*. It is common to write (2) in the informal "differential" form

$$dS_t = \mu_t dt + \sigma_t dB_t; \qquad S_0 = x.$$

One often thinks intuitively of dS_t as the "increment" of S at time t, made up of two parts, the "dt" part and the "dB_t" part. In order to further interpret this differential representation of an Ito process, suppose that σ and μ have continuous sample paths and are in $\mathcal{H}^2$. It is then literally the case that for any time t,

$$\frac{d}{d\tau} E_t(S_\tau)|_{\tau=t} = \mu_t \qquad \text{almost surely} \tag{3}$$

and

$$\frac{d}{d\tau} \mathrm{var}_t(S_\tau)|_{\tau=t} = \sigma_t^2 \qquad \text{almost surely,} \tag{4}$$

where the derivatives are taken from the right, and where, for any random variable X with finite variance, $\text{var}_t(X) \equiv E_t(X^2) - [E_t(X)]^2$ is the $\mathscr{F}_t$-conditional variance of X. In this sense of (3) and (4), we can interpret μ_t as the rate of change of the expectation of S, conditional on information available at time t, and likewise interpret σ_t^2 as the rate of change of the conditional variance of S at time t. One sometimes reads the associated abuses of notation "$E_t(dS_t) = \mu_t \, dt$" and "$\text{var}_t(dS_t) = \sigma_t^2 \, dt$." Of course, dS_t is not even a random variable, so this sort of characterization is not rigorously justified and is used purely for its intuitive content. We will refer to μ and σ as the *drift* and *diffusion* processes of S, respectively. Many authors reserve the term "diffusion" for σ_t^2 or other related quantities.

For an Ito process S of the form (2), let $\mathscr{L}(S)$ denote the space consisting of any adapted process θ with $\{\theta_t \mu_t : t \geq 0\}$ in $\mathscr{L}^1$ and $\{\theta_t \sigma_t : t \geq 0\}$ in $\mathscr{L}^2$. For θ in $\mathscr{L}(S)$, we define the stochastic integral $\int \theta \, dS$ as the Ito process given by

$$\int_0^T \theta_t \, dS_t = \int_0^T \theta_t \mu_t \, dt + \int_0^T \theta_t \sigma_t \, dB_t, \qquad T \geq 0. \tag{5}$$

We also refer to $\int \theta \, dS$ as the *gain process generated by* θ, given the price process S. If $\theta \in \mathscr{L}(S)$ is such that $\{\theta_t \sigma_t : t \geq 0\}$ is in $\mathscr{H}^2$ and $E[(\int_0^T \theta_t \mu_t \, dt)^2] < \infty$, then we write that θ is in $\mathscr{H}^2(S)$. By Proposition 5B, if θ is in $\mathscr{H}^2(S)$, then $\int \theta \, dS$ is a finite-variance process.

We will have occasion to refer to adapted processes θ and φ that are equal *almost everywhere,* by which we mean that $E(\int_0^\infty |\theta_t - \varphi_t| \, dt) = 0$. In fact, we shall write "$\theta = \varphi$" whenever $\theta = \varphi$ almost everywhere. This is a natural convention, for suppose that X and Y are Ito processes with $X_0 = Y_0$ and with $dX_t = \mu_t \, dt + \sigma_t \, dB_t$ and $dY_t = a_t \, dt + b_t \, dB_t$. Since stochastic integrals are defined for our purposes as continuous-sample-path processes, it turns out that $X_t = Y_t$ for all t almost surely if and only if $\mu = a$ almost everywhere and $\sigma = b$ almost everywhere. We call this the *unique decomposition property* of Ito processes.

D. Ito's Formula

More than any other result, *Ito's Formula* is the basis for explicit solutions to asset-pricing problems in a continuous-time setting.

Ito's Formula. *Suppose X is an Ito process with $dX_t = \mu_t \, dt + \sigma_t \, dB_t$ and $f : \mathbb{R}^2 \to \mathbb{R}$ is twice continuously differentiable. Then the process Y, defined by*

$Y_t = f(X_t, t)$, *is an Ito process with*

$$dY_t = \left[f_x(X_t, t)\mu_t + f_t(X_t, t) + \frac{1}{2} f_{xx}(X_t, t)\sigma_t^2 \right] dt + f_x(X_t, t)\sigma_t \, dB_t. \quad (6)$$

A generalization of Ito's Formula (6) appears later in the chapter.

E. The Black-Scholes Option-Pricing Formula

Consider a security, to be called a *stock*, with price process

$$S_t = x \, \exp(\alpha t + \sigma B_t), \qquad t \geq 0, \tag{7}$$

where $x > 0, \alpha$, and σ are constants. Such a process, called a *geometric Brownian motion*, is often called *log-normal* because, for any t, $\log(S_t) = \log(x) + \alpha t + \sigma B_t$ is normally distributed. Moreover, since $X_t \equiv \alpha t + \sigma B_t = \int_0^t \alpha \, ds + \int_0^t \sigma \, dB_s$ defines an Ito process X with constant drift α and diffusion σ, Ito's Formula implies that S is an Ito process and that

$$dS_t = \mu S_t \, dt + \sigma S_t \, dB_t; \qquad S_0 = x,$$

where $\mu = \alpha + \sigma^2/2$. From (3) and (4), at any time t, the rate of change of the conditional mean of S_t is μS_t, and the rate of change of the conditional variance is $\sigma^2 S_t^2$, so that, per dollar invested in this security at time t, one may think of μ as the "instantaneous" expected rate of return, and σ as the "instantaneous" standard deviation of the rate of return. This sort of characterization abounds in the literature, and one often reads the associated abuses of notation "$E(dS_t/S_t) = \mu \, dt$" and "$\text{var}(dS_t/S_t) = \sigma^2 \, dt$." The coefficient σ is also known as the *volatility* of S. In any case, a geometric Brownian motion is a natural two-parameter model of a security-price process because of these simple interpretations of μ and σ.

Consider a second security, to be called a *bond*, with the price process β defined by

$$\beta_t = \beta_0 \, e^{rt}, \qquad t \geq 0, \tag{8}$$

for some constants $\beta_0 > 0$ and r. We have the obvious interpretation of r as the *continually compounding interest rate*, that is, the exponential rate at which riskless deposits accumulate with interest. Throughout, we will also refer to r as the *short rate*. Since $\{rt : t \geq 0\}$ is trivially an Ito process, β is also an Ito process with

$$d\beta_t = r\beta_t \, dt. \tag{9}$$

We can also view (9) as an ordinary differential equation with initial condition β_0 and solution (8).

We allow any trading strategies a in $\mathcal{H}^2(S)$ for the stock and b in $\mathcal{H}^2(\beta)$ for the bond. Such a trading strategy (a, b) is said to be *self-financing* if it generates no dividends (either positive or negative), meaning that for all t,

$$a_t S_t + b_t \beta_t = a_0 S_0 + b_0 \beta_0 + \int_0^t a_u \, dS_u + \int_0^t b_u \, d\beta_u. \tag{10}$$

The self-financing condition (10) is merely a statement that the current portfolio value (on the left-hand side) is precisely the initial investment plus any trading gains, and therefore that no dividend "inflow" or "outflow" is generated.

Now consider a third security, an *option*. We begin with the case of a European call option on the stock, giving its owner the right, but not the obligation, to buy the stock at a given exercise price K on a given exercise date T. The option's price process Y is as yet unknown except for the fact that $Y_T = (S_T - K)^+ \equiv \max(S_T - K, 0)$, which follows from the fact that the option is rationally exercised if and only if $S_T > K$. (See Exercise 2.1 for a discrete-time analogue.)

Suppose there exists a self-financing trading strategy (a, b) in the stock and bond with $a_T S_T + b_T \beta_T = Y_T$. If $a_0 S_0 + b_0 \beta_0 < Y_0$, then one could sell the option for Y_0, make an initial investment of $a_0 S_0 + b_0 \beta_0$ in the trading strategy (a, b), and at time T liquidate the entire portfolio $(-1, a_T, b_T)$ of option, stock, and bond with payoff $-Y_T + a_T S_T + b_T \beta_T = 0$. The initial profit $Y_0 - a_0 S_0 - b_0 \beta_0 > 0$ is thus riskless, so the trading strategy $(-1, a, b)$ would be an arbitrage. Likewise, if $a_0 S_0 + b_0 \beta_0 > Y_0$, the strategy $(1, -a, -b)$ is an arbitrage. Thus, if there is no arbitrage, $Y_0 = a_0 S_0 + b_0 \beta_0$. The same arguments applied at each date t imply that, in the absence of arbitrage, $Y_t = a_t S_t + b_t \beta_t$. A full definition of continuous-time arbitrage is given in Chapter 6, but for now we can proceed without much ambiguity at this informal level. Our objective now is to show the following.

The Black-Scholes Formula. *If there is no arbitrage, then, for all $t < T$, $Y_t = C(S_t, t)$, where*

$$C(x, t) = x\Phi(z) - e^{-r(T-t)}K\Phi(z - \sigma\sqrt{T - t}), \tag{11}$$

with

$$z = \frac{\log(x/K) + (r + \sigma^2/2)(T - t)}{\sigma\sqrt{T - t}}, \tag{12}$$

where Φ is the cumulative standard normal distribution function.

F. Black-Scholes Formula: First Try

We will eventually see many different ways to arrive at the Black-Scholes formula (11). Although not the shortest argument, the following is perhaps the most obvious and constructive. We start by assuming that $Y_t = C(S_t, t), t < T$, without knowledge of the function C aside from the assumption that it is twice continuously differentiable on $(0, \infty) \times [0, T)$ (allowing an application of Ito's Formula). This will lead us to deduce (11), justifying the assumption and proving the result at the same time.

Based on our assumption that $Y_t = C(S_t, t)$ and Ito's Formula,

$$dY_t = \mu_Y(t)\, dt + C_x(S_t, t)\sigma S_t\, dB_t, \qquad t < T, \tag{13}$$

where

$$\mu_Y(t) = C_x(S_t, t)\mu S_t + C_t(S_t, t) + \frac{1}{2}C_{xx}(S_t, t)\sigma^2 S_t^2.$$

Now suppose there is a self-financing trading strategy (a, b) with

$$a_t S_t + b_t \beta_t = Y_t, \qquad t \in [0, T], \tag{14}$$

as outlined in Section E. This assumption will also be justified shortly. Equations (10) and (14), along with the linearity of stochastic integration, imply that

$$dY_t = a_t\, dS_t + b_t\, d\beta_t = (a_t\mu S_t + b_t\beta_t r)\, dt + a_t\sigma S_t\, dB_t. \tag{15}$$

One way to choose the trading strategy (a, b) so that both (13) and (15) are satisfied is to "match coefficients separately in both dB_t and dt." In fact, the unique decomposition property of Ito processes explained at the end of Section C implies that this is the only way to ensure that (13) and (15) are consistent. Specifically, we choose a_t so that $a_t\sigma S_t = C_x(S_t, t)\sigma S_t$; for this, we let $a_t = C_x(S_t, t)$. From (14) and $Y_t = C(S_t, t)$, we then have $C_x(S_t, t)S_t + b_t\beta_t = C(S_t, t)$, or

$$b_t = \frac{1}{\beta_t}[C(S_t, t) - C_x(S_t, t)S_t]. \tag{16}$$

Finally, "matching coefficients in dt" from (13) and (15) leaves, for $t < T$,

$$-rC(S_t, t) + C_t(S_t, t) + rS_tC_x(S_t, t) + \frac{1}{2}\sigma^2 S_t^2 C_{xx}(S_t, t) = 0. \qquad (17)$$

In order for (17) to hold, it is enough that C satisfies the partial differential equation (PDE)

$$-rC(x, t) + C_t(x, t) + rxC_x(x, t) + \frac{1}{2}\sigma^2 x^2 C_{xx}(x, t) = 0, \qquad (18)$$

for $(x, t) \in (0, \infty) \times [0, T]$. The fact that $Y_T = C(S_T, T) = (S_T - K)^+$ supplies the *boundary condition*:

$$C(x, T) = (x - K)^+, \qquad x \in (0, \infty). \qquad (19)$$

By direct calculation of derivatives, one can show as an exercise that (11) is a solution to (18)–(19). All of this seems to confirm that $C(S_0, 0)$, with C defined by the Black-Scholes formula (11), is a good candidate for the initial price of the option. In order to make this solid, suppose that $Y_0 > C(S_0, 0)$, where C is defined by (11). Consider the strategy $(-1, a, b)$ in the option, stock, and bond, with $a_t = C_x(S_t, t)$ and b_t given by (16) for $t < T$. We can choose a_T and b_T arbitrarily so that (14) is satisfied; this does not affect the self-financing condition (10) because the value of the trading strategy at a single point in time has no effect on the stochastic integral. (For this, see the implications of equality "almost everywhere" at the end of Section C.) The result is that (a, b) is self-financing by construction and that $a_T S_T + b_T \beta_T = Y_T = (S_T - K)^+$. This strategy therefore nets an initial riskless profit of

$$Y_0 - a_0 S_0 - b_0 \beta_0 = Y_0 - C(S_0, 0) > 0,$$

which defines an arbitrage. Likewise, if $Y_0 < C(S_0, 0)$, the trading strategy $(+1, -a, -b)$ is an arbitrage. Thus, it is indeed a necessary condition for the absence of arbitrage that $Y_0 = C(S_0, 0)$. Sufficiency is a more delicate matter. We will see in Chapter 6 that under mild technical conditions on trading strategies, the Black-Scholes formula for the option price is also sufficient for the absence of arbitrage. One last piece of business is to show that the "option-hedging" strategy (a, b) is such that a is in $\mathcal{H}^2(S)$ and b is in $\mathcal{H}^2(\beta)$. This is true, and is left to show as an exercise.

Transactions costs play havoc with the sort of reasoning just applied. For example, if brokerage fees are any positive fixed fraction of the market value of stock trades, the stock-trading strategy a constructed above would call for infinite total brokerage fees, since, in effect, the number of shares traded is infinite! This fact and the literature on transactions costs in this setting are reviewed in the Notes of Chapters 6 and 9.

G. The PDE for Arbitrage-Free Prices

The expression $dS_t = \mu S_t\, dt + \sigma S_t\, dB_t$ for the log-normal stock-price process S of Section E is a special case of a *stochastic differential equation* (SDE) of the form

$$dS_t = \mu(S_t, t)\, dt + \sigma(S_t, t)\, dB_t; \qquad S_0 = x, \tag{20}$$

where $\mu : \mathbb{R} \times [0, \infty) \to \mathbb{R}$ and $\sigma : \mathbb{R} \times [0, \infty) \to \mathbb{R}$ are given functions. Under regularity conditions on μ and σ reviewed in Appendix E, there is a unique Ito process S solving (20) for each starting point x in $\mathbb{R}$. Assuming that such a solution S defines a stock-price process, consider the price process β defined by

$$\beta_t = \beta_0 \exp\left[\int_0^t r(S_u, u)\, du\right], \tag{21}$$

where $r : \mathbb{R} \times [0, \infty) \to \mathbb{R}$ is well enough behaved for the existence of the integral in (21). We may view β_t as the market value at time t of an investment account that is continuously reinvested at the short rate $r(S_t, t)$. This is consistent with a trivial application of Ito's Formula, which implies that

$$d\beta_t = \beta_t r(S_t, t)\, dt; \qquad \beta_0 > 0. \tag{22}$$

Rather than restricting attention to the option payoff $Y_T = (S_T - K)^+$, consider a *derivative security* defined by the payoff $Y_T = g(S_T)$ at time T, for some continuous $g : \mathbb{R} \to \mathbb{R}$. Arguments like those in Section F lead one to formulate the arbitrage-free price process Y of the derivative security as $Y_t = C(S_t, t), t \in [0, T]$, where C solves the PDE

$$-r(x, t)C(x, t) + C_t(x, t) + r(x, t)xC_x(x, t) + \frac{1}{2}\sigma(x, t)^2 C_{xx}(x, t) = 0, \tag{23}$$

for $(x, t) \in \mathbb{R} \times [0, T)$, with the boundary condition

$$C(x, T) = g(x), \qquad x \in \mathbb{R}. \tag{24}$$

In order to tie things together, suppose that C solves (23)–(24). If $Y_0 \neq C(S_0, 0)$, then an obvious extension of our earlier arguments implies that there is an arbitrage. (This extension is left as an exercise.) This is true even if C is not twice continuously differentiable, but merely $C^{2,1}(\mathbb{R} \times [0, T))$, meaning that the derivatives C_x, C_t, and C_{xx} exist and are continuous in $\mathbb{R} \times (0, T)$, and extend continuously to $\mathbb{R} \times [0, T)$. (Ito's Formula also applies to any function in this class.)

This PDE characterization of the arbitrage-free price of derivative securities is useful if there are convenient methods for solving PDEs of the form (23)–(24). Numerical solution techniques are discussed in Chapter 12. One of these techniques is based on a probabilistic representation of solutions given in the next section.

H. The Feynman-Kac Solution

A potential simplification of the PDE problem (23)–(24) is obtained as follows. For each (x, t) in $\mathbb{R} \times [0, T]$, let $Z^{x,t}$ be the Ito process defined by $Z^{x,t}_s = x, s \leq t$, and

$$dZ^{x,t}_s = r(Z^{x,t}_s, s)Z^{x,t}_s \, ds + \sigma(Z^{x,t}_s, s) \, dB_s, \qquad s > t. \tag{25}$$

That is, $Z^{x,t}$ starts at x at time t and continues from there by following the SDE (25).

Condition FK. *The functions σ, r, and g satisfy one of the technical sufficient conditions given in Appendix E for Feynman-Kac solutions.*

The FK (for "Feynman-Kac") condition is indeed only technical, and limits how quickly the functions σ, r, and g can grow or change. Referring to Appendix E, we have the following solution to the PDE (23)–(24) as an expectation of the discounted payoff of the derivative security, modified by replacing the original price process S with a *pseudo-price process* $Z^{x,t}$ whose expected rate of return is the riskless interest rate. This is sometimes known as *risk-neutral valuation*. This is not to say that agents are risk-neutral, but rather that risk-neutrality is (in this setting) without loss of generality for purposes of pricing derivative securities.

The Feynman-Kac Solution. *Under Condition FK, if there is no arbitrage, then the derivative security defined by the payoff $g(S_T)$ at time T has the price process Y with $Y_t = C(S_t, t)$, where C is the solution to (23)–(24) given by*

$$C(x, t) = E\left(\exp\left[-\int_t^T r(Z^{x,t}_s, s) \, ds\right] g(Z^{x,t}_T)\right), \qquad (x, t) \in \mathbb{R} \times [0, T]. \tag{26}$$

It can be checked as an exercise that (26) recovers the Black-Scholes option-pricing formula (11). Calculating this expectation directly is a simpler way to solve the corresponding PDE (18)–(19) than is the method originally used to discover the Black-Scholes formula. Chapter 12 presents numerical methods for solving (23)–(24), one of which involves Monte Carlo simulation of the Feynman-Kac solution (26), which bears a close resemblance to the discrete-time equivalent-martingale-measure arbitrage-free price representation of Chapter 2. This is more than a coincidence, as we shall see in Chapter 6.

I. The Multidimensional Case

Suppose that $B^1, \ldots, B^d$ are d independent standard Brownian motions on a probability space $(\Omega, \mathcal{F}, P)$. The process $B = (B^1, \ldots, B^d)$ is known as a *standard Brownian motion in* $\mathbb{R}^d$. The standard filtration $\mathbb{F} = \{\mathcal{F}_t : t \geq 0\}$ of B is defined just as in the one-dimensional case. Given $\mathbb{F}$, the subsets $\mathcal{L}^1, \mathcal{L}^2, \mathcal{H}^1$, and $\mathcal{H}^2$ of adapted processes are also as defined in Sections A and B.

In this setting, X is an Ito process if, for some x in $\mathbb{R}$, some μ in $\mathcal{L}^1$, and some $\theta^1, \ldots, \theta^d$ in $\mathcal{L}^2$,

$$X_t = x + \int_0^t \mu_s \, ds + \sum_{i=1}^d \int_0^t \theta_s^i \, dB_s^i, \qquad t \geq 0. \tag{27}$$

For convenience, (27) is also written

$$X_t = x + \int_0^t \mu_s \, ds + \int_0^t \theta_s \, dB_s, \qquad t \geq 0, \tag{28}$$

or in the convenient stochastic differential form

$$dX_t = \mu_t \, dt + \theta_t \, dB_t; \qquad X_0 = x. \tag{29}$$

If $X^1, \ldots, X^N$ are Ito processes, then we call $X = (X^1, \ldots, X^N)$ an *Ito process in* $\mathbb{R}^N$, which can be written

$$X_t = x + \int_0^t \mu_s \, ds + \int_0^t \theta_s \, dB_s, \qquad t \geq 0, \tag{30}$$

or

$$dX_t = \mu_t \, dt + \theta_t \, dB_t; \qquad X_0 = x \in \mathbb{R}^N, \tag{31}$$

where μ and θ are valued in $\mathbb{R}^N$ and $\mathbb{R}^{N \times d}$, respectively. (Here, $\mathbb{R}^{N \times d}$ denotes the space of real matrices with N rows and d columns.) Ito's Formula extends as follows.

Ito's Formula. *Suppose* X *is the Ito process in* $\mathbb{R}^N$ *given by* (30) *and* f *is in* $C^{2,1}(\mathbb{R}^N \times [0, \infty))$. *Then* $\{f(X_t, t) : t \geq 0\}$ *is an Ito process and, for any time* t,

$$f(X_t, t) = f(X_0, 0) + \int_0^t \mathcal{D}_X f(X_s, s)\, ds + \int_0^t f_x(X_s, s)\theta_s\, dB_s,$$

where

$$\mathcal{D}_X f(X_t, t) = f_x(X_t, t)\mu_t + f_t(X_t, t) + \frac{1}{2}\mathrm{tr}\big[\theta_t \theta_t^T f_{xx}(X_t, t)\big].$$

Here, f_x, f_t, and f_{xx} denote the obvious partial derivatives of f valued in $\mathbb{R}^N$, $\mathbb{R}$, and $\mathbb{R}^{N \times N}$, respectively, and $\mathrm{tr}(A)$ denotes the *trace* of a square matrix A (the sum of its diagonal elements).

If X and Y are real-valued Ito processes with $dX_t = \mu_X(t)\, dt + \sigma_X(t)\, dB_t$ and $dY_t = \mu_Y(t)\, dt + \sigma_Y(t)\, dB_t$, then Ito's Formula (for $N = 2$) implies that the product $Z = XY$ is an Ito process, with drift μ_Z given by

$$\mu_Z(t) = X_t \mu_Y(t) + Y_t \mu_X(t) + \sigma_X(t) \cdot \sigma_Y(t). \tag{32}$$

If μ_X, μ_Y, σ_X, and σ_Y are all in $\mathcal{H}^2$ and have continuous sample paths, then an application of Fubini's Theorem (Appendix C) implies that

$$\frac{d}{ds}\mathrm{cov}_t(X_s, Y_s)\big|_{s=t^+} = \sigma_X(t) \cdot \sigma_Y(t) \qquad \text{almost surely,} \tag{33}$$

where $\mathrm{cov}_t(X_s, Y_s) = E_t(X_s Y_s) - E_t(X_s)E_t(Y_s)$ and where the derivative is taken from the right, extending the intuition developed with (3) and (4).

If X is an Ito process in $\mathbb{R}^N$ with $dX_t = \mu_t\, dt + \sigma_t\, dB_t$ and $\theta = (\theta^1, \ldots, \theta^N)$ is a vector of adapted processes such that $\theta \cdot \mu$ is in $\mathcal{L}^1$ and, for each i, $\theta \cdot \sigma^i$ is in $\mathcal{L}^2$, then we say that θ is in $\mathcal{L}(X)$, which implies that

$$\int_0^T \theta_t\, dX_t \equiv \int_0^T \theta_t \cdot \mu_t\, dt + \int_0^T \theta_t^T \sigma_t\, dB_t, \qquad T \geq 0,$$

is well defined as an Ito process. If $E[(\int_0^T \theta_t \cdot \mu_t\, dt)^2] < \infty$ and, for each i, $\theta \cdot \sigma^i$ is also in $\mathcal{H}^2$, then we say that θ is in $\mathcal{H}^2(X)$, which implies that $\int \theta\, dX$ is a finite-variance process.

Suppose that $S = (S^1, \ldots, S^N)$ is an Ito process in $\mathbb{R}^N$ specifying the prices of N given securities, and that S satisfies the stochastic differential equation

$$dS_t = \mu(S_t, t)\, dt + \sigma(S_t, t)\, dB_t; \qquad S_0 = x \in \mathbb{R}^N, \tag{34}$$

where $\mu : \mathbb{R}^N \times [0, \infty) \to \mathbb{R}^N$ and $\sigma : \mathbb{R}^N \times [0, \infty) \to \mathbb{R}^{N \times d}$ satisfy enough regularity (conditions are given in Appendix E) for existence and uniqueness of a solution to (34). Let

$$\beta_t = \beta_0 \exp\left[\int_0^t r(S_u, u) \, du\right], \qquad \beta_0 > 0, \tag{35}$$

define the price process of a bond, where $r : \mathbb{R}^N \times [0, \infty) \to \mathbb{R}$ defines a continuously compounding short rate, sufficiently well behaved that (35) is a well-defined Ito process. We can also use Ito's Formula to write

$$d\beta_t = \beta_t r(S_t, t) \, dt, \qquad \beta_0 > 0. \tag{36}$$

Finally, let some continuous $g : \mathbb{R}^N \to \mathbb{R}$ define the payoff $g(S_T)$ at time T of a derivative security whose price at time zero is to be determined.

Once again, the arguments of Section F can be extended to show that, under technical regularity conditions and in the absence of arbitrage, the price process Y of the derivative security is given by $Y_t = C(S_t, t)$, where C solves the PDE:

$$\mathscr{D}_Z C(x, t) - r(x, t)C(x, t) = 0, \qquad (x, t) \in \mathbb{R}^N \times [0, T), \tag{37}$$

with boundary condition

$$C(x, T) = g(x), \qquad x \in \mathbb{R}^N, \tag{38}$$

where

$$\mathscr{D}_Z C(x, t) = C_x(x, t)r(x, t)x + C_t(x, t)$$
$$+ \frac{1}{2} \, \text{tr} \left[\sigma(x, t)\sigma(x, t)^\top C_{xx}(x, t)\right]. \tag{39}$$

We exploit once again the technical condition FK on (r, σ, g) reviewed in Appendix E for existence of a probabilistic representation of solutions to the PDE (37)–(38).

The Feynman-Kac Solution. *Under Condition FK, if there is no arbitrage, then the derivative security with payoff $g(S_T)$ at time T has the price process Y given by $Y_t = C(S_t, t)$, where C is the solution to the PDE (37)–(38) given, at each $(x, t) \in \mathbb{R}^N \times [0, T]$, by*

$$C(x, t) = E\left[\exp\left(-\int_t^T r(Z_s^{x,t}, s) \, ds\right) g(Z_T^{x,t})\right], \tag{40}$$

where $Z^{x,t}$ is the Ito process defined by $Z_s^{x,t} = x$, $s \leq t$, and

$$dZ_s^{x,t} = r(Z_s^{x,t}, s)Z_s^{x,t} \, ds + \sigma(Z_s^{x,t}, s) \, dB_s, \qquad s \geq t. \tag{41}$$

The exercises provide applications and additional extensions of this approach to the arbitrage-free valuation of derivative securities, allowing for intermediate dividends and for an underlying Markov state process. Chapter 6 further extends arbitrage-free pricing to a non-Markovian setting using more general methods. Chapters 7 and 8 give further applications, including futures, forwards, American options, and the term structure of interest rates.

Exercises

5.1 Fixing a probability space $(\Omega, \mathcal{F}, P)$ and a filtration $\{\mathcal{F}_t : t \geq 0\}$, a process X is *Markov* if, for any time t and any integrable random variable Y that is measurable with respect to the tribe generated by $\{X_s : s \geq t\}$, we have $E(Y \mid \mathcal{F}_t) = E(Y \mid X_t)$ almost surely. In particular, for any measurable $f : \mathbb{R} \to \mathbb{R}$ such that $f(X_t)$ has finite expectation, we have $E[f(X_t) \mid \mathcal{F}_s] = E[f(X_t) \mid X_s]$ for $s \leq t$. It is a fact, which we shall not prove, that standard Brownian motion B is a Markov process with respect to its standard filtration. Use this fact to show that B is a martingale with respect to its standard filtration. Suppose that θ is a bounded adapted process. Show, as stated in Section B, that the discrete-time process X defined by $X_0 = 0$ and $X_t = \sum_{s=0}^{t-1} \theta_s \Delta^1 B_s, t \geq 1$, is a martingale with respect to $\{\mathcal{F}_0, \mathcal{F}_1, \dots\}$.

5.2 Suppose that S is defined by (7). Use Ito's Formula to show that, as claimed, $dS_t = \mu S_t\, dt + \sigma S_t\, dB_t$, where $\mu = \alpha + \sigma^2/2$.

5.3 Verify that the ordinary differential equation (9), with initial condition β_0, is solved by (8).

5.4 Verify by direct calculation of the derivatives that the PDE (18)–(19) is solved by the Black-Scholes formula (11).

5.5 Derive the PDE (23) for the arbitrage-free value of the derivative security. Hint: Use arguments analogous to those used to derive the PDE (18) for the Black-Scholes formula.

5.6 Suppose the PDE (37) for the arbitrage-free value of the derivative security is not satisfied, in that the initial price Y_0 of the security is not equal to $C(S_0, 0)$, where C solves (37)–(38). Construct an arbitrage that nets an initial risk-free profit of m units of account, where m is an arbitrary number chosen by you.

5.7 Suppose that the stock, whose price process S is given by (20), pays dividends at a rate $\delta(S_t, t)$ at time t, where a continuous function $\delta : \mathbb{R} \times [0, \infty) \to \mathbb{R}$ defines a *cumulative dividend process* D by $D_t = \int_0^t \delta(S_u, u)\, du$. The total gain process G for the security is defined by $G_t = S_t + D_t$, and a trading strategy θ in $\mathcal{L}(G)$ generates the gain process $\int \theta\, dG$, the sum of capital and dividend gains. Derive a new PDE generalizing (23) for the arbitrage-free value of the derivative security defined by g. Provide regularity conditions for the associated Feynman-Kac solution, extending (25)–(26).

5.8 Suppose that S is a stock-price process defined by (20), β is a bond-price process defined by (21), and a derivative security is defined by the lump-sum payoff $g(S_T)$ at time T, as in Section G, and also by the cumulative dividend process H defined by $H_t = \int_0^t h(S_\tau, \tau) \, d\tau$, for some continuous $h : \mathbb{R} \times [0, T] \to \mathbb{R}$. By definition, a trading strategy (a, b) in $\mathcal{H}^2(S, \beta)$ *finances* this derivative security if

$$a_t S_t + b_t \beta_t = a_0 S_0 + b_0 \beta_0 + \int_0^t a_u \, dS_u + \int_0^t b_u \, d\beta_u - H_t, \qquad t \le T, \qquad (42)$$

and

$$a_T S_T + b_T \beta_T = g(S_T). \qquad (43)$$

Relation (42) means that the current value of the portfolio is, at any time, the initial value, plus trading gains to date, less the payout to date of the derivative dividends. If (a, b) finances the derivative security in this sense and the derivative security's initial price Y_0 is not equal to $a_0 S_0 + b_0 \beta_0$, then there is an arbitrage. For example, if $Y_0 > a_0 S_0 + b_0 \beta_0$, then the strategy $(-1, a, b)$ in derivative security, stock, and bond generates the cumulative dividend process $-H + H = 0$ and the final payoff $-g(S_T) + g(S_T) = 0$, with the initial riskless profit $Y_0 - a_0 S_0 - b_0 \beta_0 > 0$. Derive an extension of the PDE (23)–(24) for the derivative security price, as well as an extension of the Feynman-Kac solution (25)–(26).

5.9 Suppose that X is the Ito process in $\mathbb{R}^K$ solving the SDE

$$dX_t = \mu(X_t, t) \, dt + \sigma(X_t, t) \, dB_t; \qquad X_0 = x.$$

We could refer to X, by analogy with Chapter 3, as the "shock process." Suppose the price process S for the N "stocks" is defined by $S_t = \mathcal{S}(X_t, t)$, where $\mathcal{S}$ is in $C^{2,1}(\mathbb{R}^K \times [0, \infty))$, and that the bond-price process β is the Ito process defined by $d\beta_t = \beta_t r(X_t, t) \, dt$, $\beta_0 > 0$, where $r : \mathbb{R}^K \times [0, \infty) \to \mathbb{R}$ is bounded and continuous.

(A) State regularity conditions that you find appropriate in order to derive a PDE analogous to (37)–(38) for the price of an additional security defined by the payoff $g(X_T)$ at time T, where $g : \mathbb{R}^K \to \mathbb{R}$. Then provide the Feynman-Kac solution, analogous to (40)–(41), including a sufficient set of technical conditions based on Appendix E.

(B) Extend part (A) to the case in which the stocks pay a cumulative dividend process D that is an Ito process in $\mathbb{R}^N$ well defined by $D_t = \int_0^t \delta(X_s, s) \, ds$, where $\delta : \mathbb{R}^K \times [0, \infty) \to \mathbb{R}^N$, and in which the additional security has the lump-sum payoff of $g(X_T)$ at time T, as well as a cumulative-dividend Ito process H well defined by $H_t = \int_0^t h(X_s, s) \, ds$, where $h : \mathbb{R}^K \times [0, T] \to \mathbb{R}$.

5.10 Suppose the short-rate process r is given by a bounded continuous function $r : [0, T] \to \mathbb{R}$. Consider a security with price process S defined by

$$dS_t = \mu(S_t) \, dt + \sigma(S_t) \, dB_t,$$

where μ and σ satisfy a Lipschitz condition. Suppose this security has the cumulative-dividend process D defined by $D_t = \int_0^t \delta_u S_u \, du$, where $\delta : [0, T] \to \mathbb{R}$ is a continuous function. (Such a function δ is often called the "dividend yield.")

(A) (Put-Call Parity) Suppose there are markets for European call and put options on the above security with exercise price K and exercise date T. Let C_0 and P_0 denote the call and put prices at time zero. Give an explicit expression for P_0 in terms of C_0, in the absence of arbitrage and transactions costs.

(B) Suppose, for all t, that $r_t = 0.10$ and that $\delta_t = 0.08$. Consider a European option expiring in $T = 0.25$ years. Suppose that $K = 50$ and $S_0 = 45$. If the call sells for 4.75, what is the put price? (Give a specific dollar price, to the nearest penny, showing how you calculated it.)

(C) Suppose, instead, that the dividend process D is defined by $D_t = \int_0^t \delta_\tau \log(S_\tau) \times S_\tau \, d\tau$. Suppose $\sigma(x) = \epsilon x$, for some constant $\epsilon > 0$. Solve part (A) again. Then calculate the price of a European call with exercise price $K = 35$ given initial stock price $S_0 = 40$, assuming, for all t, that $\delta_t = 0.08$, $r_t = 0.10$, and $\epsilon = 0.35$. Assume expiration in 0.6 years. Justify your answer.

5.11 Suppose the price of haggis (an unusually nasty food served in Scotland) follows the process H defined by

$$dH_t = H_t \mu_H \, dt + H_t \sigma_H \, dB_t, \qquad H_0 > 0,$$

in British pounds per pint, where μ_H is a constant, σ_H is a constant vector in $\mathbb{R}^2$, and B is a standard Brownian motion in $\mathbb{R}^2$. A trader at a Wall Street investment bank, Gold in Sacks, Incorporated, has decided that since there are options on almost everything else, there may as well be options on haggis. Of course, there is the matter of selling the options in the United States, denominated in U.S. dollars. It has been noted that the price of the U.S. dollar, in British pounds per dollar, follows the process

$$dD_t = D_t \mu_D \, dt + D_t \sigma_D \, dB_t, \qquad D_0 > 0,$$

where μ_D is a constant and σ_D is a constant vector in $\mathbb{R}^2$. The continuously compounding short rate in U.S. funds is r_D, a constant. Although there are liquid markets in Edinburgh for haggis and for U.S. dollars, there is not a liquid market for haggis options. Gold in Sacks has therefore decided to sell call options on haggis at a U.S. dollar strike price of 6.50 per pint expiring in three months, and cover its option position with a replicating strategy in the other instruments, so as to earn a riskless profit equal to the markup in the sale price of the options over the initial investment cost to Gold in Sacks for the replicating strategy.

(A) What replicating strategy would you recommend?

(B) If the options are sold at a 10 percent profit markup, give an explicit formula for the option price Gold in Sacks should charge its customers.

(C) Suppose borrowing in U.S. funds is too clumsy, since the other two parts of the strategy (dollar and haggis trading) are done at Gold in Sacks's Edinburgh office. If the British pound borrowing rate is r_P, a constant, is it possible, under some conditions, to answer parts (A) and (B), using British pound borrowing (and lending) rather than U.S. dollar borrowing (and lending)? If so, provide the conditions. If not, say why not. If you find it useful, you may use any arbitrage conditions relating the various coefficients $(\mu_H, \mu_D, \sigma_H, \sigma_D, r_D, r_P)$, if indeed there are any such coefficients precluding arbitrage.

5.12 Show, in the setting of Section E, that (26) recovers the Black-Scholes formula (11).

5.13 Show that the Black-Scholes option-hedging strategy (a, b) of Section F is such that $a \in \mathcal{H}^2(S)$ and $b \in \mathcal{H}^2(\beta)$, as assumed.

Notes

(A) The Brownian model was introduced to the study of option pricing by Bachelier (1900).

(B–D) Karatzas and Shreve (1988) is a standard source for stochastic calculus for Brownian motion. Proposition 5B can be found, for example, in Protter (1990).

(E–I) The Black and Scholes (1973) formula was extended by Merton (1973b, 1977) and subsequently given literally hundreds of further extensions and applications. The line of exposition here is based on Gabay (1982) and Duffie (1988a). Andreasen, Jensen, and Poulsen (1998) provide numerous alternative methods of deriving the Black-Scholes formula. The basic approach of using continuous-time self-financing strategies as the basis for making arbitrage arguments is due to Merton (1977) and Harrison and Kreps (1979). The basic idea of risk-neutral valuation, via adjustment of the underlying stock-price process, is due to Cox and Ross (1976). This is extended to the notion of equivalent martingale measures, found in Chapter 6, by Harrison and Kreps (1979).

Additional Topics: Cox and Rubinstein (1985) is a standard reference on options, while Hull (2000) has further applications and references. The impact of variations in the "volatility" on the Black-Scholes option-pricing formula is shown, in two different senses, by El Karoui, Jeanblanc, and Shreve (1998), Bergman, Grundy, and Wiener (1996a), Johnson and Shanno (1987), and Reisman (1986). For "stochastic volatility" models, see Section E and references cited in the Notes to Chapter 8.

Alternative approaches to the standard methods of stochastic calculus have been developed by Cutland, Kopp, and Willinger (1991, 1993a,b), who apply nonstandard analysis; by Bick and Willinger (1994) and Willinger and Tacqu (1989), who use a pathwise integral established by Föllmer (1981); and by Kunitomo (1993) and Cutland, Kopp, and Willinger (1991, 1993a), who exploit fractional Brownian motion. See Rogers (1998) for a discussion of the use of fractional Brownian motion in this setting. Lacoste (1995) proposes a Wiener-Chaos version of derivative calculations.

Part (C) of Exercise 5.10 was related to the author by Bruce Grundy. For the case of transactions costs and other market "imperfections," see the Notes of Chapter 6.

6

State Prices and Equivalent
Martingale Measures

THIS CHAPTER SUMMARIZES arbitrage-free security pricing theory in the continuous-time setting introduced in Chapter 5. The main idea is the equivalence between no arbitrage, the existence of state prices, and the existence of an equivalent martingale measure, paralleling the discrete-state theory of Chapter 2. This extends the Markovian results of Chapter 5, which are based on PDE methods. For those interested mainly in applications, the first sections of Chapters 7 and 8 summarize the major conclusions of this chapter as a "black box," making it possible to skip this chapter on a first reading.

The existence of a state-price deflator is shown to imply the absence of arbitrage. Then a state-price "beta" model of expected returns is derived. Turning to equivalent martingale measures, we begin with the sufficiency of an equivalent martingale measure for the absence of arbitrage. Girsanov's Theorem (Appendix D) gives conditions under which there exists an equivalent martingale measure. This approach generates another proof of the Black-Scholes formula. State prices are then connected with equivalent martingale measures; the two concepts are more or less the same. They are literally equivalent in the analogous finite-state model of Chapter 2, and we will see that the distinction here is purely technical.

A. Arbitrage

We fix a standard Brownian motion $B = (B^1, \ldots, B^d)$ in $\mathbb{R}^d$, restricted to some time interval $[0, T]$, on a given probability space $(\Omega, \mathcal{F}, P)$. We also fix the standard filtration $\mathbb{F} = \{\mathcal{F}_t : t \in [0, T]\}$ of B, as defined in Section 5I. For simplicity, we take $\mathcal{F}$ to be $\mathcal{F}_T$. Suppose the price processes of N given securities form an Ito process $X = (X^{(1)}, \ldots, X^{(N)})$ in $\mathbb{R}^N$. We suppose that each security price process is in the space H^2 containing any Ito process Y with $dY_t = a(t) \, dt + b(t) \, dB(t)$ for which

$$E\left[\left(\int_0^t a(s) \, ds\right)^2\right] < \infty \quad \text{and} \quad E\left[\int_0^t b(s) \cdot b(s) \, ds\right] < \infty.$$

Until later in the chapter, we will suppose that the securities pay no dividends during the time interval $[0, T)$, and that X_T is the vector of cum-dividend security prices at time T.

A trading strategy θ, as we recall from Chapter 5, is an $\mathbb{R}^N$-valued process θ in $\mathcal{L}(X)$, as defined in Section 5I. This means simply that the stochastic integral $\int \theta \, dX$ defining trading gains is well defined. A trading strategy θ is *self-financing* if

$$\theta_t \cdot X_t = \theta_0 \cdot X_0 + \int_0^t \theta_s \, dX_s, \qquad t \leq T. \tag{1}$$

If there is some process r with the property that $\int_0^T |r_t| \, dt$ is finite almost surely and, for some security with strictly positive price process β we have

$$\beta_t = \beta_0 \exp\left(\int_0^t r_s \, ds\right), \qquad t \in [0, T], \tag{2}$$

then we call r the *short-rate process*. In this case, $d\beta_t = r_t \beta_t \, dt$, allowing us to view r_t as the riskless short-term continuously compounding rate of interest, in an instantaneous sense, and to view β_t as the market value of an account that is continually reinvested at the short-term interest rate r.

A self-financing strategy θ is an *arbitrage* if $\theta_0 \cdot X_0 < 0$ and $\theta_T \cdot X_T \geq 0$, or $\theta_0 \cdot X_0 \leq 0$ and $\theta_T \cdot X_T > 0$. (Recall, "$\theta_T \cdot X_T > 0$" means that $\theta_T \cdot X_T$ is non-negative and is non-zero with positive probability.) Our main goal in this chapter is to characterize the properties of a price process X that admits no arbitrage, at least after placing some reasonable restrictions on trading strategies.

B. Numeraire Invariance

It is often convenient to renormalize all security prices, sometimes relative to a particular price process. This section shows that such a renormalization has essentially no economic effects. A *deflator* is a strictly positive Ito process. We can deflate the previously given security price process X by a deflator Y to get the new price process X^Y defined by $X_t^Y = X_t Y_t$.

Numeraire Invariance Theorem. *Suppose Y is a deflator. Then a trading strategy* θ *is self-financing with respect to X if and only if* θ *is self-financing with respect to* X^Y.

Proof: Let $W_t = \theta_0 \cdot X_0 + \int_0^t \theta_s \, dX_s$, $t \in [0, T]$. Let W^Y be the process defined by $W_t^Y = W_t Y_t$. Because W and Y are Ito processes, Ito's Formula implies, letting σ_X, σ_W, and σ_Y denote the respective diffusions of X, W, and Y, that

$$
\begin{aligned}
dW_t^Y &= Y_t \, dW_t + W_t \, dY_t + \sigma_W(t) \cdot \sigma_Y(t) \, dt \\
&= Y_t \theta_t \, dX_t + (\theta_t \cdot X_t) \, dY_t + [\theta_t^\top \sigma_X(t)] \sigma_Y(t) \, dt \\
&= \theta_t \cdot \left[Y_t \, dX_t + X_t \, dY_t + \sigma_X(t) \sigma_Y(t) \, dt \right] \\
&= \theta_t \, dX_t^Y.
\end{aligned}
$$

Thus, $\theta_t \cdot X_t^Y = \theta_0 \cdot X_0^Y + \int_0^t \theta_s \, dX_s^Y$ if and only if $\theta_t \cdot X_t = \theta_0 \cdot X_0 + \int_0^t \theta_s \, dX_s$, completing the proof. ∎

We have the following corollary, which is immediate from the Numeraire Invariance Theorem, the strict positivity of Y, and the definition of an arbitrage.

Corollary. *Suppose Y is a deflator. A trading strategy is an arbitrage with respect to X if and only if it is an arbitrage with respect to the deflated price process* X^Y.

C. State Prices and Doubling Strategies

Paralleling the terminology of Section 2C, a *state-price deflator* is a deflator π with the property that the deflated price process X^π is a martingale. Other terms used for this concept in the literature are *state-price density*, *marginal rates of substitution*, and *pricing kernel*. In the discrete-state, discrete-time setting of Chapter 2, we found that there is a state-price deflator if and only if there is no arbitrage. In this chapter, we will see a sense in which this result is "almost" true, up to some technical issues. First, however, we need to establish some mild restrictions on trading strategies, as the following example shows.

Suppose we take B to be a single Brownian motion ($d = 1$) and take the price process $X = (S, \beta)$, where $\beta_t = 1$ for all t and $dS_t = S_t \, dB_t$, with $S_0 = 1$. Even though X is a martingale and S is a log-normal process as typically used in the Black-Scholes option-pricing model, we are able to construct an arbitrage that produces any desired constant payoff $\alpha > 0$ at T, with no initial investment. For this, consider the stopping time

$$\tau = \inf\left\{ t : \int_0^t (T - s)^{-1/2} \, dB_s = \alpha \right\}.$$

A source cited in the Notes shows that $0 < \tau < T$ almost surely. This is not surprising given the rate at which $(T - s)^{-1/2}$ "explodes" as s approaches T. Now consider the trading strategy θ defined by $\theta_t = (a_t, b_t)$, where

$$
\begin{aligned}
a_t &= \frac{1}{S_t \sqrt{T - t}}, & t \leq \tau \\
&= 0, & t > \tau,
\end{aligned}
\tag{3}
$$

and

$$b_t = -a_t S_t + \int_0^t a_u \, dS_u. \tag{4}$$

In effect, a places a larger and larger "bet" on the risky asset as T approaches, with b chosen so as to make $\theta = (a, b)$ self-financing. It is also clear that $\theta_0 \cdot X_0 = 0$ and that $\theta_T \cdot X_T = \alpha$ almost surely. Thus θ is indeed an arbitrage, despite the natural assumptions on security prices. Some technical restrictions on trading strategies must be added if we are to expect any reasonable model of prices to preclude arbitrage.

For intuition, one may think of an analogy between the above example and a series of bets on fair and independent coin tosses at times $1/2$, $3/4$, $7/8$, and so on. Suppose one's goal is to earn a riskless profit of α by time 1, where α is some arbitrarily large number. One can bet α on heads for the first coin toss at time $1/2$. If the first toss comes up heads, one stops. Otherwise, one owes α to one's opponent. A bet of 2α on heads for the second toss at time $3/4$ produces the desired profit if heads comes up at that time. In that case, one stops. Otherwise, one is down 3α and bets 4α on the third toss, and so on. Because there is an infinite number of potential tosses, one will eventually stop with a riskless profit of α (almost surely), because the probability of losing on every one of an infinite number of tosses is $(1/2) \cdot (1/2) \cdot (1/2) \cdots = 0$. This is a classic "doubling strategy" that can be ruled out either by a technical limitation, such as limiting the total number of coin tosses, or by a credit restriction limiting the total amount that one is allowed to owe.

For the case of continuous-time trading strategies, we will eliminate the possibility of "doubling strategies" by either of two approaches. One approach requires some extra integrability condition on θ; the other requires a credit constraint, limiting the extent to which the market value $\theta_t \cdot X_t$ of the portfolio may become negative. Given a state-price deflator π, a sufficient integrability condition is that $\theta \in \mathcal{H}^2(X^\pi)$, as defined in Section 5I. The credit constraint is that $\theta_t \cdot X_t^\pi$, the deflated market value of the trading strategy, is bounded below, in that there is some constant k with $\theta_t \cdot X_t^\pi \geq k$ for all t almost surely. We let $\Theta(X^\pi)$ denote the space of such credit-constrained trading strategies. In the above example (3)–(4) of an arbitrage, $\pi \equiv 1$ defines a state-price deflator because X is itself a martingale. The trading strategy θ defined by (3)–(4), however, is neither in $\mathcal{H}^2(X)$ nor in $\Theta(X)$.

Proposition. *For any state-price deflator π, there is no arbitrage in $\mathcal{H}^2(X^\pi)$ or in $\Theta(X^\pi)$.*

Proof: Suppose π is a state-price deflator. Let θ be any self-financing trading strategy.

Suppose, to begin, that θ is in $\mathcal{H}^2(X^\pi)$. Because X^π is a martingale, we have $dX_t^\pi = v_t\, dB_t$, for some $\mathbb{R}^{N \times d}$-valued process that is provided by the Martingale Representation Theorem of Appendix D. The condition $\theta \in \mathcal{H}^2(X^\pi)$ means that $E(\int_0^T \|\theta_t v_t\|^2\, dt) < \infty$, so Proposition 5B implies that $E(\int_0^T \theta_t\, dX_t^\pi) = 0$. By numeraire invariance, θ is self-financing with respect to X^π, and we have

$$\theta_0 \cdot X_0^\pi = E\left(\theta_T \cdot X_T^\pi - \int_0^T \theta_t\, dX_t^\pi\right) = E\left(\theta_T \cdot X_T^\pi\right).$$

If $\theta_T \cdot X_T^\pi \geq 0$, then $\theta_0 \cdot X_0^\pi \geq 0$. Likewise, if $\theta_T \cdot X_T^\pi > 0$, then $\theta_0 \cdot X_0^\pi > 0$. It follows that θ cannot be an arbitrage for X^π. The Corollary to Theorem B implies that θ is not an arbitrage for X.

Now suppose that θ is in $\Theta(X^\pi)$. Because X^π is a martingale, $\int \theta\, dX^\pi$ is a local martingale (as defined in Appendix D). By the Numeraire Invariance Theorem, because θ is self-financing with respect to X, θ is also self-financing with respect to X^π. From this and the self-financing condition (1), we see that the deflated wealth process W, defined by $W_t = \theta_t \cdot X_t^\pi$, is a local martingale. Because $\theta \in \Theta(X^\pi)$, we know that W is also bounded below. Because a local martingale that is bounded below is a supermartingale (Appendix D), we know that $E(W_T) \leq W_0$. From this, if $\theta_T \cdot X_T > 0$, then $W_T > 0$, so $W_0 > 0$ and thus $\theta_0 \cdot X_0 > 0$. Likewise, if $\theta_T \cdot X_T \geq 0$, then $W_T \geq 0$, so $W_0 \geq 0$ and thus $\theta_0 \cdot X_0 \geq 0$. This implies that θ is not an arbitrage. ∎

D. Expected Rates of Return

Suppose that π is a state-price deflator for X, and consider an arbitrary security with price process S. Because a state-price deflator is an Ito process, we can write $d\pi_t = \mu_\pi(t)\,dt + \sigma_\pi(t)\,dB_t$ for appropriate μ_π and σ_π. Because S is an Ito process, we can also write $dS_t = \mu_S(t)\,dt + \sigma_S(t)\,dB_t$ for some μ_S and σ_S. As S^π is a martingale, its drift is zero. It follows from Ito's Formula that, almost everywhere,

$$0 = \mu_\pi(t)S_t + \mu_S(t)\pi_t + \sigma_S(t) \cdot \sigma_\pi(t).$$

We suppose that S is a strictly positive process, and can therefore rearrange to get

$$\frac{\mu_S(t)}{S_t} = \frac{-\mu_\pi(t)}{\pi_t} - \frac{\sigma_S(t) \cdot \sigma_\pi(t)}{\pi_t S_t}. \tag{5}$$

The *cumulative-return process* of this security is the Ito process R defined by $R_0 = 0$ and

$$dR_t = \mu_R(t)\,dt + \sigma_R(t)\,dB_t \equiv \frac{\mu_S(t)}{S_t}\,dt + \frac{\sigma_S(t)}{S_t}\,dB_t.$$

We can now write $dS_t = S_t\,dR_t$. Looking back at equations (5.3) and (5.4), μ_R may be viewed as the conditional expected rate of return, and $\sigma_R(t) \cdot \sigma_R(t)$ as the rate of change in the conditional variance of the return. We re-express (5) as

$$\mu_R(t) - \hat{r}_t = -\frac{1}{\pi_t}\sigma_R(t) \cdot \sigma_\pi(t), \tag{6}$$

where $\hat{r}_t = -\mu_\pi(t)/\pi_t$. In the sense of equation (5.33), $\sigma_R(t) \cdot \sigma_\pi(t)$ is a notion of "instantaneous covariance" of the increments of R and π. Thus (6) is reminiscent of the results of Section 1F. If $\sigma_R(t) = 0$, then $\mu_R(t) = \hat{r}_t$, so the short-term riskless rate process, if there is one, must be $\hat{r}$. In summary, (6) implies a sense in which excess expected rates of return are proportional to the "instantaneous" conditional covariance between returns and state prices. The constant of proportionality, $-1/\pi_t$, does not depend on the security. This interpretation is a bit loose, but (6) itself is unambiguous.

We have been unnecessarily restrictive in deriving (6) only for a particular security. The same formula applies in principle to the return on an arbitrary self-financing trading strategy θ. In order to define this return, let W^θ denote the associated *market-value process*, defined by $W_t^\theta = \theta_t \cdot X_t$.

If W^θ is strictly positive, then the cumulative-return process R^θ for θ is defined by

$$R^\theta_t = \int_0^t \frac{1}{W^\theta_s} \, dW^\theta_s, \qquad t \in [0, T].$$

It can be verified as an exercise that the drift μ_θ and diffusion σ_θ of R^θ satisfy the return restriction extending (6), given by

$$\mu_\theta(t) - \hat{r}_t = -\frac{1}{\pi_t} \sigma_\theta(t) \cdot \sigma_\pi(t). \tag{7}$$

We will now see that (7) leads to a "beta model" for expected returns, analogous to that of Chapter 2. We can always find adapted processes φ and ϵ valued in $\mathbb{R}^N$ and $\mathbb{R}^d$, respectively, such that

$$\sigma_\pi(t) = \sigma_X(t)^\top \varphi_t + \epsilon_t \qquad \text{and} \qquad \sigma_X(t)\epsilon_t = 0, \qquad t \in [0, T],$$

where σ_X is the $\mathbb{R}^{N \times d}$-valued diffusion of the price process X. For each (ω, t) in $\Omega \times [0, T]$, the vector $\sigma_X(\omega, t)^\top \varphi(\omega, t)$ is the orthogonal projection in $\mathbb{R}^d$ of $\sigma_\pi(\omega, t)$ onto the span of the rows of the matrix $\sigma_X(\omega, t)$. Suppose $\theta = (\theta^{(1)}, \ldots, \theta^{(N)})$ is a self-financing trading strategy with $\sigma_X^\top \theta = \sigma_X^\top \varphi$. (For example, if $X_t^{(1)} = \exp(\int_0^t r_s \, ds)$ for a short-rate process r, we can construct θ by letting $\theta_t^{(j)} = \varphi_t^{(j)}$, $j > 1$, and by choosing $\theta^{(1)}$ so that the self-financing condition is met.) The market-value process W^θ of θ is an Ito process because θ is self-financing. We suppose that the initial portfolio θ_0 can be chosen so that W^θ is also strictly positive, implying that the associated return process $R^* \equiv R^\theta$ is well defined. Because the diffusion of W^θ is $\sigma_X^\top \varphi$, the diffusion of R^* is $\sigma^* \equiv \sigma_X^\top \varphi / W^\theta$. For an arbitrary Ito return process R, (6) implies that

$$\mu_R(t) - \hat{r}_t = -\frac{1}{\pi_t} \sigma_R(t) \cdot \sigma_\pi(t)$$

$$= -\frac{1}{\pi_t} \sigma_R(t) \cdot [\sigma_X(t)^\top \varphi_t + \epsilon_t]$$

$$= -\frac{W^\theta_t}{\pi_t} \sigma_R(t) \cdot \sigma^*_t,$$

using the fact that $\sigma_R(\omega, t)$ is (in each state ω) a linear combination of the rows of $\sigma_X(\omega, t)$. This in turn implies that $\sigma_R(t) \cdot \epsilon_t = 0$. In particular, for the return process R^*, we have

$$\mu^*_t - \hat{r}_t = \frac{-W^\theta_t}{\pi_t} \sigma^*_t \cdot \sigma^*_t,$$

where μ^* is the drift (expected rate of return) of R^*. Substituting back into (6) the resulting expression for W_t^θ/π_t leaves the *state-price beta model of returns* given by

$$\mu_R(t) - \hat{r}_t = \beta_R(t)(\mu_t^* - \hat{r}_t), \tag{8}$$

where

$$\beta_R(t) = \frac{\sigma_R(t) \cdot \sigma_t^*}{\sigma_t^* \cdot \sigma_t^*}.$$

In the "instantaneous sense" in which $\sigma_t^* \cdot \sigma_t^*$ stands for the conditional variance of dR_t^* and $\sigma_R(t) \cdot \sigma_t^*$ stands for the conditional covariance between dR_t and dR_t^*, we can view (8) as the continuous-time analogue to the state-price beta models of Section 1F and Exercise 2.6(C). Likewise, we can loosely think of R^* as a return process whose increments have maximal conditional correlation with the increments of the state-price deflator π. Chapter 10 develops a special case, the *consumption-based capital asset pricing model*.

E. Equivalent Martingale Measures

A probability measure Q on $(\Omega, \mathcal{F})$ is said to be *equivalent* to P provided, for any event A, we have $Q(A) > 0$ if and only if $P(A) > 0$. An equivalent probability measure Q is an *equivalent martingale measure* for the price process X of N given securities if X is a martingale with respect to Q, and if the Radon-Nikodym derivative $\frac{dQ}{dP}$ (defined in Appendix C) has finite variance. The finite-variance condition is a technical convenience that is not uniformly adopted in the literature cited in the Notes on equivalent martingale measures. An equivalent martingale measure is sometimes referred to as a "risk-neutral" measure.

In the finite-state setting of Chapter 2, it was shown that the existence of a state-price deflator is equivalent to the existence of an equivalent martingale measure (after some deflation). Later in this chapter, we will see technical conditions sustaining that equivalence in this continuous-time setting. Aside from offering a conceptual simplification of some asset-pricing and investment problems, the use of equivalent martingale measures is justified by the large body of useful properties of martingales that can be applied to simplify reasoning and calculations.

First, we establish the sufficiency of an equivalent martingale measure for the absence of arbitrage. We later show that a technical strengthening of the no-arbitrage condition of the following theorem implies the existence of an equivalent martingale measure. Aside from technical issues, the arguments are the same as those used to show this equivalence in Chapter 2. As in Section C, we need to apply an integrability condition or a credit constraint to trading strategies.

Theorem. *If the price process X admits an equivalent martingale measure, then there is no arbitrage in $\mathcal{H}^2(X)$ or in $\underline{\Theta}(X)$.*

Proof: The proof is quite similar to that of Proposition C. Let Q be an equivalent martingale measure. Let θ be any self-financing trading strategy.

The idea of the proof is based on the case in which θ is bounded, which we assume for the moment. The fact that X is a martingale under Q implies that $E^Q(\int_0^T \theta_t \, dX_t) = 0$. The self-financing condition (1) therefore implies that

$$\theta_0 \cdot X_0 = E^Q\left(\theta_T \cdot X_T - \int_0^T \theta_t \, dX_t\right) = E^Q(\theta_T X_T).$$

Thus, if $\theta_T \cdot X_T \geq 0$, then $\theta_0 \cdot X_0 \geq 0$. Likewise, if $\theta_T \cdot X_T > 0$, then $\theta_0 \cdot X_0 > 0$. An arbitrage is therefore impossible using bounded trading strategies.

For the case of any self-financing trading strategy $\theta \in \mathcal{H}^2(X)$, additional technical arguments are needed to show that $E^Q(\int_0^T \theta_t \, dX_t) = 0$. As X is an Ito process, we can write $dX_t = \mu_t \, dt + \sigma_t \, dB_t$ for appropriate μ and σ. By the Diffusion Invariance Principle (Appendix D), there is a standard Brownian motion B^Q in $\mathbb{R}^d$ under Q such that $dX_t = \sigma_t \, dB_t^Q$. Let $Y = \int_0^T \|\theta_t \sigma_t\|^2 \, dt$. Because θ is in $\mathcal{H}^2(X)$, Y has finite expectation under P. The product of two random variables of finite variance is of finite expectation, so $\frac{dQ}{dP}\sqrt{Y}$ is also of finite expectation under P. Thus, $E^Q(\sqrt{Y}) < \infty$. Proposition 5B then implies that $\int \theta \, dX$ is a Q-martingale, so $E^Q(\int_0^T \theta_t \, dX_t) = 0$. The remainder of the proof for this case is covered by the arguments used for bounded θ.

For the case of $\theta \in \underline{\Theta}(X)$, the arguments used in the proof of Proposition C imply that the wealth process W, defined by $W_t = \theta_t \cdot X_t$, is a supermartingale under Q, so that $E^Q(\theta_T \cdot X_T) \leq \theta_0 \cdot X_0$, implying that θ cannot be an arbitrage. ∎

In most cases, the theorem is applied along the lines of the following corollary, a consequence of the corollary to the Numeraire Invariance Theorem of Section B.

Corollary. *If there is a deflator Y such that the deflated price process X^Y admits an equivalent martingale measure, then there is no arbitrage in $\mathscr{H}^2(X^Y)$ or in $\Theta(X^Y)$.*

If there is a short-rate process r, it is typical in applications to take the deflator Y defined by $Y_t = \exp(-\int_0^t r_s \, ds)$. If r is bounded, then we have $\mathscr{H}^2(X^Y) = \mathscr{H}^2(X)$ and $\Theta(X^Y) = \Theta(X)$, so the previous result can be stated in a more natural form.

F. State Prices and Martingale Measures

We now investigate the relationship between equivalent martingale measures and state-price deflators. They turn out to be effectively the same concept. We take as given the setup of Section A, including a price process X for N securities.

For a probability measure Q equivalent to P, the *density process* ξ for Q is the martingale defined by

$$\xi_t = E_t\left(\frac{dQ}{dP}\right), \qquad t \in [0, T], \tag{9}$$

where $\frac{dQ}{dP}$ is the Radon-Nikodym derivative of Q with respect to P. As stated in Appendix C, for any times t and $s > t$, and any $\mathscr{F}_s$-measurable random variable W such that $E^Q(|W|) < \infty$,

$$E_t^Q(W) = \frac{E_t(\xi_s W)}{\xi_t}, \qquad t \in [0, T]. \tag{10}$$

Proposition. *Suppose there is a short-rate process r and let Y be defined by $Y_t = \exp(-\int_0^t r_s \, ds)$. Suppose, after deflation by Y, that there is an equivalent martingale measure with density process ξ. Then a state-price deflator π is defined by $\pi_t = \xi_t Y_t$, provided $\mathrm{var}(\pi_t) < \infty$ for all t. Conversely, suppose π is a state-price deflator and let ξ be defined by*

$$\xi_t = \exp\left(\int_0^t r_s \, ds\right) \frac{\pi_t}{\pi_0}, \qquad t \in [0, T]. \tag{11}$$

Then, provided $\mathrm{var}(\xi_T)$ is finite, ξ is the density process for an equivalent martingale measure.

Proof: Suppose, after deflation by Y, that there is an equivalent martingale measure Q with density process ξ. Let $\pi = \xi Y$. Then, for any times t and $s > t$, using (10),

$$E_t(\pi_s X_s) = E_t(\xi_s X_s^Y) = \xi_t E_t^Q(X_s^Y) = \xi_t X_t^Y = \pi_t X_t. \tag{12}$$

(These expectations exist because both X_s and π_s have finite variances.) This shows that X^π is a martingale, so π is indeed a state-price deflator.

Conversely, suppose π is a state-price deflator, and let ξ be defined by (11). By applying the definition of a state-price deflator to the price process $\beta = 1/Y$, we see that ξ is a strictly positive martingale with

$$E(\xi_T) = \frac{1}{\pi_0} E(\beta_T \pi_T) = \beta_0 = 1,$$

so ξ is indeed the density of some equivalent probability measure Q. It is provided in the statement of the proposition that $\xi_T = \frac{dQ}{dP}$ has finite variance. We need only show that X^Y is a Q-martingale, but this follows by applying (12). ∎

The general equivalence between state-price deflators and equivalent martingale measures was shown in the simpler setting of Chapter 2 without technical qualification. An exercise further pursues the equivalence in this setting.

G. Girsanov and Market Prices of Risk

We now look for convenient conditions on X supporting the existence of an equivalent martingale measure. We will also see how to calculate such a measure, and conditions for the uniqueness of such a measure.

Suppose Q is any given probability measure equivalent to P, with density process ξ. By the Martingale Representation Theorem (Appendix D), we can express ξ as a stochastic integral of the form

$$d\xi_t = \gamma_t \, dB_t,$$

for some adapted process $\gamma = (\gamma^{(1)}, \ldots, \gamma^{(d)})$ with $\int_0^T \gamma_t \cdot \gamma_t \, dt < \infty$ almost surely. *Girsanov's Theorem* (Appendix D) states that a standard Brownian motion B^Q in $\mathbb{R}^d$ under Q is defined by $B_0^Q = 0$ and $dB_t^Q = dB_t + \eta_t \, dt$, where $\eta_t = -\gamma_t/\xi_t$. Because X is an Ito process, we can write $dX_t = \mu_t \, dt + \sigma_t \, dB_t$, and therefore

$$dX_t = (\mu_t - \sigma_t \eta_t)dt + \sigma_t \, dB_t^Q.$$

As X is in H^2, it is necessary and sufficient for X to be a Q-martingale that its drift is zero, which means that, almost everywhere,

$$\sigma(\omega, t)\eta(\omega, t) = \mu(\omega, t), \qquad (\omega, t) \in \Omega \times [0, T]. \qquad (13)$$

Thus, the existence of a solution η to the system (13) of linear equations (almost everywhere) is necessary for the existence of an equivalent martingale measure for X. Under additional technical conditions, we will find that it is also sufficient.

We can also view a solution η to (13) as providing a proportional relationship between mean rates of change of prices (μ) and the amounts (σ) of "risk" in price changes stemming from the underlying d Brownian motions. For this reason, any such solution η is called a *market-price-of-risk process* for X. The idea is that $\eta_i(t)$ is the "unit price," measured in price drift, of bearing exposure to the increment of $B^{(i)}$ at time t.

A *numeraire deflator* is a deflator that is the reciprocal of the price process of one of the securities. It is usually the case that one first chooses some numeraire deflator Y, and then calculates the market price of risk for the deflated price process X^Y. This is technically convenient because one of the securities, the "numeraire," has a price that is always 1 after such a deflation. If there is a short-rate process r, a typical numeraire deflator is given by Y, where $Y_t = \exp(-\int_0^t r_s \, ds)$.

If there is no market price of risk, one may guess that something is "wrong," as the following result confirms.

Lemma. *Suppose, for some numeraire deflator Y, that there is no market-price-of-risk process for X^Y. Then there are arbitrages that are in both $\underline{\Theta}(X^Y)$ and $\mathcal{H}^2(X^Y)$, and there is no equivalent martingale measure for X^Y.*

Proof: Suppose X^Y has drift process μ^Y and diffusion σ^Y, and that there is no solution η to $\sigma^Y \eta = \mu^Y$. Then, as a matter of linear algebra, there exists an adapted process θ taking values that are row vectors in $\mathbb{R}^N$ such that $\theta \sigma^Y \equiv 0$ and $\theta \mu^Y \neq 0$. By replacing $\theta(\omega, t)$ with zero for any (ω, t) such that $\theta(\omega, t)\mu^Y(\omega, t) < 0$, we can arrange to have $\theta \mu^Y > 0$. (This works provided the resulting process θ is not identically zero; in that case, the same procedure applied to $-\theta$ works.) These properties for θ are preserved after multiplication by any strictly positive adapted "scaling" process, so we can assume without loss of generality that θ is in $\mathcal{H}^2(X^Y)$. Finally, because the numeraire security associated with the deflator has a price that is identically equal to 1 after deflation, we can also choose the trading strategy for the numeraire so that, in addition to the above properties, θ is self-financing. That is, assuming without loss of generality that the numeraire security is the last security, we can adopt the same idea used in (4) and let

$$\theta_t^{(N)} = \sum_{i=1}^{N-1} -\theta_t^{(i)} X_t^{Y,(i)} + \int_0^t \theta_s^{(i)} \, dX_s^{Y,(i)}.$$

It follows that θ is a self-financing trading strategy in $\mathcal{H}^2(X^Y)$, with $\theta_0 \cdot X_0^Y = 0$, whose wealth process W, defined by $W_t = \theta_t \cdot X_t^Y$, is increasing and not constant. In particular, θ is in $\underline{\Theta}(X^Y)$. It follows that θ is an arbitrage for X^Y, and therefore (by numeraire invariance) for X.

Finally, the reasoning leading to (13) implies that if there is no market-price-of-risk process, then there can be no equivalent martingale measure for X^Y. ∎

If $\sigma(\omega, t)$ is of rank less than d, there can be multiple solutions $\eta(\omega, t)$ to (13). There may, therefore, be more than one market-price-of-risk process. If there is at least one market price of risk, we can always single out for convenience the unique "minimum-norm" market price of risk, denoted η^X. For concreteness, we could construct η^X defined as follows. Let $\hat{\sigma}$ and $\hat{\mu}$ be obtained, respectively, by eliminating $((\omega, t)$ by $(\omega, t))$ as many linearly dependent rows from $\sigma(\omega, t)$ as possible and by eliminating the corresponding elements of $\mu(\omega, t)$. Regardless of how this is done, if X has a market price of risk, then a particular market price of risk η^X is uniquely defined by

$$\eta_t^X = \hat{\sigma}_t^\top (\hat{\sigma}_t \hat{\sigma}_t^\top)^{-1} \hat{\mu}_t.$$

For any $\mathbb{R}^d$-valued adapted process η, we let

$$\nu(\eta)_t = \frac{1}{2} \int_0^t \eta_s \cdot \eta_s \, ds,$$

and, if $\nu(\eta)_T$ is finite almost surely, we let

$$\mathcal{E}(-\eta)_t = \exp\left[-\int_0^t \eta_s \, dB_s - \nu(\eta)_t\right], \qquad 0 \le t \le T.$$

The process $\mathcal{E}(-\eta)$ is known as the *stochastic exponential* of $-\eta$. Letting ξ be defined by $\xi_t = \mathcal{E}(-\eta)_t$, Ito's Formula implies that

$$d\xi_t = -\xi_t \eta_t \, dB_t,$$

so ξ is a local martingale. Novikov's Condition (Appendix D), sufficient for ξ to be a martingale, is that $\exp[\nu(\eta)_T]$ has a finite expectation. If Novikov's Condition holds and $\mathcal{E}(-\eta)_T$ has, moreover, finite variance, then we say that η is L^2-*reducible*. For example, it suffices that η is bounded. It can be shown as an exercise that if η is L^2-reducible, then so is η^X, so it suffices to check this property for η^X.

All of this sets up L^2-reducibility as a convenient condition for the existence of an equivalent martingale measure.

Theorem. *If X has a market-price-of-risk process that is L^2-reducible (it suffices that there is a bounded market price of risk for X), then there is an equivalent martingale measure for X, and there is no arbitrage in $\mathscr{H}^2(X)$ or $\Theta(X)$.*

Proof: If X has an L^2-reducible market price of risk, we let $\xi = \mathscr{E}(-\eta^X)$. By Novikov's Condition, ξ is a positive martingale. We have $\xi_0 = \mathscr{E}(-\eta)_0 = e^0 = 1$, so ξ is indeed the density process of an equivalent probability measure Q defined by $\frac{dQ}{dP} = \xi_T$. By the definition of L^2 reducibility, the variance of $\frac{dQ}{dP}$ is finite. It remains to show that X is Q-martingale.

By Girsanov's Theorem, a standard Brownian motion B^Q in $\mathbb{R}^d$ under Q is defined by $dB_t^Q = dB_t + \eta_t \, dt$. Thus $dX_t = \sigma_t \, dB_t^Q$. As $\frac{dQ}{dP}$ has finite variance and each security price process $X^{(i)}$ is in H^2, we know that

$$E^Q\left[\left(\int_0^T \sigma^{(i)}(t) \cdot \sigma^{(i)}(t) \, dt\right)^{1/2}\right] < \infty,$$

by the same argument used in the proof of Theorem E. Thus, $X^{(i)}$ is a Q-martingale by Proposition 5B, and Q is therefore an equivalent martingale measure. The lack of arbitrage in $\mathscr{H}^2(X)$ or $\Theta(X)$ follows from Theorem E. ∎

Putting this result together with the previous lemma, we see that the existence of a market-price-of-risk process is necessary and, coupled with a technical integrability condition, sufficient for the absence of "well-behaved" arbitrages and for the existence of an equivalent martingale measure.

For uniqueness of equivalent martingale measures, we can use the fact that, for any such measure Q, Girsanov's Theorem implies that we must have $\frac{dQ}{dP} = \mathscr{E}(-\eta)_T$, for some market price of risk η. If $\sigma(\omega, t)$ is of maximal rank d, however, there can be at most one solution $\eta(\omega, t)$ to (13). This maximal-rank condition is equivalent to the condition that the span of the rows of $\sigma(\omega, t)$ is all of $\mathbb{R}^d$, which is reminiscent of the uniqueness condition for equivalent martingale measures found in Chapter 2.

Proposition. *If $rank(\sigma) = d$ almost everywhere, then there is at most one market price of risk and at most one equivalent martingale measure. If there is a unique market-price-of-risk process, then $rank(\sigma) = d$ almost everywhere.*

H. Black-Scholes Again

Suppose the given security-price process is $X = (S^{(1)}, \ldots, S^{(N-1)}, \beta)$, where, for $S = (S^{(1)}, \ldots, S^{(N-1)})$,

$$dS_t = \mu_t \, dt + \sigma_t \, dB_t$$

and

$$d\beta_t = r_t \beta_t \, dt, \qquad \beta_0 > 0,$$

where μ, σ, and r are adapted processes (valued in $\mathbb{R}^{N-1}$, $\mathbb{R}^{(N-1) \times d}$, and $\mathbb{R}$, respectively). We also suppose for technical convenience that the short-rate process r is bounded. Then $Y = \beta^{-1}$ is a convenient numeraire deflator, and we let $Z = SY$. By Ito's Formula,

$$dZ_t = \left(-r_t Z_t + \frac{\mu_t}{\beta_t} \right) dt + \frac{\sigma_t}{\beta_t} \, dB_t.$$

In order to apply Theorem G to the deflated price process $\hat{X} = (Z, 1)$, it would be enough to know that Z has an L^2-reducible market price of risk. Given this, there would be an equivalent martingale measure Q and no arbitrage in $\mathscr{H}^2(X)$ or $\Theta(X)$. Suppose, for the moment, that this is the case. By the Diffusion Invariance result of Appendix D, there is a standard Brownian motion B^Q in $\mathbb{R}^d$ under Q such that

$$dZ_t = \frac{\sigma_t}{\beta_t} \, dB_t^Q.$$

Because $S = \beta Z$, another application of Ito's Formula yields

$$dS_t = r_t S_t \, dt + \sigma_t \, dB_t^Q. \tag{14}$$

Equation (14) is an important intermediate result for arbitrage-free asset pricing, giving an explicit expression for security prices under a probability measure Q with the property that the "discounted" price process S/β is a martingale. For example, this leads to an easy recovery of the Black-Scholes formula, as follows.

Suppose that, of the securities with price processes $S^{(1)}, \ldots, S^{(N-1)}$, one is a call option on another. For convenience, we denote the price process of the call option by U and the price process of the underlying security by V, so that $U_T = (V_T - K)^+$, for expiration at time T with some given exercise price K. Because UY is by assumption a martingale under Q, we have

$$U_t = \beta_t E_t^Q \left(\frac{U_T}{\beta_T} \right) = E_t^Q \left[\exp\left(-\int_t^T r_s \, ds \right) (V_T - K)^+ \right]. \tag{15}$$

The reader is asked to verify as an exercise that this is the Black-Scholes formula for the case of $d = 1$, $N = 3$, $V_0 > 0$, and with constants $\bar{r}$ and nonzero $\bar{\sigma}$ such that, for all t, $r_t = \bar{r}$ and $dV_t = V_t \mu_V(t) \, dt + V_t \bar{\sigma} \, dB_t$, where μ_V is a bounded adapted process. Indeed, in this case, Z has an L^2-reducible market-price-of-risk process, an exercise, so the assumption of an equivalent martingale measure is justified. To be more precise, it is sufficient for the absence of arbitrage that the option-price process is given by (15). Necessity of the Black-Scholes formula for the absence of arbitrages in $\mathcal{H}^2(X)$ or $\Theta(X)$ is formally addressed in Section J. We can already see, however, that the expectation in (15) defining the Black-Scholes formula does not depend on which equivalent martingale measure Q one chooses, so one should expect that the Black-Scholes formula (15) is also necessary for the absence of arbitrage. If (15) is not satisfied, for instance, there cannot be an equivalent martingale measure for S/β. Unfortunately, and for purely technical reasons, this is not enough to imply directly the necessity of (15) for the absence of well-behaved arbitrage, because we do not have a precise equivalence between the absence of arbitrage and the existence of equivalent martingale measures. Section J shows that other methods can be used to show necessity.

In the Black-Scholes setting, we have at most one equivalent martingale measure because $\bar{\sigma}$ is nonzero, implying that σ is of maximal rank $d = 1$ almost everywhere. Thus, from Proposition G, there is exactly one equivalent martingale measure.

The detailed calculations of Girsanov's Theorem appear nowhere in the actual solution (14) for the "risk-neutral behavior" of arbitrage-free security prices, which can be given by inspection in terms of σ and r only. The results extend to the case of an infinite horizon, as discussed in Section N.

I. Complete Markets

We say that a random variable W can be *replicated* by a self-financing trading strategy θ if it is obtained as the terminal value $W = \theta_T \cdot X_T$. Our basic objective in this section is to give a simple spanning condition on the diffusion σ of the price process X under which, up to technical integrability conditions, any random variable can be replicated (without resorting to "doubling strategies").

Proposition. *Suppose Y is a numeraire deflator and Q is an equivalent martingale measure for the deflated price process X^Y. Suppose the diffusion σ^Y of X^Y is of rank d almost everywhere. Let W be any random variable with $E^Q(|WY|) < \infty$. Then there is a self-financing trading strategy θ that replicates W and whose deflated market-value process $\{\theta_t \cdot X_t^Y : 0 \le t \le T\}$ is a Q-martingale.*

Proof: We can suppose that, without loss of generality, the numeraire is the last of the N securities and write $X^Y = (Z, 1)$. Let B^Q be the standard Brownian motion in $\mathbb{R}^d$ under Q obtained by Girsanov's Theorem. Because B^Q has the martingale representation property under Q, there is some φ such that

$$E_t^Q(WY_T) = E^Q(WY_T) + \int_0^t \varphi_s \, dB_s^Q, \qquad t \in [0, T]. \tag{16}$$

By the rank assumption on σ^Y and the fact that $\sigma_{Nt}^Y = 0$, there are adapted processes $\theta^{(1)}, \ldots, \theta^{(N-1)}$ solving

$$\sum_{j=1}^{N-1} \theta_t^{(j)} \sigma_{jt}^Y = \varphi_t^\top, \qquad t \in [0, T]. \tag{17}$$

Let $\theta^{(N)}$ be defined by

$$\theta_t^{(N)} = E^Q(WY_T) + \sum_{i=1}^{N-1} \left(\int_0^t \theta_s^{(i)} \, dZ_s^{(i)} - \theta_t^{(i)} Z_t^{(i)} \right). \tag{18}$$

Then $\theta = (\theta^{(1)}, \ldots, \theta^{(N)})$ is self-financing and $\theta_T \cdot X_T^Y = WY_T$. By the Numeraire Invariance Theorem, θ is also self-financing with respect to X and $\theta_T \cdot X_T = W$. As $\int \varphi \, dB^Q$ is by construction a Q-martingale, (16)–(18) imply that $\{\theta_t \cdot X_t^Y : 0 \le t \le T\}$ is a Q-martingale. ∎

In order to further explore the dynamic spanning properties of the price process X, we let $\Theta(X)$ denote the space of self-financing trading strategies in $\mathcal{H}^2(X)$. The *marketed space* of X is

$$M(X) = \{\theta_T \cdot X_T : \theta \in \Theta(X)\}.$$

We know that $M(X)$ is a subset of $L^2(P)$, the space of all random variables with finite variance (and therefore finite expectation), because Θ is a subset of $\mathcal{H}^2(X)$. We say that markets are *complete* if the marketed space $M(X)$ is actually equal to the space $L^2(P)$. Our objective now is to extend Proposition I with necessary and sufficient conditions for complete markets.

To say that $M(X)$ is *closed* means that if $W_1, W_2, \ldots$ is a sequence in $M(X)$, and if W is some random variable such that $E[(W - W_n)^2] \to 0$, then W is also in $M(X)$. (This would mean that W is also replicated by some trading strategy in Θ.) For technical reasons, this closedness property is useful. The following result is from a source cited in the Notes.

Lemma. *Suppose that Y is a numeraire deflator and that there is a bounded market-price-of-risk process for X^Y. Then $M(X^Y)$ is closed.*

We can now exploit the previous lemma to obtain a simple condition for complete markets.

Theorem. *Let $Y_t = \exp(\int_0^t -r_s\, ds)$ for a bounded short-rate process r. For $dX_t = \mu_t\, dt + \sigma_t\, dB_t$, suppose there is a bounded market-price-of-risk process for X^Y. Then markets are complete if and only if $\mathrm{rank}(\sigma) = d$ almost everywhere.*

Proof: Let η be a bounded market-price-of-risk process for X^Y and Q be the associated equivalent martingale measure. We can take $X^Y = (Z, 1)$, for an $\mathbb{R}^{N-1}$-valued Ito process Z. Let B^Q be the standard Brownian motion in $\mathbb{R}^d$ under Q defined by $dB_t^Q = dB_t + \eta_t\, dt$. Let W be a bounded random variable.

By Ito's Formula, the diffusion σ^Y of $X^Y = XY$ has the same span as σ, (ω, t) by (ω, t), and is therefore of rank d almost everywhere. By Proposition I, there is a self-financing trading strategy θ such that $\theta_T \cdot X_T = W$, and whose deflated market-value process V is a Q-martingale. Because W is bounded and $dV_t = \varphi_t\, dB_t^Q$, where φ is given by (16), Proposition 5B implies that $\theta\sigma = \varphi$ is essentially bounded. (That is, there is a constant k such that, letting $\delta_t = 1$ whenever $\|\varphi_t\| \geq k$ and zero otherwise, we have $E(\int_0^T \delta_t\, dt) = 0$.) By the definition of a market-price-of-risk process, $\theta\mu = \theta\sigma\eta$. By assumption, η is bounded, so $\theta\mu$ is essentially bounded, and therefore θ is in $\mathcal{H}^2(X)$. This proves that any bounded W can be replicated by some θ in $\Theta(X)$.

Now suppose that W is in $L^2(P)$. For each positive integer n, we approximate W with the bounded random variable W_n defined by $W_n(\omega) = W(\omega)$ whenever $|W(\omega)| \leq n$ and $W_n(\omega) = 0$ otherwise. As W_n is in the marketed space for all n, and because $E[(W - W_n)^2] \to 0$, we have W in $M(X)$ by the previous lemma. Thus $M(X) = L^2(P)$.

Conversely, suppose that it is not true that $\mathrm{rank}(\sigma) = d$ almost everywhere. We will show that markets are not complete. By the rank assumption on σ and the fact that the diffusion σ^Y of X^Y and the diffusion σ of X

have the same span for all (ω, t), there is some bounded adapted process φ such that there is no solution $\theta^{(1)}, \ldots, \theta^{(N-1)}$ to (17). Then there is no trading strategy θ in $\mathcal{H}^2(X)$ that is self-financing with respect to $(Z, 1)$ such that $\theta_T \cdot (Z_T, 1) = \int_0^T \varphi_t \, dB_t^Q$. By the Numeraire Invariance Theorem, there is no θ in $\Theta(X)$ with $\theta_T \cdot X_T = W$, where $W = \exp(\int_0^T r_t \, dt) \int_0^T \varphi_t \, dB_t^Q$. Because φ, r, and η are bounded, W is in $L^2(P)$. $\blacksquare$

J. Redundant Security Pricing

We return to the Black-Scholes example of Section H. We recall that the underlying Brownian motion B is one-dimensional, and that there are two primitive securities with price processes V and β, where V is a geometric Brownian motion and $\beta_t = e^{\bar{r}t}$ for a constant interest rate $\bar{r}$. For a market with these two securities alone, there is a bounded market-price-of-risk process. It follows that markets are complete, that there is an equivalent martingale measure Q after deflating by β, and that there is no arbitrage in $\Theta(X)$.

Now, consider an option at strike price K, paying $(V_T - K)^+$ at time T. We would like to conclude that the Black-Scholes formula applies, meaning that the option has the price process U defined by

$$U_t = E_t^Q \left[e^{-\bar{r}(T-t)} (V_T - K)^+ \right].$$

In Section H, we showed that this pricing formula is sufficient for the absence of a well-behaved arbitrage with respect to (β, V, U). Now we show that this is the unique arbitrage-free price process for the option with that property. (This was already shown, in effect, in Chapter 5, but the following argument leads to a more general theorem.)

We proceed as follows. As V_T has finite variance, so does the option payoff $(V_T - K)^+$. Suppose, to set up a contradiction, that the actual option price process $\hat{U}$ is not U. For any constant $\epsilon > 0$, let A_ϵ^+ denote the event that $\hat{U}_t - U_t \geq \epsilon$ for some t in $[0, T]$. Let A_ϵ^- denote the event that $U_t - \hat{U}_t \geq \epsilon$ for some t in $[0, T]$. Because U and $\hat{U}$ are assumed to be different processes, there is some $\epsilon > 0$ such that at least one of the events A_ϵ^+ or A_ϵ^- has strictly positive probability. Without loss of generality, suppose that $P(A_\epsilon^+) > 0$, and let $\tau = \inf\{t : \hat{U}_t - U_t \geq \epsilon\}$, a stopping time that is valued in $[0, T]$ with strictly positive probability.

By Proposition I, there is a self-financing trading strategy $\theta = (\theta^{(0)}, \theta^{(1)})$ in $\mathcal{H}^2(\beta, V)$ that replicates $(V_T - K)^+$. From the fact that θ is self-financing, numeraire invariance, and the fact that Q is an equivalent martingale measure for $(1, V/\beta)$, we have

$$\theta_t^{(0)}\beta_t + \theta_t^{(1)}V_t = E_t^Q\big(e^{-\bar{r}(T-t)}(V_T - K)^+\big) = U_t.$$

Let φ be the $\mathbb{R}^3$-valued trading strategy defining investments at the short rate, in the underlying asset, and in the option defined by $\varphi_t = 0$, $t < \tau$, and

$$\varphi_t = (\theta_t^{(0)} + e^{\bar{r}(t-\tau)}\epsilon, \theta_t^{(1)}, -1), \qquad t \geq \tau,$$

where $(\theta^{(0)}, \theta^{(1)})$ is the option-replicating strategy described above. It can be checked that φ is self-financing and that $\varphi_T \cdot (\beta_T, V_T, \hat{U}_T) > 0$, implying that φ is an arbitrage that is in $\mathcal{H}^2(\beta, V, U)$.

   More broadly, given some general price process X for the N "primitive" securities, we say that a security with price process U is *redundant* if its final value U_T can be replicated by a trading strategy θ in $\Theta(X)$. Complete markets implies that any security (with finite-variance price process) is redundant.

Theorem. *Suppose X admits an equivalent martingale measure Q. Given X, consider a redundant security with price process U in H^2. Then $(X, U) \equiv (X^{(1)}, \ldots, X^{(N)}, U)$ admits no arbitrage in $\mathcal{H}^2(X, U)$ if and only if U is a Q-martingale.*

Proof: If U is a Q-martingale, then Q is an equivalent martingale measure for (X, U), implying no arbitrage in $\mathcal{H}^2(X, U)$ by Theorem E. Conversely, suppose U is not a Q-martingale. The arguments used for the preceding Black-Scholes case extend directly to this setting so as to imply the existence of an arbitrage in $\mathcal{H}^2(X, U)$. ∎

   One would typically apply this result after deflation. In the definition of a redundant security, one could have as easily substituted the credit-constrained class $\underline{\Theta}(X, U)$ of trading strategies for $\mathcal{H}^2(X, U)$, allowing a like condition on U in the statement of the theorem.

K. Martingale Measures from No Arbitrage

So far, we have exploited the existence of an equivalent martingale measure as a sufficient condition for the absence of well-behaved arbitrage. Now we turn to the converse issue: Does the absence of well-behaved arbitrages imply the existence of an equivalent martingale measure? In

the finite-dimensional setting of Chapter 2, we know that the answer
is always: "After a change of numeraire, yes." Only technicalities stand
between this finite-dimensional equivalence and the infinite-dimensional
case we face here. Because of these technicalities, this section can be
skipped on a first reading.

Given a price process X for the N securities, suppose there is no arbitrage in $\Theta(X)$. Then, for each W in $M(X)$ (that is, each $W = \theta_T \cdot X_T$ for
some θ in $\Theta(X)$), let $\psi(W) = \theta_0 \cdot X_0$ denote the unique initial investment
required to obtain the payoff W. We know that this function $\psi : M(X) \to$
$\mathbb{R}$ is uniquely well defined because, if there are two trading strategies θ
and φ in $\Theta(X)$ with $\theta_T \cdot X_T = \varphi_T \cdot X_T$ and $\theta_0 \cdot X_0 > \varphi_0 \cdot X_0$, then $\varphi - \theta$ is an
arbitrage. The function ψ is linear because stochastic integration is linear.
Finally, again from the absence of arbitrage, ψ is strictly increasing, meaning that $\psi(W) > \psi(W')$ whenever $W > W'$. The marketed space $M(X)$ is
a *linear subspace* of $L^2(P)$ because, whenever $Z = \theta_T \cdot X_T$ and $W = \varphi_T \cdot X_T$
are in $M(X)$, then $aZ + bW$ is also in M for any constants a and b. (This
follows from the fact that $a\theta + b\varphi$ is a self-financing strategy, using the
linearity of stochastic integration.)

Because of technicalities, the existence of an equivalent martingale
measure does not follow from the absence of arbitrage in $\mathscr{H}^2(X)$, alone.
Indeed, some sources cited in the Notes provide counterexamples. We
can resort, however, to a slightly stronger condition. An *approximate arbitrage* is a sequence $\{Z_n\}$ in $M(X)$ with $\psi(Z_n) \leq 0$ for all n, such that
there exists some sequence $\{Z'_n\}$ in $L^2(P)$ with $Z'_n \leq Z_n$ for all n, and with
$E[(Z'_n - Z')^2] \to 0$ for some $Z' > 0$. The idea is that no Z_n has positive
market value, yet Z_n is larger than Z'_n, which in turns converges to a positive, nonzero, random value. For example, suppose θ is an arbitrage in
$\Theta(X)$ with $\theta_T \cdot X_T > 0$. Then the (trivial) sequence $\{Z_n\}$ defined by $Z_n =$
$\theta_T \cdot X_T$ for all n is an approximate arbitrage. (Just take $Z'_n = \theta_T \cdot X_T$ for
all n.) Provided there is a bounded short-rate process, or under other weak
assumptions, the absence of approximate arbitrage is indeed a stronger
assumption than the absence of arbitrage in $\Theta(X)$, and the difference is
only important (for technical reasons) in this infinite-dimensional setting.
If we strengthen the assumption of no arbitrage in $\mathscr{H}^2(X)$ to the assumption of no approximate arbitrage, we can recover the existence of an
equivalent martingale measure. Variants of the following result are cited
in the Notes.

Proposition. *Suppose $X^{(1)} \equiv 1$. Then there is no approximate arbitrage for X if
and only if there is an equivalent martingale measure for X.*

Proof: Suppose there is no approximate arbitrage. Then there is no arbitrage, and the pricing functional $\psi : M(X) \to \mathbb{R}$ for X is well defined, linear, and strictly increasing. By a technical result cited in the Notes, a variant of the Hahn-Banach Theorem that is sometimes called the Kreps-Yan Theorem, ψ can be extended to a strictly increasing linear functional $\Psi : L^2(P) \to \mathbb{R}$. By "extension," we mean that for any W in $M(X)$, $\Psi(W) = \psi(W)$. Because Ψ is increasing and linear, the Riesz Representation Theorem for $L^2(P)$ implies that there is a unique π in $L^2(P)$ such that

$$\Psi(W) = E(\pi W), \qquad W \in L^2(P).$$

Because $X^{(1)} \equiv 1$, we have $E(\pi X_T^{(1)}) = X_0^{(1)} = 1$, so $E(\pi) = 1$. Let Q be the probability measure defined by $\frac{dQ}{dP} = \pi$. Because Ψ is strictly increasing, $\pi \gg 0$, so Q is equivalent to P.

Obviously $X^{(1)}$ is a martingale. To show that $X^{(i)}$ is a Q-martingale for each $i > 1$, let τ be an arbitrary stopping time valued in $[0, T]$, and let θ be the trading strategy defined by

(a) $\theta^j = 0$ for $j \neq i$ and $j \neq 1$.
(b) $\theta_t^i = 1$ for $t \leq \tau$, and $\theta_t^i = 0$ for $t > \tau$.
(c) $\theta_t^1 = 0$ for $t \leq \tau$, and $\theta_t^1 = X_\tau^i$ for $t > \tau$.

This means that θ is the strategy of buying the i-th security at time 0 and selling it at time τ, holding the proceeds of the sale in the numeraire security. It is easily seen that θ is in $\Theta(X)$ and that $\theta_T \cdot X_T = X_\tau^{(i)}$, with initial investment $X_0^{(i)} = \psi(X_\tau^{(i)}) = E(\pi X_\tau^{(i)}) = E^Q(X_\tau^{(i)})$. This characterizes $X^{(i)}$ as a Q-martingale, by Doob's Optional Sampling Theorem (Appendix C). Thus, because $\frac{dQ}{dP}$ is of finite variance, Q is an equivalent martingale measure for X.

Conversely, if there is an equivalent martingale measure Q, then there is no arbitrage in $\mathcal{H}^2(X)$ by Theorem E, and the linear functional $\Psi : L^2(P) \to \mathbb{R}$ defined by $\Psi(W) = E^Q(W)$ is an extension of the pricing functional ψ. Suppose, for purposes of contradiction, that $\{W_n\}$ is an approximate arbitrage. Then there is some sequence $\{W_n'\}$ in $L^2(P)$ such that $E^Q(W_n') \leq E^Q(W_n) \leq 0$ and $E^Q(W_n')$ converges to a strictly positive number. This is impossible, so there is no approximate arbitrage. ∎

Corollary. Suppose there is a bounded short-rate process r. Then there is no approximate arbitrage for X if and only if there is an equivalent martingale measure for the deflated price process X^Y, where $Y_t = \exp(-\int_0^t r_s \, ds)$.

Proof: After deflation by Y, one of the securities has a price identically equal to 1. Because r is bounded, a trading strategy θ is an approximate arbitrage for X if and only if it is an approximate arbitrage for X^Y. The theorem then applies. ∎

L. Arbitrage Pricing with Dividends

This section and the next extend the basic arbitrage-pricing approach to securities with dividends paid during $[0, T]$. Consider an Ito process D for the *cumulative dividend* of a security. This means that the cumulative total amount of dividends paid by the security until time t is D_t. For example, if $D_t = \int_0^t \delta_s \, ds$, then δ represents the *dividend-rate process*, as treated in Exercises 5.7, 5.8, and 5.9. Given a cumulative-dividend process D and the associated security-price process X, the *gain process* $G = X + D$ measures the total (capital plus dividend) gain generated by holding the security. A trading strategy is now defined to be a process θ in $\mathcal{L}(G)$, allowing one to define the stochastic integral $\int \theta \, dG$ representing the total gain generated by θ. By the linearity of stochastic integrals, if $\int \theta \, dX$ and $\int \theta \, dD$ are well defined, then $\int \theta \, dG = \int \theta \, dX + \int \theta \, dD$, the sum of capital gains and dividend gains.

Suppose we are given N securities defined by the price process $X = (X^{(1)}, \ldots, X^{(N)})$ and cumulative-dividend process $D = (D^{(1)}, \ldots, D^{(N)})$, with the associated gain process $G = X + D$. For now, we assume, for each j, that $X^{(j)}$ and $D^{(j)}$ are Ito processes in H^2. A trading strategy θ is *self-financing*, extending our earlier definition, if

$$\theta_t \cdot X_t = \theta_0 \cdot X_0 + \int_0^t \theta_s \, dG_s, \qquad t \in [0, T].$$

As before, an *arbitrage* is a self-financing trading strategy θ with $\theta_0 \cdot X_0 \leq 0$ and $\theta_T \cdot X_T > 0$, or with $\theta_0 \cdot X_0 < 0$ and $\theta_T \cdot X_T \geq 0$.

We can extend our earlier results characterizing security prices in the absence of arbitrages that satisfy some integrability or credit constraint. An equivalent martingale measure for the dividend-price pair (D, X) is defined as an equivalent probability measure Q under which $G = X + D$ is a martingale, and such that $\frac{dQ}{dP}$ has finite variance. The existence of an equivalent martingale measure implies, by the same arguments used in the proof of Theorem E, that there is no arbitrage in $\mathcal{H}^2(G)$ or in $\Theta(X)$.

Given a trading strategy θ, if there is an Ito process D^θ such that

$$D_t^\theta = \theta_0 \cdot X_0 + \int_0^t \theta_s \, dG_s - \theta_t \cdot X_t, \qquad t \in [0, T],$$

then we say that D^θ is the cumulative-dividend process *generated* by θ. Suppose there exists an equivalent martingale measure Q for (D, X), and consider an additional security defined by the cumulative-dividend process H and price process V. Both H and V are assumed to be in H^2. Suppose that the additional security is *redundant*, in that there exists some trading strategy θ in $\mathcal{H}^2(G)$ such that $D^\theta = H$ and $\theta_T \cdot X_T = V_T$. The absence of arbitrage in $\mathcal{H}^2((G, H))$ implies that, for all t, we have $V_t = \theta_t \cdot X_t$ almost surely. From this, the gain process $V + H$ of the redundant security is also a martingale under Q. The proof is a simple extension of that of Theorem J.

Under an equivalent martingale measure Q for (D, X), we have, for any time $t \in [0, T]$,

$$X_t + D_t = G_t = E_t^Q(G_T) = E_t^Q(X_T + D_T),$$

which implies that $X_t = E_t^Q(X_T + D_T - D_t)$. For example, if D is defined by $D_t = \int_0^t \delta_s \, ds$, then

$$X_t = E_t^Q\left(X_T + \int_t^T \delta_s \, ds\right). \tag{19}$$

Given the dividend-price pair (D, X), there should be no economic effect, in principle, from a change of numeraire given by a deflator Y. We can write $dY_t = \mu_Y(t) \, dt + \sigma_Y(t) \, dB_t$ for appropriate μ_Y and σ_Y, and $dD_t = \mu_D(t) \, dt + \sigma_D(t) \, dB_t$ for appropriate μ_D and σ_D. The *deflated cumulative-dividend process* D^Y is defined by $dD_t^Y = Y_t \, dD_t + \sigma_D(t) \cdot \sigma_Y(t) \, dt$. The *deflated gain process* G^Y is defined by $G_t^Y = D_t^Y + X_t Y_t$. This leads to a slightly more general version of numeraire invariance, whose proof is left as an exercise.

Lemma (Numeraire Invariance). *Suppose θ is a trading strategy with respect to (D, X) that generates an Ito dividend process D^θ. If Y is a deflator, then the deflated dividend process $(D^\theta)^Y$ is the dividend process generated by θ with respect to (D^Y, X^Y).*

The term "$\sigma_D(t) \cdot \sigma_Y(t) \, dt$" in the definition of dD_t^Y might seem puzzling at first. This term is in fact dictated by numeraire invariance. In all applications that appear in this book, however, we have either $\sigma_D = 0$ or $\sigma_Y = 0$, implying the more "obvious" definition $dD_t^Y = Y_t \, dD_t$, which can be intuitively treated as the dividend "increment" dD_t deflated by Y_t.

Suppose that $X = (S, \beta)$, with $S = (S^{(1)}, \ldots, S^{(N-1)})$ and

$$\beta_t = \beta_0 \exp\left(\int_0^t r_s \, ds\right), \qquad \beta_0 > 0,$$

where r is a bounded short-rate process. Consider the deflator Y defined by $Y_t = \beta_t^{-1}$. If, after deflation by Y, there is an equivalent martingale measure Q, then (19) implies the convenient pricing formula

$$S_t = E_t^Q\left[\exp\left(\int_t^T -r_u\,du\right)S_T + \int_t^T \exp\left(\int_t^s -r_u\,du\right)dD_s\right]. \qquad (20)$$

Proposition I and Theorem J extend in the obvious way to this setting.

M. Lumpy Dividends and Term Structures

One can extend (20) to the case of finite-variance cumulative-dividend process of the form $D = Z + V - W$, for an Ito process Z and increasing adapted processes V and W that are right continuous with left limits. By *increasing*, we mean that $V_s \geq V_t$ whenever $s \geq t$. By *right continuous*, we mean that for any t, $\lim_{s\downarrow t} V_s = V_t$. The *jump* ΔV_t of V at time t, as depicted in Figure 6.1, is defined by $\Delta V_t = V_t - V_{t-}$, where $V_{t-} \equiv \lim_{s\uparrow t} V_s$ denotes the left limit. By convention, $V_{0-} = V_0 = 0$. The jump $\Delta D_t \equiv D_t - D_{t-}$ of the total dividend process D represents the lump-sum dividend paid at time t.

Each of the above implications of the absence of arbitrage for security prices has a natural extension to this case of "lumpy" dividends. In particular, (20) applies as stated, with $\int \theta\,dD$ defined by $\int \theta\,dZ + \int \theta\,dV - \int \theta\,dW$ whenever all three integrals are well defined, the first as a stochastic integral and the latter two as *Stieltjes integrals*. A reader unfamiliar with the Stieltjes integral may consult sources given in the Notes. Happily, the

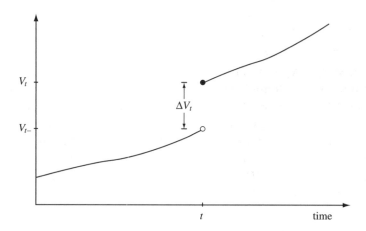

Figure 6.1. *A Right-Continuous Left-Limits Increasing Sample Path*

stochastic integral and the Stieltjes integral coincide whenever both are well defined. In this book, we only consider applications that involve the following two trivial examples of the Stieltjes integral $\int \theta \, dV$.

(a) For the first example of a Stieltjes integral, we let $V = \int \delta_t \, dt$ for some δ in $\mathcal{L}^1$, in which case $\int_0^t \theta_s \, dV_s = \int_0^t \theta_s \delta_s \, ds$.

(b) In the second case, for some stopping time τ, we have $V_t = 0$, $t < \tau$, and $V_t = v$, $t \geq \tau$, where $v = \Delta V_\tau$ is the jump of V at time τ. For this second case, we have $\int_0^t \theta_s \, dV_s = 0$, $t < \tau$, and $\int_0^t \theta_s \, dV_s = \theta_\tau \Delta V_\tau$, $t \geq \tau$, which is natural for our purposes.

We continue to take (D, X) to be a dividend-price pair if $X + D$ is an Ito process. Because of the possibility of jumps in dividends, it is now necessary to take an explicit stance, however, on whether security prices will be measured *ex dividend* or *cum dividend*. We opt for the former convention, which means that for a dividend-price pair (D, X), a trading strategy θ is self-financing if

$$\theta_t \cdot (X_t + \Delta D_t) = \theta_0 \cdot X_0 + \int_0^t \theta_s \, dG_s, \qquad t \in [0, T],$$

where $G = X + D$. With this, an *arbitrage* is defined as self-financing trading strategy θ with $\theta_0 \cdot X_0 \leq 0$ and $\theta_T \cdot (X_T + \Delta D_T) > 0$, or with $\theta_0 \cdot X_0 < 0$ and $\theta_T \cdot (X_T + \Delta D_T) \geq 0$.

Extending our earlier definition to allow for lumpy dividends, a trading strategy θ finances a dividend process D^θ if D^θ is a right-continuous process whose left limit D^θ_{t-} exists for each t, satisfying

$$\theta_t \cdot (X_t + \Delta D_t) = \theta_0 \cdot X_0 + \int_0^t \theta_s \, dG_s - D^\theta_{t-}, \qquad t \in [0, T],$$

with $\Delta D^\theta_T = \theta_T \cdot (X_T + \Delta D_T)$.

With these new definitions in place, the *term structure* can be characterized from (20) as follows. Given a bounded short-rate process r, suppose that Q is an equivalent martingale measure after deflation by Y, where $Y_t = \exp(-\int_0^t r_s \, ds)$. A unit zero-coupon riskless bond maturing at time τ is defined by the cumulative-dividend process H with $H_s = 0$, $s < \tau$, and $H_s = 1$, $s \geq \tau$. Because $dH_s = 0$ for $s \neq \tau$, and because $\Delta H_\tau = 1$, we know from case (b) of the Stieltjes integral that

$$\int_t^T \exp\left(\int_t^s -r_u \, du\right) dH_s = \exp\left(\int_t^\tau -r_u \, du\right).$$

Then (20) implies that the price at time t of a unit zero-coupon riskless bond maturing at time $\tau > t$ is given by

$$\Lambda_{t,\tau} = E_t^Q\left[\exp\left(\int_t^\tau -r_u \, du\right)\right].$$ (21)

The solution for the term structure given by (21) is based on the implicit assumption that the price of a bond after its maturity date is zero. This is also consistent with our earlier analysis of option prices, where we have implicitly equated the terminal cum-dividend price of an option with its terminal dividend payment. For example, with an option expiring at T on a price process S with exercise price K, we set the terminal option price at its expiration value $(S_T - K)^+$. This seems innocuous. Had we actually allowed for the possibility that the terminal cum-dividend option price might be something other than $(S_T - K)^+$, however, we would have needed a more complicated model and further analysis to conclude from the absence of arbitrage that the $(S_T - K)^+$ is indeed the cum-dividend expiration value. This issue of terminal security prices is further pursued in a source cited in the Notes.

N. Martingale Measures, Infinite Horizon

There are some applications for which we will want a version of Girsanov's Theorem for the case of an infinite time horizon. Care must be taken. For example, on a given probability space $(\Omega, \mathcal{F}, P)$, let $\{\mathcal{F}_t : t \geq 0\}$ be the standard filtration of a standard Brownian motion B, and suppose that there is a constant short rate r. The only other security has a geometric Brownian price process S given by

$$dS_t = \mu S_t \, dt + \sigma S_t \, dB_t,$$

for constants μ and σ. The security pays dividends at the rate δS_t at time t, for some constant δ. This setup is completely standard.

We are naturally led to define

$$B_t^Q = B_t + \eta t,$$

where $\eta = (\mu + \delta - r)/\sigma$, and re-express S in the form

$$dS_t = S_t(r - \delta) \, dt + \sigma S_t \, dB_t^Q.$$

While, there may exist a probability measure Q under which, as required by "risk-neutral pricing," B^Q is a standard Brownian motion under Q, such a measure Q and P cannot be equivalent!

We can, however, rely on the fact, cited in the Notes, that a probability space $(\Omega, \mathcal{F}, P)$ on which there is a standard Brownian motion B in $\mathbb{R}^d$ can be constructed with the following properties:

For any adapted process η in $\mathbb{R}^d$ such that $\int_0^t \eta_s \cdot \eta_s \, ds < \infty$, and such that the local martingale ξ defined by

$$\xi_t = \exp\left(\int_0^t - \eta_s \, dB_s - \frac{1}{2} \int_0^t \eta_s \cdot \eta_s \, ds \right)$$

satisfies $E(\xi_t) = 1$ for all t, there exists a probability measure Q on $(\Omega, \mathcal{F})$ such that:

- *For any time t, P and Q assign zero probability to the same events in $\mathcal{F}_t$. That is, the restrictions of these two probability measures to $\mathcal{F}_t$ are equivalent.*
- *Restricted to $(\Omega, \mathcal{F}_t)$, we have $\frac{dQ}{dP} = \xi_t$.*
- *A standard Brownian motion B^Q in $\mathbb{R}^d$ for $(\Omega, \mathcal{F}, Q)$ and $\{\mathcal{F}_t : t \geq 0\}$ is defined by*

$$B_t^Q = B_t + \int_0^t \eta_s \, ds.$$

- *Under Q, B^Q has the martingale representation property. That is, for any process M that is a local martingale under Q, there exists an adapted $\mathbb{R}^d$-valued process θ such that $\int_0^t \theta_s \cdot \theta_s \, ds < \infty$ almost surely and such that $M_t = M_0 + \int_0^t \theta_s \, dB_s^Q, \ t \geq 0$.*

Somewhat more on this issue, including a sense in which Q is uniquely defined, can be found in sources cited in the Notes.

Exercises

6.1 Provide the details left out of the proof provided for Lemma G.

6.2 Verify relation (14).

6.3 In the setting of this chapter, suppose $d = 1$, and there is a bounded short-rate process r. Suppose the price process V of an underlying asset is V, where

$$dV_t = V_t \mu_t \, dt + V_t \sigma_t \, dB_t,$$

where μ and σ are bounded, and σ is bounded away from zero.

(A) Let Y be the numeraire deflator defined by $Y_t = \exp(-\int_0^t r_s \, ds)$. Show that there is an equivalent martingale measure Q for $(V^Y, 1)$. Compute $\frac{dQ}{dP}$, and provide the drift of V under Q.

(B) Consider a European call option on the underlying asset, with expiration at T and strike K. Provide an expression for the price process U of the option in the absence of of arbitrages in $\mathcal{H}^2(V, 1/Y, U)$. Hint: Construct an arbitrage that would apply if your proposed price process were not equal to the actual price process U.

(C) For the price process U that you found in part (B), show that

$$U_0 = c_1 Q_1(A) - c_2 K Q_2(A),$$

where A is the event that the option expires in the money, Q_1 and Q_2 are probability measures equivalent to P, and c_1 and c_2 are constants. All of c_1, c_2, Q_1, and Q_2 do not depend on the strike price K. For each i, provide $\frac{dQ_i}{dQ}$ and the constant c_i, and explain how c_i can be obtained from market data without calculation.

(D) Show that the solution U_0 for the option price given in part (C) corresponds to the Black-Scholes option-pricing formula in the case of constant r and σ. Hint: For each i, use Girsanov's formula for the distribution of $\log V_T$ under Q_i.

(E) Provide an explicit solution U_0 for the option price given in part (C), for the case in which r and σ are deterministic (but not necessarily constant), expressing the solution in terms of the Black-Scholes formula with an adjusted interest rate parameter and volatility parameter.

6.4   Prove Theorem J.

6.5   Suppose that the return process R^θ for a self-financing trading strategy θ is well defined as an Ito process, as at the end of Section D. Show, as claimed there, that R^θ satisfies the state-price restriction (6).

6.6   Extend the arguments of Section E to the case of intermediate dividends, as follows. First, consider a particular security with a dividend-rate process δ in $\mathcal{H}^2$. The cumulative-dividend process H is thus defined by $H = \int_0^t \delta_s\, ds$, $t \in [0, T]$. Suppose that the security's price process V satisfies $V_T = 0$. Suppose that Q is an equivalent martingale measure with density ξ. Let π be defined by $\pi_0 = 1$ and (11). The fact that $H^Y + V^Y$ is a Q-martingale is equivalent to

$$V_t = \frac{1}{Y_t} E_t^Q \left(\int_t^T Y_s \delta_s\, ds \right), \qquad t \in [0, T].$$

(A) From the definition of ξ, Fubini's Theorem, the law of iterated expectations, and the fact that ξ is a martingale, show each of the equalities

$$V_t = \frac{1}{\xi_t Y_t} E_t \left(\xi_T \int_t^T Y_s \delta_s\, ds \right)$$

$$= \frac{1}{\xi_t Y_t} E_t \left(\int_t^T \xi_T Y_s \delta_s\, ds \right)$$

$$= \frac{1}{\xi_t Y_t} \int_t^T E_t(\xi_T Y_s \delta_s)\, ds$$

$$= \frac{1}{\xi_t Y_t} \int_t^T E_t[E_s(\xi_T Y_s \delta_s)] \, ds$$

$$= \frac{1}{\xi_t Y_t} \int_t^T E_t(\xi_s Y_s \delta_s) \, ds$$

$$= \frac{1}{\xi_t Y_t} E_t \left(\int_t^T \xi_s Y_s \delta_s \, ds \right)$$

$$= \frac{1}{\pi_t} E_t \left(\int_t^T \pi_s \delta_s \, ds \right).$$

This calculation shows that $H^\pi + V^\pi$ is a martingale, consistent with the definition of π as a state-price deflator. Reversing the calculations shows that if π is a state-price deflator and $\mathrm{var}(\pi_T) < \infty$, then $H^Y + V^Y$ is a Q-martingale, where Q is the probability measure defined by its density process ξ from (11).

(B) Extend to the case of V_T not necessarily zero. That is, suppose Q is an equivalent probability measure whose density process ξ is of finite variance. Show that $V^Y + H^Y$ is a Q-martingale if and only if $V^\pi + H^\pi$ is a P-martingale.

(C) Extend to the case of a cumulative-dividend process H that is a bounded Ito process. (Although beyond our scope here, an extension of Ito's Formula applying to general dividend processes that are not necessarily Ito processes shows that one need not assume that H is an Ito process.)

6.7 (State-Price Beta Again).   Recall that the cumulative-dividend process D^θ generated by a trading strategy θ is defined by $\Delta D_T^\theta = W_T^\theta$ and $W_t^\theta = W_0^\theta + \int_0^t \theta_s \, dG_s - D_{t-}^\theta$, where $W_t^\theta = \theta_t \cdot (X_t + \Delta D_t)$ and G is the gain process of the given securities. Let G^θ denote the gain process generated by θ, defined by $G_t^\theta = W_t^\theta + D_{t-}^\theta$. Assuming that an Ito return process R^θ for θ is well defined by $dR_t^\theta = (W_t^\theta)^{-1} \, dG_t^\theta$, show that R^θ satisfies the return restriction (6).

6.8   Extend the proof of Proposition K to allow for general dividend processes. Add technical conditions as necessary.

6.9   In the setting of Section A, a probability measure Q equivalent to P is called a *local martingale measure* for X if X is a local martingale under Q. Show that if there is a local martingale measure for the deflated price process X^Y, for some deflator Y, then there is no arbitrage θ for X whose market-value process $\{\theta_t \cdot X_t : t \geq 0\}$ is nonnegative, a slightly stronger credit constraint than that of $\Theta(X)$.

6.10   Suppose, for some numeraire deflator Y, that X^Y has a market-price-of-risk process η such that $\int_0^T \eta_t \cdot \eta_t \, dt < \infty$. Prove that there is no arbitrage for X whose market-value process is nonnegative. Add no regularity conditions.

6.11   Prove numeraire invariance with dividends, in the form of Lemma L.

Notes

The basic approach of this chapter is from Harrison and Kreps (1979) and Harrison and Pliska (1981), who coined most of the terms and developed most of the techniques and basic results. Huang (1985b, c) generalized the basic theory. The development here differs in some minor ways. Most of the results in this chapter extend to an abstract filtration, not necessarily generated by Brownian motion.

(A–B) The notion of a self-financing trading strategy is from Harrison and Kreps (1979). On numeraire invariance in more general settings, see Huang (1985b) and Protter (1999), and on the role of numeraire, see Geman, El Karoui, and Rochet (1995).

(C) The idea of a doubling strategy, as described here in terms of coin tosses, appears in Harrison and Kreps (1979). The actual continuous-time "doubling" strategy (3)–(4), and proof that the associated stopping time τ is valued in $(0, T)$, is from Karatzas (1993), as is a version of Lemma G. The relevance of the credit-constrained class $\underline{\Theta}(X)$ of trading strategies and related results such as Proposition C originate with Dybvig and Huang (1988). Hindy (1995) explores further the implications of a nonnegative wealth constraint.

(D) The beta version of the state-pricing results may be original.

(E) Equivalent martingale measures were developed in Harrison and Kreps (1979), who also developed the equivalence, up to technical issues, of the absence of arbitrage and the existence of equivalent martingale measures. This section presents only one direction of that result.

(F) The relationship between state prices and equivalent martingale measures is standard.

(G–H) Girsanov's Theorem was brought into this application by Harrison and Kreps (1979). Huang and Pagès (1992) give an extension to the case of an infinite-time horizon. Choulli, Krawczyk, and Stricker (1998) address the role of martingales that are stochastic exponentials (such as a density process) in financial applications. Loewenstein and Willard (1998, 1999) treat the implications of local martingale versions of a "density process" for what would, as a martingale, define an equivalent martingale measure.

(I–J) The relationship between complete markets and the uniqueness of an equivalent martingale measure was initiated by Harrison and Kreps (1979) and Harrison and Pliska (1981). More on this can be found in Artzner and Heath (1990, 1995), Jarrow and Madan (1991), Müller (1985), Protter (1999), and Stricker (1984). Delbaen, Monat, Schachermayer, Schweizer, and Stricker (1994) and Monat and Stricker (1994, 1995) provide conditions for L^2-closedness of the marketed space of contingent claims, a property used in the last section and in the proof of Proposition I. Rydberg (1997) discusses uniqueness in a Markovian setting. On preserving market completeness under a change of measure with abstract filtrations, see Duffie (1985).

(K) The main technical result used in Section K, on the extension of positive linear functionals, is inspired by Kreps (1981) and can be found specifically in Clark (1993). The notion of an approximate arbitrage is a slight variation on the notion of a *free lunch*, introduced by Kreps (1981). Related results leading to technical conditions for the existence of an equivalent martingale measure are based on Harrison and Kreps (1979) and Harrison and Pliska (1981). The result applies without technical qualification in discrete-time settings, as shown by Dalang, Morton, and Willinger (1990). For a simpler proof, see Kabanov and Stricker (2000). Delbaen and Schachermayer (1999) offer a definitive result in continuous-time settings, based on the notion of a *free lunch with vanishing risk*, which is closely related to that of an approximate arbitrage. They show the equivalence, after deflation by a numeraire deflator, between no free lunch with vanishing risk and the existence of a local martingale measure. For previous and related results, see Ansel and Stricker (1992, 1994b), Back and Pliska (1987), Cassese (1996) Delbaen (1992), Delbaen and Schachermayer (1994a, b, 1995a, b, c, 1996a, b, 1998), Duffie and Huang (1986), El Karoui and Quenez (1995), Frittelli and Lakner (1995), Jacod and Shiryaev (1998), Kabanov (1996), Kabanov and Kramkov (1994, 1995), Kusuoka (1992a), Lakner (1993a, b), Levental and Skorohod (1995), Rogers (1994), Schachermayer (1992, 1994, 1998), Schweizer (1992), and Stricker (1990).

For various notions of counterexamples to the existence of an equivalent martingale measure in the absence of arbitrage, see Stricker (1990), Back and Pliska (1991), Delbaen and Schachermayer (1994b), Schachermayer (1993), and Levental and Skorohod (1995).

(L–M) The extensions to handle dividends and jumps is routine. The Stieltjes integral, mentioned in Section M, can be found in an analysis text such as Royden (1968). In order to see a sense in which the absence of arbitrage implies that terminal ex-dividend prices are zero, see Ōhashi (1991). This issue is especially delicate in non-Brownian information settings, since the event that $X_T \neq 0$, in some informational sense not explored here, can be suddenly revealed at time T, and therefore be impossible to exploit with a simultaneous trade. For further discussion of the terminal arbitrage issue, see Ōhashi (1991).

(N) The motivation here is from Huang and Pagès (1992). The results extending Girsanov's Theorem are based on Revuz and Yor (1991), Section VIII.1.

Additional Topics: Banz and Miller (1978) and Breeden and Litzenberger (1978) deduce state prices from the valuation of derivative securities.

Amendinger (1999) treats martingale representation for enlarged filtrations. Imkeller, Pontier, and Weisz (1999) address the existence of arbitrage after enlarging the filtration to include some "advanced" information.

Dritschel and Protter (1998) apply martingale representation in a financial setting involving Azema's martingale.

Babbs and Selby (1996), Bühlmann, Delbaen, Embrechts, and Shiryaev (1998), and Föllmer and Schweizer (1990) suggest some criteria or parameterization for the selection of an equivalent martingale measure in incomplete markets. In particular, Artzner (1995), Bajeux-Besnainou and Portait (1997), Dijkstra (1996), Johnson (1994), and Long (1990) address the *numeraire portfolio*, also called *growth-optimal portfolio*, as a device for selecting a state-price deflator.

Carr and Jarrow (1990) show a connection between *local time* and the Black-Scholes model. See also Bick (1995).

Analogues to some of the results in Chapter 5 or in this chapter for the case of market imperfections such as portfolio constraints or transactions costs are provided by Ahn, Dayal, Grannan, and Swindle (1995), Avellaneda and Parás (1994a), Bergman (1995), Boyle and Vorst (1992), Carassus and Jouini (1998), Chen (1994), Clewlow and Hodges (1996), Constantinides (1993), Constantinides and Zariphopoulou (1999), Cvitanić and Karatzas (1993), Davis and Clark (1993), Davis and Panas (1991), Davis, Panas, and Zariphopoulou (1993), Edirisinghe, Naik, and Uppal (1993), Grannan and Swindle (1996), Henrotte (1991), Jouini and Kallal (1993a, 1995), Karatzas and Kou (1998), Korn (1995), Kusuoka (1992b, 1993), Leland (1985), Levental and Skorohod (1997), Luttmer (1996), Munk (1997), Soner, Shreve, and Cvitanić (1994), Taleb (1997), and Whalley and Wilmott (1997). Many of these results are asymptotic, for "small" proportional transactions costs, based on the approach of Leland (1985). Additional implications of transactions costs and portfolio constraints for optimal portfolio and consumption choice are cited in the Notes of Chapter 9.

An application to international markets is given by Delbaen and Shirakawa (1996).

General treatments of some of the issues covered in this chapter can be found in Babbs and Selby (1996), Back and Pliska (1991), Christensen (1987, 1991), Conze and Viswanathan (1991b), Dothan (1990), El Karoui and Quenez (1991), El Karoui and Quenez (1995), Jarrow and Madan (1999), Jouini and Kallal (1995), Karatzas (1993), Müller (1985), Protter (1999), and Rady (1993).

7

Term-Structure Models

THIS CHAPTER REVIEWS models of the term structure of interest rates that are used for the pricing and hedging of fixed-income securities, those whose future payoffs are contingent on future interest rates. Term-structure modeling is one of the most active and sophisticated areas of application of financial theory to everyday business problems, ranging from managing the risk of a bond portfolio to the design and pricing of collateralized mortgage obligations.

Included in this chapter are such standard examples as the Merton, Ho-Lee, Dothan, Brennan-Schwartz, Vasicek, Black-Derman-Toy, Black-Karasinski, and Cox-Ingersoll-Ross models, and variations of these "single-factor" term-structure models, so named because they treat the entire term structure of interest rates at any time as a function of a single state variable, the short rate of interest. We will also review multifactor models, including multifactor affine models, extending the Cox-Ingersoll-Ross and Vasicek models.

All of the named single-factor and multifactor models can be viewed in terms of marginal forward rates rather than directly in terms of interest rates, within the Heath-Jarrow-Morton (HJM) term-structure framework. The HJM framework allows, under technical conditions, any initial term structure of forward interest rates and any process for the conditional volatilities and correlations of these forward rates.

Numerical tractability is essential for practical applications. The "calibration" of model parameters and the pricing of term-structure derivatives are typically done by such numerical methods as "binomial trees" (Chapter 3), Fourier transform methods (Chapter 8), Monte Carlo simulation (Chapter 12), and finite-difference solution of PDEs (Chapter 12).

This chapter makes little direct use of the pricing theory developed in Chapter 6 beyond the basic idea of an equivalent martingale measure,

which can therefore be treated as a "black box." One need only remember
that, with probabilities assigned by an equivalent martingale measure, the
expected rate of return on any security is the short rate of interest. Since
the existence of an equivalent martingale measure is, except for purely
technical conditions, equivalent to the absence of arbitrage, we find it safe
and convenient to work almost from the outset under an assumed equivalent martingale measure. Sufficient conditions for an equivalent martingale measure are reviewed in Chapter 6. An equilibrium example is given
in Chapter 10. In empirical applications, it is often convenient to specify
the probabilistic properties of a term-structure model under an equivalent martingale measure and also under a probability measure reflecting
actual data generation.

A. The Term Structure

We fix a standard Brownian motion $B = (B^1, \ldots, B^d)$ in $\mathbb{R}^d$, for some
dimension $d \geq 1$, restricted to some time interval $[0, T]$, on a given prob-
ability space $(\Omega, \mathcal{F}, P)$. We also fix the standard filtration $\mathbb{F} = \{\mathcal{F}_t : 0 \leq t \leq T\}$ of B, as defined in Section 5I.

We take as given an adapted short-rate process r with $\int_0^T |r_t| \, dt < \infty$.
Conceptually, r_t is the continually compounding rate of interest on riskless
securities at time t. This is formalized by supposing that, for any time t,
one can invest one unit of account and achieve a market value at any
future time s of $\exp(\int_t^s r_u \, du)$. This may be viewed as the proceeds of
continual reinvestment at the short rate r.

Consider a *zero-coupon bond* maturing at some future time $s > t$. By
definition, the bond pays no dividends before time s, and offers a fixed
lump-sum payment at time s that we can take without loss of generality
to be 1 unit of account. Although it is not always essential to do so, we
assume throughout the chapter that such a bond exists for each maturity
date s. One of our main objectives is to characterize the price $\Lambda_{t,s}$ at time
t of the s-maturity bond, and its behavior over time.

In the absence of arbitrage, purely technical conditions reviewed in
Chapter 6 are required for the existence of an equivalent martingale measure. Such a probability measure Q has the property that any security
whose dividend is in the form of a lump-sum payment of Z at some time
s has a price, at any time $t < s$, of

$$E_t^Q \left[\exp\left(\int_t^s -r_u \, du \right) Z \right], \tag{1}$$

where E_t^Q denotes $\mathcal{F}_t$-conditional expectation under Q. Here, Z would be $\mathcal{F}_s$-measurable, and such that the expectation (1) is well defined. A review of Theorem 2G justifies the easy finite-dimensional version of (1). In particular, taking $Z = 1$ in (1), the price at time t of the zero-coupon bond maturing at s is

$$\Lambda_{t,s} \equiv E_t^Q\left[\exp\left(\int_t^s -r_u \, du\right)\right]. \tag{2}$$

The doubly indexed process Λ is sometimes known as the *discount function,* or more loosely as the *term structure of interest rates.* The term structure is often expressed in terms of the *yield curve.* The *continuously compounding yield* $y_{t,\tau}$ on a zero-coupon bond maturing at time $t + \tau$ is defined by

$$y_{t,\tau} = -\frac{\log(\Lambda_{t,t+\tau})}{\tau}.$$

The term structure can also be represented in terms of forward interest rates, as explained in Section J.

In most of this chapter, we review conventional models of the behavior of the short rate r under a fixed equivalent martingale measure Q. In each case, r is modeled in terms of the standard Brownian motion B^Q in $\mathbb{R}^d$ under Q that is obtained from B via Girsanov's Theorem (Appendix D). The Notes cite more general models. We will characterize the term structure and the pricing of term-structure derivatives, securities whose payoffs depend on the term structure.

B. One-Factor Term-Structure Models

We begin with *one-factor term-structure models,* by which we mean models of the short rate r given by an SDE of the form

$$dr_t = \mu(r_t, t) \, dt + \sigma(r_t, t) \, dB_t^Q, \tag{3}$$

where $\mu : \mathbb{R} \times [0, T] \to \mathbb{R}$ and $\sigma : \mathbb{R} \times [0, T] \to \mathbb{R}^d$ satisfy technical conditions guaranteeing the existence of a solution to (3) such that for all t and $s \geq t$, the price $\Lambda_{t,s}$ of the zero-coupon bond maturing at s is finite and well defined by (2). For simplicity, we can take $d = 1$.

The one-factor models are so named because the Markov property (under Q) of the solution r to (3) implies from (2) that the short rate is the only state variable, or "factor," on which the current yield curve

Table 7.1. *Common Single-Factor Model Parameters*

Model	K_0	K_1	K_2	H_0	H_1	ν
Cox-Ingersoll-Ross	•	•			•	0.5
Pearson-Sun	•	•		•	•	0.5
Dothan					•	1.0
Brennan-Schwartz	•	•			•	1.0
Merton (Ho-Lee)	•			•		1.0
Vasicek	•	•		•		1.0
Black-Karasinski		•	•		•	1.0
Constantinides-Ingersoll					•	1.5

depends. That is, for all t and $s \geq t$, we can write $\Lambda_{t,s} = F(t, s, r_t)$, for some fixed $F : [0, T] \times [0, T] \times \mathbb{R} \to \mathbb{R}$.

Table 7.1 shows many of the parametric examples of one-factor models appearing in the literature, with their conventional names. Each of these models is a special case of the SDE

$$dr_t = \left[K_0(t) + K_1(t)r_t + K_2(t)r_t \log(r_t)\right] dt + \left[H_0(t) + H_1(t)r_t\right]^\nu dB_t^Q,$$

for continuous functions $K_0, K_1, K_2, H_0,$ and H_1 on $[0, T]$ into $\mathbb{R}$, and for some exponent $\nu \in [0.5, 1.5]$. Coefficient restrictions, and restrictions on the space of possible short rates, are needed for the existence and uniqueness of solutions. For each model, Table 7.1 shows the associated exponent ν, and uses the symbol "•" to indicate those coefficients that appear in nonzero form. We can view a negative coefficient function K_1 as a *mean-reversion* parameter, in that a higher short rate generates a lower drift, and vice versa. Empirically speaking, mean reversion is widely believed to be a useful attribute to include in single-factor short-rate models.

In most cases, the original versions of these models had constant coefficients, and were only later extended to allow $K_i(t)$ and $H_i(t)$ to depend on t, for practical reasons, such as calibration of the model to a given set of bond and option prices, as described in Section 12M. For example, with time-varying coefficients, the *Merton model* of the term structure is often called the *Ho-Lee model.* A popular special case of the *Black-Karasinski model* is the *Black-Derman-Toy model,* defined in Exercise 7.1. References to the literature are given in the Notes.

Each of these single-factor models has its own desirable properties, some of which will be reviewed below. It tends to depend on the application which of these, if any, is used in practice. The Notes cite some of the empirical evidence regarding these single-factor models, in some cases strongly pointing toward multifactor extensions, to which we will turn later in this chapter.

For essentially any single-factor model, the term structure can be computed (numerically, if not explicitly) by taking advantage of the Feynman-Kac relationship between PDEs and SDEs given in Appendix E. Fixing for convenience the maturity date s, the Feynman-Kac approach implies from (2), under technical conditions on μ and σ, that for all t,

$$\Lambda_{t,s} = f(r_t, t), \tag{4}$$

where $f \in C^{2,1}(\mathbb{R} \times [0, T])$ solves the PDE

$$\mathscr{D}f(x, t) - xf(x, t) = 0, \qquad (x, t) \in \mathbb{R} \times [0, s), \tag{5}$$

with boundary condition

$$f(x, s) = 1, \qquad x \in \mathbb{R}, \tag{6}$$

where

$$\mathscr{D}f(x, t) = f_t(x, t) + f_x(x, t)\mu(x, t) + \frac{1}{2}f_{xx}(x, t)\sigma(x, t)^2.$$

According to the results in Appendix E, in order for (4)–(6) to be consistent, it is enough that r is nonnegative and that μ and σ satisfy Lipschitz conditions in x and have derivatives μ_x, σ_x, μ_{xx}, and σ_{xx} that are continuous and satisfy growth conditions in x. These conditions are not necessary and can be weakened. We note that the Lipschitz condition is violated for several of the examples considered in Table 7.1, such as the Cox-Ingersoll-Ross model, which must be treated on a case-by-case basis.

The PDE (5)–(6) can be quickly solved using numerical algorithms described in Chapter 12. If μ and σ do not depend on t, then, for any calendar time t and any time $u < s$ remaining to maturity, we can also view the solution f to (5)–(6) as determining the price $f(r_t, s - u) = \Lambda_{t,t+u}$ at time t of the zero-coupon bond maturing at $t + u$, so that a single function f describes the entire term structure at any time.

C. The Gaussian Single-Factor Models

A subset of the models considered in Table 7.1, those with $K_2 = H_1 = 0$, are *Gaussian*, in that the short rates $\{r(t_1), \ldots, r(t_k)\}$ at any finite set $\{t_1, \ldots, t_k\}$ of times have a joint normal distribution under Q. This follows from the properties of linear stochastic differential equations reviewed in Appendix E. Special cases are the Merton (often called "Ho-Lee") and Vasicek models.

For the Gaussian model, we can show that bond-price processes are log-normal (under Q) by defining a new process y satisfying $dy_t = -r_t \, dt$, and noting that (r, y) is the solution of a two-dimensional linear stochastic differential equation, in the sense of Appendix E. Thus, for any t and $s \geq t$, the random variable $y_s - y_t = -\int_t^s r_u \, du$ is normally distributed. Under Q, the mean $m(t, s)$ and variance $v(t, s)$ of $-\int_t^s r_u \, du$, conditional on $\mathcal{F}_t$, are easily computed in terms of r_t, K_0, K_1, and H_0. From the results for linear SDEs in Appendix E, the conditional variance $v(t, s)$ is deterministic and the conditional mean $m(t, s)$ is of the form $a(t, s) + \beta(t, s)r_t$, for coefficients $a(t, s)$ and $\beta(t, s)$ whose calculation is left as an exercise. It follows that

$$
\begin{aligned}
\Lambda_{t, s} &= E_t^Q \left[\exp\left(-\int_t^s r_u \, du \right) \right] \\
&= \exp\left(m(t, s) + \frac{v(t, s)}{2} \right) \\
&= e^{\alpha(t, s) + \beta(t,s)r(t)},
\end{aligned}
\tag{7}
$$

where $\alpha(t, s) = a(t, s) + v(t, s)/2$. Because r_t is normally distributed under Q, this means that any zero-coupon bond price is log-normally distributed under Q. Using this property, a further exercise requests explicit computation of bond-option prices in this setting, along the lines of the original Black-Scholes formula. Aside from the simplicity of the Gaussian model, this explicit computation is one of its main advantages in applications.

An undesirable feature of the Gaussian model is that it implies (for H_0 everywhere nonzero) that the short rate and yields on bonds of any maturity are negative with positive probability at any future date. While negative interest rates are sometimes plausible when expressed in "real" (consumption numeraire) terms, it is common in practice to express term structures in nominal terms, relative to the price of money. In nominal terms, negative bond yields imply a kind of arbitrage. In order to describe this arbitrage, we can formally view *money* as a security with no dividends whose price process is identically equal to 1. If a particular zero-coupon bond were to offer a negative yield, consider a short position in the bond (that is, borrowing) and a long position of an equal number of units of money, both held to the maturity of the bond. With a negative bond yield, the initial bond price is larger than 1, implying that this position is an arbitrage. Of course, the proposed alternative of everywhere positive interest rates, along with money, implies that the opposite strategy is an arbitrage if money can be freely shorted. One normally assumes that money is a special kind of security that cannot be shorted. (Indeed, the fact that money has a strictly positive price despite having no dividends means that shorting money is itself a kind of arbitrage.) To address properly the role of money in supporting nonnegative interest rates would therefore require a rather wide detour into monetary theory and the institutional features of money markets. It may suffice for our purposes to point out that money conveys certain special advantages, for example the ability to undertake certain types of transactions immediately, or with reduced transactions costs, which would imply a fee in equilibrium for the shorting of money. Let us merely leave this issue with the sense that allowing negative interest rates is not necessarily "wrong," but is somewhat undesirable. Gaussian short-rate models are nevertheless useful, and frequently used, because they are relatively tractable and in light of the low likelihood that they would assign to negative interest rates within a reasonably short time, with reasonable choices for the coefficient functions.

D. The Cox-Ingersoll-Ross Model

One of the best-known single-factor term-structure models is the *Cox-Ingersoll-Ross* (CIR) model indicated in Table 7.1. For constant coefficient functions K_0, K_1, and H_1, the CIR drift and diffusion functions, μ and σ, may be written in the form

$$\mu(x, t) = \kappa(\bar{x} - x); \qquad \sigma(x, t) = C\sqrt{x}, \qquad x \geq 0, \qquad (8)$$

for constants κ, $\bar{x}$, and C. Provided κ and $\bar{x}$ are positive, there is a nonnegative solution to the SDE (3), based on a source cited in the Notes. (Obviously, nonnegativity is important, if only for the fact of the square root in the diffusion.) Of course, we assume that $r_0 \geq 0$, and treat (5)–(6) as applying only to a short rate x in $[0, \infty)$. Given r_0, under Q, r_t has a noncentral χ^2 distribution with parameters that are known explicitly. The drift $\kappa(\bar{x} - r_t)$ indicates reversion of r_t toward a stationary risk-neutral mean $\bar{x}$ at a rate κ, in the sense that

$$E^Q(r_t) = \bar{x} + e^{-\kappa t}(r_0 - \bar{x}),$$

which tends to $\bar{x}$ as t goes to $+\infty$. Additional properties of this model are discussed later in this chapter and in Section 10I, where the coefficients

κ, $\bar{x}$, and C are calculated in a general-equilibrium setting in terms of the utility function and endowment of a representative agent. For the CIR model, it can be verified by direct computation of the derivatives that the solution for the term-structure PDE (5)–(6) is given by

$$f(x, t) = e^{\alpha(t, s) + \beta(t, s)x}, \tag{9}$$

where

$$\alpha(t, s) = \frac{2\kappa\bar{x}}{C^2}\left[\log\left(2\gamma e^{(\gamma+\kappa)(s-t)/2}\right) - \log((\gamma + \kappa)(e^{\gamma(s-t)} - 1) + 2\gamma)\right], \tag{10}$$

$$\beta(t, s) = \frac{2(1 - e^{\gamma(s-t)})}{(\gamma + \kappa)(e^{\gamma(s-t)} - 1) + 2\gamma}, \tag{11}$$

for $\gamma = (\kappa^2 + 2C^2)^{1/2}$. We will later consider multifactor versions of the CIR model.

E. The Affine Single-Factor Models

The Gaussian and Cox-Ingersoll-Ross models are special cases of single-factor models with the property that the solution f of the term-structure PDE (5)–(6) is given in the exponential-affine form (9) for some coefficients $\alpha(t, s)$ and $\beta(t, s)$ that are continuously differentiable in s. For all t, the yield $-\log[f(x, t)]/(s - t)$ obtained from (9) is affine in x. We therefore call any such model an *affine term-structure model*. (A function $g : \mathbb{R}^k \to \mathbb{R}$, for some k, is *affine* if there are constants a and b in $\mathbb{R}^k$ such that for all x, $g(x) = a + b \cdot x$.)

We can use the PDE (5) to characterize the drift and diffusion functions, μ and σ, underlying any affine model. Specifically, substituting (9) into (5) and simplifying leaves, for each $(x, t) \in \mathbb{R} \times [0, s)$,

$$\beta(t, s)\mu(x, t) = [1 - \beta_t(t, s)]x - \alpha_t(t, s) - \frac{1}{2}\beta^2(t, s)\sigma^2(x, t), \tag{12}$$

where subscripts indicate partial derivatives. We will use (12) to deduce how $\mu(x, t)$ and $\sigma(x, t)$ depend on x. Suppose, for simplicity, that $\mu(x, t)$ and $\sigma(x, t)$ do not depend on t. Applying (12) at two possible maturity dates, say s_1 and s_2, we have the two linear equations in the two unknowns $\mu(x)$ and $\sigma^2(x)$:

$$A(s_1, s_2)\begin{pmatrix} \mu(x) \\ \sigma^2(x) \end{pmatrix} = \begin{pmatrix} -\alpha_t(t, s_1) + [1 - \beta_t(t, s_1)]x \\ -\alpha_t(t, s_2) + [1 - \beta_t(t, s_2)]x \end{pmatrix}, \tag{13}$$

where

$$A(s_1, s_2) = \begin{pmatrix} \beta(t, s_1) & \beta^2(t, s_1)/2 \\ \beta(t, s_2) & \beta^2(t, s_2)/2 \end{pmatrix}.$$

Except at maturity dates s_1 and s_2 chosen so that $A(s_1, s_2)$ is singular, we can conclude from (13) that $\mu(x)$ and $\sigma^2(x)$ must themselves be affine in x.

Going the other way, suppose that μ and σ^2 are affine in x, in that

$$\mu(x, t) = K_0(t) + K_1(t)x; \qquad \sigma^2(x, t) = H_0(t) + H_1(t)x.$$

Then we can recover an affine term-structure model by showing that the solution to (5)–(6) is of the affine form (9). Such a solution applies if there exists (α, β) solving (12). The terms proportional to x in (12) must sum to zero, for otherwise we could vary x and contradict (12). This supplies us with an ordinary differential equation (ODE) for β:

$$\beta_t(t, s) = 1 - K_1(t)\beta(t, s) - \frac{1}{2}H_1(t)\beta^2(t, s); \qquad \beta(s, s) = 0, \qquad (14)$$

whose boundary condition $\beta(s, s) = 0$ is dictated by (6) and (9). The ODE (14) is a form of what is known as a *Riccati equation*. Solutions are finite given technical conditions on K_1 and H_1.

Likewise, the "intercept" term in (12), the term that is not dependent on x, must also be zero. Having solved for β from (14), this gives us

$$\alpha_t(t, s) = -K_0(t)\beta(t, s) - \frac{1}{2}H_0(t)\beta^2(t, s).$$

Again, the boundary condition $\alpha(s, s) = 0$ is from (6) and (9). Thus, by integrating $\alpha_u(u, s)$ with respect to u, we have

$$\alpha(t, s) = \int_t^s \left[K_0(u)\beta(u, s) + \frac{1}{2}H_0(u)\beta^2(u, s) \right] du. \qquad (15)$$

Thus, technicalities aside, μ and σ^2 are affine in x if and only if the term structure is itself affine in x. Sources cited in the Notes strengthen this conclusion. Numerical solutions of the ODE (14), for example by discretization methods such as Runge-Kutta, are straightforward. Then (15) can be solved by numerical integration. The special cases associated with the Gaussian model and the CIR model have explicit solutions for α and β.

We have shown, basically, that affine term-structure models are easily classified and solved. This idea is further pursued in a multifactor setting later in this chapter and in sources cited in the Notes.

From the above characterization, we know that the "affine class" of term-structure models includes those shown in Table 7.1 with $K_2 = 0$ and $\nu = 0.5$, including

(a) The *Vasicek model*, for which $H_1 = 0$.
(b) The *Cox-Ingersoll-Ross model*, for which $H_0 = 0$.
(c) The *Merton (Ho-Lee) model*, for which $K_1 = H_1 = 0$.
(d) The *Pearson-Sun model*.

For affine models with $H_1 \neq 0$, existence of a solution to the SDE (3) requires coefficients (H, K) with

$$K_0(t) - K_1(t)\frac{H_0(t)}{H_1(t)} \geq 0, \qquad t \in [0, T]. \tag{16}$$

This condition guarantees the existence of a solution r to the SDE (3) with $r(t) \geq -H_0(t)/H_1(t)$ for all t.

F. Term-Structure Derivatives

We return to the general one-factor model (3) and consider one of its most important applications, the pricing of derivative securities. Suppose a derivative has a payoff at some given time s defined by $g(r_s)$. By the definition of an equivalent martingale measure, the price at time t for such a security is

$$F(r_t, t) \equiv E_t^Q\left[\exp\left(-\int_t^s r_u\,du\right)g(r_s)\right].$$

The Feynman-Kac PDE results of Appendix E give technical conditions on μ, σ, and g under which F solves the PDE, for $(x, t) \in \mathbb{R} \times [0, s)$,

$$F_t(x, t) + F_x(x, t)\mu(x, t) + \frac{1}{2}F_{xx}(x, t)\sigma(x, t)^2 - xF(x, t) = 0, \tag{17}$$

with boundary condition

$$F(x, s) = g(x), \qquad x \in \mathbb{R}. \tag{18}$$

Some examples follow, abstracting from many institutional details.

(a) A European option expiring at time s on a zero-coupon bond maturing at some later time u, with strike price p, is a claim to $(\Lambda_{s,u} - p)^+$ at s. The valuation of the option is given, in a one-factor setting, by the solution F to (17)–(18), with $g(x) = [f(x, s) - p]^+$, where $f(x, s)$ is the price at time s of a zero-coupon bond maturing at u.

(b) A *forward-rate agreement* (FRA) calls for a net payment by the fixed-rate payer of $c^* - c(s)$ at time s, where c^* is a fixed payment and $c(s)$ is a floating-rate payment for a time-to-maturity δ, in *arrears*, meaning that $c(s) = \Lambda_{s-\delta,s}^{-1} - 1$ is the simple interest rate applying at time $s - \delta$ for loans maturing at time s. In practice, we usually have a time to maturity δ of one-quarter or one-half year. When originally sold, the fixed-rate payment c^* is usually set so that the FRA is *at market*, meaning of zero market value.

(c) An *interest-rate swap* is a portfolio of FRAs maturing at a given increasing sequence $t(1), t(2), \ldots, t(n)$ of coupon dates. The intercoupon interval $t(i) - t(i-1)$ is usually 3 months or 6 months. The associated FRA for date $t(i)$ calls for a net payment by the fixed-rate payer of $c^* - c(t(i))$, where the floating-rate payment received is $c(t(i)) = \Lambda_{t(i-1),t(i)}^{-1} - 1$, and the fixed-rate payment c^* is the same for all coupon dates. At initiation, the swap is usually *at market*, meaning that the fixed rate c^* is chosen so that the swap is of zero market value. Ignoring default risk and market imperfections, this would imply, as can be shown as an exercise, that the fixed-rate coupon c^* is the par coupon rate. That is, the at-market swap rate c^* is set at the origination date t of the swap so that

$$1 = c^* \left(\Lambda_{t,t(1)} + \cdots + \Lambda_{t,t(n)} \right) + \Lambda_{t,t(n)},$$

meaning that c^* is the coupon rate on a *par* bond, one whose face value and initial market value are the same.

(d) A *cap* can be viewed as a portfolio of "caplet" payments of the form $(c(t(i)) - c^*)^+$, for a sequence of payment dates $t(1), t(2), \ldots, t(n)$ and floating rates $c(t(i))$ that are defined as for a swap. The fixed rate c^* is set with the terms of the cap contract. Exercise 7.13 explores the valuation of caps.

(e) A *floor* is defined symmetrically with a cap, replacing $(c(t(i)) - c^*)^+$ with $(c^* - c(t(i)))^+$.

(f) A *swaption* is an option to enter into a swap at a given strike rate c^* at some exercise time. If the future time is fixed, the swaption is European. An important variant, the *Bermudan swaption*, allows exercise at any of a given set of successive coupon dates.

Path-dependent derivative securities, such as mortgage-backed securities, sometimes call for additional state variables. Some interest-rate derivative securities are based on the yields of bonds that are subject to some risk of default, in which case the approach must be modified by accounting for default risk, as illustrated in Chapter 11.

There are relatively few cases of practical interest for which the PDE (17)–(18) can be solved explicitly. Chapters 8 and 12 review some numerical solution techniques.

G. The Fundamental Solution

Based on the results of Appendix E, under technical conditions we can also express the solution F of the PDE (17)–(18) for the value of a derivative term-structure security in the form

$$F(x, t) = \int_{-\infty}^{+\infty} G(x, t, y, s)g(y)\, dy, \tag{19}$$

where G is the *fundamental solution* of the PDE (17). Some have called G the *Green's function* associated with (17), although that terminology is not rigorously justified. From (19), for any time $s > t$ and any interval $[y(1), y(2)]$,

$$\int_{y(1)}^{y(2)} G(r_t, t, y, s)\, dy$$

is the price at time t of a security that pays one unit of account at time s in the event that r_s is in $[y(1), y(2)]$. For example, the current price $\Lambda_{t,s}$ of the zero-coupon bond maturing at s is given by $\int_{-\infty}^{+\infty} G(r_t, t, y, s)\, dy$.

One can compute the fundamental solution G by solving a PDE that is "dual" to (5)–(6), in the following sense. As explained in Appendix E, under technical conditions, for each (x, t) in $\mathbb{R} \times [0, T]$, a function $\psi \in C^{2,1}(\mathbb{R} \times (0, T])$ is defined by $\psi(y, s) = G(x, t, y, s)$, and solves the *forward Kolmogorov equation* (also known as the *Fokker-Planck equation*):

$$\mathscr{D}^*\psi(y, s) - y\psi(y, s) = 0, \tag{20}$$

where

$$\mathscr{D}^*\psi(y, s) = -\psi_s(y, s) - \frac{\partial}{\partial y}\left[\psi(y, s)\mu(y, s)\right] + \frac{1}{2}\frac{\partial^2}{\partial y^2}\left[\psi(y, s)\sigma(y, s)^2\right].$$

The "intuitive" boundary condition for (20) is obtained from the role of G in pricing securities. Imagine that the current short rate at time t is x, and consider an instrument that pays one unit of account immediately, if and only if the current short rate is some number y. Presumably this contingent claim is valued at 1 unit of account if $x = y$, and otherwise has no value. From continuity in s, one can thus think of $\psi(\cdot, s)$ as the density at time s of a measure on $\mathbb{R}$ that converges as $s \downarrow t$ to a probability measure ν with $\nu(\{x\}) = 1$, sometimes called the *Dirac measure* at x. Although this initial boundary condition on ψ can be made more precise, we leave that to sources cited in Appendix E. An implementation of this boundary condition for a numerical solution of (20) is spelled out in Chapter 12. A discrete-time analogue is found in Chapter 3, where we provided an algorithm for computing the fundamental solutions for the Black-Derman-Toy and Ho-Lee models.

Given the fundamental solution G, the derivative asset price function F is more easily computed by numerically integrating (19) than from a direct numerical attack on the PDE (17)–(18). Thus, given a sufficient number of derivative securities whose prices must be computed, it may be worth the effort to compute G. Some numerical methods for calculating F and G are indicated in Chapter 12.

A lengthy argument given by a source cited in the Notes shows that the fundamental solution G of the Cox-Ingersoll-Ross model (8) is given explicitly in terms of the parameters κ, $\bar{x}$, and C by

$$G(x, 0, y, t) = \frac{\varphi(t)I_q\left(\varphi(t)\sqrt{xye^{-\gamma t}}\right)}{\exp\left[\varphi(t)(y + xe^{-\gamma t}) - \eta(x + \kappa\bar{x}t - y)\right]}\left(\frac{e^{\gamma t}y}{x}\right)^{q/2},$$

where $\gamma = (\kappa^2 + 2C^2)^{1/2}$, $\eta = (\kappa - \gamma)/C^2$,

$$\varphi(t) = \frac{2\gamma}{C^2(1 - e^{-\gamma t})}, \qquad q = \frac{2\kappa\bar{x}}{C^2} - 1,$$

and $I_q(\cdot)$ is the modified Bessel function of the first kind of order q. The same source gives explicit solutions for the fundamental solutions of other models. For time-independent μ and σ, as with the CIR model, we have, for all t and $s > t$, $G(x, t, y, s) = G(x, 0, y, s - t)$.

H. Multifactor Models

The one-factor model (3) for the short rate is limiting. Even a casual review of the empirical properties of the term structure, some of which can be found in papers cited in the Notes, shows the significant potential improvements in fit offered by a *multifactor term-structure model*. While terminology varies from place to place, by a "multifactor" model, we mean a model in which the short rate is of the form $r_t = R(X_t, t)$, $t \geq 0$, where X is an Ito process in some subset D of $\mathbb{R}^k$ solving a stochastic differential equation of the form

$$dX_t = \mu(X_t, t)\, dt + \sigma(X_t, t)\, dB_t^Q, \tag{21}$$

where the given functions R, μ, and σ on $D \times [0, \infty)$ into $\mathbb{R}$, $\mathbb{R}^k$, and $\mathbb{R}^{k \times d}$, respectively, satisfy enough technical regularity to guarantee that (21) has a unique solution and that the term structure (2) is well defined. (Sufficient conditions are given in Appendix E.) In empirical applications, one often supposes that the state process X also satisfies a stochastic differential equation under the probability measure P, in order to exploit the time-series behavior of observed prices and price-determining variables in estimating the model. Examples are indicated in the Notes.

An interpretation of the role of the "state variables" is left open for the time being. For example, in an equilibrium model such as that considered in Chapter 10, some elements of the state vector X_t are sometimes *latent*, that is, unobservable to the modeler, except insofar as they can be inferred from prices that depend on the levels of X. This latent-variable approach has been popular in much of the empirical literature on term-structure modeling. Another approach is to take some or all of the state variables to be directly observable variables, such as macroeconomic determinants of the business cycle and inflation, that are thought to play a role in determining the term structure. This approach has also been explored in the empirical literature. In many examples, one of the component processes $X^{(1)}, \ldots, X^{(k)}$ is singled out as the short-rate process r, whose drift and diffusion are allowed to depend on the levels of the other component processes.

A derivative security, in this setting, can often be represented in terms of some real-valued terminal payment function g on $\mathbb{R}^k$, for some maturity date $s \leq T$. By the definition of an equivalent martingale measure, the associated derivative security price is given from (1) by

$$F(X_t, t) = E_t^Q\left[\exp\left(-\int_t^s R(X_u, u)\, du\right) g(X_s)\right].$$

Extending (17)–(18), under technical conditions given in Appendix E, we have the PDE characterization

$$\mathcal{D}F(x, t) - R(x, t)F(x, t) = 0, \qquad (x, t) \in D \times [0, s), \qquad (22)$$

with boundary condition

$$F(x, s) = g(x), \qquad x \in D, \qquad (23)$$

where

$$\mathcal{D}F(x, t) = F_t(x, t) + F_x(x, t)\mu(x, t) + \frac{1}{2}\text{tr}\big[\sigma(x, t)\sigma(x, t)^\top F_{xx}(x, t)\big].$$

The case of a zero-coupon bond is $g(x) \equiv 1$. Under technical conditions, we can also express the solution F, as in (19), in terms of the fundamental solution G of the PDE (22), as discussed in Appendix E.

I. Affine Term-Structure Models

A rich and tractable subclass of multifactor models are the *affine term-structure models*, for which the state process X is an *affine diffusion*, defined by taking (21) with

$$\mu(x, t) = K_0 + K_1 x, \qquad (24)$$

for some $K_0 \in \mathbb{R}^k$ and $K_1 \in \mathbb{R}^{k \times k}$, and by taking, for each i and j in $\{1, \ldots, k\}$,

$$\big(\sigma(x, t)\sigma(x, t)^\top\big)_{ij} = H_{0ij} + H_{1ij} \cdot x, \qquad (25)$$

for $H_{0ij} \in \mathbb{R}$ and $H_{1ij} \in \mathbb{R}^k$. One can also allow the coefficient functions $H = (H_0, H_1)$ and $K = (K_0, K_1)$ to depend on t; we ignore that for notational simplicity.

Given the coefficients (H, K), a natural state space $D \subset \mathbb{R}^k$ for this affine model is set by the obvious requirement that $\big(\sigma(x, t)\sigma(x, t)^\top\big)_{ii} \geq 0$ for all x in D. Thus, given H, we choose the state space

$$D = \big\{x \in \mathbb{R}^k : H_{0ii} + H_{1ii} \cdot x \geq 0, \quad i \in \{1, \ldots, k\}\big\}. \qquad (26)$$

Conditions cited in the Notes on the coefficients (H, K) ensure existence of a unique solution X to (21) that is valued in D.

An example is the "multifactor CIR" model, defined by

$$dX_{it} = \kappa_i(\bar{x}_i - X_{it})\,dt + C_i\sqrt{X_{it}}\,dB_t^{Q,(i)}, \qquad X_{i0} > 0, \qquad (27)$$

where κ_i, $\bar{x}_i$, and C_i are positive constants playing the same respective roles as κ, $\bar{x}$, and C in the one-factor CIR model (8). Given the independence under Q of $B^{Q,\,(1)}, \ldots, B^{Q,\,(k)}$, if we let $R(x, t) = x_1 + \cdots + x_k$, then the multifactor CIR model generates the zero-coupon bond price $f(x, t)$ for maturity date s given by

$$f(x, t) = \exp\left[\alpha(t, s) + \beta_1(t, s)x_1 + \cdots + \beta_k(t, s)x_k\right], \tag{28}$$

where $\alpha(t, s) = \alpha_1(t, s) + \cdots + \alpha_k(t, s)$, and where $\alpha_i(t, s)$ and $\beta_i(t, s)$ are the solution coefficients of the univariate CIR model with coefficients $(\kappa_i, \bar{x}_i, C_i)$.

More generally, we suppose that

$$R(x, t) = \rho_0 + \rho_1 \cdot x, \tag{29}$$

for coefficients $\rho_0 \in \mathbb{R}$ and $\rho_1 \in \mathbb{R}^k$. For a fixed maturity date s, we expect a solution $f(X_t, t)$ for the price at time t of a zero-coupon bond maturing at time s to be of the exponential-affine form

$$f(x, t) = e^{\alpha(t)+\beta(t)\cdot x}, \tag{30}$$

for deterministic $\alpha(t)$ and $\beta(t)$. For notational simplicity, we suppress the maturity date s from the notation for α and β, and we let $\beta(t)^\top H_1(t)\beta(t)$ denote the vector in $\mathbb{R}^k$ whose n-th element is $\sum_{i,\,j} \beta_i(t) H_{1,\,ijn}\beta_j(t)$. After substituting the candidate solution (30) into the PDE (22), extending from the single-factor case, we conjecture that β satisfies the k-dimensional ordinary differential equation, analogous to (14), given by

$$\beta'(t) = \rho_1 - K_1^\top \beta(t) - \frac{1}{2}\beta(t)^\top H_1 \beta(t), \tag{31}$$

with the boundary condition $\beta(s) = 0$ determined by (30) and the requirement that $f(x, s) = 1$. We have repeatedly used a *separation-of-variables* argument: If $a + b \cdot x = 0$ for all x in some open subset of $\mathbb{R}^k$, then a and b must be zero.

The ODE (31) is, as with the single-factor affine models, a Riccati equation. Solutions are finite given technical conditions on K_1 and H_1. In some cases, an explicit solution is possible. One can alternatively apply a numerical ODE solution method, such as Runge-Kutta.

Likewise, we find that

$$\alpha'(t) = \rho_0 - K_0 \cdot \beta(t) - \frac{1}{2}\beta(t)^\top H_0 \beta(t), \tag{32}$$

with the boundary condition $\alpha(s) = 0$. One integrates (32) to get

$$\alpha(t) = \int_t^s \left[-\rho_0 + K_0 \cdot \beta(u) + \frac{1}{2}\beta(u)^\top H_0 \beta(u) \right] du. \tag{33}$$

Numerical integration is an easy and fast method for treating (33) when explicit solutions are not at hand.

This affine class of term-structure models extends to allow for time-dependent coefficients (K, H, ρ) and to cases with jumps in the state process X, as cited in the Notes. As we shall see in Chapter 8, one can also analytically solve for the transition distribution of an affine state-variable process, and for the associated prices of options on zero-coupon bonds and other securities, using Fourier-transform methods. Affine models, moreover, are used extensively in the analysis of default timing and the related valuation of defaultable bonds, as explained in Chapter 11.

J. The HJM Model of Forward Rates

In modeling the term structure, we have so far taken as the primitive a model of the short-rate process of the form $r_t = R(X_t, t)$, where (under some equivalent martingale measure) X solves a given stochastic differential equation. (In the one-factor case, one usually takes $r_t = X_t$.) This approach has the advantage of a finite-dimensional state space. For example, with this state-space approach one can compute certain derivative prices by solving PDEs. This approach is also amenable to standard econometric methods for the estimation of coefficients from time-series data, as indicated in the Notes.

An alternative approach is to directly model the stochastic behavior of the entire term structure of interest rates. This is the essence of the Heath-Jarrow-Morton (HJM) model. The remainder of this section is a summary of the basic elements of the HJM model. The following section, the exercises, and sources cited in the Notes provide many extensions and details.

The forward price at time t of a zero-coupon bond for delivery at time $\tau \geq t$ with maturity at time $s \geq \tau$ is (in the absence of arbitrage) given by $\Lambda_{t,s}/\Lambda_{t,\tau}$, the ratio of zero-coupon bond prices at maturity and delivery, respectively. Proof of this is left as an exercise. The associated *forward rate* is defined by

$$\Phi_{t,\tau,s} \equiv \frac{\log(\Lambda_{t,\tau}) - \log(\Lambda_{t,s})}{s - \tau}, \tag{34}$$

which can be viewed as the continuously compounding yield of the bond
bought forward. The *instantaneous forward rate*, when it exists, is defined
for each time t and forward delivery date $\tau \geq t$, by

$$f(t, \tau) = \lim_{s \downarrow \tau} \Phi_{t, \tau, s}. \tag{35}$$

Thus, the instantaneous forward-rate process f exists (and is an adapted
process) if and only if, for all t, the discount $\Lambda_{t,s}$ is differentiable with
respect to s.

From (34) and (35), we arrive at the ordinary differential equation

$$\frac{d}{ds} \Lambda_{t,s} = -\Lambda_{t,s} f(t, s),$$

with the boundary condition $\Lambda(t, t) = 1$, with the solution

$$\Lambda_{t,s} = \exp\left(-\int_t^s f(t, u)\, du\right). \tag{36}$$

The term structure can thus be recovered from the instantaneous forward
rates, and vice versa.

Given a stochastic model f of forward rates, we will assume that the
short-rate process r is defined by $r_t = f(t, t)$, the limit of bond yields as
maturity goes to zero. Justification of this assumption can be given under
technical conditions cited in the Notes.

We first fix a maturity date s and model the one-dimensional forward-
rate process $f(\cdot, s) = \{f(t, s) : 0 \leq t \leq s\}$. We suppose that $f(\cdot, s)$ is an
Ito process, meaning that

$$f(t, s) = f(0, s) + \int_0^t \mu(u, s)\, du + \int_0^t \sigma(u, s)\, dB_u^Q, \qquad 0 \leq t \leq s, \tag{37}$$

where $\mu(\cdot, s) = \{\mu(t, s) : 0 \leq t \leq s\}$ and $\sigma(\cdot, s) = \{\sigma(t, s) : 0 \leq t \leq s\}$
are adapted processes valued in $\mathbb{R}$ and $\mathbb{R}^d$, respectively, such that, almost
surely, $\int_0^s |\mu(t, s)|\, dt < \infty$ and $\int_0^s \sigma(t, s) \cdot \sigma(t, s)\, dt < \infty$.

There is an important consistency relationship between μ and σ.
Under purely technical conditions, it must be the case that

$$\mu(t, s) = \sigma(t, s) \cdot \int_t^s \sigma(t, u)\, du. \tag{38}$$

This risk-neutral drift restriction on forward rates will be shown at the
end of this section. For now, let us point out that knowledge of the initial
forward rates $\{f(0, s) : 0 \leq s \leq T\}$ and the forward-rate "volatility" process

σ is enough to determine all bond and interest-rate derivative price processes. That is, given (38), we can use the definition $r_t = f(t, t)$ of the short rate to obtain

$$r_t = f(0, t) + \int_0^t \sigma(v, t) \cdot \int_v^t \sigma(v, u) \, du \, dv + \int_0^t \sigma(v, t) \, dB_v^Q, \tag{39}$$

assuming that this process exists and is adapted. We can see that if σ is everywhere zero, the spot and forward rates must coincide, in that $r(t) = f(0, t)$ for all t, as one would expect from the absence of arbitrage in a deterministic bond market! From (39), we can price any term-structure related security using the basic formula (1). Aside from the Gaussian special case studied in Exercise 7.6 and certain other restrictive special cases, most valuation work in the HJM setting is done numerically. Special cases aside, there is no finite-dimensional state variable for the HJM model, so PDE-based computational methods cannot be used. Monte Carlo simulation, as explained in Chapter 12, is a common solution method. One can alternatively build an analogous model in discrete time with a finite number of states, and compute prices from "first principles." For the discrete model, the expectation analogous to (1) is obtained by constructing all sample paths for r from the discretization of (39), and by computing the probability (under Q) of each. Sources given in the Notes provide details.

It remains to confirm the key relationship (38) between the drifts and diffusions of forward rates. Consider the Q-martingale M defined by

$$M_t = E_t^Q \left[\exp\left(-\int_0^s r_u \, du \right) \right]$$

$$= \exp\left(-\int_0^t r_u \, du \right) \Lambda_{t, s}$$

$$= \exp(X_t + Y_t), \tag{40}$$

where, using (36),

$$X_t = -\int_0^t r_u \, du; \qquad Y_t = -\int_t^s f(t, u) \, du. \tag{41}$$

In order to continue, we want to show that Y, as an infinite sum of the Ito processes for forward rates over all maturities ranging from t to s, is itself an Ito process. From Fubini's Theorem for stochastic integrals (Appendix D), this is true under technical conditions on μ and σ. For example, it is certainly sufficient for Fubini's Theorem that, in addition to our previous assumptions, $\mu(t, u, \omega)$ and $\sigma(t, u, \omega)$ are uniformly bounded and, for each ω, continuous in (t, u). Under these or weaker conditions for Fubini's Theorem, we can calculate that $dY_t = \mu_Y(t)\,dt + \sigma_Y(t)\,dB_t^Q$, where

$$\mu_Y(t) = f(t, t) - \int_t^s \mu(t, u)\,du, \tag{42}$$

and

$$\sigma_Y(t) = -\int_t^s \sigma(t, u)\,du. \tag{43}$$

This is natural, given the linearity of stochastic integration explained in Chapter 5. Provided Fubini's Theorem does apply to give us (42)–(43), we can apply Ito's Formula in the usual way to $M_t = e^{X(t)+Y(t)}$ and obtain the drift under Q of M as

$$\mu_M(t) = M_t\left(\mu_Y(t) + \frac{1}{2}\sigma_Y(t) \cdot \sigma_Y(t) - r_t\right). \tag{44}$$

Because M is a Q-martingale, we must have $\mu_M = 0$, so, substituting (42) into (44), we obtain

$$\int_t^s \mu(t, u)\,du = \frac{1}{2}\left(\int_t^s \sigma(t, u)\,du\right) \cdot \left(\int_t^s \sigma(t, u)\,du\right). \tag{45}$$

Taking the derivative of each side of (45) with respect to s then leaves the risk-neutral drift restriction (38).

K. Markovian Yield Curves and SPDEs

We can view the forward-rate curve as

$$g(t, u) = \{f(t, t + u) : 0 \le u \le \infty\}, \tag{46}$$

with u indexing time to maturity, *not* date of maturity. In each state ω of Ω, we can model the term structure $g(t) = g(t, \cdot)$ at each time t as an element of some convenient state space $\mathscr{S}$ of real-valued continuously differentiable functions on $[0, \infty)$. Now, letting $v(t, u) = \sigma(t, t + u)$, the risk-neutral drift restriction on f, and enough regularity, imply the *stochastic partial differential equation* (SPDE) for g given by

$$dg(t, u) = \frac{\partial g(t, u)}{\partial u}\,dt + V(t, u)\,dt + v(t, u)\,dB_t^Q, \tag{47}$$

where

$$V(t, u) = v(t, u) \cdot \int_0^u v(t, z)\,dz. \tag{48}$$

This formulation (47) is an example of a rather delicate class of SPDEs that are called "hyperbolic." Existence conditions, in various senses, are left to sources in the Notes. The idea is rather elegant. Provided the SPDE (47) is well defined, the entire forward-rate curve $g(t)$ is a sufficient statistic for its future evolution. That is, the function-valued process $\{g(t) : t \geq 0\}$ is Markovian with some such state space $\mathscr{S}$. One may even allow the Brownian motion B^Q to be "infinite dimensional," in a sense explored in sources cited in the Notes.

Applications of the SPDE approach include the *market model*, examined in Exercise 7.14, based on results cited in the Notes, which specifies certain discrete forward rates as log-normal under related forward risk-neutral measures. This allows the use of the Black-Scholes formula for bond option pricing. This is a matter of some convenience in practice, for the prices of many caps and bond options are quoted in terms of Black-Scholes implied volatilities.

Exercises

7.1 The *Black-Derman-Toy model* is normally expressed in the form

$$r_t = U(t) \exp[\gamma(t) B^Q(t)], \tag{49}$$

for some functions U and γ in $C^1(\mathbb{R}_+)$. Find conditions on K_1, K_2, and H_2 under which the parameterization for the Black-Karasinski model shown in Table 7.1 specializes to the Black-Derman-Toy model (49).

7.2 For the Vasicek model, as specified in Table 7.1, show that

$$\Lambda_{t,s} = \exp[\alpha(t, s) + \beta(t, s) r_t],$$

and solve for $\alpha(t, s)$ and $\beta(t, s)$ in the case of time-independent K_0, K_1, and H_0.

7.3 For the Vasicek model, for time-independent K_0, K_1, and H_0, compute the price at time zero of a zero-coupon bond call option. The underlying bond matures at time s. The option is European, struck at $c \in (0, 1)$, and expiring at τ. That is, compute the price of a derivative that pays $(\Lambda_{\tau, s} - c)^+$ at time τ. Hint: Choose as a numeraire the zero-coupon bond maturing at time τ. Relative to this numeraire, the short rate is zero and the payoff of the option is unaffected since $\Lambda_{\tau, \tau} = 1$. Use Ito's Formula and the solution to the previous exercise to write a stochastic differential expression for the deflated bond price $p_t \equiv \Lambda_{t,s}/\Lambda_{t,\tau}$, $t \leq \tau$. As such, p is a "log-normal" process. Now apply the approach taken in Chapter 5 or Chapter 6. Express the solution for the bond option price in the form of the Black-Scholes option-pricing formula, replacing the usual arguments with new expressions based on K_0, K_1, and H_0. Do not forget to renormalize to the original numeraire! This exercise is extended below to the Heath-Jarrow-Morton setting.

7.4   Show, as claimed in Section J, that in the absence of arbitrage, the forward price at time t for delivery at time τ of a zero-coupon bond maturing at time $s > \tau$ is given by $\Lambda_{t,s}/\Lambda_{t,\tau}$. Show that if the short-rate process r is nonnegative, then the forward interest rates defined by (34) and the instantaneous forward rates defined by (35) are nonnegative. Finally, show (36).

7.5   Let $\lambda_{t,\tau,s}$ denote the forward price at time t for delivery at time τ of one zero-coupon bond maturing at time s. Now consider the forward price F_t at time t for delivery at time s of a security with price process S and deterministic dividend rate process δ. Show, assuming integrability as needed, that the absence of arbitrage implies that

$$F_t = \frac{S_t}{\Lambda_{t,s}} - \int_t^s \lambda_{t,\tau,s}^{-1} \delta_\tau \, d\tau.$$

Do not assume the existence of an equivalent martingale measure.

7.6   Consider the Gaussian forward-rate model, defined by taking the HJM model of Section J with coefficients $\mu(t, s)$ and $\sigma(t, s)$ of (37) that are deterministic and differentiable with respect to s. Let $d = 1$ for simplicity. Calculate the arbitrage-free price at time t of a European call option on a unit zero-coupon bond maturing at time s, with strike price K and expiration date τ, with $t < \tau < s$. To be specific, the option has payoff $(\Lambda_{\tau,s} - K)^+$ at time τ. Hint: Consider the numeraire deflator defined by normalizing prices relative to the price $\Lambda_{t,\tau}$ of the pure discount bond maturing at τ. With this deflation, compute an equivalent martingale measure $P(\tau)$ and the stochastic differential equation under $P(\tau)$ for the deflated bond-price process Z defined by $Z_t = \Lambda_{t,s}/\Lambda_{t,\tau}$, $t \leq \tau$ and $Z_t = \Lambda_{t,s}$, $t > \tau$. Show that Z_τ is log-normally distributed under $P(\tau)$. Using the fact that $\Lambda_{\tau,\tau} = 1$, show that the relevant option price is $\Lambda_{t,\tau} E_t^{P(\tau)}[(\Lambda_{\tau,s} - K)^+]$. An explicit solution is then obtained by exploiting the Black-Scholes option-pricing formula. Under $P(\tau)$, conditioning on $\mathcal{F}_t$, one needs to compute the variance of $\log \Lambda_{\tau,s}$, which is normally distributed.

7.7   Verify the claim that the at-market coupon rate c^* on a swap is the par fixed coupon rate.

7.8   In the context of the HJM model with forward-rate process f, consider a bond issued at time t that pays a dividend process $\{\delta_s : t \leq s \leq \tau\}$ until some maturity date τ, at which time it pays 1 unit of account. Suppose that, for all s, we have $\delta_s = f(t, s)$. Show that, barring arbitrage, the price at time t of this bond is 1.

7.9   We can derive the equivalent martingale measure Q for the HJM model as follows, at the same time obtaining conditions under which an arbitrage-free instantaneous forward-rate model f is defined in terms of the Brownian motion B under the original measure P, for each fixed maturity s, by

$$f(t, s) = f(0, s) + \int_0^t \alpha(u, s) \, du + \int_0^t \sigma(u, s) \, dB_u, \qquad t \leq s. \tag{50}$$

Here, $\{\alpha(t, s) : 0 \le t \le s\}$ and $\{\sigma(t, s) : 0 \le t \le s\}$ are adapted processes valued in $\mathbb{R}$ and $\mathbb{R}^d$, respectively, such that (50) is well defined as an Ito process. This proceeds as follows.

(A) For each fixed s, suppose an $\mathbb{R}^d$-valued process a^s and a real-valued process b^s are well defined by

$$a_t^s = -\int_t^s \sigma(t, v) \, dv; \qquad b_t^s = \frac{\|a_t^s\|^2}{2} - \int_t^s \alpha(t, v) \, dv, \qquad t \le s. \qquad (51)$$

Show, under additional technical conditions, that for each fixed s,

$$\Lambda_{t,s} = \Lambda_{0,s} + \int_0^t \Lambda_{u,s}(r_u + b_u^s) \, du + \int_0^t \Lambda_{u,s} \, a_u^s \, dB_u, \qquad 0 \le t \le s. \qquad (52)$$

Now, taking an arbitrary set $\{s(1), \ldots, s(d)\}$ of d different maturities, consider the deflated bond-price processes $Z^1, \ldots, Z^d$, defined by

$$Z_t^i = \exp\left(-\int_0^t r_u \, du\right) \Lambda_{t, s(i)}, \qquad t \le s(i). \qquad (53)$$

For the absence of arbitrage involving these d bonds until time $S \equiv \min\{s(i) : 1 \le i \le d\}$, Chapter 6 shows that it suffices, and in a sense is almost necessary, that there exists an equivalent martingale measure Q for $Z = (Z^1, \ldots, Z^d)$. For this, it is sufficient that Z has a market price of risk that is L^2-reducible, in the sense of Section 6G. The question of L^2-reducibility hinges on the drift and diffusion processes of Z. For the remainder of the exercise, we restrict ourselves to the time interval $[0, S]$.

(B) Show that, for all i,

$$dZ_t^i = Z_t^i b_t^{s(i)} \, dt + Z_t^i a_t^{s(i)} \, dB_t, \qquad t \in [0, S]. \qquad (54)$$

For each $t \le S$, let A_t be the $d \times d$ matrix whose (i, j)-element is the j-th element of the vector $a_t^{s(i)}$, and let λ_t be the vector in $\mathbb{R}^d$ whose i-th element is $b_t^{s(i)}$. We can then consider the system of linear equations

$$A_t \eta_t = \lambda_t, \qquad t \in [0, S], \qquad (55)$$

to be solved for an $\mathbb{R}^d$-valued process η in $\mathcal{L}^2$. Assuming such a solution η to (55) exists, and letting $\nu(Z) = \int_0^S \eta_t \cdot \eta_t \, dt / 2$ and $\xi(Z) = \exp[\int_0^S -\eta_t \, dB_t - \nu(Z)]$, Proposition 6G implies that α and σ are consistent with the absence of arbitrage, and that there exists an equivalent martingale measure for Z that is denoted $Q(S)$, provided $\exp[\nu(Z)]$ has finite expectation and $\xi(Z)$ has finite variance. In this case, we can let

$$\frac{dQ(S)}{dP} = \xi(Z). \qquad (56)$$

Provided A_t is nonsingular almost everywhere, $Q(S)$ is uniquely defined. Of course, S is arbitrary. A sufficient set of technical conditions for each of the above steps is cited in the Notes.

(C) Suppose A_t is everywhere nonsingular. Using Girsanov's Theorem of Appendix D, show that, for $t \le s$,

$$f(t, s) = f(0, s) + \int_0^t [\alpha(u, s) - \sigma(u, s)\eta_u]\, du + \int_0^t \sigma(u, s)\, dB_u^Q, \qquad (57)$$

where B^Q is the standard Brownian in $\mathbb{R}^d$ under $Q(S)$ arising from Girsanov's Theorem. That is, $dB_t^Q = dB_t + \eta_t\, dt$.

(D) Show that (57) and (38) are consistent.

7.10 (Foreign Bond Derivatives).   Suppose you are to price a foreign bond option. The underlying zero-coupon bond pays one unit of foreign currency at some maturity date T, and has a domestic-currency price process of S. For convenience, we will refer to the domestic currency as "dollars." With an expiration date for the option of τ and a strike price of K dollars, the bond option pays $(S_\tau - K)^+$ dollars at time τ. Our job is to obtain the bond option-price process C.

The foreign-currency price process, say U_t, is given. The foreign currency is defined as a security having a continuous dividend process of $U_t R_t$, where R is the foreign short-rate process. The exchange-rate process U is assumed to be a strictly positive Ito process of the form

$$dU_t = \alpha_t U_t\, dt + U_t \beta_t\, dB_t,$$

where α, a real-valued adapted process, and β, an $\mathbb{R}^d$-valued adapted process, are both bounded.

Foreign interest rates are given by a forward-rate process F, as in the HJM setting. That is, the price of the given zero-coupon foreign bond at time t, in units of foreign currency, is $\exp(\int_t^T -F(t, u)\, du)$, and we have $R_t = F(t, t)$. It follows that the foreign bond-price process, in dollars, is given by

$$S_t = U_t \exp\left(\int_t^T -F(t, u)\, du \right),$$

and that the price of the foreign bond option, in dollars, is

$$C_t = E_t^Q\left[\exp\left(\int_t^\tau -r_u\, du \right)(S_\tau - K)^+ \right], \qquad (58)$$

where r is the dollar short-rate process and Q is an equivalent martingale measure. In general, we assume that the vector X of security-price processes (in dollars) for all available securities is such that $\exp(\int_0^t -r_u\, du)X_t$ defines a Q-martingale, consistent with the definition of Q as an equivalent martingale measure. It is assumed that for each t and $s \ge t$,

$$F(t, s) = F(0, s) + \int_0^t a(u, s)\, du + \int_0^t b(u, s)\, dB_u^Q,$$

where B^Q is a standard Brownian motion in $\mathbb{R}^d$ under Q, and where the s-dependent drift process $a(\cdot, s): \Omega \times [0, T] \to \mathbb{R}$ and the s-dependent diffusion process $b(\cdot, s) : \Omega \times [0, T] \rightarrow \mathbb{R}^d$ are assumed to satisfy sufficient regularity conditions for Q to indeed be an equivalent martingale measure and for foreign bond-price processes to be well defined.

(A) Demonstrate the risk-neutral drift restriction on the foreign forward-rate process F is given by $a(t, s) = b(t, s) \cdot [\int_t^s b(t, u) \, du - \beta_t]$.

(B) Suppose the domestic forward-rate process f is also of the HJM form. That is, we have $r_t = f(t, t)$, where

$$f(t, s) = f(0, s) + \int_0^t \mu(u, s) \, du + \int_0^t \sigma(u, s) \, dB_u^Q, \qquad (59)$$

and where the s-dependent drift process $\mu(\cdot, s) : \Omega \times [0, T] \rightarrow \mathbb{R}$ and the s-dependent diffusion process $\sigma(\cdot, s) : \Omega \times [0, T] \rightarrow \mathbb{R}^d$ are assumed to satisfy regularity conditions analogous to those on a and b, respectively. Suppose the coefficient processes β, b, and σ are all deterministic. Derive a relatively explicit expression for the foreign bond-option price.

(C) A *yield-spread option* is a derivative security that promises a dollar payoff that depends on the difference $\delta = F - f$ between the foreign and domestic forward-rate curves. A model for the *spread curve* δ may be specified by

$$\delta(t, s) = \delta(0, s) + \int_0^t m(u, s) \, du + \int_0^t v(u, s) \, dB_u^Q, \qquad (60)$$

where the s-dependent drift process $m(\cdot, s) : \Omega \times [0, T] \rightarrow \mathbb{R}$ and the s-dependent diffusion process $v(\cdot, s) : \Omega \times [0, T] \rightarrow \mathbb{R}^d$ are assumed to satisfy regularity conditions analogous to a and b, respectively. Given (59), develop the drift restriction on δ. That is, obtain an expression for m that does not explicitly involve a and b. Do not assume deterministic coefficient processes β, σ, and v.

7.11 Suppose X solves the SDE (21) with the affine coefficients of (24) and (25), and that the short-rate process r is of the affine form $r_t = \rho_0 + \rho_1 \cdot X_t$.

(A) Show, under technical integrability conditions, that a claim to $e^{a+b \cdot X(s)}$ at time s has a price at any time $t < s$ of the form $e^{\alpha(t) + \beta(t) \cdot X(t)}$, where $\alpha(t)$ and $\beta(t)$ depend on t only. Provide an ordinary differential equation for β, with a boundary condition, and a solution for α in terms of β. Provide the integrability condition that you used to obtain this result.

(B) Let $f(X_s, s)$ denote the price at time s of a zero-coupon bond maturing at time $T > s$. Provide technical integrability conditions under which the futures price at time t for delivery at time s of this bond is of the form $e^{\bar{\alpha}(t) + \bar{\beta}(t) \cdot X(t)}$, where $\bar{\alpha}(t)$ and $\bar{\beta}(t)$ depend on t only. Provide an ordinary differential equation for $\bar{\beta}$, with a boundary condition, and a solution for $\bar{\alpha}$ in terms of $\bar{\beta}$.

7.12 Suppose that X is an affine state process under the "original" probability measure P, in that $dX_t = \mu(X_t) \, dt + \sigma(X_t) \, dB_t$, where B is a standard Brownian motion in $\mathbb{R}^d$ under P and $x \mapsto (\mu(x), \sigma(x)\sigma(x)^\top)$ is affine. Suppose the short-rate process r is of the form $r_t = \rho_0(t) + \rho_1(t) \cdot X_t$, for possibly-time-dependent coefficients ρ_0 and ρ_1.

(A) Consider a process ξ of the form $\xi_t = e^{\alpha(t)+\beta(t) \cdot X(t)}$, for time-dependent coefficients α and β. Provide an ordinary differential equation (ODE) for $\alpha(t)$ and $\beta(t)$, and technical integrability conditions, under which ξ is the density process of some equivalent probability measure Q.

(B) Suppose, for arbitrary t and s, the price at time t of a zero-coupon bond maturing at time s is of the form $\sum_{i=1}^n e^{a(i, t, s)+b(i,t,s) \cdot X(t)}$, for deterministic coefficients $a(i, t, s)$ and $b(i, t, s)$. Can you guess some form, under technical conditions, of an associated equivalent martingale measure Q, after some convenient deflation, that provides this type of term structure? What is the most general consistent form that you can guess?

7.13 (Cap Pricing).   Show that a claim to the caplet payoff $(c(t_i) - c^*)^+$ at time t_i, as defined in Section F, may be viewed as a European put option, exercisable at time t_{i-1}, on a zero-coupon bond maturing at time t_i. Now, in the Vasicek setting, provide a formula for the price at time 0 of a cap, which is the portfolio of caplets defined in Section F.

7.14 (The Market Model and Cap Pricing).   In the setting of Section A, let $\{\Lambda_{t,s}\}$ be a given model of the term structure of discounts, and let $\Gamma_{t,s,u} = \Lambda_{t,u}/\Lambda_{t,s}$ define the associated forward bond prices, as in Section J. For each given date s, using as a numeraire the bond maturing at date s, we know that the absence of arbitrage is tantamount to the existence of an equivalent martingale measure Q_s after deflation by $\Lambda_{t,s}$. That is, for each $u \geq s$, the bond-price process $\{\Lambda_{t,u}/\Lambda_{t,s} : 0 \leq t \leq s\}$ is a Q_s-martingale. We recall that Q_s is called the forward measure for maturity s.

(A) Suppose, for each $s \leq T$, that such a forward measure Q_s exists. Fixing s, show, under technical integrability conditions that you will supply, that for each given maturity date $u \geq s$,

$$d\Gamma_{t,s,u} = \Gamma_{t,s,u}\gamma(t, s, u) \, dW_t^s, \tag{61}$$

for some adapted $\mathbb{R}^d$-valued process $\{\gamma(t, s, u) : 0 \leq t \leq s\}$ such that the stochastic integral is well defined, where W^s is a particular standard Brownian motion in $\mathbb{R}^d$ under Q_s.

(B) Given the model (61) for forward bond-price processes, consider, for each fixed date s and tenor δ, the δ-tenor forward rate $L(t, s)$ defined by

$$1 + L(t, s)\delta = \frac{1}{\Gamma(t, s, s + \delta)}, \tag{62}$$

which is the convention by which discrete-tenor forward rates are quoted in practice. In practice, δ is typically 3 months, 6 months, or 1 year. The rate $L(s, s)$ is the spot δ-tenor rate for maturity at $s + \delta$, sometimes called the LIBOR rate, because of the quotation method used for the London Inter-Bank Offering Rate. Calculate a process $\lambda(\cdot, s) = \{\lambda(t, s) : 0 \leq t \leq s\}$ for which

$$dL(t, s) = L(t, s)\lambda(t, s) \, dW_t^{s+\delta}. \tag{63}$$

(C) Suppose that $\lambda(\cdot, s)$ is deterministic, and that $L(0, s)$ is strictly positive. Calculate explicitly the price at time t of a caplet paying $\delta(L(s, s) - \bar{L})^+$ at the settlement date $s + \delta$, for some strike rate $\bar{L}$. (This is the common payment convention in current market practice, as explained in Section F.)

Notes

General treatments of term-structure modeling and related derivative pricing issues are offered by Garbade (1996), Moreleda (1997), DeMunnik (1992), Musiela and Rutkowski (1997), and Sundaresan (1997). Van Horne (1993) describes the general institutional features of fixed-income security markets.

(B–C) The Gaussian short-rate model appears in Merton (1974), who originated much of the approach taken in this chapter. Pye (1966) has an early precursor of modern term-structure modeling. Ho and Lee (1986) extended the model and developed the idea of calibration of the model to the current yield curve. Option evaluation and other applications of the Gaussian model are provided by Carverhill (1988), Jamshidian (1989a, b, d, 1991a, 1993b), and El Karoui and Rochet (1989). Jamshidian (1989b) developed the forward-measure approach for this purpose. See also Davis (1998), El Karoui and Rochet (1989), Elliot and der Hoek (1999), and Schroder (1999). The calibration idea, reviewed in Section 12M, has been further developed by Black, Derman, and Toy (1990), Hull and White (1990a, 1993), and Black and Karasinski (1991), among others. The Black-Derman-Toy model was shown in a discrete-time version in Exercise 3.12. Exercise 12.6 shows convergence of the discrete-time Black-Derman-Toy model, with appropriate parameters, to the continuous-time "log-normal" model shown in Exercise 7.1. Other models include that of Courtadon (1982).

(D) The CIR term-structure model of Cox, Ingersoll, and Ross (1985b) was developed in a general-equilibrium setting, as explained in Chapter 10. It was also later developed as a primitive arbitrage-based term-structure model by Richard (1978). One can see that the associated CIR short-rate process exists from the results of Yamada and Watanabe (1971) reviewed in Appendix E. In order to apply their results, we can let $\sigma(x) = 0$ for $x < 0$. The nonnegativity of solutions is then implied by the fact that zero is a natural boundary, in the sense of Gihman and Skorohod (1972). Feller (1951) solved for the Laplace transform of the distribution of the CIR interest rate r_t. The associated density was calculated by Yao, according to a footnote of Richard (1978). Further characterization is given in Cox, Ingersoll, and Ross (1985b), Cherubini (1993), Cherubini and Esposito (1992), Deelstra and Delbaen (1994, 1995), Delbaen (1993), Gibbons and Sun (1986), Jamshidian (1995), Nelson and Ramaswamy (1989), and Rogers (1993).

Sun (1992) provides a discrete-time model that converges with shrinking period length to the CIR model. For additional results in a CIR setting, including analytic treatment of time-varying coefficients, see Maghsoodi (1996a, b, 1997a, b).

(E) The idea that an affine term-structure model is typically associated with affine drift and squared diffusion is foreshadowed in Cox, Ingersoll, and Ross (1985b) and Hull and White (1990a), and is explicit in Brown and Schaefer (1994a).

Filipović (1999a) provides a definitive result for affine term-structure models in a one-dimensional state space, based in part on the characterization of continuous-branching processes with immigration by Kawazu and Watanabe (1971).

Examples of the one-dimensional affine class include those of Carverhill (1988), Chen (1996), Cox, Ingersoll, and Ross (1985b), Dybvig (1988), Frachot (1996), Jamshidian (1989a, b, d, 1991a), Pearson and Sun (1994), Selby and Strickland (1993), and Vasicek (1977). Pearson and Sun (1994) refer to their model as the translated CIR model, for obvious reasons.

(F) Applied general treatments of term-structure derivatives include those of Garbade (1996), Moreleda (1997), DeMunnik (1992), Musiela and Rutkowski (1997), and Sundaresan (1997). Swap markets are analyzed by Brace and Musiela (1994b), Carr (1993b), Duffie and Huang (1996), El Karoui and Geman (1994), and Sundaresan (1997). For institutional and general economic features of the swap markets, see Lang, Litzenberger, and Liu (1996) and Litzenberger (1992). For the valuation of caps, see, for example, Chen and Scott (1995), Clewlow, Pang, and Strickland (1997), Miltersen, Sandmann, and Sondermann (1997), and Scott (1996b). Jamshidian (1999) and Rutkowski (1996, 1998) offer general treatments of LIBOR (London Interbank Offering Rate) derivative modeling.

On the valuation of other specific forms of term-structure derivatives, see Artzner and Roger (1993), Bajeux-Besnainou and Portait (1998), Brace and Musiela (1994b), Chacko and Das (1998), Chen and Scott (1992b, 1993b), Cherubini and Esposito (1995), Chesney, Elliott, and Gibson (1993), Cohen (1995), Daher, Romano, and Zacklad (1992), Décamps and Rochet (1997), El Karoui, Lepage, Myneni, Roseau, and Viswanathan (1991a, b), Turnbull (1993), Fleming and Whaley (1994) (wildcard options), Ingersoll (1977) (convertible bonds), Jamshidian (1993a, 1994) (diff swaps and quantos), Jarrow and Turnbull (1994), Longstaff (1990) (yield options), and Turnbull (1994).

On the valuation of American bond options, see Andersen and Andreasen (1999), Büttler (1995), Büttler and Waldvogel (1996), Gatarek and Musiela (1995), Grosen and Jorgensen (1995), Jamshidian (1989a, c), Jorgensen (1996), Longstaff and Schwartz (1998), Pedersen (1999), and Tanudjaja (1995).

Cox, Ingersoll, and Ross (1981b), Duffie and Stanton (1988), and Grinblatt and Jegadeesh (1996) consider the relative pricing of futures and forwards. Apelfeld and Conze (1990) study the term structure under imperfect information using filtering theory, extending the work of Dothan and Feldman (1986). Additional fixed-income derivative pricing issues are considered in Chapter 8. Derivative hedging issues are also considered by Jarrow and Turnbull (1997a), and Jaschke (1997).

(G) Applications to term-structure modeling of the fundamental solution, sometimes erroneously called the Green's function, are illustrated by Büttler and Waldvogel (1996), Dash (1989), Beaglehole (1990), Beaglehole and Tenney (1991), Dai (1994), and Jamshidian (1991c). The fundamental solution for the Dothan (log-normal) short-rate model can be deduced from the form of the solution by Hogan (1993a) of what he calls the "conditional discounting function." Chen (1996) provides the fundamental solution for his three-factor affine model. Steenkiste and Foresi (1999) provide a general treatment of fundamental solutions of the PDE for affine models. The summary here is standard. For more on technical details and references, see, for example, Karatzas and Shreve (1988).

(H–I) Duffie and Kan (1996) provide a characterization of multifactor affine term-structure models. Affine multifactor term-structure models include those of Balduzzi, Das, and Foresi (1998), Balduzzi, Das, Foresi, and Sundaram (1996), Berardi and Esposito (1999), Chen (1996), Cox, Ingersoll, and Ross (1985b), Dai and Singleton (2000), Heston (1988b), Langetieg (1980), Longstaff and Schwartz (1992, 1993), Pang and Hodges (1995), and Selby and Strickland (1993).

Filipović (1999a) offers an example in a multidimensional setting of a term-structure model in which yields are affine in diffusion state variables that do not solve an affine stochastic differential equation.

The valuation of discount bond options and caps in an affine setting, using Fourier-transform methods, is pursued by Chen and Scott (1995), Duffie, Pan, and Singleton (2000), Nunes, Clewlow, and Hodges (1999), and Scaillet (1996). The valuation of path-dependent derivatives in an affine setting is considered by Leblanc and Scaillet (1998). Steenkiste and Foresi (1999) provide a general treatment of fundamental solutions of the PDE for affine models. For a Runge-Kutta method of numerically solving an ODE such as (31), see Press, Flannery, Teukolsky, and Vetterling (1993). For additional general discussion of affine term-structure models, see Dai and Singleton (2000), Duffee (1999b), Duffie, Pan, and Singleton (2000), Pedersen (1997), and Steenkiste and Foresi (1999).

Empirical estimation of various forms of affine term-structure models is pursued by Brown and Schaefer (1994b), Chan, Karolyi, Longstaff, and Saunders (1992), Chen and Scott (1992a, 1993a), Dai (1995, 1996), Dai and Singleton (2000), Duan and Simonato (1993), Duffee (1999b), Duffie and Singleton (1997), Gibbons and Ramaswamy (1993), Heston (1989), DeMunnik (1992), Lesne (1995), Longstaff and Schwartz (1993), Pearson and Sun (1994), Pennacchi (1991), Rogers and Stummer (1994), Singh (1995), Stambaugh (1988), and Vasicek (1995). Further analysis of the affine model with regard to transform methods for option valuation and other applications is provided in Chapter 8 and by Duffie, Pan, and Singleton (2000), Liu, Pan, and Pedersen (1999), and Singleton (1999).

Cherif, El Karoui, Myneni, and Viswanathan (1995), Constantinides (1992), El Karoui, Myneni, and Viswanathan (1992), Jamshidian (1996a), and Rogers (1993) characterize a model in which the short rate is a linear-quadratic form in a multivariate Markov Gaussian process. This model clearly overlaps with the general affine model, under a change of variables, although the extent to which a model can be developed that fully nests both affine and quadratic Gaussian models remains to be seen. Piazzesi (1999) offers extensions that include both quadratic-Gaussian and affine-non-Gaussian features.

The consol-rate multifactor model of Brennan and Schwartz (1979, 1980c, 1982) is further analyzed by Nelson and Schaefer (1983), Schaefer and Schwartz (1984), Hogan (1993b), and Duffie, Ma, and Yong (1995).

Other multifactor models include those of Black, Derman, and Kani (1992), Chan (1992), Kraus and Smith (1993), and Platten (1994).

(J) The idea of using the instantaneous forward-rate process appears in Richard (1978). The forward-rate model of Heath, Jarrow, and Morton (1992a) has been extensively treated in the case of Gaussian instantaneous forward rates Jamshidian (1989a, b, d, 1991a), El Karoui and Rochet (1989), El Karoui, Lepage, Myneni, Roseau, and Viswanathan (1991a, b), El Karoui and Lacoste (1992), Frachot (1995), Frachot, Janci, and Lacoste (1993), Frachot and Lesne (1993a, b, c), Miltersen (1994), and DeMunnik (1992). The illustration of the basic HJM drift restriction (38) is based on Rogers (1993). A quicker alternative derivation, based on an assumption that bond-price diffusions are differentiable with respect to maturity, is given by Hull (2000). The original derivation of (38) by Heath, Jarrow, and Morton (1992a) is based on the approach in Exercise 7.12. This exercise is useful as a means of establishing the relationship between the behavior of forward rates under the original measure P and under the equivalent martingale measure Q. Technical conditions justifying the calculations leading to (38) and the relationship $r_t = f(t, t)$ between the short rate and forward rates are found in Carverhill (1995), Heath, Jarrow, and Morton (1992a), and Miltersen (1994).

Exercise 7.6, on bond-option pricing in a Gaussian forward-rate setting, is from several of the above papers on the HJM model. Heath, Jarrow, and Morton (1992a) provide a model for forward rates in the form

$$f(t, s) = f(0, s) + \int_0^t \nu[u, s, f(u, s)]\, du + \int_0^t v[u, s, f(u, s)]\, dB_u^Q, \qquad (64)$$

for $0 \le t \le s$, where $\nu : [0, T] \times [0, T] \times \mathbb{R} \to \mathbb{R}$ and $v : [0, T] \times [0, T] \times \mathbb{R} \to \mathbb{R}^d$ are bounded and Lipschitz continuous. Under additional regularity, the solution for the forward-rate process is nonnegative. The HJM model has been extended by Miltersen (1994). For related work, derivative pricing, and computational methods in the HJM setting, see Babbs (1991), Brace and Musiela (1995b), Baxter (1996), Carverhill and Pang (1995), Heath, Jarrow, and Morton (1990, 1992b), Jeffrey (1995a, b), Miltersen and Persson (1997), and Rutkowski (1995, 1996).

Markovian versions of the HJM model are presented by Au and Thurston (1993), Bhar and Chiarella (1995), Brace and Musiela (1994a), Cheyette (1995), Jeffrey (1995c), Musiela (1994b), Ritchken and Sankarasubramanian (1992), and Ritchken and Trevor (1993).

(K) Musiela (1994b) developed a version of the HJM model in which the forward-rate curve is a Markov process. For related work in this setting, sometimes called a string, random field, or SPDE model of the term structure, see Cont (1998), Jong and Santa-Clara (1999), Goldstein (1997, 2000), Goldys and Musiela (1996), Hamza and Klebaner (1995), Kennedy (1994), Kusuoka (2000), Musiela and Sondermann (1994), Pang (1996), Santa-Clara and Sornette (1997), and Sornette (1998).

Additional Topics: Cox, Ingersoll, and Ross (1981a) and Cheng (1991) give examples of what can go wrong if one begins with a model for the stochastic behavior of bond prices without first verifying conditions for the absence of arbitrage. See also Campbell (1986b). Amin and Morton (1994a) show how to estimate implied volatilities of interest rates from term-structure models. Theoretical arbitrage problems with the calibration approach, as often applied in practice, are explained by Backus, Foresi, and Zin (1998).

There is a growing literature on the econometric estimation of term-structure models. In addition to papers mentioned above, this includes the work of Aït-Sahalia (1996a, b, c), Ball and Torous (1994), Broze, Scaillet, and Zakoïan (1993), Bühler, Uhrig-Homburg, Walter, and Weber (1995), Buono, Gregory-Allen, and Yaari (1992), Chan, Karolyi, Longstaff, and Saunders (1992), Danesi, Garcia, Genon-Catalot, and Laurent (1993), Das (1993a, b), Duffee (1999b), Fournié and Talay (1991), Gourieroux and Laurent (1994), Gourieroux and Scaillet (1994), Grinblatt and Jegadeesh (1996), Jegadeesh (1993), Koedijk, Nissen, Schotman, and Wolff (1994), Litterman and Scheinkman (1988), and DeMunnik (1992). For estimation in the HJM setting, see Frachot (1995), Frachot, Janci, and Lacoste (1993) Frachot and Lesne (1993a, b, c), Flesaker (1993), Jeffrey (1995b), Miltersen (1993), and Stanton (1995a).

On log-normal interest rates and on the "market model" of interest rates of Miltersen, Sandmann, and Sondermann (1997) used in Exercise 7.14, see Andersen and Andreasen (1998), Brace and Musiela (1995c), Dothan (1978), Goldberg (1998), Goldys, Musiela, and Sondermann (1994), Hansen and Jorgensen (1998), Hogan (1993a), Jamshidian (1996b, 1997b, 1999), Miltersen, Sandmann, and Sondermann (1997), Sandmann and Sondermann (1997), Musiela (1994a), and Vargiolu (1999). A related log-normal futures-price term-structure model is due to Heath (1998).

The role of jumps in term-structure modeling is examined by Baz and Das (1996), Björk, Kabanov, and Runggaldier (1995), Björk, DiMasi, Kabanov, and Runggaldier (1997), Das (1993c, 1995, 1997, 1998), Das and Foresi (1996), Duffie and Kan (1996), Eberlein and Raible (1999), Glasserman and Kou (1999), and Naik and Lee (1994).

Dybvig, Ingersoll, and Ross (1996) show that the asymptote of long-term interest rates, as maturity goes to infinity, defines a process that is nondecreasing in calendar time. Related work can be found in Carverhill (1996) and El Karoui, Frachot, and Geman (1997).

Numerical methods for solving term-structure models and the pricing of derivative securities are described in Chapter 12.

The pricing of mortgage-backed securities based on term-structure models is pursued by Boudoukh, Richardson, Stanton, and Whitelaw (1995), Cheyette (1996), Jakobsen (1992), Stanton (1995b), and Stanton and Wallace (1995, 1998), who also review some of the related literature.

For term-structure models in a foreign exchange setting, see Nielsen and Saá-Requejo (1992) and Saá-Requejo (1993). The exercise on pricing foreign bond options in the HJM setting is based on Amin and Jarrow (1993) and Amin and Bodurtha (1995). The explicit form of the drift restriction on the foreign forward rates appearing as a solution in this exercise seems to have appeared both here and in Musiela and Rutkowski (1997). Restrictions implied by monetary integration are explored by Lund (1999).

We have taken the zero-coupon yield curve throughout as though it can be directly observed in the marketplace. In fact, it is normal practice in the finance industry to estimate the current zero-coupon yield curve (or forward rates) from the prices of both zero-coupon and coupon bonds. Such curve-fitting methods as nonlinear least squares or splines of several varieties are used for this purpose. See, for example, Adams and Van Deventer (1994), Coleman, Fisher, and Ibbotson (1992), Diament (1993), Fisher, Nychka, and Zervos (1994), Jaschke (1996), Konno and Takase (1995, 1996), and Svensson and Dahlquist (1993). Consistency of the curve-fitting method with an underlying term-structure model is examined by Björk and Christensen (1999), Björk and Gombani (1999), and Filipović (1999b).

On modeling the term structure of real interest rates, see Brown and Schaefer (1996) and Pennacchi (1991). On central-bank policy effects and term-structure models, see Babbs and Webber (1994), Balduzzi, Bertola, Foresi, and Klapper (1998), and Piazzesi (1997, 1999).

On the relative yields of taxable and nontaxable bonds, see Jordan (1995) and Rumsey (1996).

The expectations hypothesis is addressed in a term-structure setting by Fisher and Gilles (1998a).

The implications of special repo rates for term-structure modeling are explored by Barone and Risa (1994), Duffie (1996), and Fisher and Gilles (1996). Grinblatt (1994) pursues a related swap-spread model.

Further general reading on arbitrage-free models of the term structure is found in Artzner and Delbaen (1990b), Babbs and Webber (1994), Back (1996), Balduzzi (1994), Björk (1996), Bossaerts (1990), Campbell (1995), Carverhill (1990, 1991), Heston (1988a, 1989), Hull and White (1993), Marsh (1994), DeMunnik (1992), Musiela and Rutkowski (1997), Pedersen and Shiu (1993), Pedersen, Shiu, and Thorlacius (1989), Rogers (1993), and Webber (1990, 1992).

Alternative approaches to modeling the term structure of interest rates are given by Backus, Foresi, and Zin (1998), Brace and Musiela (1995a), Goldstein (1995), Jin and Glasserman (1998), Kim (1992, 1993, 1994), Tice and Webber (1997), and Zheng (1994).

On term-structure modeling of forward commodity prices, see references cited in Chapter 8.

8

Derivative Pricing

THIS CHAPTER APPLIES arbitrage-free pricing techniques from Chapters 6 and 7 to derivative securities that are not always easily treated by the direct PDE approach of Chapter 5. A derivative security is one whose cash flows are contingent on the prices of other securities, or on related indices. After summarizing the essential results from Chapter 6 for this purpose, we study the valuation of forwards, futures, European and American options, and certain exotic options. Option pricing with stochastic volatility is addressed with Fourier-transform methods.

A. Martingale Measures in a Black Box

Skipping over the foundational theory developed in Chapter 6, this section reviews the properties of an equivalent martingale measure, a convenient "black-box" approach to derivative asset pricing in the absence of arbitrage. Once again, we fix a standard Brownian motion $B = (B^1, \ldots, B^d)$ in $\mathbb{R}^d$ restricted to some time interval $[0, T]$, on a given probability space $(\Omega, \mathcal{F}, P)$. The standard filtration $\mathbb{F} = \{\mathcal{F}_t : 0 \le t \le T\}$ of B is as defined in Section 5I.

We take as given an adapted short-rate process r, with $\int_0^T |r_t| \, dt < \infty$ almost surely, and an Ito security-price process S in $\mathbb{R}^N$ with

$$dS_t = \mu_t \, dt + \sigma_t \, dB_t,$$

for appropriate μ and σ. It was shown in Chapter 6 that, aside from technical conditions, the absence of arbitrage is equivalent to the existence of a probability measure Q with special "risk-neutral" properties, called an equivalent martingale measure. For this chapter, we will use a narrow definition of equivalent martingale measures under which all expected rates of return are equivalent to the riskless rate r; a broader definition is given in Chapter 6. This means that, under Q, there is a standard Brownian motion B^Q in $\mathbb{R}^d$ such that, if the given securities pay no dividends before T, then

$$dS_t = r_t S_t \, dt + \sigma_t \, dB_t^Q, \tag{1}$$

which repeats (6.14). After substituting this "risk-neutral" measure Q for P, one can thus treat every security as though its "instantaneous expected rate of return" is the short rate r.

More generally, suppose the securities with price process S are claims to a cumulative-dividend process D. (That is, D_t is the vector of cumulative dividends paid by the N securities up through time t.) In this case, we have

$$S_t = E_t^Q \left[\exp\left(\int_t^T -r_s \, ds \right) S_T + \int_t^T \exp\left(\int_t^s -r_u \, du \right) dD_s \right], \tag{2}$$

which repeats (6.20). For example, suppose that $D_t = \int_0^t \delta_s \, ds$ for some dividend-rate process δ. Then (2) implies that

$$dS_t = (r_t S_t - \delta_t) \, dt + \sigma_t \, dB_t^Q, \tag{3}$$

generalizing (1). For another example, consider a unit discount riskless bond maturing at some time s. The cumulative-dividend process, say H, of this security is characterized by $H_u = 0$ for $u < s$ and $H_u = 1$ for $u \geq s$. The price of this bond at any time $t < s$ is therefore determined by (2) as

$$\Lambda_{t,s} \equiv E_t^Q \left[\exp\left(-\int_t^s r_u \, du \right) \right].$$

This doubly indexed process Λ is sometimes known as the *discount function*, or more loosely as a *term-structure model*. Details are given in Chapter 7.

By the definition of an equivalent martingale measure given in Chapter 6, any random variable Z that has finite variance with respect to P has finite expectation with respect to Q, and

$$E_t^Q(Z) = \frac{1}{\xi_t} E_t(\xi_T Z), \tag{4}$$

where E_t^Q denotes $\mathcal{F}_t$-conditional expectation under Q and

$$\xi_t = \exp\left(-\int_0^t \eta_s \, dB_s - \frac{1}{2} \int_0^t \eta_s \cdot \eta_s \, ds \right),$$

and where η is a market-price-of-risk process, that is, an adapted process in $\mathbb{R}^d$ solving the family of linear equations

$$\sigma_t \eta_t = \mu_t - r_t S_t, \qquad t \in [0, T].$$

The remainder of this chapter applies these concepts to the calculation of derivative asset prices, going beyond the simple cases treated in Chapter 5.

B. Forward Prices

Sections B through D address the pricing of forward and futures contracts, an important class of derivatives. A discrete-time primer on this topic is given in Exercise 2.17. The forward contract is the simpler of these two closely related securities. Let W be an $\mathscr{F}_T$-measurable finite-variance random variable underlying the claim payable to a holder of the forward contract at its delivery date T. For example, with a forward contract for delivery of a foreign currency at time T, the random variable W is the market value at time T of the foreign currency. The forward-price process F is an Ito process defined by the fact that one forward contract at time t is a commitment to pay the net amount $F_t - W$ at time T, with no other cash flows at any time. In particular, the true price of a forward contract, at the contract date, is zero.

We fix a bounded short-rate process r and an equivalent martingale measure Q. The dividend process H defined by the forward contract made at time t is given by $H_s = 0$, $s < T$, and $H_T = W - F_t$. Because the true price of the forward contract at t is zero, (2) implies that

$$0 = E_t^Q\left[\exp\left(-\int_t^T r_s \, ds\right)(W - F_t)\right].$$

Solving for the forward price,

$$F_t = \frac{E_t^Q\left[\exp(-\int_t^T r_s \, ds)W\right]}{E_t^Q\left[\exp(-\int_t^T r_s \, ds)\right]}.$$

If we assume that there exists at time t a zero-coupon riskless bond maturing at time T, then

$$F_t = \frac{1}{\Lambda_{t,T}} E_t^Q\left[\exp\left(-\int_t^T r_s \, ds\right)W\right]. \tag{5}$$

From this, we see that the forward-price process F is indeed an Ito process.

If r and W are statistically independent with respect to Q, we have the simplified expression $F_t = E_t^Q(W)$, implying that the forward price is a Q-martingale. This would be true, for instance, if the short-rate process r is deterministic.

As an example, suppose that the forward contract is for delivery at time T of one unit of a particular security with price process S and dividend process D. In particular, $W = S_T$. We can obtain a more concrete representation of the forward price than (5), as follows. From (5) and (2),

$$F_t = \frac{1}{\Lambda_{t,T}} \left(S_t - E_t^Q \left[\int_t^T \exp\left(-\int_t^s r_u \, du\right) dD_s \right] \right). \tag{6}$$

If the short-rate process r is deterministic, we can simplify further to

$$F_t = \frac{S_t}{\Lambda_{t,T}} - E_t^Q \left[\int_t^T \exp\left(\int_s^T r_u \, du\right) dD_s \right]. \tag{7}$$

which is known as the *cost-of-carry formula* for forward prices.

For deterministic r and D, the cost-of-carry formula (7) can be recovered from a direct and simple arbitrage argument. As an alternative to buying a forward contract at time t, one could instead buy the underlying security at t and borrow the required cost S_t by selling riskless zero-coupon bonds maturing at T. If one lends out the dividends as they are received by buying riskless bonds maturing at T, the net payoff to this strategy at time T is the value S_T of the underlying security, less the maturity value $S_t/\Lambda_{t,T}$ of the bonds sold at t, plus the total maturity value $\int_t^T \Lambda_{s,T}^{-1} \, dD_s$ of all of the bonds purchased with the dividends received between t and T. The total is $S_T - S_t/\Lambda_{t,T} + \int_t^T \Lambda_{s,T}^{-1} \, dD_s$. The payoff of the forward contract is $S_T - F_t$. Since these two strategies have no payoffs except at T, and since both F_t and $S_t/\Lambda_{t,T} - \int_t^T \Lambda_{s,T}^{-1} \, dD_s$ are known at time t, there would be an arbitrage unless F_t and $S_t/\Lambda_{t,T} - \int_t^T \Lambda_{s,T}^{-1} \, dD_s$ are equal, consistent with (7).

We have put aside the issue of calculating the equivalent martingale measure Q. The simplest case is that in which the forward contract is redundant, for in this case, the equivalent martingale measure does not depend on the forward price. The forward contract is automatically redundant if the underlying asset is a security with deterministic dividends between the contract date t and the delivery date T, provided there is a zero-coupon bond maturing at T. In that case, the forward contract can be replicated by a strategy similar to that used to verify the cost-of-carry formula directly. Construction of the strategy is assigned as an exercise.

C. Futures and Continuous Resettlement

As with a forward contract, a futures contract with delivery date T is keyed to some delivery value W, which we take to be an $\mathcal{F}_T$-measurable random variable with finite variance. The contract is completely defined by a *futures-price process* Φ with the property that $\Phi_T = W$. As we shall see, the contract is literally a security whose price process is zero and whose cumulative-dividend process is Φ. In other words, changes in the futures price are credited to the holder of the contract as they occur. See Exercise 2.17 for an explanation in discrete time.

This definition is an abstraction of the traditional notion of a futures contract, which calls for the holder of $+1$ contract at the delivery time T to accept delivery of some asset (whose spot market value at T is represented here by W) in return for simultaneous payment of the current futures price Φ_T. Likewise, the holder of -1 contract, also known as a *short position* of 1 contract, is traditionally obliged to make delivery of the same underlying asset in exchange for the current futures price Φ_T. This informally justifies the property $\Phi_T = W$ of the futures-price process Φ given in the definition above. Roughly speaking, if Φ_T is not equal to W (and if we continue to neglect transactions costs and other details), there is a *delivery arbitrage*. We will not explicitly define a delivery arbitrage since it only complicates the following analysis of futures prices. Informally, however, in the event that $W > \Phi_T$, one could buy at time T the deliverable asset for W, simultaneously sell one futures contract, and make immediate delivery for a profit of $W - \Phi_T$. Thus the potential of delivery arbitrage will naturally equate Φ_T with the delivery value W. This is sometimes known as the principle of *convergence*.

Many modern futures contracts have streamlined procedures that avoid the delivery process. For these, the only link that exists with the notion of delivery is that the terminal futures price Φ_T is contractually equated to some such variable W, which could be the price of some commodity or security, or even some abstract variable of general economic interest such as a price deflator. This procedure, finessing the actual delivery of some asset, is known as *cash settlement*. In any case, whether based on cash settlement or the absence of delivery arbitrage, we shall always take it by definition that the delivery futures price Φ_T is equal to the given delivery value W.

The institutional feature of futures markets that is central to our analysis of futures prices is *resettlement*, the process that generates daily or even more frequent payments to and from the holders of futures contracts based on changes in the futures price. As with the expression "forward price," the term "futures price" can be misleading in that the futures price Φ_t at time t is not at all the price of the contract. Instead, at each reset-tlement time t, an investor who has held $\bar{\theta}$ futures contracts since the last resettlement time, say s, receives the resettlement payment $\bar{\theta}(\Phi_t - \Phi_s)$, following the simplest resettlement recipe. More complicated resettlement arrangements often apply in practice. The continuous-time abstraction is to take the futures-price process Φ to be an Ito process and a *futures position process* to be some θ in $\mathcal{H}^2(\Phi)$ generating the resettlement gain $\int \theta \, d\Phi$ as a cumulative-dividend process. In particular, as we have already stated in its definition, the futures-price process Φ is itself, formally speaking, the cumulative dividend process associated with the contract. The true price process is zero, since (again ignoring some of the detailed institutional procedures) there is no payment against the contract due at the time a contract is bought or sold.

D. Arbitrage-Free Futures Prices

The futures-price process Φ can now be characterized as follows. We suppose that the short-rate process r is bounded. For all t, let $Y_t = \exp(-\int_0^t r_s \, ds)$. Because Φ is strictly speaking the cumulative-dividend process associated with the futures contract, and since the true-price process of the contract is zero, from (2) we see that

$$0 = E_t^Q \left(\int_t^T Y_s \, d\Phi_s \right), \qquad t \leq T,$$

from which it follows that the stochastic integral $\int Y \, d\Phi$ is a Q-martingale. Because r is bounded, there are constants $k_1 > 0$ and k_2 such that $k_1 \leq Y_t \leq k_2$ for all t. The process $\int Y \, d\Phi$ is therefore a Q-martingale if and only if Φ is also a Q-martingale. (This seems obvious; proof is assigned as an exercise.) Since $\Phi_T = W$, we have deduced a convenient representation for the futures-price process:

$$\Phi_t = E_t^Q(W), \qquad t \in [0, T]. \tag{8}$$

If r and W are statistically independent under Q, the futures-price process Φ given by (8) and the forward-price process F given by (5) are thus identical. In particular, if r is deterministic, the cost-of-carry formula (7) applies as well to futures prices.

As for how to calculate an equivalent martingale measure Q, it is most convenient if the futures contract is redundant, for then a suitable Q can be calculated directly from the other available securities. We shall work on this approach, originating with an article cited in the Notes, and fix for the remainder of the section such an equivalent martingale measure Q. Aside from the case of complete markets, it is not obvious how to establish the redundancy of a futures contract since the futures-price process Φ is itself the cumulative-dividend process of the contract, so any argument might seem circular. Suppose, however, that there is a self-financing strategy (in securities other than the futures contract) whose value at the delivery date T is

$$Z_T = W \exp\left(\int_t^T r_s \, ds\right).$$

We will give an example of such a strategy shortly. From the definition of Q, the market value of this strategy at time t is $Z_t = E_t^Q(W)$. We claim that if Φ_t is not equal to Z_t, then there is an arbitrage. In order to show this, we will construct a trading strategy, involving only the futures contract and borrowing or lending at the short rate, such that the strategy pays off exactly Z_T at time T and requires the investment of Φ_t at time t. It will be clear from this that the absence of arbitrage equates Φ_t and Z_t. The strategy is constructed as follows. Let θ be the (bounded) futures position process defined by $\theta_s = 0, s < t$, and $\theta_s = \exp(\int_t^s r_u \, du), s \geq t$. Let V_t be the amount invested at the short rate at time t, determined as follows. Let $V_s = 0, s < t$, and $V_t = \Phi_t$. After t, let all dividends generated by the futures position be invested at the short rate and "rolled over." That is, let

$$dV_s = r_s V_s \, ds + \theta_s \, d\Phi_s, \qquad s \in [t, T].$$

The total market value at any time $s \geq t$ of this self-financing strategy in futures and investment at the short rate is the amount V_s invested at the short rate, since the true price of the futures contract is zero. We can calculate by Ito's Formula that

$$V_T = \Phi_T \exp\left(\int_t^T r_s \, ds\right) = W \exp\left(\int_t^T r_s \, ds\right) = Z_T, \qquad (9)$$

which verifies the claim that the futures contract is redundant.

Summarizing, the futures-price process is uniquely defined by (8) provided there is a self-financing strategy with value $Z_T = W \exp(\int_t^T r_s \, ds)$ at the delivery date T. It remains to look for examples in which Z_T is indeed the value at time T of some self-financing strategy. That is the case, for instance, if the futures contract delivers a security that pays no dividends before T and if the short-rate process is deterministic. With this, the purchase of $\exp(\int_t^T r_s\,ds)$ units of the underlying security at time t would suffice. More general examples can easily be constructed.

There is one loose end to tidy up. The assumption that the futures-price process Φ is an Ito process played a role in our analysis, yet we have not confirmed that the solution (8) for Φ is actually an Ito process. This can be shown as an application of Girsanov's Theorem (Appendix D).

E. Stochastic Volatility

The Black-Scholes option-pricing formula, as we recall from Chapter 5, is of the form $C(x, p, \bar{r}, t, \bar{\sigma})$, for $C : \mathbb{R}_+^5 \to \mathbb{R}_+$, where x is the current underlying asset price, p is the exercise price, $\bar{r}$ is the short interest rate, t is the time to expiration, and $\bar{\sigma}$ is the volatility coefficient for the underlying asset. For each fixed $(x, p, \bar{r}, t)$ with nonzero x and t, the map from $\bar{\sigma}$ to $C(x, p, \bar{r}, t, \bar{\sigma})$ is strictly increasing, and its range is unbounded. We may therefore invert and obtain the volatility from the option price. That is, we can define an *implied volatility* function $I : \mathbb{R}_+^5 \to \mathbb{R}_+$ by

$$c = C(x, p, \bar{r}, t, I(x, p, \bar{r}, t, c)), \tag{10}$$

for all sufficiently large $c \in \mathbb{R}_+$.

If c_1 is the Black-Scholes price of an option on a given asset at strike p_1 and expiration t_1, and c_2 is the Black-Scholes price of an option on the same asset at strike p_2 and expiration t_2, then the associated implied volatilities $I(x, p_1, \bar{r}, t_1, c_1)$ and $I(x, p_2, \bar{r}, t_2, c_2)$ must be identical, if indeed the assumptions underlying the Black-Scholes formula apply literally, and in particular if the underlying price process has the constant volatility of a geometric Brownian motion. It has been widely noted, however, that actual market prices for European options on the same underlying asset have associated Black-Scholes implied volatilities that vary with both exercise price and expiration date. For example, in certain markets at certain times, implied volatilities of options with a given exercise date depend on strike prices in a manner that is often termed a *smile curve*. Figure 8.1, for example, illustrates the dependence of Black-Scholes implied volatilities on moneyness (the ratio of strike price to futures price), for various S&P 500 index options on November 2, 1993. Other forms of systematic deviation away from constant implied volatilities have been noted, both over time and across various derivatives at a point in time.

Three major lines of modeling address these systematic deviations from the assumptions underlying the Black-Scholes model. In all of these,

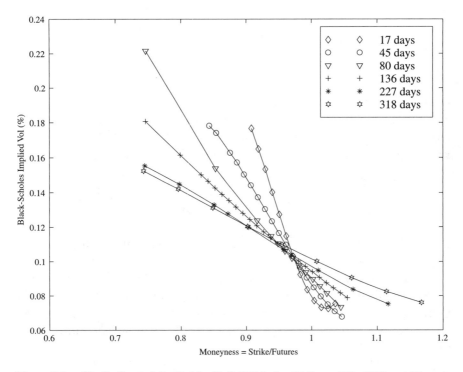

Figure 8.1. *"Smile Curves" Implied by S&P 500 Index Options of Six Different Times to Expiration, from Market Data for November 2, 1993*

the underlying log-normal price process is generalized by replacing the constant-volatility parameter $\bar{\sigma}$ of the Black-Scholes model with a *volatility process*, an adapted nonnegative process V with $\int_0^T V_t \, dt < \infty$ such that the underlying asset price process S satisfies

$$dS_t = r_t S_t \, dt + S_t \sqrt{V_t} \, d\epsilon_t^S, \qquad (11)$$

where $\epsilon^S = c_S \cdot B^Q$ is a standard Brownian motion under Q obtained from any c_S in $\mathbb{R}^d$ with unit norm.

In the first class of models, $V_t = v(S_t, t)$, for some function $v : \mathbb{R} \times [0, T] \to \mathbb{R}$ satisfying technical regularity conditions. In practical applications, the function v, or its discrete-time, discrete-state analogue, is often "calibrated" to the available option prices. This approach, sometimes referred to as the *implied-tree* model, is explored in literature cited in the Notes of this chapter and of Chapter 3.

For a second class of models, called *generalized autoregressive conditional heteroscedastic*, or GARCH, the volatility depends on the path of squared returns. The model was originally formulated in a discrete-time setting by constructing the volatility V_t at time t of the return $R_{t+1} = \log S_{t+1} - \log S_t$ according to the recursive formula

$$V_t = a + bV_{t-1} + cR_t^2, \tag{12}$$

for fixed coefficients a, b, and c satisfying regularity conditions. By taking a time period of length h, normalizing in a natural way, and taking limits, a natural continuous-time limiting behavior for volatility is simply a deterministic mean-reverting process V satisfying the ordinary differential equation

$$\frac{dV(t)}{dt} = \kappa(\bar{v} - V(t)). \tag{13}$$

(Discussion of the nature of the continuous-time limit can be found in sources cited in the Notes.)

In a third approach, the increments of the volatility process V depend on Brownian motions (or more general random processes) that are not perfectly correlated with ϵ^S. For example, in a simple "one-factor" setting the volatility process V satisfies a stochastic differential equation of the form

$$dV_t = \mu_V(V_t)\,dt + \sigma_V(V_t)\,d\epsilon_t^V, \tag{14}$$

where $\epsilon^V = c_V \cdot B^Q$ is a standard Brownian motion under Q, for some constant vector c_V of unit norm. As we shall see, the correlation parameter $c_{SV} = c_S \cdot c_V$ has an important influence on option prices.

The Feynman-Kac approach illustrated in Chapter 5 leads, under technical conditions, to a partial differential equation to be solved for a function $f : \mathbb{R}_+ \times \mathbb{R} \times [0, t] \to \mathbb{R}$ that determines the price at time s of a European option at exercise price p and expiration at time t as

$$f(S_s, V_s, s) = E_s^Q[e^{-\bar{r}(t-s)}(S_t - p)^+].$$

Methods for solving such a PDE by discretization are cited in Chapter 12.

A special case of the stochastic-volatility model that has sometimes been applied takes the correlation parameter c_{SV} to be zero. This implies that the volatility process V is independently distributed (under Q) with the return-driving Brownian motion ϵ^S. One can then more easily calculate the value of an option (or another derivative) on the underlying asset by noting that, conditional on the volatility process V, the underlying asset price process is log-normal under Q. That is, the distribution under Q of

$\log S_t$ conditional on the entire volatility process $\{V_s : s \in [0, t]\}$ is normal with standard deviation $\sigma(V)\sqrt{t}$, where

$$\sigma(V) = \frac{1}{\sqrt{t}}\left(\int_0^t V_s \, ds\right)^{1/2},$$

and with mean $\bar{r}t - \sigma(V)^2 t/2$. By the law of iterated expectations, the initial European call-option price, with expiration date t and strike p, is given by

$$\begin{aligned}
f(S_0, V_0, t) &= E^Q\left[e^{-\bar{r}t}(S_t - p)^+\right] \\
&= E^Q(E^Q[e^{-\bar{r}t}(S_t - p)^+ \mid \{V_s : s \in [0, t]\}]) \\
&= E^Q[C(S_0, p, \bar{r}, t, \sigma(V))],
\end{aligned} \quad (15)$$

where $C(\cdot)$ as usual denotes the Black-Scholes formula. Given a particular stochastic model for V, one could evaluate the option price (15) by several numerical methods mentioned in the Notes. One finds that the implied smile curve is indeed "smile-shaped," although it is difficult to reconcile this special case with the empirical behavior of many types of options. In particular, in many settings, a pronounced *skew* to the smile, as in Figure 8.1, indicates an important potential role for correlation between the increments of the return-driving and volatility-driving Brownian motions, ϵ^S and ϵ^V. This role is borne out directly by the correlation apparent from time-series data on implied volatilities and returns for certain important asset classes, as indicated in sources cited in the Notes.

A tractable model that allows for the skew effects of correlation is the *Heston model*, the special case of (14) for which

$$dV_t = \kappa(\bar{v} - V_t) \, dt + \sigma_v\sqrt{V_t} \, d\epsilon_t^V, \quad (16)$$

for positive coefficients κ, $\bar{v}$, and σ_v that play the same respective roles for V as for a Cox-Ingersoll-Ross interest-rate model. (Indeed, (16) is sometimes called a "CIR model" for volatility.) In the original Heston model, the short rate was assumed to be a constant, say $\bar{r}$, and option prices can be computed analytically, using transform methods explained in the next section, in terms of the parameters $(\bar{r}, c_{SV}, \kappa, \bar{v}, \sigma_v)$ of the Heston model, as well as the initial volatility V_0, the initial underlying price S_0, the strike price, and the expiration time. Figure 8.2 shows the "smile curves" for the options illustrated in Figure 8.1, for parameters, including V_0, chosen to minimize the sum of squared differences between actual and theoretical

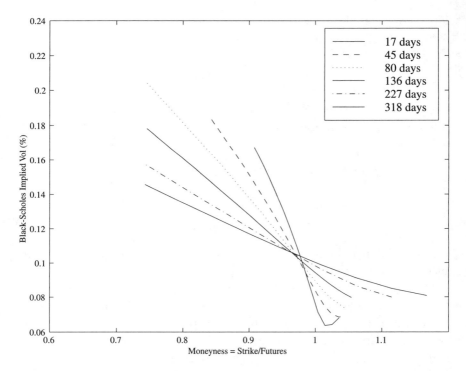

Figure 8.2. *"Smile Curves" Calculated for S&P 500 Index Options of Six Different Exercise Dates, November 2, 1993, using the Heston Model*

option prices. Notably, the distinctly downward slopes, often called skews, are captured with a negative correlation coefficient c_{SV}. Taking the short rate $\bar{r} = 0.0319$, the remaining coefficients of the Heston model are calibrated as $c_{SV} = -0.66$, $\kappa = 19.66$, $\bar{v} = 0.017$, $\sigma_v = 1.516$, and $\sqrt{V_0} = 0.094$. The Notes cite literature that uses time-series data on both options and underlying prices to fit the parameters, indicating evidence that the Heston model is overly restrictive for these data. This transform approach, however, also accommodates stochastic interest rates, jumps, and more general volatility models.

F. Option Valuation by Transform Analysis

This section is devoted to the calculation of option prices with stochastic volatility, in a setting with affine state dynamics of the type introduced for term-structure modeling in Chapter 7. We use transform analysis, allowing for relatively rich and tractable specifications of stochastic interest rates and volatility, and, eventually, for jumps. Repeating from Chapter 7, a state process X in state space $D \subset \mathbb{R}^k$ is affine (under Q) if

$$dX_t = \mu(X_t)\,dt + \sigma(X_t)\,dB_t^Q, \tag{17}$$

where $\mu(x) = K_0 + K_1 x$ for some $K_0 \in \mathbb{R}^k$ and $K_1 \in \mathbb{R}^{k \times k}$ and, for each i and j in $\{1, \ldots, k\}$,

$$\left(\sigma(x)\sigma(x)^\top\right)_{ij} = H_{0ij} + H_{1ij} \cdot x, \tag{18}$$

for some $H_{0ij} \in \mathbb{R}$ and $H_{1ij} \in \mathbb{R}^k$, for the state space

$$D = \{x : H_{0ii} + H_{1ii} \cdot x \geq 0, \ 1 \leq i \leq n\}. \tag{19}$$

The Notes cite technical conditions on the coefficients (H, K) ensuring the existence of a unique solution X to (17). For time-series empirical studies, it is often convenient to suppose that the state process X is also affine under the original data-generating probability measure P, albeit with a different set $K^P = (K_0^P, K_1^P)$ of drift-related coefficients in place of K. Conditions for this, and extensions to time-dependent coefficients, are explored in exercises.

In this setting, the short-rate process r is assumed to be of the affine form $r_t = \rho_0 + \rho_1 \cdot X_t$, for coefficients ρ_0 in $\mathbb{R}$ and ρ_1 in $\mathbb{R}^k$. Finally, we suppose that the price process S underlying the options in question is of the exponential-affine form $S_t = \exp(a_t + b_t \cdot X_t)$, for potentially time-dependent coefficients a_t in $\mathbb{R}$ and b_t in $\mathbb{R}^k$. An example would be the price of an equity, a foreign currency, or, as shown in Chapter 7, the price of a zero-coupon bond.

The Heston model (16) is a special case of an affine process $X = (X^{(1)}, X^{(2)})$, with $X_t^{(1)} = Y_t \equiv \log(S_t)$, and $X_t^{(2)} = V_t$. The short rate is assumed constant $\bar{r} = \rho_0$. From Ito's Formula,

$$dY_t = \left(\bar{r} - \frac{1}{2}V_t\right)dt + \sqrt{V_t}\,d\epsilon_t^S, \tag{20}$$

which indeed makes the state vector $X_t = (Y_t, V_t)$ an affine process, whose state space is $D = \mathbb{R} \times [0, \infty)$, and whose coefficients (H, K) can be chosen in terms of the parameters $(\bar{r}, c_{SV}, \kappa, \bar{v}, \sigma_v)$ of the Heston model. The underlying asset price is of the desired exponential-affine form because $S_t = e^{Y(t)}$. We will return to the Heston model shortly with some explicit results on option valuation.

For the general affine case, suppose we are interested in valuing a European call option on the underlying security, with strike price p and exercise date t. We have the initial option price

$$U_0 = E^Q\left[\exp\left(-\int_0^t r_u\, du\right)(S_t - p)^+\right].$$

Letting A denote the event $\{\omega : S(\omega, t) \geq p\}$ that the option is in the money at expiration, we have the option price

$$U_0 = E^Q\left[\exp\left(-\int_0^t r_s\, ds\right)\left(S_t 1_A - p 1_A\right)\right].$$

Because $S(t) = e^{a(t) + b(t)\cdot X(t)}$, we have

$$U_0 = e^{a(t)} G(-\log p + a(t); t, b(t), -b(t))$$
$$- p G(-\log p + a(t); t, 0, -b(t)), \tag{21}$$

where, for any $y \in \mathbb{R}$ and for any coefficient vectors d and δ in $\mathbb{R}^k$,

$$G(y; t, d, \delta) = E^Q\left[\exp\left(-\int_0^t r_s\, ds\right) e^{d\cdot X(t)} 1_{\delta\cdot X(t) \leq y}\right]. \tag{22}$$

So, if we can compute the function G, we can obtain the prices of options of any strike and exercise date. Likewise, the prices of European puts, interest-rate caps, chooser options, and many other derivatives can be derived in terms of G, as shown in exercises and sources cited in the Notes.

We note, for fixed (t, d, δ), assuming $E^Q(\exp(\int_0^t -r_s\, ds)e^{d\cdot X(t)}) < \infty$, that $G(\cdot; t, d, \delta)$ is a bounded increasing function. For any such function $g : \mathbb{R} \to [0, \infty)$, an associated *transform* $\hat{g} : \mathbb{R} \to \mathbb{C}$, where $\mathbb{C}$ is the set of complex numbers, is defined by

$$\hat{g}(z) = \int_{-\infty}^{+\infty} e^{izy}\, dg(y), \tag{23}$$

where i is the usual imaginary number, often denoted $\sqrt{-1}$. (Appendix H summarizes a few minimal elements of complex arithmetic.) Depending on one's conventions, one may refer to $\hat{g}$ as the *Fourier transform* of g. Under the technical condition that $\int_{-\infty}^{+\infty} |\hat{g}(z)|\, dz < \infty$, we have the *Lévy Inversion Formula*

$$g(y) = \frac{\hat{g}(0)}{2} - \frac{1}{\pi}\int_0^\infty \frac{1}{z}\, \mathrm{Im}[e^{-izy}\hat{g}(z)]\, dz, \tag{24}$$

where $\mathrm{Im}(c)$ denotes the imaginary part of a complex number c.

For the case $g(\cdot) = G(\cdot; t, d, \delta)$, with transform $\hat{G}(\cdot; t, d, \delta)$, we can compute $G(y; t, d, \delta)$ from (24), typically by computing the integral in (24) numerically, and thereby obtain option prices from (21). Our final objective is therefore to compute the transform $\hat{G}$. Fixing z, an application of Fubini's Theorem to (23) implies that $\hat{G}(z; t, d, \delta) = f(X_0, 0)$, where $f : D \times [0, t] \to \mathbb{C}$ is defined by

$$f(X_s, s) = E^Q\left[\exp\left(-\int_s^t r_u \, du\right) e^{d \cdot X(t)} e^{iz\delta \cdot X(t)} \ \Big| \ X_s\right]. \tag{25}$$

From (25), the same separation-of-variables arguments used in Chapter 7 imply, under technical regularity conditions, that

$$f(x, s) = e^{\alpha(s) + \beta(s) \cdot x}, \tag{26}$$

where β solves the Riccati ordinary differential equation (ODE)

$$\beta'(s) = \rho_1 - K_1^\top \beta(s) - \frac{1}{2}\beta(s)^\top H_1 \beta(s), \tag{27}$$

with the boundary condition

$$\beta(t) = d + iz\delta, \tag{28}$$

and where

$$\alpha(s) = \int_s^t \left[-\rho_0 + K_0 \cdot \beta(u) + \frac{1}{2}\beta(u)^\top H_0 \beta(u)\right] du. \tag{29}$$

The ODE (27) is identical to that arising in the affine term-structure calculations of Chapter 7, but the solutions for $\alpha(t)$ and $\beta(t)$ are complex numbers, in light of the complex boundary condition (28) for $\beta(t)$. One must keep track of both the real and imaginary parts of $\alpha(s)$ and $\beta(s)$, following the usual rules of complex arithmetic outlined in Appendix H.

Thus, under technical conditions, we have our transform $\hat{G}(z; t, d, \delta)$, evaluated at a particular z. We then have the option-pricing formula (21), where $G(y; t, d, \delta)$ is obtained from the inversion formula (24) applied to the transforms $\hat{G}(\cdot; t, b(t), -b(t))$ and $\hat{G}(\cdot; t, 0, -b(t))$, obtained by solving the Ricatti equation (27) with the respective boundary conditions $b(t) - izb(t)$ and $-izb(t)$. For cases in which the ODE (27) cannot be solved explicitly, its numerical computation, followed by numerical integration to obtain (24), is somewhat burdensome. Direct PDE or Monte Carlo numerical methods would typically, however, be even more computationally intensive.

For option pricing with the Heston model, we require only the transform $\psi(u) = e^{-\bar{r}t} E^Q[e^{uY(t)}]$, for some particular choices of $u \in \mathbb{C}$. Solving (27) for this case, we have

$$\psi(u) = e^{\bar{\alpha}(t,u) + uY(0) + \bar{\beta}(t,u)V(0)},$$

where, letting $b = u\sigma_v c_{SV} - \kappa$, $a = u(1 - u)$, and $\gamma = \sqrt{b^2 + a\sigma_v^2}$, we find that

$$\bar{\beta}(t, u) = -\frac{a(1 - e^{-\gamma t})}{2\gamma - (\gamma + b)(1 - e^{-\gamma t})},$$

$$\bar{\alpha}(t, u) = \bar{r}t(u - 1) - \kappa\bar{v}\left(\frac{\gamma + b}{\sigma_v^2} t + \frac{2}{\sigma_v^2} \log\left[1 - \frac{\gamma + b}{2\gamma}(1 - e^{-\gamma t})\right]\right).$$

Other special cases for which one can compute explicit solutions are cited in the Notes, or treated in exercises.

G. American Security Valuation

This section addresses the valuation of American securities, those whose cash flows are determined by the stopping time at which the owner of the American security decides to exercise. As our setup for primitive securities, we take a bounded short-rate process r and suppose that the price process S of the other securities satisfies (1), where B^Q is a standard Brownian motion under a probability measure Q equivalent to P. We also suppose for this section that rank$(\sigma) = d$ almost everywhere, so that any random payoff with finite risk-neutral expectation can be replicated without resorting to "doubling strategies," as shown by Proposition 6I. As indicated in Chapter 2, some sort of dynamic-spanning property of this type is important for the valuation of American securities.

An *American security*, defined by an adapted process U and an expiration time $\bar{\tau}$, is a claim to the payoff U_τ at a stopping time $\tau \leq \bar{\tau}$ chosen by the holder of the security. Such a stopping time is an *exercise policy*. As with the discrete-time treatment in Chapter 2, our objective is to calculate the price process V of the American security and to characterize rational exercise policies. The classic example is the case of a put option on a stock in the Black-Scholes setting of constant-volatility stock prices and constant short rates. In that case, we have $U_t = (p - S_t)^+$, where p is the exercise price and S is the underlying asset price process. More generally, we will rely on the following technical condition.

American Regularity Condition. *U is a adapted continuous process, bounded below, with $E^Q(U_*) < \infty$, where $U_* = \sup_{t \in [0, T]} U_t$.*

This regularity is certainly satisfied for an American put option in standard settings for which the underlying price process is an Ito process.

Given some particular exercise policy τ, Proposition 6I implies that the claim to $U_\tau \exp(\int_\tau^T r_s\, ds)$ at T can be replicated by a self-financing trading strategy θ whose market-value process V^τ is given by

$$V_t^\tau = E_t^Q(\varphi_{t,\tau} U_\tau),$$

where $\varphi_{t,\tau} \equiv \exp(\int_t^\tau -r_s\, ds)$. This implies that the payoff of U_τ at time τ is replicated by the trading strategy θ^τ that is θ until time τ, and zero afterward, generating a lump-sum payment of U_τ at τ.

Following the approach taken in Section 2I, we therefore define a *rational exercise policy* as a solution to the *optimal-stopping problem*

$$V_0^* = \sup_{\tau \in \mathcal{T}(0)} V_0^\tau, \tag{30}$$

where $\mathcal{T}(t)$ denotes the set of stopping times valued in $[t, \bar{\tau}]$. This is the problem of maximizing the initial cost of replication. We will show that there is in fact a stopping time τ^* solving (30), and that the absence of "nonpathological" arbitrages implies that the American security must sell initially for V_0^*.

If $V_0 < V_0^*$, then purchase of the American security for V_0, adoption of a rational exercise policy τ^*, and replication of the payoff $-U(\tau^*)$ at τ^* at an initial payoff of V_0^*, together generate a net initial profit of $V_0^* - V_0 > 0$ and no further cash flow. This is an arbitrage.

In order to rule out the other possibility, that $V_0 > V_0^*$, we will exploit the notion of a *super-replicating trading strategy*, a self-financing trading strategy whose market-value process Y dominates the exercise-value process U, in that $Y_t \geq U_t$ for all t in $[0, \bar{\tau}]$. We will show the existence of a super-replicating trading strategy with initial market value $Y_0 = V_0^*$. If $V_0 > V_0^*$, then sale of the American security and adoption of a super-replicating strategy implies an initial profit of $V_0 - V_0^* > 0$ and the ability to cover the payment U_τ demanded by the holder of the American security at exercise with the market value Y_τ of the super-replicating strategy, regardless of the exercise policy τ used by the holder of the American security. This constitutes an arbitrage. Indeed, then, the unique arbitrage-free American security price would be given by (30). (We have implicitly extended the definition of an arbitrage slightly in order to handle American securities.)

Let $\hat{U}$ be the deflated exercise-value process, defined by

$$\hat{U}_t = \exp\left(\int_0^t -r_s\, ds\right) U_t.$$

Let W be the *Snell envelope* of $\hat{U}$ under Q, meaning that

$$W_t = \operatorname*{ess\,sup}_{\tau \in \mathcal{T}(t)} E_t^Q(\hat{U}_\tau), \qquad t \le \bar{\tau}, \tag{31}$$

where ess sup denotes *essential supremum*. [In other words, for all τ in $\mathcal{T}(t)$, $P(W_t \ge E_t^Q(\hat{U}_\tau)) = 1$, and if $\hat{W}_t$ is any other $\mathcal{F}_t$-measurable random variable satisfying $P(\hat{W}_t \ge E_t^Q(\hat{U}_\tau)) = 1$ for all τ in $\mathcal{T}(t)$, then $P(W_t \le \hat{W}_t) = 1$.]

We recall from Chapter 6 that a trading strategy whose market-value process is bounded below cannot take advantage of certain "pathological" varieties of arbitrage, such as doubling strategies.

Proposition. *There is a super-replicating trading strategy θ^* whose market-value process Y is bounded below, with inital market value $Y_0 = V_0^*$. A rational exercise policy is given by $\tau^0 = \inf\{t : Y_t = U_t\}$.*

Proof: Under the American Regularity Conditions, a source cited in the Notes shows that the Snell envelope W of $\hat{U}$ is a continuous super-martingale under Q, and can therefore be decomposed in the form $W = Z - A$, where Z is a Q-martingale and A is an increasing adapted process with $A_0 = 0$. By Proposition 6I and numeraire invariance, there is a self-financing trading strategy whose market-value process Y has the final market value $Y_T = Z_{\bar{\tau}} \exp(\int_{\bar{\tau}}^T r_t \, dt)$ and satisfies

$$Y_t = E_t^Q\left[\exp\left(\int_t^T -r_t \, dt\right) Y_T\right].$$

A Q-martingale $\hat{Y}$ is thus defined by $\hat{Y}_t = Y_t \exp(\int_0^t -r_s \, ds)$. Because Z is also a Q-martingale, for $t \le \bar{\tau}$ we have

$$\begin{aligned}
Y_t &= \exp\left(\int_0^t r_s \, ds\right) E_t^Q\left[\exp\left(-\int_0^T r_s \, ds\right) Y_T\right] \\
&= \exp\left(\int_0^t r_s \, ds\right) E_t^Q[Z(\bar{\tau})] \\
&= \exp\left(\int_0^t r_s \, ds\right) Z_t \\
&= \exp\left(\int_0^t r_s \, ds\right)(W_t + A_t). \tag{32}
\end{aligned}$$

Taking $t = 0$ in (32), we have $Y_0 = W_0 = V_0^*$, as asserted. From (32),

$$Y_t \ge \exp\left(\int_0^t r_s \, ds\right) W_t \ge U_t, \tag{33}$$

using the fact that A_t is nonnegative, the definition of $\hat{U}_t$, and the fact that $W_t \geq \hat{U}_t$. Thus the underlying trading strategy is super-replicating. Because U is bounded below, (33) implies that the replicating market-value process Y is bounded below. Moreover, τ^0 is a rational exercise policy because

$$V_0^* = Y_0 = E^Q\left[\exp\left(\int_0^{\tau^0} -r_t \, dt\right)Y(\tau^0)\right] = V_0^{\tau^0},$$

from noting that $\hat{Y}$ is a Q-martingale and that $Y(\tau^0) = U(\tau^0)$. ∎

Putting the various pieces of the story together, the "arbitrage-pricing" result is summarized as follows. If the initial price V_0 of the American security $(U, \bar{\tau})$ is strictly larger than

$$V_0^* = \sup_{\tau \in \mathcal{J}(0)} E^Q\left[\exp\left(\int_0^{\tau} -r(s) \, ds\right)U_\tau\right], \tag{34}$$

then an arbitrage consists of sale of the option and adoption of the super-replicating trading strategy θ^* until whatever exercise time τ chosen by the option holder. Conversely, if $V_0 < V_0^*$, then an arbitrage is made by purchase of the option at time 0, exercise of the option at the rational time τ^0, and adoption of the trading strategy $-\theta^*$ until liquidation at τ^0. Neither of these arbitrage strategies are "doubling strategies" of the type discussed in Chapter 6; the implied pricing is indeed consistent with the given equivalent martingale measure Q.

All of our assumptions are satisfied in the case of an American put in the "Black-Scholes" setting, with a constant short rate $\bar{r}$, and an underlying price process S solving

$$dS_t = \bar{r}S_t \, dt + \bar{\sigma}S_t \, d\epsilon_t^S; \qquad S_0 = x, \tag{35}$$

where ϵ^S is a standard Brownian motion under Q. Thus, an American put with exercise price p and expiration at time $\bar{\tau}$ has the initial arbitrage-free price

$$V_0^* = \max_{\tau \in \mathcal{J}(0)} E^Q[e^{-\bar{r}\tau}(p - S_\tau)^+]. \tag{36}$$

In Chapter 12 we review some numerical recipes for approximating this value. There need not in fact be complete markets for our results to apply in this simple setting, for even if the underlying Brownian motion is of dimension $d > 1$, the super-replicating strategy of Proposition 8G can be constructed in terms of the underlying security with price process S and with funds invested at the short rate $\bar{r}$, and has a market-value process Y

that dominates the exercise value $(p - S_\tau)^+$ at any stopping time τ, *even a stopping time τ that is determined by information not generated by the Brownian motion ϵ^S of the underlying price process S.*

By extending our arguments, we can handle an American security that promises a cumulative-dividend process H until exercised at a stopping time $\tau \leq \bar{\tau}$ for a final payoff of U_τ. The same arguments applied previously lead to an initial price of the American security $(H, U, \bar{\tau})$ given, under similar technical regularity, by

$$V_0^* = \sup_{\tau \in \mathcal{T}(0)} E^Q \left(\int_0^\tau e^{\int_0^s -r(u)\,du}\,dH_s + e^{\int_0^\tau -r(u)\,du} U_\tau \right).$$

H. American Exercise Boundaries

We take the case of an American security $(U, \bar{\tau})$ with $U_t = g(X_t, t)$, where $g : \mathbb{R}^k \times [0, T] \to \mathbb{R}$ is continuous and X is a state process in $\mathbb{R}^k$ satisfying the SDE

$$dX_t = a(X_t)\,dt + b(X_t)\,dB_t^Q, \tag{37}$$

for continuous functions a and b satisfying Lipschitz conditions. For simplicity, we take the interest-rate process r to be zero, and later show that, aside from technicalities, this is without loss of generality. We adopt the American regularity conditions and again assume redundancy of the American security for any exercise policy. Starting at time t with initial condition $X_t = x$ for (37), the arbitrage-free value is given by

$$h(x, t) \equiv \sup_{\tau \in \mathcal{T}(t)} E_t^Q [g(X_\tau, \tau)]. \tag{38}$$

By inspection, $h \geq g$. From Proposition G, an optimal exercise policy is given by

$$\tau^0 = \inf\{t \in [0, T] : h(X_t, t) = g(X_t, t)\}. \tag{39}$$

By (39), $h(X_t, t) > g(X_t, t)$ for all $t < \tau^0$. Letting

$$\mathscr{E} = \{(x, t) \in \mathbb{R}^k \times [0, T] : h(x, t) = g(x, t)\}, \tag{40}$$

we can write $\tau^0 = \inf\{t : (X_t, t) \in \mathscr{E}\}$, and safely call $\mathscr{E}$ the *exercise region*, and its complement

$$\mathscr{C} = \{(x, t) \in \mathbb{R}^k \times [0, T) : h(x, t) > g(x, t)\}$$

the *continuation region*. In order to solve the optimal exercise problem, it is enough to break $\mathbb{R}^k \times [0, T]$ into these two sets. An optimal policy is then to exercise whenever (X_t, t) is in $\mathcal{E}$, and otherwise to wait. Typically, solving for the exercise region $\mathcal{E}$ is a formidable problem.

For a characterization of the solution in terms of the solution of a partial differential equation, suppose that h is sufficiently smooth for an application of Ito's Formula. Then

$$h(X_t, t) = h(X_0, 0) + \int_0^t \mathcal{D}h(X_s, s) \, ds + \int_0^t h_x(X_s, s)b(X_s) \, dB_s^Q,$$

where

$$\mathcal{D}h(x, t) = h_t(x, t) + h_x(x, t)a(x) + \frac{1}{2} \operatorname{tr}[h_{xx}(x, t)b(x)b(x)^\top].$$

For any initial conditions (x, t) and any stopping time $\tau \geq t$, we know from the definition of h that $E^Q[h(X_\tau, \tau)] \leq h(x, t)$. From this, it is natural to conjecture that $\mathcal{D}h(x, t) \leq 0$ for all (x, t). Moreover, we can see that $\mathcal{D}h(x, t) = 0$ for all (x, t) in $\mathcal{C}$. We summarize these conjectured necessary conditions on h, suppressing the arguments (x, t) everywhere for brevity. On $\mathbb{R}^k \times [0, T)$,

$$h \geq g, \qquad \mathcal{D}h \leq 0, \qquad (h - g)(\mathcal{D}h) = 0. \tag{41}$$

The last of these three conditions means that $\mathcal{D}h = 0$ wherever $h > g$, and conversely that $h = g$ wherever $\mathcal{D}h < 0$. Intuitively, this is a Bellman condition prescribing a policy of not exercising so long as the expected rate of change of the value function is not strictly negative. We also have the boundary condition

$$h(x, T) = g(x, T), \qquad x \in \mathbb{R}^k. \tag{42}$$

Under strong technical assumptions that can be found in sources cited in the Notes, it turns out that these necessary conditions (41)–(42) are also sufficient for h to be the value function. This characterization (41)–(42) of the value function lends itself to a finite-difference algorithm for numerical solution of the value function h.

In order to incorporate nonzero interest rates, suppose that the short-rate process r can be written in the form $r_t = R(X_t)$ for some bounded $R(\cdot)$. By similar arguments, the variational inequality (41)–(42) for the value function h can then be written exactly as before, with the exception that $\mathcal{D}h(x, t)$ is replaced everywhere by $\mathcal{D}h(x, t) - R(x)h(x, t)$.

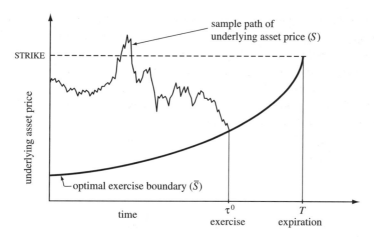

Figure 8.3. *Optimal Exercise Boundary for American Put*

For the special case of the American put with a constant short rate and the constant-volatility underlying process S given by (35), a series of advances cited in the Notes has led to the following characterization of the solution, taking the state process X to be the underlying price process S. Because S is nonnegative, the continuation region $\mathscr{C}$ can be treated as a subset of $\mathbb{R}_+ \times [0, T)$. It turns out that there is an increasing continuously differentiable function $\bar{S} : [0, T) \to \mathbb{R}$, called the *optimal exercise boundary*, such that $\mathscr{C} = \{(x, t) : x > \bar{S}_t\}$. Letting $\bar{S}_T = K$, the optimal exercise policy τ^* is then to exercise when (and if) the stock price S "hits the optimal exercise boundary," as illustrated in Figure 8.3. That is, $\tau^0 = \inf\{t : S_t \le \bar{S}_t\}$.

Unfortunately, there is no explicit solution available for the optimal-stopping boundary $\bar{S}$. There are, however, numerical methods for estimating the value function h and exercise boundary $\bar{S}$. One is the simple algorithm (3.23) for the "binomial" model, which as we see in Chapter 12 can be taken as an approximation of the Black-Scholes model. The other is a direct finite-difference numerical solution of the associated *partial differential inequality* (41)–(42), which in this case can be written, with the change of variables from stock price x to its logarithm $y = \log(x)$: On $\mathbb{R} \times [0, T)$,

$$h(y, t) - (K - e^y)^+ \ge 0,$$

$$\mathscr{D}h(y, t) - \bar{r}h(y, t) \le 0, \tag{43}$$

$$\left[h(y, t) - (K - e^y)^+\right]\left[\mathscr{D}h(y, t) - \bar{r}h(y, t)\right] = 0,$$

with the boundary condition

$$h(y, T) = (K - e^y)^+, \qquad y \in \mathbb{R}, \tag{44}$$

where

$$\mathcal{D}h(y, t) = h_t(y, t) + \left(\bar{r} - \frac{\bar{\sigma}^2}{2}\right)h_y(y, t) + \frac{\bar{\sigma}^2}{2}h_{yy}(y, t). \tag{45}$$

Not all of the indicated derivatives of h may exist, but it turns out, from sources cited in the Notes, that there is no essential difficulty in treating (43)–(44) as written for computational purposes.

I. Lookback Options

Certain classes of derivative securities are said to be *path dependent*, in that the payoff of the derivative security at a given time depends on the path taken by the underlying asset price up until that time. An important and illustrative class of examples is given by *lookback options*.

Consider the case of a *sell-at-the-max option*, with exercise date T. Let S be an Ito process defining the price of a security, and let r be a bounded adapted short-rate process. For any times t and $s \geq t$, let $S_{t,s}^* = \max\{S_u : t \leq u \leq s\}$ denote the maximum level achieved by the price process between times t and s. This option offers the right to sell the stock at time T for $S_{0,T}^*$. Of course, $S_{0,T}^* \geq S_T$, so the option is always exercised for a payoff of $S_{0,T}^* - S_T$. Given an equivalent martingale measure Q, the market value of the option at time t is then

$$V_t = E_t^Q\left[\exp\left(-\int_t^T r_s \, ds\right)(S_{0,T}^* - S_T)\right]. \tag{46}$$

For the case of a log-normal security-price process satisfying (35) and a constant short interest rate $\bar{r}$, a closed-form solution can be obtained for the lookback-option price process V. We know that $S_t = S_0 \exp(\alpha t + \bar{\sigma}\epsilon_t^S)$, where ϵ^S is a standard Brownian motion under Q and $\alpha = \bar{r} - \bar{\sigma}^2/2$. Thus

$$S_{0,T}^* = \max(S_{0,t}^*, S_{t,T}^*)$$

$$= \max\left[S_{0,t}^*, S_t \exp(Z_{t,T})\right], \tag{47}$$

where

$$Z_{t,T} = \max_{u \in [t, T]} \alpha(u - t) + \bar{\sigma}(\epsilon_u^S - \epsilon_t^S). \tag{48}$$

The cumulative distribution function F_{T-t} of $Z_{t,T}$ is known, based on sources cited in the Notes, to be given by

$$F_\tau(z) = 1 - \Phi\left(\frac{z - \alpha\tau}{\bar\sigma\sqrt{\tau}}\right) + e^{2\alpha z/\bar\sigma^2}\Phi\left(\frac{-z - \alpha\tau}{\bar\sigma\sqrt{\tau}}\right), \qquad z > 0, \qquad (49)$$

where Φ is the standard normal cumulative distribution function. From (47),

$$E_t^Q\left(S_{0,T}^*\right) = F_{T-t}(z^*)S_{0,t}^* + [1 - F_{T-t}(z^*)]S_t \int_{z^*}^\infty e^z F_{T-t}'(z)\, dz, \qquad (50)$$

where $z^* = \log(S_{0,t}^*) - \log(S_t)$.

Because there are no dividends, the payment of S_T at T has a market value at time t of S_t. From (46), we thus have

$$V_t = E_t^Q\left(e^{-\bar r(T-t)}S_{0,T}^*\right) - S_t.$$

After computing the integral in (50), we have the lookback sell-at-the-max put option price $V_t = v(S_t, S_{0,t}^*; T - t)$, where

$$v(x, y; \tau) = -x\Phi(-D) + e^{-\bar r\tau} y\,\Phi(-D + \bar\sigma\sqrt{\tau})$$

$$+ \frac{\bar\sigma^2}{2\bar r}e^{-\bar r\tau}x\left[-\left(\frac{x}{y}\right)^{-2\bar r/\bar\sigma^2}\Phi\left(D - \frac{2\bar r}{\bar\sigma}\sqrt{\tau}\right) + e^{\bar r\tau}\Phi(D)\right], \quad (51)$$

and where

$$D = \frac{1}{\bar\sigma\sqrt{\tau}}\left(\log\left(\frac{x}{y}\right) + \bar r\tau + \frac{1}{2}\bar\sigma^2\tau\right).$$

The analogous arbitrage-free *buy-at-the-min* lookback price is also known in closed form. This is the derivative paying $S_T - S_{*,0,T}$ at time T, where

$$S_{*,t,s} = \min\{S_u : t \le u \le s\}. \qquad (52)$$

Other varieties of path-dependent derivatives include

- *knock-outs*, whose payoff is zero if the underlying asset price touches a given boundary before expiration. (See Exercise 2.1.)
- *knock-ins*, whose payoff is zero unless the underlying asset price touches a given boundary before expiration.
- *barrier* derivatives, which pay off at the point in time at which a given process, usually the underlying asset price, touches some boundary.
- *Asians*, whose payoff depends on the average over time of the sample path of the underlying asset price before expiration.

Path-dependent options are sometimes called *exotic options,* despite the fact that some are commonplace in the market. Exotic options include, however, a much wider variety of options that need not be path dependent. Some relevant sources are indicated in the Notes.

Exercises

8.1 Show by use of Girsanov's Theorem that the futures-price process Φ defined by (8) is an Ito process (under the original measure P).

8.2 Verify (9) with Ito's Formula.

8.3 Show, as claimed in Section D, that if Φ is an Ito process and Y is bounded and bounded away from zero, then $\int Y \, d\Phi$ is a martingale if and only if Φ is a martingale. Hint: Use the unique decomposition property of Ito processes.

8.4 Suppose there are three traded securities. Security 1 has the price process X given by $X_t = x \exp(\alpha t + \beta \cdot B_t)$, where $\alpha \in \mathbb{R}$, $\beta \in \mathbb{R}^2$, and B is a standard Brownian motion in $\mathbb{R}^2$. Security 2 has the price process Y given by $Y_t = y \exp(at + b \cdot B_t)$, where $a \in \mathbb{R}$, $b \in \mathbb{R}^2$. Security 3 has the price process e^{rt}, where r is a constant. None of the securities pay dividends during $[0, T]$. Consider a contract paying, at some time $T > 0$, either k units of security 1 or one unit of security 2, whichever is preferred by the owner of the contract at that time. Calculate the arbitrage-free price of that contract.

8.5 Consider the *rolling spot futures contract,* defined as follows. The contract promises to pay, continually, changes in the spot price S_t of the underlying asset as well as futures resettlement payments. That is, the rolling spot futures-price process associated with the contract, say U, contractually satisfies $U_T = S_T$, and the total gain for the contract between any two times t and $s \geq t$ is $G_s - G_t$, where $G_t = U_t + S_t$. Show that, given the existence of an equivalent martingale measure (which is essentially equivalent to no arbitrage), the rolling spot futures-price process is given by $U_t = 2\Phi_t - S_t$, where Φ_t is the conventional futures price.

8.6 Compute the value of the buy-at-the-min lookback option defined in Section I under the same assumptions used to derive the price (50) of the sell-at-the-max option.

8.7 Consider an underlying asset price process S satisfying (35), the log-normal model, and a futures option on the asset. That is, we let f be the futures price for delivery of the underlying asset at time T, and consider a security that pays $(f_\tau - K)^+$ at some given time $\tau < T$. Compute the initial price of this futures option.

8.8 Suppose the short-rate process r is given by the Cox-Ingersoll-Ross model, defined in Section 7D. Compute the futures price and the forward price that would apply at time zero for delivery at time $\tau < T$ of a zero-coupon bond maturing at time T. Hint: For the futures price, conjecture the form $f(r_t, t) = e^{\alpha(t) + \beta(t)r(t)}$, for $t < \tau$, for time-dependent coefficients α and β. You will determine an ordinary differential equation for β, with a boundary condition at τ. Consider the change of variables given by $b(t) = \beta(t)^{-1}$. Solve for b, then β, then α.

8.9 (A Market-Timing Option Valuation Formula).   Consider an economy with a constant short rate of r, and a firm whose equity price process is a geometric Brownian motion S. We assume, as usual, that for given real parameters α and σ, $S_t = S_0 \exp(\alpha t + \sigma B_t)$, where B is a standard Brownian motion. A constant-proportional investment strategy is defined by the fraction $b \in \mathbb{R}$ of the value of a portfolio of the riskless and risky securities that is invested in the risky asset, with rebalancing to maintain this fraction constantly over time. (In Chapter 9, for example, we find that under HARA utility and technical regularity, such a policy is optimal.)

The wealth process $W(b)$ associated with such a policy coefficient b, with initial wealth $W(b)_0 = 1$, is unambiguously defined for each $b \in \mathbb{R}$.

If one had advance knowledge at time zero of the path of the underlying share price, one could take advantage of this knowledge in choosing from among different available constant-proportional policies. Such an advanced-knowledge policy is defined by a constant risky-investment fraction b that is an $\mathcal{F}_T$-measurable random variable. Of course, we assume that such advance knowledge is not available. Nevertheless, a broker-dealer decides to offer for a sale a derivative security that pays off the value of the constant-proportional investment strategy that would have been chosen with advance knowledge. The broker-dealer calls this a *market-timing option*. This market-timing option pays off $W(b^*)_T$ at a fixed time T, where, for each ω, the fraction $b^*(\omega)$ solves the problem

$$\max_{b \in [0, 1]} W(b, \omega)_T.$$

The requirement that b be chosen in $[0, 1]$ means no short sales of either asset. In other words, the broker-dealer will give the investor the payoff associated with a constant-proportional investment policy whose risky fraction is chosen at time T *after seeing what happened!*

(A) Compute the market value of the market-timing option, assuming the absence of arbitrage. In this setting, the type of arbitrage to rule out would be in the form of a self-financing trading strategy $\theta \in \mathcal{H}^2(S, e^{-rt})$ for stock and bank account, combined with a fixed position in the market-timing option. Show that there is no such arbitrage at the price that you propose, and that there is such an arbitrage at any other price.

(B) Suppose that the broker-dealer offers to sell a market-timing option with the one change being that the risky-asset proportion b is not constrained to $[0, 1]$, but is completely unconstrained. If there is a finite arbitrage-free price for the market-timing option, compute it and show why, as above. If not, show why not.

8.10 (Gold Delivery Contract Pricing).   The spot price process S of gold is assumed to be a geometric Brownian motion with constant volatility parameter v.

The interest rate is assumed to be a constant $r \geq 0$. We assume for simplicity that gold can be stored costlessly, and pays no dividends. That is, the usual assumptions underlying the Black-Scholes model apply.

A gold-mining firm offers the following delivery contract to special customers. For a price of p, set and paid on date 0, the customer receives the right, but not the obligation, to buy n ounces of gold from the mining firm on dates chosen by the customer between dates $T > 0$ and $U > T$, inclusive, at the spot price S_T set on date T. For each date t between T and U, the decision of whether or not to purchase gold on date t at the price S_T can be made based on all information available on date t. At most k ounces can be purchased per day. (Purchase decisions can be made at a fixed time, say noon, each day.) For notational simplicity, you may assume that n/k is an integer and that $U - T \geq n/k$.

(A) Provide, and justify, an explicit formula for the unique arbitrage-free price p of the gold delivery contract.

(B) For an extra fee of f, set and paid on date 0, the customer can elect on a given date T_0, between 0 and T, to double the size of the contract to $2n$ ounces by making an additional payment of p on date T_0. State explicitly the arbitrage-free level of f. You may assume for notational simplicity that $U - T \geq 2n/k$.

8.11 For the Heston model with parameter vector $(\bar{r}, c_{SV}, \kappa, \bar{v}, \sigma_v)$, this exercise explores a variation on the transform solution method. For a real coefficient h and a fixed time t, let U solve the SDE

$$dU_t = (\bar{r} + hV_t)\, dt + \sqrt{V_t}\, d\epsilon_t^S; \qquad U_0 = \log S_0.$$

For each real number y and time t, let

$$g(y) = Q(U_t \leq y). \tag{53}$$

(A) Show that the transform $\hat{g}$ of $g(\cdot)$ is given by

$$\hat{g}(z) = \exp\big[C(t, z) + D(t, z)V_0 + izU_0\big], \tag{54}$$

where

$$C(t, z) = \bar{r}izt + \frac{\kappa \bar{v}}{\sigma_v^2}\left[(\kappa - c_{SV}\,\sigma_v zi + \varphi)t - 2\log\left(\frac{1 - \zeta e^{t\varphi}}{1 - \zeta}\right)\right],$$

$$D(t, z) = \frac{\kappa - c_{SV}\,\sigma_v zi + \varphi}{\sigma_v^2} \cdot \left(\frac{1 - e^{t\varphi}}{1 - \zeta e^{t\varphi}}\right),$$

for

$$\zeta = \frac{\kappa - c_{SV}\,\sigma_v zi + \varphi}{\kappa - c_{SV}\,\sigma_v zi - \varphi},$$

with

$$\varphi = \sqrt{(c_{SV}\,\sigma_v zi - \kappa)^2 - \sigma_v^2(2hzi - z^2)}.$$

Hint: Verify that the coefficients $C(\cdot, z)$ and $D(\cdot, z)$ satisfy the appropriate Riccati equations.

(B) Provide the price of a call option on the underlying, expiring at time t and struck at p. Hint: In order to compute the term $G(y; t, b(t), -b(t))$ of the option-pricing formula (21), consider treating the underlying price process S as a numeraire. Consider that h and the parameters of the SDE solved by V depend on the probability measure used. Use the Lévy inversion formula, taking $\hat{g}(0) = 0.5$, rather than evaluating $\hat{g}(0)$ directly from the transform solution form above.

(C) For the Heston model with parameters

$$(\bar{r}, c_{SV}, \kappa, \bar{v}, \sigma_v) = (0.05, -0.5, 0.5, 0.09, 0.09),$$

let $S_0 = 100$ and $V_0 = 0.09$. Plot or tabulate (at least 10 points) the smile curve (Black-Scholes implied volatilities) for European call options with expiration at time $t = 0.25$. Now replot for the correlation parameter $c_{SV} = 0$. You may compute (24) with any convenient numerical-integration software.

8.12 (Volatility Hedging).   As we know from Chapter 5, the implied-tree model has the property that an option can be replicated, and therefore hedged, by a self-financing trading strategy involving the underlying asset and funds invested at the short rate r. The stochastic-volatility model does not generally have this property. Under regularity conditions, however, one can replicate a given option with a self-financing trading strategy involving the underlying asset, *a different option*, and funds invested at the riskless rate r.

(A) To be specific, consider the model (11) for the underlying price process S and (14) for the volatility process V, with correlation coefficient $c_{SV} \in (0, 1)$. Let $\Phi_t = f(S_t, V_t, t)$ and $\Gamma_t = g(S_t, V_t, t)$ denote the prices at time t of options for expiration at a future time τ, and different strike prices p_1 and p_2, respectively. Suppose that f and g solve the PDEs suggested by the Feynman-Kac approach. Suppose the short rate is a constant $\bar{r}$. Let $\theta = (a, b, c)$ denote a self-financing trading strategy in the price process $(S_t, \Phi_t, e^{\bar{r}t})$ that replicates the payoff of the option with strike p_2 and price process Γ. Solve for θ_t explicitly in terms of f and g and their partial derivatives, making minimal assumptions.

(B) For the Heston model, with parameters

$$(\bar{r}, c_{SV}, \kappa, \bar{v}, \sigma_v) = (0.05, -0.5, 0.5, 0.09, 0.09),$$

let $S_0 = 100$, $V_0 = 0.09$, and $p_1 = 100$. Tabulate (or plot) estimates of the initial replicating portfolio (a_0, b_0, c_0) as the exercise price p_2 of the option to be replicated ranges from 60 to 150, showing at least 10 points. In order to estimate partial derivatives, you may use either analytic methods (show your work) or take the usual discretization approximation, under which, for small Δ, we have $F'(x) \simeq [F(x + \Delta) - F(x - \Delta)]/2\Delta$.

8.13 (Option Valuation in an Affine Term-Structure Model).   This problem shows how to calculate the prices of options on bonds in a setting with affine state dynamics. We start slightly differently than in Section 7I by beginning with the behavior of the state process X, not under an equivalent martingale measure Q, but rather under the originally given measure P, assuming that X solves a stochastic differential equation of the form

$$dX_t = [K_0^P + K_1^P X_t] \, dt + \sigma(X_t) \, dB_t, \qquad X_0 \in D \subset \mathbb{R}^k, \qquad (55)$$

where B is a standard Brownian motion in $\mathbb{R}^d$ under P, and σ satisfies (18). We assume additional conditions on the coefficients $K^P = (K_0^P, K_1^P)$ and $H = (H_{0ij}, H_{1ij})$ that ensure existence of a unique solution X to (55) in the state space D defined by (19). You may assume for simplicity that D contains an open set.

(A) The state-price deflator π for the given economy is assumed to be the process π defined by $\pi_t = \exp(X_t^{(1)})$, the exponential of the first coordinate of the state process $X = (X^{(1)}, \ldots, X^{(k)})^\top$. This implies that the short-rate process r is defined by $r_t = \rho_0 + \rho_1 \cdot X_t$ for some $\rho_0 \in \mathbb{R}$ and $\rho_1 \in \mathbb{R}^k$. Compute ρ_0 and ρ_1.

(B) The price at time t of a zero-coupon bond maturing at a given time $s \geq t$ is by definition of π given by $f(X_t, t, s) = E_t(\pi_s)/\pi_t$. Extending the ideas in Section 7I, conjecture the ordinary differential equation (ODE) solved by some $a : [0, s] \to \mathbb{R}$ and $b : [0, s] \to \mathbb{R}^k$ such that $f(x, t, s) = \exp[a(s - t) + b(s - t) \cdot x]$. Do not forget to provide boundary conditions. This sort of ordinary differential equation (which we shall see again below) is easy to solve numerically, provided a solution exists (which we assume). Perform a verification of your candidate solution for f under technical integrability conditions provided by you. Hint: If an Ito process is a martingale, its drift process must be zero.

(C) Suppose there are $n > 0$ such zero-coupon bonds available for trade, with maturity dates $T_1, T_2, \ldots, T_n$. Provide a spanning condition under which, in principle, an additional security with payoff at some time T given by a bounded $\mathcal{F}_T$-measurable random variable Z is redundant, given the opportunity to trade the n bonds and to borrow or lend continuously at the short rate r. Develop notation as you need it.

(D) We are now interested in pricing a zero-coupon bond option that provides the opportunity, but not the obligation, to *sell* at time τ for a given price $p > 0$ the zero-coupon bond maturing at a given time $s > \tau$ (paying one unit of account at maturity). The option is in the money at expiration if and only if $\exp[a(s - \tau) + b(s - \tau) \cdot X_\tau] \leq p$, which is the event A that $b(s - \tau) \cdot X_\tau \leq \log p - a(s - \tau)$. It can be seen under integrability conditions that the price of the option at time 0 is therefore of the form $c_1 Q_1(A) - c_2 Q_2(A)$, for some coefficients c_1 and c_2 and some probability measures Q_1 and Q_2 equivalent to P. Provide the integrability conditions, the Radon-Nikodym derivatives of Q_1 and Q_2 with respect to P, and the definitions of c_1 and c_2. Explain how to obtain these coefficients c_1 and c_2 from market data.

(E) For each $i \in \{1, 2\}$, the density process ξ_i of Q_i can be shown (under technical integrability conditions) to be of the form $\xi_i(t) = \exp[\alpha_i(t) + \beta_i(t) \cdot X_t]$, for α_i and β_i solving ordinary differential equations. Provide these ordinary differential equations, their boundary conditions, and technical integrability conditions justifying this solution.

(F) Under Q_i, for each $i \in \{1, 2\}$, provide a new stochastic differential equation for the state-vector process X driven by a standard Brownian motion $B^{Q(i)}$ in $\mathbb{R}^d$ under Q_i. Define $B^{Q(i)}$.

(G) By virtue of the previous steps, you have shown that the bond option price can be easily computed if one can compute any probability of the form $Q_i(\gamma \cdot X_T \leq y)$, for any $\gamma \in \mathbb{R}^d$ and any y. One can compute $P(Z \leq z)$, for a given random variable Z and number z, if one knows the characteristic function $\psi : \mathbb{R} \to \mathbb{R}$ of Z, defined by $\psi(u) = E[\exp(iuZ)]$, where $i = \sqrt{-1}$ is the usual imaginary number. Thus, option pricing in this setting can be reduced to the calculation of the characteristic function (sometimes called the Fourier transform—the Fourier transform and the characteristic function are identical up to a scalar multiple) of $Z = \gamma \cdot X_T$ under Q_1 and Q_2. Based on the results of Section F, we conjecture that, fixing u and d, and defining $\psi(X_t, t) = E_t[\exp(iud \cdot X_T)]$, we have

$$\psi(x, t) = \exp[\alpha(t) + \beta(t) \cdot x],$$

where α and β are complex-valued coefficient functions that solve ordinary differential equations (ODEs). Taking as given the time-dependent coeffcients $(K(t), H(t))$ for X appropriate to the probability measure at hand, your task is now to provide these ODEs for α and β, *with their boundary conditions*, and to confirm the conjecture under integrability conditions *provided by you* that will arise as you verify your solution with Ito's Formula. Hint: Remember that $\psi(x, t)$ is a complex number, and apply Ito's Formula to get the drift (both the real and imaginary parts). You will see a restriction on the drift that will give you the desired ODEs. Express the ODEs as tidily as possible. Note: In practice, at this point, you would compute the solutions of the differential equation for each u, separately (there are tricks that can speed this up), and from the resulting characteristic function, numerically compute the needed numbers c_1, c_2, $Q_1(A)$, and $Q_2(A)$.

Notes

General reviews of options, futures, or other derivative markets include those of Avellaneda and Laurence (2000), Cox and Rubinstein (1985), Daigler (1993), Duffie (1989), Hull (2000), Jarrow and Rudd (1983), Jarrow and Turnbull (1999), Lamberton and Lapeyre (1997), Musiela and Rutkowski (1997), Prisman (2000), Rubinstein (1999), Siegel and Siegel (1990), and Stoll and Whaley (1993). For computational issues, see Chapter 12, Tavella and Randall (2000), and Wilmott, Dewynne, and Howison (1993). Dixit and Pindyck (1993) is a thorough treatment, with references, of the modeling of real options, which arise in the theory of production planning and capital budgeting under uncertainty.

(B–D) The relationship between forwards and futures in Sections B, C, and D was developed by Cox, Ingersoll, and Ross (1981b). The derivation given here for the martingale property (8) of futures prices is original, although the formula itself is due to Cox, Ingersoll, and Ross (1981b), as is the subsequent replication strategy. For additional work in this vein, see Bick (1994), Dezhbakhsh (1994), Duffie and

Stanton (1988), and Myneni (1992b). An explicit Gaussian example is given by Jamshidian (1993b) and Jamshidian and Fein (1990). Grinblatt and Jegadeesh (1996) derived the futures prices for bonds in the setting of a Cox-Ingersoll-Ross model of the term structure. Carr (1989) provides option-valuation models for assets with stochastic dividends, in terms of the stochastic model for forward prices on the underlying asset.

Bick (1997), Carr (1993b), Carr and Chen (1993), and Hemler (1990) value the option to deliver various grades of the underlying asset against the futures contract, sometimes called the *cheapest-to-deliver option* or *quality option*, and the associated problem of determining the futures price. This problem is related to that of valuing compound options, and options on the maximum or minimum of several assets, which was solved (in the Black-Scholes setting) by Geske (1979), Johnson (1987), Margrabe (1978), Selby and Hodges (1987), and Stulz (1982). For the related wildcard option, see Fleming and Whaley (1994).

Black (1976) showed how to extend the Black-Scholes option-pricing formula to the case of futures options. See also Bick (1988).

On put-call parity and symmetry, see Carr (1993a). The forward and futures prices for bonds in the Cox-Ingersoll-Ross model, addressed in Exercise 8.8, are found in Grinblatt (1994). A related problem, examined by Carr (1989), is the valuation of options when carrying costs are unknown.

(E–F) Beckers (1981) developed and promoted the idea of using implied volatility as a measure of the market volatility implicit in options prices. A generalized version of implied volatility is discussed by Bick and Reisman (1993). Cherian and Jarrow (1998) explore a related "rationality" issue.

Derman and Kani (1994), Dupire (1994a, b), Jackwerth (1997, 2000), Jackwerth and Rubinstein (1996a, b, c), Rubinstein (1994, 1995) and Toft and Brown (1996) treat implied-tree models for option pricing, calibrating to a given family of smile curves or "risk-neutral" probability distributions. Andersen and Brotherton-Ratcliffe (1995) take an "implied finite-difference" approach to the analysis of smiles. A general calibration approach is pursued by Lagnado and Osher (1996).

Breeden and Litzenberger (1978) described how one can invert for the state-price deflator, in certain settings, from the prices of options at each exercise price. This topic is further pursued by Aït-Sahalia and Lo (1998, 2000), Rady (1995), Rosenberg and Engle (1999).

Option pricing with stochastic volatility was proposed as an answer to the "smile curve," and analyzed, by Hull and White (1987), Scott (1987, 1992), and Wiggins (1987), and since has been addressed by Amin (1993b), Amin and Ng (1993), Amin and Morton (1994b), Ball and Roma (1994), Barles, Romano, and Touzi (1993), Duan (1995), Heston (1993), Hofmann, Platen, and Schweizer (1992), Lu and Yu (1993), Madan and Chang (1996), Platen and Schweizer (1994), Renault, Pastorello, and Touzi (2000), Renault and Touzi (1992), and Touzi (1993, 1995).

Amin and Jarrow (1993) treat the problem of option valuation with stochastic interest rates, in a Heath-Jarrow-Morton setting. Melino and Turnbull (1990) illustrate an application to foreign-exchange option pricing. Heynen and Kat (1993) and Heynen, Kemna, and Vorst (1994) provide formulas for prediction of volatility in a Markovian setting. Nelson (1990, 1991, 1992) treat the convergence of ARCH, GARCH, and EGARCH models to stochastic-volatility models of the style considered in Section E, as well as related issues. Corradi (2000), however, shows that a more natural notion of convergence leaves a limiting volatility process defined by (13) that is degenerate. Bollerslev, Chou, and Kroner (1992) and Taylor (1994) survey applications in finance for ARCH and ARCH-related models, originated by Engle (1982). Heston and Nandi (1997) offered an option-pricing model in a GARCH setting. Harvey, Ruiz, and Shephard (1994), Harvey and Shephard (1993), and Lamoureux and Lastrapes (1993) present related econometric techniques and results. Hobson and Rogers (1993) describe a model for endogenous stochastic volatility, while Hobson and Rogers (1998) show how markets can be complete with stochastic volatility. This is further pursued by Romano and Touzi (1997), who also provide for monotonicty of option prices with respect to the stochastic-volatility state variable.

Proposition E can be deduced from results in Karatzas and Shreve (1988).

Based on early work by Clark (1973), Geman, Madan and Yor (1999), Ghysels, Gourieroux, and Jasiak (1995), Maghsoodi (1998), Redekop (1995), and Redekop and Fisher (1995) treat stochastic volatility through the effects of a random time change, sometimes called "market time." Bergman, Grundy, and Wiener (1996b), El Karoui, Jeanblanc, and Shreve (1998), Frey and Sin (1997), and Romano and Touzi (1997) characterize the dependence of the option price on the underlying price and on the coefficients of the model, including volatility. Some of these results give conditions for convexity of the option price with respect to the underlying asset, using the method of stochastic flows.

Attempts have also been made to extend the econometric modeling in a time-series setting to include observations on option prices in the data set used to estimate the parameters of the stochastic volatility process, as in Aït-Sahalia, Wang, and Yared (1998), Benzoni (1998), Chernov and Ghysels (2000), Guo (1998), Pan (1999), Poteshman (1998), and Renault and Touzi (1992). Exploiting options data improves the econometric efficiency of the estimation, given the one-to-one relationship between V_t and a given option price at time t. Other econometric approaches built around stochastic volatility include those of Pouque, Papanicolaou, and Sircar (1999a, b, c).

Figure 8.1 is reproduced from Duffie, Pan, and Singleton (2000). The options data used to plot this figure are from the home page of Professor Yacine Aït-Sahalia of Princeton University. The figure represents a total of 87 options with maturities (times to exercise date) ranging from 17 days to 318 days, and strike prices ranging from 0.74 to 1.17 times the underlying futures price.

The transform approach of Section F was originated by Stein and Stein (1991). The first explicit results along these lines were by Heston (1993). Transform results for general affine models of Duffie, Pan, and Singleton (2000) extend those of Bakshi, Cao, and Chen (1997), Bakshi and Madan (1997), Bates (1996), Bates (1997), and Scott (1997). Option pricing by fast Fourier transform is illustrated by Carr and Madan (1999).

Option pricing in a jump-diffusion setting was originated by Merton (1976), and more recently treated by Amin (1993a), Andersen and Andreasen (1999),

Ball and Torous (1985), Bates (1997), Carr and Madan (1999), Eberlein and Jacod (1997), Eberlein and Keller (1995), Eberlein, Keller, and Prause (1998), Jorion (1988), Kou (1999), Lando (1995), Madan and Milne (1991), Madan, Milne, and Shefrin (1989), Pappalardo (1996), Scott (1997), and Zhang (1994). Pan (1999), Barndorff-Nielsen (1997), and Eraker, Johannes, and Polson (1999) offer econometric evidence on jump behavior.

(G–H) McKean (1965), Merton (1973b), Harrison and Kreps (1979), and Bensoussan (1984) did important early work on American option pricing. Proposition G is from Karatzas (1988), although his technical conditions are slightly different. Karatzas defines the *fair price* of an American security, which turns out to be equal to the arbitrage-free price when both exist, and also extends Merton's analysis of *perpetual options*, those with no expiration. Jaillet, Lamberton, and Lapeyre (1988, 1990) review the treatment of the optimal-stopping valuation problem as a variational inequality, which can be written in the form (41). A decomposition of the American option in terms of an *early exercise premium* was proposed in a collection of papers by Jamshidian (1989c), Jacka (1991), Kim (1990), and Carr, Jarrow, and Myneni (1992), working from the formulation by McKean (1965) of the free-boundary problem, sometimes called a Stefan problem. Van Moerbeke (1976) was the first to demonstrate, among other results, that the optimal stopping boundary S^* is continuously differentiable. In this regard, see also Ait-Sahlia (1995). Jorgensen (1994) and Myneni (1992a) survey this and other literature on American put option pricing in the Black-Scholes setting.

Numerical or approximate solutions to the American option price or the optimal exercise boundary are given by Ait-Sahlia and Lai (1997a, b, 1998), Allegretto, Barles, Burdeau, Romano, and Samsoen (1995), Barone-Adesi, and Elliott (1993), Barone-Adesi and Elliott (1991), Broadie and Detemple (1996), Carr (1994), Carr and Faguet (1996), Geske and Johnson (1984), Huang, Subrahmanyam, Yu (1996), and Longstaff and Schwartz (1998). See, also, the Notes of Chapter 12. The behavior of the optimal exercise boundary near expiration is treated by Ait-Sahlia (1995), Barles, Burdeau, Romano, and Samsoen (1993), Lamberton (1993), and Charretour, Elliott, Myneni, and Viswanathan (1992). Buckdahn and Hu (1995), Gukhal (1995a, b), Pham (1995), and Zhang (1993) treat American options with jumps in the underlying. Additional general work on optimal stopping in the setting of American options is offered by Beibel and Lerche (1995, 1997) and Kusuoka (1996).

de Matos (1993) gives a simulated-method-of-moments estimation technique for American options. Yu (1993) provides additional results on American option valuation. Broadie and Detemple (1995, 1997) provide pricing for American capped call options, and for options on multiple assets. Haug (1999) treats American barrier options.

Kifer (2000), McConnell and Schwartz (1986), and Pikovsky and Shreve (1996b) analyze the valuation of securities for which both the buyer and the seller retain American options, such as callable convertible debt.

(I) The sell-at-the-max and buy-at-the-min lookback option valuation is from Goldman, Sosin, and Gatto (1979). The particular representation of the sell-at-the-max put formula is copied from Conze and Viswanathan (1991a). The distribution of the maximum of a Brownian motion path between two dates, and related results on the distribution of first passage times, can be found in Chuang (1994), Dassios (1994), Harrison (1985), and Ricciardi and Sato (1998). For other lookback option valuation results, see Conze and Viswanathan (1991a), Davydov and Linetsky (1999a, b), Duffie and Harrison (1993), Hobson (1998), Ju (1997b), and Shepp and Shiryaev (1993).

The Asian option, based on an arithmetic average of the underlying price process, is analyzed by Décamps and Koehl (1994), Geman and Yor (1993), Oliveira (1994), Rogers and Shi (1995), and Yor (1991). Akahari (1993) and Yor (1993) treat the related problem of median-price options. Bakshi and Madan (2000), He and Takahashi (1995), and Ju (1997a) consider average-rate options.

The hedging of Asian and lookback options is analyzed by Kat (1993). For hedging under leverage constraints, see Naik and Uppal (1994). For hedging with a "minimax" criterion, see Howe and Rustem (1994a, b).

Forms of *barrier options*, which are variously known as *knock-outs*, *knock-ins*, *down-and-outs*, *up-and-ins*, *limited-risk options*, and *lock-in options*, are covered by Carr (1995), Carr and Ellis (1994), Conze and Viswanathan (1991a), Haug (1999), Merton (1973b), Sbuelz (1998), and Yu (1993).

Nahum (1998) treats options dependent on a maximum over a discrete set of times.

Andersen, Andreasen, and Brotherton-Ratcliffe (1998) and Delbaen and Yor (1999) consider passport options.

For additional methods for the analysis of path-dependent options, see Kind, Lipster, and Runggaldier (1991), Zhou (1997a), and Zou and Derman (1996).

Chesney, Jeanblanc, and Yor (1997) and Schröder (1999a, b, c, d) use advanced transform methods to analyze path-dependent options, such as Asian, barrier, and "Parisian options," a form of barrier option. Jamshidian (1997a) provides methods for the valuation of double-barrier options.

Additional Topics: Term-structure models such as those applied in Chapter 7 have been applied to commodity option valuation by Grauer and Litzenberger (1979), Jamshidian (1991b, 1993b), Miltersen and Schwartz (1998), and in other sources cited in Chapter 7. Grabbe (1983) developed a foreign-exchange version of the Black-Scholes model. Nielsen and Saá-Requejo (1992) further treat foreign-exchange option valuation.

The hedging coefficients, "delta," "gamma," and so on, associated with derivative securities are studied by Carr (1991).

On option pricing with transactions costs and constraints, see Barles and Soner (1998), Bergman (1985a), Frey (1996), Ma and Cvitanić (1996), Subramanian (1997), and references cited in the Notes of Chapter 6. Johnson and Shanno (1987) and Rich (1993) deal with the impact of default risk on the Black-Scholes approach, a topic revisited in Chapter 11. Brennan and Schwartz (1980b) present a model for the valuation of convertible bonds.

The definition and pricing result for the market-timing option is from Ordentlich (1996). Gerber and Shiu (1994) describe a computational approach to option pricing based on the Escher transform. Heston (1997) considers option pricing with infinitely divisible distributions for the underlying.

Andersen (1995) considers bivariate binary options. Davydov and Linetsky (1998) and Linetsky (1999) treat step options and double-step options. Flesaker (1991) considers cases in which the underlying is unobservable at expiration.

Frey and Stremme (1997) consider feedback effects, allowing for hedging activity to influence the price of the option.

Based on early work by Jamshidian (1989b) for bond option pricing under the forward measure, Geman, El Karoui, and Rochet (1995) and Schroder (1999) treat changes of numeraire in the valuation of futures, forwards, and options.

9

Portfolio and Consumption Choice

THIS CHAPTER PRESENTS basic results on optimal portfolio and consumption choice, first using dynamic programming, then using general martingale and utility-gradient methods. We begin with a review of the Hamilton-Jacobi-Bellman equation for stochastic control, and then apply it to Merton's problem of optimal consumption and portfolio choice in finite- and infinite-horizon settings. Then, exploiting the properties of equivalent martingale measures from Chapter 6, Merton's problem is solved once again in a non-Markovian setting. Finally, we turn to the general utility-gradient approach from Chapter 2, and show that it coincides with the approach of equivalent martingale measures.

A. Stochastic Control

Dynamic programming in continuous time is often called *stochastic control* and uses the same basic ideas applied in the discrete-time setting of Chapter 3. The existence of well-behaved solutions in a continuous-time setting is a delicate matter, however, and we shall focus mainly on necessary conditions. This helps us to conjecture a solution that, if correct, can often be validated.

Given is a standard Brownian motion $B = (B^1, \ldots, B^d)$ in $\mathbb{R}^d$ on a probability space $(\Omega, \mathcal{F}, P)$. We fix the standard filtration $\mathbb{F} = \{\mathcal{F}_t : t \geq 0\}$ of B and begin with the time horizon $[0, T]$ for some finite $T > 0$. The primitive objects of a stochastic-control problem are

- a set $A \subset \mathbb{R}^m$ of *actions*, for some integer $m \geq 1$.
- a set $\mathcal{Y} \subset \mathbb{R}^K$ of *states*, for some integer $K \geq 1$.
- a set $\mathcal{C}$ of A-valued adapted processes, called *controls*.
- a *controlled drift function* $g : A \times \mathcal{Y} \to \mathbb{R}^K$.

- a *controlled diffusion function* $h : A \times \mathcal{Y} \to \mathbb{R}^{K \times d}$.
- a *running reward function* $f : A \times \mathcal{Y} \times [0, T] \to \mathbb{R}$.
- a *terminal reward function* $F : \mathcal{Y} \to \mathbb{R}$.

The state space $\mathcal{Y}$ is not to be confused with the underlying set Ω of "states of the world." A control c in $\mathscr{C}$ is *admissible* given an initial state y in $\mathcal{Y}$ if there is a unique Ito process Y^c valued in $\mathcal{Y}$ with

$$dY_t^c = g(c_t, Y_t^c)\, dt + h(c_t, Y_t^c)\, dB_t; \qquad Y_0^c = y. \tag{1}$$

For admissibility, technical conditions are required of c, g, and h.

Let $\mathscr{C}_a(y)$ denote the set of admissible controls given initial state y. We assume that the primitives $(A, \mathcal{Y}, \mathscr{C}, g, h, f, F)$ are such that, given any initial state $y \in \mathcal{Y}$, the utility of any admissible control c is well defined as

$$V^c(y) = E\left[\int_0^T f(c_t, Y_t^c, t)\, dt + F(Y_T^c)\right],$$

which we allow to take the values $-\infty$ or $+\infty$. The *value* of an initial state y in $\mathcal{Y}$ is then

$$V(y) = \sup_{c \in \mathscr{C}_a(y)} V^c(y), \tag{2}$$

with $V(y) = -\infty$ if there is no admissible control given initial state y. If $V^c(y) = V(y)$, then c is an *optimal control* at y. (One may note that this formulation allows for the possibility that an optimal control achieves infinite utility.)

One usually proceeds by conjecturing that $V(y) = J(y, 0)$ for some J in $C^{2,1}(\mathcal{Y} \times [0, T))$ that solves the Bellman equation:

$$\sup_{a \in A} \{\mathscr{D}^a J(y, t) + f(a, y, t)\} = 0, \qquad (y, t) \in \mathcal{Y} \times [0, T), \tag{3}$$

where

$$\mathscr{D}^a J(y, t) = J_y(y, t) g(a, y) + J_t(y, t) + \frac{1}{2} \mathrm{tr}[h(a, y) h(a, y)^\top J_{yy}(y, t)],$$

with the boundary condition

$$J(y, T) = F(y), \qquad y \in \mathcal{Y}. \tag{4}$$

An intuitive justification of (3) is obtained from an analogous discrete-time, discrete-state, discrete-action setting, in which the Bellman equation would be something like

$$J(y, t) = \max_{a \in A} \{f(a, y, t) + E[J(Y_{t+1}^c, t + 1) \mid Y_t^c = y, c_t = a]\},$$

where $f(a, y, t)$ is the running reward per unit of time. (The reader is invited to apply imagination liberally here. A complete development and rigorous justification of this analogy goes well beyond the goal of illustrating the idea. Sources that give such a justification are cited in the Notes.) For any given control process c, this discrete-time Bellman equation of Chapter 3 implies that

$$E_t\big[J(Y_{t+1}^c, t+1) - J(Y_t^c, t)\big] + f(c_t, Y_t^c, t) \le 0,$$

which, for a model with intervals of length Δt, may be rewritten

$$E_t\big[J(Y_{t+\Delta t}^c, t+\Delta t) - J(Y_t^c, t)\big] + f(c_t, Y_t^c, t)\Delta t \le 0.$$

Now, returning to the continuous-time setting, dividing the last equation by Δt, and taking limits as $\Delta t \to 0$ leaves, under technical conditions described in Chapter 5,

$$\frac{d}{ds} E_t\big[J(Y_s^c, s)\big]\Big|_{s=t+} + f(c_t, Y_t^c, t) = \mathscr{D}^{c(t)} J(Y_t^c, t) + f(c_t, Y_t^c, t) \le 0,$$

with equality if c_t attains the supremum in the discrete version of the Bellman equation. This leads, again only by this incomplete heuristic argument, to the Bellman equation (3).

The continuous-time Bellman equation (3) is often called the *Hamilton-Jacobi-Bellman (HJB)* equation. One may think of $J(y, t)$ as the optimal utility remaining at time t in state y. Given a solution J to (3)–(4), suppose that a measurable function $C : \mathcal{Y} \times [0, T] \to A$ is defined so that, for each (y, t), the action $C(y, t)$ solves (3). The intuitive idea is that if the time is t and the state is y, then the optimal action is $C(y, t)$. In order to verify the optimality of choosing actions in this manner for the original problem (2), we turn this feedback form of control policy function C into a control in the sense of problem (2), that is, a process in the set $\mathcal{C}$. For this, suppose that there is a $\mathcal{Y}$-valued solution Y^* to the stochastic differential equation (SDE)

$$dY_t^* = g\big[C(Y_t^*, t), Y_t^*\big] dt + h\big[C(Y_t^*, t), Y_t^*\big] dB_t; \qquad Y_0^* = y.$$

Conditions on the primitives of the problem sufficient for the existence of a unique solution Y^* to this SDE are often difficult to formulate because C depends on J, which is not usually an explicit function. Sources indicated in the Notes address this existence issue. Given Y^*, we can conjecture that an optimal control c^* is given by $c_t^* = C(Y_t^*, t)$, and attempt to verify this conjecture as follows. Let $c \in \mathscr{C}_a(y)$ be an arbitrary admissible control. We want to show that $V^{c^*}(y) \geq V^c(y)$. By (3),

$$\mathscr{D}^{c(t)} J(Y_t^c, t) + f(c_t, Y_t^c, t) \leq 0, \qquad t \in [0, T]. \qquad (5)$$

By Ito's Formula,

$$J(Y_T^c, T) = J(y, 0) + \int_0^T \mathscr{D}^{c(t)} J(Y_t^c, t) \, dt + \int_0^T \beta_t \, dB_t, \qquad (6)$$

where $\beta_t = J_y(Y_t^c, t)h(c_t, Y_t^c)$. Supposing that the local martingale $\int \beta \, dB$ is in fact a martingale (which is usually verified on a problem-by-problem basis or circumvented by special tricks), we know that $E(\int_0^T \beta_t \, dB_t) = 0$. We could then take the expectation of each side of (6) and use the boundary condition (4) and inequality (5) to see that

$$V^c(y) = E\left[\int_0^T f(c_t, Y_t^c, t) \, dt + F(Y_T^c)\right] \leq J(y, 0). \qquad (7)$$

The same calculation would apply with $c = c^*$, except that the inequalities in (5) and (7) may be replaced with equalities, implying that

$$J(y, 0) = V^{c^*}(y). \qquad (8)$$

Then (7) and (8) would imply that $V(y) = J(y, 0)$, and that c^* is indeed optimal.

This is only a sketch of the general approach, with several assumptions made along the way. These assumptions can be replaced by strong technical regularity conditions on the primitives $(A, \mathscr{Y}, \mathscr{C}, g, h, f, F)$, but the known general conditions are too restrictive for most applications in finance. Instead, one typically uses the Bellman equation (3)–(4) as a means of guessing an explicit solution that, if correct, can often be validated by some variation of the above procedure. In some cases, the Bellman equation can also be used as the basis for a finite-difference numerical solution, as indicated in sources cited in the Notes of Chapter 12.

B. Merton's Problem

We now apply the stochastic-control approach to the solution of a "classic" optimal-consumption and investment problem in continuous time.

Suppose $X = (X^{(0)}, X^{(1)}, \ldots, X^{(N)})$ is an Ito process in $\mathbb{R}^{N+1}$ for the prices of $N + 1$ securities. For each $i \geq 1$, we assume that

$$dX_t^{(i)} = \mu_i X_t^{(i)} \, dt + X_t^{(i)} \sigma^{(i)} \, dB_t, \qquad X_0^{(i)} > 0, \tag{9}$$

where σ^i is the i-th row of a matrix σ in $\mathbb{R}^{N \times d}$ with linearly independent rows, and where μ_i is a constant. This implies, in particular, that each process $X^{(i)}$ is a geometric Brownian motion of the sort used in the Black-Scholes model of option pricing. We suppose that $\sigma^{(0)} = 0$, so that $r = \mu_0$ is the short rate.

Utility is defined over the space D of *consumption* pairs (c, Z), where c is an adapted nonnegative consumption-rate process with $\int_0^T c_t \, dt < \infty$ almost surely and Z is an $\mathcal{F}_T$-measurable nonnegative random variable describing terminal lump-sum consumption. Specifically, $U : D \to \mathbb{R}$ is defined by

$$U(c, Z) = E\left[\int_0^T u(c_t, t) \, dt + F(Z) \right], \tag{10}$$

where

- $F : \mathbb{R}_+ \to \mathbb{R}$ is increasing and concave with $F(0) = 0$;
- $u : \mathbb{R}_+ \times [0, T] \to \mathbb{R}$ is continuous and, for each t in $[0, T]$, $u(\cdot, t) :$ $\mathbb{R}_+ \to \mathbb{R}$ is increasing and concave, with $u(0, t) = 0$;
- F is strictly concave or zero, or for each t in $[0, T]$, $u(\cdot, t)$ is strictly concave or zero;
- at least one of u and F is nonzero.

A trading strategy is a process $\theta = (\theta^{(0)}, \ldots, \theta^{(N)})$ in $\mathcal{L}(X)$. (As defined in Chapter 5, this means merely that the stochastic integral $\int \theta \, dX$ exists.) Given an initial wealth $w > 0$, we say that (c, Z, θ) is *budget-feasible*, denoted $(c, Z, \theta) \in \Lambda(w)$, if (c, Z) is a consumption choice in D and $\theta \in \mathcal{L}(X)$ is a trading strategy satisfying

$$\theta_t \cdot X_t = w + \int_0^t \theta_s \, dX_s - \int_0^t c_s \, ds \geq 0, \qquad t \in [0, T], \tag{11}$$

and

$$\theta_T \cdot X_T \geq Z. \tag{12}$$

The first restriction (11) is that the current market value $\theta_t \cdot X_t$ of the trading strategy is nonnegative and equal to its initial value w, plus any gains from security trade, less the cumulative consumption to date. The non-negative wealth restriction can be viewed as a credit constraint, as in

Section 6C. The second restriction (12) is that the terminal portfolio value is sufficient to cover the terminal consumption. We now have the problem, for each initial wealth w,

$$\sup_{(c,Z,\theta)\in\Lambda(w)} U(c, Z). \qquad (13)$$

In order to convert this problem statement (13) into one that is more easily addressed within the stochastic-control formulation set up in Section A, we represent trading strategies in terms of the fractions $\varphi^{(1)}, \ldots, \varphi^{(N)}$ of total wealth held in the "risky" securities, those with price processes $X^{(1)}, \ldots, X^{(N)}$, respectively. Because wealth is restricted to be nonnegative, this involves no loss of generality. That is, for a given trading strategy θ in the original sense, we can let

$$\varphi_t^{(n)} = \frac{\theta_t^{(n)} X_t^{(n)}}{\theta_t \cdot X_t}, \qquad \theta_t \cdot X_t \neq 0, \qquad (14)$$

with $\varphi_t^{(n)} = 0$ if $\theta_t \cdot X_t = 0$.

Problem (13) is converted into a standard control problem of the variety in Section A by first defining a state process. Using portfolio fractions to define trading strategies allows one to leave the security-price process X out of the definition of the state process for the control problem. Instead, we can define a one-dimensional state process W for the investor's total wealth. As a notational convenience, we let $\lambda \in \mathbb{R}^N$ denote the vector in $\mathbb{R}^N$ with $\lambda_i = \mu_i - r$, the "excess expected rate of return" on security i. Given a consumption process c and an adapted process $\varphi = (\varphi^{(1)}, \ldots, \varphi^{(N)})$ defining fractions of total wealth held in the risky securities, we can pose the question of existence of a nonnegative Ito process for wealth W satisfying

$$dW_t = [W_t(\varphi_t \cdot \lambda + r) - c_t]\, dt + W_t \varphi_t^\top \sigma\, dB_t; \qquad W_0 = w. \qquad (15)$$

One may notice that in order for W to remain nonnegative, an admissible control (c, φ) has the property that $\varphi_t = 0$ and $W_t = c_t = 0$ for t larger than the stopping time $\inf\{s : W_s = 0\}$. Thus nonzero investment and consumption are ruled out once there is no remaining wealth.

The control problem associated with (13) is thus fixed by defining the primitives $(A, \mathcal{Y}, \mathcal{C}, g, h, f, F)$ as follows:

- $A = \mathbb{R}_+ \times \mathbb{R}^N$, with typical element $(\bar{c}, \bar{\varphi})$ representing the current consumption rate $\bar{c}$ and the fractions $\bar{\varphi}_1, \ldots, \bar{\varphi}_N$ of current wealth invested in the risky securities.

- $\mathscr{Y} = \mathbb{R}_+$, with typical element w representing current wealth.
- $\mathscr{C}$ is the set of adapted processes (c, φ) valued in $\mathbb{R}_+$ and $\mathbb{R}^N$, respectively, with $\int_0^T c_t \, dt < \infty$ almost surely and $\int_0^T \varphi_t \cdot \varphi_t \, dt < \infty$ almost surely.
- $g[(\bar{c}, \bar{\varphi}), w] = w\bar{\varphi} \cdot \lambda + rw - \bar{c}.$
- $h[(\bar{c}, \bar{\varphi}), w] = w\bar{\varphi}^\top \sigma.$
- $f[(\bar{c}, \bar{\varphi}), w, t] = u(\bar{c}, t)$, where u is as specified by (10).
- $F(w)$ is as specified by (10).

An admissible control given initial wealth w is a control (c, φ) in $\mathscr{C}$ for which there is a unique nonnegative Ito process W satisfying (15).

The control problem $(A, \mathscr{Y}, \mathscr{C}, g, h, f, F)$ is equivalent to the original problem (13), with the small exception that the control formulation forces the investor to consume all terminal wealth, whereas the original budget constraint (12) allows the investor to leave some terminal wealth unconsumed. Because the terminal utility function F is increasing, however, this distinction is not important. Indeed, one can see that (c, Z, θ) is in $\Lambda(w)$ if and only if the wealth process $\{W_t = \theta_t \cdot X_t : t \in [0, T]\}$ is nonnegative, satisfies (15), and $W_T \geq Z$, where φ is defined from θ by (14).

C. Solution to Merton's Problem

The Bellman equation (3) for Merton's problem, at a current level $w > 0$ of wealth, is

$$\sup_{(\bar{c}, \bar{\varphi}) \in A} \left\{ \mathscr{D}^{\bar{c}, \bar{\varphi}} J(w, t) + u(\bar{c}, t) \right\} = 0, \tag{16}$$

where

$$\mathscr{D}^{\bar{c}, \bar{\varphi}} J(w, t) = J_w(w, t)(w\bar{\varphi} \cdot \lambda + rw - \bar{c}) + J_t(w, t) + \frac{w^2}{2} \bar{\varphi}^\top \sigma \sigma^\top \bar{\varphi} J_{ww}(w, t),$$

with the boundary condition

$$J(w, T) = F(w), \qquad w \geq 0. \tag{17}$$

For any t, one may think of $J(\cdot, t)$ as the investor's *indirect utility function for wealth* at time t. We note that

$$J(0, t) = \int_t^T u(0, s) \, ds + F(0), \qquad t \in [0, T], \tag{18}$$

from our remark regarding the nonnegativity of solutions to (16).

If, for each t, $u(\cdot, t)$ is strictly concave and twice continuously differentiable on $(0, \infty)$, then the first-order condition for interior optimal choice of $\bar{c}$ in (16) implies that $\bar{c} = C(w, t)$, where

$$C(w, t) = I[J_w(w, t), t],$$

and where $I(\cdot, t)$ inverts $u_c(\cdot, t)$, meaning that $I[u_c(x, t), t] = x$ for all x and t. We let $I = 0$ if $u = 0$. Assuming that the indirect utility function $J(\cdot, t)$ for wealth is strictly concave, the first-order condition for optimal choice of $\bar{\varphi}$ in (16) implies that $\bar{\varphi} = \Phi(w, t)$, where

$$\Phi(w, t) = \frac{-J_w(w, t)}{w J_{ww}(w, t)} (\sigma \sigma^\top)^{-1} \lambda. \qquad (19)$$

We remark that the optimal portfolio fractions are given by a fixed vector $\tilde{\varphi} = (\sigma \sigma^\top)^{-1} \lambda$ of portfolio weights multiplied by the Arrow-Pratt measure of relative risk tolerance (reciprocal of relative risk aversion) of the indirect utility function $J(\cdot, t)$. This means effectively that, in this setting of time-homogeneous Gaussian returns and additive utility, it is enough for purposes of optimal portfolio choice for any investor to replace all risky investments with investments in a single "mutual fund," a security that invests in the given risky securities, trading among them so as to maintain the given proportions $\tilde{\varphi}$ of total asset value in each. Every investor would be content to invest in only this mutual fund and in riskless borrowing and lending, although different investors would have different fractions of wealth in the mutual fund, depending on the risk aversion of their indirect utility for wealth. This would not necessarily be consistent with market clearing, and therefore with equilibrium.

We focus for now on the special case of $u = 0$ and $F(w) = w^\alpha / \alpha$ for some coefficient $\alpha \in (0, 1)$. The associated *relative risk aversion* is $1 - \alpha$. This is an example of a utility function that is often called *hyperbolic absolute risk averse (HARA)*. Because we take $u = 0$ and F strictly increasing, any optimal intermediate consumption choice c^* must be zero. An explicit value function J for this HARA utility example is conjectured as follows. Suppose Z is the optimal terminal consumption for initial wealth level 1. Now consider a new level w of initial wealth, for some fixed $w \in (0, \infty)$. One may see that wZ must be the associated optimal terminal consumption. Certainly, wZ can be obtained in a budget-feasible manner, for if $Z = \theta_T \cdot X_T$ can be obtained from initial wealth 1 with a trading strategy θ, then, given the linearity of stochastic integrals, $w\theta$ is a budget-feasible strategy for initial wealth w, and we have $w\theta_T \cdot X_T = wZ$. If there were some alternative terminal consumption $\hat{Z}$ that is budget-feasible with initial wealth w and with the higher utility

$$E\left(\frac{\hat{Z}^\alpha}{\alpha}\right) > E\left[\frac{(wZ)^\alpha}{\alpha}\right], \tag{20}$$

then we would have a contradiction, as follows. First, dividing (20) through by w^α/α leaves

$$E\left[\left(\frac{\hat{Z}}{w}\right)^\alpha\right] > E(Z^\alpha). \tag{21}$$

By the above reasoning, $\hat{Z}/w$ can be financed with initial wealth 1, but then (21) contradicts the optimality of Z for initial wealth 1. Thus, as asserted, for any initial level of wealth w, the optimal terminal consumption is wZ. It follows that

$$J(w, 0) = E\left[\frac{(wZ)^\alpha}{\alpha}\right] = \frac{w^\alpha}{\alpha}K,$$

where $K = E(Z^\alpha)$. Up to a constant K, which depends on all of the basic parameters $(\lambda, r, \sigma, \alpha, T)$ of the model, we have a reasonable conjecture for the initial indirect utility function $J(\cdot, 0)$. For $t \in (0, T)$, the optimal remaining utility can be conjectured in exactly the above manner, treating the problem as one with a time horizon of $T - t$ rather than T. We therefore conjecture that $J(w, t) = k(t)w^\alpha/\alpha$ for some function $k : [0, T] \to \mathbb{R}$. In order for J to be sufficiently differentiable for an application of Ito's Formula, we conjecture that k is itself continuously differentiable.

   With this conjecture for J in hand, we can solve (19) to get, for all (w, t),

$$\Phi(w, t) = \frac{(\sigma\sigma^\top)^{-1}\lambda}{1 - \alpha}, \tag{22}$$

or fixed portfolio fractions. The total fraction of wealth invested in risky assets is therefore decreasing in the relative risk aversion $1 - \alpha$. Because $u = 0$, we have

$$C(w, t) = 0. \tag{23}$$

We can substitute (22)–(23) into the Bellman equation (16), using our conjecture $J(w, t) = k(t)w^\alpha/\alpha$ to obtain the ordinary differential equation

$$k'(t) = -\epsilon k(t), \tag{24}$$

where

$$\epsilon = \frac{\alpha \lambda^\top (\sigma \sigma^\top)^{-1} \lambda}{2(1-\alpha)} + r\alpha, \tag{25}$$

with the boundary condition from (17):

$$k(T) = 1. \tag{26}$$

Solving (24)–(26), we have

$$k(t) = e^{\epsilon(T-t)}, \qquad t \in [0, T].$$

We have found that the function J defined by $J(w, t) = e^{\epsilon(T-t)} w^\alpha / \alpha$ solves the Bellman equation (16) and the boundary condition (17), so J is therefore a logical candidate for the value function.

We now verify this candidate for the value function, and also that the conjectured optimal control (c^*, φ^*), which is given by $c_t^* = 0$ and $\varphi_t^* = (\sigma \sigma^\top)^{-1} \lambda / (1 - \alpha)$, is indeed optimal. Let (c, φ) be an arbitrary admissible control for initial wealth w, and let W be the associated wealth process solving (15). From the Bellman equation (16), Ito's Formula, and the boundary condition (17), we have

$$J(w, 0) + \int_0^T \beta_t \, dB_t \geq F(W_T), \tag{27}$$

where $\beta_t = J_w(W_t, t) W_t \varphi_t^\top \sigma$. Because J is nonnegative, the Bellman equation (16) and Ito's Formula also imply that a nonnegative process M is defined by $M_t = J(w, 0) + \int_0^t \beta_s \, dB_s$. We also know that M is a local martingale (as defined in Appendix D). A nonnegative local martingale is a supermartingale (a fact also stipulated in Appendix D). By taking expectations of each side of (27), this implies that for an arbitrary admissible control, $J(w, 0) \geq E[F(W_T)]$.

It remains to show that for the candidate optimal control (c^*, φ^*), with associated wealth process W^*, we have $J(w, 0) = E[F(W_T^*)]$, verifying optimality. For the candidate optimal control (c^*, φ^*), the Bellman equation and the same calculations leave us with

$$J(w, 0) + \int_0^T \beta_t^* \, dB_t = F(W_T^*), \tag{28}$$

where $\beta_t^* = J_w(W_t^*, t) W_t^* \lambda^\top (\sigma \sigma^\top)^{-1} \sigma / (1 - \alpha)$. An equality appears in place of the inequality in (27) because the proposed optimal control achieves the supremum in the Bellman equation. Because $J_w(W_t^*, t) \times W_t^* = e^{\epsilon(T-t)} (W_t^*)^\alpha$, it can be seen as an exercise that $E(\int_0^T \beta_t^* \cdot \beta_t^* \, dt) < \infty$, implying by Proposition 5B that $\int \beta^* \, dB$ is a martingale. Taking expectations through (28) then leaves $J(w, 0) = E[F(W_T^*)]$, verifying the optimality of (c^*, φ^*) and confirming that the problem has optimal initial utility $J(w, 0) = e^{\epsilon T} w^\alpha / \alpha$.

D. The Infinite-Horizon Case

The primitives $(A, \mathcal{Y}, \mathcal{C}, g, h, f)$ of an infinite-horizon control problem are just as described in Section A, dropping the terminal reward F. The running reward function $f : A \times \mathcal{Y} \times [0, \infty) \to \mathbb{R}$ is usually defined, given a *discount rate* $\rho \in (0, \infty)$, by $f(a, y, t) = e^{-\rho t} v(a, y)$, for some $v : A \times \mathcal{Y} \to \mathbb{R}$. Given an initial state y in $\mathcal{Y}$, the value of an admissible control c in $\mathcal{C}$ is

$$V^c(y) = E\left[\int_0^\infty e^{-\rho t} v(c_t, Y_t^c) \, dt\right], \tag{29}$$

assuming that the expectation exists, where Y^c is given by (1). The supremum value $V(y)$ is as defined by (2). The finite-horizon Bellman equation (3) is replaced with

$$\sup_{a \in A}\{\mathscr{D}^a J(y) - \rho J(y) + v(a, y)\} = 0, \qquad y \in \mathcal{Y}, \tag{30}$$

for J in $C^2(\mathcal{Y})$, where

$$\mathscr{D}^a J(y) = J_y(y) g(a, y) + \frac{1}{2} \, \text{tr}\big[h(a, y) h(a, y)^\top J_{yy}(y)\big].$$

Rather than the boundary condition (4), one can add technical conditions yielding the so-called *transversality condition*

$$\lim_{T \to \infty} E\big(e^{-\rho T} |J(Y_T^c)|\big) = 0, \tag{31}$$

for any given initial state $Y_0^c = y$ in $\mathcal{Y}$ and any admissible control c. With this, the same arguments and technical assumptions applied in Section A imply that a solution J to the Bellman equation (30) defines the value $J(y) = V(y)$ of the problem. The essential difference is the replacement of (7) with

$$J(y) \geq E\left[\int_0^T e^{-\rho t} v(c_t, Y_t^c) \, dt + e^{-\rho T} J(Y_T^c)\right], \qquad T > 0,$$

from which $J(y) \geq V^c(y)$ for an arbitrary admissible control c by taking the limit of the right-hand side as $T \to \infty$, using (31). Similarly, a candidate optimal control is defined in feedback form by a function $C : \mathcal{Y} \to A$

with the property that for each y, the action $C(y)$ solves the Bellman equation (30). Once again, technical conditions on the primitives guarantee the existence of an optimal control, but such conditions are often too restrictive in practice, and the Bellman equation is frequently used more as an aid in conjecturing a solution.

In Merton's problem, for example, with $v(\bar{c}, w) = \bar{c}^\alpha/\alpha$, $\alpha \in (0, 1)$, it is natural to conjecture that $J(w) = Kw^\alpha/\alpha$ for some constant K. With some calculations, the Bellman equation (30) for this candidate value function J leads to $K = \gamma^{\alpha-1}$, where

$$\gamma = \frac{\rho - r\alpha}{1 - \alpha} - \frac{\alpha\lambda^\top(\sigma\sigma^\top)^{-1}\lambda}{2(1-\alpha)^2}. \tag{32}$$

The associated consumption-portfolio policy (c^*, φ^*) is given by $\varphi_t^* = (\sigma\sigma^\top)^{-1}\lambda/(1 - \alpha)$ and $c_t^* = \gamma W_t^*$, where W^* is the wealth process generated by (c^*, φ^*). In order to confirm the optimality of this policy, the transversality condition (31) must be checked, and is satisfied provided $\gamma > 0$. This verification is left as an exercise.

E. The Martingale Formulation

The objective now is to use the martingale results of Chapter 6 as the basis of a new method for solving Merton's problem (13). First, we state an extension of numeraire invariance (Lemma 6L).

Lemma. Let Y be any deflator. Given an initial wealth $w \geq 0$, a strategy (c, Z, θ) is budget-feasible given price process X if and only if

$$\theta_t \cdot X_t^Y = wY_0 + \int_0^t \theta_s \, dX_s^Y - \int_0^t Y_s c_s \, ds \geq 0, \qquad t \in [0, T], \tag{33}$$

and

$$\theta_T \cdot X_T^Y \geq ZY_T. \tag{34}$$

For simplicity, we suppose that $N = d$. By Girsanov's Theorem (Appendix D), there is an equivalent martingale measure Q for the deflated price process $\hat{X}$, defined by $\hat{X}_t = e^{-rt}X_t$, and Q is defined by the density process ξ, in that

$$E_t^Q(Z) = \frac{1}{\xi_t} E_t^P(Z\xi_T), \tag{35}$$

for any random variable Z with $E^Q(|Z|) < \infty$, where

$$\xi_t = \exp\left(-\eta^\top B_t - \frac{t}{2}\eta^\top \eta\right), \qquad t \in [0, T], \tag{36}$$

and where η is the market price of risk for $\hat{X}$ defined by

$$\eta = \sigma^{-1}\lambda. \tag{37}$$

(The invertibility of σ is implied by our earlier assumption that the rows of σ are linearly independent. The fact that ξ satisfies the Novikov condition and that $\text{var}(\xi_T) < \infty$, as demanded by the definition of an equivalent martingale measure, are easily shown as an exercise.) As shown in Proposition 6F, the associated state-price deflator π is defined by $\pi_t = \xi_t e^{-rt}$.

Proposition. *Given a consumption choice (c, Z) in D and some initial wealth w, there exists a trading strategy θ such that (c, Z, θ) is budget-feasible if and only if*

$$E\left(\pi_T Z + \int_0^T \pi_t c_t \, dt\right) \leq w. \tag{38}$$

Proof: Suppose (c, Z, θ) is budget-feasible. Applying the previous numeraire invariance lemma to the state-price deflator π, and using the fact that $\pi_0 = \xi_0 = 1$, we have

$$w + \int_0^T \theta_t dX_t^\pi \geq \pi_T Z + \int_0^T \pi_t c_t \, dt. \tag{39}$$

Because X^π is a martingale under P, the process M, defined by $M_t = w + \int_0^t \theta_s \, dX_s^\pi$, is a local martingale under P. Moreover, by (33), M is nonnegative, and therefore a supermartingale (Appendix D). Taking expectations through (39) leaves (38).

Conversely, suppose (c, Z) satisfies (38), and let M be the Q-martingale defined by

$$M_t = E_t^Q\left(e^{-rT}Z + \int_0^T e^{-rt}c_t \, dt\right), \qquad t \in [0, T].$$

By Girsanov's Theorem (Appendix D), a standard Brownian motion B^Q in $\mathbb{R}^d$ under Q is defined by $B_t^Q = B_t + \eta t$, and B^Q has the martingale representation property. We thus know there is some $\varphi = (\varphi^{(1)}, \ldots, \varphi^{(d)})$ with components in $\mathscr{L}^2$ such that

$$M_t = M_0 + \int_0^t \varphi_s \, dB_s^Q, \qquad t \in [0, T],$$

where $M_0 \leq w$. For the deflator Y defined by $Y_t = e^{-rt}$, we also know that $\hat{X} = X^Y$ is a Q-martingale. From the definitions of the market price of risk η and of B^Q,

$$d\hat{X}_t^{(i)} = \hat{X}_t^{(i)}\sigma^{(i)} \, dB_t^Q, \qquad 1 \leq i \leq N.$$

Because σ is invertible and $\hat{X}$ is strictly positive with continuous sample paths, we can choose adapted processes $(\theta^{(1)}, \ldots, \theta^{(N)})$ such that

$$(\theta_t^{(1)}\hat{X}_t^{(1)}, \ldots, \theta_t^{(N)}\hat{X}_t^{(N)})\sigma = \varphi_t^\top, \qquad t \in [0, T].$$

This implies that

$$M_t = M_0 + \sum_{i=1}^{N} \int_0^t \theta_s^{(i)} \, d\hat{X}_s^{(i)}.$$

We can also let

$$\theta_t^{(0)} = w + \sum_{i=1}^{N} \int_0^t \theta_s^{(i)} d\hat{X}_s^{(i)} - \sum_{i=1}^{N} \theta_t^{(i)} \hat{X}_t^{(i)} - \int_0^t e^{-rs}c_s \, ds. \qquad (40)$$

Because φ has components in $\mathcal{L}^2$, we know that $\theta = (\theta^{(0)}, \ldots, \theta^{(N)})$ is in $\mathcal{L}(\hat{X})$. From (38), Fubini's Theorem, and the fact that $\xi_t = \pi_t e^{rt}$ defines the density process for Q, we have

$$M_0 = E^Q\left(e^{-rT}Z + \int_0^T e^{-rt}c_t \, dt\right) \leq w. \qquad (41)$$

From (40), for any $t \leq T$,

$$\theta_t \cdot \hat{X}_t = w + \int_0^t \theta_s d\hat{X}_s - \int_0^t e^{-rs}c_s \, ds$$

$$= w + M_t - M_0 - \int_0^t e^{-rs}c_s \, ds$$

$$= w - M_0 + E_t^Q\left(\int_t^T e^{-rs}c_s \, ds + e^{-rT}Z\right) \geq 0,$$

using from (41) the fact that $w \geq M_0$. Restating this inequality in terms of the deflator, $Y_t = e^{-rt}$, we have (33). We can also use the same inequality for $t = T$ and the fact that $E_T^Q(e^{-rT}Z) = e^{-rT}Z$ to obtain (34). Thus, by numeraire invariance in the form of Lemma E, (c, Z, θ) is budget-feasible. ∎

Corollary. *Given a consumption choice (c^*, Z^*) in D and some initial wealth w, there exists a trading strategy θ^* such that (c^*, Z^*, θ^*) solves Merton's problem (13) if and only if (c^*, Z^*) solves the problem*

$$\sup_{(c, Z) \in D} U(c, Z) \quad \text{subject to } E\left(\int_0^T \pi_t c_t \, dt + \pi_T Z\right) \leq w. \tag{42}$$

F. Martingale Solution

We are now in a position to obtain a relatively explicit solution to Merton's problem (13) in the form of the equivalent formulation (42).

By the Saddle Point Theorem (which can be found in Appendix B) and the strict monotonicity of u or F, (c^*, Z^*) solves (42) if and only if there is a scalar Lagrange multiplier $\gamma^* > 0$ such that, *first*, (c^*, Z^*) solves the unconstrained problem

$$\sup_{(c, Z) \in D} \mathcal{L}(c, Z; \gamma^*), \tag{43}$$

where, for any $\gamma \geq 0$,

$$\mathcal{L}(c, Z; \gamma) = U(c, Z) - \gamma E\left(\pi_T Z + \int_0^T \pi_t c_t \, dt - w\right), \tag{44}$$

and *second*, the complementary-slackness condition,

$$E\left(\pi_T Z^* + \int_0^T \pi_t c_t^* \, dt\right) = w, \tag{45}$$

is satisfied. Applying Corollary E, we can thus summarize our progress on Merton's problem (13) as follows.

Proposition. *Given some (c^*, Z^*) in D, there is a trading strategy θ^* such that (c^*, Z^*, θ^*) solves Merton's problem (13) if and only if there is a constant $\gamma^* > 0$ such that (c^*, Z^*) solves (43), and $E(\pi_T Z^* + \int_0^T \pi_t c_t^* \, dt) = w$.*

In order to obtain intuition for the solution of (43), we begin with some arbitrary $\gamma > 0$ and treat $U(c, Z) = E[\int_0^T u(c_t, t) \, dt + F(Z)]$ intuitively by thinking of "E" and "$\int$" as finite sums, in which case the first-order conditions for optimality of $(c^*, Z^*) \gg 0$ for the problem $\sup_{(c, Z)} \mathcal{L}(c, Z; \gamma)$, assuming differentiability of u and F, are

$$u_c(c_t^*, t) - \gamma \pi_t = 0, \qquad t \in [0, T], \tag{46}$$

and

$$F'(Z^*) - \gamma\pi_T = 0. \tag{47}$$

Solving, we have

$$c_t^* = I(\gamma\pi_t, t), \qquad t \in [0, T], \tag{48}$$

and

$$Z^* = I_F(\gamma\pi_T), \tag{49}$$

where, as we recall, $I(\cdot, t)$ inverts $u_c(\cdot, t)$, and where $I_F = 0$ if $F = 0$ and otherwise I_F inverts F'. We will confirm these conjectured forms (48) and (49) of the solution in the next theorem. Under strict concavity of u or F, the inversions $I(\cdot, t)$ and I_F, respectively, are continuous and strictly decreasing. A decreasing function $\hat{w} : (0, \infty) \to \overline{\mathbb{R}}$ is therefore defined by

$$\hat{w}(\gamma) = E\left[\int_0^T \pi_t I(\gamma\pi_t, t)\, dt + \pi_T I_F(\gamma\pi_T)\right]. \tag{50}$$

(We have not yet ruled out the possibility that the expectation may be $+\infty$.) All of this implies that (c^*, Z^*) of (48)–(49) maximizes $\mathcal{L}(c, Z; \gamma)$ provided the required initial investment $\hat{w}(\gamma)$ is equal to the endowed initial wealth w. This leaves an equation $\hat{w}(\gamma) = w$ to solve for the "correct" Lagrange multiplier γ^*, and with that an explicit solution to the optimal-consumption policy for Merton's problem.

We can be a little more systematic about the properties of u and F in order to guarantee that $\hat{w}(\gamma) = w$ can be solved for a unique $\gamma^* > 0$. A strictly concave increasing function $F : \mathbb{R}_+ \to \mathbb{R}$ that is differentiable on $(0, \infty)$ satisfies *Inada conditions* if $\inf_x F'(x) = 0$ and $\sup_x F'(x) = +\infty$. If F satisfies these Inada conditions, then the inverse I_F of F' is well defined as a strictly decreasing continuous function on $(0, \infty)$ whose image is $(0, \infty)$.

Condition A. *Either F is zero or F is differentiable on $(0, \infty)$, strictly concave, and satisfies Inada conditions. Either u is zero or, for all t, $u(\cdot, t)$ is differentiable on $(0, \infty)$, strictly concave, and satisfies Inada conditions. For each $\gamma > 0$, $\hat{w}(\gamma)$ is finite.*

We recall the standing assumption that at least one of u and F is nonzero. The assumption of finiteness of $\hat{w}(\cdot)$ can be shown under regularity conditions on utility cited in the Notes.

Theorem. *Under Condition A, for any $w > 0$, Merton's problem (13) has a solution (c^*, Z^*, θ^*), where (c^*, Z^*) is given by (48)–(49) for a unique $\gamma \in (0, \infty)$.*

Proof: Under Condition A, the Dominated Convergence Theorem implies that $\hat{w}(\cdot)$ is continuous. Because one or both of $I(\cdot, t)$ and $I_F(\cdot)$ have $(0, \infty)$ as their image and are strictly decreasing, $\hat{w}(\cdot)$ inherits these two properties. From this, given any initial wealth $w > 0$, there is a unique γ^* with $\hat{w}(\gamma^*) = w$. Let (c^*, Z^*) be defined by (48)–(49), taking $\gamma = \gamma^*$. Proposition E tells us there is a trading strategy θ^* such that (c^*, Z^*, θ^*) is budget-feasible. Let (θ, c, Z) be any budget-feasible choice. Proposition E also implies that (c, Z) satisfies (38). For each (ω, t), the first-order conditions (46) and (47) are sufficient (by concavity of u and F) for optimality of $c^*(\omega, t)$ and $Z^*(\omega)$ in the problems

$$\sup_{\bar{c} \in [0, \infty)} u(\bar{c}, t) - \gamma^* \pi(\omega, t)\bar{c}$$

and

$$\sup_{\bar{Z} \in [0, \infty)} F(\bar{Z}) - \gamma^* \pi(\omega, T)\bar{Z},$$

respectively. Thus,

$$u(c_t^*, t) - \gamma^* \pi_t c_t^* \geq u(c_t, t) - \gamma^* \pi_t c_t, \qquad 0 \leq t \leq T, \tag{51}$$

and

$$F(Z^*) - \gamma^* \pi_T Z^* \geq F(Z) - \gamma^* \pi_T Z. \tag{52}$$

Integrating (51) from 0 to T, adding (52), and taking expectations, and then applying the complementary-slackness condition (45) and the budget constraint (38), leaves $U(c^*, Z^*) \geq U(c, Z)$. As (c, Z, θ) is arbitrary, this implies the optimality of (c^*, Z^*, θ^*). ∎

This result, giving a relatively explicit consumption solution to Merton's problem, has been extended in many directions, including relaxing the regularity conditions on utility in Condition A, and indeed even generalizing the assumption of additive utility to allow for habit-formation or recursive utility, as indicated in the Notes. In the next section, we will show that one can also extend to allow general Ito security-price processes, under technical conditions.

For a specific example, we once again consider terminal consumption only, taking $u \equiv 0$ and $F(w) = w^\alpha/\alpha$ for $\alpha \in (0, 1)$. Then $c^* = 0$ and the calculations above imply that $\hat{w}(\gamma) = E[\pi_T(\gamma \pi_T)^{1/(\alpha-1)}]$. Solving $\hat{w}(\gamma^*) = w$ for γ^* leaves

$$\gamma^* = w^{\alpha-1} E(\pi_T^{\alpha/(\alpha-1)})^{1-\alpha}.$$

It is left as an exercise to check that (49) can be reduced explicitly to

$$Z^* = I_F(\gamma^* \pi_T) = W_T,$$

where

$$dW_t = W_t(r + \bar{\varphi} \cdot \lambda) \, dt + W_t \bar{\varphi}^\top \sigma \, dB_t; \qquad W_0 = w,$$

where $\bar{\varphi} = (\sigma \sigma^\top)^{-1} \lambda / (1 - \alpha)$ is the vector of fixed optimal portfolio fractions found previously from the Bellman equation.

G. A Generalization

We generalize the security-price process $X = (X^{(0)}, X^{(1)}, \ldots, X^{(N)})$ to be of the form

$$dX_t^{(i)} = \mu_t^{(i)} X_t^{(i)} \, dt + X_t^{(i)} \sigma_t^{(i)} \, dB_t, \qquad X_0^{(i)} > 0, \tag{53}$$

where $\mu = (\mu^{(0)}, \ldots, \mu^{(N)})$ and the $\mathbb{R}^{N \times d}$-valued process σ whose i-th row is $\sigma^{(i)}$ are bounded adapted processes. We suppose that $\sigma^{(0)} = 0$, so that again $r = \mu^{(0)}$ is the short-rate process. We assume for simplicity that $N = d$. The excess expected returns of the "risky" securities are defined by an $\mathbb{R}^N$-valued process λ given by $\lambda_t^{(i)} = \mu_t^{(i)} - r_t$. The deflated price process $\hat{X}$ is defined by $\hat{X}_t = X_t \exp(-\int_0^t r_s \, ds)$. We assume that σ is invertible (almost everywhere) and that the market-price-of-risk process η for $\hat{X}$, defined by $\eta_t = \sigma_t^{-1} \lambda_t$, is bounded. It follows from the results of Chapter 6 that markets are complete (at least in the sense of Proposition 6I) and that there are no arbitrages that are well behaved, in the sense of Chapter 6.

In this setting, a state-price deflator π is defined by

$$\pi_t = \exp\left(-\int_0^t r_s \, ds\right) \xi_t, \tag{54}$$

where

$$\xi_t = \exp\left(-\frac{1}{2} \int_0^t \eta_s \cdot \eta_s \, ds - \int_0^t \eta_s \, dB_s\right).$$

The reformulation of Merton's problem given by Proposition F and the form (48)–(49) of the solution (when it exists) still apply, substituting only the state-price deflator π of (54) for that given in the earlier special case of constant r, λ, and σ. Once again, the only difficulty to overcome is a solution γ^* to $\hat{w}(\gamma^*) = w$, where $\hat{w}$ is again defined by (50). This is guaranteed by the same Condition A of the previous section. The proof of Theorem F thus suffices for the following extension.

Proposition. *Suppose that* μ *and* σ *are bounded adapted processes, that* $rank(\sigma) = d$ *almost everywhere, and that* $\eta = \sigma^{-1}\lambda$ *is bounded. Under Condition A, for any* $w > 0$, *Merton's problem has the optimal-consumption policy given by* (48)–(49) *for a unique scalar* $\gamma > 0$.

Although this approach generates an explicit solution for the optimal-consumption policy up to an unknown scalar γ, it does not say much about the form of the optimal trading strategy, beyond its existence. The Notes cite sources in which an optimal strategy is represented in terms of the *Malliavin calculus*. The original stochastic-control approach, in a Markov setting, gives explicit solutions for the optimal trading strategy in terms of the derivatives of the value function. Although there are few examples in which these derivatives are known explicitly, they can be approximated by a numerical solution of the Hamilton-Jacobi-Bellman equation, by extending the finite-difference methods given in Chapter 12.

H. The Utility-Gradient Approach

The martingale approach can be simplified, at least under technical conditions, by adopting the utility-gradient approach of Chapter 2. Although conceptually easy, this theory has only been developed to the point of theorems under restrictive conditions, and with proofs beyond the scope of this book, so we shall merely sketch out the basic ideas and refer to the Notes for sources with proofs and more details.

We let L_+ denote the set of nonnegative adapted consumption processes satisfying the integrability condition $E(\int_0^T c_t\, dt) < \infty$. We adopt a concave utility function $U : L_+ \to \mathbb{R}$, not necessarily of the additive form

$$U(c) = E\left[\int_0^T u(c_t, t)\, dt\right]. \tag{55}$$

We fix the security-price process X of Section G. Fixing also the initial wealth w, we say that a consumption process c in L_+ is budget-feasible if there is some trading strategy θ such that

$$\theta_t \cdot X_t = w + \int_0^t \theta_s\, dX_s - \int_0^t c_s\, ds \geq 0, \qquad t \in [0, T],$$

with $\theta_T \cdot X_T = 0$. A budget-feasible consumption process c is optimal if it solves the problem

$$\sup_{c \in \mathcal{A}} U(c),$$

where $\mathscr{A}$ denotes the set of budget-feasible consumption processes. If c^* is budget-feasible and the gradient $\nabla U(c^*)$ (defined in Appendix B) of U at c^* exists, the gradient approach to optimality reviewed in Appendix B leads to the first-order condition for optimality:

$$\nabla U(c^*; c - c^*) \leq 0, \qquad c \in \mathscr{A}.$$

We suppose that c^* is budget-feasible and that $\nabla U(c^*)$ exists, with a Riesz representation π that is an Ito process. That is,

$$\nabla U(c^*; c - c^*) = E\left[\int_0^T (c_t - c_t^*)\pi_t \, dt \right], \qquad c \in \mathscr{A}.$$

As shown in Appendix G, this is true for the additive model (55), under natural conditions, taking $\pi_t = u_c(c_t^*, t)$. Appendix G also gives Riesz representations of the utility gradients of other forms of utility functions, such as continuous-time versions of the habit-formation and recursive utilities considered in Exercises 2.8 and 2.9.

Based on Proposition 2D and the results of Section G, it is natural to conjecture that c^* is optimal if and only if the Riesz representation π of $\nabla U(c^*)$ is in fact a state-price deflator. In order to explore this conjecture, we suppose that π is indeed a state-price deflator; that is, X^π is a martingale. Numeraire invariance implies that c is budget-feasible if and only if there is some trading strategy θ with

$$\theta_t \cdot X_t^\pi = w\pi_0 + \int_0^t \theta_s \, dX_s^\pi - \int_0^t c_s \pi_s \, ds \geq 0, \qquad t \in [0, T], \tag{56}$$

and $\theta_T \cdot X_T^\pi = 0$. For any budget-feasible strategy (c, θ), because $\int \theta \, dX^\pi$ is a local martingale that is bounded below, and therefore a supermartingale, (56) implies that

$$E\left(\int_0^T c_t \pi_t \, dt \right) \leq w\pi_0.$$

Applying this in particular to c^*, where we expect it to hold with strict equality under technical conditions, we have

$$\nabla U(c^*; c - c^*) = E\left[\int_0^T \pi_t (c_t - c_t^*) \, dt \right] \leq 0, \qquad c \in \mathscr{A}. \tag{57}$$

Thus, assuming some technical conditions along the way, we have shown that the first-order condition for optimality of a budget-feasible choice c is essentially that the Riesz representation π of the utility gradient at c

is a state-price deflator. (This was precisely what we found in the finite-dimensional setting of Chapter 2.) We would next like to see how to deduce an optimal choice c^* from this first-order condition (57). We may have a significant amount of structure with which to determine c^* on this basis. First, from Chapter 6, we know that a state-price deflator π is given, under regularity, by

$$\pi_t = \pi_0 \exp\left(-\int_0^t r_s \, ds\right)\xi_t, \tag{58}$$

where ξ is the density process for some equivalent martingale measure, which implies that $d\xi_t = -\xi_t \eta_t \, dB_t$ for a market-price-of-risk process η for $\hat{X}$. Second, U may be one of the popular utility functions for which we can calculate the gradient $\nabla U(c)$ at any c. Finally, we can attempt to invert for an optimal c^* by matching the Riesz representation of $\nabla U(c^*)$ to one of the state-price deflators that we can calculate from (58).

In the case of additive utility, for example, if c^* is optimal, then a state-price deflator π can be chosen, for some scalar $k > 0$, by $k\pi_t = u_c(c_t^*, t)$, so that $c_t^* = I(k\pi_t, t)$, where $I(\cdot, t)$ inverts $u_c(\cdot, t)$. Finally, we need to choose k so that c^* is budget-feasible. For the case of complete markets, it suffices, by the same numeraire invariance argument made earlier, that

$$\pi_0 w = E\left(\int_0^T c_t^* \pi_t \, dt\right) = E\left[\int_0^T I(k\pi_t, t)\pi_t \, dt\right]. \tag{59}$$

Provided $I(\cdot, t)$ has range $(0, \infty)$ for all t, the arguments used in Section F can be applied for the existence of some scalar $k > 0$ satisfying (59). It is enough, for instance, that a market-price-of-risk process η can be chosen to be bounded, and that I satisfies a uniform growth condition in its first argument. The Notes cite examples of a nonadditive utility function U with the property that for each deflator π in a suitably general class, one can recover a unique consumption process c^* with the property that $\nabla U(c^*)$ has π as its Riesz representation. Subject to regularity conditions, the habit-formation and recursive-utility functions have this property.

For the case of incomplete markets (for which it is not true that rank$(\sigma) = d$ almost everywhere), all of the above steps can be carried out in the absence of arbitrage, except that there need not be a trading strategy θ^* that finances the candidate solution c^*. Papers cited in the Notes have taken the following approach. With incomplete markets, there is a family of different market-price-of-risk processes. The objective is to choose a market-price-of-risk process η^* with the property that, when matching the Riesz representation of the utility gradient to $k\eta^*$, we can choose k so that c^* can be financed. This can be done under technical regularity conditions.

Exercises

9.1 For the candidate optimal portfolio control $\varphi_t^* = \bar{\varphi}$ given by the right-hand side of (22), verify that (28) is indeed a martingale as asserted.

9.2 Solve Merton's problem in the following cases. Add any regularity conditions that you feel are appropriate.

(A) Let T be finite, $F = 0$, and $u(c, t) = e^{-\rho t} c^\alpha / \alpha$, $\alpha \in (0, 1)$.

(B) Let T be finite, $F = 0$, and $u(c, t) = \log c$.

(C) Let $T = +\infty$ and $u(c, t) = e^{-\rho t} c^\alpha / \alpha$, $\alpha \in (0, 1)$. Verify the solution given by $c_t^* = \gamma W_t^*$ and $\varphi_t^* = (\sigma \sigma^\top)^{-1} \lambda / (1 - \alpha)$, where γ is given by (32). Verify the so-called transversality condition (31) with $\gamma > 0$.

9.3 Extend the example in Section D, with $v(\bar{c}, w) = \bar{c}^\alpha / \alpha$, to the case without a riskless security. Add regularity conditions as appropriate.

9.4 The rate of growth of capital stock in a given production technology is determined by a "random shock" process Y solving the stochastic differential equation

$$dY_t = (b - \kappa Y_t)\, dt + k\sqrt{Y_t}\, dB_t; \qquad Y_0 = y \in \mathbb{R}_+, \qquad t \geq 0,$$

where b, κ, and k are strictly positive scalars with $2b > k^2$, and where B is a standard Brownian motion. Let $\mathscr{C}$ be the space of nonnegative adapted consumption processes satisfying $\int_0^T c_t\, dt < \infty$ almost surely for all $T \geq 0$. For each c in $\mathscr{C}$, a capital stock process K^c is defined by

$$dK_t^c = (K_t^c h Y_t - c_t)\, dt + K_t^c \epsilon \sqrt{Y_t}\, dB_t; \qquad K_0^c = x > 0,$$

where h and ϵ are strictly positive scalars with $h > \epsilon^2$. Consider the control problem

$$V(x, y) = \sup_{c \in \mathscr{C}} E\left[\int_0^T e^{-\rho t} \log(c_t)\, dt \right],$$

subject to $K_t^c \geq 0$ for all t in $[0, T]$.

(A) Let $C : \mathbb{R}_+ \times [0, T] \to \mathbb{R}_+$ be defined by

$$C(x, t) = \frac{\rho x}{1 - e^{-\rho(T-t)}},$$

and let K be the solution of the SDE

$$dK_t = [K_t h Y_t - C(K_t, t)]\, dt + K_t \epsilon \sqrt{Y_t}\, dB_t; \qquad K_0 = x > 0.$$

Finally, let c^* be the consumption process defined by $c_t^* = C(K_t, t)$. Show that c^* is the unique optimal-consumption control. Hint: Verify that $V(x, y) = J(x, y, 0)$, where J is of the form

$$J(x, y, t) = A_1(t) \log(x) + A_2(t)y + A_3(t), \qquad (x, y, t) \in \mathbb{R}_+ \times \mathbb{R} \times [0, T),$$

where A_1, A_2, and A_3 are (deterministic) real-valued functions of time. State the function A_1 and differential equations for A_2 and A_3.

(B) State the value function and the optimal consumption for the infinite-horizon case. Add regularity conditions as appropriate.

9.5 An agent has the objective of maximizing $E[u(W_T)]$, where W_T denotes wealth at some future time T and $u : \mathbb{R} \to \mathbb{R}$ is increasing and strictly concave. The wealth W_T is the sum of the market value of a fixed portfolio of assets and the terminal value of the margin account of a futures trading strategy, as elaborated below. This problem is one of characterizing optimal futures hedging. The first component of wealth is the spot market value of a fixed portfolio $p \in \mathbb{R}^M$ of M different assets whose price processes $S^{(1)}, \dots, S^{(M)}$ satisfy the respective stochastic differential equations

$$dS_t^{(m)} = \mu_m(t)\, dt + \sigma_m(t)\, dB_t; \quad t \geq 0, \quad S_0^{(m)} = 1, \quad m \in \{1, \dots, M\},$$

where, for each $m, \mu_m : [0, T] \to \mathbb{R}$ and $\sigma_m : [0, T] \to \mathbb{R}^d$ are continuous. There are futures contracts for K assets with delivery at some date $\tau > T$, having futures-price processes $F^{(1)}, \dots, F^{(K)}$ satisfying the stochastic differential equations

$$dF_t^{(k)} = m_k(t)\, dt + v_k(t)\, dB_t; \qquad t \in [0, T], \qquad 1 \leq k \leq K,$$

where m_k and v_k are continuous on $[0, T]$ into $\mathbb{R}$ and $\mathbb{R}^d$, respectively. For simplicity, we assume that there is a constant short rate r for borrowing or lending. One takes a futures position merely by committing oneself to mark a margin account to market. Conceptually, that is, if one holds a long (positive) position of, say, ten futures contracts on a particular asset and the price of the futures contract goes up by a dollar, then one receives ten dollars from the short side of the contract. (In practice, the contracts are largely insured against default by the opposite side, and it is normal to treat the contracts as default-free for modeling purposes.) The margin account earns interest at the riskless rate (or, if the margin account balance is negative, one loses interest at the riskless rate). We ignore margin calls or borrowing limits. Formally, as described in Section 8C, the futures-price process is actually the cumulative-dividend process of a futures contract; the true price process is zero. Given any bounded adapted process $\theta = (\theta^{(1)}, \dots, \theta^{(K)})$ for the agent's futures-position process, the agent's wealth at time T is $p \cdot S_T + X_T$, where X is the Ito process for the agent's margin account value, defined by $X_0 = 0$ and $dX_t = rX_t\, dt + \theta_t\, dF_t$.

(A) Set up the agent's dynamic hedging problem for choice of futures-position process θ in the framework of continuous-time stochastic control. State the Bellman equation and first-order conditions. Derive an explicit expression for the optimal futures position θ_t involving the (unknown) value function. Make regularity assumptions such as differentiability and nonsingularity. Hint: Let $W_t = p \cdot S_t + e^{r(T-t)}X_t$, $t \in [0, T]$.

(B) Solve for the optimal policy θ in the case $m \equiv 0$, meaning no expected futures-price changes. Add any regularity conditions needed to prove optimality.

(C) Solve the problem explicitly for the case $u(w) = -e^{-\alpha w}$, where $\alpha > 0$ is a scalar risk-aversion coefficient. Prove optimality.

9.6 In the setting of Section B, consider the special case of the utility function

$$U(c, Z) = E\left[\int_0^T \log(c_t) \, dt + \sqrt{Z}\right].$$

Obtain a closed-form solution for Merton's problem (13). Hint: The mixture of logarithm and power function in the utility makes this a situation in which the martingale approach has an advantage over the Bellman approach, from which it might be difficult to conjecture a value function. Once the optimal-consumption policy is found, do not forget to calculate the optimal portfolio trading strategy.

9.7 (Utility-Gradient Example).   Suppose B is a standard Brownian motion and there are two securities with price processes S and β given by

$$dS_t = \mu_t S_t \, dt + \sigma_t S_t \, dB_t, \qquad S_0 > 0,$$

$$d\beta_t = r_t \beta_t \, dt, \qquad \beta_0 > 0,$$

where μ, σ, and r are bounded adapted processes with $\mu_t > r_t$ for all t. We take the infinite-horizon case, with utility function U defined by

$$U(c) = E\left(\int_0^\infty e^{-\rho t} c_t^\alpha \, dt\right),$$

where $\alpha \in (0, 1)$ and $\rho \in (0, \infty)$. Taking the utility-gradient approach of Section H, c^* is, in principle, an optimal choice if and only if

$$E\left(\int_0^\infty \pi_t c_t^* \, dt\right) = w,$$

where $\nabla U(c^*)$ has Riesz representation π, and S^π and β^π are martingales. Assuming that the solution c^* is an Ito process with

$$dc_t^* = c_t^* \mu_t^* \, dt + c_t^* \sigma_t^* \, dB_t,$$

we can write

$$d\pi_t = \pi_t \mu_\pi(t) \, dt + \pi_t \sigma_\pi(t) \, dB_t$$

for processes μ_π and σ_π that can be solved explicitly in terms of μ^* and σ^* from Ito's Formula and the fact that $\pi_t = \alpha e^{-\rho t}(c_t^*)^{\alpha-1}$. Assuming that S^π and β^π are indeed martingales, solve for μ^* and σ^* explicitly.

9.8 Verify that, as defined by (35) and (36), Q is indeed an equivalent martingale measure, including the property that $\text{var}(\xi_T) < \infty$.

9.9 (Constrained Investment Behavior). Security markets are characterized by price processes $S = (S^{(1)}, \ldots, S^{(N)})$ and β, with

$$d\beta_t = \beta_t r_t \, dt, \qquad \beta_0 > 0,$$

for a bounded adapted process r, and with

$$dS_t^{(i)} = S_t^{(i)} \mu_t^{(i)} \, dt + S_t^{(i)} \sigma_t^{(i)} \, dB_t,$$

where, for each i, $\mu^{(i)}$ and $\sigma^{(i)}$ are bounded adapted processes in $\mathbb{R}$ and $\mathbb{R}^d$, respectively. We also assume that $\Gamma_t = (\sigma_t \sigma_t^\top)^{-1}$ is well defined and bounded. With a trading strategy specified in terms of a bounded adapted process φ valued in $\mathbb{R}^N$ with $\int_0^T \varphi_t \cdot \varphi_t \, dt < \infty$, and with a nonnegative consumption process c, the wealth process $W^{(\varphi, c)}$ of an investor is defined by

$$dW_t^{(\varphi, c)} = \left[W_t^{(\varphi, c)}(\varphi_t \cdot \lambda_t + r_t) - c_t \right] dt + W_t^{(\varphi, c)} \varphi_t^\top \sigma_t \, dB_t; \quad W_0^{(\varphi, c)} = w,$$

where $\lambda_t^i = \mu_t^i - r_t$ and where $w > 0$ is a given constant. The investment-consumption strategy (φ, c) is admissible if $W_t^{(\varphi, c)} \geq 0$ for all t. Consider an investor with the utility criterion

$$U(c) = E\left[\int_0^T e^{-\rho t} \log c_t \, dt \right],$$

where $\rho > 0$ is a constant, and c is chosen from the set of nonnegative adapted processes such that $U(c)$ is well defined.

(A) (Unconstrained Case). Let $\mathscr{C}^*(r, \mu, \sigma)$ denote the set of solutions to the investor's optimization problem,

$$\sup_{(\varphi, c) \in \mathscr{C}(w)} U(c),$$

where $\mathscr{C}(w)$ is the set of admissible strategies. Calculate $\mathscr{C}^*(r, \mu, \sigma)$.

(B) (Leverage Constraints). Let $\mathscr{C}(w, \ell) = \{(\varphi, c) \in \mathscr{C}(w) : \sum_{i=1}^N \varphi_t^i \leq \ell_t\}$, where ℓ is a nonnegative bounded adapted process that sets an upper bound on the leverage of the investment strategy. The investor's problem is now

$$\sup_{(\varphi, c) \in \mathscr{C}(w, \ell)} U(c).$$

Solve this leverage-constrained problem. Hint: Reduce the problem to that of the unconstrained case by an adjustment of the interest rate r, to reflect the shadow price of the leverage constraint, so that the problem may be effectively solved unconstrained.

(C) (Leverage and Short-Sales Constraints).   Let

$$\mathscr{C}(w, \ell, b) = \{(\varphi, c) \in \mathscr{C}(w, \ell) : \varphi_t \geq -b_t\},$$

where ℓ is as above and $b = (b^{(1)}, \ldots, b^{(N)})$, where $b^{(i)}$ is for each i a nonnegative bounded adapted process that places, in addition to a leverage constraint, a bound on short sales as a fraction of portfolio value. Now, solve:

$$\sup_{(\varphi, c) \in \mathscr{C}(w, \ell, b)} U(c).$$

Hint: Again, reduce to the unconstrained case, this time by suitable adjustment of all of the return coefficients (r, μ) to reflect the shadow prices of the constraints.

9.10 (Investment and Price Behavior with Jumps).   The objective of this exercise is to extend the basic results for consumption-investment models and asset pricing to an economy in which the volatilities and expected rates of return of the available securities may change suddenly, and depend on a "regime" state process defined by a two-state Markov chain Z, as defined in Appendix F. When a regime switch occurs, the price may jump as well, for example to reflect the sudden change in the distribution of returns on equilibrium asset values.

We fix a probability space on which is defined a standard Brownian motion B in $\mathbb{R}^d$ and the two-state continuous-time Markov chain Z, as defined in Appendix F, with states 0 and 1, and transition intensities $\lambda(0)$ and $\lambda(1)$. We let M denote the compensated version of Z.

Suppose $X = (X^{(0)}, X^{(1)}, \ldots, X^{(N)})$ is an adapted process in $\mathbb{R}^{N+1}$ for the prices of $N + 1$ securities. For each $i \geq 1$, we assume that

$$dX_t^{(i)} = \mu_i(Z_t)X_t^{(i)} \, dt + X_t^{(i)}\sigma^{(i)}(Z_t) \, dB_t + X_{t-}^{(i)}\beta_i(Z_{t-})dM_t, \qquad X_0 > 0,$$

where, for each $j \in \{0, 1\}$,

   $\sigma^{(i)}(j)$ is the i-th row of a constant matrix $\sigma(j)$ in $\mathbb{R}^{N \times d}$.
   $\mu_i(j)$ is a constant.
   $\beta_i(j)$ is a constant strictly less than 1 in absolute value.

This implies, in particular, that within a "regime," each process $X^{(i)}$ behaves as a geometric Brownian motion of the sort used in the Black-Scholes model of option pricing. When the regime changes, the price process jumps and its drift and diffusion parameters change. When the regime changes from 0 to 1, for example, the price of risky security i jumps by a multiplicative factor of $\beta_i(0)$. When the regime changes from 1 to zero, the price of risky security i jumps by a multiplicative factor of $-\beta_i(1)$.

Given a short-rate process $\{R(Z_t) : t \geq 0\}$, for given constants $R(0)$ and $R(1)$, the market value of an investment rolled over at the short rate defines a value process $X^{(0)}$ by

$$dX_t^{(0)} = R(Z_t)X_t^{(0)} \, dt; \qquad X_0^{(0)} > 0.$$

The filtration of tribes generated by (B, Z), and augmented with null sets, as above, defines the information available to investors. A trading strategy is a predictable $\mathbb{R}^{N+1}$-valued process θ such that the stochastic integral $\int \theta \, dX$ exists. (Note the informational restriction to predictable trading strategies, as defined in Appendix F. With merely the requirement of adapted trading strategies, a position could be taken at a jump time τ based on information associated with the outcome of the jump.) A trading strategy θ is self-financing if

$$\theta_t \cdot X_t = \theta_0 \cdot X_0 + \int_0^t \theta_s \, dX_s, \qquad 0 \le t \le T.$$

(A) (Complete Markets and Equivalent Martingale Measure). Find conditions on the primitive functions $(\sigma, \mu, r, \beta, \lambda)$ defining asset returns that are sufficient for the existence of a unique equivalent martingale measure Q for the deflated price process $X_t / X_t^{(0)}$. (Do not assume that λ or β are trivial.) Show, under these conditions, that for any bounded $\mathscr{F}_T$-measurable random variable Y, there is a self-financing trading strategy θ with bounded market value $\theta_t \cdot X_t$, with $\theta_T \cdot X_T = Y$, and with

$$\theta_0 \cdot X_0 = E^Q\left[\exp\left(\int_0^T -R(Z_t) \, dt\right) Y\right].$$

Also, given the existence of an equivalent martingale measure, show that any self-financing trading strategy θ satisfying $\theta_t \cdot X_t \ge 0$ for all t cannot be an arbitrage. Hint: For a given equivalent probability measure Q, let

$$\xi_t = E_t\left(\frac{dQ}{dP}\right), \qquad t \le T.$$

Because ξ is a martingale, it has a martingale representation in the form

$$d\xi_t = \xi_t \sigma_\xi(t) \, dB_t + \xi_{t-}\beta_\xi(t) dM_t,$$

for some adapted processes σ_ξ and β_ξ. For Q to be an equivalent martingale measure under the numeraire deflator $X^{(0)}$, it must be the case that a P-martingale is defined by the process whose value at time t is

$$\frac{\xi_t X_t^{(i)}}{X_t^{(0)}}.$$

Using Ito's Formula from Appendix F for the case of a product of processes of this form, compute restrictions on σ_ξ and β_ξ in terms of the primitives, and then provide restrictions on the asset-return coefficient functions μ, r, σ, λ, and β under which ξ, and therefore Q, are uniquely well defined. Please do not forget that ξ should be of finite variance.

(B) (Martingale Formulation of Optimality). Utility is defined over the space L_+ of nonnegative adapted consumption processes satisfying the restriction that $\int_0^T c_t \, dt < \infty$ almost surely. Specifically, $U : L_+ \to \mathbb{R}$ is defined by

$$U(c) = E\left[\int_0^T e^{-\rho t} u(c_t) \, dt\right].$$

For this part of the problem, T is a fixed finite time and $u : \mathbb{R}_+ \to \mathbb{R}$ is strictly concave and increasing.

Given an initial wealth $w > 0$, we say that (c, θ) is *budget-feasible*, denoted $(c, \theta) \in \Lambda(w)$, if $c \in L_+$ and if $\theta \in \mathcal{L}(X)$ is a trading strategy satisfying

$$\theta_t \cdot X_t = w + \int_0^t \theta_s \, dX_s - \int_0^t c_s \, ds \geq 0, \qquad t \in [0, T],$$

where $w > 0$ is a given constant and

$$\theta_T \cdot X_T \geq 0.$$

We now have the problem, for each initial wealth w and each initial regime $i \in \{0, 1\}$,

$$J(i, w, 0) = \sup_{(c, \theta) \in \Lambda(w)} U(c). \tag{60}$$

Using the martingale approach, compute the optimal-consumption process up to a missing scalar Lagrange multipler. Justify your answer, making technical assumptions as needed.

(C) (Parametric Example). We change the formulation in part (B) by letting $T = +\infty$ and by considering the special case $u(c) = c^\alpha$, for some α in $(0, 1)$. A consumption process c is nonnegative and adapted, with $\int_0^t c_s \, ds < \infty$ for each $t > 0$. We also simplify the problem by assuming that $\beta_i = 0$ for all i, meaning that a regime shift causes no jump in asset prices, but may cause a change in expected rates of returns, volatilities, and correlations. State the solution to (60), proving its optimality by reducing the supremum value function J defined by (60) to two unknown coefficients, k_0 and k_1, one for each initial regime. Using your extension of the Hamilton-Jacobi-Bellman equation for optimal control in this setting, obtain two nonlinear restrictions on these two unknown coefficients. Assume existence of a solution to this system of equations for k_0 and k_1. Compute the candidate optimal-consumption and portfolio fraction policies as explicitly as possible. Verify your candidate solution, under additional explicit regularity conditions on the primitive parameters as well as k_0 and k_1. Please be extremely careful to provide a complete proof of optimality, given k_0 and k_1.

(D) (Robinson Crusoe). Let $d = 1$ (one-dimensional Brownian motion). Robinson must consume at each time t from a physical stock K_t of consumption commodity, satisfying the production equation

$$dK_t = [\eta(Z_t)K_t - c_t] \, dt + K_t \zeta(Z_t) \, dB_t + K_{t-} \delta(Z_{t-}) dZ_t, \tag{61}$$

where η, ζ, and δ are real-valued functions on $\{0, 1\}$ and c is a nonnegative adapted consumption process to be chosen by Robinson. We assume that $|\delta| < 1$. Robinson's utility for consumption is defined by

$$U(c) = E\left[\int_0^\infty e^{-\rho t} c_t^\alpha \, dt\right],$$

for a given $\alpha \in (0, 1)$. Robinson's problem is

$$\sup_{c \in \mathscr{A}} U(c), \tag{62}$$

where $\mathscr{A}$ is the space containing any consumption process c such that the stock K_t of commodity solving (61) remains nonnegative for all t. Solve (62). Hint: Conjecture the form of the value function. Now, for each initial state $i \in \{0, 1\}$, consider the stopping time τ of first transition to the other state. Begin your calculation of the unknown coefficients of the solution by conditioning on this stopping time τ.

(E) (Incomplete Information and Filtering). We now consider the special case of a single risky asset ($N = 1$) for which, with each change in regime, there is no jump in the risky asset price (that is, $\beta = 0$), no change in the interest rate (that is, $R(1) = R(0) = \bar{r}$ for some constant $\bar{r}$), and no jumps in the volatility (that is, $\sigma(1) = \sigma(2) = q$ for some constant q). With a change in regime, however, there is a change in the mean-rate-of-return coefficient. That is, $\mu(1) \neq \mu(0)$. For simplicity, we will assume that $\lambda(0) = \lambda(1) = \bar{\lambda}$, for some constant $\bar{\lambda} > 0$, so that the arrival intensity of a change in regime is the same in both regimes.

Suppose, however, that the investor is *not able to observe the regime state process Z*, but can only observe the risky asset's price process $S = X^{(1)}$. This means that, for the investor, the relevant filtration of tribes describing the available information is $\{\mathscr{F}_t^S = \sigma(\{S_u : u \leq t\})\}$.

Now solve the optimal portfolio investment strategy for an investor with the utility criterion

$$U(c) = E\left[\int_0^\infty e^{-\rho t} \log c_t \, dt\right],$$

where $\rho > 0$ is a constant, and c is chosen from the set of nonnegative adapted processes such that $U(c)$ is well defined. Hint: It may assist you to work with a stochastic differential model for asset price behavior given the limited information available. For this, let $p_t = P(Z_t = 1 \mid \mathscr{F}_t^S)$ denote the conditional probability at time t that $Z_t = 1$, given the observed asset prices to that time. By adding and subtracting the same thing from the stochastic differential expression for S, we have

$$dS_t = S_t m(p_t) \, dt + S_t q \, d\bar{B}_t,$$

where

$$d\bar{B}_t = \frac{1}{q}[\mu(Z_t) - m(p_t)] \, dt + dB_t,$$

and where, for any $\alpha \in [0, 1]$,

$$m(\alpha) = \alpha\mu(1) + (1 - \alpha)\mu(0)$$

defines the conditional expectation of the mean rate of return on the risky asset given probability α that the unknown regime is 1. It can be shown, for the probability space $(\Omega, \mathcal{F}, P)$ and the limited filtration $\{\mathcal{F}_t^S : t \geq 0\}$ available to the investor, that $\bar{B}$ is a standard Brownian motion. It turns out, moreover, that

$$dp_t = \bar{\lambda}(1 - 2p_t)\, dt + kp_t(1 - p_t)d\bar{B}_t,$$

where $k = [\mu(1) - \mu(0)]/q$. The initial condition p_0 is the investor's prior probability assessment that $Z(0) = 1$. We have therefore effectively reduced the original investment problem to one of complete observation, with a stochastic mean rate of return $m(p_t)$ determined by a separate Markov process p satisfying its own stochastic differential equation.

Notes

A comprehensive treatment of the topic is provided by Karatzas and Shreve (1998). Other surveys include those of Quenez (1992) and Karatzas (1989).

(A) Standard treatments of stochastic control in this setting are given by Fleming and Rishel (1975), Krylov (1980), Bensoussan (1983), Lions (1981, 1983), and Fleming and Soner (1993). The book of Fleming and Soner (1993) treats *viscosity solutions* of the Hamilton-Jacobi-Bellman (HJB) equation. Among other advantages of this approach, it allows one to characterize the continuous-time stochastic-control problem as the limit of discrete Markov control problems of the sort considered in Chapter 3. Other work using viscosity methods includes that of Benth, Karlsen, and Reikvam (1999).

(B–D) Merton (1969, 1971), in perhaps the first successful application of stochastic control methods in an economics application, formulated and solved the problem described in Section B. (Another early example is Mirrlees [1974].) Extensions and improvements of Merton's result have been developed by Aase (1984), Fleming and Zariphopoulou (1991), Karatzas, Lehoczky, Sethi, and Shreve (1986), Lehoczky, Sethi, and Shreve (1983, 1985), Sethi and Taksar (1988), Fitzpatrick and Fleming (1991), Richard (1975), Jacka (1984), Ocone and Karatzas (1991) (who apply the Malliavin calculus), and Merton (1990).

(E–G) The martingale approach to optimal investment described in Section E has been developed in a series of papers. Principal among these are Cox and Huang (1989) and, subsequently, Karatzas, Lehoczky, and Shreve (1987). This literature includes Cox (1983), Pliska (1986), Cox and Huang (1991), Back (1986), Back and Pliska (1987), Huang and Pagès (1992), Lakner and Slud (1991), Pagès (1987), Jeanblanc and Pontier (1990), Richardson (1989), and Xu and Shreve (1992a, b). For applications of duality techniques and other methods to multiperiod investment with constraints including incomplete markets, see Broadie, Cvitanić, and Soner (1998), Cuoco (1997), Cvitanić (1995, 1997, 1999), Cvitanić and Karatzas (1992, 1993, 1995, 1996a, b), Cvitanić, Karatzas, and Soner (1998), Derviz (1996), He and Pagès (1993), He and Pearson (1991a, b), Karatzas, Lehoczky, Shreve, and Xu (1991), El Karoui and Quenez (1991), Ruegg (1996), and Tepla (1996).

For additional results with incomplete markets, see Adler and Detemple (1988), Cuoco (1994), Cvitanić and Karatzas (1992, 1995), Cvitanić, Schacher-mayer, and Wang (1999), Duffie, Fleming, Soner, and Zariphopoulou (1997), Duffie and Zariphopoulou (1993), Dybvig (1989), El Karoui and Jeanblanc (1998), He and Pagès (1993), Koo (1998, 1999), Munk (2000b), Pagès (1987), Scheinkman and Weiss (1986), and Svensson and Werner (1993).

For the case of short-sales constraints and other forms of portfolio restric-tions, see Back and Pliska (1986), Brennan, Schwartz, and Lagnado (1997), Cuoco (1994), Cvitanić and Karatzas (1992, 1995), Dybvig (1995), Fleming and Zariphopoulou (1991), He and Pagès (1993), Hindy (1995), Shirakawa (1994), Vila and Zariphopoulou (1997), Xu and Shreve (1992a, b), and Zariphopoulou (1992, 1994).

(H) The utility-gradient approach to optimal investment of Section H is based on work by Harrison and Kreps (1979), Kreps (1981), Huang (1985c), Foldes (1978a, b, 1990, 1991a, b, 1992, 1996), Back (1991), and Duffie and Skiadas (1994), and is extended in these sources to an abstract setting with more general information and utility functions. Appendix G provides some additional information on the existence and calculation of utility gradients.

Additional Topics: For problems with mean-variance criteria in a continuous-time setting, see Ansel and Stricker (1994a), Bajeux-Besnainou and Portait (1993), Bossaerts and Hillion (1997), Bouleau and Lamberton (1989), Duffie and Jackson (1990), Duffie and Richardson (1991), Föllmer and Schweizer (1990), Föllmer and Sondermann (1986), Gourieroux, Laurent, and Pham (1998), Lakner (1994a), Lioui(1995), Schweizer (1994a, b, c, d), and Sekine (1998).

For optimality under various habit-formation utilities, see Chapman (1997), Constantinides (1990), Detemple and Zapatero (1992), Ingersoll (1992), Ryder and Heal (1973), Schroder and Skiadas (1999), and Sundaresan (1989).

A model involving local substitution for consumption was developed by Hindy and Huang (1992, 1993a), and Hindy, Huang, and Kreps (1992). See also Bank and Riedel (1999) and Hindy, Huang, and Zhu (1997).

Ekern (1993) is an example of a model of irreversible investment. Dixit and Pindyck (1993) review many other models of optimal production under uncer-tainty using stochastic-control methods. See, also, Chapter 11 and its Notes.

For a development of recursive utility in continuous-time settings, called stochastic differential utility, see Duffie and Epstein (1992b) (with Skiadas), and for related work including portfolio and consumption choice, see Ahn (1993), Bergman (1985b), Duffie and Epstein (1992a), Duffie and Lions (1990), Duffie and Skiadas (1994), Duffie, Schroder, and Skiadas (1997), El Karoui, Peng, and Quenez (1997), Fisher and Gilles (1998b), Lazrak and Quenez (1999), Ma (1991, 1993a, b), Schroder and Skiadas (1999), Svensson (1989), and Uzawa (1968). For the related problem of backward stochastic differen-tial equations (BSDE), see Pardoux and Peng (1990) and Peng (1993b) for their seminal work, and for subsequent developments, see Alvarez and Tourin (1996), Bally (1995), Barles, Buckdahn, and Pardoux (1997), Barles and Lesigne (1997), Buckdahn (1995a, b), Cvitanić, Karatzas, and Soner (1998), Darling (1995), El Karoui (1997), El Karoui and Huang (1997), El Karoui, Kapoudjian,

Pardoux, Peng, and Quenez (1997), El Karoui, Peng, and Quenez (1997) Gegout-Petit and Pardoux (1996), Pardoux and Peng (1994), Pardoux (1997), Peng (1993a), Pontier (1997), and Quenez (1997). For developments and applications of forward-backward stochastic differential equations (FBSDE), see Antonelli (1993), Cvitanić and Ma (1996), Duffie, Geoffard, and Skiadas (1994), Ma, Protter, and Yong (1994), and Ma and Yong (1995, 1999).

For an elegant extension of Merton's problem that allows for proportional transactions costs, see Davis and Norman (1990). Other work on optimal investment problems in the case of transactions costs includes that of Akian, Menaldi, and Sulem (1996), Akian, Sulem, and Taksar (1999), Alvarez (1991), Arntzen (1994), Avellaneda and Parás (1994b), Balduzzi and Lynch (1997, 1999), Cadenillas and Pliska (1999), Chang (1993), Clewlow and Hodges (1996), Constantinides (1986), Cuoco and Liu (2000), Davis and Panas (1991), Duffie and Sun (1990), Dumas and Luciano (1989), Edirisinghe, Naik, and Uppal (1993), Fleming, Grossman, Vila, and Zariphopoulou (1989), Huang (1999), Jouini and Kallal (1993a, b), Lynch and Balduzzi (1998), Pliska and Selby (1994), Schroder (1993), Shreve and Soner (1994), Shreve, Soner, and Xu (1991), Taksar, Klass, and Assaf (1988), Vayanos and Vila (1999), Weerasinghe (1998), and Zariphopoulou (1992). See also the references cited in the Notes of Chapter 6.

On the existence of additive or other particular forms of utility consistent with given asset prices, sometimes called "integrability," or an "inverse problem," see Bick (1986), Cuoco and Zapatero (2000), He and Huang (1994), He and Leland (1993), Hodges and Carverhill (1992), and Wang (1993b). On turnpike problems, see Cox and Huang (1991, 1992), Dybvig, Rogers, and Back (1999), and Huang and Zariphopoulou (1999). For problems in settings with incomplete information, usually requiring filtering of the state, see Detemple (1986, 1991), Detemple and Murthy (1994a), Dothan and Feldman (1986), Gennotte (1986), Duffie, Schroder, and Skiadas (1997), Föllmer and Schweizer (1990), Honda (1997c), Karatzas (1991), Karatzas and Xue (1990), Kuwana (1994, 1995), Lakner (1994b, 1995), Ocone and Karatzas (1991), Pikovsky and Karatzas (1996), and Schweizer (1994d). Exercise 9.10 is based on Honda (1997b, c). For more on portfolio choice with regime switching, see Honda (1996, 1997b). For the results on filtering used in Exercise 9.10, see Lipster and Shiryaev (1977).

For optimal investment with "advance information" (that is, based on enlargement of filtrations), see Amendinger, Imkeller, and Schweizer (1998) and Pikovsky and Karatzas (1996).

On portfolio and consumption choice with stochastic return distributions, see Liu (1999) and Schroder and Skiadas (1999).

Exercise 9.4 is from Cox, Ingersoll, and Ross (1985b). Exercise 9.9 is based in part on Cvitanić and Karatzas (1992, 1995) and Tepla (2000).

For optimal behavior of a "large investor," that is, one who considers the impact of trading on prices, see Cuoco and Cvitanić (1998) and Sircar (1996).

On portfolio insurance, see Grossman and Zhou (1996). On optimal portfolio choice with logarithmic additive utility, there is a long history. A recent general treatment is given by Goll and Kallsen (1999). On the related growth-optimal policies, see Iyengar and Cover (1997) and work cited therein.

On policies allowing for a payoff with bankruptcy, see Sethi and Taksar (1992) and Sethi, Taksar, and Prisman (1992).

10

Equilibrium

THIS CHAPTER REVIEWS security market equilibrium in a continuous-time setting and derives several implications for security prices and expected returns. These include Breeden's consumption-based capital asset pricing model (in both complete- and incomplete-market settings) as well as the Cox-Ingersoll-Ross model of the term structure.

A. The Primitives

As usual, we let $B = (B^1, \ldots, B^d)$ denote a standard Brownian motion in $\mathbb{R}^d$ on a probability space $(\Omega, \mathscr{F}, P)$, and let $\mathbb{F} = \{\mathscr{F}_T : t \geq 0\}$ denote the standard filtration of B. The consumption space is the set L of adapted processes satisfying $E(\int_0^T c_t^2 \, dt) < \infty$ for some fixed time horizon $T > 0$.

There are m agents. Agent i is defined by a nonzero consumption endowment process e^i in the set L_+ nonnegative processes in L, and by a strictly increasing utility function $U_i : L_+ \to \mathbb{R}$.

As in Section 6L, a cumulative-dividend process is a finite-variance process of the form $C = Z + V - W$, where $Z = \int \theta \, dB$ for some $\theta \in \mathscr{L}(B)$, and where V and W are increasing adapted right-continuous processes. For any time t, the jump $\Delta C_t \equiv C_t - C_{t-}$ represents the lump-sum payment at time t. For example, if the security is a unit zero-coupon bond that matures at time τ, then $C_t = 0$, $t < \tau$, and $C_t = 1$, $t \geq \tau$. By convention, any dividend process C satisfies $C_{0-} = C_0 = 0$. For example, a dividend-rate process δ in L defines the cumulative-dividend process $C = V - W$ with $V_t = \int_0^t \max(\delta_s, 0) \, ds$ and $W_t = \int_0^t \max(-\delta_s, 0) \, ds$. There are $N + 1$ securities, numbered 0 through N, defined by a cumulative-dividend process $D = (D^{(0)}, D^{(1)}, \ldots, D^{(N)})$.

Mainly for expositional reasons, we assume that the given dividend processes are measured in nominal units of account, and will shortly define the price process for consumption in terms of the same nominal units of account. We later normalize by the price of consumption in order to recover continuous-time versions of the utility-based asset pricing results of Chapter 2. Altogether, the set of primitives of the economy is

$$\mathcal{E} = \{(\Omega, \mathcal{F}, \mathbb{F}, P); B; \{(e^i, U_i) : 1 \le i \le m\}; D\}. \tag{1}$$

B. Security-Spot Market Equilibrium

The dividend process $D = (D^{(0)}, \ldots, D^{(N)})$ is assigned a price process $X = (X^{(0)}, \ldots, X^{(N)})$ such that the gain process $G = D + X$ is an Ito process in $\mathbb{R}^{N+1}$. We treat X_t as the ex-dividend price at time t, that is, the price without including the current dividend jump ΔD_t. There is also a process p in L for the price of the single consumption commodity. A trading strategy is a process $\theta = (\theta^{(0)}, \ldots, \theta^{(N)})$ in $\mathcal{H}^2(G)$. Given the consumption-price process p, a trading strategy θ *finances a consumption process c* if

$$\theta_t \cdot (X_t + \Delta D_t) = \int_0^t \theta_s \, dG_s - \int_0^t p_s c_s \, ds, \quad t \in [0, T], \tag{2}$$

and

$$\theta_T \cdot (X_T + \Delta D_T) = 0. \tag{3}$$

Relation (2) is an accounting restriction, stating that the market value of the current portfolio is generated entirely by security trading gains, net of the cost of consumption purchases. The terminal budget constraint (3) requires that there be no remaining obligations at time T.

Given a security-price process X and a consumption-price process p, agent i faces the problem

$$\sup_{(c, \theta) \in \Lambda(i)} U_i(c), \tag{4}$$

where $\Lambda(i) = \{(c, \theta) \in L_+ \times \mathcal{H}^2(G) : \theta \text{ finances } c - e^i\}$.

A *security-spot market equilibrium* for the economy $\mathcal{E}$ of (1) is a collection

$$\{X; p; (c^i, \theta^i), 1 \le i \le m\} \tag{5}$$

such that, given the security-price process X and the consumption-price process p, for each agent i, (c^i, θ^i) solves (4), and markets clear:

$$\sum_{i=1}^m \theta^i = 0; \quad \sum_{i=1}^m c^i - e^i = 0.$$

C. Arrow-Debreu Equilibrium

A related notion of equilibrium is one in which any consumption process c in L can be purchased at time zero for some $\Pi(c)$ that is given by a nonzero linear *price function* $\Pi : L \to \mathbb{R}$. Paralleling the definitions given in Chapter 2, an allocation $(c^1, \ldots, c^m) \in (L_+)^m$ of consumption processes is feasible if $\sum_{i=1}^m c^i \le \sum_{i=1}^m e^i$. An Arrow-Debreu equilibrium is a collection $[\Pi, (c^1, \ldots, c^m)]$ consisting of a price function Π and a feasible allocation $(c^1, \ldots, c^m)$ such that, for each i, c^i solves

$$\sup_{c \in L_+} U_i(c) \quad \text{subject to } \Pi(c) \le \Pi(e^i). \tag{6}$$

Conditions for the existence of an Arrow-Debreu equilibrium are given in Section G and cited in the Notes.

Lemma. *If $\Pi : L \to \mathbb{R}$ is linear and strictly increasing, then there is a unique π in L such that*

$$\Pi(c) = E\left(\int_0^T \pi_t c_t \, dt \right), \quad c \in L. \tag{7}$$

Moreover, π is strictly positive.

A proof of this continuous-time analogue of Lemma 2C is found in the Notes. Since U_i is strictly increasing by assumption, any Arrow-Debreu equilibrium price function Π is strictly increasing and therefore has a representation of the form (7) for a unique process $\pi \gg 0$, which is known as the Riesz representation of Π.

If feasible, an allocation $(c^1, \ldots, c^m)$ is Pareto optimal if there is no feasible allocation $(b^1, \ldots, b^m)$ such that $U_i(b^i) \ge U_i(c^i)$ for all i, with strict inequality for at least one i.

The First Welfare Theorem. *Any Arrow-Debreu equilibrium allocation is Pareto optimal.*

Proof: Let $[\Pi, (c^1, \ldots, c^m)]$ be an Arrow-Debreu equilibrium, and let π denote the Riesz representation of Π. Suppose $(b^1, \ldots, b^m)$ is a feasible allocation with $U_i(b^i) \ge U_i(c^i)$ for all i, with at least one strict inequality, say for agent j. We need a contradiction to complete the proof. Since $U_j(b^j) > U_j(c^j)$, we know that

$$\Pi(b^j) > \Pi(c^j). \tag{8}$$

If for some i, $\epsilon \equiv \Pi(c^i) - \Pi(b^i) > 0$, we could let

$$\hat{c}^i = b^i + \frac{\epsilon}{\Pi(\pi)}\pi, \qquad (9)$$

from which $\Pi(\hat{c}^i) = \Pi(c^i)$. But then, since U_i is strictly increasing and $\pi > 0$, we would have $U_i(\hat{c}^i) > U_i(c^i)$, which is impossible by the definition of an equilibrium. Thus

$$\Pi(b^i) \geq \Pi(c^i), \quad 1 \leq i \leq m. \qquad (10)$$

Combining (8), (10), and feasibility produces the contradiction

$$\Pi\left(\sum_{i=1}^{m} e^i\right) \geq \Pi\left(\sum_{i=1}^{m} b^i\right) > \Pi\left(\sum_{i=1}^{m} c^i\right) = \Pi\left(\sum_{i=1}^{m} e^i\right), \qquad (11)$$

which proves the result. ∎

The following result is shown with the Separating Hyperplane Theorem in exactly the same manner as for Lemma 1E.

Proposition. *Suppose, for all i, that U_i is concave. Then $(c^1, \ldots, c^m)$ is a Pareto optimal allocation if and only if there is a nonzero vector λ in $\mathbb{R}_+^m$ such that $(c^1, \ldots, c^m)$ solves the problem*

$$\sup_{(b^1, \ldots, b^m)} \sum_{i=1}^{m} \lambda_i U_i(b^i) \quad \text{subject to } b^1 + \cdots + b^m \leq e^1 + \cdots + e^m. \qquad (12)$$

D. Implementing Arrow-Debreu Equilibrium

In this section we fix an Arrow-Debreu equilibrium $[\Pi, (c^1, \ldots, c^m)]$ and examine spanning conditions on the cumulative-dividend process D under which there exists a security-spot market equilibrium with the same consumption allocation. We assume throughout the following that $D_t^{(0)} = 0$, $t < T$, with $D_T^{(0)} = 1$, meaning that $D^{(0)}$ is a (nominal) zero-coupon unit bond maturing at T. This assumption can be relaxed at a cost in notational complexity.

An Ito process $M = (M^1, \ldots, M^k)$ in $\mathbb{R}^k$, for some integer $k \geq 1$, is called a *martingale generator* if M is a martingale and if, for any martingale Y, we can write

$$Y_t = Y_0 + \int_0^t \theta_s \, dM_s,$$

for some $\theta \in \mathcal{L}(M)$. For example, the underlying standard Brownian motion B is itself a martingale generator. From this, one can verify that a martingale M is a martingale generator if and only if $dM_t = \eta_t \, dB_t$, where η is an $\mathbb{R}^{k \times d}$-valued process that is of rank d almost everywhere.

The following spanning condition on the cumulative-dividend process D is unnecessarily restrictive (in a sense discussed in the Notes), but simplifies the following exposition. We will fix the martingale $M(D)$ in $\mathbb{R}^{N+1}$ defined by $M(D)_t = E_t(D_T)$.

Dynamic Spanning Condition. *$D^{(0)}$ is a nominal zero-coupon unit bond maturing at T and $M(D)$ is a martingale generator.*

Obviously, $D^{(0)}$ makes no contribution toward meeting the condition that $M(D)$ is a martingale generator. The dynamic spanning condition therefore requires at least $d + 1$ securities. An example of a cumulative-dividend process D for which $M(D)$ is a martingale generator is one for which $D_T^{(j)} = \int_0^T \sigma_t^{(j)} \, dB_t$, where $\sigma^{(1)}, \ldots, \sigma^{(N)}$ are the rows of a matrix process σ that has rank d almost everywhere. This means that $d + 1$ is also a sufficient number of securities.

Theorem. *Suppose that the cumulative-dividend process D satisfies the dynamic spanning condition. Let $[\Pi, (c^1, \ldots, c^m)]$ be an Arrow-Debreu equilibrium. Let p denote the Riesz representation of Π and let*

$$X_t = E_t(D_T - D_t), \quad t \in [0, T]. \tag{13}$$

If p is bounded, then $\{X; p; (c^i, \theta^i), 1 \le i \le m\}$ is a security-spot market equilibrium for some $(\theta^1, \ldots, \theta^m)$.

Proof: Given the security-price process X defined by (13) and the dynamic spanning condition on D, we know that $G = X + D = M(D)$ is a martingale generator. We pick an arbitrary agent i and let Y be the martingale defined by

$$Y_t = E_T \left[\int_0^T (c_s^i - e_s^i) p_s \, ds \right], \quad t \in [0, T]. \tag{14}$$

Since $\Pi(c^i - e^i) = 0$ and p is the Riesz representation of Π, we know that $Y_0 = 0$. The dynamic spanning condition implies that $M(D) = G$ is a martingale generator, so that there is some $\theta = (\theta^{(0)}, \theta^{(1)}, \ldots, \theta^{(N)})$ in $\mathscr{L}(G)$ with

$$Y_t = \int_0^t \theta_s \, dG_s, \quad t \in [0, T]. \tag{15}$$

Since p is bounded and c^i and e^i are in L, $E(Y_T^2) < \infty$. Thus $\theta \in \mathcal{H}^2(G)$ by Proposition 5B. Since $G^0 \equiv 1$, $\int \theta \, dG$ is unaffected by redefining $\theta^{(0)}$ so that

$$\theta_t^{(0)} = \sum_{j=1}^N \left[\int_0^t \theta_s^{(j)} \, dG_s^{(j)} - \theta_t^{(j)} (X_t^{(j)} + \Delta D_t^{(j)}) \right] - \int_0^t p_s (c_s^i - e_s^i) \, ds. \qquad (16)$$

Simple algebra and (14)–(16) imply that $\theta_T \cdot (X_T + \Delta D_T) = 0$ and that

$$\theta_t \cdot (X_t + \Delta D_t) = \int_0^t \theta_s \, dG_s - \int_0^t (c_s^i - e_s^i) p_s \, ds, \quad t \in [0, T]. \qquad (17)$$

That is, θ finances $c^i - e^i$.

If, for some agent i, $\hat{\theta}$ is a trading strategy financing $\hat{c} - e^i$ for some consumption process $\hat{c}$, we claim that $U_i(\hat{c}) \leq U_i(c^i)$. If, on the contrary, $U_i(\hat{c}) > U_i(c^i)$, then we have $\Pi(\hat{c}) > \Pi(c^i) = \Pi(e^i)$ by the properties of an Arrow-Debreu equilibrium, so $E\left[\int_0^T (\hat{c}_t - e_t^i) p_t \, dt\right] > 0$. This, however, is inconsistent with the requirement of the financing condition that

$$0 = \theta_T \cdot (X_T + \Delta D_T) = \int_0^T \hat{\theta}_t \, dG_t - \int_0^T (\hat{c}_t - e_t^i) p_t \, dt, \qquad (18)$$

as can be seen by taking expectations through (18) and using the fact that $E(\int_0^T \hat{\theta}_t \, dG_t) = 0$. Thus (c^i, θ) solves agent i's problem (4).

Let θ^i be chosen in this fashion for each agent $i > 1$, and let $\theta^1 = -\sum_{i=2}^m \theta^i$. It can be checked from the linearity of stochastic integration that θ^1 finances $c^1 - e^1$, so (c^1, θ^1) is a solution to problem (4) for agent 1. By construction, $\sum_{i=1}^m \theta^i = 0$. By the feasibility of $(c^1, \ldots, c^m)$, we conclude that $\{X; p; (c^i, \theta^i), 1 \leq i \leq m\}$ is an equilibrium. ∎

E. Real Security Prices

The equilibrium $\{X; p; (c^i, \theta^i), 1 \leq i \leq m\}$ shown in the last theorem has a nominal security-price process X that is "risk-neutral," in the sense of (13). Relative to the price of the consumption commodity, or in *real* terms, security prices are not generally risk-neutral. For example, consider a particular security paying the nominal cumulative-dividend process C defined by $C_t = \int_0^t \delta_s \, ds$, for some nonnegative dividend-rate process δ in L. We let Y denote the nominal price process of this security. By (13), $Y_t = E_t(\int_t^T \delta_s \, ds)$. The *real* price process S, defined by $S_t = Y_t/p_t$, and the real dividend-rate process $\hat{\delta}$, defined by $\hat{\delta}_t = \delta_t/p_t$, are therefore related by

$$S_t = \frac{1}{p_t} E_t \left(\int_t^T p_s \hat{\delta}_s \, ds \right), \quad t \in [0, T]. \qquad (19)$$

We can consider a more general cumulative-dividend process C that is increasing and right-continuous, allowing for the payment of lump-sum amounts at points in time, as for a coupon bond. Since the real dividend process $\hat{C}$ corresponding to C is given by $\hat{C}_t = \int_0^t p_s^{-1} dC_s$, the real price process S for a security promising the real cumulative-dividend process $\hat{C}$ is given from (13) by

$$S_t = \frac{1}{p_t} E_t \left(\int_t^T p_s \, d\hat{C}_s \right), \quad t \in [0, T]. \tag{20}$$

A simple example is a real zero-coupon unit bond maturing at some time τ in $(0, T]$, for which we have $\hat{C}_t = 0$, $t < \tau$, and $\hat{C}_t = 1$, $t \geq \tau$. The real bond-price process is then given from (20) by

$$\Lambda_{t,\tau} \equiv \frac{1}{p_t} E_t(p_t), \quad t < \tau, \tag{21}$$

with $\Lambda_{t,\tau} = 0$, $t \geq \tau$. This defines the term structure of interest rates. Although we will have no need for it, the extension of (20) for a cumulative-dividend process $\hat{C}$ that is an Ito process may be calculated from the general formula given in Chapter 6 for the deflation of Ito dividend processes.

The central issue, to which we now turn, is a characterization of the consumption-price process p. For example, we will give sufficient conditions for p to be an Ito process. After the above normalization to real prices, this will imply that p is a state-price deflator in the sense of Chapter 6.

F. Optimality with Additive Utility

For most of the remainder of the chapter, we will be exploiting the properties of *smooth-additive* utility functions, defined as follows.

Definition. *A utility function* $U : L_+ \to \mathbb{R}$ *is smooth-additive* (u) *if*

$$U(c) = E \left[\int_0^T u(c_t, t) \, dt \right], \tag{22}$$

where $u : \mathbb{R}_+ \times [0, T] \to \mathbb{R}$ *is smooth on* $(0, \infty) \times [0, T]$ *and, for each* t *in* $[0, T]$, $u(\cdot, t) : \mathbb{R}_+ \to \mathbb{R}$ *is increasing, strictly concave, with an unbounded derivative* $u_c(\cdot, t)$ *on* $(0, \infty)$.

For the purposes of this definition, we call a function "smooth" if it can be extended to an open set with continuous derivatives of any order. (In our applications, the order required will sometimes be as high as three). A special case of a utility function U that is smooth-additive (u) is that given by $u(c, t) = e^{-\rho t} c^\alpha / \alpha$, with $\alpha < 1$ and $\alpha \neq 0$. If the consumption-price process p is bounded, the Inada condition of unbounded u_c guarantees that consumption will be strictly positive.

Consider the choice problem in an Arrow-Debreu equilibrium with smooth-additive utility:

$$\sup_{c \in L_+} E\left[\int_0^T u(c_t, t)\, dt\right] \quad \text{subject to } E\left(\int_0^T p_t c_t\, dt\right) \leq w, \qquad (23)$$

where p is the Riesz representation of the equilibrium price function Π and $w > 0$ is the market value $\Pi(\hat{e})$ of the agent's endowment $\hat{e}$. Given the strict monotonicity and concavity of utility, the Saddle Point Theorem implies that a necessary and sufficient condition for c^* to solve (23) is the existence of a Lagrange multiplier $\gamma > 0$ such that c^* solves the unconstrained problem

$$\sup_{c \in L_+} E\left(\int_0^T [u(c_t, t) - \gamma p_t c_t]\, dt\right), \qquad (24)$$

along with the complementary slackness condition $E(\int_0^T p_t c_t^*\, dt) = w$.

Naturally, one can do no better than to maximize $u(c_t, t) - \gamma p_t c_t$ separately for each t and each state of the world. Since $u_c(\cdot, t)$ is unbounded, this implies, for optimal c^*, that $c^* \gg 0$ and that

$$u_c(c_t^*, t) = \gamma p_t, \quad t \in [0, T]. \qquad (25)$$

In fact, this leads directly to a method for solving (23) that is described in Section 9G, but that is not needed here. Relation (25) gives us our first characterization of the state-price deflator p in the security-spot market equilibrium studied in Sections D and E. We know, for some $\gamma > 0$, that

$$p_t = \frac{1}{\gamma} u_c(c_t^*, t), \quad t \in [0, T], \qquad (26)$$

assuming that one of the agents has the optimal consumption process c^* and a utility function that is smooth-additive (u). The fact that the Lagrange multiplier γ is unknown is of no consequence, since $\{\gamma p_t : t \in [0, T]\}$ is also a state-price deflator for any constant $\gamma > 0$. This characterization of the state-price deflator is in terms of an individual agent's consumption process. Now we work toward a like characterization of p in terms of aggregate consumption, which is arguably more easily studied from empirical data.

G. Equilibrium with Additive Utility

This section further characterizes state-price deflators under the assumption of smooth-additive utility. A proof of the following theorem is cited in the Notes.

Theorem. *Suppose that the aggregate endowment process e is bounded away from zero and that, for each i, U_i is smooth-additive (u_i). Then there is an Arrow-Debreu equilibrium $[\Pi, (c^1, \dots, c^m)]$ for which Π has a bounded Riesz representation p, and such that for all i, c^i is bounded away from zero.*

Coupling this result with Theorem D, we have conditions for the existence of a security-spot market equilibrium under smooth-additive utility.

Corollary. *Suppose, in addition, that the cumulative-dividend process D satisfies the dynamic spanning condition. Let X be given by (13). Then there are trading strategies $(\theta^1, \dots, \theta^m)$ such that $[X; p; (c^i, \theta^i), 1 \leq i \leq m]$ is a security-spot market equilibrium.*

We fix the equilibrium consumption allocation $(c^1, \dots, c^m)$ and consumption-price process p of this result for the remainder of this section and the next. By Theorem C, $(c^1, \dots, c^m)$ is a Pareto optimal allocation. By Proposition C, there exists a nonzero "weight" vector $\lambda \in \mathbb{R}^m_+$ such that $(c^1, \dots, c^m)$ solves the problem

$$\sup_{(b^1, \dots, b^m)} \sum_{i=1}^m \lambda_i E\left[\int_0^T u_i(b^i_t, t)\, dt\right] \quad \text{subject to } b^1 + \dots + b^m \leq e. \quad (27)$$

Because of the additive nature of utility, one can solve this problem separately for each time t in $[0, T]$ and state ω in Ω. In order to see this, let $u_\lambda : \mathbb{R}_+ \times [0, T] \to \mathbb{R}$ be defined by

$$u_\lambda(y, t) = \sup_{x \in \mathbb{R}^m} \sum_{i=1}^m \lambda_i u_i(x_i, t) \quad \text{subject to } x_1 + \dots + x_m \leq y. \quad (28)$$

Since $(c^1, \dots, c^m)$ solves (27), it follows that $[c^1(\omega, t), \dots, c^m(\omega, t)]$ solves problem (28) for $y = e(\omega, t)$, except perhaps for (ω, t) in a null subset. (A set $A \subset \Omega \times [0, T]$ is *null* if $E(\int_0^T 1_A(t)\, dt) = 0$, where $1_A(t)$ is the random variable whose outcome is 1 if (ω, t) is in A, and is zero otherwise.) This is shown as follows. Suppose not, and let $(b^1, \ldots, b^m)$ be a feasible allocation and A be a nonnull subset of $\Omega \times [0, T]$ such that, for all (ω, t) in A,

$$\sum_{i=1}^{m} \lambda_i u_i[b^i(\omega, t), t] > \sum_{i=1}^{m} \lambda_i u_i[c^i(\omega, t), t]. \tag{29}$$

Let $(a^1, \ldots, a^m)$ be the feasible allocation defined by

$$a^i(\omega, t) = b^i(\omega, t), \quad (\omega, t) \in A,$$

$$= c^i(\omega, t), \quad \text{otherwise.}$$

Then

$$\sum_{i=1}^{m} \lambda_i U_i(a^i) > \sum_{i=1}^{m} \lambda_i U_i(c^i),$$

contradicting the fact that $(c^1, \ldots, c^m)$ solves (27).

An exercise in applying the Implicit Function Theorem shows that the utility function $U_\lambda : L_+ \to \mathbb{R}$, defined by

$$U_\lambda(c) = E\left[\int_0^T u_\lambda(c_t, t) \, dt\right], \tag{30}$$

is smooth-additive (u_λ). With $y > 0$, the first-order conditions for optimality of x^* in (28) imply that

$$\lambda_i u_{ic}(x_i^*, t) = u_{\lambda c}(y, t), \quad i \in \{1, \ldots, m\}, \tag{31}$$

where the subscript "c" indicates a derivative in the customary way. This implies that, almost everywhere and for all i,

$$\lambda_i u_{ic}(c_t^i, t) = u_{\lambda c}(e_t, t). \tag{32}$$

Joining (32) with the first-order condition (26) for individual optimality implies that the Riesz representation p of Π is given by

$$k p_t = u_{\lambda c}(e_t, t), \quad t \in [0, T], \tag{33}$$

for a constant $k > 0$ that can be taken to be 1 by rescaling p.

We have thus characterized a nominal consumption-price process p in terms of the "marginal utility of a representative agent." It should be kept in mind that the weights $\lambda_1, \ldots, \lambda_m$ generally depend on the original endowment $(e^1, \ldots, e^m)$, and indeed on the particular equilibrium if there is more than one. (Uniqueness of equilibrium is implied by a gross-substitutes condition cited in the Notes.) Despite these limitations,

(33) is a useful representation of state prices on intuitive grounds, and the smoothness of u_λ is also important for future applications of Ito's Formula.

Returning to the security-spot market equilibrium of Theorem D, we can rewrite the security valuation equation (20) using the consumption numeraire in the form

$$S_t = \frac{1}{u_{\lambda c}(e_t, t)} E_t\left[\int_t^T u_{\lambda c}(e_s, s)\, d\hat{C}_s\right], \quad t \in [0, T], \tag{34}$$

which should strike a familiar note from a reading of Chapter 2.

H. The Consumption-Based CAPM

In Section G we showed that, in terms of a numeraire that is a zero-coupon bond paying one unit of account at time T, the consumption-price process p of Theorem G is given by $p_t = u_{\lambda c}(e_t, t)$, where u_λ is defined by (28) for some fixed utility weight vector $\lambda \in \mathbb{R}^m_+$. We henceforth assume that e is an Ito process of the form $de_t = \mu_e(t)\, dt + \sigma_e(t)dB_t$, which implies by Ito's Formula and the smoothness of u_λ that p is also an Ito process with

$$dp_t = \mu_p(t)\, dt + \sigma_p(t)\, dB_t, \tag{35}$$

where $\sigma_p(t) = \mu_{\lambda cc}(e_t, t)\sigma_e(t)$ and

$$\mu_p(t) = u_{\lambda cc}(e_t, t)\mu_e(t) + u_{\lambda ct}(e_t, t) + \frac{1}{2}u_{\lambda ccc}(e_t, t)\sigma_e(t) \cdot \sigma_e(t). \tag{36}$$

In view of (20) and the fact that p is an Ito process, p is in fact a state-price deflator (relative to the consumption numeraire). Based on a review of Section 6D, the associated short-rate process r, sometimes called the *real short rate* must be given by $r_t = -\mu_p(t)/p_t$. We can thus think of the real short rate r_t at time t as the expected exponential rate of decline of the representative agent's "marginal utility," which is $p_t = u_{\lambda c}(e_t, t)$. Also from Section 6D, if the cumulative return of a given security is given by an Ito process R, then the fact that p is a state-price deflator implies that

$$\mu_R(t) - r_t = -\frac{1}{p_t}\sigma_R(t) \cdot \sigma_p(t) = \gamma_t\sigma_R(t) \cdot \sigma_e(t), \tag{37}$$

where $\gamma_t \equiv -u_{\lambda cc}(e_t, t)/u_{\lambda c}(e_t, t)$ is the *Arrow-Pratt measure* of risk aversion of $u_\lambda(\cdot, t)$ at e_t. In other words, excess expected returns are increasing in the "instantaneous covariance" of returns with aggregate consumption changes, and are increasing in "representative risk aversion." Moreover, these relationships are linear. Under stronger technical conditions,

Section J extends this *consumption-based capital asset pricing model* (CCAPM) to incomplete markets. Within the restrictive setting of smooth-additive utility, the CCAPM is thus quite general. Without going into details, however, its empirical support is weak, as indicated in sources cited in the Notes.

We can also view the CCAPM from a traditional "beta" perspective. The required calculations are shown in Section 6D. Since $\sigma_p(\omega, t)$ and $\sigma_e(\omega, t)$ are co-linear vectors for all (ω, t), the beta calculations in Section 6D apply equivalently to both e and p. These calculations lead to the "beta" formula

$$\mu_R(t) - r_t = \beta_R(t)(\mu_t^* - r_t), \tag{38}$$

where

$$\beta_R(t) = \frac{\sigma_R(t) \cdot \sigma_t^*}{\sigma_t^* \cdot \sigma_t^*} \tag{39}$$

is the instantaneous analogue to the beta coefficient of the CAPM, and where μ^* and σ^* are the drift and diffusion of a return process R^* with the property that $\sigma_t^* = k_t \sigma_e(t)$ for some strictly positive real-valued process k. In the sense of Section 6D, R^* is a return process with perfect instantaneous correlation with the aggregate consumption process e.

I. The CIR Term Structure

We will work out an equilibrium justification of the Cox-Ingersoll-Ross (CIR) model of the term structure that was introduced in Section 7D. Our starting point is the solution to Exercise 9.4 involving the optimal-consumption process δ from a technology with a capital-stock process K. For a given "discount rate" $\rho \in (0, \infty)$, let

$$U(c) \equiv E\left[\int_0^T e^{-\rho t} \log(c_t) \, dt\right], \quad c \in L_+. \tag{40}$$

The single agent in the economy has the utility function $U : L_+ \to \overline{\mathbb{R}}$ defined by (40).

For simplicity, we take the Brownian motion B to be one-dimensional. Repeating the solution to Exercise 9.4, the optimal capital-stock process K is the Ito process defined by

$$dK_t = (K_t h Y_t - \delta_t) \, dt + K_t \epsilon \sqrt{Y_t} \, dB_t, \quad K_0 > 0, \tag{41}$$

where

$$\delta_t = \frac{\rho K_t}{1 - e^{-\rho(T-t)}}, \quad t \in [0, T], \tag{42}$$

and where Y solves the SDE

$$dY_t = (b - \kappa Y_t)\, dt + k\sqrt{Y_t}\, dB_t, \quad Y_0 > 0, \tag{43}$$

for strictly positive scalars κ, b, k, h, and ϵ such that $2b > k^2$ and $h > \epsilon^2$. We can think of Y as a "shock" process that affects the productivity of capital. The existence and nonnegativity of the process Y is treated in the Notes of Chapter 7. The existence of the process K defined by (41)–(42) follows by expressing K_t in terms of Y, which can be done by expanding $\log(K_t)$ with the aid of Ito's formula.

We will start by assuming that the single agent's endowment process e is the optimal "drawdown" rate δ on the capital stock defined by (42). From this point, despite some differences in technical assumptions, we can reproduce the asset pricing results developed earlier in the chapter.

The equilibrium proposed here does not fit into the technical framework of the model provided earlier in the chapter because the logarithmic utility function is not "smooth-additive" in the sense defined above, being unbounded below. We nevertheless proceed under the assumption that failure of the technical conditions does not invalidate the essential aspects of the model.

We take the state-price deflator p defined in the usual way for the one-agent ($\lambda = 1$) case of $u_\lambda(x, t) = e^{-\rho t} \log x$ by

$$p_t = u_{\lambda c}(\delta_t, t) = \frac{e^{-\rho t}}{\delta_t}, \quad t \in [0, T). \tag{44}$$

The real price process S of any security promising an increasing right-continuous real cumulative-dividend process $\hat{C}$ is then given by (20).

With the aid of Ito's Formula, we have

$$dp_t = (\epsilon^2 - h)Y_t p_t\, dt - p_t \epsilon \sqrt{Y_t}\, dB_t. \tag{45}$$

The short-rate process r is given as in Section H by

$$r_t = \frac{-\mu_p(t)}{p_t} = (h - \epsilon^2)Y_t. \tag{46}$$

Since $dr_t = (h - \epsilon^2)\, dY_t$, we calculate that

$$dr_t = \kappa(r^* - r_t)\, dt + \sigma_r \sqrt{r_t}\, dB_t, \tag{47}$$

where $r^* = b(h - \epsilon^2)/\kappa$ and $\sigma_r = k\sqrt{h - \epsilon^2}$. This is the form of the short rate assumed in the CIR model of the term structure studied in Section 7D in a "risk-neutral" setting. It is a convenient fact, to be shown shortly, that for the equilibrium state-price deflator p of (45), the associated "risk-neutral" stochastic differential equation for the short-rate process is of the same form as (47), although with different coefficients.

For $r_t > r^*$, the drift of r is negative; for $r_t < r^*$, the drift of r is positive. We can therefore view r as a *mean-reverting* process, reverting toward r^*. We can be more precise about this, as follows. It has been shown, as indicated in the Notes, that $\bar{r}_t \equiv E(r_t)$ is finite and continuous in t. It follows from Fubini's Theorem (Appendix C) that $E(\int_0^T r_t \, dt) < \infty$, and therefore, by Proposition 5B, that the stochastic integral $\int_0^T \sigma_r \sqrt{r_t} \, dB_t$ has zero expectation. Thus

$$\bar{r}_t = r_0 + E\left[\int_0^t \kappa(r^* - r_s) \, ds\right].$$

Applying Fubini's Theorem again, $\bar{r}_t = r_0 + \int_0^t \kappa(r^* - \bar{r}_s) \, ds$, which is equivalent to the ordinary differential equation

$$\frac{d\bar{r}_t}{dt} = \kappa(r^* - \bar{r}_t); \quad \bar{r}_0 = r_0,$$

with solution $\bar{r}_t = r^* + (r_0 - r^*)e^{-\kappa t}$. Thus, $E(r_t) \to r^*$ exponentially with t, and r^* is the "long-run mean" of the short-rate process. By using Fubini's Theorem for conditional expectations, we can show likewise that, for any times t and $s \geq t$,

$$E_t(r_s) = r^* + (r_t - r^*)e^{-\kappa(s-t)} \quad \text{almost surely.}$$

As we know from Chapter 7, in order to price term-structure instruments, it is enough to be able to represent the short-rate process r under an equivalent martingale measure. We can apply Ito's Formula to represent p in the form

$$p_t = p_0 \exp\left(\frac{h - \epsilon^2/2}{\epsilon^2 - h} \int_0^t r_s \, ds - \frac{\epsilon}{\sqrt{h - \epsilon^2}} \int_0^t \sqrt{r_s} \, dB_s\right). \tag{48}$$

Based on equation (6.15), under technical integrability conditions that we simply assume, the density process ξ of an equivalent martingale measure Q is given by

$$
\xi_t = \exp\left(\int_0^t r_s \, ds\right) \frac{p_t}{p_0}
$$

$$
= \exp\left(\frac{\epsilon^2/2}{\epsilon^2 - h} \int_0^t r_s \, ds - \frac{\epsilon}{\sqrt{h - \epsilon^2}} \int_0^t \sqrt{r_s} \, dB_s\right). \tag{49}
$$

From Girsanov's Theorem of Appendix D, a standard Brownian motion $\hat{B}$ under the equivalent martingale measure Q is defined by

$$
d\hat{B}_t = dB_t + \frac{\epsilon}{\sqrt{h - \epsilon^2}} \sqrt{r_t} \, dt. \tag{50}
$$

Thus, under the equivalent martingale measure Q, we can represent the short-rate process r in the same square-root mean-reverting form

$$
dr_t = \kappa(r^* - r_t) \, dt + \sigma_r \sqrt{r_t} \left(d\hat{B}_t - \frac{\epsilon}{\sqrt{h - \epsilon^2}} \sqrt{r_t} \, dt\right)
$$

$$
= [b(h - \epsilon^2) - (k\epsilon + \kappa)r_t] \, dt + \sigma_r \sqrt{r_t} \, d\hat{B}_t.
$$

In particular, $\Lambda_{t,s} = E_t^Q[\exp(\int_t^s -r_u \, du)]$, which is solved explicitly in Section 7D. Chapter 7 gives multifactor extensions, applications to derivative term-structure pricing, and an explicit solution of the fundamental solution of the PDE associated with r.

J. The CCAPM in Incomplete Markets

We can recover a version of the CCAPM without assuming complete markets, although more demanding technical assumptions are required and there is as yet no set of conditions that is sufficient for the existence of equilibrium except in trivial or simple parametric examples. We will pass over most of the technical details, which are handled in papers cited in the Notes, and take as an assumption the first-order conditions for individual optimality.

Section 9H shows that in principle, if the gradient $\nabla U_i(c^i)$ of the utility of agent i at an optimal-consumption process c^i exists and has a Riesz representation given by a deflator π^i, then π^i is a state-price deflator. The discrete-time analogue of this result in Proposition 2D. As shown in Appendix G, the gradient of a utility function U that is smooth-additive (u) at a consumption process c that is bounded away from zero has a Riesz representation π given by $\pi_t = u_c(c_t, t)$.

Let us assume that, for each agent i, the utility function U_i is smooth-additive (u_i) and that the equilibrium consumption process c^i is an Ito process bounded away from zero, so that

$$dc_t^i = \mu_c^i(t)\, dt + \sigma_c^i(t)\, dB_t,$$

for appropriate processes μ_c^i and σ_c^i. The Riesz representation π^i of $\nabla U_i(c^i)$ exists and is given by $\pi_t^i = u_{ic}(c_t^i, t)$. This implies that π^i is an Ito process, with $d\pi_t^i = \mu_\pi^i(t)\, dt + \sigma_\pi^i(t)\, dB_t$, where

$$\mu_\pi^i(t) = u_{icc}(c_t^i, t)\mu_c^i(t) + u_{ict}(e_t, t) + \frac{1}{2}u_{iccc}(e_t, t)\sigma_c^i(t) \cdot \sigma_c^i(t)$$

and $\sigma_\pi^i(t) = u_{icc}(c_t^i, t)\sigma_c^i(t)$.

From this point, the calculations in Section H for the representative agent can be repeated for agent i. This replaces (37) with

$$\mu_R(t) - r_t = \gamma_t^i \sigma_R(t) \cdot \sigma_c^i(t), \tag{51}$$

where $r_t = -\mu_\pi^i(t)/\pi_t^i$, and where $\gamma_t^i = -u_{icc}(c_t^i, t)/u_{ic}(c_t^i, t)$ is the "risk aversion" of agent i at time t. If there exists a return process R with $\sigma_R = 0$, then r is the short-rate process. In any case, r_t is the expected return on any trading strategy whose return process R has $\sigma_R(t) \cdot \sigma_c^i(t) = 0$.

Assuming that there is indeed a short-rate process r, we can divide each side of (51) by γ_t^i and then sum the resulting expression over the m agents. Since $\sigma_e(t) = \sigma_c^1(t) + \cdots + \sigma_c^m(t)$, we get

$$\mu_R(t) - r_t = \Gamma_t \sigma_R(t) \cdot \sigma_e(t), \tag{52}$$

where

$$\Gamma_t \equiv \left(\frac{1}{\gamma_t^1} + \cdots + \frac{1}{\gamma_t^m}\right)^{-1}$$

is referred to as the *market risk aversion*. Thus, (52) extends (37), showing that excess expected rates of return on any security are proportional to the "instantaneous covariance" of the return with aggregate consumption increments, with a "market-risk-aversion" constant of proportionality. A "beta" form of the CCAPM can now be derived, as shown in Section 6D.

Exercises

10.1 Prove Proposition C.

10.2 Show the calculations verifying relations (45) through (50).

10.3 Let $\tilde{r} = \{\tilde{r}_t : 0 \le t \le T\}$ be an arbitrary nonnegative bounded adapted process. This question allows you to prove the existence of a continuous-time security-spot market equilibrium with classical preferences in which the short-rate process is $\tilde{r}$.

First, for the model of preferences, suppose there is a single agent with a utility function that is smooth-additive (u), where $u(x, t) = e^{-\rho t} x^\alpha$, for $\alpha \in (0, 1)$. Next, suppose that the consumption endowment process e is defined by $e_t = \exp(Z_t)$, where

$$Z_t = Z_0 + \int_0^t (a + b\tilde{r}_s) \, ds + \int_0^t \sqrt{\tilde{r}_s} \, \sigma \, dB_s, \tag{53}$$

where a and b are constants, and where σ is a constant vector in $\mathbb{R}^d$.

(A) Choose the constants a and b so that the equilibrium short-rate process is $\tilde{r}$.

(B) Suppose there are heterogeneous agents with utility functions defined, for $i \in \{1, \ldots, m\}$, by

$$U_i(c) = E\left(\int_0^T \exp\left[-\int_0^t \rho_i(s) \, ds \right] c_t^\alpha \, dt \right),$$

where ρ_i is a bounded adapted process. The endowment for agent i is a process e^i such that $e = \sum_{i=1}^m e^i$ is the process defined above in terms of $\tilde{r}$. Assume the existence of an equilibrium with dynamic spanning. Calculate the short-rate process r in terms of the vector $\lambda \in \mathbb{R}_+^m$ (of "weights" on the m agents' utility functions) that defines the representative agent.

(C) Repeat part (B) in the special case that $\rho_i = \bar{\rho}$ for all i, where $\bar{\rho}$ is a constant. Do not assume complete markets (dynamic spanning), but do assume that, for all i, the endowment process e^i is financed by some trading strategy whose market value is bounded below. That is, calculate the short-rate process once again. Can you choose a and b so that the short-rate process is $\tilde{r}$? Support your answer.

10.4 This is an alternative to the CIR model of the term structure found in Section I. In the CIR model, the equilibrium interest rate has an attractive mean-reverting property. Here we derive a less attractive term structure because of a cruder model for adjustment of the capital stock. Although one must make some minor technical assumptions, there is only one natural closed-form solution.

The capital stock K solves the stochastic integral equation

$$K_t = K_0 + \int_0^t (hK_s - \delta_s) \, ds + \int_0^t \epsilon K_s \, dB_s, \qquad t \ge 0,$$

where h and ϵ are strictly positive scalars, B is a standard Brownian motion in $\mathbb{R}$, and $\delta = \{\delta_t : t \geq 0\}$ is a nonnegative dividend process. As in Exercise 9.4, the single firm in question depletes its capital stock K_t at the rate δ_t. We take an infinite-horizon setting and assume that the firm depletes its stock so as to maximize the agent's utility $U(\delta)$, with

$$U(\delta) = E\left(\int_0^\infty e^{-\rho t} \delta_t^\alpha \, dt\right),$$

where $\rho > 0$ is a scalar discount rate and $\alpha \in (0, 1)$.

(A) Solve the firm's dividend control problem.

The consumer ignores what the firm is trying to do and merely takes it that the firm's common share sells for $\mathscr{S}(K_t)$, $t \geq 0$, where $\mathscr{S}$ is a C^2 strictly increasing function, and that each share pays the dividend process δ that the firm determines. The consumer is free to purchase any number of these shares (or to short-sell them), and is also able to borrow or lend at a short-rate process r given by $r_t = R(K_t)$, for some function R of the current capital stock. These are the only two securities available. The consumer has one share of the firm's stock as an initial endowment. Let W_t denote the consumer's total wealth at any time t in stock and bond. The consumer must choose at any time t the fraction of wealth to hold in the firm's share (with the remainder reinvested continually at the short rate) and must also decide at what rate to consume. (Consumption is the numeraire.)

(B) Briefly formulate the consumer's portfolio-consumption control problem. Derive the Bellman equation and first-order conditions, assuming differentiability and interior optima.

(C) Choose a stock-pricing function $\mathscr{S}$ and an interest-rate function R at which the consumer optimally holds none of the bond and one share of the firm. In other words: State an equilibrium security-price process and an interest-rate process, both as functions of the current capital stock K_t.

(D) Calculate the initial equilibrium market value of a zero-net-supply bond paying one unit of real wealth at a given time $\tau > 0$. Supply also the equilibrium market value of a *consol*, a pure income bond paying consumption perpetually at a fixed rate of one unit of consumption per unit of time.

(E) State a differential equation for the equilibrium market value of a security paying dividends at a rate given by a bounded C^2 function f (with bounded derivative) of the current capital stock. Include a boundary condition.

10.5 Consider the following continuous-time analogue to the Markov single-agent asset pricing model of Chapter 4. Let X be the Ito process in $\mathbb{R}^N$ solving the stochastic differential equation

$$dX_t = \nu(X_t) \, dt + \eta(X_t) \, dB_t; \qquad X_0 = x \in \mathbb{R}^N, \tag{54}$$

where $\nu : \mathbb{R}^N \to \mathbb{R}^N$ and $\eta : \mathbb{R}^N \to \mathbb{R}^{N \times d}$ are sufficiently well behaved for existence. There are N securities in total supply of one each, paying dividends according to a bounded measurable function $f : \mathbb{R}^N \to \mathbb{R}^N_+$. That is, security n pays dividends at the rate $f_n(X_t)$ at time t. The security-price process is an Ito process S in $\mathbb{R}^N$. The single agent chooses a nonnegative real-valued bounded adapted consumption process c and a bounded trading strategy $\theta = (\theta^{(1)}, \ldots, \theta^{(N)})$. The wealth process $W^{c\theta}$ of an agent initially endowed with all of the securities and adopting the consumption-portfolio strategy (c, θ) is thus given by

$$W_T^{c\theta} = \mathbf{1} \cdot S_0 + \int_0^T \left[\theta_t \cdot f(X_t) - c_t \right] dt + \int_0^T \theta_t \, dS_t, \qquad T \geq 0,$$

where $\mathbf{1} = (1, 1, \ldots, 1)^\top \in \mathbb{R}^N$. The agent's utility function U is defined by

$$U(c) = E\left[\int_0^\infty e^{-\rho t} u(c_t) \, dt \right],$$

where $\rho \in (0, \infty)$ and $u : \mathbb{R}_+ \to \mathbb{R}$ is increasing and strictly concave. An equilibrium for this economy is a security-price process S such that the problem $\sup_{c, \theta} U(c)$ has a solution (c, θ) with $c_t = \mathbf{1} \cdot f(X_t)$ and $\theta_t = \mathbf{1}$ for all $t \in [0, \infty)$.

(A) Suppose the security-price process S is given by $S_t = \mathscr{S}(X_t)$ for all t, for some twice continuously differentiable function $\mathscr{S} : \mathbb{R}^N \to \mathbb{R}^N$. Provide the Bellman equation for the agent's stochastic control problem. A verification argument is not required.

(B) Based on your understanding of this model, give an expression for the term structure of interest rates. That is, provide a conjecture for the market value at time t of a T-period pure discount bond, which is a zero-net-supply contract to pay one unit of the consumption numeraire at time $t + T$. No verification argument is required here. The expression should involve only the primitives of the model, ν, η, d, u, ρ, the initial state $x \in \mathbb{R}^N$, and future states, $X_t, t \geq 0$.

(C) Provide a PDE for the market value of any security as a necessary condition for an equilibrium, under stated regularity conditions, using the following infinite-horizon version of the Feynman-Kac formula. (We drop the argument $x \in \mathbb{R}^N$ from all functions for simplicity.) We do not supply the "strong regularity conditions" referred to in the result; there is a range of possible assumptions that are cumbersome and mainly of mathematical interest.

A Version of the Feynman-Kac Formula. *Suppose* $R : \mathbb{R}^N \to \mathbb{R}$ *and* $h : \mathbb{R}^N \to \mathbb{R}$ *are measurable, and that* (ν, η, h, R) *satisfies the "strong regularity conditions." Suppose* $F \in C^2(\mathbb{R}^N)$ *satisfies a growth condition. Then* F *satisfies the partial differential equation* $\mathscr{D}F - RF + h = 0$ *if and only if*

$$F(x) = E\left(\int_0^\infty \exp\left[-\int_0^t R(X_s) \, ds \right] h(X_t) \, dt \right), \qquad x \in \mathbb{R}^N,$$

where $\mathscr{D}F = F_x \nu + \frac{1}{2}\mathrm{tr}(\eta^\top F_{xx} \eta)$.

(D) Solve for the term structure of interest rates in the special case of $N = 1$ and

$$u(y) = \frac{y^{(\alpha+1)} - 1}{\alpha + 1}, \qquad \alpha \in (-1, 0),$$

$$\nu(x) = Ax, \qquad A \in \mathbb{R},$$

$$\eta(x) = D, \qquad D \in \mathbb{R}^d,$$

$$f(x) = e^{bx}, \qquad b \in \mathbb{R}.$$

Also, solve for the current equilibrium short-rate process r in this economy.

(E) For this last part, a further extension of the Black-Scholes model, we do not take the parametric assumptions of part (D). Suppose the short-rate process is given by $r_t = R(X_t)$ for all t, where $R : \mathbb{R}^N \to \mathbb{R}$, and that the security-price process is given by $S_t = \mathscr{S}(X_t)$ for all t, for some twice continuously differentiable function $\mathscr{S} : \mathbb{R}^N \to \mathbb{R}^N$. Give a PDE for the arbitrage-free value of an additional security defined by a dividend process $\{h(X_t) : t \geq 0\}$, where $h : \mathbb{R}^N \to \mathbb{R}$ is bounded and measurable. In particular, state regularity conditions implying redundancy of this additional security. Finally, give a solution to the PDE you suggest, in the form of an expectation, and provide the corresponding regularity conditions.

10.6 This exercise is to verify that the CIR model of the term structure given in Section I can be embedded in a stock-market equilibrium with decentralized production decisions. The objective is to construct an equilibrium $[(S, \pi), \delta, (c, \theta)]$ of the following form:

  (a) δ is the optimal real output rate process of a firm controlling the capital-stock production process and maximizing its share price;
  (b) π is a state-price deflator;
  (c) S is the real stock-price process of the firm that is taken as given by the agent, and is equal to the share-price process generated as the market value of the firm's solution to the problem of maximizing its real market value, given the state-price deflator π;
  (d) $(c_t, \theta_t) = (\delta_t, 1)$ solves the agent's optimal-consumption and trading strategy problem, given (S, δ) as the price process and real dividend-rate process of the firm. (Note that, as opposed to the pure-exchange economy studied in the body of the chapter, for which securities are held in zero net supply, the total supply of the firm's shares is 1. The market clearing condition is thus that the agent optimally holds one share in equilibrium.)

(A) Formally define a stochastic equilibrium consistent with the loose description just given. In particular, state precisely the agent's problem and the firm's problem.

(B) In the setting of Exercise 9.4, show that the (real) stock-price process $S = K$, the capital-stock process of (41), and the dividend rate δ given by (42) are consistent with equilibrium. Add any technical regularity conditions that you find appropriate. Hint: Be careful about real versus nominal values.

10.7 Given the Markov shock process X of (54) and an equilibrium characterized by Theorem G and its corollary, suppose that the aggregate endowment process e is defined by $e_t = g(X_t, t)$, where $g \in C^{2,1}(\mathbb{R}^N \times [0, T])$. Express a state-price deflator p and the short rate r in the form $p_t = \varphi(X_t, t)$ and $r_t = R(X_t, t)$, for measurable functions φ and R on $\mathbb{R}^N \times [0, T]$. Under technical conditions, the density process ξ of an equivalent martingale measure Q for real security prices is defined by $\xi_t = \exp(\int_0^t r_s \, ds) p_t$. Show that $d\xi_t = -\xi_t \Theta(X_t, t) \, dB_t$ for some $\mathbb{R}^d$-valued function Θ on $\mathbb{R}^N \times [0, T]$. Show that there is a standard Brownian motion $\hat{B}$ in $\mathbb{R}^d$ under Q such that X solves an SDE of the form

$$dX_t = \alpha(X_t, t) \, dt + \eta(X_t, t) \, d\hat{B}_t,$$

and state the function α. Show that, under technical regularity conditions, the price of a security promising a real dividend-rate process of the form $\{h(X_t, t) : t \in [0, T]\}$ is given as the solution to a PDE of the Cauchy type examined in Appendix E. State the PDE.

Notes

The basic framework of this chapter is standard. The seminal continuous-time equilibrium asset pricing model is due to Merton (1973a).

(C) Section C is standard in general-equilibrium theory. Existence of Arrow-Debreu equilibria in infinite-dimensional settings similar to the one treated in this chapter was first shown by Bewley (1972). The first result that applies directly to the case of square-integrable functions, treated here, is due to Mas-Colell (1986a). Developments in general-equilibrium modeling in infinite-dimensional spaces are surveyed by Mas-Colell and Zame (1992). Theorem G is from Duffie and Zame (1989). Other proofs of essentially the same result are given by Araujo and Monteiro (1989), Karatzas, Lakner, Lehoczky, and Shreve (1991), Dana and Pontier (1990), and Dana (1993a, b), who studies the uniqueness of equilibria. Dana and Le Van (1996) pursue duality-based equilibrium results. An extension showing existence with recursive utility is given in Duffie, Geoffard, Skiadas (1994). (A sense in which this formulation is restrictive is given in Araujo and Monteiro [1987] and Monteiro [1994].) Dumas, Uppal, and Wang (2000) provide a characterization of efficient allocations with recursive utility, and applications to asset pricing.

On Pareto optimality in infinite-dimensional economies, see Mas-Colell (1986b). Colell and He (1992b) provide a notion of "local" agent weights associated with the locally Pareto optimal allocation of securities to agents.

Lemma C is proved as follows. First, L is a Banach lattice under the norm

$$c \mapsto \left[E\left(\int_0^T c_t^2 \, dt \right) \right]^{1/2}.$$

Any increasing linear function $\Pi : L \to \mathbb{R}$ on a Banach lattice is continuous, as shown, for example, by Aliprantis and Burkinshaw (1985). Under the given norm, L is a Hilbert space with inner product $(p, c) \mapsto E(\int_0^T p_t c_t \, dt)$. Since Π

is continuous, there is a unique π in L such that Π has the representation $\Pi(c) = E(\int_0^T \pi_t c_t \, dt)$, based on the same reasoning used in Exercise 1.17. Since Π is strictly increasing, π is strictly positive.

(D–G) Section D is based on Duffie and Huang (1985) and Duffie (1986). The dynamic spanning condition and the assumption that securities are defined in nominal terms can be weakened, as explained by Duffie and Zame (1989). The remainder of Section G is based on Huang (1987). Christensen, Graversen, and Miltersen (1996) also relax the dynamic-spanning assumption.

(H–J) Section H presents the consumption-based capital asset pricing model of Breeden (1979), whose discrete-time antecedent is Rubinstein (1976). The line of proof shown here, however, is from Duffie and Zame (1989). Section J contains Breeden's consumption-based CAPM once again, this time without complete markets. The general line of proof is from Grossman and Shiller (1982) and Back (1991); the latter has a more general information filtration. For further development of this model, see Cornell (1981) and Madan (1988). Breeden's original proof is based on the assumed existence of smooth solutions to each agent's value function for stochastic control in a Markov setting. Breeden follows Merton (1973a) in this regard. The impact of transactions costs on the consumption-based CAPM is studied by Grossman and Laroque (1990). See also He and Modest (1995), Marshall (1999), and Vayanos (1998). Related results are found in Black (1990), Delgado and Dumas (1993), and Heston (1990). For an empirical analysis of the consumption-based CAPM, see Breeden, Gibbons, and Litzenberger (1989).

(I) Section I is condensed from Cox, Ingersoll, and Ross (1985b). For empirical analyses of the Cox, Ingersoll, and Ross (1985a) term-structure model, see Chen and Scott (1992a, b, 1993a), Gibbons and Ramaswamy (1993), and Pearson and Sun (1994). A discrete-time analogue of the Cox, Ingersoll, and Ross term-structure model is due to Gibbons and Sun (1986). For further analysis in a Markov setting, see Cox, Ingersoll, and Ross (1985a) and Breeden (1986). For more on the CIR term-structure model, and related models, see Chapter 7. Goldstein and Zapatero (1996) present a model supporting the Vasicek term-structure model.

Additional Topics: Karatzas, Lakner, Lehoczky, and Shreve (1991) and Karatzas, Lehoczky, and Shreve (1990) have relatively explicit solutions of equilibrium with additive utility. Karatzas, Lehoczky, and Shreve (1991) show the existence of equilibrium with *singular price* behavior, meaning that the state-price deflator is not an Ito process. This implies, for example, that there is no short-rate process.

Asset-pricing models, or related theory, based on habit-formation utility models are given by Dai (2000), Detemple and Zapatero (1991), Sundaresan (1989), Constantinides (1990), Chapman (1998a), and Shrikhande (1995). The equilibrium or asset-pricing implications of recursive-utility models in continuous time, called stochastic differential utility, are developed by Duffie and Epstein (1992a), Duffie and Skiadas (1994), Duffie, Schroder, and Skiadas (1997), Dumas, Uppal, and Wang (2000), Epstein and Melino (1995), Fisher and Gilles (1997), and

Ma (1991). For the impact of disappointment aversion on security valuation, see Bonomo and Garcia (1993). Chen and Epstein (1999) and (in discrete time) Epstein and Wang (1994) explore the effects, and representation, of ambiguity aversion in the face of Knightian uncertainty. Heaton (1993) examines the implications of time-nonseparable preferences and time aggregation of data. See also Campbell (1993).

Some examples of models with incomplete information, or heterogeneous beliefs, or asymmetric information are provided by Back, Cao, and Willard (2000), Detemple (1986, 1995), Detemple and Murthy (1994b, 1997b), Dothan and Feldman (1986), Gennotte (1986), Ghysels (1986), Honda (1997a), Pikovsky and Karatzas (1998), Wang (1993a), and Zapatero (1993, 1998).

Dumas (1989) and Delgado and Dumas (1993) work out explicit solutions for examples of equilibrium models with additive utility. Bajeux-Besnainou and Portait (1997) and Johnson (1994) give a characterization of state-price deflators in terms of a log-utility-based numeraire deflator, initially developed by Long (1990).

Chamberlain (1988) gives sufficient conditions for the Capital Asset Pricing Model, based on the market portfolio.

For an equilibrium model of portfolio insurance, see Basak (1995). Föllmer (1993) describes an alternative to the standard general-equilibrium approach to asset pricing. Pham and Touzi (1993) examine an equilibrium model of the risk premium associated with stochastic volatility. For applications to foreign exchange rates, see Nielsen and Saá-Requejo (1992) and Zapatero (1995).

Bick (1986), Hodges and Carverhill (1992), and Hodges and Selby (1996) present equilibrium models supporting the Black-Scholes option-pricing formula.

Exercise 10.3 is based partly on Heston (1988b). See also Nakagawa (1999). For interest-rate behavior with heterogeneous agents, see Wang (1996). Part (D) of Exercise 10.5 is from Hansen and Singleton (1996). Exercise 10.7 is based on Cox, Ingersoll, and Ross (1985a), Huang (1987), and Duffie and Zame (1989).

Basak (1997) and Frey and Stremme (1997) treat agents who understand that they have market power. Basak and Cuoco (1999), Detemple and Murthy (1997a), Detemple and Serrat (1999), Saito (1998), and Serrat (1995) address equilibrium with portfolio constraints and incomplete markets. In particular, Loewenstein and Willard (1999) treat collateral constraints.

Equilibrium in international asset markets is treated, for example, by Serrat (2000).

For applications to insurance, see, for example, Aase (1999) and Zuasti (1999).

11
Corporate Securities

THIS CHAPTER OFFERS a basic review of the valuation of equities and corporate liabilities, beginning with some standard issues regarding the capital structure of a firm. Then, we turn to models of the valuation of defaultable debt that are based on an assumed stochastic arrival intensity of the stopping time defining default. The work presented in this chapter is widely extended in work cited in the Notes.

We begin in the first few sections with an extremely simple model of the stochastic behavior of the market values of assets, equity, and debt. We may think of equity and debt, at this first pass, as derivatives with respect to the total market value of the firm, and priced accordingly. Later, we introduce market imperfections and increase the degree of control that may be exercised by holders of equity and debt. With this, the theory becomes more complex and less like a derivative valuation model. There are many more interesting variations than could be addressed well in the space available here. Our objective is merely to convey some sense of the types of issues and standard modeling approaches.

We let B be a standard Brownian motion in $\mathbb{R}^d$ on a complete probability space $(\Omega, \mathcal{F}, P)$, and fix the standard filtration $\{\mathcal{F}_t : t \geq 0\}$ of B. Later, we allow for information revealed by "Poisson-like arrivals," a significant departure from our usual case of Brownian information.

A. The Black-Scholes-Merton Model

For a simple start, we outline the classic Black-Scholes-Merton model of corporate debt and equity valuation. We suppose that the firm's future cash flows have a total market value at time t given by A_t, where A is a

259

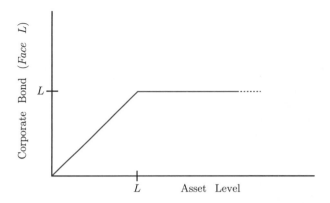

Figure 11.1. *Corporate Bond as a Derivative on the Firm's Assets*

geometric Brownian motion, satisfying

$$dA_t = \varphi A_t \, dt + \sigma A_t \, dB_t,$$

for constants φ and $\sigma > 0$, and where we have taken $d = 1$ as the dimension of the underlying Brownian motion B. One sometimes refers to A_t as the *assets* of the firm. We will suppose for simplicity that the firm produces no cash flows before a given time T. In order to justify this valuation of the firm, we could assume that there is some other security (or self-financing trading strategy) whose market value at any time t is A_t.

We take it that the original owners of the firm have chosen a capital structure consisting of pure equity and of debt in the form of a single zero-coupon bond maturing at time T, of face value L. In the event that the total value A_T of the firm at maturity is less than the contractual payment L due on the debt, the firm defaults, giving its future cash flows, worth A_T, to debtholders. That is, debtholders receive $\min(L, A_T)$ at T, as depicted in Figure 11.1. Equityholders receive the residual $\max(A_T - L, 0)$. We suppose for simplicity that there are no other distributions (such as dividends) to debt or equity. We will shortly confirm the natural conjecture that the market value of equity is given by the Black-Scholes option-pricing formula, treating the firm's asset value as the price of the underlying security.

Bond and equity investors have already paid the original owners of the firm for their respective securities. The absence of well-behaved arbitrage implies that at any time $t < T$, the total of the market values S_t of equity and Y_t of debt must be the market value A_t of the assets. (The result seems obvious; an exercise asks for proof.)

Markets are complete, in the sense of Chapter 6, given riskless borrowing or lending at a constant rate r and access to a self-financing trading strategy whose value process is A. This implies that there is at most one equivalent martingale measure.

Letting $B_t^Q = B_t + \eta t$, where $\eta = (\varphi - r)/\sigma$, we have

$$dA_t = rA_t\, dt + \sigma A_t\, dB_t^Q.$$

By Girsanov's Theorem, B^Q defines a standard Brownian motion under the equivalent probability measure Q defined by

$$\frac{dQ}{dP} = e^{-\eta B(T) - \eta^2 T/2}.$$

By Ito's Formula, $\{e^{-rt}A_t : t \in [0, T]\}$ is a Q-martingale. It follows that, after deflation by e^{-rt}, Q is the equivalent martingale measure. As Q is unique in this regard, we have the unique price process S of equity in the absence of well-behaved arbitrage, as explained in Chapter 6, given by

$$S_t = E_t^Q\big[e^{-r(T-t)} \max(A_T - L, 0)\big].$$

Thus, the equity price S_t is computed by the Black-Scholes option-pricing formula, treating A_t as the underlying asset price, σ as the volatility coefficient, the face value L of debt as the strike price, and $T - t$ as the time remaining to exercise. The market value of debt at time t is the residual, $A_t - S_t$.

When the original owners of the firm sold the debt with face value L and the equity, they realized a total initial market value of $S_0 + Y_0 = A_0$, which does not depend on the chosen face value L of debt. This is one aspect of the *Modigliani-Miller Theorem*. The same irrelevance of capital structure for the total valuation of the firm applies much more generally, and has nothing to do with geometric Brownian motion, nor with the specific nature of debt and equity. Once we consider market imperfections, however, the design of the capital structure can be important in this regard.

Fixing the current value A_t of the assets, the market value S_t of equity is increasing in the asset volatility parameter σ, due to the usual Jensen effect in the Black-Scholes formula. Thus, equity owners, were they to be given the opportunity to make a switch to a "riskier technology," one with a larger asset volatility parameter, would increase their market valuation by doing so, at the expense of bondholders, provided the total initial market value of the firm is not reduced too much by the switch. This is a simple example of what is sometimes called "asset substitution."

Given the time value of the option embedded in equity, bondhold-ers would prefer to advance the maturity date of the debt; equityholders would prefer to extend it.

Equityholders (or managers acting as their agents) typically hold the power to make decisions on behalf of the firm, subject to legal and con-tractual restrictions such as debt covenants. This is natural in light of equity's position as the residual claim on the firm's cash flows. Later, in both the body of the chapter and in the exercises, we consider the oppor-tunity that equityholders may have to issue additional debt, to call debt, or to make changes in production technologies. We will also consider certain rights of debtholders.

B. Endogenous Default Timing

We shift now to a slightly more elaborate setting for the valuation of debt and equity, and consider the endogenous timing of default. We take as given a martingale measure Q, in the infinite-horizon sense of Section 6N, after deflation by e^{-rt}.

The resources of a given firm are assumed to consist of cash flows at the rate δ_t for each time t. We suppose that δ is an adapted process with $\int_0^t |\delta_s| ds < \infty$ almost surely for all t. The market value of the assets of the firm at time t is defined as the market value A_t of the future cash flows. That is,

$$A_t = E_t^Q \left[\int_t^\infty e^{-r(s-t)} \delta_s ds \right]. \tag{1}$$

We assume that A_t is well defined and finite for all t. The martingale-representation part of Girsanov's Theorem then implies that

$$dA_t = (rA_t - \delta_t)dt + \sigma_t \, dB_t^Q, \tag{2}$$

where σ is an adapted $\mathbb{R}^d$-valued process such that $\int_0^T \sigma_t \cdot \sigma_t \, dt < \infty$ for all $T \in [0, \infty)$, and where B^Q is the standard Brownian motion in $\mathbb{R}^d$ under Q obtained from B and Girsanov's Theorem.

We suppose that the original owners of the firm chose its capital struc-ture to consist of a single bond as its debt, and pure equity, defined in detail below. The bond and equity investors have already paid the origi-nal owners for these securities. Before we consider the effects of market imperfections, the total of the market values of equity and debt must be the market value A of the assets, which is a given process, so the design of the capital structure is again irrelevant from the viewpoint of maximizing the total value received by the original owners of the firm.

For simplicity, we suppose that the bond promises to pay coupons at a constant total rate c, continually in time, until default. This sort of bond is sometimes called a *consol*. Equityholders receive the residual cash flow in the form of dividends at the rate $\delta_t - c$ at time t, until default. At default, the firm's future cash flows are assigned to debtholders.

The equityholders' dividend rate, $\delta_t - c$, may have negative outcomes. It is commonly stipulated, however, that equity claimants have *limited liability*, meaning that they should not experience negative cash flows. One can arrange for limited liability by dilution of equity. That is, so long as the market value of equity remains strictly positive, newly issued equity can be sold into the market so as to continually finance the negative portion $(c - \delta_t)^+$ of the residual cash flow. (Alternatively, the firm could issue debt, or other forms of securities, to finance itself, which we pursue in exercises.) When the price of equity reaches zero, and the financing of the firm through equity dilution is no longer possible, the firm is in any case in default, as we shall see. While dilution increases the quantity of shares outstanding, it does not alter the total market value of all shares, and so is a relatively simple modeling device. Moreover, dilution is irrelevant to individual shareholders, who would in any case be in a position to avoid negative cash flows by selling their own shares as necessary to finance the negative portion of their dividends, with the same effect as if the firm had diluted their shares for this purpose. We are ignoring here any frictional costs of equity issuance or trading. This is another aspect of the Modigliani-Miller theory, that part of it dealing with the irrelevance of dividend policy.

Equityholders are assumed to have the contractual right to declare default at any stopping time T, at which time equityholders give up to debtholders the rights to all future cash flows, a contractual arrangement termed *strict priority*, or sometimes *absolute priority*. We assume that equityholders are not permitted to delay liquidation after the value A of the firm reaches 0, so we ignore the possibility that $A_T < 0$. Only later do we consider the option of equityholders to change the firm's production technology, or to call in the debt for some price.

The bond contract conveys to debtholders, under a *protective covenant*, the right to force liquidation at any stopping time τ at which the asset value A_τ is as low or lower than some stipulated level, which we take for now to be the face value L of the debt. Debtholders would receive A_τ at such a time τ; equityholders would receive nothing. We later treat other covenants.

Assuming that $A_0 > L$, we first consider the total coupon payment rate c that would be chosen at time 0 in order that the initial market value of the bond is its face value L. Such a bond is said to be "at par," and the corresponding coupon rate per unit of face value, c/L, is the *par yield*. If bondholders rationally enforce their protective covenant, we claim that the par yield must be the riskless rate r. We also claim that, until default, the bond paying coupons at the total rate $c = rL$ is always priced at its face value L, and that equity is always priced at the residual value, $A - L$. Finally, equityholders have no strict preference to declare default on a par-coupon bond before $\tau(L) = \inf\{t : A_t \leq L\}$, which is the first time allowed for in the protective covenant, and bondholders rationally force liquidation at $\tau(L)$.

If the total coupon rate c is strictly less than the par rate rL, then equityholders never gain by exercising the right to declare default (or, if they have it, the right to call the debt at its face value) at any stopping time T with $A_T \geq L$, because the market value at time T of the future cash flows to the bond is strictly less than L if liquidation occurs at a stopping time $U > T$ with $A_U \leq L$. Avoiding liquidation at T would therefore leave a market value for equity that is strictly greater than $A_T - L$. With $c < rL$, bondholders would liquidate at the first time $\tau(L)$ allowed for in their protective covenant, for by doing so they receive L at $\tau(L)$ for a bond that, if left alive, would be worth less than L. In summary, with $c < rL$, the bond is liquidated at $\tau(L)$, and trades at a "discount" price at any time t before liquidation, given by

$$Y_t = E_t^Q\left[\int_t^{\tau(L)} e^{-r(s-t)} c \, ds + e^{-r(\tau(L)-t)} L\right] \tag{3}$$

$$= \frac{c}{r} + E_t^Q\left[e^{-r(\tau(L)-t)}\right]\left(L - \frac{c}{r}\right) < L. \tag{4}$$

C. Example: Brownian Dividend Growth

As an example, suppose the cash-flow rate process δ is a geometric Brownian motion under Q, in that

$$d\delta_t = \mu\delta_t \, dt + \sigma\delta_t \, dB_t^Q,$$

for constants μ and σ, where B^Q is a standard Brownian motion under Q. We assume throughout that $\mu < r$, so that, from (1), A is finite and

$$dA_t = \mu A_t \, dt + \sigma A_t \, dB_t^Q.$$

We calculate that $\delta_t = (r - \mu)A_t$.

For any given constant $K \in (0, A_0)$, the market value of a security that claims one unit of account at the hitting time $\tau(K) = \inf\{t : A_t \leq K\}$ is, at any time $t < \tau(K)$,

$$E_t^Q\left[e^{-r(\tau(K)-t)}\right] = \left(\frac{A_t}{K}\right)^{-\gamma}, \tag{5}$$

where

$$\gamma = \frac{m + \sqrt{m^2 + 2r\sigma^2}}{\sigma^2}, \tag{6}$$

and where $m = \mu - \sigma^2/2$. An exercise provides guidance on the verification of (5), a pricing formula that will prove useful in what follows.

Let us consider for simplicity the case in which bondholders have no protective covenant. Then equityholders declare default at a stopping time that solves the maximum-equity-valuation problem

$$w(A_0) \equiv \sup_{T \in \mathcal{T}} E^Q\left[\int_0^T e^{-rt}(\delta_t - c)\,dt\right], \tag{7}$$

where $\mathcal{T}$ is the set of stopping times.

We naturally conjecture that the maximization problem (7) is solved by a hitting time of the form $\tau(A_B) = \inf\{t : A_t \leq A_B\}$, for some default-triggering level A_B of assets, to be determined. Given this conjecture, we further conjecture from Ito's Formula that the function $w : (0, \infty) \to [0, \infty)$ defined by (7) solves the ODE

$$\mathcal{D}w(x) - rw(x) + (r - \mu)x - c = 0, \qquad x > A_B, \tag{8}$$

where

$$\mathcal{D}w(x) = w'(x)\mu x + \frac{1}{2}w''(x)\sigma^2 x^2, \tag{9}$$

with the absolute-priority boundary condition

$$w(x) = 0, \qquad x \leq A_B. \tag{10}$$

Finally, we conjecture the *smooth-pasting condition*

$$w'(A_B) = 0, \tag{11}$$

based on (10) and continuity of the first derivative $w'(\cdot)$ at A_B. Although not an obvious requirement for optimality, the smooth-pasting condition, sometimes called the *high-order-contact* condition, has proven to be a fruit-ful method by which to conjecture solutions, as follows.

If we are correct in conjecturing that the optimal default time is of the form $\tau(A_B) = \inf\{t : A_t \leq A_B\}$, then, given an initial asset level $A_0 = x > A_B$, the value of equity must be

$$w(x) = x - A_B\left(\frac{x}{A_B}\right)^{-\gamma} - \frac{c}{r}\left[1 - \left(\frac{x}{A_B}\right)^{-\gamma}\right]. \tag{12}$$

This conjectured value of equity is merely the market value x of the total future cash flows of the firm, less a deduction equal to the market value of the debtholders' claim to A_B at the default time $\tau(A_B)$ using (5), less another deduction equal to the market value of coupon payments to bond-holders before default. The market value of those coupon payments is easily computed as the present value c/r of coupons paid at the rate c from time 0 to time $+\infty$, less the present value of coupons paid at the rate c from the default time $\tau(A_B)$ until $+\infty$, again using (5). In order to com-plete our conjecture, we apply the smooth-pasting condition $w'(A_B) = 0$ to this functional form (12), and by calculation obtain the conjectured default-triggering asset level as

$$A_B = \beta c, \tag{13}$$

where

$$\beta = \frac{\gamma}{r(1 + \gamma)}. \tag{14}$$

We are ready to state and verify the result.

Proposition. *The default-timing problem* (7) *is solved by* $\inf\{t : A_t \leq \beta c\}$. *The associated initial market value* $w(A_0)$ *of equity is* $W(A_0, c)$, *where*

$$W(x, c) = 0, \qquad x \leq \beta c, \tag{15}$$

and

$$W(x, c) = x - \beta c\left(\frac{x}{\beta c}\right)^{-\gamma} - \frac{c}{r}\left[1 - \left(\frac{x}{\beta c}\right)^{-\gamma}\right], \qquad x \geq \beta c. \tag{16}$$

The initial value of debt is $A_0 - W(A_0, c)$.

Proof: First, it may be checked by calculation that $W(\cdot, c)$ satisfies the differential equation (8) and the smooth-pasting condition (11). Ito's

Formula applies to C^2 (twice continuously differentiable) functions. In our case, although $W(\cdot, c)$ need not be C^2, it is convex, is C^1, and is C^2 except at βc, where $W_x(\beta c, c) = 0$. Under these conditions, we obtain the result, as though from a standard application of Ito's Formula, that

$$W(A_s, c) = W(A_0, c) + \int_0^s \mathscr{D}W(A_t, c)\, dt + \int_0^s W_x(A_t, c)\sigma A_t\, dB_t^Q, \qquad (17)$$

where

$$\mathscr{D}W(x, c) = W_x(x, c)\mu x + \frac{1}{2}W_{xx}(x, c)\sigma^2 x^2, \qquad (18)$$

except at $x = \beta c$, where we may replace "$W_{xx}(\beta c, c)$" with zero. This slight extension of Ito's Formula is based on sources cited in the Notes.

For each time t, let

$$q_t = e^{-rt}W(A_t, c) + \int_0^t e^{-rs}((r - \mu)A_s - c)\, ds.$$

From Ito's Formula,

$$dq_t = e^{-rt}f(A_t)\, dt + e^{-rt}W_x(A_t, c)\sigma A_t\, dB_t^Q, \qquad (19)$$

where

$$f(x) = \mathscr{D}W(x, c) - rW(x, c) + (r - \mu)x - c.$$

Because W_x is bounded, the last term of (19) defines a Q-martingale, by Proposition 5B. For $x \leq \beta c$, we have both $W(x, c) = 0$ and $(r - \mu)x - c \leq 0$, so $f(x) \leq 0$. For $x > \beta c$, we have (8), and therefore $f(x) = 0$. The drift of q is therefore never positive, and for any stopping time T we have $q_0 \geq E^Q(q_T)$, or equivalently,

$$W(A_0, c) \geq E^Q\left[\int_0^T e^{-rs}(\delta_s - c)\, ds + e^{-rT}W(A_T, c)\right]. \qquad (20)$$

For the particular stopping time $\tau(\beta c)$, we have

$$W(A_0, c) = E^Q\left[\int_0^{\tau(\beta c)} e^{-rs}(\delta_s - c)\, ds\right], \qquad (21)$$

using the boundary condition (15) and the fact that $f(x) = 0$ for $x > \beta c$. So, for any stopping time T,

$$
\begin{aligned}
W(A_0, c) &= E^Q \left[\int_0^{\tau(\beta c)} e^{-rs}(\delta_s - c)\, ds \right] \\
&\geq E^Q \left[\int_0^T e^{-rs}(\delta_s - c)\, ds + e^{-rT} W(A_T, c) \right] \qquad (22) \\
&\geq E^Q \left[\int_0^T e^{-rs}(\delta_s - c)\, ds \right],
\end{aligned}
$$

using the nonnegativity of W for the last inequality. This implies the optimality of the stopping time $\tau(\beta c)$ and verification of the proposed solution $W(A_0, c)$ of (7). ∎

D. Taxes and Bankruptcy Costs

In order to see how the original owners of the firm may have a strict but limited incentive to issue debt, we introduce two market imperfections:

- A tax deduction, at a tax rate of θ, on interest expense, so that the after-tax effective coupon rate paid by the firm is $(1 - \theta)c$.
- Bankruptcy costs, so that, with default at time t, the assets of the firm are disposed of at a salvage value of $\hat{A}_t \leq A_t$, where $\hat{A}$ is a given continuous adapted process.

We also consider more carefully the formulation of an equilibrium, in which equityholders and bondholders each exercise their own rights so as to maximize the market values of their own securities, given correct conjectures regarding the equilibrium policy of the other claimant. Because the total of the market values of equity and debt is not the fixed process A, new considerations arise.

As equityholders and bondholders maximize the market values of their respective securities, without considering the total value of the firm, inefficiencies may arise. That is, in an equilibrium, the total of the market values of equity and bond may be strictly less than maximal, for example because of default that is premature from the viewpoint of maximizing the total value of the firm. An unrestricted central planner could in such a case split the firm's cash flows between equityholders and bondholders so as to achieve strictly larger market values for each than the equilibrium values of their respective securities.

Absent the tax shield on debt, the original owner of the firm, who selects a capital structure at time 0 so as to maximize the total initial market value of all corporate securities, would have avoided a capital structure that involves an inefficiency of this type. For example, an all-equity firm would avoid bankruptcy costs.

We suppose that the bond contract conveys to bondholders a protective covenant allowing liquidation whenever $A_t \leq K$, for some given $K \in [0, L]$. Bondholders force liquidation under their protective covenant at some stopping time τ. Equityholders default at some stopping time T. The market value of equity at any time $t < \tau \wedge T \equiv \min(\tau, T)$ is

$$\mathcal{S}_t(T, \tau) = E_t^Q \left(\int_t^{T \wedge \tau} e^{-r(s-t)} (\delta_s - (1 - \theta)c) \, ds \right).$$

The bond valuation is

$$\mathcal{Y}_t(T, \tau) = E_t^Q \left(\int_t^{T \wedge \tau} e^{-r(s-t)} c \, ds + e^{-r((T \wedge \tau)-t)} \hat{A}(\tau \wedge T) \right).$$

An equilibrium is a pair (T^*, τ^*) of liquidation times solving the respective optimal-stopping problems

$$S_0 = \sup_{T \in \mathcal{T}} \mathcal{S}_0(T, \tau^*),$$

and

$$Y_0 = \sup_{\tau \in \mathcal{T}_K} \mathcal{Y}_0(T^*, \tau),$$

where $\mathcal{T}_K = \{\tau \in \mathcal{T} : A_\tau \leq K\}$. This situation is sometimes called a *stochastic game*, or more specifically a *stopping game*. In general, there need not be a unique equilibrium, or indeed any equilibrium.

E. Endogenous Capital Structure

In order to illustrate the endogenous choice of capital structure based on the trade-off between the values of tax shields and of bankruptcy losses, we extend the example of Section C by assuming a tax rate of $\theta \in (0, 1)$ and bankruptcy recovery $\hat{A} = (1 - \alpha)A$, for a constant distress rate $\alpha \in [0, 1]$. For simplicity, we again suppose that $K = 0$, or no protective covenant.

The equity valuation and optimal default timing problem is identical to (7), except that equityholders treat the effective coupon rate as the after-tax rate $c(1 - \theta)$. Thus, the optimal equity market value is

$W(A_0, c(1 - \theta))$, where $W(x, y)$ is given by (15)–(16). The optimal default time is

$$T^* = \inf\{t : A_t \leq \beta(1 - \theta)c\}.$$

For a given coupon rate c, the bankruptcy distress-cost rate α has no effect on the equity value. The market value $U(A_0, c)$ of debt, at asset level A_0 and coupon rate c, is indeed affected by distress costs, in that

$$U(x, c) = (1 - \alpha)x, \qquad x \leq \beta(1 - \theta)c, \qquad (23)$$

and, for $x \geq \beta(1 - \theta)c$,

$$U(x, c) = (1 - \alpha)\beta c(1 - \theta)\left(\frac{x}{\beta c(1 - \theta)}\right)^{-\gamma}$$

$$+ \frac{c}{r}\left[1 - \left(\frac{x}{\beta c(1 - \theta)}\right)^{-\gamma}\right]. \qquad (24)$$

The first term of (24) is the market value of the payment of the recovery value $(1 - \alpha)A(T^*) = (1 - \alpha)\beta c(1 - \theta)$ at default, using (5). The second term is the market value of receiving the coupon rate c until T^*.

The capital structure that maximizes the market value received by the initial owners for sale of equity and debt can now be determined from the coupon rate c^* solving

$$\sup_c \left\{U(A_0, c) + W(A_0, (1 - \theta)c)\right\}. \qquad (25)$$

An explicit solution for c^* is cited in the Notes, and allows one to easily examine the resolution of the trade-off between the market value

$$H(A_0, c) = \frac{\theta c}{r}\left[1 - \left(\frac{A_0}{\beta c(1 - \theta)}\right)^{-\gamma}\right]$$

of tax shields and the market value

$$h(A_0, c) = \alpha \beta c(1 - \theta)\left(\frac{A_0}{\beta c(1 - \theta)}\right)^{-\gamma}$$

of financial distress costs associated with bankruptcy. The coupon rate that solves (25) is that which maximizes $H(A_0, c) - h(A_0, c)$, the benefit-cost difference. Although the tax shield is valuable to the firm, it is merely a transfer from somewhere else in the economy. The bankruptcy distress cost, however, involves a net social cost, illustrating an inefficiency caused by taxes.

F. Technology Choice

Suppose that, rather than being faced with a fixed cash-flow rate process until liquidation, the firm may switch over time among a set $\{\delta_1, \ldots, \delta_m\}$ of m alternative cash-flow rate processes. The lump-sum cost of switching from technology i, with associated cash-flow process δ_i, to a different technology j is assumed to be some constant $\varphi(i, j)$, with $\varphi(i, i) = 0$.

A technology-choice process is a right-continuous, left-limits adapted process ζ taking values in $\{1, \ldots, m\}$. The initial technology ζ_0 is given. A time t at which $\zeta(t) \neq \zeta(t-) \equiv \lim_{s \uparrow t} \zeta(s)$ corresponds to a switch from technology $\zeta(t-)$ to $\zeta(t)$, at an associated cost of $\varphi(\zeta(t-), \zeta(t))$. We can restrict technology-choice processes to some admissible subset Z.

Given an admissible technology-choice process ζ, the firm's total cumulative cash flow by time t is D_t^ζ, where $D_0^\zeta = 0$ and

$$dD_t^\zeta = \delta_{\zeta(t)}(t)\, dt - \varphi(\zeta(t-), \zeta(t)).$$

We assume that the market value of the firm's total future cash flows at time t is well defined by

$$A_t^\zeta = E_t^Q \left[\int_t^\infty e^{-r(s-t)} dD_s^\zeta \right].$$

An all-equity firm would have an initial market value of

$$A_0^* = \sup_{\zeta \in Z} A_0^\zeta.$$

With debt at a coupon rate c and a corporate tax rate of θ, the initial valuation of equity is

$$S_0 = \sup_{\zeta \in Z,\, T \in \mathcal{T}} E^Q \left(\int_0^T e^{-rt} dD_t^\zeta - \int_0^T e^{-rt}(1 - \theta)c\, dt \right).$$

Given the technology-choice process ζ and the default stopping time T of equityholders, the valuation of debt at any time t before default is

$$Y_t = E_t^Q \left(\int_t^T e^{-r(s-t)} c\, ds + e^{-r(T-t)} \hat{A}_T^\zeta \right),$$

where $\hat{A}_T^\zeta$ denotes the debt recovery value at default, given a technology-choice process ζ. (For simplicity, we have assumed no covenants.)

We do not generally anticipate efficient equilibria, given the competing interests of bond- and equityholders. Inefficiencies can arise, for example, from *asset substitution*, meaning a choice by equityholders of a risky and inefficient technology, one that does not maximize the total market value of debt and equity.

An often-studied inefficiency is *debt overhang*, meaning an optimal technology choice ζ for equityholders that fails to switch to a "more efficient" technology, one that would increase the total market value of the firm, because the cost $\varphi(\zeta(t-), i)$ of switching at an appropriate time t, which would be immediately paid by equityholders, exceeds the resulting increase in the post-adoption market value of equity. With debt overhang, while a new technology may increase the total market value of the firm (after accounting for the adoption costs), the market value of debt may go up by an even greater amount, leaving a negative impact on equityholders. Examples of asset substitution and debt overhang are explored in exercises.

For a simple example, consider the case of $m = 2$ technologies. The first is trivial, in that $\delta_1 \equiv 0$. The second generates dividends at the rate $\delta_{2t} = X_t$ at time t, where

$$dX_t = \mu X_t \, dt + \sigma X_t \, dB_t^Q,$$

for constants μ and σ.

The firm begins as "inactive," in technology $\zeta(0) = 1$, and can switch to the "active" technology, producing dividends at the rate X_t, by making an investment of $\varphi(1, 2) = I > 0$. The optimal switch time is of the form $\inf\{t : X_t \geq \bar{x}\}$, for some trigger level $\bar{x}$. Once having made the investment to become active, there is no reason for an all-equity firm to stop producing, unless there is a "salvage value," that is, unless $\varphi(2, 1) < 0$. An exercise calls for a solution of this investment problem, and for the associated valuations of equity and debt. The presence of debt may generate an inefficiency, in that the timing of activation may be delayed (debt overhang) and the timing of abandonment for the salvage value may (by "asset substitution") be inefficient, generating a lower total value than that of an all-equity firm, absent tax shields. The Notes cite sources with many variants of this *real-option* problem.

G. Other Market Imperfections

A "perfect" debt covenant forces equity owners to follow the production and financing strategy that maximizes the total market value of the firm, including the initial sale value of debt. Such a covenant, while theoretically maximizing the initial owners' total market value, may in practice be prohibitively costly to formulate, monitor, and enforce. This section offers an informal discussion of the monitoring and renegotiation of debt, and a brief list of potential extensions of our modeling approach.

An inability of bondholders to perfectly monitor the firm implies that, with some probability, equityholders, unless otherwise prohibited, may have a valuable option to violate the covenant, for example to continue to operate the firm after the asset value drops below protective levels set in the covenant. If monitoring by bondholders can be improved at some cost, then bondholders might restore some of the value that would have been "expropriated" by equityholders. The total of the market values of debt and equity is lowered, however, by the market value of future monitoring costs. It may be fruitful for the initial owner of the firm, before issuance of debt, to put in place a low-cost monitoring system, so as to raise the total initial market value of the firm. After the debt has been issued, however, it may in some cases be to the advantage of equityholders to take actions that increase the cost of monitoring.

Another common market imperfection is an inability to enforce strict priority. While equityholders may be contractually entitled to nothing in the event of their failure to meet the bond covenants or to make timely payments on the debt contracts, they may attempt to renegotiate this absolute priority. For example, equityholders may be in a position to influence the level of financial distress costs, or to delay giving up the firm to debtholders. In order to entice equityholders to make efforts to arrange for low financial distress costs, bondholders may negotiate to convey some portion of the remaining value of the firm to equityholders. If any action by equityholders can only reduce financial distress costs, then, under reasonable conditions, this ability to negotiate a deviation from absolute priority presumably raises the pre-default market values of both debt and equity above the values that would prevail if strict priority were always enforced. If, however, equityholders can, by actions that they are entitled to make, increase financial distress costs (that is, "destroy" value), then the opportunity to renegotiate can raise the market value of equity at the expense of bondholders, relative to the values that would apply with strict priority.

One may extend the models that we have seen so as to treat bonds of finite maturity, or with discrete coupons. One can also allow for multiple classes of debtholders, each with its own contractual cash flows and rights, by generalizing the definition of an equilibrium in a relatively straightforward way. For example, bonds are conventionally classified by priority, so that, at liquidation, senior bondholders are contractually entitled to cash flows resulting from liquidation up to the total face value of senior debt (in proportion to the face values of the respective senior bonds, and normally without regard to maturity dates). If the most senior class of debtholders can be paid off in full, the next most senior class is assigned liquidation cash flows, and so on, to the lowest subordination class. Some bonds may be secured by certain identified assets, or *collateralized,* in effect giving them seniority over the liquidation value resulting from those cash flows, before any unsecured bonds may be paid according to the seniority of unsecured claims. In practice, the overall priority structure may be rather complicated. Some implications of seniority and of relative maturity for bond valuation are explored in exercises.

Corporate bonds are often callable, within certain time restrictions. Not infrequently, corporate bonds may be converted to equity at prearranged conversion ratios (number of shares for a given face value) at the timing option of bondholders. Such *convertible bonds* present a challenging set of valuation issues, some reviewed in sources cited in the Notes. Occasionally, corporate bonds are *puttable,* that is, may be sold back to the issuer at a prearranged price at the option of bondholders.

One can also allow for adjustments in capital structure, normally instigated by equityholders, that result in the issuing and retiring of securities, subject to legal restrictions, some of which may be embedded in debt contracts.

H. Intensity-Based Modeling of Default

This section introduces a model for a default time as a stopping time τ with a given intensity process λ, as defined below. From the joint behavior of λ, the short-rate process r, the promised payment of the security, and the model of recovery at default, as well as risk premia, one can characterize the stochastic behavior of the term structure of yields on defaultable bonds.

In applications, default intensities are allowed to depend on observable variables that are linked with the likelihood of default, such as debt-to-equity ratios, asset volatility measures, other accounting measures of indebtedness, market equity prices, bond yield spreads, industry performance measures, and macroeconomic variables related to the business cycle. This dependence could, but in practice does not usually, arise endogenously from a model of the ability or incentives of the firm to make payments on its debt. Because the approach presented here does not depend on the specific setting of a firm, it has also been applied to the valuation of defaultable sovereign debt, as indicated in the Notes.

We fix a complete probability space $(\Omega, \mathcal{F}, P)$ and a filtration $\{\mathcal{G}_t : t \geq 0\}$ satisfying the usual conditions, which are listed in Appendix I. This will be our first extensive use, for reasons that will become clear, of continuous-time filtrations that are not purely Brownian. As we depart from the case of purely Brownian information, it is important to make a distinction between an adapted process and a *predictable process*. As defined in Appendix I, a predictable process is, intuitively speaking, one whose value at any time s depends only on the information in the underlying filtration that is available up to, but not including, time s.

As defined in Appendix I, a nonexplosive counting process K (for example, a Poisson process) has an intensity λ if λ is a predictable nonnegative process satisfying $\int_0^t \lambda_s \, ds < \infty$ almost surely for all t, with the property that a local martingale M, the *compensated counting process*, is given by

$$M_t = K_t - \int_0^t \lambda_s \, ds. \tag{26}$$

The compensated counting process M is a martingale if, for all t, we have $E(\int_0^t \lambda_s \, ds) < \infty$, as elaborated in Appendix I.

We will say that a stopping time τ has an *intensity* λ if τ is the first jump time of a nonexplosive counting process whose intensity process is λ. The accompanying intuition is that, at any time t and state ω with $t < \tau(\omega)$, the $\mathcal{G}_t$-conditional probability that $\tau \leq t + \Delta$ is approximately $\lambda(\omega, t)\Delta$, for small Δ. This intuition is justified in the sense of derivatives if λ is bounded and continuous, and under weaker conditions.

A stopping time τ is *nontrivial* if $P(\tau \in (0, \infty)) > 0$. If a stopping time τ is nontrivial and if the filtration $\{\mathcal{G}_t : t \geq 0\}$ is the standard filtration of some Brownian motion B in $\mathbb{R}^d$, then τ could not have an intensity. We know this from the fact that, if $\{\mathcal{G}_t : t \geq 0\}$ is the standard filtration of B, then the associated compensated counting process M of (26) (indeed, any local martingale) could be represented as a stochastic integral with respect to B, and therefore cannot jump, but M must jump at τ. In order to have an intensity, a stopping time must be *totally inaccessible*, a property whose definition, cited in the Notes, suggests arrival as a "sudden surprise," but there are no such surprises on a Brownian filtration!

As an illustration, we could imagine that the firm's equityholders or managers are equipped with some Brownian filtration for purposes of determining their optimal default time τ, as in Section C, but that bondholders have imperfect monitoring, and may view τ as having an intensity with respect to the bondholders' own filtration $\{\mathcal{G}_t : t \geq 0\}$, which contains less information than the Brownian filtration. Such a situation arises in a model cited in the Notes.

We say that τ is *doubly stochastic* with intensity λ if the underlying counting process whose first jump time is τ is doubly stochastic with intensity λ, as defined in Appendix I. The doubly stochastic property implies that

$$P(\tau > s \,|\, \mathcal{G}_t) = E_t\left[\exp\left(-\int_t^s \lambda_u \, du\right)\right], \qquad t < \min(\tau, s), \qquad (27)$$

where E_t denotes $\mathcal{G}_t$-conditional expectation. This property (27) is convenient for calculations, as evaluating the expectation in (27) is computationally equivalent to the pricing of a default-free zero-coupon bond, treating λ as a short rate and "E_t" as risk-neutral. Indeed, this analogy is also quite helpful for intuition.

It would be sufficient for (27) that $\lambda_t = \Lambda(X_t, t)$ for some measurable $\Lambda : \mathbb{R}^n \times [0, \infty) \to [0, \infty)$, where X in $\mathbb{R}^d$ solves a stochastic differential equation of the form

$$dX_t = \mu(X_t, t) \, dt + \sigma(X_t, t) \, dB_t, \qquad (28)$$

for some $(\mathcal{G}_t)$-standard Brownian motion B in $\mathbb{R}^d$.

More generally, (27) follows from assuming that the doubly stochastic counting process K whose first jump time is τ is *driven by some filtration* $\{\mathcal{F}_t : t \geq 0\}$, a concept defined in Appendix I. (Included in the definition is the condition that $\mathcal{F}_t \subset \mathcal{G}_t$, and that $\{\mathcal{F}_t : t \geq 0\}$ satisfies the usual conditions.) The idea of the doubly stochastic assumption is that the intensity λ is $(\mathcal{F}_t)$-predictable and that, conditional on λ, K is a Poisson process with (conditionally deterministic) time-varying intensity $\{\lambda_t : t \geq 0\}$. In particular, for any time $s > t$, conditional on the tribe $\mathcal{G}_t \vee \mathcal{F}_s$ generated by the events in $\mathcal{G}_t \cup \mathcal{F}_s$, the number $K_s - K_t$ of arrivals between t and s is distributed as a Poisson random variable with parameter $\int_t^s \lambda_u \, du$. (A random variable q has the *Poisson distribution with parameter β* if $P(q = k) = e^{-\beta}\beta^k/k!$ for any nonnegative integer k.) Thus, letting A be the event that $K_s - K_t = 0$, the law of iterated expectations implies that, for $t < \tau$,

$$
\begin{aligned}
P(\tau > s \,|\, \mathcal{G}_t) &= E(1_A \,|\, \mathcal{G}_t) \\
&= E[E(1_A \,|\, \mathcal{G}_t \vee \mathcal{F}_s) \,|\, \mathcal{G}_t] \\
&= E[P(K_s - K_t = 0 \,|\, \mathcal{G}_t \vee \mathcal{F}_s) \,|\, \mathcal{G}_t] \\
&= E\left[\exp\left(\int_t^s -\lambda_u \, du\right)\Big| \, \mathcal{G}_t\right],
\end{aligned}
\qquad (29)
$$

consistent with (27). This is only a sketch of the idea; sources cited in the Notes offer a proper development of the theory. Appendix I connects the intensity to the probability density and hazard rate of the underlying stopping time.

As we proceed, we will repeatedly use the following natural result. We have not defined here a stochastic integral with respect to a martingale in the case of our general filtration, but that is done in sources cited in the Notes.

Lemma. *Suppose M is a martingale and H is a bounded predictable process. Then the stochastic integral $\int H \, dM$ is well defined and is a martingale.*

I. Risk-Neutral Intensity Process

For purposes of the market valuation of bonds and other securities whose cash flows are sensitive to default timing, we would want to have an equivalent martingale measure Q and a *risk-neutral intensity process*, that is, an intensity process λ^Q for the default time τ that is associated with $(\Omega, \mathcal{F}, Q)$ and the given filtration $\{\mathcal{G}_t : t \geq 0\}$. In this case, we call λ^Q the *Q-intensity* of τ. (As usual, there may be more than one equivalent martingale measure.) As we shall see later in this section, the ratio λ^Q/λ (for λ strictly positive) is in some sense a multiplicative risk premium for the uncertainty associated with the timing of default. The Notes cite the following convenient result.

Proposition. *Suppose a nonexplosive counting process K has a P-intensity process and Q is any probability measure equivalent to P. Then K has a Q-intensity process.*

A version of Girsanov's Theorem provides conditions suitable for calculating the change of probability measure associated with a change of intensity, by analogy with the "change in drift" of a Brownian motion. Suppose K is a nonexplosive counting process with intensity λ, and that φ is a strictly positive predictable process such that, for some fixed time horizon T, $\int_0^T \varphi_s \lambda_s \, ds$ is finite almost surely. A local martingale ξ is then well defined by

$$\xi_t = \exp\left(\int_0^t (1 - \varphi_s)\lambda_s \, ds\right) \prod_{\{i : T(i) \leq t\}} \varphi_{T(i)}, \qquad t \leq T.$$

Girsanov's Theorem. *Suppose the local martingale ξ is in fact a martingale. Then an equivalent probability measure Q is defined by $\frac{dQ}{dP} = \xi(T)$. Restricted to the time interval $[0, T]$, the counting process K has Q-intensity $\lambda\varphi$.*

Care must be taken with assumptions, for the convenient doubly stochastic property need not be preserved with a change to an equivalent probability measure. Illustrative counterexamples are cited in the Notes. A proof of Girsanov's Theorem is cited in Appendix I, which also gives sufficient conditions for the martingale property of ξ, and for K to be doubly stochastic under both P and Q.

Under certain conditions on the filtration $\{\mathcal{G}_t : t \geq 0\}$ that are outlined in Appendix I, the martingale representation property applies, and for any equivalent probability measure Q, one can obtain the associated Q-intensity of K from the martingale representation of the associated density process.

J. Zero-Recovery Bond Pricing

We fix a short-rate process r and an equivalent martingale measure Q after deflation by $\exp(\int_0^t -r_u \, du)$. We consider the valuation of a security that pays $F1_{\{\tau > s\}}$ at a given time $s > 0$, where F is a $\mathcal{G}_T$-measurable bounded random variable. As $1_{\{\tau > s\}}$ is the random variable that is 1 in the event of no default by s and zero otherwise, we may view F as the contractually promised payment of the security at time s, with default by s leading to no payment. The case of a defaultable zero-coupon bond is treated by letting $F = 1$. In the next section, we will consider recovery at default.

From the definition of Q as an equivalent martingale measure, the price S_t of this security at any time $t < s$ is given by

$$S_t = E_t^Q\left[\exp\left(-\int_t^s r_u \, du\right) 1_{\{\tau > s\}} F\right], \tag{30}$$

where E_t^Q denotes $\mathcal{G}_t$-conditional expectation under Q. From (30) and the fact that τ is a stopping time, S_t must be zero for all $t \geq \tau$.

Under Q, the default time τ is assumed to have an intensity process λ^Q.

Theorem. *Suppose that F, r, and λ^Q are bounded and that τ is doubly stochastic under Q driven by a filtration $\{\mathcal{F}_t : t \geq 0\}$ such that r is $(\mathcal{F}_t)$-adapted and F is $\mathcal{F}_s$-measurable. Fix any $t < s$. Then, for $t \geq \tau$, we have $S_t = 0$, and for $t < \tau$,*

$$S_t = E_t^Q\left[\exp\left(-\int_t^s (r_u + \lambda_u^Q) \, du\right) F\right]. \tag{31}$$

The idea of this representation (31) of the pre-default price is that discounting for default that occurs at an intensity is analogous to discounting at the short rate r.

Proof: From (30), the law of iterated expectations, and the assumption that r is $(\mathcal{F}_t)$-adapted and F is $\mathcal{F}_s$-measurable,

$$S_t = E^Q\left(E^Q\left[\exp\left(-\int_t^s r_u\, du\right)1_{\{\tau>s\}}F\,\Big|\,\mathcal{F}_s \vee \mathcal{G}_t\right]\Big|\,\mathcal{G}_t\right)$$

$$= E^Q\left(\exp\left(-\int_t^s r_u\, du\right)FE^Q\left[1_{\{\tau>s\}}\,\Big|\,\mathcal{F}_s \vee \mathcal{G}_t\right]\Big|\,\mathcal{G}_t\right).$$

The result then follows from the implication of double stochasticity that $Q(\tau > s\,|\,\mathcal{F}_s \vee \mathcal{G}_t) = \exp(\int_t^s -\lambda_u^Q\, du)$. ∎

As a special case, suppose the filtration $\{\mathcal{F}_t : t \geq 0\}$ is generated by B^Q, a $(\mathcal{G}_t)$-standard Brownian motion in $\mathbb{R}^d$ under Q. Consider a "state" process X valued in some subset D of $\mathbb{R}^n$ and solving a stochastic differential equation of the form

$$dX_t = \mu(X_t)\, dt + \sigma(X_t)\, dB_t^Q. \tag{32}$$

It is natural to allow dependence of λ^Q, r, and F on the state process X in the sense that

$$\lambda_t^Q = \Lambda(X_t), \qquad r_t = \rho(X_t), \qquad F = f(X_T), \tag{33}$$

where Λ, ρ, and f are real-valued measurable functions on D.

Relation (31) then states that for $t < \tau$, we have $S_t = g(X_t, t)$, for a function $g : D \times [0, s] \to \mathbb{R}$ that, under the Feynman-Kac technical conditions (Appendix E), solves the PDE

$$\mathcal{D}g(x, t) - [\Lambda(x) + \rho(x)]g(x, t) = 0, \tag{34}$$

for $(x, t) \in D \times [0, s)$, with the boundary condition

$$g(x, T) = f(x), \tag{35}$$

where

$$\mathcal{D}g(x, t) = g_t(x, t) + g_x(x, t)\mu(x) + \frac{1}{2}\,\text{tr}[\Sigma(x)g_{xx}(x, t)],$$

for $\Sigma(x) = \sigma(x)\sigma(x)^\top$.

For computationally tractable examples, suppose that the functions μ, Σ, ρ, Λ, and $\log f(\cdot)$ are affine. (For a zero-coupon defaultable bond, we take $f(x) \equiv 1$.) In this "affine" setting, as shown in Chapter 7, we can readily compute a solution to (34)–(35) of the form $g(x, t) = e^{\alpha(t)+\beta(t)\cdot x}$, for deterministic coefficients $\alpha(t)$ and $\beta(t)$ that are explicitly known or easily computed in practice.

K. Pricing with Recovery at Default

The next step is to consider the recovery of some random payoff W at the default time τ, if default occurs before the maturity date s of the security. We adopt the assumptions of Theorem J, and add the assumption that $W = w_\tau$, where w is a bounded predictable process that is also adapted to the filtration $\{\mathcal{F}_t : t \geq 0\}$ that appears in the theorem statement.

The market value at any time $t < \min(s, \tau)$ of any default recovery is, by definition of the equivalent martingale measure Q, given by

$$J_t = E_t^Q \left[\exp\left(\int_t^\tau -r_u \, du \right) 1_{\{\tau \leq s\}} w_\tau \right]. \tag{36}$$

The doubly stochastic assumption implies that τ has a probability density under Q, at any time u in $[t, s]$, conditional on $\mathcal{G}_t \vee \mathcal{F}_s$, and on the event that $\tau > t$, of

$$q(t, u) = \exp\left(\int_t^u -\lambda_z^Q \, dz \right) \lambda_u^Q.$$

Thus, using the same iterated-expectations argument of the proof of Theorem J, we have, on the event that $\tau > t$,

$$J_t = E^Q \left(E^Q \left[\exp\left(\int_t^\tau -r_z \, dz \right) 1_{\{\tau \leq s\}} w_\tau \,\middle|\, \mathcal{F}_s \vee \mathcal{G}_t \right] \,\middle|\, \mathcal{G}_t \right)$$

$$= E^Q \left(\int_t^s \exp\left(\int_t^u -r_z \, dz \right) q(t, u) w_u \, du \,\middle|\, \mathcal{G}_t \right)$$

$$= \int_t^s \Phi(t, u) \, du,$$

using Fubini's Theorem, where

$$\Phi(t, u) = E_t^Q \left[\exp\left(\int_t^u -(\lambda_z^Q + r_z) \, dz \right) \lambda_u^Q w_u \right]. \tag{37}$$

We summarize the main defaultable valuation result as follows.

Theorem. Consider a security that pays F at s if $\tau > s$, and otherwise pays w_τ at τ. Suppose that w, F, λ^Q, and r are bounded. Suppose that τ is doubly stochastic under Q driven by a filtration $\{\mathcal{F}_t : t \geq 0\}$ with the property that r and w are $(\mathcal{F}_t)$-adapted and F is $\mathcal{F}_s$-measurable. Then, for $t \geq \tau$, we have $S_t = 0$, and for $t < \tau$,

$$S_t = E_t^Q \left[\exp\left(-\int_t^s (r_u + \lambda_u^Q) \, du \right) F \right] + \int_t^s \Phi(t, u) \, du. \tag{38}$$

In the affine state-space setting described at the end of the previous section, $\Phi(t, u)$ can be computed by our usual "affine" methods, provided that w is of form $w_t = e^{a(t)+b(t) \cdot X(t)}$ for deterministic $a(t)$ and $b(t)$. In this case, it is an exercise to show that, under technical regularity,

$$\Phi(t, u) = e^{\alpha(t,u)+\beta(t,u) \cdot X(t)}[c(t, u) + C(t, u) \cdot X(t)], \tag{39}$$

for readily computed deterministic coefficients α, β, c, and C. This still leaves the task of numerical computation of the integral $\int_t^s \Phi(t, u)\, du$.

For the price of a typical defaultable bond promising periodic coupons followed by its principal at maturity, one may sum the prices of the coupons and of the principal, treating each of these payments as though it were a separate zero-coupon bond. An often-used assumption, although one that need not apply in practice, is that there is no default recovery for coupons, and that bonds of different maturities have the same recovery of principal. In any case, convenient parametric assumptions, based for example on an affine driving process X, lead to straightforward computation of a term structure of defaultable bond yields that may be applied in practical situations, such as the valuation of *credit derivatives*, a class of derivative securities designed to transfer credit risk that is treated in sources cited in the Notes.

For the case of defaultable bonds with embedded American options, the most typical cases being callable or convertible bonds, the usual resort is valuation by some numerical implementation of the associated dynamic programming problems.

L. Default-Adjusted Short Rate

In the setting of Theorem K, a particularly simple pricing representation can be based on the definition of a predictable process ℓ for the fractional loss in market value at default, defined by

$$(1 - \ell_\tau)(S_{\tau-}) = w_\tau. \tag{40}$$

Manipulation that is left as an exercise shows that, under the conditions of Theorem K, for $t < \min(\tau, s)$,

$$S_t = E_t^Q\left[\exp\left(\int_t^s -(r_u + \ell_u \lambda_u^Q)\, du\right)F\right]. \tag{41}$$

This valuation model (41) is particularly convenient if we take ℓ as an exogenously given fractional loss process, as it allows for the application of standard valuation methods, treating the payoff F as default-free, but accounting for the intensity and severity of default losses through the "default-adjusted" short-rate process $r + \ell\lambda^Q$. The adjustment $\ell\lambda^Q$ is in fact the risk-neutral mean rate of proportional loss in market value due to default.

Notably, the dependence of the bond price on the intensity λ^Q and fractional loss ℓ at default is only through the product $\ell\lambda^Q$. Thus, for any bounded strictly positive predictable process θ, the bond price is invariant to a substitution for ℓ and λ^Q of $\theta\ell$ and λ^Q/θ, respectively. For example, doubling λ^Q and halving ℓ has no effect on the bond-price process before default.

Suppose, for example, that τ is doubly stochastic driven by X, and we take $r_t + \ell_t\lambda_t^Q = R(X_t)$ and $F = f(X_T)$, for a state process X satisfying (32). Then, under Feynman-Kac regularity conditions, we obtain at each time t before default the bond price $S_t = g(X_t, t)$, for a solution g of the PDE

$$\mathscr{D}g(x, t) - R(x)g(x, t) = 0, \qquad (x, t) \in D \times [0, s), \qquad (42)$$

with boundary condition $g(x, s) = f(x)$. Sources cited in the Notes, as well as exercises, provide examples. As a special case, if the driving process X is affine, if $f(x) = e^{d \cdot x}$ for some $c. \in \mathbb{R}^n$, and if $R(x) = a + b \cdot x$ for some $a \in \mathbb{R}$ and b in $\mathbb{R}^n$, then we have $g(x, t) = e^{\alpha(t)+\beta(t)\cdot x}$ for deterministic and readily computed coefficients $\alpha(t)$ and $\beta(t)$.

There are also interesting cases, some cited in the Notes, in which λ_t^Q or ℓ_t (or both) are naturally dependent on the pre-default bond price itself. In a Markovian setting, the PDE (42) would be generalized to one of the nonlinear form

$$\mathscr{D}g(x, t) - R(x, g(x, t))g(x, t) = 0. \qquad (43)$$

Exercises

11.1 In the setting of Section A, suppose "equity" and "debt" are defined by an arbitrary sharing rule, subject only to the feasibility condition $S_T + Y_T = A_T$. Suppose there is a stopping time τ such that $P(\tau \le T) > 0$ and $A_\tau \ne Y_\tau + S_\tau$. Show that there is an arbitrage whose market value is bounded below.

11.2 Show that (2) is implied by (1).

11.3 In the setting of Section B, an asset-valuation process A is fixed, and we consider the contractual right of debtholders to force liquidation at any stopping time T at which $A_T \leq K$, where $K \leq L$ is a constant. We assume for simplicity that $A_0 \geq L$. We also suppose that equityholders have the right to call the debt at par, meaning that, at a stopping time selected by equityholders, the obligation to pay coupons can be extinguished in return for a payment of L to bondholders.

(A) Show that the bond is always liquidated by $\tau(K)$, assuming that equityholders and bondholders optimally time their covenant exercise, default, and call decisions and that each knows the other's policy.

(B) Suppose $K = L$ and $c \leq rL$. Show that the bond sells at a discount to its face value (that is, $Y_t \leq L$) until bondholders optimally force liquidation at $\tau(L)$. The bond price Y_t at any time t before $\tau(L)$ is thus

$$Y_t = E_t^Q \left[\int_t^{\tau(L)} e^{-r(s-t)} c \, ds + e^{-r(\tau(K)-t)} L \right]. \tag{3}$$

Show that the par yield is the riskless rate r.

(C) Suppose $K \geq L$ and $c > rL$. Show that equityholders immediately liquidate, and the bond is worth its face value, L.

11.4 Verify (5). Hint: Let $M_t = e^{-rt}(A_t/K)^\gamma$. Show that M is a Q-martingale.

11.5 Solve the real-options example at the end of Section F, in the following cases.

(A) First, for an all-equity firm ($c = 0$), calculate the optimal time to invest in the active technology for the case of no salvage value, that is, with $\varphi(2, 1) = 0$. Provide a full verification argument.

(B) Extending part (A) to the case with salvage value, conjecture the parametric functional form of the solution, with conditions determining the parameters. A full verification proof of the solution may be omitted.

(C) Now, suppose that the firm has debt paying coupons at the constant total after-tax rate of c. For the case of no salvage value, $\varphi(2, 1) = 0$, provide boundary trigger policies characterizing the solution of the problem of when to invest and when to declare default. Please determine the appropriate boundaries. A full verification proof may be omitted.

(D) Now, suppose that the active technology has a constant cost rate of $k > 0$, for a net cash-flow rate of $X_t - k$. For an all-equity firm ($c = 0$), characterize·the optimal times to activate and deactivate the dividend-producing technology for the case of no salvage value, that is, with $\varphi(2, 1) \geq 0$. A full verification proof may be omitted.

11.6 (Subordinated Debt). Suppose equity and debt investors are informed according to the standard filtration of a standard Brownian motion B. Riskless borrowing is available at constant rate $r > 0$. The capital structure of a given firm, Zinc, is made up of three claims on the assets: equity and two different zero-coupon bonds. The first of the two bonds to mature is a promise to pay F_1 at time $T_1 > 0$, subject to available assets and prioritization. The second to mature pays F_2 at $T_2 > T_1$, subject to available assets. Assuming there are any assets remaining, Zinc is liquidated at $T_3 > T_2$, with all proceeds of liquidation going to its equity owners. All bond payments are made out of current assets. The production technology of Zinc is such that an asset stock of any amount x at time t is translated into an asset stock of $x \exp[m(T - t) + \sigma(B_T - B_t)]$ at any $T > t$, where $m > r$ and $\sigma > 0$, provided there were no bond payments between t and T. The initial level of assets is $x > 0$. No investment in assets is made after time 0. Let A_t denote the level of assets at any time $t > 0$. At the first maturity date T_1, the assets are reduced so as to pay down as much as possible of the face value F_1 of the bond maturing at T_1. That is, if $A(T_1-) \geq F_1$, then the asset level at T_1 is $A(T_1) = A(T_1-) - F_1$. These assets are then reinvested in the same technology until T_2, and the second bond is likewise paid down, if possible. If the second bond is fully paid down at T_2, then the remaining assets are reinvested until T_3 and then paid out to equity. If, however, there is an insufficient amount of assets to pay down the first bond at T_1, then the issuer defaults. Priority in default is given to the second bond, that maturing at T_2. That is, if $A(T_1-) < F_1$, then Zinc is immediately liquidated at time T_1, with $\min(F_2, A(T_1-))$ paid immediately to the second bond (that maturing at T_2), and with any remainder $[A(T_1-) - F_2]^+$ going to the first bond, that maturing at T_1. Thus, the first bond to mature is "junior," as it is subordinated to the second bond to mature. The second bond to mature is senior. Equity owners get nothing in this scenario. Likewise, in the event at T_2 that $A(T_2-) < F_2$, the firm is immediately liquidated, with $A(T_2-)$ going to the second bond holder, and nothing to equity.

A separate firm, Zonk, with an identical technology (that is, with the same coefficients (m, σ) and driven by the same Brownian motion B), is fully equity funded (no bonds), pays no dividends, receives no new investment, and is liquidated at T_3. The market value of Zonk's equity at any time t before T_3 is Zonk's level of assets. All securities, equities and bonds, can be traded, long or short, and there are no transactions costs, taxes, or other market imperfections. We suppose that there is no arbitrage whose market value is bounded below, in the usual sense.

(A) Suppose that Zinc's equity owners can purchase or sell units of additional assets at time 0 (only), at a price of 1 unit of account per unit of assets. Any purchase is funded by issuing additional equity. (This is called "dilution.") The purchasers of new equity pay a "fair market value" for their shares. For example, suppose the total initial assets of the firm are increased by 100 units of account. The new initial level of assets, $x + 100$, is invested in the given (m, σ) technology, and after paying down the bonds at T_1 and T_2, any residual assets, say Z, at T_3 are split, with some fraction $\varphi \in (0, 1)$ going to the original equity shares, and the remaining fraction $1 - \varphi$ going to the new equity shares purchased at time zero. It must be the case that the market value of the claim to $Z(1 - \varphi)$ at time T_3 is worth 100 at time 0. In this scenario, the total market value of the bonds would increase by some amount, and the total market value of the equity, new combined with old, would increase by some amount. Any proceeds from a sale of assets at time 0 is paid immediately to initial equity owners as a dividend. This decision, to purchase or sell some amount of assets at time 0, is the only decision ever made by equity owners. The bond contracts have a protective covenant, however, stipulating that Zinc cannot sell assets so as to reduce current assets below the total face value $F_1 + F_2$ of the two bonds. (Assets may, however, go below $F_1 + F_2$ after time 0 if the production technology has a sufficiently low outcome. If $x < F_1 + F_2$, assets may be purchased in a nonnegative amount, even if the total assets after the purchase are less than $F_1 + F_2$.) State, and rigorously justify, an optimal (equity-market-value maximizing) level of recapitalization. That is, calculate the amount C of assets to be purchased (or sold, for the case $C < 0$) so as to maximize the market value of the shares held by the original equity owners, as it depends on $(x, F_1, T_1, F_2, T_2, T_3, r, m, \sigma)$, subject to $x + C \geq F_1 + F_2$ for the case $x > F_1 + F_2$.

(B) Suppose the protective covenant described in part (A) is modified so that the owners of the senior bonds (those maturing at T_2) can reset the minimum level to which assets may be reduced through an equity dividend at time zero (only), from $F_1 + F_2$ to a new minimum level $F < F_1 + F_2$, selected by senior bondholders. Assume that the objective of senior bondholders in resetting the protective covenant is to maximize the initial market value of their own bonds. Could there be a situation in which senior bondholders would choose to exercise their option to allow equity owners to reduce assets (by sale and equity dividend) as far as some level $F < F_1 + F_2$? In one sentence, only, provide a reason why it could be, or could not be, optimal for senior bondholders to do so. If it could be, construct such an example, giving explicit numbers for $x, r, m, \sigma, (F_1, T_1), (F_2, T_2)$, and T_3. If you wish, you may take $\sigma = 0$. Provide, for your example, an optimal lower bound F on initial assets that would be chosen by senior bondholders in the revised protective covenant. Assume common knowledge of rationality by both bondholders and equity owners. In particular, bondholders assume that, if they reset the protective covenant, then equity owners will optimally buy or sell assets subject to the new covenant.

(C) Now, fixing the initial level x of assets, suppose that Zinc's equity owners can substitute the current technology with an alternative technology that has the same mean-growth parameter m, but has a higher volatility parameter $\hat{\sigma} > \sigma$. The same Brownian motion B drives asset growth. Would Zinc's equity owners choose to do so in all cases? Please bear in mind that, while the all-equity firm Zonc remains as described above, there may not be another firm that uses the riskier technology characterized by $(m, \hat{\sigma})$. Please justify your answer theoretically. Please be precise, by giving a proof or counterexample.

11.7 (Floating-Rate Notes). Fix a probability space and a filtration. Consider an arbitrage-free market in which, for each t and $s > t$, there is available for purchase or sale a unit zero-coupon default-free bond maturing at s with a bounded price at t of $\Lambda_{t,s}$ with outcomes in $(0, 1)$. A floating-rate note, with a given maturity T, a face value of 1, and a spread K_T, is defined as a claim to payment of the face value 1 at the maturity date T, and payment at each integer date $i \in \{1, \ldots, T\}$ of the spread K_T plus the one-period default-free floating rate L_{i-1} established at the previous integer date. The one-period default-free floating rate L_{i-1} established at date $i - 1$ is $\Lambda^{-1}_{i-1,\, i} - 1$, the simple interest rate on one-period default-free loans. (In practice, the calendar length of the interpayment time interval associated with a given note may vary from case to case. You may assume for concreteness that one unit of time is one calendar year, and that bounded positions in zero-coupon bonds and floating-rate notes are permitted. All prices and trading strategies are adapted.)

(A) A *par floating-rate note* is a floating-rate note whose market value at the issue date is equal to its face value. Prove, without the benefit of assuming the existence of a state-price deflator, short-rate process, or equivalent martingale measure, that for any integer maturity T, the unique arbitrage-free default-free par floating-rate spread K_T is zero. (You may assume that the issue date is 0.)

(B) Now, suppose there is a complete probability space $(\Omega, \mathscr{F}, P)$, and a filtration $\{\mathscr{G}_t\}$ satisfying the usual conditions. There is an adapted nonnegative short-rate process r, and an equivalent martingale measure Q after deflation by $\exp(- \int_0^t r_u \, du)$. A corporation, Zank, defaults at a stopping time τ that, under Q, is doubly stochastic with an intensity process λ^Q.

For simplicity, we suppose that any floating-rate note issued by Zank has no cash flows at or after default. This is sometimes called a "zero-recovery" assumption. One can price a defaultable floating-rate note of maturity T at any given spread K_T by pricing each of the promised payments at times 1 through T, and then adding up the prices. For an "explicit" model, we now suppose that there is an $\mathbb{R}^n$-valued process X that is "affine" under Q, in the sense that, for any

$$c = (a, \hat{a}, b, \hat{b}) \in \mathbb{R} \times \mathbb{R} \times \mathbb{R}^n \times \mathbb{R}^n,$$

and for any times t and $s > t$, there exist a scalar $\alpha(t, s, c)$ and some $\beta(t, s, c)$ in $\mathbb{R}^n$ such that

$$e^{\alpha(t,\, s,\, c) + \beta(t,\, s,\, c) \cdot X(t)} = E_t^Q \left[e^{\int_t^s -(a + b \cdot X(u))\, du} e^{\hat{a} + \hat{b} \cdot X(s)} \right].$$

These coefficients $\alpha(t, s, c)$ and $\beta(t, s, c)$ are typically computable in applications from certain ordinary differential equations, and in certain cases are explicit. You may take these coefficients as given in terms of any (t, s, c).

Assume that $r_t = a + b \cdot X(t)$ and that $\lambda_t^Q = a^Q + b^Q \cdot X(t)$, for given scalars a and a^Q, and given b and b^Q in $\mathbb{R}^n$. Assuming the pricing rule (31) applies, price the coupon payment $L_{i-1} + K_T$ promised at date i. Finally, give a formula for the par spread K_T.

11.8 (Valuation of Options with Bankruptcy). We fix a complete probability space $(\Omega, \mathscr{F}, P)$ and a filtration $\{\mathscr{G}_t : t \geq 0\}$ satisfying the usual conditions. Suppose, in a given economy, that there is a constant short rate r. Consider a firm whose equity price process is a geometric Brownian motion X, until bankruptcy.

We assume that there is an equivalent martingale measure Q (after deflation by e^{-rt}) such that, for given real parameters m and σ, we have

$$X_t = X_0 \exp(mt + \sigma B_t^Q),$$

where B^Q is a standard Brownian motion under Q. Bankruptcy occurs with constant Q-intensity λ^Q. Specifically, bankruptcy occurs at the stopping time $\tau = \inf\{t : K_t = 1\}$, where, under Q, K is a Poisson process, independent of B^Q, with constant intensity λ^Q. When bankruptcy occurs, the price of the equity jumps to zero.

(A) Compute the price of a European call option on the equity for expiration at time T and for strike price $x > 0$. Hint: The point of the exercise is that the firm may go bankrupt before expiration. The option pays off if the firm does not go bankrupt, and if the price of the equity is above the strike.

(B) Compute the price of a European put option on the equity for expiration at time T and for strike price $x > 0$, without using put-call parity. Now show that put-call parity holds.

11.9 Fixing a probability space and a filtration satisfying the usual conditions, consider a market in which there exists a short-rate process r and an equivalent martingale measure Q after deflation by $\exp(\int_0^t -r_s \, ds)$, with $dr_t = a(t) \, dt + b(t) \, dB_t^Q$, for continuous functions a and b of time alone, where B^Q is a standard Brownian motion in $\mathbb{R}^2$ under Q, and b is therefore valued in $\mathbb{R}^2$.

(A) For a given maturity T_1, show that the price process U of a zero-coupon bond maturing at T_1 satisfies $dU_t = r_t U_t \, dt + U(t)v(t) \, dB_t^Q$, $t < T_1$, and provide a formula for $v(t)$ in terms of a and b. Hint: Use the fact that $\int_0^{T_1} r_t \, dt$ is normally distributed under Q. Alternatively, use the fact that this is an affine term-structure model.

(B) Consider a firm whose total market-value process A satisfies $dA_t = r_t A_t \, dt + A_t \sigma_A \, dB_t^Q$, $A_0 > 0$, where $\sigma_A \in \mathbb{R}^2$. There are no dividends, and the drift, $r_t A_t$, is therefore dictated by the definition of an equivalent martingale measure. The firm has issued L bonds maturing at T_1, each promising to pay 1 unit of account at maturity unless the value A_T of the firm is not large enough to cover the debt, in which case the bonds share the value of the firm on a pro rata basis, meaning a default payment of A_T/L to each bondholder. Letting Z_0 denote the price of a bond at time zero, compute explicitly the *default risk premium* $U_0 - Z_0$, showing it to be of the form of a Black-Scholes put option price with explicitly stated coefficients. Hint: Take U as a deflator.

11.10 Suppose that τ is a stopping time with intensity λ, in the sense of Section H, and let $N_t = 1_{\{\tau \geq t\}}$. Show that N is a nonexplosive counting process with intensity $\{\lambda_t 1_{\{\tau \leq t\}} : t \geq 0\}$. Hint: Use the local martingale characterization of intensity.

11.11 Under the conditions of Theorem K and the assumption that $w_\tau = (1 - \ell_\tau)(S_{\tau-})$, obtain the representation (41) of defaultable bond prices based on the default-adjusted short rate. The following exercise asks for a bit more, taking ℓ as a primitive rather than w.

11.12 Suppose that ℓ is a given predictable process valued in $[0, 1]$, to be treated as a fractional loss in market value at default. Suppose, in the setting of Section I, that the promised payoff F, the short-rate process r, and the intensity λ^Q of the default time τ are bounded, and let

$$Y_t = E_t^Q \left[\exp\left(\int_t^s -(r_u + \ell_u \lambda_u^Q) \, du \right) F \right], \qquad t \le s. \tag{44}$$

Suppose that Y does not jump at τ, almost surely. (Conditions for this are analogous to those of Theorem I.) Show that there is a unique bounded adapted process S with the property that S is the price process for a security that pays $(1 - \ell_\tau) S_{\tau-}$ at τ if $\tau \le s$ and pays F at s if $\tau > s$. Show, moreover, that for $t < \tau$, we have $S_t = Y_t$, and that for $t \ge \tau$, we have $S_t = 0$.

11.13 Certain credit derivatives are based on the *first to default*, meaning that they are based on the first $\min(\tau_1, \ldots, \tau_n)$ of n default (stopping) times $\tau_1, \ldots, \tau_n$. In the setting of Section H, suppose that, for each i, the stopping time τ_i has intensity λ_i, and that there is no simultaneous default, meaning that for any i and $j \ne i$, we have $P(\tau_i = \tau_j) = 0$. Show that $\min(\tau_1, \ldots, \tau_n)$ has intensity $\lambda_1 + \cdots + \lambda_n$.

11.14 On a given complete probability space $(\Omega, \mathcal{F}, P)$, let N be a Poisson process with constant intensity γ. Let W be a random variable, independent of N, with outcomes 1 and 0, with respective probabilities p and $1 - p$. Let $K = NW$, and let $\mathcal{G}_t$ be the completion of the tribe generated by $\{(K_s, N_s) : 0 \le s \le t\}$. Let τ be the first jump time of K. Show that K is a nonexplosive counting process, and calculate its intensity process λ. Calculate, for an arbitrary given time s, the survival probability $P(\tau > s)$, and show that the convenient formula (27) does not apply. In particular, K is not doubly stochastic.

11.15 Derive the formula (39), under an affine model for X under Q, and affine dependence of λ^Q and r on X. You may assume that (37) applies, and adopt integrability conditions as needed.

Notes

(A) This model of debt and equity pricing is based on Black and Scholes (1973) and Merton (1970, 1973b, 1974). Pitts and Selby (1983) further characterize the implied shape of the term structure of credit spreads. Modigliani and Miller (1958) is the classic treatment of irrelevance of capital structure in perfect capital markets. Geske (1977) uses compound option modeling so as to extend to debt at various maturities.

(B–E) These sections are based on the model proposed by Fisher, Heinkel, and Zechner (1989), and explicitly solved by Leland (1994) for optimal default timing and for the valuation of equity and debt with taxes and bankruptcy distress costs. The model was further elaborated to treat coupon debt of finite maturity in Leland and Toft (1996), endogenous calling of debt and recapitalization in Leland (1998) and Uhrig-Homburg (1998), incomplete observation by bond investors, with default intensity, in Duffie and Lando (1998), and alternative approaches to default recovery in Anderson and Sundaresan (1996), Anderson, Pan, and Sundaresan (1995), Fan and Sundaresan (1997), Mella-Barral (1999), and Mella-Barral and Perraudin (1997).

The optimality verification proof of Section C is adapted from Duffie and Lando (1998). For this proof, we use a version of Ito's Formula that can be applied to a real-valued function that is C^1 and is C^2 except at a point, as, for example, in Karatzas and Shreve (1988), page 219.

Cvitanić and Karatzas (1996b) and Kifer (2000) treat stopping games that might be adapted to some of the games considered in this chapter.

Black and Cox (1976) developed the idea of first-passage-based default timing, but used an exogenous default boundary. Longstaff and Schwartz (1995a) developed a similar first-passage defaultable bond pricing model with stochastic default-free interest rates. (See also Nielsen, Saá-Requejo, and Santa-Clara (1993) and Collin-Dufresne and Goldstein (1999).) Zhou (2000) bases pricing on first passage of a jump-diffusion.

(F) Examples based on the switching approach here have been developed and solved repeatedly in the literature. A standard model that fits literally into the setting of this section is that of Dixit (1989). Further sources to the literature are cited by Dixit and Pindyck (1994), who summarize a significant amount of modeling in this topic area, which is sometimes called *real options*. Boyarchenko and Levendorskii (2000a,b) and Marcozzi (2000) offer some related results on perpetual options.

(G) On renegotiation and pricing, see Anderson and Sundaresan (1996), Anderson, Pan, and Sundaresan (1995), Décamps and Faure-Grimaud (1998, 1999), Fan and Sundaresan (1997), Mella-Barral (1999), and Mella-Barral and Perraudin (1997).

Huang, Subrahmanyam, and Sundaram (1999) address the valuation of corporate debt with costly refinancing.

Acharya and Carpenter (1999) treat callable defaultable bonds. On convertible bond valuation, see Brennan and Schwartz (1980a), Davis and Lischka (1999), Loshak (1996), Nyborg (1996), and Tsiveriotis and Fernandes (1998). On the timing of call and conversion options on convertible bonds, see Ederington, Caton, and Campbell (1997).

On credit derivatives, see Chen and Sopranzetti (1999), Cooper and Martin (1996), Davis and Mavroidis (1997), Duffie (1998b), Longstaff and Schwartz (1995b), and Pierides (1997).

(H–I) A standard reference on counting processes is Brémaud (1981). Additional sources include Daley and Vere-Jones (1988) and Karr (1991). Meyer (1966) defines totally inaccessible stopping times. Appendix I contains a summary of some of the key results on counting processes that we use here. Lemma H and the definition of a stochastic integral with respect to a martingale can be found in Protter (1990), among other sources. Proposition I is from Artzner and Delbaen (1995). Theorem I is simplified from Brémaud (1981), as summarized in Appendix I. Duffie and Lando (1998) show how default intensity can arise in the model of Section C with incomplete information. Elliott, Jeanblanc, and Yor (1999) give a new proof of this intensity result, which is generalized by Song (1998) to the multidimensional case. Kusuoka (1999b) provides an example of this intensity result that is based on unobservable drift of assets.

Kusuoka (1999b) also gives examples in which the doubly stochastic property is not preserved under a change of measure.

(J) The use of intensity-based defaultable bond pricing models was instigated by Artzner and Delbaen (1990a, 1992, 1995), Lando (1994, 1998), and Jarrow and Turnbull (1995). Theorem J is based on results from Duffie, Schroder, and Skiadas (1996) and Lando (1998). Additional work in this vein is by Bielecki and Rutkowski (1999a,b, 2000), Cooper and Mello (1991, 1992), Das and Sundaram (2000), Das and Tufano (1995), Davydov, Linetsky, and Lotz (1999), Duffie (1998a), Duffie and Huang (1996), Duffie and Singleton (1999), Elliott, Jeanblanc, and Yor (1999), Hull and White (1992, 1995), Jarrow and Yu (1999), Jarrow, Lando, and Yu (1999), Jeanblanc and Rutkowski (1999), Madan and Unal (1998), and Nielsen and Ronn (1995).

Intensity-based debt pricing models based on stochastic transition among credit ratings were developed by Arvantis, Gregory, and Laurent (1999), Jarrow, Lando, and Turnbull (1997), Kijima and Komoribayashi (1998), Kijima (1998), and Lando (1998).

(K) These results are based on Duffie, and Schroder, and Skiadas (1996) and Lando (1994, 1998). Schönbucher (1998) extends to treat the case of recovery W which is not of the form w_τ for some predictable process w, but rather allows the recovery to be revealed just at the default time τ.

(L) Debt pricing models based on a default-adjusted short-rate process were developed by Duffie and Singleton (1999), based on precursors due to Pye (1974) and Litterman and Iben (1991). For empirical work on default-adjusted short rates, see Duffee (1999a) for an application to corporate bonds, and Duffie, Pedersen, and Singleton (2000) and Pagès (2000) for work on sovereign debt. For more on sovereign debt valuation, see Gibson and Sundaresan (1999) and Merrick (1999).

Applications of price-dependent default-adjusted short rates determined by the nonlinear PDE (43) include the case of defaultable swaps, as addressed by Duffie and Huang (1996). For more on the valuation of defaultable swaps, see Abken (1993), Artzner and Delbaen (1990a), Cooper and Mello (1991), Jarrow and Turnbull (1997b), Li (1995), Huge and Lando (1999), and Sorenson and Bollier (1995). For institutional background on defaultable swaps, see Litzenberger (1992). On the impact of credit risk on derivative pricing, see Martin (1997).

Additional Topics: The exercise on corporate bond pricing under Gaussian interest rates is based on Décamps and Rochet (1997) and Shimko, Tejima, and Van Deventer (1993). On the impact of illiquidity on defaultable debt prices, see Ericsson and Renault (1999). Models of default correlation and collateralized debt obligations include those of Davis and Lo (1999, 2000), Duffie and Gârleanu (1999), and Finger (2000).

Bensoussan, Crouhy, and Galai (1995a,b) analyze compound options and complex options, examples of which include options on an equity, which in turn can be viewed as an option on the underlying assets of the firm. Galai and Schneller (1978) and Schwartz (1997) treat warrant valuation.

12

Numerical Methods

THIS CHAPTER REVIEWS three numerical approaches to pricing securities in a continuous-time setting: "binomial" approximation, Monte Carlo simulation, and finite-difference solution of the associated partial differential equation.

A. Central Limit Theorems

It is well known that a normal random variable can be represented as the limit of normalized sums of Bernoulli trials, that is, $i.i.d.$ binomial random variables. This idea, a version of the Central Limit Theorem, leads to the characterization given in this section of the Black-Scholes option-pricing formula (equation [5.11]) as the limit of the binomial option-pricing formula (equation [2.16]), letting the number of trading periods per unit of time go to infinity. Aside from making an interesting connection between the discrete- and continuous-time settings, this also suggests a numerical recipe for calculating continuous-time arbitrage-free derivative security prices.

A sequence $\{X_n\}$ of random variables *converges in distribution* to a random variable X, denoted $X_n \Rightarrow X$, if, for any bounded continuous function $f : \mathbb{R} \to \mathbb{R}$, we have $E[f(X_n)] \to E[f(X)]$. We could allow X and each of $X_1, X_2, \ldots$ to be defined on different probability spaces. A standard version of the Central Limit Theorem reads along the following lines. A random variable is *standard normal* if it has the standard normal cumulative distribution function.

Central Limit Theorem. *Suppose $Y_1, Y_2, \ldots$ is a sequence of independent and identically distributed random variables on a probability space, each with expected* *value μ and finite variance $\sigma^2 > 0$. For each n, let $Z_n = Y_1 + \cdots + Y_n$. Then, for any standard normal random variable X,*

$$\frac{Z_n - n\mu}{\sigma\sqrt{n}} \Rightarrow X.$$

Proofs are cited in the Notes. This version of the Central Limit Theorem is not general enough to handle convergence of the binomial option-pricing formula of Exercise 2.1 to the Black-Scholes formula. In order to set up the required extension, we say that a collection

$$Y = \{Y_1^n, Y_2^n, \ldots, Y_{k(n)}^n : n \in \{1, 2, \ldots\}\},$$

with $k(n) \to \infty$ as $n \to \infty$, is a *triangular array* if, for each n, $Y_1^n, \ldots, Y_{k(n)}^n$ are independently distributed random variables on some probability space. The following version of the Central Limit Theorem is sufficient for our purposes here, and can be proved as an easy corollary of the Lindeberg-Feller Central Limit Theorem given in Appendix C.

Proposition. *Suppose Y is a triangular array of random variables such that $Y_1^n, \ldots, Y_{k(n)}^n$ are bounded in absolute value by a constant y_n, with $y_n \to 0$. Let $Z_n = Y_1^n + \cdots + Y_{k(n)}^n$. If $E(Z_n) \to \mu$ and $\mathrm{var}(Z_n) \to \sigma^2 > 0$, then Z_n converges in distribution to a normally distributed random variable with mean μ and variance σ^2.*

B. Binomial to Black-Scholes

Recall the setup from Section 5E of the Black-Scholes model for pricing a European put option:

- a probability space $(\Omega, \mathcal{F}, P)$ on which there is a standard Brownian motion B;
- a stock-price process S defined by $S_t = x \exp(\alpha t + \sigma B_t)$ and a bond-price process β defined by $\beta_t = \beta_0 e^{rt}$, for constants α, σ, and r;
- the put-option payoff $(K - S_T)^+$, defined by the expiration time T and exercise price K.

The solution of the "arbitrage-free" put price, in the sense of Chapter 6, is

$$\varphi = E^Q\big[e^{-rT}(K - xe^{X_T})^+\big], \tag{1}$$

where $X_t = (r - \sigma^2/2)t + \sigma B_t^Q$ for any $t \leq T$, where B^Q is a standard Brownian motion under the equivalent martingale measure Q.

In the binomial setting of Exercise 2.1, the stock has a binomial return in each period with outcomes D and $U > D$, while a riskless bond has a constant return given by some $R \in (D, U)$. The risk-neutralized probabilistic representation of the put price is given, as with the call-price formula of Chapter 2, by

$$E^Q\left[R^{-T}(K - xe^\rho)^+\right], \tag{2}$$

where $\rho = Y_1 + \cdots + Y_T$, and where $Y_1, \ldots, Y_T$ are, under Q, i.i.d. binomial random variables (called *Bernoulli trials*) having outcomes $u = \log(U)$ and $d = \log(D)$ with respective "risk-neutral" probabilities $p = (R - D)/(U - D)$ and $1 - p$. We can calibrate the binomial stock returns U and D, as well as the bond return R, to our model of the continuous-time stock- and bond-price processes as follows. Obviously, we set the bond return at $R = e^r$. The stock returns U and D require more thought. To maintain some probabilistic similarity between the continuous-time and binomial models, we will explicitly model an exogenously given probability q of an up-return U, and choose U and D so that the "actual" (under P) mean and standard deviation of the continuously compounding stock returns are the same in the two settings. The probability q should not be confused with the "risk-neutralized" probability p constructed from the returns. Let us arbitrarily choose $q = 0.50$, and then select $u = \alpha + \sigma$ and $d = \alpha - \sigma$. With this, the continuously compounding stock returns in both the discrete- and continuous-time models have, under P, mean α and variance σ^2 per unit of time. Many other combinations of q, u, and d would work.

Let "Model n" refer to the binomial model with n trading periods per unit of time and with returns U_n, D_n, and R_n per trading period. We will allow n to approach infinity, always calibrating, as above, the binomial returns to the continuous-time returns. In order to maintain the mean and variance (under P) of total returns per unit of time at the continuously compounding levels α and σ^2, respectively, we reset the per-trading-period continuously compounding returns $u_n = \log(U_n)$ and $d_n = \log(D_n)$ to $u_n = \alpha/n + \sigma/\sqrt{n}$ and $d_n = \alpha/n - \sigma/\sqrt{n}$. We leave q_n fixed at 0.50. With i.i.d. returns, the per-unit-of-time risk-neutral mean and variance of the continuously compounding returns are then, respectively,

$$n\left[q_n u_n + (1 - q_n)d_n\right] = \alpha$$

and

$$nq_n(1 - q_n)(u_n - d_n)^2 = \sigma^2,$$

precisely as required. The per-trading-period return on the bond is $R_n = e^{r/n}$. The number of trading periods required for passage of T units of calendar time is Tn. We can therefore rewrite the put-price formula (2) for Model n as

$$\varphi_n = E^Q\left(e^{-rT}[K - xe^{\rho(n)}]^+\right), \tag{3}$$

where $\rho(n) = Y_1^n + \cdots + Y_{Tn}^n$ and where $Y_1^n, \ldots, Y_{Tn}^n$ are *i.i.d.* binomial with outcomes u_n and d_n at respective risk-neutralized (Q) probabilities of p_n and $1 - p_n$, where

$$p_n = \frac{R_n - D_n}{U_n - D_n}. \tag{4}$$

The per-unit-of-time risk-neutralized mean and variance of returns are, respectively,

$$M_n = n\left[p_n u_n + (1 - p_n)d_n\right]$$

and

$$V_n = np_n(1 - p_n)(u_n - d_n)^2.$$

An exercise shows that $M_n \to r - \sigma^2/2$ and $V_n \to \sigma^2$. Thus, $E^Q[\rho(nT)] \to (r - \sigma^2/2)T$ and $\text{var}_Q[\rho(nT)] \to \sigma^2 T$, where var_Q denotes variance under Q. Because u_n and d_n each converge to zero, the version of the Central Limit Theorem given by Proposition A implies that $\rho(n) \Rightarrow X_T$. Because the function $h : \mathbb{R} \to \mathbb{R}$ defined by $h(y) = (K - xe^y)^+$ is bounded and continuous, the binomial put price φ_n of (3) converges to the Black-Scholes put price φ given in (1) as the number n of trading intervals per unit of time goes to infinity.

The only properties of the put payoff function h used above are its continuity and its boundedness. The same arguments therefore allow one to conclude that, for any bounded continuous g, the arbitrage-free price of a claim to $g(S_{Tn})$ in the binomial setting with n trading periods per unit of time converges to the corresponding continuous-time "arbitrage-free" price $E^Q[e^{-rT}g(Z_T)]$ obtained from the Feynman-Kac formula, where $Z_T = x\exp[(r - \sigma^2/2)T + \sigma B_T^Q]$.

By put-call parity, the binomial call-pricing formula converges to the Black-Scholes call-pricing formula in the same sense. That is, put-call parity implies both that

$$C_n = x + \varphi_n - e^{-rT}K$$

and that

$$C(x, 0) = x + \varphi - e^{-rT}K.$$

Since $\varphi_n \to \varphi$, we have $C_n \to C(x, 0)$.

C. Binomial Convergence for Unbounded Derivative Payoffs

By now, it may be apparent why we began with the case of put options and only then treated calls by put-call parity. The call payoff function $x \mapsto (e^x - K)^+$ is not bounded! By a slightly more tedious argument, we could have shown convergence for the call-price formula directly, without applying put-call parity, by using the following results. This section is not essential and can be skipped on a first reading. Uniformly integrable random variables are defined in Appendix C.

Continuous Mapping Theorem. *Suppose $X_n \Rightarrow X$ and g is a continuous function. Then $g(X_n) \Rightarrow g(X)$.*

Proposition. *Suppose $X_n \Rightarrow X$. If $\{X_n\}$ is uniformly integrable, then $E(X_n) \to E(X)$. Conversely, if $X, X_1, X_2, \ldots$ are nonnegative and have finite expectations with $E(X_n) \to E(X)$, then $\{X_n\}$ is uniformly integrable.*

It can be shown as an exercise that, for $\rho(n)$ as defined in the previous section, the sequence of call payoffs $\{[xe^{\rho(n)} - K]^+\}$ is uniformly integrable, from which the above two results imply directly convergence of the binomial call-price formula to the Black-Scholes formula.

More generally, consider any derivative security with payoff function g such that $\{V_n\}$ is uniformly integrable when defined by $V_n = g[xe^{\rho(n)}]$. Suppose, moreover, that g is continuous and satisfies a polynomial growth condition, as defined in Appendix E, so that the Feynman-Kac pricing formula (5.26) applies. We then have convergence of the binomial price $E^Q(e^{-rT}V_n)$ to the continuous-time price $E^Q[e^{-rT}g(Z_T)]$, where

$$Z_t = x \exp\left[\left(r - \frac{\sigma^2}{2}\right)t + \sigma B_t^Q\right], \qquad t \leq T. \tag{5}$$

D. Discretization of Asset Price Processes

The Feynman-Kac solution (5.40) for derivative asset prices is typically difficult to calculate explicitly. This section and the following two address the numerical solution of (5.40) by Monte Carlo simulation of a discrete-time approximation of the stochastic differential equation (5.41).

We begin with a probability space on which is defined a standard Brownian motion B in $\mathbb{R}^d$, along with its standard filtration. The SDE to be approximated is assumed to be of the form

$$dX_t = a(X_t, t)\, dt + b(X_t, t)dB_t; \qquad X_0 = x \in \mathbb{R}^N, \qquad (6)$$

where $a : \mathbb{R}^N \times [0, \infty) \to \mathbb{R}^N$ and $b : \mathbb{R}^N \times [0, \infty) \to \mathbb{R}^{N \times d}$ have, for any k, bounded k-th derivatives. Referring to Appendix E, this is more than enough to ensure the existence of a unique Ito process X in $\mathbb{R}^N$ satisfying (6). A natural scheme for approximating (6) is the *Euler approximation*: For n periods per unit of time, let $\hat{X}^n$ be the discrete-time $\mathbb{R}^N$-valued process defined on some (possibly different) probability space $(\Omega, \mathscr{F}, P)$ by

$$\hat{X}^n_{k+1} - \hat{X}^n_k = \frac{1}{n} a\left(\hat{X}^n_k, \frac{k}{n}\right) + \frac{1}{\sqrt{n}} b\left(\hat{X}^n_k, \frac{k}{n}\right) \epsilon_{k+1}; \qquad \hat{X}^n_0 = x, \qquad (7)$$

where $\epsilon_1, \epsilon_2, \ldots$ is an *i.i.d.* sequence of standard normal vectors valued in $\mathbb{R}^d$. This is known as the Euler approximation of (6).

Our objective is to approximate an expression of the form $E[f(X_T)]$, where T is a fixed time, X is the solution of (6), and $f : \mathbb{R}^N \to \mathbb{R}$ satisfies a polynomial growth condition (defined in Appendix E) and has derivatives of any order. Our tentative approximation is $f_n = E[f(\hat{X}^n_{Tn})]$. The issue is: How good is this approximation? Let $e_n = E[f(X_T)] - f_n$ denote the approximation error. It can be shown that $e_n \to 0$. Even better, we can give an *order of convergence*. A sequence $\{y_n\}$ has *order-k convergence* if $y_n n^k$ is bounded in n. The Euler approximation is said to be a *first-order scheme* in that e_n has order-1 convergence. More precisely, there is a constant C such that $e_n + C/n$ has order-2 convergence. The error coefficient C may be positive or negative, and gives a notion of bias in the approximation. Although C is usually unknown, it turns out that C can itself be approximated to first order by $C_n = 2(f_n - f_{2n})$.

The Notes give a source for these properties of the Euler approximation as well as references to more complicated schemes with order-2 error. For instance, with $N = 1$ and under technical conditions, an order-2 scheme is given by the *Milshtein approximation*. Given μ and σ in $C^2(\mathbb{R})$ such that, for all t, we have $a(x, t) = \mu(x)$ and $b(x, t) = \sigma(x)$, the Milshtein approximation is given by

$$\hat{X}_{k+1}^n - \hat{X}_k^n = \frac{1}{n}\left[\mu(\hat{X}_k^n) - \frac{1}{2}\sigma(\hat{X}_k^n)\sigma'(\hat{X}_k^n)\right]$$

$$+ \frac{1}{\sqrt{n}}\sigma(\hat{X}_k^n)\epsilon_{k+1} + \frac{1}{2n}\sigma(\hat{X}_k^n)\sigma'(\hat{X}_k^n)\epsilon_{k+1}^2$$

$$+ \frac{1}{n^{3/2}}\nu(\hat{X}_k^n)\epsilon_{k+1} + \frac{1}{n^2}\eta(\hat{X}_k^n), \tag{8}$$

where

$$\nu(x) = \frac{1}{2}\mu(x)\sigma'(x) + \frac{1}{2}\mu'(x)\sigma(x) + \frac{1}{4}\sigma(x)^2\sigma''(x)$$

and

$$\eta(x) = \frac{1}{2}\mu(x)\mu'(x) + \frac{1}{4}\mu''(x)\sigma(x)^2.$$

E. Monte Carlo Simulation

Of course, we do not generally know even the approximation $E[f(\hat{X}_{Tn}^n)]$, but we can in turn estimate this quantity by Monte Carlo simulation. The law of large numbers states: If $Y_1, Y_2, \ldots$ is an *i.i.d.* sequence of random variables of finite expectations, then $(Y_1 + \cdots + Y_k)/k \to E(Y_1)$ almost surely.

Let $Y_1 = f(\hat{X}_{Tn}^n)$ be defined as above. This is the first simulation of the random variable whose mean is to be computed. For each i, let Y_i be defined in the same manner, with the exception that we substitute a sequence $\{\epsilon^{(i)}\}$ of standard normal vectors in $\mathbb{R}^d$ for the original, standard normal vectors $\epsilon = (\epsilon_1, \ldots, \epsilon_{Tn})$ of (7). We let $\epsilon^{(1)}, \epsilon^{(2)}, \ldots$ itself be *i.i.d.* The sequence $Y_1, Y_2, \ldots$ is therefore *i.i.d.*, and qualifies for an application of the law of large numbers, leaving

$$f(n, k) \equiv \frac{Y_1 + \cdots + Y_k}{k} \to E\left[f(\hat{X}_{Tn}^n)\right] \quad \text{a.s.} \tag{9}$$

In practice, one often substitutes *pseudo-random* numbers for $\{\epsilon^{(i)}\}$, using some deterministic scheme. There are a number of methods, called *variance reduction techniques*, such as *importance sampling*, that can improve the convergence properties of Monte Carlo simulation. For example, rather than choosing $\epsilon^{(1)}, \epsilon^{(2)}, \ldots$ to be *i.i.d.*, one can use $\epsilon^{(i)}$ for even i, and for odd i, let $\epsilon^{(i)} = -\epsilon^{(i-1)}$. Under conditions, this *antithetic sampling* method improves the convergence properties of the simulation. Further variance reduction methods are found in sources cited in the Notes.

At this point, (9) gives us an approximation $f(n, k)$ of $E[f(X_T)]$ based on a discrete-time approximation $\hat{X}^n$ of the Ito process X with n periods per unit of time, and with k simulations of the process $\hat{X}^n$. The number of additions required to compute $f(n, k)$ is roughly proportional to $N^2 Tnk$. Since N and T are presumably fixed for a given problem, we are concerned about the size of nk, given limited computation time. The Central Limit Theorem will provide us with an asymptotic trade-off between the number n of time points per unit of time and the number k of simulated sample paths. This is illustrated in the following section, based on research cited in the Notes.

F. Efficient SDE Simulation

Consider the following conditions on a sequence $\{Z(1), Z(2), \ldots \}$ of random variables that converges in distribution to some random variable Z. For our problem of calculating $E[f(X_T)]$, we may think of $Z(n)$ as $f(\hat{X}^n_{Tn})$ and Z as $f(X_T)$.

Condition A. *Let $\alpha = E(Z)$ and $\alpha(n) = E[Z(n)]$.*

   (i) $Z(n) \Rightarrow Z$ as $n \to \infty$.
   (ii) $E[Z^2(n)] \to E(Z^2) < \infty$ as $n \to \infty$.
   (iii) $\alpha(n) = \alpha + \beta n^{-p} + o(n^{-p})$ as $n \to \infty$, where $\beta \neq 0$ and $p > 0$.

Conditions (i) and (ii) will be sufficient for an application of the Central Limit Theorem. In our application, p is the order of convergence of the discretization scheme and β is a coefficient of the bias of the estimator $\alpha(n)$. For a sequence x_n of nonzero real numbers, the property "$o(x_n)$" means simply that $o(x_n)/x_n$ converges with n to zero. In our application, n is the number of time periods per sample path.

Consider the estimator for $E(Z)$ given by

$$a_n = \frac{1}{k_n} \sum_{i=1}^{k_n} Z_i(n),$$

where $Z_1(n), Z_2(n), \ldots$ is an *i.i.d.* sequence of random variables with the same distribution as $Z(n)$, and k_n is a positive integer that may depend on n. In our application, k_n is the number of sample paths simulated, given n. For our application, the amount of computer resources used to compute a_n is proportional to nk_n. The following result shows that, as this computing budget grows to infinity, the approximation error $z_n = a_n - \alpha$ has an asymptotically normal distribution provided k_n grows with n

like n^{2p}. If k_n does not grow at this rate, then the asymptotic distribution is "infinite," meaning a loss in efficiency. For instance, with the Euler scheme ($p = 1$), the number of simulations should quadruple (at least asymptotically) with each doubling of the number of time intervals. With a second-order scheme such as (8), the number of simulations should be on the order of the number of time intervals to the fourth power, and so on. Sharper results concerning the asymptotic distribution can be found with the original source for this result, cited in the Notes.

Theorem 1. *Suppose Condition A holds.*

(A) *If* $k_n/n^{2p} \to +\infty$ *or if* $k_n/n^{2p} \to 0$ *as* $nk_n \to \infty$, *then*

$$(k_n n)^{p/(1+2p)}|a_n - \alpha| \Rightarrow +\infty. \tag{10}$$

(B) *If* k_n/n^{2p} *converges to a nonzero constant* c *as* $nk_n \to \infty$, *then*

$$(k_n n)^{p/(1+2p)}(a_n - \alpha) \Rightarrow \frac{\sigma}{C^{1/2}}W + \beta C^p, \tag{11}$$

where $C = c^{1/(1+2p)}$, W *is standard normal, and* $\sigma^2 = \mathrm{var}(Z)$.

Proof: Note that

$$a_n - \alpha = \frac{1}{k_n}\sum_{i=1}^{k_n}\hat{Z}_i(n) + \alpha(n) - \alpha,$$

where $\hat{Z}_i(n) = Z_i(n) - \alpha(n)$. Then,

$$(k_n n)^{p/(1+2p)}(a_n - \alpha) = (k_n n)^{p/(1+2p)}k_n^{-1/2}\left(\sum_{i=1}^{k_n}\frac{\hat{Z}_i(n)}{\sqrt{k_n}}\right)$$

$$+(k_n n)^{p/(1+2p)}(\alpha(n) - \alpha).$$

Parts (i) and (ii) of Condition A allow an application of the Lindeberg-Feller Central Limit Theorem (Appendix C). Thus, as $n \to \infty$,

$$\sum_{i=1}^{k_n}\frac{\hat{Z}_i(n)}{\sqrt{k_n}} \Rightarrow \sigma W,$$

where W is standard normal and $\sigma^2 = \mathrm{var}(Z)$. Applying part (iii) of Condition A and some algebra completes the proof. ∎

G. Applying Feynman-Kac

Consider the solution given by (5.40) for the price $C(x, 0)$ of a derivative asset paying $g(S_T)$ at time T, where S is defined by (5.34) and where the short rate at time t is given by $r(S_t, t)$. To repeat, we have

$$C(x, 0) = E[Y_T g(Z_T)], \tag{12}$$

where $Y_t = \exp[\int_0^t -r(Z_s, s)\, ds]$ and where

$$dZ_t = r(Z_t, t)Z_t\, dt + \sigma(Z_t, t)dB_t; \quad Z_0 = x.$$

Since $dY_t = -r(Z_t, t)Y_t\, dt$, the $\mathbb{R}^{N+1}$-valued process X defined by $X_t = (Y_t, Z_t)$ solves an SDE of the same form as (6). We assume that the associated coefficient functions a and b satisfy the technical regularity conditions imposed with (6) of Section D. This calls for r to be bounded with bounded derivatives of every order and for σ to have bounded derivatives of every order. The Feynman-Kac solution (12) can be written in the form $E[f(X_T)]$, where $f : \mathbb{R}^{N+1} \to \mathbb{R}$ is defined by $f(y, z_1, \ldots, z_N) = yg(z_1, \ldots, z_N)$. If g has bounded derivatives of every order, then the derivative asset price $C(x, 0)$ can be approximated as suggested in the previous section. (Weaker conditions will suffice.)

The case of options requires special handling. The payoff function g of a call, defined by $g(x) = (x - K)^+$, is not even once differentiable. The "kink" at K is the only issue to overcome. The function g can be satisfactorily approximated by g_α, where, for any $\alpha > 0$,

$$g_\alpha(x) = \frac{x - K + \sqrt{(x - K)^2 + \alpha}}{2}. \tag{13}$$

Indeed, g_α has continuous derivatives of any order, satisfies a growth condition, and converges uniformly and monotonically from above to g as $\alpha \to 0$. The Dominated Convergence Theorem therefore implies that the associated Feynman-Kac solution also converges to $C(x, 0)$ as $\alpha \to 0$.

H. Finite-Difference Methods

This section reviews a simple finite-difference method for the PDE associated with asset prices. After reviewing the basic idea, we will work out an example based on the Cox-Ingersoll-Ross model of the term structure.

We will treat the *Cauchy problem*: Given real-valued functions r, g, h, μ, and σ on $\mathbb{R} \times [0, T]$, find a function f in $C^{2,1}(\mathbb{R} \times [0, T))$ solving

$$\mathscr{D}f(x, t) - r(x, t)f(x, t) + h(x, t) = 0, \qquad (x, t) \in \mathbb{R} \times [0, T), \tag{14}$$

with boundary condition

$$f(x, T) = g(x, T), \qquad x \in \mathbb{R}, \tag{15}$$

where

$$\mathscr{D}f(x, t) = f_t(x, t) + f_x(x, t)\mu(x, t) + \frac{1}{2}\sigma(x, t)^2 f_{xx}(x, t).$$

As we have seen in Chapter 5, we can interpret the solution f to (14)–(15) as the arbitrage-free market value of a security that promises the dividend rate $h(x, t)$ at time t when the state is x, assuming that the security has a terminal value of $g(x, T)$ at time T when the state is x. The short rate is $r(x, t)$ at time t when the state is x, and the "primitive" securities have prices and dividends determining the functions μ and σ in the manner described in Chapter 5. Alternatively, μ and σ could be determined directly from the equilibrium approach shown in Chapter 10 (see Exercise 10.7). Regularity conditions that ensure the existence and uniqueness of solutions are treated in Appendix E, where probabilistic Feynman-Kac solutions are also treated.

The basic idea of the finite-difference method for solving (14)–(15) is to choose a *grid*

$$\big\{(x_i, t_j) : i \in \{1, \dots, N\}, j \in \{1, \dots, M\}\big\} \subset \mathbb{R} \times [0, T],$$

and to find an approximate solution of (14)–(15) in the form of an $N \times M$ matrix F whose (i, j)-element F_{ij} is to be an approximation of $f(x_i, t_j)$. We always take $t_1 = 0$ and $t_M = T$. We take constants Δx and Δt to define the *mesh sizes* of the grid, so that $x_i - x_{i-1} = \Delta x$ for all $i > 1$ and $t_j - t_{j-1} = \Delta t$ for all $j > 1$, as depicted in Figure 12.1. In principle, increasing the number N of space points or the number $M = T/\Delta t$ of time points increases the accuracy of the approximation, although the convergence and stability properties of finite-difference methods can be a delicate issue. Various finite-difference methods could be suitable for the Cauchy problem, depending on the properties of (μ, σ, r, h, g). We will merely describe one of these, sometimes known as the *Crank-Nicholson method*, which has reasonable properties. We leave a characterization of the accuracy and stability of this and other finite-difference schemes to sources cited in the Notes.

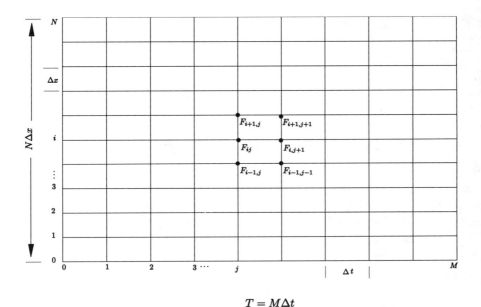

$$T = M\Delta t$$

Figure 12.1. *A Finite-Difference Grid*

The basis of the Crank-Nicholson method is the following approximation of the derivatives of f given F:

$$f_t(x_i, t_j) \sim \frac{F_{i,j+1} - F_{ij}}{\Delta t},$$

$$f_x(x_i, t_j) \sim \frac{F_{i+1,j+1} - F_{i-1,j+1} + F_{i+1,j} - F_{i-1,j}}{4\Delta x},$$

$$f_{xx}(x_i, t_j) \sim \frac{F_{i+1,j+1} - 2F_{i,j+1} + F_{i-1,j+1} + F_{i+1,j} - 2F_{ij} + F_{i-1,j}}{2(\Delta x)^2}.$$

It may be seen that the Crank-Nicholson method actually takes $(F_{i,j+1} + F_{i,j})/2$ as our approximation of $f(x_i, t_j)$. Accordingly, as we substitute these approximations of the derivatives of f into (14), we obtain at (x_i, t_j), for $1 < i < N$, the expression

$$a_{ij}F_{i-1,j} + b_{ij}F_{ij} + c_{ij}F_{i+1,j} = -a_{ij}F_{i-1,j+1} + \beta_{ij}F_{i,j+1} - c_{ij}F_{i+1,j+1} + e_{ij}, \quad (16)$$

where

$$a_{ij} = -\frac{\mu(x_i, t_j)}{4\Delta x} + \frac{\sigma(x_i, t_j)^2}{4(\Delta x)^2},$$

$$b_{ij} = -\frac{r(x_i, t_j)}{2} - \frac{1}{\Delta t} - \frac{\sigma(x_i, t_j)^2}{2(\Delta x)^2},$$

$$c_{ij} = \frac{\mu(x_i, t_j)}{4\Delta x} + \frac{\sigma(x_i, t_j)^2}{4(\Delta x)^2},$$

$$\beta_{ij} = -\frac{1}{\Delta t} + \frac{\sigma(x_i, t_j)^2}{2(\Delta x)^2} + \frac{r(x_i, t_j)}{2},$$

$$e_{ij} = -h(x_i, t_j).$$

Of course, (16) is not defined at $i = 1$ or $i = N$, for which we substitute with equations of the form

$$b_{1j}F_{1j} + c_{1j}F_{2j} = d_{1j}; \qquad a_{Nj}F_{N-1,j} + b_{Nj}F_{Nj} = d_{Nj}, \tag{17}$$

for suitable coefficients $b_{1j}, c_{1j}, d_{1j}, a_{Nj}, b_{Nj}$, and d_{Nj} that may depend on the particular problem at hand.

We can combine (16) and (17) to obtain a backward difference equation for the columns $F_1, F_2, \ldots, F_M$ of F, given by

$$A_j F_j = d_j, \tag{18}$$

with terminal boundary condition

$$F_{iM} = g(x_i, T), \qquad i \in \{1, \ldots, N\}, \tag{19}$$

where A_j is the *tridiagonal matrix* given by

$$A_j = \begin{bmatrix} b_{1j} & c_{1j} & 0 & 0 & 0 & \cdots & 0 \\ a_{2j} & b_{2j} & c_{2j} & 0 & 0 & \cdots & 0 \\ 0 & a_{3j} & b_{3j} & c_{3j} & 0 & \cdots & 0 \\ 0 & 0 & a_{4j} & b_{4j} & c_{4j} & \cdots & 0 \\ \vdots & & & \ddots & & & \vdots \\ 0 & \cdots & 0 & 0 & a_{N-1,j} & b_{N-1,j} & c_{N-1,j} \\ 0 & \cdots & 0 & 0 & 0 & a_{Nj} & b_{Nj} \end{bmatrix} \tag{20}$$

and where $d_j \in \mathbb{R}^N$ is the vector with i-th element

$$d_{ij} = -a_{ij}F_{i-1,j+1} + \beta_{ij}F_{i,j+1} - c_{ij}F_{i+1,j+1} + e_{ij}. \qquad (21)$$

Standard "staircase" algorithms for solving linear equations of the tridiagonal form (18) can be found in off-the-shelf software packages. (Code is provided in Appendix J.) Such algorithms exploit the special structure of A_j, avoiding a "brute-force" calculation of its inverse.

To summarize, the basic finite-difference algorithm (18)–(19) begins by fixing F_M according to the terminal boundary condition (19). Then d_{M-1} is computed from F_M by (21). Then F_{M-1} is computed by solving the tridiagonal equation (18) with $j = M - 1$. Next, d_{M-2} is computed from F_{M-1}, (18) is solved for F_{M-2}, and so on, until F_1 is solved. If the functions μ, σ, and r do not depend on the time parameter, then the matrix A_j does not depend on j, and can be computed once before the backward difference solution is propagated. The boundary equations given by (17) usually call for special treatment.

Sources indicated in the Notes treat finite-difference methods for more than one state variable. The number of computations grows exponentially with the number of state variables, as opposed to the linear growth of computations with the Monte Carlo approach. The finite-difference approach can also be more difficult to implement, and its convergence is a more delicate issue. For problems with one or two state variables, however, it is typically the case that the finite-difference approach requires fewer computations in total than the Monte Carlo approach in order to obtain similar accuracy.

I. Term-Structure Example

Consider a model for the short rate r given by the stochastic differential equation

$$dr_t = \mu(r_t, t)dt + \sigma(r_t, t)d\hat{B}_t, \qquad r_0 \geq 0, \qquad (22)$$

where $\hat{B}$ is a standard Brownian motion under an equivalent martingale measure and where μ and σ satisfy regularity conditions.

Consider the problem of solving for the term structure. For a given time T and any $t < T$, we would like to solve for the price $f(x, t)$ of a security paying one unit of account at time T, when the current time is t and the current short rate is x. Since the short rate is itself the state variable x, and since there are no intermediate dividends to consider, the PDE (14) specializes to

$$\mathscr{D}f(x, t) - xf(x, t) = 0, \tag{23}$$

with boundary condition

$$f(x, T) = 1, \qquad x \in \mathbb{R}. \tag{24}$$

If the functions μ and σ do not depend on t, we can also view $f(x, t)$ as the price at time zero for a unit bond maturing at $T - t$, so the solution of (23)–(24) characterizes the entire term structure up to maturity T.

It would be easy to implement the finite-difference algorithm (18)–(19) directly, although practical considerations often suggest a change of state variables. For example, suppose that μ and σ are continuous and that, for all t, we have $\mu(0, t) \geq 0$ and $\sigma(0, t) = 0$. Then the solution of (22) is nonnegative, as indicated in the Notes to Chapter 7. In that case, we can treat the original state space as $[0, \infty)$, and consider a change of state variables, which has been used in the literature cited in the Notes, given by a function $Y : [0, \infty) \rightarrow (0, 1]$, with

$$Y(x) = \frac{1}{1 + \gamma x}, \qquad x \in [0, \infty), \tag{25}$$

for some $\gamma > 0$. In other words, the short rate x corresponds to a new state $y = Y(x)$.

We can extend the range of Y to $[0, 1]$ by treating $Y(+\infty)$ as 0. A grid

$$\{(y_i, t_j) : i \in \{1, \ldots, N\}, j \in \{1, \ldots, M\}\} \subset [0, 1] \times [0, T],$$

with fixed mesh size Δy in the new state variable generates a solution with varying mesh size in the old short-rate state variable x, and with greater grid point concentration at lower interest-rate levels, in a fashion dictated by the coefficient γ. This may be a desirable feature of this change of variables. We take $y_1 = 0$ and $y_N = 1$.

Inverting (25), we can write the short rate as a function of the new state variable given by

$$X(y) = \frac{1 - y}{\gamma y}, \qquad y \in (0, 1].$$

If we let $\hat{f}(y, t) = f[X(y), t]$ for all y and t, the PDE (23)–(24) may be written

$$\widehat{\mathscr{D}}\hat{f}(y, t) - X(y)\hat{f}(y, t) = 0; \qquad \hat{f}(y, T) = 1, \tag{26}$$

where

$$\mathcal{D}\hat{f}(y, t) = \hat{f}_y(y, t)\hat{\mu}(y, t) + \hat{f}_t(y, t) + \frac{1}{2}\hat{\sigma}(y, t)^2\hat{f}_{yy}(y, t),$$

and where, using Ito's Formula,

$$\hat{\mu}(y, t) = Y'[X(y)]\mu[X(y, t)] + \frac{1}{2}Y''[X(y)]\sigma[X(y), t]^2,$$

$$\hat{\sigma}(y, t) = Y'[X(y)]\sigma[X(y), t].$$

The value equation (26) also applies for other well-behaved changes of variables given by some C^2 function Y with an inverse X. The Notes cite a source proposing a special change of variables with the property that $\hat{\sigma} \equiv 1$, which has computational advantages.

Solving for an approximation F_{ij} to the bond price $f[X(y_i), t_j]$ is now easily accomplished by the Crank-Nicholson solution (18)–(19) corresponding to (26). Throughout, we take $F_{1j} = 0$, corresponding to a zero bond price at an "infinite" interest rate. This determines the boundary equation of (17) for $i = 1$. For $i = N$, we use the fact that $\sigma(0, t) = 0$ and evaluate (26) at $y = 1$ ($x = 0$), leaving

$$\hat{f}_y(1, t)\hat{\mu}(1, t) + \hat{f}_t(1, t) = 0.$$

Replacing the usual Crank-Nicholson approximation for $\hat{f}_y(y_N, t_j)$ with the nonsymmetric approximation

$$\hat{f}_y(y_N, t_j) \sim \frac{F_{N,j} - F_{N-1,j}}{\Delta y},$$

the boundary equations (17) are then specified by the coefficients $b_{1j} = 1$, $c_{1j} = 0$, $d_{1j} = 0$, and

$$a_{Nj} = -\frac{\hat{\mu}(1)}{\Delta y}; \qquad b_{Nj} = -\frac{1}{\Delta t} + \frac{\hat{\mu}(1)}{\Delta y}; \qquad d_{Nj} = -\frac{1}{\Delta t}F_{N,j+1}. \qquad (27)$$

For a coupon bond, or any other security promising lump-sum payments during $[0, T]$, the finite-difference equation (18) should be replaced by

$$F_j = F_{j+} + D_j; \qquad A_j F_{j+} = d_j, \qquad (18')$$

where D_j is the vector in $\mathbb{R}^N$ whose i-th element is the lump-sum dividend paid at time t_j if the state is between $x_i - \Delta x/2$ and $x_i + \Delta x/2$, so that we can treat F_{j+} as the ex-dividend approximation and F_j as the cum-dividend

Table 12.1. **Numerical Error (parts per million) of Crank-Nicholson Algorithm**

Number of State Points	Number of Time Points		
	40	80	160
40	176	186	188
80	35	44	46
120	8	18	20
160	−1	9	11
200	−5	4	6
240	−7	2	4

The instrument priced is a 10-year 7-percent-coupon default-free bond (with semi-annual coupons of 3.5 percent of face value). The algorithm is Crank-Nicholson, as described in the text. The CIR short-rate model is used with coefficients $A = 0.5$, $\bar{x} = 0.0719$, and $C = 0.1664$. The initial short rate is chosen so as to price the bond at par. The parameters are chosen so that, as measured in an instantaneous sense, the initial volatility of the yield is 15 percent. The table shows the difference between the numerical estimate of the bond price and the theoretical price, as a fraction of the theoretical price, in parts per million.

approximation. Linear approximations could be made in the obvious fashion if the lump-sum payments do not occur exactly as suggested in terms of the grid points.

Table 12.1 shows the accuracy of this finite-difference scheme for zero-coupon bond prices for the CIR example

$$\mu(x, t) = A(\bar{x} - x); \qquad \sigma(x, t) = C\sqrt{x}, \tag{28}$$

where A, $\bar{x}$, and C are positive constants. The table shows the difference between the exact solution (whose explicit solution for this case is given in Chapter 7) and the approximate solution. This approximation error, as a fraction of the exact solution, is shown in Table 12.1, in parts per million. Computer code for this solution is given in Appendix J.

J. Finite-Difference Algorithms with Early Exercise Options

Suppose the security whose value is to be determined has an early exercise feature, so that at any time t, the security can be exercised at a payoff of $g(x, t)$ if the state is x. For example, if the state x represents a primitive security price and the derivative security in question is an American put option at strike K, then $g(x, t) = (K - x)^+$ for all x and t, as discussed in Sections 8I and 8E. With an early exercise feature, it is natural to conjecture that the finite-difference algorithm given in the previous section can be adjusted merely by replacing the backward difference step (18) with

$$F_{ij} = \max[\hat{F}_{ij}, g(x_i, t_j)], \qquad i \in \{1, \ldots, N\}, \tag{29}$$

where $\hat{F}_j$ is the vector in $\mathbb{R}^N$ solving $A_j\hat{F}_j = d_j$. In other words, at each step, the value of the American security is taken to be the larger of its exercised value and its unexercised value, in line with the analysis of Section 3G. Computer code for bond-option prices, based on this algorithm, is shown in Appendix J.

A delicate issue is the convergence, and rate of convergence, of this algorithm (29) to the solution of the associated continuous-time optimal-stopping problem that is shown in Section 8I to characterize the American security's true arbitrage-free value. Some of the literature dealing with this convergence issue is cited in the Notes.

K. The Numerical Solution of State Prices

Returning to the setting of the PDE (14)–(15) for security valuation, suppose there are many different securities to be valued, all based on the same functions r, μ, and σ. Only the functions h and g differ from security to security. In this case, given a grid $\{(x_i, t_j)\}$ defined by mesh sizes Δx and Δt, it makes sense to find an approximation Ψ_{ij} of the market value at time 0 of a security that pays $1/\Delta x$ units of account at time t_j in the event that the state is between $x_i + \Delta x/2$ and $x_i - \Delta x/2$. With this, it is reasonable to approximate the market value at time 0 of the security with payoff functions h for dividend rate and g for terminal value by

$$V(h, g) \equiv \Delta t \Delta x \sum_{j=1}^{M} \left[\sum_{i=1}^{N} \Psi_{ij} h(x_i, t_j) \right] + \Delta x \sum_{i=1}^{N} \Psi_{iM} g(x_i, T). \qquad (30)$$

We will show how the same finite-difference approach used to calculate F in Section H can be modified to calculate the "approximate state prices" specified by Ψ. This is based on the fundamental solution of the PDE (14), reviewed in Appendix E. Under technical conditions, for each initial state x^* in $\mathbb{R}$, there is a function $\psi \in C^{2,1}(\mathbb{R} \times (0, T])$ with the following (almost equivalent) properties:

(a) ψ satisfies

$$\mathcal{D}^*\psi(x, t) - r(x, t)\psi(x, t) = 0, \qquad (x, t) \in \mathbb{R} \times (0, T], \qquad (31)$$

where

$$\mathcal{D}^*\psi(x, t) = -\psi_t(x, t) - \frac{\partial}{\partial x}\big[\psi(x, t)\mu(x, t)\big]$$

$$+ \frac{1}{2}\frac{\partial^2}{\partial x^2}\big[\sigma(x, t)^2\psi(x, t)\big],$$

with an initial boundary condition requiring essentially that $\psi(\cdot, t)$ is the density of a measure that converges as $t \to 0$ to a probability measure ν with $\nu(\{x^*\}) = 1$; and

(b) for any (g, h) satisfying technical conditions, the solution f of the PDE (14)–(15) satisfies

$$f(x^*, 0) = \int_0^T \int_{-\infty}^{+\infty} \psi(x, t)h(x, t)dxdt + \int_{-\infty}^{+\infty} \psi(x, T)g(x, T)dx,$$

$$(32)$$

which is the integral analogous to the sum given by (30).

The PDE (31) is sometimes called the *Fokker-Planck equation*, or the forward Kolmogorov equation, to distinguish it from the backward Kolmogorov equation (14). For the case $r \equiv 0$, one can literally treat $\psi(\cdot, t)$ as the probability density of X_t, where X solves the underlying stochastic differential equation $dX_t = \mu(X_t, t)dt + \sigma(X_t, t)dB_t$, with $X_0 = x^*$. Much more can be said on this point, as indicated in sources cited in the Notes. The initial boundary condition for (31) stated above corresponds naturally to this interpretation of ψ. An explicit solution for ψ for the Cox-Ingersoll-Ross model (28) is given in Section 7G.

Now, given (32) and the equivalence between (a) and (b), in order to solve for $f(x^*, 0)$ we would like to approximate ψ with a finite-difference solution Ψ of the PDE (31). The same Crank-Nicholson approach can be applied, generating the forward difference equation for the columns $\Psi_1, \Psi_2, \ldots, \Psi_M$ of Ψ given by

$$A_j^* \Psi_j = d_j^*, \tag{33}$$

with boundary condition for a given initial state $x_k = x^*$ of

$$\Psi_{k1} = \frac{1}{\Delta x}; \qquad \Psi_{i1} = 0, \quad i \neq k, \tag{34}$$

where the tridiagonal matrix A_j^* and the vector d_j^* can be calculated for each j in the same manner as for the backward difference equation, using the Crank-Nicholson approximations for the derivatives of ψ in terms of Ψ. Specifically, for σ twice continuously differentiable with respect to x and μ continuously differentiable with respect to x, we have

$$d_{ij}^* = -a_{ij}^* \Psi_{i-1, j-1} + \beta_{ij}^* \Psi_{i, j-1} - c_{ij}^* \Psi_{i+1, j-1} \tag{35}$$

and

$$A_j^* = \begin{bmatrix} b_{1j}^* & c_{1j}^* & 0 & 0 & 0 & \cdots & 0 \\ a_{2j}^* & b_{2j}^* & c_{2j}^* & 0 & 0 & \cdots & 0 \\ 0 & a_{3j}^* & b_{3j}^* & c_{3j}^* & 0 & \cdots & 0 \\ 0 & 0 & a_{4j}^* & b_{4j}^* & c_{4j}^* & \cdots & 0 \\ \vdots & & & & \ddots & & \vdots \\ 0 & \cdots & 0 & 0 & a_{N-1,j}^* & b_{N-1,j}^* & c_{N-1,j}^* \\ 0 & \cdots & 0 & 0 & 0 & a_{Nj}^* & b_{Nj}^* \end{bmatrix}, \tag{36}$$

where

$$a_{ij}^* = \frac{\mu(x_i, t_j) - 2\sigma(x_i, t_j)\sigma_x(x_i, t_j)}{4\Delta x} + \frac{\sigma(x_i, t_j)^2}{4(\Delta x)^2},$$

$$b_{ij}^* = -\frac{1}{\Delta t} - \frac{\sigma(x_i, t_j)^2}{2(\Delta x)^2}$$
$$- \frac{r(x_i, t_j) + \mu_x(x_i, t_j) - \sigma_x(x_i, t_j)^2 - \sigma_{xx}(x_i, t_j)\sigma(x_i, t_j)}{2},$$

$$c_{ij}^* = \frac{2\sigma(x_i, t_j)\sigma_x(x_i, t_j) - \mu(x_i, t_j)}{4\Delta x} + \frac{\sigma(x_i, t_j)^2}{4(\Delta x)^2},$$

$$\beta_{ij}^* = \frac{r(x_i, t_j) + \mu_x(x_i, t_j) - \sigma_{xx}(x_i, t_j)\sigma(x_i, t_j) - \sigma_x(x_i, t_j)^2}{2}$$
$$- \frac{1}{\Delta t} + \frac{\sigma(x_i, t_j)^2}{2(\Delta x)^2}.$$

The cases of $i = 1$ and $i = N$ again require special consideration.

One begins with the initial condition (34) for Ψ_1, and then propagates the solution forward, calculating Ψ_j at each stage by (33), given d_j^* in terms of Ψ_{j-1}. (In fact, in application, stability of solutions may be more easily achieved by initial conditions that are not so "concentrated" at the initial condition as suggested by (34), but rather by an initial condition at Δt later in time that is, for example, a low-variance Gaussian density suggested by the parameters. There is in any case a certain "art" to obtaining reasonable approximate solutions.)

Given Ψ, the approximate value of any security with dividend rate h and terminal value g is given by (30). If there is but a single security to value, (30) involves an extra set of computations that is not required with the backward approach. With many securities to value, however, the "forward approach" can involve significant savings in computations.

The astute reader will notice that we could have avoided the scaling factors Δx and $1/\Delta x$ in (30) and (34), respectively, in which case Ψ would not be an approximation for ψ, but rather for $\Delta x \psi$.

L. Numerical Solution of the Pricing Semi-Group

In the tridiagonal system (33)–(35), we have $d_j^* = C_j^* \Psi_{j-1}$ for the tridiagonal matrix

$$
C_j^* = \begin{bmatrix}
\beta_{1j}^* & -c_{1j}^* & 0 & 0 & 0 & \cdots & 0 \\
-a_{2j}^* & \beta_{2j}^* & -c_{2j}^* & 0 & 0 & \cdots & 0 \\
0 & -a_{3j}^* & \beta_{3j}^* & -c_{3j}^* & 0 & \cdots & 0 \\
0 & 0 & -a_{4j}^* & \beta_{4j}^* & -c_{4j}^* & \cdots & 0 \\
\vdots & & & & \ddots & & \vdots \\
0 & \cdots & 0 & 0 & -a_{N-1,j}^* & \beta_{N-1,j}^* & -c_{N-1,j}^* \\
0 & \cdots & 0 & 0 & 0 & -a_{Nj}^* & \beta_{Nj}^*
\end{bmatrix}.
$$

Thus (33) can be re-expressed in the recursive form

$$
\Psi_j = \Pi_j \Psi_{j-1}, \tag{37}
$$

where $\Pi_j = (A_j^*)^{-1} C_j^*$. It follows that, for any j and $k \geq j$,

$$
\Psi_k = \Pi_{jk} \Psi_j, \tag{38}
$$

where

$$
\Pi_{jk} = \Pi_{j+1} \Pi_{j+2} \cdots \Pi_k, \tag{39}
$$

and where Π_{jj} denotes the identity matrix. The collection $\Pi = \{\Pi_{jk} : 1 \leq j \leq k \leq M\}$ of $N \times N$ matrices is a semi-group since it has the property: Whenever $j \leq k \leq m$, we have $\Pi_{jm} = \Pi_{jk}\Pi_{km}$. We will describe some of the useful properties of the semi-group Π.

First, for any initial state x_k in the grid, the associated approximate state-price matrix Ψ is given by

$$
\Psi_j = \Pi_{1j} \Psi_1, \tag{40}
$$

where Ψ_1 is given by (34). This means that, given the semi-group Π, the state prices associated with any given initial state can be obtained without repeated solution of the tridiagonal equations (37).

Second, given any payoff functions h and g, the $N \times M$ matrix F^* approximating the solution f to (14)–(15) is easily characterized as follows. For any j and $k \geq j$, we have

$$F_j^* = \Pi_{jk} F_k^* + \sum_{m=j+1}^{k} \Pi_{jm} H_m, \tag{41}$$

where H_j is the vector in $\mathbb{R}^N$ with $h(x_i, t_j)\Delta t$ as its i-th element. In particular, (41) applies with $k = M$ and the boundary condition $F_{iM}^* = g(x_i, T)$.

Although solving for the semi-group Π can be computationally intensive, there are obvious compensations. For the case in which μ, σ, and r do not depend on t, the matrices A_j^* and C_j^* do not depend on j, so there is but a single matrix $\overline{\Pi}$ to compute, with $\Pi_j = \overline{\Pi}$ for all j.

The close parallel between (41) and the Markov chain valuation equation (3.17) is not an accident. One can indeed approximate the solution X to the SDE $dX_t = \mu(X_t, t)\, dt + \sigma(X_t, t)dB_t$ with that of an N-state Markov chain having transition matrix $q^{(j)}$ at period $j \in \{1, \ldots, M\}$ given by

$$q_{ik}^{(j)} = [1 + r(x_i, t_j)\Delta t]\Pi_{ik}. \tag{42}$$

A source given in the Notes gives the sense of this approximation and further details on this connection between continuous and discrete pricing.

The parallel with the discrete-time case extends to the pricing of American securities. Using the semi-group approach, one can replace the backward difference equation (29) for the American security described in Section J with the backward equation

$$F_j^* = \max[\Pi_{j+1}(F_{j+1} + H_{j+1}), G_j], \tag{43}$$

where the maximum is taken element-wise and where G_j is the vector in $\mathbb{R}^N$ whose i-th element is $g(x_i, t_j)$. Equation (3.21) gives the exact discrete-time version of this American valuation algorithm.

M. Fitting the Initial Term Structure

In the context of the term-structure model (22), there are many practical applications in which the initial term structure is given from market data in the form of a vector p in $\mathbb{R}^N$, with p_j denoting the price at time 0 of a unit pure discount bond maturing at t_j. (In practice, p is often obtained from the prices of coupon bonds by spline methods cited in the Notes of Chapter 7.) Since a model rarely coincides with reality, the functions μ and σ determining the risk-neutral behavior of the short rate will not, in general, generate a term structure consistent with the market data p. Suppose, however, that for each t, the functions $\mu(\cdot, t)$ and $\sigma(\cdot, t)$ depend on a free parameter $\lambda(t)$. One can imagine choosing the function λ in order to match the solution of the term structure to that given by p. For example, one could extend the CIR model (28) by replacing the constant $\bar{x}$ with $\lambda(t)$, and then choose $\lambda(t_1), \lambda(t_2), \ldots, \lambda(t_M)$ so that the solution given in Section I for the term structure is consistent with p.

One can imagine a number of different numerical approaches to this term-structure matching procedure. One that has been suggested by a source cited in the Notes is based on the numerical solution Ψ for state prices. Using the fact that $\sum_{i=1}^{N} \Psi_{ij}$ approximates p_j, the proposed algorithm for λ is given by the following steps.

(a) Let $j = 2$.
(b) Search for that number $\lambda(t_j)$ such that, given Ψ_{j-1}, we have

$$\hat{p}_j[\lambda(t_j), \Psi_{j-1}] = p_j, \tag{44}$$

where $\hat{p}_j[\lambda(t_j), \Psi_{j-1}] = \sum_{i=1}^{N} \Psi_j$ is notation indicating the dependence of the solution Ψ_j of (33) on Ψ_{j-1} and $\lambda(t_j)$ given by (35) and (36). This one-dimensional search could be conducted by a Newton-Raphson iterative method.
(c) Let j be increased by 1, and return to step (b) if $j \leq M$. Otherwise, stop.

In order for the numerical search for $\lambda(t_j)$ in step (44) to succeed, and for the solution to be uniquely defined, the model should be such that $\hat{p}_j(\cdot, \Psi_{j-1})$ is a strictly monotonic continuous function with range $(0, 1)$. This is true for the CIR example given above, in which $\bar{x}$ is replaced in (28) with $\lambda(t)$.

One could match additional parameters to market data on the prices of derivative securities, such as options. The idea is to obtain better "calibration" with the market in order, in principle, to obtain higher accuracy in the pricing of derivative securities. For example, one can extend by taking λ to be an $\mathbb{R}^2$-valued function specifying two free parameters, to be matched against the initial term structure of bond prices as well as the initial "volatility structure" implicit in bond-option prices, an approach taken in papers cited in the Notes.

Of course, with the passage of time, the "matched" model will fall out of calibration, implying that the free parameter vector λ was in fact inappropriate. In typical practice, a new set of free parameters is chosen, and valuation proceeds again. This process of routine reparameterization is theoretically inconsistent (and, to the author's knowledge, has been applied with relatively little econometric sophistication), but seems to some degree unavoidable. The "name of the game" is apparently to specify an accurate term-structure model that is both tractable and relatively stable over time.

Exercises

12.1 Prove Proposition A, using the Lindeberg-Feller Central Limit Theorem given in Appendix C.

12.2 Show, as claimed in Section B, that the per-unit-of-time risk-neutralized mean M_n and variance V_n converge to $r - \sigma^2/2$ and σ^2, respectively.

12.3 Show that the sequence $\{[xe^{\rho(n)} - K]^+\}$ of "binomial" call-option payoffs constructed in Section C is uniformly integrable. Hint: Use the converse part of Theorem C.

12.4 Show how the Lindeberg-Feller Central Limit Theorem is invoked in order to obtain the limiting normal distribution asserted in the proof of Theorem F.

12.5 Verify the Crank-Nicholson equation (16) from (14) and the Crank-Nicholson derivative approximations.

12.6 (Binomial Approximation of the Black-Derman-Toy Term-Structure Model). The continuous-time version of the Black-Derman-Toy model shown in Exercise 7.1 has the short-rate process r given by

$$r_t^c = U(t) \exp\big[\beta(t)\hat{B}(t)\big],$$

where $\hat{B}$ is a standard Brownian motion under an equivalent martingale measure Q, and where $U : [0, \infty) \to \mathbb{R}_{++}$ and $\beta : [0, \infty) \to \mathbb{R}_{++}$ are continuously differentiable. The discrete-time version of the Black-Derman-Toy model given in Exercise 3.11 has the short-rate process r given by $r_t^d = a_t \exp(b_t X_t)$, where, for each time $t \in \{0, 1, \dots\}$, a_t and b_t are strictly positive constants, and X_t is a shock process with the property that, for all t,

$$Q\big(X_{t+1} - X_t = 1 \mid X_0, \dots, X_t\big) = Q\big(X_{t+1} - X_t = 0 \mid X_0, \dots, X_t\big) = \frac{1}{2}.$$

This exercise calls for the construction, at each t, of sequences $\{a_t^n\}$ and $\{b_t^n\}$ of coefficients for the discrete-time Black-Derman-Toy model with the property that, for each $t \in \{1, 2, \ldots\}$,

$$r_t^n \equiv a_t^n \exp(b_t^n X_{tn}) \Rightarrow r_t^c,$$

or convergence in distribution of the discrete-time model with n time periods per unit of calendar time to the continuous-time model. Hint: Use the Continuous Mapping Theorem, and the fact that $z \mapsto U(t)\exp(\beta(t)z)$ defines a continuous function on $\mathbb{R}$ into $\mathbb{R}$. We can write

$$r_t^n = U(t)\exp\left[\beta_t\left(X_{tn}b_t^n - \log\left[\frac{a_t^n}{U(t)}\right]\right)\right].$$

Show that it is therefore enough to choose $\{a_t^n\}$ and $\{b_t^n\}$ so that

$$X_{tn}b_t^n - \log\left[\frac{a_t^n}{U(t)}\right] \Rightarrow Z,$$

where Z is normally distributed with mean zero and variance t. Make use of the Central Limit Theorem to design $\{a_t^n\}$ and $\{b_t^n\}$ accordingly.

Notes

(A) Standard references on probability theory include Chung (1974), Chow and Teicher (1978), Billingsley (1986), and Durrett (1991), all of which include the law of large numbers and the Central Limit Theorem.

(B–C) The convergence of the binomial model of option pricing to the Black-Scholes model is due to Cox, Ross, and Rubinstein (1979). Extensions of this approach can be found in Amin (1991, 1993b), Bertsimas, Kogan, and Lo (1998), Clewlow and Carverhill (1995), Cutland, Kopp, and Willinger (1991, 1993a), Diener and Diener (1999), Duffie (1988c), Duffie and Protter (1988), He (1990, 1991), Heston and Zhou (1997), Hubalek and Schachermayer (1998), Lamberton and Pagès (1990), Lamberton (1997), Lesne, Prigent, and Scaillet (2000), Lee (1991), Madan, Milne, and Shefrin (1989), Nelson and Ramaswamy (1989), Prigent (1995), Rogers and Stapleton (1998), Willinger and Tacqu (1991), and Eberlein (1991), among many other papers.

For other numerical procedures, see Gerber and Shiu (1994) and Levy, Avellaneda, and Parás (1994). Broadie, Glasserman, and Kou (1997, 1999) treat discretization errors for path-dependent options and barrier options. Curran (1996) and Glasserman, Heidelberger, and Shahabuddin (1999) discuss importance sampling for path-dependent option valuation. Fournié and Lasry (1996) and Fournié, Lasry, and Touzi (1996) also treat importance sampling with pricing applications. On approximatization methods for Asian options, see Chalasani, Jha, and Varikooty (1998), Fu, Madan, and Wang (1999), and Zvan, Forsyth, and Vetzal (1998).

(D–E) This section is based on Talay and Tubaro (1990). Milshtein (1974, 1978) introduced second-order discretization schemes such as (8). Bally and Talay (1996), and Talay (1984, 1986, 1990) provide more advanced second-order schemes for discretization of stochastic differential equations in $\mathbb{R}^n$. See also Bernard, Talay, and Tubaro (1994), Kusuoka (1999a), Newton (1990), and Török (1993) in this regard. On discretization of backward SDEs, see Chevance (1995, 1996) and Douglas, Ma, and Protter (1996).

(F) This section is based on Duffie and Glynn (1995), where additional details may be found. The first edition of this book took a different approach to the trade-off between number of simulations and number of time steps, based on the Large Deviations Theorem, which is described by Durrett (1991).

(G) Boyle, Broadie, and Glasserman (1997) offer a general survey of pricing by Monte Carlo simulation. The smooth approximation g_α in Section G of the call payoff function appears in Duffie (1988c), and was related to the author by Stephen Smale. Various applications of the Monte Carlo estimation of derivative asset prices and hedging are given by Andersen (1996), Avellaneda, Buff, Friedman, Grandchamp, Kruk, and Newman (1999), Barraquand (1993), Boyle (1977, 1988, 1990), Boyle, Evnine, and Gibbs (1989), Glasserman and Zhao (1999), Fournié (1993), Jones and Jacobs (1986), and Schoenmakers and Heemink (1996). For the simulation of hedging coefficients, or "deltas" and other derivatives, see Clewlow and Carverhill (1992) and Broadie and Glasserman (1996). For "quasi-Monte Carlo" simulation methods, with finance applications, see Caflisch and Morokoff (1995, 1996), Caflisch, Morokoff, and Owen (1997), Chidambaran and Figlewski (1995), Joy, Boyle, and Tan (1996), Morokoff and Caflisch (1993, 1994, 1995), and Moskowitz and Caflisch (1994).
    Owen (1996, 1997) and Owen and Tavella (1996) apply scrambled-net methods to pricing and risk calculations.

(H) Tavella and Randall (2000) review the solution of derivative pricing by finite-difference methods. Mitchell and Griffiths (1980), Smith (1985), and Strikwerda (1989) are basic treatments of the finite-difference solution of PDEs. Computer code for the solution of tridiagonal systems of equations such as (18) is given by Press, Flannery, Teukolsky, and Vetterling (1993). An example of a more advanced finite-difference approach is given by Lawson and Morris (1978). Schwartz (1977) introduced the use of finite-difference methods to the solution of asset pricing in finance. Andreasen (1998) applies finite-difference methods to lookback options. For more examples of finite-difference methods with financial applications, see Clewlow (1990) and Druskin, Knizhnerman, Tamarchenko, and Kostek (1997).

(I) The term-structure example of Section I is based on Courtadon (1982) and Stanton (1995b). Jamshidian (1991c) gives an alternate change of variables under which the diffusion is a constant. The literature in finance is reviewed and summarized by Clewlow (1990). The Crank-Nicholson approximation is known as an *implicit* method. Hull and White (1990b) show how the range of the simpler *explicit* methods can be extended. Hull and White (1993) review some of the simpler implicit and explicit methods. Dewynne and Wilmott (1994) provide example applications to exotic options. Barles, Daher, and Romano (1992) examine the general issue of convergence of finite-difference schemes in finance applications. Nelson and Ramaswamy (1989) treat finite-difference methods that are based on replacing the underlying stochastic differential equation with a Markov chain that has binomial transitions, extending the range of application of the binomial approach. Kishimoto (1989), Stanton (1990), and Stanton and Wallace (1995) numerically solve path-dependent security prices, such as mortgage-backed securities. Willard (1996) treats path-dependent valuation in a multifactor setting.

Dengler and Jarrow (1996) examine the implications of variable time steps in numerical option-pricing solutions.

(J) Justification of the valuation algorithm (29) for securities with early exercise options is a delicate issue that is treated by Jaillet, Lamberton, and Lapeyre (1988, 1990). An early variation of this algorithm for the Black-Scholes (log-normal) put option problem is found in Brennan and Schwartz (1977). The methods of Chernoff and Petkau (1984) also give a practical accurate numerical approximation to the American put value. For further results on the numerical valuation of American-style securities, see Ait-Sahlia and Lai (1996), Amin (1991), Amin and Khanna (1994), Andreasen and Gruenewald (1996), Barraquand and Pudet (1996), Barraquand and Martineau (1995), Bjerksund and Stensland (1993), Broadie and Detemple (1994), Broadie and Glasserman (1996, 1997, 1998), Bunch and Johnson (1993), Büttler (1995), Büttler and Waldvogel (1996), Carr (1994, 1998), Carr and Faguet (1994), Clarke and Parrott (1996), Dempster (1994), Dempster and Hutton (1997), Gandhi, Kooros, and Salkin (1993), Gao, Huang, and Subrahmanyam (1996), Ibanez and Zapatero (1999), Lamberton (1997), Lee (1990), Longstaff and Schwartz (1998), Wu (1996), and Zhang (1993).

(K–L) The valuation of securities in terms of the fundamental solution also appears in the literature under such labels as *path integrals*, as in Dash (1989), or Green's function, as in Beaglehole (1990) who calculates the fundamental solution G explicitly for the Cox-Ingersoll-Ross model (28), or Jamshidian (1991c). The idea of using pricing semi-groups goes back at least to Garman (1985). See also Huang (1985a).

(M) The issue of matching parameters to the initial term structure apparently originated with Ho and Lee (1986) in their "binomial" model of the term structure. Subsequent work in this vein can be found in Black, Derman, and Toy (1990), Dybvig (1988), Hull and White (1990a, 1994), and Jamshidian (1991c). Further references are given in the Notes to Chapter 7. The Newton-Raphson search, and other numerical optimization techniques, can be found in Luenberger (1984) and Press, Flannery, Teukolsky, and Vetterling (1993).

Additional Topics: On numerical methods for valuation of interest-rate options, in addition to sources cited in Chapter 7, see Clewlow and Strickland (1996), Clewlow, Pang, and Strickland (1997), Kunitomo and Takahashi (1996), Li, Ritchken, and Sankarasubramanian (1995), Nielsen and Sandmann (1996), Scott

(1996a), and Topper (1997). For numerical methods for HJM models in particular, see Brace (1996), Chiarella and Hassan (1997), Heath, Jarrow, and Morton (1990, 1992a, b), and Ritchken and Trevor (1999).

On the numerical valuation of convertible debt, see Pikovsky and Shreve (1996a) and Zhu and Sun (1999).

An important topic that we have not treated is numerical solution of dynamic programming problems. Examples in the literature include Judd (1989), Tauchen and Hussey (1991), and Gagnon and Taylor (1990), who treat discrete-time models, and Fitzpatrick and Fleming (1991), Fleming and Soner (1993), Munk (2000a), and Prigent (1994). A free-boundary problem that arises with investment under durability is treated by Hindy, Huang, and Zhu (1993, 1997).

Numerical computation of equilibria is treated by Kubler and Schmedders (1997), Marcet (1993), and Marcet and Marshall (1994).

Fourier transform methods for derivative pricing are discussed in Chapter 8. See also Carr and Madan (1998) and Rebonato and Cooper (1996). Applications of Malliavin calculus to asset pricing and hedging are addressed by Fournié, Lasry, Lebuchoux, Lions, and Touzi (1999).

Eydeland (1994a, b) provides alternative numerical methods for some of the derivative valuation problems addressed here. Bouleau and Lépingle (1994) is a general treatment of numerical methods for stochastic problems.

Appendixes

A
Finite-State Probability

SUPPOSE Ω is a finite set. A *tribe* on Ω is a collection $\mathcal{F}$ of subsets of Ω that includes the empty set $\varnothing$ and that satisfies the following two conditions:

(a) if B is in $\mathcal{F}$, then its *complement* $\{\omega \in \Omega : \omega \notin B\}$ is also in $\mathcal{F}$;

(b) if A and B are in $\mathcal{F}$, their union $A \cup B$ is in $\mathcal{F}$.

A tribe $\mathcal{F}$ is also known as an *algebra* or *field*, among other terms. When Ω is to be thought of as the states of the world, the elements of $\mathcal{F}$ are called *events*. Conditions (a) and (b) allow for simple logical rules regarding the probabilities of events. Specifically, a *probability measure* is a function $P : \mathcal{F} \to [0, 1]$ satisfying $P(\varnothing) = 0$, $P(\Omega) = 1$, and, for any disjoint events A and B,

$$P(A \cup B) = P(A) + P(B).$$

Under P, an event B has *probability* $P(B)$. A pair $(\Omega, \mathcal{F})$ consisting of a finite set Ω and a tribe $\mathcal{F}$ on Ω is called a measurable space. With the addition of a probability measure P on $\mathcal{F}$, the triple $(\Omega, \mathcal{F}, P)$ is a called a *probability space*.

Fixing a measurable space $(\Omega, \mathcal{F})$, a *random variable* is a function $X : \Omega \to \mathbb{R}$ with the following property: For any $x \in \mathbb{R}$, the set $\{\omega \in \Omega : X(\omega) = x\}$ is in $\mathcal{F}$. Intuitively, X is a random variable if, for any possible outcome x, we will know whether X has this outcome from knowing the outcomes (true or false) of the events in $\mathcal{F}$. If X is a random variable with respect to $(\Omega, \mathcal{F})$, we also say that X is $\mathcal{F}$-*measurable*.

Since Ω is finite, for any random variable X there are events $B_1, \ldots, B_n$ and some α in $\mathbb{R}^n$ such that $X = \alpha_1 1_{B_1} + \cdots + \alpha_n 1_{B_n}$, where the *indicator function* 1_B for an event B is defined by $1_B(\omega) = 1$ for ω in B, and $1_B(\omega) = 0$ otherwise. Given a probability measure P, the *expectation* of X is then defined by

$$E(X) = \alpha_1 P(B_1) + \cdots + \alpha_n P(B_n), \tag{A.1}$$

merely the probability-weighted average of the outcomes.

For a probability space $(\Omega, \mathscr{F}, P)$ with Ω finite, if $\mathscr{G}$ is a tribe on Ω that is contained by $\mathscr{F}$, then $\mathscr{G}$ represents in some sense "less information," and is known as a *subtribe* of $\mathscr{F}$. For any $\mathscr{F}$-measurable random variable X, the *conditional expectation* of X given a subtribe $\mathscr{G}$ of $\mathscr{F}$ is defined as any $\mathscr{G}$-measurable random variable Y, satisfying the property that $E(XZ) = E(YZ)$ for any $\mathscr{G}$-measurable random variable Z. We let $E(X \mid \mathscr{G})$ denote this conditional expectation. The *law of iterated expectations*, also called the *tower property*, states that if $\mathscr{G}$ is a subtribe of another subtribe $\mathscr{H}$, then for any random variable X, $E[E(X \mid \mathscr{H}) \mid \mathscr{G}] = E(X \mid \mathscr{G})$.

If Y is a nonnegative random variable with $E(Y) = 1$, then we can create a new probability measure Q from the old probability measure P by defining $Q(B) = E(1_B Y)$ for any event B. In this case, we write $\frac{dQ}{dP} = Y$, and call Y the *Radon-Nikodym derivative* of Q with respect to P. It also follows that, for any random variable X,

$$E^Q(X) = E^P(YX),$$

where E^Q denotes expectation under Q, and likewise for E^P. If $Q(B) > 0$ whenever $P(B) > 0$, and vice versa, then P and Q are said to be *equivalent measures*; they have the same events of probability zero.

If $\mathscr{G}$ is a subtribe of $\mathscr{F}$ and Q is equivalent to P, then

$$E^Q(Z \mid \mathscr{G}) = \frac{1}{E^P(\xi \mid \mathscr{G})} E^P(\xi Z \mid \mathscr{G}), \tag{A.2}$$

where $\xi = \frac{dQ}{dP}$.

The tribe *generated* by a set Z of random variables is the smallest subtribe, often denoted $\sigma(Z)$, with respect to which each random variable in Z is measurable. It is enough to think of $\sigma(Z)$ as the set of events that can be ascertained as true or false by observing the outcomes of all of the random variables in Z.

Suppose there are multiple periods given by a set $\mathscr{T}$ of times such as $\{0, 1, \ldots, T\}$ or $\{0, 1, \ldots\}$. A *filtration* $\mathbb{F} = \{\mathscr{F}_t : t \in \mathscr{T}\}$ of subtribes of $\mathscr{F}$ is usually given, as described in Section 2A. We always assume that $\mathscr{F}_t \subset \mathscr{F}_s$ whenever $t \leq s$. Given $\mathbb{F}$, a *stopping time* is a random variable τ taking values in $\mathscr{T} \cup \{+\infty\}$ such that, for any time t in $\mathscr{T}$, the event $\{\omega \in \Omega : \tau(\omega) \leq t\}$

is in $\mathcal{F}_t$. The event $\tau = +\infty$ is allowed for convenience. For example, if two processes X and Y are not the same, then the stopping time $\tau = \inf\{t : X_t \neq Y_t\}$ has a strictly positive probability of being finite valued, but may also have a strictly positive probability of being $+\infty$. (We follow the usual convention that the infimum of the empty set is $+\infty$.) A stopping time τ is nontrivial if $P(\tau = +\infty) < 1$. A martingale can be defined as in Section 2A, or alternatively as any $\mathbb{F}$-adapted process X such that, for any bounded stopping time τ, we have $E(X_\tau) = E(X_1)$.

The tribe $\mathcal{F}_\tau$ of events known at a finite-valued stopping time τ allows us to define the conditional expectation $E_\tau(\cdot) \equiv E(\cdot \mid \mathcal{F}_\tau)$. We define $\mathcal{F}_\tau$ to include any event A with the property that, for any time t, the event $A \cap \{\omega : \tau(\omega) \leq t\}$ is in $\mathcal{F}_t$.

A *supermartingale* is an adapted process X with the property that $X_t \geq E_t(X_s)$ for all t and $s \geq t$. It is known that a supermartingale X can be decomposed as the sum $X = M - A$, where M is a martingale and A is an increasing process with $A_0 = 0$, and such that, for each $t < T$, A_{t+1} is $\mathcal{F}_t$-measurable. Likewise, a *submartingale* is an adapted process X such that $-X$ is a supermartingale.

B

Separating Hyperplanes and Optimality

THIS APPENDIX REVIEWS some applications of the following result. Basic references are Rockafeller (1973) and Luenberger (1984).

Separating Hyperplane Theorem. *Suppose that A and B are convex disjoint subsets of $\mathbb{R}^n$. There is some nonzero linear functional F such that $F(x) \leq F(y)$ for each x in A and y in B. Moreover, if x is in the interior of A or y is in the interior of B, then $F(x) < F(y)$. Furthermore, if A is closed and B is compact, then F can be chosen so that $F(x) < F(y)$ for all x in A and y in B.*

Our first application of the Separating Hyperplane Theorem is a special case for separation of cones that is applied in Theorem 1A.

Linear Separation of Cones. *Suppose M and K are closed convex cones in $\mathbb{R}^n$ that intersect precisely at zero. If K does not contain a linear subspace other than $\{0\}$, then there is a nonzero linear functional F such that $F(x) < F(y)$ for each x in M and each nonzero y in K.*

Proof: We can assume without loss of generality that $K \neq \{0\}$. Let C be the convex hull (that is, the set of all convex combinations) of $\{y \in K : \|y\| = 1\}$.

As C is a compact subset of K, and K contains no lines, we know that C and M are disjoint. By the Separating Hyperplane Theorem, there is a nonzero linear functional F such that $F(x) < F(y)$ for all x in M and y in C. As 0 is in M, we have $F(y) > 0$ for all y in C. For any nonzero element z of K, we have $z = \lambda y$ for some y in C and some strictly positive scalar λ. The result[1] follows. ∎

---

[1]This proof, due to Lasse Pedersen, is simpler than that of the second edition.

Our next application of the Separating Hyperplane Theorem is the Saddle Point Theorem for optimality. A *concave program* is a triple (U, X, g) of the form

$$\sup_{x \in X} U(x) \qquad \text{subject to } g(x) \leq 0, \qquad (\text{B.1})$$

where X is a convex subset of some vector space, $U : X \to \mathbb{R}$ is concave, and $g : X \to \mathbb{R}^m$ is convex for some integer m. The *Lagrangian* for (U, X, g) is the function $\mathcal{L} : X \times \mathbb{R}_+^m \to \mathbb{R}$ defined by $\mathcal{L}(x, \lambda) = U(x) - \lambda \cdot g(x)$. A pair (x_0, λ_0) in $X \times \mathbb{R}_+^m$ is a *saddle point* of $\mathcal{L}$ if, for all (x, λ) in $X \times \mathbb{R}_+^m$, we have $\mathcal{L}(x, \lambda_0) \leq \mathcal{L}(x_0, \lambda_0) \leq \mathcal{L}(x_0, \lambda)$. If (x_0, λ_0) is a saddle point, we often term λ_0 a *Lagrange multiplier* for problem (B.1). The following version of the conditions for optimality is proved with the Separating Hyperplane Theorem. The existence of some $\underline{x}$ in X with $g(\underline{x}) \ll 0$ is known as the *Slater condition*.

Saddle Point Theorem. *Let (U, X, g) be a concave program.*

    I. *(Necessity) Suppose the Slater condition is satisfied. If x_0 solves* (B.1), *then there exists $\lambda_0 \in \mathbb{R}_+^m$ such that (x_0, λ_0) is a saddle point of the Lagrangian $\mathcal{L}$. Moreover, $\lambda_0 \cdot g(x_0) = 0$, which is called the* complementary slackness condition.

    II. *(Sufficiency) If (x_0, λ_0) is a saddle point of $\mathcal{L}$, then x_0 solves* (B.1).

Proof: For the first part of the result, let $L = \mathbb{R} \times \mathbb{R}^m$, let

$$C(r, z) = \{x \in X : r \leq U(x), z \geq g(x)\},$$

and let

$$A = \{(r, z) : C(r, z) \neq \varnothing\}$$

and

$$B = \{(r, z) : r > U(x_0), z \ll 0\}.$$

Both A and B are convex. By the fact that x_0 solves (B.1), the sets A and B are disjoint. By the Separating Hyperplane Theorem, there is a linear functional $F : L \to \mathbb{R}$ such that $F(v) < F(w)$ for each v in A and w in B. It follows, for any v in A and w in the closure of B, that $F(v) \leq F(w)$. There is some scalar α and λ in $\mathbb{R}^m$ such that, for any (r, z) in L, we have $F(r, z) = \alpha r + \lambda \cdot z$. Using the Slater condition, we can check that $\alpha > 0$ and $\lambda \leq 0$. Let $\lambda_0 = -\lambda/\alpha$. It follows, using the fact that $[U(x_0), 0]$

is in both A and the closure of B, that (x_0, λ_0) is a saddle point, and that complementary slackness holds.

The second part of the result is easy to show. ∎

Now we turn to first-order conditions for optimality. Consider

$$\sup_{x \in X} U(x), \tag{B.2}$$

where X is a convex subset of a vector space L and $U : X \to \mathbb{R}$ is some function. We are interested in necessary and sufficient conditions for x^* to solve (B.2). For $x \in X$, let

$$\mathcal{Y}(x, y) = \sup\{\epsilon \in [0, 1) : x + \alpha y \in X, \ \alpha \in [0, \epsilon]\}$$

and

$$F(x) = \{y \in L : \mathcal{Y}(x, y) > 0\},$$

the set of *feasible directions* from x. The derivative of U at some x in X in the direction $y \in F(x)$, if it exists, is defined as the limit

$$\delta U(x; y) \equiv \lim_{\alpha \downarrow 0} \frac{U(x + \alpha y) - U(x)}{\alpha}. \tag{B.3}$$

This is sometimes known as the *directional* or *Gateaux* derivative. If $y \mapsto \delta U(x; y)$ defines a linear function on $F(x)$, this function is called the *gradient* of U at x, and is denoted $\nabla U(x)$. In that case, we write $\nabla U(x; y) = \delta U(x; y)$ for the value of $\nabla U(x)$ at y. If $U : \mathbb{R}^n \to \mathbb{R}$ is a continuously differentiable function, then the gradient $\nabla U(x)$ exists at any x and $\nabla U(x; y) = \partial U(x) \cdot y$, where $\partial U(x)$ is the vector of partial derivatives of U at x.

Suppose x^* solves (B.2) and $\nabla U(x^*)$ exists. Then $\nabla U(x^*; y) \leq 0$ for all y in $F(x^*)$, for if not, there is some feasible direction y with $\nabla U(x^*; y) > 0$, in which case there is some $\alpha > 0$ with $U(x^* + \alpha y) - U(x^*) > 0$, which contradicts the optimality of x^*. If $F(x^*)$ is the entire vector space L, it follows that $\nabla U(x^*) \equiv 0$ is necessary for the optimality of x^*, for if $\nabla U(x^*; y) < 0$, then $-y$ is a feasible direction of strict improvement.

If U is concave, $\nabla U(x^*)$ exists, and $F(x^*) = L$, then it is both necessary and sufficient for the optimality of x^* that $\nabla U(x^*) \equiv 0$. Necessity has been shown. For sufficiency, concavity of U implies that for any x and $y \in X$,

$$U(y) - U(x) \leq \nabla U(x; y - x). \tag{B.4}$$

Taking $x = x^*$, we have $U(y) \leq U(x^*)$ for all y. There are extensions of these results to the case of nondifferentiable U.

C
Probability

THIS APPENDIX EXTENDS the definitions of Appendix A to handle probability spaces with possibly infinitely many distinct events. We also add some useful general results, such as the Dominated Convergence Theorem, the Central Limit Theorem, and Fubini's Theorem. A standard reference is Billingsley (1986).

Given a set Ω of states, a *tribe* on Ω is a collection $\mathscr{F}$ of subsets of Ω that includes the empty set $\varnothing$ and that satisfies the following two conditions:

(a) if B is in $\mathscr{F}$, then its *complement* $\{\omega \in \Omega : \omega \notin B\}$ is also in $\mathscr{F}$;
(b) for any sequence $\{B_1, B_2, \ldots\}$ in $\mathscr{F}$, the union $B_1 \cup B_2 \cup \cdots$ is in $\mathscr{F}$.

A tribe is also known in this general context as a *σ-algebra* or *σ-field*. For any collection $\mathscr{A}$ of subsets of Ω, the tribe *generated* by $\mathscr{A}$ is the intersection of all tribes containing $\mathscr{A}$. An important example is to take $\Omega = \mathbb{R}^n$ and to let $\mathscr{F}$ be the tribe generated by the open sets of $\mathbb{R}^n$. In this case, $\mathscr{F}$ is known as the *Borel* tribe on $\mathbb{R}^n$, and is denoted $\mathscr{B}(\mathbb{R}^n)$.

Suppose Ω is a set with tribe $\mathscr{F}$. A *random variable* is a function $X : \Omega \to \mathbb{R}$ with the following property: For any set A in the Borel tribe $\mathscr{B}(\mathbb{R})$, the set $\{\omega \in \Omega : X(\omega) \in A\}$ is in $\mathscr{F}$. A *probability measure* is a function $P : \mathscr{F} \to [0, 1]$ satisfying $P(\varnothing) = 0$, $P(\Omega) = 1$, and, for any sequence $B_1, B_2, \ldots$ of disjoint events,

$$P(B_1 \cup B_2 \cup \cdots) = \sum_{n=1}^{\infty} P(B_n).$$

The triple $(\Omega, \mathscr{F}, P)$ is a probability space.

An event B is said to be *almost sure* if $P(B) = 1$. For example, "$X = Y$ *almost surely*" means, in formal notation, that $P(\{\omega \in \Omega : X(\omega) = Y(\omega)\}) = 1$. We sometimes write instead, more informally, that "$P(X = Y) = 1$."

It is our practice throughout to take "$X = Y$" to mean merely that $X = Y$ almost surely, but the phrase "almost surely" is sometimes added for emphasis.

Given a probability space $(\Omega, \mathcal{F}, P)$, a *null set* is a subset of an event of zero probability. In order to assign zero probability to null sets, the probability space can be *completed*, which means that we can replace $\mathcal{F}$ with the tribe $\mathcal{F}^\sim$ generated by the union of $\mathcal{F}$ and the set of all null sets. The probability measure P then extends uniquely to a probability measure $P^\sim$ on $(\Omega, \mathcal{F}^\sim)$ with the property that $P^\sim(A) = P(A)$ for all A in $\mathcal{F}$ and $P^\sim(A) = 0$ for any null set A. The space $(\Omega, \mathcal{F}^\sim, P^\sim)$ is called the *completion* of $(\Omega, \mathcal{F}, P)$.

Suppose X is a random variable that can be written as a linear combination, $X = \alpha_1 1_{B_1} + \cdots + \alpha_n 1_{B_n}$, of indicator functions. In this case, X is called *simple*. As in the finite-state case, the *expectation* of X given a probability measure P on $(\Omega, \mathcal{F})$ is defined by

$$E(X) = \alpha_1 P(B_1) + \cdots + \alpha_n P(B_n),$$

merely the probability-weighted average of the outcomes. If X is not necessarily simple, but is a nonnegative random variable, then the expectation of X is defined as

$$E(X) \equiv \sup_{Y \in \mathcal{S}} E(Y) \qquad \text{subject to } Y \le X, \tag{C.1}$$

where $\mathcal{S}$ is the set of simple random variables. More generally, any random variable X may be written as $X = X^+ - X^-$, where $X^+ \equiv \max(X, 0)$ and $X^- \equiv \max(-X, 0)$; that is, X is the difference between its positive and negative parts. If both $E(X^+)$ and $E(X^-)$ are finite, then X is said to be *integrable*, and its expectation is defined by

$$E(X) \equiv E(X^+) - E(X^-), \tag{C.2}$$

which coincides with the definition for simple random variables when X is itself simple. If X^+ is integrable and X^- is not, we define $E(X) = -\infty$, and symmetrically define $E(X) = +\infty$ when X^- is integrable and X^+ is not.

Fixing a probability space $(\Omega, \mathcal{F}, P)$, a sequence $\{X_n\}$ of random variables *converges in distribution* to a random variable X if, for any bounded continuous $f : \mathbb{R} \to \mathbb{R}$, we have $E[f(X_n)] \to E[f(X)]$. The sequence $\{X_n\}$ *converges in probability* to X if, for all $\epsilon > 0$, $P(|X_n - X| \ge \epsilon) \to 0$. The sequence $\{X_n\}$ converges almost surely to X if there is an event B of probability 1 such that $X_n(\omega) \to X(\omega)$ for all ω in B. The definition of convergence in distribution extends as given to the case of X_n defined on a (possibly different) probability space $(\Omega_n, \mathcal{F}_n, P_n)$ for each n.

Dominated Convergence Theorem. *Suppose $\{X_n\}$ is a sequence of random variables on a probability space with $|X_n| \le Y$ for all n, where Y is a random variable with $E(|Y|) < \infty$. Suppose, almost surely, or in probability, or in distribution, that X_n converges to X. Then $E(X_n) \to E(X)$.*

Convergence almost surely implies convergence in probability, which in turn implies convergence in distribution, so we could have stated the Dominated Convergence Theorem just for convergence in distribution and had the same result.

A sequence $\{X_n\}$ of random variables on a given probability space is *independently distributed* if, for any finite subset $\{X_1, \ldots, X_k\}$ and any bounded measurable functions $f_i : \mathbb{R} \to \mathbb{R}$, $1 \le i \le k$, we have

$$E[f_1(X_1)f_2(X_2) \cdots f_k(X_k)] = E[f_1(X_1)]E[f_2(X_2)] \cdots E[f_k(X_k)].$$

A sequence $\{X_n\}$ of random variables on a given probability space is *uniformly integrable* if

$$\lim_{\alpha \to \infty} \sup_n E(Y_{\alpha n}) = 0,$$

where $Y_{\alpha n}(\omega) = |X_n(\omega)|$ if $|X_n(\omega)| \ge \alpha$ and otherwise $Y_{\alpha n}(\omega) = 0$.

We next describe a version of the Central Limit Theorem. For this, we define

$$Y = \left\{ Y_1^n, Y_2^n, \ldots, Y_{k(n)}^n : n \in \{1, 2, \ldots\} \right\},$$

with $k(n) \to \infty$, to be a *triangular array* if, for each n, $Y_1^n, \ldots, Y_{k(n)}^n$ are independently distributed random variables on some probability space. For any constant $\epsilon > 0$, let $U(\epsilon)$ denote the "ϵ-truncated" triangular array defined by $U_j^n(\epsilon) = 0$ for $|Y_j^n| \le \epsilon$ and $U_j^n(\epsilon) = Y_j^n$ for $|Y_j^n| > \epsilon$. The array Y satisfies the *Lindeberg-Feller condition* if, for any $\epsilon > 0$,

$$\lim_{n \to \infty} \text{var}\left[U_1^n(\epsilon) + \cdots + U_{k(n)}^n(\epsilon) \right] = 0.$$

The Lindeberg-Feller Central Limit Theorem. *Suppose Y is a triangular array of random variables, all with zero expectations, satisfying the Lindeberg-Feller condition. For each n, let $Z_n = Y_1^n + \cdots + Y_{k(n)}^n$ and let $s_n^2 = \text{var}(Z_n)$. If $s_n^2 \to \sigma^2 > 0$, then Z_n converges in distribution to a normal random variable with mean zero and variance σ^2.*

For any integrable random variable X, the *conditional expectation* of X given a subtribe $\mathcal{G}$ of $\mathcal{F}$ is denoted $E(X \mid \mathcal{G})$, and is defined as any $\mathcal{G}$-measurable random variable Y with the property $E(XZ) = E(YZ)$ for any $\mathcal{G}$-measurable random variable Z such that XZ is integrable. The existence of this conditional expectation is assured, but we do not show that here. The *law of iterated expectations* applies as in the finite-state case.

As in the finite-state setting, Q and P are equivalent probability measures on $(\Omega, \mathcal{F})$ if, for any event A, $P(A) = 0$ if and only if $Q(A) = 0$. In this case, there is always a strictly positive random variable ξ called the *Radon-Nikodym* derivative of Q with respect to P, with the following property: If Z is such that $E^Q(|Z|) < \infty$, then $E^Q(Z) = E^P(\xi Z)$. Under the same assumptions, if $\mathcal{G}$ is a subtribe of $\mathcal{F}$, then

$$E^Q(Z \mid \mathcal{G}) = \frac{1}{E^P(\xi \mid \mathcal{G})} E^P(\xi Z \mid \mathcal{G}). \tag{C.3}$$

It is common to denote ξ by $\frac{dQ}{dP}$.

If there are multiple periods, we fix a set of times denoted $\mathcal{T}$, usually with $\mathcal{T} = \{0, 1, \ldots, T\}$, or $\mathcal{T} = \{0, 1, \ldots\}$, or $\mathcal{T} = [0, T]$, or $\mathcal{T} = [0, \infty)$. A filtration $\mathbb{F} = \{\mathcal{F}_t : t \in \mathcal{T}\}$ of subtribes of $\mathcal{F}$ is usually given, as in the finite-state case. We always assume that $\mathcal{F}_t \subset \mathcal{F}_s$ whenever $t \leq s$.

For the case $\mathcal{T} = [0, T]$ or $[0, \infty)$, we often require a family $X = \{X_t : t \in \mathcal{T}\}$ of random variables to be measurable when treated as a function $X : \Omega \times \mathcal{T} \to \mathbb{R}$. "Measurable" here means *product measurable*, sometimes called *jointly measurable*, that is, measurable with respect to the smallest tribe on $\Omega \times \mathcal{T}$ containing all sets of the form $A \times B$, where $A \in \mathcal{F}$ and B is in the Borel tribe on $\mathcal{T}$. In fact, we always take it as a matter of definition, given at the beginning of Chapter 5, that a *process* $X : \Omega \times \mathcal{T} \to \mathbb{R}$ is product measurable so as to avoid continually referring to product measurability.

A process X is *adapted* if, for all t, the random variable X_t is measurable with respect to $\mathcal{F}_t$. A *martingale* is an adapted process X that is *integrable*, in the sense that X_t is integrable for each t, and such that $E(X_t \mid \mathcal{F}_s) = X_s$ whenever $t \geq s$.

A *stopping time* is a random variable $\tau : \Omega \to \mathcal{T} \cup \{+\infty\}$ with the property that for each time t, the event $\{\omega : \tau(\omega) \geq t\}$ is in $\mathcal{F}_t$. As in the finite-state case, a martingale can also be defined as an adapted integrable process such that for any bounded stopping time τ, we have $E(X_\tau) = E(X_0)$.

Fubini's Theorem states the following. Suppose $(\Omega, \mathcal{F}, P)$ is a probability space and $X : \Omega \times [0, T] \to \mathbb{R}$ is product measurable. If

$$E\left(\int_0^T |X_t|\, dt\right) < \infty,$$

then $E\left(\int_0^T X_t\, dt\right) = \int_0^T E(X_t)\, dt$. That is, we can reverse the order of the expectation and the time integral. More generally, if $\mathcal{G}$ is a subtribe of $\mathcal{F}$, then the conditions above for Fubini's Theorem imply that

$$E\left(\int_0^T X_t\, dt \mid \mathcal{G}\right) = \int_0^T E(X_t \mid \mathcal{G})\, dt \qquad \text{almost surely.} \qquad \text{(C.4)}$$

Fubini's Theorem also applies as stated with $T = +\infty$. This version can be found in Either and Kurtz (1986), page 74.

D

Stochastic Integration

THIS APPENDIX SUMMARIZES the definition and properties of the stochastic integral and reviews two useful related results, Girsanov's Theorem and the Martingale Representation Theorem. Standard references are Chung and Williams (1990), Karatzas and Shreve (1988), and Revuz and Yor (1991). For the case of a general information filtration, see Protter (1990).

We fix a standard Brownian motion $B = (B^1, \ldots, B^d)$ in $\mathbb{R}^d$ on a complete probability space $(\Omega, \mathscr{F}, P)$, as well as the standard filtration $\mathbb{F} = \{\mathscr{F}_t : t \geq 0\}$ of B, as defined in Section 5I. We remind the reader that a "process" has been defined for the purposes of this book as a jointly measurable function on $\Omega \times [0, \infty)$ into some Euclidean space (or some Borel measurable subset of a Euclidean space). We also recall that B is defined by the fact that it is an $\mathbb{R}^d$-valued process with continuous sample paths such that

(a) $P(B_0 = 0) = 1$;

(b) for any times t and $s > t$, $B_s - B_t$ is normally distributed in $\mathbb{R}^d$ with mean zero and covariance matrix $(s - t)I$;

(c) for any times $t_0, \ldots, t_n$ with $0 < t_0 < t_1 < \cdots < t_n < \infty$, the random variables $B(t_0), B(t_1) - B(t_0), \ldots, B(t_n) - B(t_{n-1})$ are independently distributed.

Finally, recall that $\mathscr{F}_t$ is the tribe (often called the σ-algebra) generated by the union of the tribe $\sigma(\{B_s : 0 \leq s \leq t\})$ and the null sets of $\mathscr{F}$.

In order to define the stochastic integral, we fix a time interval $[0, T]$ and take M to be one of the processes $B^1, \ldots, B^d$, say B^i. An adapted process $\theta : \Omega \times [0, T] \to \mathbb{R}$ is *simple* if there is a partition of $[0, T]$ given by times $0 = t_0 < t_1 < \cdots < t_N = T$ such that for all $n > 0$,

$$\theta(t) = \theta(t_n), \qquad t \in (t_{n-1}, t_n].$$

334

For a simple process θ, it is natural to define the stochastic integral $\int \theta \, dM$, at any time $t \in [t_n, t_{n+1})$, for any $n < N$, by

$$\int_0^t \theta_s \, dM_s \equiv \sum_{i=0}^{n-1} \theta(t_{i+1})[M(t_{i+1}) - M(t_i)] + \theta(t_{n+1})[M(t) - M(t_n)].$$

For $t = t_N = T$, we let $\int_0^T \theta_s \, dM_s = \sum_{i=0}^{N-1} \theta(t_{i+1})[M(t_{i+1}) - M(t_i)]$. We let $\mathcal{L}$ denote the set of adapted processes. We recall the notation from Chapter 5:

$$\mathcal{L}^1 = \left\{ \theta \in \mathcal{L} : \int_0^T |\theta_t| \, dt < \infty \quad \text{a.s.} \right\},$$

$$\mathcal{L}^2 = \left\{ \theta \in \mathcal{L} : \int_0^T \theta_t^2 \, dt < \infty \quad \text{a.s.} \right\},$$

$$\mathcal{H}^2 = \left\{ \theta \in \mathcal{L}^2 : E\left(\int_0^T \theta_t^2 \, dt \right) < \infty \right\}.$$

An important fact that we shall not prove here is that for any $\theta \in \mathcal{H}^2$, there is a sequence $\{\theta_n\}$ of adapted simple processes approximating θ in the sense that

$$E\left(\int_0^T [\theta_n(t) - \theta(t)]^2 \, dt \right) \to 0. \tag{D.1}$$

It also turns out that for each θ in $\mathcal{H}^2$, there is a unique random variable Y_θ with the property that for any such sequence $\{\theta_n\}$ approximating θ in the sense of (D.1),

$$E\left(\left[Y_\theta - \int_0^T \theta_n(t) \, dM_t \right]^2 \right) \to 0.$$

(To be more precise, Y_θ is uniquely defined in the sense that if another random variable Y has the same property, then $Y = Y_\theta$ almost surely.) This random variable Y_θ is denoted $\int_0^T \theta_t \, dM_t$. Since T and $M = B^i$ are arbitrary, we have defined the stochastic integral $\int_0^T \theta_t \, dB_t \equiv \sum_{i=1}^d \int_0^T \theta_t^i \, dB_t^i$ for any $\theta = (\theta^1, \ldots, \theta^d)$ in $(\mathcal{H}^2)^d$ and any T. The fact that this definition of the stochastic integral is possible, and the fact that the process $\int \theta \, dB$ satisfies the properties laid out in Chapter 5, are both shown, for example, in Karatzas and Shreve (1988), Section 3.2. In particular, this stochastic integral is defined so that every sample path is continuous. Karatzas and Shreve have taken special care to extend the usual definition of $\int \theta \, dB$ for "progressively measurable" θ in $(\mathcal{H}^2)^d$ to allow any θ in $(\mathcal{H}^2)^d$.

We also wish to define $\int \theta \, dB \equiv \sum_i \int \theta^i \, dB^i$ for some given $\theta = (\theta^1, \ldots, \theta^d) \in (\mathcal{L}^2)^d$. This is done as follows. For any given positive integer n, let $\tau(n) = \inf\{t : \int_0^t \theta_s \cdot \theta_s \, ds = n\}$. Let $\theta_t^{(n)} = \theta_t 1_{t \leq \tau(n)}$. Then $\theta^{(n)}$ is in $(\mathcal{H}^2)^d$, so we can define $\int \theta^{(n)} \, dB$. Since θ is in $(\mathcal{L}^2)^d$, we know that $\tau(n) \to T$ almost surely, and we can therefore define $\int_0^t \theta_s \, dB_s$ for any t in $[0, T]$ as the limit of $\int_0^t \theta_s^{(n)} \, dB_s$ as $n \to \infty$.

Bick and Willinger (1994) point out that for some of the applications treated in this book, such as the Black-Scholes option-pricing formula, the stochastic integral simplifies to the usual Stieltjes integral.

We will sometimes need to work with the notion of a *local martingale*, an adapted process X with the property that there exists an increasing sequence $\tau(n)$ of stopping times converging to T almost surely such that for each n, the *stopped process* $X^{\tau(n)}$ is a martingale when defined by $X_t^{\tau(n)} = X_{\min(t, \tau(n))}$. For example, in the previous paragraph, since $\int \theta^{(n)} \, dB$ is a martingale (Proposition 5B), $\int \theta \, dB$ is a local martingale. Of course, a martingale is a local martingale.

A *supermartingale* is an adapted integrable process X with the property that for any times t and $s > t$, $E_t(X_s) \leq X_t$. A *right-continuous process* is a process X such that for all $t < T$, we have $X_t = \lim_{s \downarrow t} X_s$, that is, whose sample paths are continuous from the right. For example, any stochastic integral is right-continuous since its sample paths are continuous! The following two results are frequently applied:

(a) A nonnegative local martingale is a supermartingale.

(b) *Doob-Meyer Decomposition*: A right-continuous supermartingale X may be expressed in the form $X = M - A$, where M is a martingale and A is an increasing adapted process with $A_0 = 0$. (In general, the Doob-Meyer decomposition actually says more about the nature of the process A, but the stated properties are enough for our purposes in this "Brownian" setting.)

The Martingale Representation Theorem. *If M is a local martingale, then there exists θ in $(\mathcal{L}^2)^d$ such that*

$$M_t = M_0 + \int_0^t \theta_s \, dB_s, \qquad t \geq 0. \tag{D.2}$$

The following result is closely related.

Dudley's Theorem. *Fix $T > 0$ and let X be any $\mathcal{F}_T$-measurable random variable. Suppose $d = 1$ or $E(|X|) < \infty$. Then there exists a constant x and some θ in $(\mathcal{L}^2)^d$ such that*

$$X = x + \int_0^T \theta_t \, dB_t \qquad almost\ surely.$$

We move now to Girsanov's Theorem, which deals with the construction of a Brownian motion under a change of probability measure. We restrict ourselves for the remainder of the appendix to a fixed time horizon $T < \infty$. In particular, the probability space is $(\Omega, \mathcal{F}_T, P)$ and the standard filtration $\mathbb{F} = \{\mathcal{F}_t : 0 \le t \le T\}$ of $B = \{B_t : 0 \le t \le T\}$ is as previously defined, with all defining conditions restricted to $[0, T]$. A vector $\theta = (\theta^1, \ldots, \theta^d)$ of processes in $\mathcal{L}^2$ satisfies *Novikov's condition* if

$$E\left[\exp\left(\frac{1}{2}\int_0^T \theta_s \cdot \theta_s \, ds\right)\right] < \infty. \tag{D.3}$$

Proposition. *If θ satisfies Novikov's condition, then a martingale ξ^θ is defined by*

$$\xi_t^\theta = \exp\left(-\int_0^t \theta_s \, dB_s - \frac{1}{2}\int_0^t \theta_s \cdot \theta_s \, ds\right), \qquad t \in [0, T].$$

Suppose θ satisfies Novikov's condition. Because ξ^θ is a martingale and $\xi_0^\theta = 1$, we know that $E(\xi_T^\theta) = 1$. Since ξ_T^θ is strictly positive, we saw in Appendix C that an equivalent probability measure $Q(\theta)$ can be defined by

$$\frac{dQ(\theta)}{dP} = \xi_T^\theta.$$

It is sometimes useful to exploit Ito's Lemma and write $d\xi_t^\theta = -\xi_t^\theta \theta_t \, dB_t$.

For any local martingales Y and Z, there is a unique continuous adapted process, denoted $\langle Y, Z \rangle$, such that $\langle Y, Z \rangle_0 = 0$ and $YZ - \langle Y, Z \rangle$ is a local martingale. One sometimes calls $\langle X, Y \rangle$ the *sharp-brackets process*. Evidently, by the Martingale Representation Theorem and Ito's Formula, for some $\mathbb{R}^d$-valued adapted processes σ_Y and σ_Z, we have $dY_t = \sigma_Y(t) \, dB_t$, $dZ_t = \sigma_Z(t) \, dB_t$, and $d\langle Y, Z \rangle_t = \sigma_Y(t) \cdot \sigma_Z(t) \, dt$.

Next, we state Lévy's characterization of Brownian motion. The result actually applies for any filtration $(\mathcal{F}_t)$ satisfying the usual conditions, stated in Appendix F, as stated in Revuz and Yor (1991).

Lévy's Characterization Theorem. *Suppose X is an $\mathbb{R}^k$-valued adapted process. Then X is a standard Brownian motion in $\mathbb{R}^k$ if and only if $X_0 = 0$ and X is a continuous local martingale in $\mathbb{R}^k$ with $\langle X^{(i)}, X^{(j)} \rangle_t = t\delta_{ij}$, where $\delta_{ii} = 1$ and, for distinct i and j, $\delta_{ij} = 0$.*

Girsanov's Theorem. *Given $\theta \in (\mathcal{L}^2)^d$, suppose that ξ^θ is a martingale. (Novikov's condition suffices.) Then a standard Brownian motion B^θ that is a martingale under $Q(\theta)$ is defined by*

$$B_t^\theta = B_t + \int_0^t \theta_s \, ds, \qquad 0 \le t \le T. \tag{D.4}$$

Moreover, B^θ has the martingale representation property under $Q(\theta)$. That is, for any local $Q(\theta)$-martingale M, there is some φ in $(\mathcal{L}^2)^d$ such that

$$M_t = M_0 + \int_0^t \varphi_s \, dB_s^\theta, \qquad t \leq T.$$

The martingale representation aspect of Girsanov's Theorem is not usually emphasized, but is particularly useful in finance applications. By direct calculation, Girsanov's Theorem has the following useful corollary.

Corollary. *Let X be an Ito process in $\mathbb{R}^N$ of the form*

$$X_t = x + \int_0^t \mu_s \, ds + \int_0^t \sigma_s \, dB_s, \qquad 0 \leq t \leq T.$$

Suppose $v = (v^1, \ldots, v^N)$ is a vector of processes in $\mathcal{L}^1$ such that there exists some θ in $(\mathcal{L}^2)^d$ satisfying

$$\sigma_t \theta_t = \mu_t - v_t, \qquad 0 \leq t \leq T.$$

If ξ^θ is a martingale (Novikov's condition suffices), then X is also an Ito process with respect to $(\Omega, \mathcal{F}, \mathbb{F}, Q(\theta))$, and

$$X_t = x + \int_0^t v_s \, ds + \int_0^t \sigma_s \, dB_s^\theta, \qquad 0 \leq t \leq T.$$

In short, Girsanov's Theorem gives us a way to adjust probability assessments so that a given Ito process can be rewritten as an Ito process with almost arbitrary drift.

For any probability measure Q equivalent to P, we can define a martingale M by

$$M_t = E_t \left(\frac{dQ}{dP} \right), \qquad t \leq T.$$

The Martingale Representation Theorem implies that there is some $\varphi \in (\mathcal{L}^2)^d$ such that $dM_t = \varphi_t \, dB_t$. In particular, M is a continuous process. Since Q is equivalent to P, it can be shown that M is a strictly positive process, and we can define θ in $(\mathcal{L}^2)^d$ by $\theta_t = -\varphi_t / M_t$. It follows that $M = \xi^\theta$, and that $Q = Q(\theta)$. Given the unique decomposition property of Ito processes, this implies the following convenient result, showing that the diffusion of an Ito process does not change with a change to an equivalent probability measure. (The drift process can of course change, as we have just seen.)

Diffusion Invariance Principle. *Let Q be a probability measure equivalent to P. There is a standard Brownian motion B^Q in $\mathbb{R}^d$ under Q with the martingale representation property under Q. Let X be an Ito process (under P) with $dX_t = \mu_t \, dt + \sigma_t \, dB_t$. Then X is also an Ito process under Q, and $dX_t = \mu^Q(t) \, dt + \sigma_t \, dB_t^Q$, where μ^Q is the drift of X under Q.*

Finally, we review a version of Fubini's Theorem for stochastic integrals that was used in deriving the Heath-Jarrow-Morton model for forward rates. Suppose X is an Ito process and, for some bounded real interval $[a, b]$, $H : [a, b] \times \Omega \times [0, T] \to \mathbb{R}$ is jointly measurable and, for each u in $[a, b]$, $H^u \equiv H(u, \cdot, \cdot)$ defines an adapted process such that the stochastic integral $\int H_t^u \, dX_t$ exists. Let $h(\omega, t) = [\int_a^b [H(u, \omega, t)]^2 \, du]^{0.5}$, and suppose that the stochastic integral $\int h_t \, dX_t$ exists. Letting $g(\omega, t) = \int_a^b H^u(\omega, t) \, du$, we get a result analogous to Fubini's Theorem in its classical form of Appendix C, namely that, for each time s, $\int_a^b \int_0^s H_t^u \, dX_t \, du = \int_0^s g_t \, dX_t$. This follows from Theorem 46, page 160, of Protter (1990).

E

SDE, PDE, and Feynman-Kac

THIS APPENDIX TREATS the existence of solutions to stochastic differential equations (SDEs) and shows how SDEs can be used to represent solutions to partial differential equations (PDEs) of the parabolic type. Standard references include Karatzas and Shreve (1988).

As usual, a standard Brownian motion B in $\mathbb{R}^d$ is given on some probability space $(\Omega, \mathcal{F}, P)$, along with the standard filtration $\mathbb{F}$ of B, as defined in Appendix D. An SDE is an expression of the form

$$dX_t = \mu(X_t, t)\, dt + \sigma(X_t, t)\, dB_t, \qquad (E.1)$$

where $\mu : \mathbb{R}^N \times [0, \infty) \to \mathbb{R}^N$ and $\sigma : \mathbb{R}^N \times [0, \infty) \to \mathbb{R}^{N \times d}$ are given functions. We are interested in conditions on μ and σ under which, for each x in $\mathbb{R}^N$, there is a unique Ito process X satisfying (E.1) with $X_0 = x$. In this case, we say that X solves (E.1) with initial condition x. A process such as X is often called a *diffusion*, although there is no generally accepted definition for "diffusion." By saying "unique," we mean as usual that any other Ito process with the same properties is equal to X almost everywhere. A unique solution in this sense is sometimes called a *strong solution*. We will have no need for what is known as a *weak solution*.

Sufficient conditions for a solution to (E.1) are *Lipschitz* and *growth* conditions on μ and σ. In order to explain these, we first define a norm on matrices by letting $\|A\| = [\mathrm{tr}(AA^\top)]^{1/2}$ for any matrix A, where "$\mathrm{tr}(\cdot)$" denotes trace. (This coincides with the usual Euclidean norm when A has one row or column.) We then say that σ satisfies a Lipschitz condition in x if there is a constant k such that, for any x and y in $\mathbb{R}^N$ and any time t,

$$\|\sigma(x, t) - \sigma(y, t)\| \leq k\|x - y\|. \qquad (E.2)$$

Similarly, σ satisfies a growth condition in x if there is a constant k such that, for any x in $\mathbb{R}^N$ and any time t,

$$\|\sigma(x, t)\|^2 \le k(1 + \|x\|^2). \tag{E.3}$$

Note that these conditions apply *uniformly in t*, in that the constants apply for all t simultaneously. The same conditions (E.2) and (E.3), substituting μ for σ, define Lipschitz and growth conditions, respectively, on μ.

SDE Proposition. *Suppose μ and σ are measurable and satisfy Lipschitz and growth conditions in x. Then, for each x in $\mathbb{R}^N$, there is a unique Ito process X in $\mathbb{R}^N$ satisfying the SDE (E.1) with initial condition x. Moreover, X is a Markov process, and for each time t there is a constant C such that*

$$E(\|X_t\|^2) \le Ce^{Ct}(1 + \|x\|^2).$$

The conclusion that X is a Markov process can be strengthened to the conclusion that X is a strong Markov process, a property that we do not define here. One can weaken somewhat the Lipschitz conditions for solutions to (E.1). We say that σ is *locally Lipschitz* in x if, for each positive constant K, there is a constant k such that (E.2) is satisfied for all t and for all x and y bounded in norm by K.

SDE Theorem. *Suppose μ and σ are measurable, satisfy growth conditions in x, and are locally Lipschitz in x. Then, for each x in $\mathbb{R}^N$, there is a unique Ito process X in $\mathbb{R}^N$ satisfying the SDE (E.1) with initial condition x. Moreover, X is a Markov process. If, in addition, μ and σ are continuous functions, then X is a finite-variance process.*

Even these weaker conditions do not cover the case of "square root" diffusions of the type used in the Cox-Ingersoll-Ross model, and more general "affine" processes of the type appearing in Chapters 7 and 8. For these special cases, we can rely on the following result for the one-dimensional case ($N = d = 1$), reported in Karatzas and Shreve (1988), page 291. It is enough that μ is continuous and satisfies a Lipschitz condition in X, and that σ is continuous with the property that

$$|\sigma(x, t) - \sigma(y, t)| \le \rho(|x - y|),$$

for all x and y and all t, where $\rho : [0, \infty) \to [0, \infty)$ is a strictly increasing function with $\rho(0) = 0$ such that for any $\epsilon > 0$,

$$\int_{(0,\epsilon)} \rho^{-2}(x) \, dx = +\infty.$$

It is enough to take $\rho(x) = \sqrt{x}$, which covers the CIR model (taking $\sigma(x) = 0$ for $x < 0$). While even these weak conditions can be further weakened, it should be noted that there are counterexamples to the uniqueness of solutions for the case $\sigma(x) = |x|^\alpha$ for $\alpha < 1/2$.

These SDE existence results can be gleaned from such sources as Ikeda and Watanabe (1981) or Karatzas and Shreve (1988). The conditions of these results also imply that for any given time τ and any x in $\mathbb{R}^N$, there is a unique Ito process X satisfying (E.1) for $t \geq \tau$ with $X_t = x$, $t \leq \tau$. In this case, we say that X solves (E.1) with initial condition x at time τ.

An important special case of the SDE is the *linear stochastic differential equation*

$$dX_t = [a(t)X_t + b(t)]\, dt + c(t)\, dB_t, \qquad (E.4)$$

where $a : [0, \infty) \to \mathbb{R}^{N \times N}$, $b : [0, \infty) \to \mathbb{R}^N$, and $c : [0, \infty) \to \mathbb{R}^{N \times d}$ are continuous. We can express the solution to a linear SDE quite explicitly. First, let Φ denote the solution of the ordinary differential equation

$$\frac{d\Phi(t)}{dt} = a(t)\Phi(t), \qquad \Phi(0) = I_{N \times N}.$$

It can be shown that for all t, the matrix $\Phi(t)$ is nonsingular, and the solution of (E.4) is

$$X_t = \Phi(t)\left[X_0 + \int_0^t \Phi^{-1}(s)b(s)\, ds + \int_0^t \Phi^{-1}(s)c(s)\, dB_s \right], \qquad t \geq 0.$$

In particular, X is *Gaussian*, meaning that for any finite times $t_1, \ldots, t_k$, $\{X(t_1), \ldots, X(t_k)\}$ has a joint normal distribution. For any t, the mean vector $m(t)$ and covariance matrix $V(t)$ for X_t are given as solutions to the ordinary differential equations

$$\frac{dm(t)}{dt} = a(t)m(t) + b(t), \qquad\qquad m_0 = X_0,$$

$$\frac{dV(t)}{dt} = a(t)V(t) + V(t)a(t)^\top + c(t)c(t)^\top, \qquad V(0) = 0.$$

Further details, and generalizations, can be found in Karatzas and Shreve (1988).

We next consider the *Cauchy problem*, for given $T > 0$: Find $f \in C^{2,1}(\mathbb{R}^N \times [0, T))$ solving

$$\mathscr{D}f(x, t) - r(x, t)f(x, t) + h(x, t) = 0, \qquad (x, t) \in \mathbb{R}^N \times [0, T), \qquad (E.5)$$

with the boundary condition

$$f(x, T) = g(x), \qquad x \in \mathbb{R}^N, \tag{E.6}$$

where

$$\mathscr{D}f(x, t) = f_t(x, t) + f_x(x, t)\mu(x, t) + \frac{1}{2}\mathrm{tr}\big[\sigma(x, t)\sigma(x, t)^\top f_{xx}(x, t)\big], \tag{E.7}$$

and where $r : \mathbb{R}^N \times [0, T] \to \mathbb{R}$, $h : \mathbb{R}^N \times [0, T] \to \mathbb{R}$, $g : \mathbb{R}^N \to \mathbb{R}$, $\mu : \mathbb{R}^N \times [0, T] \to \mathbb{R}^N$, and $\sigma : \mathbb{R}^N \times [0, T] \to \mathbb{R}^{N \times d}$.

The Feynman-Kac solution to (E.5)–(E.6), should it exist, is given by

$$f(x, t) = E_{x, t}\left[\int_t^T \varphi_{t, s}\, h(X_s, s)\, ds + \varphi_{t, T}\, g(X_T)\right], \tag{E.8}$$

where

$$\varphi_{t, s} = \exp\left[-\int_t^s r(X_\tau, \tau)\, d\tau\right],$$

and where $E_{x, t}$ indicates that X is assumed to solve the SDE (E.1) with initial condition x at time t. The term "Feynman-Kac" is widely considered a misnomer in that it originally referred to the probabilistic representation of the solution to a narrower class of parabolic equations than the Cauchy problem. Typically, (E.8) would be called a *probabilistic solution* of the PDE (E.5)–(E.6).

Momentarily putting aside the delicate issue of existence of solutions to the Cauchy problem, the Feynman-Kac representation of a given solution is itself not difficult to verify under technical assumptions. In order to see this, suppose that X solves (E.1) and that f is a solution to the Cauchy problem. For an arbitrary (x, t) in $\mathbb{R}^N \times [0, T]$, let Y be the Ito process defined by $Y_s = f(x, t)$, $s < t$, and

$$Y_s = f(X_s, s)\varphi_{t, s}, \qquad s \in [t, T],$$

where X solves (E.1) with initial condition x at time t. By Ito's Formula,

$$Y_T = f(x, t) + \int_t^T \varphi_{t,s}\big[\mathscr{D}f(X_s, s) - r(X_s, s)f(X_s, s)\big]\, ds$$

$$+ \int_t^T \varphi_{t, s} f_x(X_s, s)\sigma(X_s, s)\, dB_s.$$

Taking expectations through each side, rearranging, and assuming enough technical conditions for integrability and (from Proposition 5B) for the integral with respect to B to be a martingale, we have

$$f(x, t) = E_{x, t}\left(\varphi_{t, T} f(X_T, T) - \int_t^T \varphi_{t, s}[\mathscr{D}f(X_s, s) - r(X_s, s)f(X_s, s)]\, ds\right),$$

from which (E.8) follows with substitution of (E.5) and (E.6). Sufficient technical conditions are

    (a) all of r, g, h, μ, σ, and f are continuous;

    (b) the solution f satisfies a *polynomial growth condition* in x, meaning that for some positive constants M and ν,

$$|f(x, t)| \le M(1 + \|x\|^{\nu}), \qquad (x, t) \in \mathbb{R}^N \times [0, T];$$

    (c) g and h are each either nonnegative or satisfy a polynomial growth condition in x;

    (d) r is nonnegative; and

    (e) μ and σ satisfy Lipschitz and growth conditions in x.

We state this more formally.

Proposition. *Suppose conditions (a)–(e) above are satisfied and that f solves (E.5)–(E.6). Then (E.5)–(E.6) is solved by (E.8). There is no other solution to (E.5)–(E.6) that satisfies a polynomial growth condition.*

A proof is found in Karatzas and Shreve (1988), page 366. Reducing the PDE solution to an expectation in this fashion can sometimes ease the computation of the solution, as is the case for the Black-Scholes formula. The expectation can also be used as the basis for a numerical solution by Monte Carlo methods, a topic considered in Chapter 12. The Feynman-Kac approach can also be applied to other types of parabolic and elliptic PDEs.

The previous proposition does not resolve whether or not a solution to the PDE actually exists. For this, stronger technical conditions are typically imposed. Different sets of conditions are available in the literature; we will give some of these from different sources. A function $F : \mathbb{R}^N \to \mathbb{R}^K$ is *Hölder continuous* if there is some $\alpha \in (0, 1]$ such that

$$\sup_{x, y, x \ne y} \frac{\|F(x) - F(y)\|}{\|x - y\|^{\alpha}} < \infty.$$

A function has a property (such as Hölder continuity) *locally* if it has the property when restricted to any compact subset of its domain.

Condition 1. *The functions μ, σ, g, h, and r are all continuous and*

(a) μ *and* σ *are bounded and locally Lipschitz in* (x, t);

(b) σ *is Hölder continuous in* x, *uniformly in* t;

(c) r *is bounded and, locally, r is Hölder continuous in x, uniformly in t;*

(d) h *is Hölder continuous in x, uniformly in t, and satisfies a polynomial growth condition in x;*

(e) $\sigma\sigma^\top$ *is uniformly parabolic, in that there is some scalar $\epsilon > 0$ such that the eigenvalues of $\sigma(x, t)\sigma(x, t)^\top$ are larger than ϵ for all $(x, t) \in \mathbb{R}^N \times [0, T]$; and*

(f) g *satisfies a polynomial growth condition.*

We can substitute strong smoothness conditions for some of the stringent bounding and uniform ellipticity properties of Condition 1.

Condition 2. *All of μ, σ, g, r, and h satisfy a Lipschitz condition in x, and r is nonnegative. All of μ, σ, g, r, h, μ_x, σ_x, g_x, r_x, h_x, μ_{xx}, σ_{xx}, g_{xx}, r_{xx}, and h_{xx} exist, are continuous, and satisfy a growth condition in x.*

Theorem. *Under Condition 1 or Condition 2, there is a unique solution of (E.5)–(E.6) that satisfies a polynomial growth condition in x, and this solution is given by (E.8).*

Condition 1 is from Friedman (1975), while Condition 2 is a special case from Krylov (1980). Kuwana (1994) offers improvements on Krylov's result. Unfortunately, neither Condition 1 nor Condition 2 includes the exact case of the Black-Scholes option-pricing formula, simply because the option payoff is not differentiable in the stock price.

Under technical conditions on μ, σ, and r, there is a function $G : \mathbb{R}^N \times [0, T] \times \mathbb{R}^N \times [0, T] \to \mathbb{R}$, called the *fundamental solution* of (E.5)–(E.6), or sometimes the *Green's function*, that has the following useful properties:

(a) For any $(x_0, t_0) \in \mathbb{R}^N \times [0, T)$, the function ψ defined by $\psi(x, t) = G(x_0, t_0, x, t)$ is in $C^{2,1}(\mathbb{R}^N \times (t_0, T])$ and solves the PDE

$$\mathscr{D}^*\psi(x, t) - r(x, t)\psi(x, t) = 0, \quad (x, t) \in \mathbb{R}^N \times (t_0, T], \quad \text{(E.9)}$$

where

$$\mathscr{D}^*\psi(x, t) = -\psi_t(x, t) - \sum_{i=1}^{N} \frac{\partial}{\partial x_i}\big[\psi(x, t)\mu_i(x, t)\big]$$

$$+ \frac{1}{2}\sum_{i=1}^{N}\sum_{j=1}^{N} \frac{\partial^2}{\partial x_i x_j}\big[a_{ij}(x, t)\psi(x, t)\big],$$

where $a(x, t) = \sigma(x, t)\sigma(x, t)^\top$. The PDE (E.9) is sometimes called the *Fokker-Planck equation*, or the *forward Kolmogorov equation*, distinguishing it from the *backward Kolmogorov equation* (E.5)–(E.6).

(b) Under technical conditions on g and h, the solution to (E.5)–(E.6) is given by

$$
\begin{aligned}
f(x_0, t_0) = &\int_{t_0}^{T} \int_{\mathbb{R}^N} G(x_0, t_0, x, t) h(x, t)\, dx\, dt \\
&+ \int_{\mathbb{R}^N} G(x_0, t_0, x, T) g(x)\, dx.
\end{aligned}
\tag{E.10}
$$

A sufficient set of technical conditions, as well as boundary conditions for (E.9), are given by Friedman (1964) and Friedman (1975). Knowledge of the fundamental solution G is valuable since particular solutions of the PDE (E.5)–(E.6) can be computed from (E.10) for each of a number of different cases for g and h. In the case of $N = 1$, numerical solution of G is briefly discussed in Chapter 12.

Further work on probabilistic solutions of PDEs has been done by Freidlin (1985).

F

Ito's Formula with Jumps

THIS APPENDIX DEVELOPS Ito's Formula in somewhat more generality, allowing for certain simple settings with jumps. A standard source, with further generality, is Protter (1990).

We first establish some preliminary definitions. We fix a complete probability space $(\Omega, \mathcal{F}, P)$ and a filtration $\{\mathcal{G}_t : t \geq 0\}$ satisfying the *usual conditions*:

- For all t, $\mathcal{G}_t$ contains all of the null sets of $\mathcal{F}$.
- For all t, $\mathcal{G}_t = \bigcap_{s>t} \mathcal{G}_s$, a property called *right-continuity*.

A function $Z : [0, \infty) \to \mathbb{R}$ is *left-continuous* if, for all t, we have $Z_t = \lim_{s \uparrow t} Z_s$; the process has *left limits* if $Z_{t-} = \lim_{s \uparrow t} Z_s$ exists; and finally the process is *right-continuous* if $Z_t = \lim_{s \downarrow t} Z_s$. The *jump* ΔZ of Z at time t is $\Delta Z_t = Z_t - Z_{t-}$.

Under the usual conditions, we can without loss of generality for our applications assume that a martingale has sample paths that are almost surely right-continuous with left limits. See, for example, Protter (1990), page 8. This is sometimes taken as a defining property of martingales, for example by Jacod and Shiryaev (1987).

Lemma 1. *Suppose Q is equivalent to P, with density process ξ. Then an adapted process Y that is right-continuous with left limits is a Q-martingale if and only if ξY is a P-martingale.*

The proof is immediate from the calculation shown in Appendix C for $E^Q(\cdot | \mathcal{G}_t)$.

A process X is a *finite-variation process* if $X = U - V$, where U and V are right-continuous increasing adapted processes with left limits. For example, X is finite-variation if $X_t = \int_0^t \delta_s \, ds$, where δ is an adapted process such that the integral exists. The next lemma is a variant of Ito's Formula.

Lemma 2. *Suppose X is a finite-variation process and $f : \mathbb{R} \to \mathbb{R}$ is continuously differentiable. Then*

$$f(X_t) = f(X_0) + \int_{0+}^t f'(X_{s-}) \, dX_s + \sum_{0 < s \leq t} [f(X_s) - f(X_{s-}) - f'(X_{s-})\Delta X_s].$$

This can be found, for example, in Protter (1990), page 71.

We now record a version of Ito's Formula that is only occasionally used in this book. For proofs and extensions, see Protter (1990). A *semimartingale* is a process of the form $V + M$, where V is a finite-variation process and M is a local martingale.

Lemma 3. *Suppose X and Y are semimartingales and at least one of them is a finite-variation process. Let $Z = XY$. Then Z is a semimartingale and*

$$dZ_t = X_{t-} \, dY_t + Y_{t-} \, dX_t + \Delta X_t \Delta Y_t. \tag{F.1}$$

We now extend the last two lemmas. From this point, B denotes a standard Brownian motion in $\mathbb{R}^d$.

Lemma 4. *Suppose $X = M + A$, where A is a finite-variation process and $M_t = \int_0^t \sigma_u \, dB_u$, where σ is an adapted process in $\mathbb{R}^d$ with $\int_0^t \sigma_s \cdot \sigma_s \, ds < \infty$ almost surely for all t. Suppose $f : \mathbb{R} \to \mathbb{R}$ is twice continuously differentiable. Then*

$$f(X_t) = f(X_0) + \int_{0+}^t f'(X_{s-}) \, dX_s + \sum_{0 < s \leq t} [f(X_s) - f(X_{s-}) - f'(X_{s-})\Delta X_s]$$

$$+ \frac{1}{2} \int_0^t f''(X_s) \, \sigma_s \cdot \sigma_s \, ds.$$

Lemma 5. *Suppose $dX_t = dA_t + \sigma_t \, dB_t$ and $dY_t = dC_t + v_t \, dB_t$, where A and C are finite-variation processes, and σ and v are adapted processes in $\mathbb{R}^d$ such that $\int_0^t \sigma_s \cdot \sigma_s \, ds$ and $\int_0^t v_s \cdot v_s \, ds$ are finite almost surely for all t. Let $Z = XY$. Then Z is a semimartingale and*

$$dZ_t = X_{t-} \, dY_t + Y_{t-} \, dX_t + \Delta X_t \Delta Y_t + \sigma_t \cdot v_t \, dt. \tag{F.2}$$

One can easily define a stochastic integral with respect to a Poisson process N, or any counting process, as defined in Appendix I. For any adapted process θ, we can let

$$\int_0^T \theta_t \, dN_t = \sum_{\{i \, : \, 0 < T_i \leq T\}} \theta(T_i). \tag{F.3}$$

Based on the notion of a Poisson process, we can define a *continuous-time Markov chain*. We will look only at the case of such a process Z with two possible states, say 0 and 1. When in state 0, the process Z moves to state 1 after a time whose probability distribution is exponential with parameter $\lambda(0)$. When in state 1, the process moves to state 0 after a time whose probability distribution is exponential with parameter $\lambda(1)$. More precisely, Z solves the stochastic differential equation

$$dZ_t = \gamma_0(Z(t-)) \, dN_t^{(0)} + \gamma_1(Z(t-)) \, dN_t^{(1)}, \tag{F.4}$$

where $N^{(0)}$ and $N^{(1)}$ are independent Poisson processes with intensity parameters $\lambda(0)$ and $\lambda(1)$, respectively, and where

$$\gamma_0(0) = -\gamma_1(1) = 1; \qquad \gamma_0(1) = \gamma_1(0) = 0.$$

The initial condition, Z_0, is either 0 or 1. This is easily generalized to the n-state case.

One can see that the "compensated" process M, defined by

$$dM_t = -\lambda(Z_t)\gamma_{Z(t)}(Z_t) \, dt + dZ_t,$$

is a martingale. Moreover, as above, (B, M) has the martingale representation property, as defined in Appendix I, for the filtration generated by (B, Z).

We remark that, because Z has a countable number of jumps (almost surely), it makes no difference, for any f, whether we write $\int f(Z_t) \, dt$ or $\int f(Z_{t-}) \, dt$, as $f(Z_t)$ and $f(Z_{t-})$ differ at most at a countable set of points. This remark applies similarly below for all integrals with respect to t.

We now develop some simple applications of Ito's Formula. Here, Z is either a Poisson process with parameter λ, or Z is the continuous-time Markov chain described above. Suppose that S and U are processes with

$$dS_t = \mu_S(t) \, dt + \sigma_S(t) \, dB_t + \beta_S(t) \, dZ(t),$$
$$dU_t = \mu_U(t) \, dt + \sigma_U(t) \, dB_t + \beta_U(t) \, dZ(t),$$

where $\mu_S, \mu_U, \sigma_S, \sigma_U, \beta_S,$ and β_U are adapted processes such that these integrals exist, with β_S and β_U left-continuous.

Let $f : \mathbb{R} \times [0, T] \to \mathbb{R}$ be twice continuously differentiable and let $U_t = f(S_t, t)$. Lemma 4 implies that

$$dU_t = \delta(t) \, dt + f_x(S_t, t) \, \sigma_S(t) \, dB_t + f(S_t, t) - f(S_{t-}, t), \tag{F.5}$$

where

$$\delta(t) = f_t(S_t, t) + f_x(S_t, t)\mu_S(t) + \frac{1}{2}f_{xx}(S_t, t)\|\sigma_S(t)\|^2.$$

One may note that δ is not generally the rate of change of the conditional expectation of U, for the "jump" term $f(S_t, t) - f(S_{t-}, t)$ in (F.5) introduces another source of expected change. Indeed, provided f satisfies a growth condition in its first (S_t) argument, we have

$$dU_t = \mu_U(t)\, dt + dY_t,$$

where Y is a local martingale and, for the case in which Z is a Poisson with arrival intensity λ,

$$\mu_U(t) = \delta(t) + \lambda[f(S_{t-} + \beta_S(t), t) - f(S_{t-}, t)]. \tag{F.6}$$

The last term in (F.6) represents the expected rate of arrival of jumps multiplied by the size of a jump at time t, assuming that a jump occurs at time t. If Z is instead the continuous-time Markov chain (F.4), then

$$\mu_U(t) = \delta(t) + \lambda(Z_{t-})[f(S(t-) + \beta_S(t)\gamma_{Z(t-)}(Z_{t-}), t) - f(S_{t-}, t)]. \tag{F.7}$$

More generally, let $f: \{0, 1\} \times \mathbb{R} \times [0, T] \to \mathbb{R}$ be twice continuously differentiable with respect to its last two arguments, and let $U_t = f(Z_t, S_t, t)$. We let f_x and f_{xx} denote partials with respect to the second (S_t) argument. Then

$$dU_t = \delta(t)\, dt + f_x(Z_t, S_t, t)\,\sigma_S(t)\, dB_t + f(Z_t, S_t, t) - f(Z_{t-}, S_{t-}, t), \tag{F.8}$$

where

$$\delta = f_t(Z_t, S_t, t) + f_x(Z_t, S_t, t)\mu_S(t) + \frac{1}{2}f_{xx}(Z_t, S_t, t)\|\sigma_S(t)\|^2.$$

Moreover, $dU_t = \mu_U(t)\, dt + dY_t$, for Y a local martingale and

$$\mu_U(t) = \delta(t) + \lambda(Z_{t-})J_t,$$

where

$$J_t = f(Z_{t-} + \gamma_{Z(t-)}(Z_{t-}), S_{t-} + \gamma_{Z(t-)}(Z_{t-})\beta_S(t), t) - f(Z_{t-}, S_{t-}, t)$$

is the size of a jump at time t given that a jump occurs.

G

Utility Gradients

THIS APPENDIX GIVES some examples of the calculation of utility gradients in a continuous-time setting. Further examples are found in Duffie and Skiadas (1994). For further work in this direction, see Schroder and Skiadas (1997, 1999, 2000).

First recall the Mean Value Theorem: If $f : [a, b] \to \mathbb{R}$ is continuous on the interval $[a, b]$ and has a derivative on (a, b), then there is some $c \in (a, b)$ such that $f(b) - f(a) = f'(c)(b - a)$.

We fix a probability space and the time interval $[0, T]$. A process $c : \Omega \times [0, T] \to \mathbb{R}$ is *square-integrable* if $E(\int_0^T c_t^2 dt) < \infty$. Let L denote the space of square-integrable processes and L_+ the space of nonnegative processes in L. We recall from Appendix B that the gradient of a function $U : L_+ \to \mathbb{R}$, when well defined at $c \in L_+$, is given by

$$\nabla U(c; h) = \lim_{\alpha \to 0} \frac{U(c + \alpha h) - U(c)}{\alpha}, \quad h \in F(c),$$

where $F(c)$ is the set of feasible directions at c.

Consider first the additive-utility function U defined by

$$U(c) = E\left[\int_0^T u(c_t, t)\, dt\right],$$

where u is continuous and, for each t, $u(\cdot, t)$ is continuously differentiable on $(0, \infty)$ with a derivative $u_c(\cdot, t)$ satisfying a growth condition $|u_c(y, t)| \le k + ky$, for some constant k independent of t. Let $c \in L_+$ and $h \in F(c)$. Let $\{\alpha_n\}$ be any sequence of strictly positive scalars smaller than 1 and converging to zero. For each n, ω, and t, let $\zeta_{n, t}(\omega)$ be chosen, by the Mean Value Theorem, so that

$$u_c[c_t(\omega) + \zeta_{n, t}(\omega), t]\alpha_n h_t(\omega) = u[c_t(\omega) + \alpha_n h_t(\omega), t] - u[c_t(\omega), t].$$

In fact, this can be done so that ζ_n is a process in L_+. It follows that for all n,

$$\left| \frac{u(c_t + \alpha_n h_t, t) - u(c_t, t)}{\alpha_n} \right| = |u_c(c_t + \zeta_{n,t}, t) h_t|$$

$$\leq (k + k|c_t + \zeta_{n,t}|)|h_t|$$

$$\leq (k + k|c_t| + k\alpha_n|h_t|)|h_t|$$

$$\leq y_t \equiv (k + k|c_t| + |h_t|)|h_t|.$$

Moreover, $E(\int_0^T |y_t|\, dt) < \infty$ by the Cauchy-Schwartz inequality since both c and h are in L. The Dominated Convergence Theorem implies that

$$\lim_{n \to \infty} \frac{u(c + \alpha_n h) - U(c)}{\alpha} = E\left[\int_0^T \lim_n u_c(c_t + \zeta_{n,t}, t) h_t\, dt \right]$$

$$= E\left[\int_0^T u_c(c_t, t) h_t\, dt \right],$$

since $\zeta_{n,t}(\omega)$ converges with n to 0 for all (ω, t). Thus, for any $h \in F(c)$,

$$\nabla U(c; h) = E\left(\int_0^T \pi_t h_t\, dt \right),$$

where $\pi_t = u_c(c_t, t)$. This implies that the gradient of U at c exists and has the Riesz representation π.

Suppose, for any $\epsilon > 0$, that u_c satisfies the growth condition given above restricted to $(\epsilon, \infty) \times [0, T]$, but not necessarily on the whole domain $[0, \infty) \times [0, T]$. This is important, for example, in dealing with Inada conditions, as in the example $u(x, t) = e^{-\rho t} x^\alpha$. In that case, the above calculations extend to obtain the same solution for utility gradients so long as the given consumption process c is bounded away from zero. That is, suppose for some $\epsilon > 0$ that $c_t \geq \epsilon$ for all t. In order to be a feasible direction, $c + \delta h \geq 0$ for some $\delta \in (0, 1)$, so $c + \alpha h$ must be bounded away from zero for all $\alpha \in (0, \delta/2)$, and all of the above calculations carry through to this case. This situation covers the equilibrium described by Theorem 10G, in which the consumption process c^i of an arbitrary agent i is indeed bounded away from zero.

We now extend this approach to calculating utility gradients to continuous-time versions of recursive and habit-forming utilities. For these, we fix a filtration $\mathbb{F} = \{\mathscr{F}_t : t \in [0, T]\}$ of tribes satisfying the usual conditions, which are given in Appendix F. We let $f : \Omega \times [0, T] \times \mathbb{R}^n \times \mathbb{R} \to \mathbb{R}$ be a jointly measurable function satisfying the following conditions:

(a) For each fixed (z, v), $f(\cdot, \cdot, z, v)$ is an adapted process.

(b) Uniform Lipschitz condition in utility: For all (ω, t, z, u, v), there exists a constant K such that $|f(\omega, t, z, u) - f(\omega, t, z, v)| \leq K|u - v|$.

(c) Uniform growth condition: There exists a constant K such that for all (ω, t, z), we have $|f(\omega, t, z, 0)| \leq K(1 + \|z\|)$.

The function f is a "felicity" function. Its first and second generic arguments, "ω" and "t," allow dependence of felicity on state and time. The third "z" argument allows dependence on current or past consumption through n different variables. The final argument, "v," allows dependence of the felicity on utility itself. The additive model has felicity $f(\omega, t, z, v) = u(z, t)$, where z stands for current consumption. Fixing a given consumption process c in L_+, we wish to define a utility process V, an Ito process whose current level V_t corresponds to current utility for remaining consumption. For example, with the additive model, we have $V_t = E_t[\int_t^T u(c_s, s) \, ds]$. In general, we will define the utility for c with felicity f to be $U(c) = V_0$.

We use the following existence result of Duffie and Epstein (1992b).

Theorem. *Given any* $Z = (Z_1, \ldots, Z_n)$ *in* L^n, *there is a unique process* V *such that*

$$V_t = E_t \left(\int_t^T f(s, Z_s, V_s) \, ds \right), \quad t \in [0, T].$$

In writing "$f(s, Z_s, V_s)$," we have suppressed ω from the notation.

For the continuous-time case of recursive utility, called *stochastic differential utility*, developed in Duffie and Epstein (1992b), this result is applied with $n = 1$ and $Z = c$, the consumption process. For the continuous-time version of the habit-formation model, developed by Ryder and Heal (1973) and Sundaresan (1989), and applied by Constantinides (1990) and Detemple and Zapatero (1991, 1992), we take $n = 2$ and let

$$Z_{1t} = c_t,$$

$$Z_{2t} = Z_{20} + \int_0^t H(c_s, Z_s) \, ds, \quad t \in [0, T],$$

for some measurable $H : \mathbb{R}^2 \to \mathbb{R}$ that is uniformly Lipschitz in its second argument and satisfies a growth condition in its first argument. (See Chapman (1997) on the question of monotonicity.) It is not difficult to extend this example to cases in which H is state and time dependent. We can compute the Riesz representation of the gradients of the new utilities just defined. For this, we assume that f is continuously differentiable with respect to (z, v), and that there exists a constant K such that

$$\|f_z(\omega, t, z, v)\| \leq K(1 + \|z\|), \quad (\omega, t, z, v) \in [0, T] \times \Omega \times \mathbb{R}^n \times \mathbb{R},$$

where, here and below, subscripts denote partial derivatives with respect to the indicated arguments. For the habit-formation case, we also assume that H is continuously differentiable, that its partial derivative H_c with respect to consumption satisfies a uniform growth condition, and that H_z is bounded. That is, there is a constant K such that $|H_c(c, z)| \leq K(1 + |c|)$ for all (c, z).

With these new utilities, and under the stated assumptions, for any strictly positive consumption process c we again have a utility gradient of the form

$$\nabla U(c; h) = E\left(\int_0^T \pi_t h_t \, dt\right),$$

for a Riesz representation π that is given for stochastic differential utility by

$$\pi_t = Y_t f_z(t, Z_t, V_t),$$

where $Y_t \equiv \exp(\int_0^t f_v(s, Z_s, V_s) \, ds)$, and for habit-formation utility by

$$\pi_t = Y_t\left[E_t\left(\int_t^T f_z(s, Z_s, V_s) \exp\left(\int_s^t (f_v(u) + H_z(u)) \, du\right) ds\right) H_c(t) + f_c(t)\right],$$

where the obvious arguments have been omitted. Proofs of these gradient representations, and extensions to more general models, can be found in Duffie and Skiadas (1994).

Another formulation of habit formation is suggested by Hindy and Huang (1992), extending the work of Hindy, Huang, and Kreps (1992). Their model is incorporated into this setting by taking $n = 1$ and $Z_t = \int_0^t k_{t-s} \, dC_s$, where k is a bounded adapted process and C is an increasing right-continuous adapted process defining *cumulative consumption*. For the case of absolutely continuous cumulative consumption, we have $C_t = \int_0^t c_s \, ds$ for some $c \in L_+$. In general, consumption may occur with "lumps." A gradient calculation for this case is given by Duffie and Skiadas (1994).

H

Ito's Formula for Complex Functions

THIS APPENDIX GIVES some minimal rules necessary for applying Ito's Formula to the types of complex-valued functions that arise in the transform calculations of Chapter 8.

With an imaginary number traditionally denoted $i = \sqrt{-1}$, a *complex number* is an object of the form $z = a + bi$, for some real numbers a and b. The *real part* of z is a; the *imaginary part* of z is ib. The set of complex numbers, denoted $\mathbb{C}$, is a vector space by pairwise calculations, in that $(a + bi) + (c + di) = (a + c) + (b + d)i$ and $k(a, bi) = (ka, kbi)$ for any real scalar k. Complex multiplication is given by

$$(a + bi) \times (c + di) = ac + adi + bci + bdi^2 = (ac - bd) + (ad + bc)i.$$

We have the definition $e^{i\theta} = \cos(\theta) + i\sin(\theta)$ (which can be justified by deeper axioms). For a complex number $z = a + bi$, one treats e^z as the complex number $e^{a+bi} = e^a e^{bi}$. One can check that, for two complex numbers z and w, we have $e^w e^z = e^{w+z}$ and $e^w / e^z = e^{w-z}$.

The norm of a complex number $a + bi$ is defined by $|a + bi| = \sqrt{a^2 + b^2}$. The square root $\gamma = \sqrt{a + bi}$ is defined by $\gamma = |\gamma^2|^{1/2} \times \exp(i \arg(\gamma^2)/2)$, where $\gamma^2 = a + bi$ and, for any $z \in \mathbb{C}$, $\arg(z)$ is defined such that $z = |z| \exp(i \arg(z))$, with $-\pi < \arg(z) \leq \pi$. For any $z \in \mathbb{C}$, $\ln(z) = \ln|z| + i \arg(z)$, as defined on the "principal branch."

There are certain definitions and rules for differentiation of an appropriate class of complex-valued functions called *analytic*. Of these, we will need only the facts:

(a) $z \mapsto e^z$ is analytic with $\frac{d}{dz} e^z = e^z$.

(b) For integer $n \geq 1$, $z \mapsto z^n$ is analytic with $\frac{d}{dz} z^n = nz^{n-1}$.

(c) The chain rule $\frac{d}{dz} f(g(z)) = f'(g(z))g'(z)$ applies whenever f and g are analytic.

If an Ito process Y is complex valued (that is, $Y = (Y_R + Y_I i)$, for real-valued Ito processes Y_R and Y_I), then we can apply Ito's Formula to see that $g(Y_t)$ is a complex-valued Ito process for any analytic g. The only such g that we need consider here are of the exponential and polynomial forms (a) and (b), above. In particular, we will be interested in characterizing the process $Z = e^Y$ for $Y(t) = \alpha(t) + \beta(t) \cdot X(t)$, where X is a (real) Ito process valued in $\mathbb{R}^k$, and $\alpha : [0, T] \to \mathbb{C}$ and $\beta : [0, T] \to \mathbb{C}^d$ are analytic. In general, if $Y = Y^{(a)} + iY^{(b)}$ for real Ito processes $Y^{(a)}$ and $Y^{(b)}$, with respective diffusions σ_a and σ_b, then we denote the diffusion of Y by $\sigma_Y = \sigma_a + i\sigma_b$, and Ito's Formula is that

$$g(Y_t) = g(Y_0) + \int_0^t g'(Y_s) \, dY_s + \int_0^t \frac{1}{2} g''(Y_s) \sigma_Y(s) \cdot \sigma_Y(s) \, ds.$$

This follows from Theorem 35, page 76, of Protter (1990).

I

Counting Processes

This appendix reviews the basic theory of intensity-based models of counting processes. Brémaud (1981) is a standard source.

All properties below are with respect to a probability space $(\Omega, \mathcal{F}, P)$ and a given filtration $\{\mathcal{G}_t : t \geq 0\}$ satisfying the usual conditions (Appendix F) unless otherwise indicated. We sometimes use the usual shorthand, as in "$(\mathcal{F}_t)$-adapted," to specify a property with respect to some alternative filtration $\{\mathcal{F}_t : t \geq 0\}$.

A process Y is *predictable* if $Y : \Omega \times [0, \infty) \to \mathbb{R}$ is measurable with respect to the tribe on $\Omega \times [0, \infty)$ generated by the set of all left-continuous adapted processes. The idea is that one can "foretell" Y_t based on all of the information available up to, but not including, time t. Of course, any left-continuous adapted process is predictable, as is, in particular, any continuous process.

A *counting process* N, also known as a *point process*, is defined via an increasing sequence $\{T_0, T_1, \dots\}$ of random variables valued in $[0, \infty]$, with $T_0 = 0$ and with $T_n < T_{n+1}$ whenever $T_n < \infty$, according to

$$N_t = n, \qquad t \in [T_n, T_{n+1}), \qquad (\text{I.1})$$

where we define $N_t = +\infty$ if $t \geq \lim_n T_n$. We may treat T_n as the n-th jump time of N, and N_t as the number of jumps that have occurred up to and including time t. The counting process is *nonexplosive* if $\lim T_n = +\infty$ almost surely.

Definitions of "intensity" vary slightly from place to place. One may refer to Section II.3 of Brémaud (1981), in particular Theorems T8 and T9, to compare other definitions of intensity with the following. Let λ be a nonnegative predictable process such that, for all t, we have $\int_0^t \lambda_s \, ds < \infty$

almost surely. Then a nonexplosive adapted counting process N has λ as its *intensity* if $\{N_t - \int_0^t \lambda_s \, ds : t \geq 0\}$ is a local martingale.

From Brémaud's Theorem T12, without an important loss of generality for our purposes, we can require an intensity to be predictable, as above, and we can treat an intensity as essentially unique, in that: If λ and $\tilde{\lambda}$ are both intensities for N, as defined above, then

$$\int_0^\infty |\lambda_s - \tilde{\lambda}_s| \lambda_s \, ds = 0 \quad \text{a.s.} \tag{I.2}$$

We note that if λ is strictly positive, then (I.2) implies that $\lambda = \tilde{\lambda}$ almost everywhere.

We can get rid of the annoying "localness" of the above local martingale characterization of intensity under the following technical condition, which can be verified from Theorems T8 and T9 of Brémaud (1981).

Proposition 1. *Suppose N is an adapted counting process and λ is a nonnegative predictable process such that, for all t, $E(\int_0^t \lambda_s \, ds) < \infty$. Then the following are equivalent*:

   (i) *N is nonexplosive and λ is the intensity of N.*
   (ii) *$\{N_t - \int_0^t \lambda_s \, ds : t \geq 0\}$ is a martingale.*

Proposition 2. *Suppose N is a nonexplosive adapted counting process with intensity λ, with $\int_0^t \lambda_s \, ds < \infty$ almost surely for all t. Let M be defined by $M_t = N_t - \int_0^t \lambda_s \, ds$. Then, for any predictable process H such that $\int_0^t |H_s| \lambda_s \, ds$ is finite almost surely for all t, a local martingale Y is well defined by*

$$Y_t = \int_0^t H_s \, dM_s = \int_0^t H_s \, dN_s - \int_0^t H_s \lambda_s \, ds.$$

If, moreover, $E\left[\int_0^t |H_s| \lambda_s \, ds\right] < \infty$, then Y is a martingale.

In order to define a Poisson process, we first recall that a random variable K with outcomes $\{0, 1, 2, \ldots\}$ has the *Poisson distribution* with parameter β if

$$P(K = k) = e^{-\beta} \frac{\beta^k}{k!},$$

with the convention that $0! = 1$. A *Poisson process* is an adapted nonexplosive counting process N with deterministic intensity λ such that $\int_0^t \lambda_s \, ds$ is finite almost surely for all t, with the property that, for all t and $s > t$, conditional on $\mathcal{G}_t$, the random variable $N_s - N_t$ has the Poisson distribution with parameter $\int_t^s \lambda_u \, du$. (See Brémaud (1981), page 22.)

We recall that $\{\mathcal{G}_t : t \in [0, T]\}$ is the *augmented filtration of a process* Y valued in some Euclidean space if, for all t, $\mathcal{G}_t$ is the completion of $\sigma(\{Y_s : 0 \leq s \leq t\})$.

Suppose N is a nonexplosive counting process with intensity λ, and $\{\mathcal{F}_t : t \geq 0\}$ is a filtration satisfying the usual conditions, with $\mathcal{F}_t \subset \mathcal{G}_t$. We say that N is *doubly stochastic driven by* $\{\mathcal{F}_t : t \geq 0\}$ if λ is $(\mathcal{F}_t)$-predictable and if, for all t and $s > t$, conditional on the tribe $\mathcal{G}_t \vee \mathcal{F}_s$ generated by $\mathcal{G}_t \cup \mathcal{F}_s$, $N_s - N_t$ has the Poisson distribution with parameter $\int_t^s \lambda_u \, du$. For conditions under which a filtration $\{\mathcal{F}_t : t \geq 0\}$ generated by a Markov process X satisfies the usual conditions, see Chung (1982), Theorem 4, page 61.

It is to be emphasized that the filtration $\{\mathcal{G}_t : t \geq 0\}$ has been fixed in advance for purposes of the above definitions. In applications involving doubly stochastic processes, it is often the case that one constructs the underlying filtration $\{\mathcal{G}_t : t \geq 0\}$ as follows. First, one has a filtration $\{\mathcal{F}_t : t \geq 0\}$ satisfying the usual conditions, and an $(\mathcal{F}_t)$-predictable process λ such that $\int_0^t \lambda_s \, ds < \infty$ almost surely for all t. We then let $Z_1, Z_2, \ldots$ be independent standard exponential random variables (that is, with $P(Z_i > z) = e^{-z}$) that, for all t, are independent of $\mathcal{F}_t$. We let $T_0 = 0$ and, for $n \geq 1$, we let T_n be defined recursively by

$$T_n = \inf \left\{ t \geq T_{n-1} : \int_{T_{n-1}}^t \lambda_u \, du = Z_n \right\}. \tag{I.3}$$

Now, we can define N by (I.1). (This construction can also be used for Monte Carlo simulation of the jump times of N.) Finally, for each t, we let $\mathcal{G}_t$ be the tribe generated by $\mathcal{F}_t$ and $\{N_s : 0 \leq s \leq t\}$. By this construction, relative to the filtration $\{\mathcal{G}_t : t \geq 0\}$, N is a nonexplosive counting process with intensity λ that is doubly stochastic driven by $\{\mathcal{F}_t : t \geq 0\}$. In examples, $\{\mathcal{F}_t : t \geq 0\}$ is usually the filtration generated by a state process, such as the solution of a stochastic differential equation.

Next, we review the martingale representation theorem in this setting, restricting attention to a fixed time interval $[0, T]$. We say that a local martingale $M = (M^{(1)}, \ldots, M^{(k)})$ in $\mathbb{R}^k$ has the *martingale representation property* if, for any martingale Y, there exist predictable processes $H^{(1)}, \ldots, H^{(k)}$ such that the stochastic integral $\int H^{(i)} \, dM^{(i)}$ is well defined for each i and

$$Y_t = Y_0 + \sum_{i=1}^k \int_0^t H_s^{(i)} \, dM_s^{(i)}, \quad \text{a.s.}, \quad t \in [0, T].$$

The following representation result is from Brémaud (1981).

Proposition 3. *Suppose that $N = (N^{(1)}, \ldots, N^{(k)})$, where $N^{(i)}$ is a nonexplosive counting process that has the intensity $\lambda^{(i)}$ relative to the augmented filtration $\{\mathcal{G}_t : t \in [0, T]\}$ of N. Let $M_t^{(i)} = N_t^{(i)} - \int_0^t \lambda_s^{(i)} \, ds$. Then $M = (M^{(1)}, \ldots, M^{(k)})$ has the martingale representation property for $\{\mathcal{G}_t : t \in [0, T]\}$.*

Proposition 4. *For a given probability space, let $N = (N^{(1)}, \ldots, N^{(k)})$, where $N^{(i)}$ is a Poisson process with intensity $\lambda^{(i)}$ relative to the augmented filtration generated by N itself. Let B be a standard Brownian motion in $\mathbb{R}^d$, independent of N, and let $\{\mathcal{G}_t : t \geq 0\}$ be the augmented filtration generated by (B, N). Then $N^{(i)}$ has the $(\mathcal{G}_t)$-intensity $\lambda^{(i)}$, a $(\mathcal{G}_t)$-martingale $M^{(i)}$ is defined by $M_t^{(i)} = N_t^{(i)} - \int_0^t \lambda_s^{(i)} \, ds$, and $(B^{(1)}, \ldots, B^{(d)}, M^{(1)}, \ldots, M^{(k)})$ has the martingale representation property for $\{\mathcal{G}_t : t \geq 0\}$.*

We can also extend this result as follows. We can let $N^{(i)}$ be doubly stochastic driven by the standard filtration of a standard Brownian motion B in $\mathbb{R}^d$. For the augmented filtration generated by (B, N), defining $M^{(i)}$ as the compensated counting process of $N^{(i)}$, $(B^{(1)}, \ldots, B^{(d)}, M^{(1)}, \ldots, M^{(k)})$ has the martingale representation property. For details and technical conditions, see, for example, Kusuoka (1999b). For more on martingale representation, see Jacod and Shiryaev (1987).

Next, we turn to Girsanov's Theorem. Suppose N is a nonexplosive counting process with intensity λ, and φ is a strictly positive predictable process such that, for some fixed time horizon T, $\int_0^T \varphi_s \lambda_s \, ds$ is finite almost surely. A local martingale ξ is then well defined by

$$\xi_t = \exp\left(\int_0^t (1 - \varphi_s) \lambda_s \, ds\right) \prod_{\{i : T(i) \leq t\}} \varphi_{T(i)}, \qquad t \leq T, \qquad (I.4)$$

where $T(i)$ denotes the i-th jump time of K.

Proposition 5. *Suppose that the local martingale ξ is a martingale. For this, it suffices that λ is bounded and deterministic and that φ is bounded. Then an equivalent probability measure Q is defined by letting $\frac{dQ}{dP} = \xi(T)$. Restricted to the time interval $[0, T]$, under the probability measure Q, N is a nonexplosive counting process with intensity $\lambda\varphi$.*

The proof is essentially the same as that found in Brémaud (1981), page 168, making use of Lemmas 1 and 2 of Appendix F.

By an extra measurability condition, we can specify a change of probability measure associated with a given change of intensity, under which the doubly stochastic property is preserved.

Proposition 6. *Suppose N is doubly stochastic driven by $\{\mathcal{F}_t : t \geq 0\}$ with intensity λ, where $\mathcal{G}_t$ is the completion of $\mathcal{F}_t \vee \sigma(\{N_s : 0 \leq s \leq t\})$. For a fixed time $T > 0$, let φ be an $(\mathcal{F}_t)$-predictable process with $\int_0^T \varphi_t \lambda_t \, dt < \infty$ almost surely. Let ξ be defined by (I.4), and suppose that ξ is a martingale. (For this, it suffices that λ and φ are bounded.) Let Q be the probability measure with $\frac{dQ}{dP} = \xi_T$. Then, restricted to the time interval $[0, T]$, under the probability measure Q and with respect to the filtration $\{\mathcal{G}_t : 0 \leq t \leq T\}$, N is doubly stochastic driven by $\{\mathcal{F}_t : t \in [0, T]\}$, with intensity $\lambda\varphi$.*

For a proof, we note that, under Q, N is, by Proposition 5, a non-explosive counting process with $(\mathcal{G}_t)$-intensity $\lambda\varphi$, which is $(\mathcal{F}_t)$-predictable. Further, ξ is a P-martingale with respect to the filtration $\{\mathcal{H}_t : t \in [0, T]\}$ defined by letting $\mathcal{H}_t$ be the completion of $\sigma(\{N_s : s \leq t\}) \vee \mathcal{F}_T$. (To verify the stated sufficient condition for martingality, we can apply the argument of Brémaud (1981), page 168, the doubly stochastic property under P, and the law of iterated expectations.) Now, we can use the characterization (1.8), page 22, of Brémaud (1981) and apply Ito's Formula (Appendix F) to see that, under Q with respect to $\{\mathcal{H}_t : t \in [0, T]\}$, the counting process N is doubly stochastic, driven by $\{\mathcal{F}_t : t \geq 0\}$, with intensity $\lambda\varphi$. Finally, the result follows by noting that, whenever $s > t$, we have

$$Q(N_s - N_t = k \mid \mathcal{G}_t \vee \mathcal{F}_s) = Q(N_s - N_t = k \mid \sigma\{N_u : 0 \leq u \leq t\} \vee \mathcal{F}_s)$$
$$= Q(N_s - N_t = k \mid \mathcal{H}_t),$$

using the definition of $\mathcal{G}_t$, and the fact that $\mathcal{F}_t \subset \mathcal{F}_s$.

Finally, we calculate, under some regularity conditions, the density and *hazard rate* of a doubly stochastic stopping time τ with intensity λ, driven by some filtration.

Letting $p(t) = P(\tau > t)$ define the *survival function* $p : [0, \infty) \to [0, 1]$, the density of the stopping time τ is $\pi(t) = -p'(t)$, if it exists, and the *hazard function* $h : [0, \infty) \to [0, \infty)$ is defined by

$$h(t) = \frac{\pi(t)}{p(t)} = -\frac{d}{dt} \log p(t),$$

so that we can then write

$$p(t) = e^{-\int_0^t h(u) \, du}.$$

One can similarly define the $\mathcal{G}_t$-conditional density and hazard rate.

Now, because $p(t) = E(e^{-\int_0^t \lambda(u)\,du})$, if differentiation through this expectation is justified, then we would have the natural result that

$$p'(t) = E\left(-e^{-\int_0^t \lambda(u)\,du}\lambda(t)\right), \tag{I.5}$$

from which $\pi(t)$ and $h(t)$ would be defined as above. Grandell (1976), pages 106–107, has shown that (I.5) is correct provided that:

1. There is a constant C such that, for all t, $E(\lambda_t^2) < C$.
2. For any $\epsilon > 0$ and almost every time t,

$$\lim_{\delta \to 0} P(|\lambda(t + \delta) - \lambda(t)| \geq \epsilon) = 0.$$

These properties are satisfied in many typical models. For affine models, in the sense of Chapter 11, we have an explicit expression for the density and hazard rate under these conditions. For $\mathcal{G}_t$-conditional density and hazard-rate calculations, analogous results apply.

J
Finite-Difference Code

THIS APPENDIX GIVES computer code written in C by Ravi Myneni and revised by Michael Boulware, at the author's direction, for the numerical solution of coupon-bond and coupon-bond option prices for the Cox-Ingersoll-Ross model of the term structure, using the Crank-Nicholson finite-difference algorithm given in Chapter 12. Zero-coupon bond prices, of course, are also given directly in terms of the explicit solution shown in Chapter 7, from which coupon-bond prices can be computed by treating a coupon bond as a portfolio of zero-coupon bonds of different maturities. This code is merely for the pedagogic purposes of Chapter 12, and is not intended for commercial or other uses. Although this code has been successfully applied by the author to various examples, neither the author, Ravi Myneni, nor Michael Boulware accept any liability for any losses related to its use, or misuse, for any purpose. This code is "faster" than that of the first edition.

The code should be linked with the following copyrighted subroutines from *Numerical Recipes in C*, by Press, Flannery, Teukolsky, and Vetterling (1993).

(a) ivector(),
(b) dvector(),
(c) free_ivector(),
(d) free_dvector().

These subroutines are also normally sold with copies of *Numerical Recipes in C*. Neither the author of this book nor Ravi Myneni accept any liability for the use or misuse of these subroutines.

The code requires the use of so-called "include" files. Because such files vary from system to system, they are not included here.

```
/****************************************************************
This code was written by Ravi Myneni under the direction
of the author, and revised by Michael Boulware.
****************************************************************/
#define MAX(a,b) (a,b, a > b ? a : b)
 fdi_bond_option(number_space_points,number_time_points,parameters,
                 coupon,par,bond_maturity,option_maturity,call_put,
                 american_european,strike,spot_rates,bond_prices,
                 accrued_interest,option_prices)
  /****************************************************************
fdi_bond_option() is an implicit finite difference algorithm
        for valuing bond options in the CIR model with constant
        speed of adjustment, long term mean and volatility
        parameters.
        ------------------------------------------------------------
     int    number_time_points  = number of time points
                 (Note: actual number of temporal steps is one less.)
     int    number_space_points = number of space points
                 (Note: actual number of spatial steps is one less.)
         double *parameters        = model parameters vector:
                                      0 <-> speed of adjustment
                                      1 <-> long term mean
                                      2 <-> volatility parameter
         double coupon            = coupon rate (annual % par)
         double par               = bond's par value (%)
     double bond_maturity     = bond time to maturity (in years)
     double option_maturity   = option time to maturity (in years)
         char   call_put          = call ('C') or put ('P')
         char   american_european = american ('A') or european ('E')
         double strike            = option strike on flat price
         double *spot_rates       = vector of spot rates
         double *bond_prices      = vector of flat bond prices
         double *accrued_interest = accrued interest on bond
         double *option_prices    = vector of option prices
     -------------------------------------------------------------
     ****************************************************************/
    int number_space_points,number_time_points;
    double *parameters,coupon,par,bond_maturity,option_maturity, strike;
    char call_put,american_european;
    double *spot_rates,*bond_prices,*accrued_interest,*option_prices;
    {
     int error;
     int i,j,k,option_expiration_period,*coupon_flows,*ivector();
     double r,s,t,semi_annual_coupon,accrued,*mu,*sigma,gamma;
     double *a,*b,*c,*y_bond,*y_option,*dvector();
     double time_delta,space_delta;
     void free_ivector(),free_dvector();
```

```
/**** Some useful checks ****/
if (number_space_points < 10 || number_space_points > 3000)
  { printf("! number_space_points out of bounds\n"); return(1);}
if (number_time_points < 10 || number_time_points > 5000)
  { printf("! number_time_points out of bounds\n"); return(2); }
if (bond_maturity < 2.0/365.0 || bond_maturity > 50.0)
  { printf("! bond_maturity invalid\n"); return(3); }
if (option_maturity < 1.0/365.0 || option_maturity > 50.0)
  { printf("! option_maturity invalid\n"); return(4); }
if (option_maturity >= bond_maturity)
  { printf("! option_maturity exceeds bond_maturity\n");
    return(5); }
if (strike < 0.0)
  { printf("! strike is negative\n"); return(6); }
/**** Initialization of parameters ****/
space_delta= 1.0 / (double)(number_space_points-1);
time_delta= bond_maturity / (double)(number_time_points-1);
if (time_delta >= 0.5)
  { printf("! number_space_points too small\n"); error= 7; goto
    fre; }
gamma= 12.5;
/**** Calculation of semi-annual coupon ****/
semi_annual_coupon= coupon * par / 200.0;
/**** Calculation of option expiration node ****/
option_expiration_period= (int)((option_maturity / time_delta)
    + 0.5);
if (option_expiration_period == 0 || option_expiration_period ==
number_time_points-1)
  { printf("! option_maturity out of bounds\n"); error= 8; goto
    fre; }
/**** Allocation of memory ****/
a= dvector(0,number_space_points-1);
b= dvector(0,number_space_points-1);
c= dvector(0,number_space_points-1);
y_bond= dvector(0,number_space_points-1);
y_option= dvector(0,number_space_points-1);
mu= dvector(0,number_space_points-1);
sigma= dvector(0,number_space_points-1);
coupon_flows= ivector(0,number_time_points-1);
/**** Calculation of semi-annual coupon nodes ****/
for (j=number_time_points-1,i=0 ; j >= 0 ; j--)
  {
    k= (int)(((double)(i)*0.5 / time_delta) + 0.5);
    if (j == number_time_points-k-1)
      { coupon_flows[j]= 1; i++; }
    else
      { coupon_flows[j]= 0; }
  }
```

```
/**** Initialization of terminal bond price ****/
for (i=0 ; i < number_space_points ; i++)
   { bond_prices[i]= par; }
/**** Calculation of pde parameters ****/
for (i=1 ; i < number_space_points ; i++)
  {
    error= fdi_sdv(i,gamma,space_delta,parameters,&spot_rates[i],
    &mu[i], &sigma[i]);
    if (error)
      { printf("! error %d occurred in fdi_sdv()\n",error);
        error= 9; goto fre; }
  }
/**** Main valuation loop until option expiration ****/
for (j=number_time_points-1 ; j > option_expiration_period; j--)
   {
    /**** Addition of semi-annual coupon ****/
    if (coupon_flows[j])
      {
        for (i=0 ; i < number_space_points ; i++)
    { bond_prices[i] += semi_annual_coupon; }
      }
    /**** Highest spot rate case is treated differently ****/
    spot_rates[0]= 1.0e+12;
    a[0]= 0.0;
    b[0]= 1.0;
    c[0]= 0.0;
    if (j == number_time_points-1)
      { y_bond[0]= bond_prices[0] / time_delta; }
    else
      { y_bond[0]= 0.0; }
    /****Lowest spot rate case is also treated differently ****/
    a[number_space_points-1]= -mu[number_space_points-1] /
                              space_delta;
    b[number_space_points-1]= mu[number_space_points-1] /
                              space_delta
                              - 1.0 / time_delta;
    c[number_space_points-1]= 0.0;
    y_bond[number_space_points-1]
          = -bond_prices [number_space_points-1] / time_delta;

    /**** Now do the intermediate points ****/
    for (i=1 ; i < number_space_points-1 ; i++)
       {
         r= mu[i] / (4.0 * space_delta);
         s= sigma[i] / (2.0 * pow(space_delta,2.0));
         a[i]= (s - r);
         b[i]= -((1.0 / time_delta) + (2.0 * s)+ 0.5*spot_rates[i]);
```

```
            c[i]= (s + r);
            y_bond[i]= (r - s) * bond_prices[i-1] + ((2.0 * s)
                    -(1.0 / time_delta) - 0.5*spot_rates[i])
                    * bond_prices[i] - (r + s) * bond_prices[i+1];
        }
    /**** Solution of tridiagonal system ****/
    tridagm(a,b,c,bond_prices,y_bond,number_space_points);
    }
/**** Initialization of terminal value of option ****/
if (coupon_flows[option_expiration_period])
  { accrued= 0.0; }
else
  {
    for (i=option_expiration_period ; !coupon_flows[i]; i++) {;}
    accrued= (1.0 - ((double)(i - option_expiration_period)
            * time_delta / 0.5)) * semi_annual_coupon;
  }
for (i=0 ; i < number_space_points ; i++)
    {
      if (call_put == 'C' || call_put == 'c')
        { option_prices[i]= MAX(bond_prices[i]-accrued
                            -strike,0.0); }
      else
        { option_prices[i]= MAX(strike-bond_prices[i]
                            +accrued,0.0); }
    }
/**** Main valuation loop until initial period ****/
for (j=option_expiration_period ; j > 0 ; j--)
    {
    /**** Addition of semi-annual coupon ****/
    if (coupon_flows[j])
        {
          for (i=0 ; i < number_space_points ; i++)
    { bond_prices[i] += semi_annual_coupon; }
        }

    /**** Highest spot rate case is treated differently ****/
    spot_rates[0]= 1.0e+12;
    a[0]= 0.0;
    b[0]= 1.0;
    c[0]= 0.0;
    if (j == number_time_points-1)
      {
        y_bond[0]= bond_prices[0] / time_delta;
        y_option[0]= option_prices[0] / time_delta;
      }
```

```
else
  {
    y_bond[0]= 0.0;
    y_option[0]= 0.0;
  }
/**** Lowest spot rate case is also treated separately ****/
a[number_space_points-1]= -mu[number_space_points-1] /
                                space_delta;
b[number_space_points-1]= mu[number_space_points-1] /
                                space_delta - 1.0 / time_delta;
c[number_space_points-1]= 0.0;
y_bond[number_space_points-1]
        = -bond_prices[number_space_points-1] / time_delta;
y_option[number_space_points-1]
        = -option_prices[number_space_points-1] / time_delta;
/**** Now do the intermediate points ****/
for (i=1 ; i < number_space_points-1 ; i++)
  {
    r= mu[i] / (4.0 * space_delta);
    s= sigma[i] / (2.0 * pow(space_delta,2.0));
    a[i]= (s - r);
    b[i]= -((1.0 / time_delta) + (2.0 * s) + 0.5*
            spot_rates[i]);
    c[i]= (s + r);
    y_bond[i]= (r - s) * bond_prices[i-1] + ((2.0 * s) -
    (1.0 / time_delta) -0.5*spot_rates[i])
              * bond_prices[i] - (r + s) * bond_prices[i+1];
    y_option[i]= (r - s) * option_prices[i-1] + ((2.0 * s) -
    (1.0 / time_delta) -0.5*spot_rates[i])
                  * option_prices[i] - (r + s)
                  * option_prices[i+1];
  }
/**** Solution of tridiagonal system ****/
tridagm(a,b,c,bond_prices,y_bond,number_space_points);
tridagm(a,b,c,option_prices,y_option,number_space_points);
/**** American feature is handled by the Wald-Bellman
                                    equation ****/
if (american_european == 'A' || american_european == 'a')
  {
    if (coupon_flows[j-1])
      { accrued= 0.0; }
    else
      {
        for (i=j-1 ; !coupon_flows[i] ; i++) {;}
        accrued= (1.0 - ((double)(i - j + 1)
                * time_delta / 0.5)) * semi_annual_coupon;
      }
```

```
        for (i=0 ; i < number_space_points ; i++)
           {
             if (call_put == 'C' || call_put == 'c')
               { option_prices[i]= MAX(option_prices[i],
                               bond_prices[i]-accrued-strike); }
             else
               { option_prices[i]= MAX(option_prices[i],
                               strike-bond_prices[i]+
                  accrued); }
          }
        }
     }
   if (coupon_flows[0])
     { *accrued_interest= 0.0; }
   else
     {
       *accrued_interest= (1.0 - ((double)(coupon_flows[0])
                        * time_delta
                        / 0.5)) * semi_annual_coupon;
       for (i=0 ; i < number_space_points ; i++)
       { bond_prices[i] -= *accrued_interest; }
     }
   /**** Cleanup ****/
   error= 0;
 fre:
   free_dvector(a,0,number_space_points-1);
   free_dvector(b,0,number_space_points-1);
   free_dvector(c,0,number_space_points-1);
   free_dvector(y_bond,0,number_space_points-1);
   free_dvector(y_option,0,number_space_points-1);
   free_dvector(mu,0,number_space_points-1);
   free_dvector(sigma,0,number_space_points-1);
   free_ivector(coupon_flows,0,number_time_points-1);
   return(error);
}
fdi_sdv(position,gamma,space_delta,parameters,spot_rate,mu,sigma)
  /****************************************************************
fdi_sdv() computes the coefficients for fdi_bond_option().
   ------------------------------------------------------------
   long   position    = position along the space axis.
      double gamma        = scaling factor (usually 12.5).
      double space_delta = one interval of space axis.
      double *parameters          = model parameters vector:
                          0 <-> speed of adjustment
                          1 <-> long term mean
                          2 <-> volatility parameter
      double *spot_rate  = spot rate (in decimal).
```

```
              double *mu          = drift rate modified by gamma
                                    (in decimal).
              double *sigma       = variance modified by gamma
                                    (in decimal).
      ----------------------------------------------------------------
   ****************************************************************/
int position;
double gamma,space_delta,*parameters,*spot_rate,*mu,*sigma;
{
  int error;
  int i,j,k;
  double r,s,y;
      /**** Some useful checks ****/
      if (position < 0)
        { printf("! position invalid\n"); return(1); }
      if (gamma < 1.0 || gamma > 100.0)
        { printf("! gamma out of bounds\n"); return(2); }
      if (space_delta <= 0)
        { printf("! space_delta invalid\n"); return(3); }
      /**** Compute spot rate ****/
      y= (double)(position) * space_delta;
      *spot_rate= (1.0 - y)/ (gamma * y);
      /**** Useful calculation ****/
      s= *spot_rate * pow(parameters[2],2.0);
      /**** Compute drift ****/
      r= parameters[0] * (parameters[1] - *spot_rate);
      r *= -gamma * pow(y,2.0);
      r += pow(gamma,2.0) * pow(y,3.0) * s;
      *mu= r;
      /**** Compute variance/2.0 ****/
      r= 0.5 * pow(gamma,2.0) * pow(y,4.0) * s;
      *sigma= r;

  return(0);
}
tridagm(a,b,c,x,y,number)
  /****************************************************************
      tridagm() is a variant  Numerical Recipes' routine of the
      same name.
      ----------------------------------------------------------------
   ****************************************************************/
  long number;
  double *a,*b,*c,*x,*y;
{
  int error;
  int i,j,k;
  double r,s,t,bet,*gam,*vec;
```

```
   double *dvector();
   gam= dvector(0,number-1);
   if (b[0] == 0.0)
     { error= 1; goto fre; }
   x[0]= y[0] / (bet=b[0]);
   for (j=1 ; j < number ; j++)
     {
        gam[j]= c[j-1] / bet;
        bet= b[j] - a[j] * gam[j];
        if (bet == 0.0)
          { error= 2; goto fre; }
        x[j]= (y[j] -a[j] * x[j-1]) / bet;
     }
   for (j=(number-2) ; j >= 0 ; j--)
     { x[j] -= gam[j+1] * x[j+1]; }
  error= 0;
  fre:
   free_dvector(gam,0,number-1);
   return(error);
}
```

Bibliography

Aase, K. (1984). "Optimum Portfolio Diversification in a General Continuous Time Model." *Stochastic Processes and Their Application* 18: 81–98.

Aase, K. (1999). "An Equilibrium Model of Catastrophe Insurance Futures and Spreads." *Geneva Papers on Risk and Insurance Theory* 24: 69–96.

Abel, A. (1988). "Stock Prices under Time-Varying Dividend Risk: An Exact Solution in an Infinite-Horizon General Equilibrium Model." *Journal of Monetary Economics* 22: 375–393.

Abken, P. (1993). "Valuation of Default-Risky Interest-Rate Swaps." *Advances in Futures and Options Research* 6: 93–116.

Acharya, S., and D. Madan. (1993). "Arbitrage-Free Econometric Option Pricing Models in an Incomplete Market with a Locally Risky Discount Factor." Working Paper, Federal Reserve Board.

Acharya, V., and J. Carpenter. (1999). "Corporate Bonds: Valuation, Hedging, and Optimal Exercise Boundaries." Working Paper, Department of Finance, Stern School of Business.

Adams, K., and D. Van Deventer. (1994). "Fitting Yield Curves and Forward Rate Curves with Maximum Smoothness." *Journal of Fixed Income* 4 (June): 52–62.

Adler, M., and J. Detemple. (1988). "On the Optimal Hedge of a Non-Traded Cash Position." *Journal of Finance* 43: 143–153.

Ahn, H. (1993). "A Review on Stochastic Differential Utility." Working Paper, Mathematics Department, Purdue University.

Ahn, H., M. Dayal, E. Grannan, and G. Swindle. (1995). "Hedging with Transaction Costs." *Annals of Applied Probability* 8: 341–366.

Aït-Sahalia, Y. (1996a). "Do Interest Rates Really Follow Continuous-Time Markov Diffusions?" Working Paper, Graduate School of Business, University of Chicago and NBER.

Aït-Sahalia, Y. (1996b). "Nonparametric Pricing of Interest Rate Derivative Securities." *Econometrica* 64: 527–560.

Aït-Sahalia, Y. (1996c). "Testing Continuous-Time Models of the Spot Interest Rate." *Review of Financial Studies* 9: 385–342.

Aït-Sahalia, Y., and A. Lo. (1998). "Nonparametric Estimation of State-Price Densities Implicit in Financial Asset Prices." *Journal of Finance* 53: 499–547.

Aït-Sahalia, Y., and A. Lo. (2000). "Nonparametric Risk Management and Implied Risk Aversion." *Journal of Econometrics* 94: 9–51.

Aït-Sahalia, Y., Y. Wang, and F. Yared. (1998). "Do Option Markets Correctly Price the Probabilities of Movement of the Underlying Asset?" Working Paper, Graduate School
of Business, University of Chicago. Forthcoming in *Journal of Econometrics.*

Ait-Sahlia, F. (1995). "Optimal Stopping and Weak Convergence Methods for Some Problems in Financial Economics." Working Paper, Ph.D. Dissertation, Operations
Research Department, Stanford University.

Ait-Sahlia, F., and T. Lai. (1997a). "Random Walk Duality and the Valuation of Discrete
Lookback Options." Working Paper, Hewlett-Packard Laboratories.

Ait-Sahlia, F., and T. Lai. (1997b). "Valuation of Discrete Barrier and Hindsight Options."
Working Paper, Hewlett-Packard Laboratories.

Ait-Sahlia, F., and T.-L. Lai. (1996). "Approximations for American Options." Working Paper,
School of Operations Research and Industrial Engineering, Cornell University.

Ait-Sahlia, F., and T.-L. Lai. (1998). "Efficient Approximations to American Option Prices,
Hedge Parameters and Exercise Boundaries." Working Paper, Hewlett-Packard
Laboratories, Palo Alto, CA.

Aiyagari, S., and M. Gertler. (1991). "Asset Returns with Transaction Costs and Uninsured
Individual Risk: A Stage III Exercise." *Journal of Monetary Economics* 27: 311–331.

Akahari, J. (1993). "Some Formulas for a New Type of Path-Dependent Option." Working
Paper, Department of Mathematics, University of Tokyo.

Akian, M., J.-L. Menaldi, and A. Sulem. (1996). "On an Investment-Consumption Model with
Transaction Costs." *SIAM Journal on Control and Optimization* 34: 329–364.

Akian, M., A. Sulem, and M. Taksar. (1999). "Dynamic Optimisation of a Long Term Growth
Rate for a Mixed Portfolio with Transaction Costs. The Logarithmic Utility Case."
Working Paper, INRIA Rocquencourt.

Aliprantis, C., and O. Burkinshaw. (1985). *Positive Operators.* Orlando: Academic Press.

Allegretto, W., G. Barone-Adesi, and R. Elliott. (1993). "Numerical Evaluation of the Critical Price and American Options." Working Paper, Department of Mathematics,
University of Alberta.

Allingham, M. (1991). "Existence Theorems in the Capital Asset Pricing Model." *Econometrica*
59: 1169–1174.

Alvarez, O. (1991). "Gestion de Portefeuille avec Coût de Transaction." Working Paper, École
Polytechnique.

Alvarez, O., and A. Tourin. (1996). "Viscosity Solutions of Nonlinear Integro-Differential
Equations." *Annales de l'Institut Henri Poincaré Analyse Non Lineaire* 13: 293–317.

Amendinger, J. (1999). "Martingale Representation Theorems for Initially Enlarged Filtrations." Working Paper, Technische Universität Berlin.

Amendinger, J., P. Imkeller, and M. Schweizer. (1998). "Additional Logarithmic Utility of an
Insider." *Stochastic Processes and Their Applications* 75: 263–286.

Amin, K. (1991). "On the Computation of Continuous Time Option Prices Using Discrete
Approximations." *Journal of Financial and Quantitative Analysis* 26: 477–495.

Amin, K. (1993a). "Jump-Diffusion Option Valuation in Discrete-Time." *Journal of Finance* 48:
1833–1863.

Amin, K. (1993b). "Option Valuation with Systematic Stochastic Volatility." *Journal of Finance*
48: 881–910.

Amin, K., and J. Bodurtha. (1995). "Discrete-Time Valuation of American Options with
Stochastic Interest Rates." *Review of Financial Studies* 8: 193–234.

Amin, K., and R. Jarrow. (1993). "Pricing Options on Risky Assets in a Stochastic Interest Rate Economy." *Mathematical Finance* 2: 217–237.

Amin, K., and A. Khanna. (1994). "Convergence of American Option Values from Discrete to Continuous-Time Financial Models." *Mathematical Finance* 4: 289–304.

Amin, K., and A. Morton. (1994). "Implied Volatility Functions in Arbitrage-Free Term Structure Models." *Journal of Financial Economics* 35: 141–180.

Amin, K., and V. Ng. (1993). "Options Valuation with Systematic Stochastic Volatility." *Journal of Finance* 48: 881–909.

Andersen, L. (1995). "Bivariate Binary Options." Working Paper, Research General Re Financial Products Corp.

Andersen, L. (1996). "Monte Carlo Simulation of Barrier and Lookback Options with Continuous or High-Frequency Monitoring of the Underlying Asset." Working Paper, General Re Financial Products Corp.

Andersen, L., and J. Andreasen. (1998). "Volatility Skew and Extensions of the Libor Market Model." Working Paper, General Re Financial Products, New York. Forthcoming in *Applied Mathematical Finance.*

Andersen, L., and J. Andreasen. (1999). "Jump-Diffusion Processes: Volatility Smile Fitting and Numerical Methods for Pricing." Working Paper, General Re Financial Products. Forthcoming in *Review of Derivatives Research.*

Andersen, L., J. Andreasen, and R. Brotherton-Ratcliffe. (1998). "The Passport Option." *Journal of Computational Finance* 1 (3).

Andersen, L., and R. Brotherton-Ratcliffe. (1995). "The Equity Option Volatility Smile: An Implicit Finite Difference Approach." Working Paper, General Re Financial Products Corp.

Anderson, R., Y. Pan, and S. Sundaresan. (1995). "Corporate Bond Yield Spreads and the Term Structure." Working Paper, CORE, Belgium.

Anderson, R., and S. Sundaresan. (1996). "Design and Valuation of Debt Contracts." *Review of Financial Studies* 9: 37–68.

Andreasen, J. (1998). "Fast and Accurate Pricing of Path Dependent Options: A Finite Difference Approach." *Journal of Computational Finance* 2 (Fall).

Andreasen, J., and B. Gruenewald. (1996). "American Option Pricing in the Jump-Diffusion Model." Working Paper, Aarhus University, Denmark.

Andreasen, J., B. Jensen, and R. Poulsen. (1998). "Eight Valuation Methods in Financial Mathematics: The Black-Scholes Formula as an Example." *Mathematical Scientist* 23: 18–40.

Ansel, J., and C. Stricker. (1992). "Quelques Remarques sur un Theoreme de Yan." Working Paper, Université de Franche-Comté.

Ansel, J., and C. Stricker. (1994a). "Couverture des Actifs Contingents et Prix Maximum." *Annales de l'Institut Henri Poincaré Probabilites Statistiques* 30: 303–315.

Ansel, J., and C. Stricker. (1994b). "Lois de Martingale, Densités et Decomposition de Föllmer Schweizer." Working Paper, Université de Franche-Comté.

Antonelli, F. (1993). "Backward-Forward Stochastic Differential Equations." *Annals of Applied Probability* 3: 777–793.

Apelfeld, R., and A. Conze. (1990). "The Term Structure of Interest Rates: The Case of Imperfect Information." Working Paper, Department of Economics, University of Chicago.

Araujo, A., and P. Monteiro. (1987). "Generic Non-Existence of Equilibria in Finance Models." *Journal of Mathematical Economics* 20: 489–501.

Araujo, A., and P. Monteiro. (1989). "Equilibrium Without Uniform Conditions." *Journal of Economic Theory* 48: 416–427.

Araujo, A., P. Monteiro, and M. Páscoa. (1996). "Infinite Horizon Incomplete Markets with a Continuum of States." *Mathematical Finance* 6: 119–132.

Arntzen, H. (1994). "Solution to a Class of Stochastic Investment Problems Involving Finite Variation Controls." Working Paper, Mathematics Institute, University of Oslo.

Arrow, K. (1951). "An Extension of the Basic Theorems of Classical Welfare Economics." In J. Neyman (Ed.), *Proceedings of the Second Berkeley Symposium on Mathematical Statistics and Probability*, pp. 507–532. Berkeley: University of California Press.

Arrow, K. (1953). "Le Rôle des Valeurs Boursières pour la Repartition la Meillure des Risques." *Econometrie*. Colloq. Internat. Centre National de la Recherche Scientifique 40 (Paris 1952), pp. 41–47; discussion, pp. 47–48, C.N.R.S. (Paris 1953). English Translation in *Review of Economic Studies* 31 (1964): 91–96.

Arrow, K. (1970). *Essays in the Theory of Risk Bearing*. London: North-Holland.

Arrow, K., and G. Debreu. (1954). "Existence of an Equilibrium for a Competitive Economy." *Econometrica* 22: 265–290.

Artzner, P. (1995). "References for the Numeraire Portfolio." Working Paper, Institut de Recherche Mathématique Avancée Université Louis Pasteur et CNRS, et Laboratoire de Recherche en Gestion.

Artzner, P., and F. Delbaen. (1990a). "'Finem Lauda' or the Risk of Swaps." *Insurance: Mathematics and Economics* 9: 295–303.

Artzner, P., and F. Delbaen. (1990b). "Term Structure of Interest Rates: The Martingale Approach." *Advances in Applied Mathematics* 10: 95–129.

Artzner, P., and F. Delbaen. (1992). "Credit Risk and Prepayment Option." *ASTIN Bulletin* 22: 81–96.

Artzner, P., and F. Delbaen. (1995). "Default Risk and Incomplete Insurance Markets." *Mathematical Finance* 5: 187–195.

Artzner, P., and D. Heath. (1990). "Completeness and Non-Unique Pricing." Working Paper, Department of Operations Research, Cornell University.

Artzner, P., and D. Heath. (1995). "Approximate Completeness with Multiple Martingale Measures." *Mathematical Finance* 5: 1–11.

Artzner, P., and P. Roger. (1993). "Definition and Valuation of Optional Coupon Reinvestment Bonds." *Finance* 14: 7–22.

Arvantis, A., J. Gregory, and J.-P. Laurent. (1999). "Building Models for Credit Spreads." *Journal of Derivatives* 6 (3): 27–43.

Au, K., and D. Thurston. (1993). "Markovian Term Structure Movements." Working Paper, School of Banking and Finance, University of New South Wales.

Avellaneda, M., R. Buff, C. Friedman, N. Grandchamp, L. Kruk, and J. Newman. (1999). "Weighted Monte Carlo: A New Technique for Calibrating Asset-Pricing Models." Working Paper, Courant Institute of Mathematical Sciences.

Avellaneda, M., and A. Parás. (1994). "Dynamic Hedging Strategies for Derivative Securities in the Presence of Large Transaction Costs." *Applied Mathematical Finance* 1: 165–194.

Avelleneda, M., and P. Laurence. (2000). *Financial Models and Derivative Securities*. Forthcoming.

Babbs, S. (1991). "A Family of Ito Process Models for the Term Structure of Interest Rates." Working Paper, Financial Options Research Centre, University of Warwick.

Babbs, S., and M. Selby. (1996). "Pricing by Arbitrage in Incomplete Markets." *Mathematical Finance* 8: 163–168.

Babbs, S., and N. Webber. (1994). "A Theory of the Term Structure with an Official Short Rate." Working Paper, Midland Global Markets and University of Warwick.

Bachelier, L. (1900). "Théorie de la Speculation." *Annales Scientifiques de L'École Normale Supérieure* 3d ser., 17: 21–88. Translation in *The Random Character of Stock Market Prices*, ed. Paul Cootner, pp. 17–79. Cambridge, MA: MIT Press, 1964.

Back, K. (1986). "Securities Market Equilibrium without Bankruptcy: Contingent Claim Valuation and the Martingale Property." Working Paper, Center for Mathematical Studies in Economics and Management Science, Northwestern University.

Back, K. (1991). "Asset Pricing for General Processes." *Journal of Mathematical Economics* 20: 371–396.

Back, K. (1996). "Yield Curve Models: A Mathematical Review." Working Paper, Olin School of Business, Washington University in St. Louis, St. Louis.

Back, K., H. Cao, and G. Willard. (2000). "Imperfect Competition among Informed Traders." *Journal of Finance* 55: 2117–2155.

Back, K., and S. Pliska. (1986). "Discrete versus Continuous Trading in Securities Markets with Net Worth Constraints." Working Paper, Center for Mathematical Studies in Economics and Management Science, Northwestern University.

Back, K., and S. Pliska. (1987). "The Shadow Price of Information in Continuous Time Decision Problems." *Stochastics* 22: 151–186.

Back, K., and S. Pliska. (1991). "On the Fundamental Theorem of Asset Pricing with an Infinite State Space." *Journal of Mathematical Economics* 20: 1–18.

Backus, D., S. Foresi, and S. Zin. (1998). "Arbitrage Opportunities in Arbitrage-Free Models of Bond Pricing." *Journal of Business and Economic Statistics* 16: 13–26.

Bajeux-Besnainou, I., and R. Portait. (1993). "Dynamic Asset Allocation in a Mean-Variance Framework." Working Paper, ESSEC and Laboratoire d'Econométrie de L'École Polytechnique.

Bajeux-Besnainou, I., and R. Portait. (1997). "The Numeraire Portfolio: A New Methodology for Financial Theory." *European Journal of Finance* 3: 291–309.

Bajeux-Besnainou, I., and R. Portait. (1998). "Pricing Derivative Securities with a Multi-Factor Gaussian Model." *Applied Mathematical Finance* 5: 1–19.

Bajeux-Besnainou, I., and J.-C. Rochet. (1996). "Dynamic Spanning: Are Options an Appropriate Instrument?" *Mathematical Finance* 6: 1–16.

Bakshi, G., C. Cao, and Z. Chen. (1997). "Empirical Performance of Alternative Option Pricing Models." *Journal of Finance* 52: 2003–2049.

Bakshi, G., and D. Madan. (1997). "Pricing Average-Rate Contingent Claims." Working Paper, Department of Finance, College of Business and Management, University of Maryland.

Bakshi, G., and D. Madan. (2000). "Spanning and Derivative Security Valuation." *Journal of Financial Economics* 55: 205–238.

Balasko, Y. (1989). *Foundations of the Theory of General Equilibrium.* New York: Academic Press.

Balasko, Y., and D. Cass. (1986). "The Structure of Financial Equilibrium with Exogenous Yields: The Case of Incomplete Markets." *Econometrica* 57: 135–162.

Balasko, Y., D. Cass, and P. Siconolfi. (1990). "The Structure of Financial Equilibrium with Exogenous Yields: The Case of Restricted Participation." *Journal of Mathematical Economics* 19: 195–216.

Balduzzi, P. (1994). "A Second Factor in Bond Yields." Working Paper, Department of Finance, Stern School of Business, New York University.

Balduzzi, P., G. Bertola, S. Foresi, and L. Klapper. (1998). "Interest Rate Targeting and the Dynamics of Short-Term Interest Rates." *Journal of Money, Credit, and Banking* 30: 26–50.

Balduzzi, P., S. Das, and S. Foresi. (1998). "The Central Tendency: A Second Factor in Bond Yields." *Review of Economics and Statistics* 80: 62–72.

Balduzzi, P., S. Das, S. Foresi, and R. Sundaram. (1996). "A Simple Approach to Three Factor Affine Term Structure Models." *Journal of Fixed Income* 6 (December): 43–53.

Balduzzi, P., and A. Lynch. (1997). "Samuelson's Irrelevance Result Reconsidered: The Case of Transaction Costs." Working Paper, New York University.

Balduzzi, P., and A. Lynch. (1999). "Transaction Costs and Predictability: Some Utility Cost Calculations." *Journal of Financial Economics* 52: 47–78.

Ball, C., and A. Roma. (1994). "Stochastic Volatility Option Pricing." *Journal of Financial and Quantitative Analysis* 29: 589–607.

Ball, C., and W. Torous. (1985). "On Jumps in Common Stock Prices and their Impact on Call Option Pricing." *Journal of Finance* 40: 155–173.

Ball, C., and W. Torous. (1994). "Regime Shifts in Short-Term Interest Rate Dynamics." Working Paper, Owen Graduate School of Management, Vanderbilt University.

Bally, V. (1995). "An Approximation Scheme for BSDE's and Applications to Control and Nonlinear PDE's." Working Paper, Laboratoire De Statistique et Processus, Universités du Maine et D'Angers.

Bally, V., and D. Talay. (1996). "The Law of the Euler Scheme for Stochastic Differential Equations: II. Convergence Rate of the Density." *Monte Carlo Methods and Applications* 2: 93–128.

Bank, P., and F. Riedel. (1999). "Optimal Consumption Choice under Uncertainty with Intertemporal Substitution." Working Paper, Mathematics Department, Humboldt-University of Berlin.

Banz, R., and M. Miller. (1978). "Prices for State-Contingent Claims: Some Evidence and Applications." *Journal of Business* 51: 653–672.

Barberis, N., M. Huang, and T. Santos. (2001). "Prospect Theory and Asset Prices." *Quarterly Journal of Economics*, 116: 1–53.

Barles, G., R. Buckdahn, and E. Pardoux. (1997). "Backward Stochastic Differential Equations and Integral-Partial Differential Equations." *Stochastics and Stochastics Reports* 60: 57–83.

Barles, G., J. Burdeau, M. Romano, and N. Samsoen. (1993). "Estimation de la Frontière Libre des Options Américaines au Voisinage de l'Echéance." *Comtes Rendus de l'Academie de Science de Paris* 316-I: 171–174.

Barles, G., J. Burdeau, M. Romano, and N. Samsoen. (1995). "Critical Stock Price Near Expiration." *Mathematical Finance* 2: 77–96.

Barles, G., C. Daher, and M. Romano. (1992). "Convergence of Numerical Schemes for Parabolic Equations Arising in Finance Theory." Working Paper, Cahier 9244, CEREMADE, Université de Paris.

Barles, G., and E. Lesigne. (1997). "SDE, BSDE and PDE." In N. El Karoui and L. Mazliak (Eds.), *Backward Stochastic Differential Equations*, pp. 47–80. Essex: Addison Wesley Longman Ltd.

Barles, G., M. Romano, and N. Touzi. (1993). "Contingent Claims and Market Completeness in a Stochastic Volatility Model." Working Paper, Département de Mathématiques, Université de Tours, France.

Barles, G., and M. Soner. (1998). "Option Pricing with Transaction Costs and a Nonlinear Black-Scholes Equation." *Finance and Stochastics* 2: 369–397.

Barndorff-Nielsen, O. (1997). "Normal Inverse Gaussian Distributions and Stochastic Volatility Modelling." *Scandinavian Journal of Statistics* 24: 1–13.

Barone, E., and S. Risa. (1994). "Valuation of Floaters and Options on Floaters under Special Repo Rates." Working Paper, Instituto Mobiliare Italiano, Rome.

Barone-Adesi, G., and R. Elliott. (1991). "Approximations for the Values of American Options." *Stochastic Analysis and Applications* 9: 115–131.

Barraquand, J. (1993). "Numerical Valuation of High Dimensional Multivariate European Securities." Working Paper, Digital Research Laboratory, Paris.

Barraquand, J., and D. Martineau. (1995). "Numerical Valuation of High Dimensional Multivariate American Securities." *Journal of Financial and Quantitative Analysis* 30: 383–405.

Barraquand, J., and T. Pudet. (1996). "Pricing of American Path-Dependent Contingent Claims." *Mathematical Finance* 6: 17–51.

Bartle, R. (1976). *The Elements of Real Analysis* (2nd ed.). New York: Wiley.

Basak, S. (1995). "A General Equilibrium Model of Portfolio Insurance." *Review of Financial Studies* 8: 1059–1090.

Basak, S. (1997). "Consumption Choice and Asset Pricing with a Non-Price-Taking Agent." *Economic Theory* 10: 437–462.

Basak, S., and D. Cuoco. (1999). "An Equilibrium Model with Restricted Stock Market Participation." *Review of Financial Studies* 11: 309–341.

Bates, D. (1996). "Jumps and Stochastic Volatility: Exchange Rate Processes Implicit in Deutsche Mark Option." *Review of Financial Studies* 9: 69–107.

Bates, D. (1997). "Post-87' Crash Fears in S-and-P 500 Futures Options." Working Paper, Finance Department, Wharton School, University of Pennsylvania.

Baxter, M. (1996). "General Interest-Rate Models and the Universality of HJM." Working Paper, Statistical Laboratory, University of Cambridge, Cambridge.

Baz, J., and S. Das. (1996). "Analytical Approximations of the Term Structure for Jump-Diffusion Processes: A Numerical Analysis." *Journal of Fixed Income* 6 (1): 78–86.

Beaglehole, D. (1990). "Tax Clientele and Stochastic Processes in the Gilt Market." Working Paper, Graduate School of Business, University of Chicago.

Beaglehole, D., and M. Tenney. (1991). "General Solutions of Some Interest Rate Contingent Claim Pricing Equations." *Journal of Fixed Income* 1: 69–84.

Becker, R., and J. Boyd. (1993). "Recursive Utility: Discrete Time Theory." *Hitotsubashi Journal of Economics* 34: 49–98.

Beckers, S. (1981). "Standard Deviations Implied in Option Process as Predictors of Future Stock Price Variability." *Journal of Banking and Finance* 5: 363–382.

Beibel, M., and H. Lerche. (1995). "A New Look at Warrant Pricing and Related Optimal Stopping Problems." Working Paper, Institut für Mathematische Stochastik, University of Bonn.

Beibel, M., and H. Lerche. (1997). "A New Look at Optimal Stopping Problems Related to Mathematical Finance." *Statistica Sinica* 7: 93–108.

Bellman, R. (1957). *Dynamic Programming*. Princeton, N.J.: Princeton University Press.

Bensoussan, A. (1983). "Lectures on Stochastic Control." In S. Mitter and A. Moro (Eds.), *Nonlinear Filtering and Stochastic Control*, Lecture Notes in Mathematics 972, pp. 1–62. New York: Springer-Verlag.

Bensoussan, A. (1984). "On the Theory of Option Pricing." *Acta Applicandae Mathematicae* 2: 139–158.

Bensoussan, A., M. Crouhy, and D. Galai. (1995a). "Black-Scholes Approximation of Complex Option Values: The Cases of European Compound Call Options and Equity Warrants." Working Paper, Université Paris Dauphine and INRIA, France.

Bensoussan, A., M. Crouhy, and D. Galai. (1995b). "Stochastic Equity Volatility Related to the Leverage Effect II: Valuation of European Equity Options and Warrants." *Applied Mathematical Finance* 2: 43–59.

Benth, R., K. Karlsen, and K. Reikvam. (1999). "Optimal Portfolio Selection with Consumption and Nonlinear Integro-Differential Equations with Gradient Constraint: A Viscosity Solution Approach." Working Paper, Centre for Mathmatical Physics and Stochastics.

Benveniste, L., and J. Scheinkman. (1979). "On the Differentiability of the Value Function in Dynamic Models of Economics." *Econometrica* 47: 727–732.

Benzoni, L. (1998). "Pricing Options under Stochastic Volatility: An Econnometric Analysis." Working Paper, J.L. Kellog Graduate School of Management, Northwestern University.

Berardi, A., and M. Esposito. (1999). "A Base Model for Multifactor Specifications of the Term Structure." *Economic Notes* 28: 145–170.

Bergman, Y. (1985b). "Time Preference and Capital Asset Pricing Models." *Journal of Financial Economics* 14: 145–159.

Bergman, Y. (1995). "Option Pricing with Differential Interest Rates." *Reveiw of Financial Studies* 8: 475–500.

Bergman, Y., B. Grundy, and Z. Wiener. (1996). "Generalized Theory of Rational Optional Pricing." *Journal of Finance* 51: 1573–1610.

Berk, J. (1992). "The Necessary and Sufficient Conditions that Imply the CAPM." Working Paper, Faculty of Commerce, University of British Columbia, Canada.

Berk, J. (1997). "Necessary Conditions for the CAPM." *Journal of Economic Theory* 73: 245–257.

Berk, J., and H. Uhlig. (1993). "The Timing of Information in a General Equilibrium Framework." *Journal of Economic Theory* 59: 275–287.

Bernard, P., D. Talay, and L. Tubaro. (1994). "Rate of Convergence of a Stochastic Particle Method for the Kolmogorov Equation with Variable Coefficients." *Mathematics of Computation* 63: 555–587.

Bertsekas, D. (1976). *Dynamic Programming and Stochastic Control*. New York: Academic Press.

Bertsekas, D., and S. Shreve. (1978). *Stochastic Optimal Control: The Discrete Time Case*. New York: Academic Press.

Bertsimas, D., L. Kogan, and A. Lo. (1998). "When is Time Continuous?" Working Paper, MIT Sloan School of Management. Forthcoming in *Journal of Financial Economics*.

Bewley, T. (1972). "Existence of Equilibria in Economies with Infinitely Many Commodities." *Journal of Economic Theory* 4: 514–540.

Bewley, T. (1982). "Thoughts on Volatility Tests of the Intertemporal Asset Pricing Model." Working Paper, Department of Economics, Northwestern University.

Bhar, R., and C. Chiarella. (1995). "Transformation of Heath-Jarrow-Morton Models to Markovian Systems." Working Paper, School of Finance and Economics, University of Technology, Sydney.

Bick, A. (1986). "On Viable Diffusion Price Processes." *Journal of Finance* 45: 673–689.

Bick, A. (1988). "Producing Derivative Assets with Forward Contracts." *Journal of Financial and Quantitative Analysis* 2: 153–160.

Bick, A. (1994). "Futures Pricing via Futures Strategies." Working Paper, Faculty of Business Administration, Simon Fraser University, Vancouver, Canada.

Bick, A. (1995). "Quadratic Variation Based Dynamic Strategies." *Management Science* 41: 722–732.

Bick, A. (1997). "Two Closed-Form Formulas for the Futures Price in the Presence of a Quality Option." *European Finance Review* 1: 81–104.

Bick, A., and H. Reisman. (1993). "Generalized Implied Volatility." Working Paper, Faculty of Business Administration, Simon Fraser University, Vancouver, Canada.

Bick, A., and W. Willinger. (1994). "Dynamic Spanning without Probabilities." *Stochastic Processes and Their Applications* 50: 349–374.

Bielecki, T., and M. Rutkowski. (1999a). "Credit Risk Modelling: A Multiple Ratings Case." Working Paper, Northeastern Illinois University and Technical University of Warsaw.

Bielecki, T., and M. Rutkowski. (1999b). "Modelling of the Defaultable Term Structure: Conditionally Markov Approach." Working Paper, Northeastern Illinois University and Technical University of Warsaw.

Bielecki, T., and M. Rutkowski. (2000). "Credit Risk Modelling: Intensity Based Approach." Working Paper, Department of Mathematics, Northeastern Illinois University.

Billingsley, P. (1986). *Probability and Measure* (2d ed.). New York: Wiley.

Bjerksund, P., and G. Stensland. (1993). "Closed-Form Approximation of American Options." *Scandinavian Journal of Management* 9: S87–S99.

Björk, T. (1996). "Interest Rate Theory." Working Paper, Department of Finance, Stockholm School of Economics.

Björk, T. (1998). *Arbitrage Theory in Continuous Time.* New York: Oxford University Press.

Björk, T., and B. Christensen. (1999). "Interest Rate Dynamics and Consistent Forward Rate Curves." *Mathematical Finance* 22: 17–23.

Björk, T., G. DiMasi, Y. Kabanov, and W. Runggaldier. (1997). "Towards a General Theory of Bond Markets." *Finance and Stochastics* 1: 141–174.

Björk, T., and A. Gombani. (1999). "Minimal Realizations of Interest Rate Models." *Finance and Stochastics* 3: 413–432.

Björk, T., Y. Kabanov, and W. Runggaldier. (1995). "Bond Markets where Prices are Driven by a General Marked Point Process." Working Paper, Optimization and Systems Theory, Department of Mathematics, Royal Institute of Technology, Stockholm.

Black, F. (1972). "Capital Market Equilibrium with Restricted Borrowing." *Journal of Business* 45: 444–454.

Black, F. (1976). "The Pricing of Commodity Contracts." *Journal of Financial Economics* 3: 167–179.

Black, F. (1990). "Mean Reversion and Consumption Smoothing." *Review of Financial Studies* 3: 107–114.

Black, F. (1995). *Exploring General Equilibrium.* Cambridge, MA: MIT Press.

Black, F., and J. Cox. (1976). "Valuing Corporate Securities: Liabilities: Some Effects of Bond Indenture Provisions." *Journal of Finance* 31: 351–367.

Black, F., E. Derman, and I. Kani. (1992). "A Two-Factor Model of Interest Rates." Working Paper, Goldman, Sachs and Company, New York.

Black, F., E. Derman, and W. Toy. (1990). "A One-Factor Model of Interest Rates and Its Application to Treasury Bond Options." *Financial Analysts Journal* January–February: 33–39.

Black, F., and P. Karasinski. (1991). "Bond and Option Pricing when Short Rates are Lognormal." *Financial Analysts Journal* (July–August): 52–59.

Black, F., and M. Scholes. (1973). "The Pricing of Options and Corporate Liabilities." *Journal of Political Economy* 81: 637–654.

Blackwell, D. (1965). "Discounted Dynamic Programming." *Annals of Mathematical Statistics* 36: 226–235.

Blume, L., D. Easley, and M. O'Hara. (1982). "Characterization of Optimal Plans for Stochastic Dynamic Programs." *Journal of Economic Theory* 28: 221–234.

Bollerslev, T., R. Chou, and K. Kroner. (1992). "ARCH Modeling in Finance: A Review of the Theory and Empirical Evidence." *Journal of Econometrics* 52: 5–59.

Bonomo, M., and R. Garcia. (1993). "Disappointment Aversion as a Solution to the Equity Premium and the Risk-Free Rate Puzzles." Working Paper, CRDE 2793, Université de Montréal.

Bossaerts, P. (1990). "Modern Term Structure Theory." Working Paper, California Institute of Technology, Pasadena.

Bossaerts, P., E. Ghysels, and C. Gouriéroux. (1996). "Arbitrage-Based Pricing when Volatility is Stochastic." Working Paper, California Institute of Technology, Pasadena.

Bossaerts, P., and P. Hillion. (1997). "Local Parametric Analysis of Hedging in Discrete Time." *Journal of Econometrics* 81: 243–272.

Bottazzi, J., T. Hens, and A. Löffler. (1994). "Market Demand Functions in the CAPM." Working Paper, Delta, Université de Paris.

Bottazzi, J.-M. (1995). "Existence of Equilibria with Incomplete Markets: The Case of Smooth Returns." *Journal of Mathematical Economics* 24: 59–72.

Bottazzi, J.-M., and T. Hens. (1996). "Excess Demand Functions and Incomplete Markets." *Journal of Economic Theory* 68: 49–63.

Boudoukh, J., M. Richardson, R. Stanton, and R. Whitelaw. (1995). "Pricing Mortgage-Backed Securities in a Multifactor Interest Rate Environment: A Multivariate Density Estimation Approach." Working Paper, Institute of Business and Economic Research, University of California at Berkeley.

Bouleau, N., and D. Lamberton. (1989). "Residual Risks and Hedging Strategies in Markovian Markets." *Stochastic Processes and Their Applications* 33: 131–150.

Bouleau, N., and D. Lépingle. (1994). *Numerical Methods for Stochastic Processes.* New York: Wiley.

Boyarchenko, S., and S. Levendorskii. (2000a). "Pricing of the Perpetual American Call Under Lévy Processes." Working Paper, Department of Mathematics, University of Pennsylvania.

Boyarchenko, S., and S. Levendorskii. (2000b). "Pricing of the Perpetual American Put Under Lévy Processes." Working Paper, Department of Mathematics, University of Pennsylvania.

Boyle, P. (1977). "Options: A Monte Carlo Approach." *Journal of Financial Economics* 4: 323–338.

Boyle, P. (1988). "A Lattice Framework for Option Pricing with Two State Variables." *Journal of Financial and Quantitative Analysis* 23: 1–12.

Boyle, P. (1990). "Valuation of Derivative Securities Involving Several Assets using Discrete Time Methods." Working Paper, Accounting Group, University of Waterloo, Waterloo, Canada.

Boyle, P., M. Broadie, and P. Glasserman. (1997). "Monte Carlo Methods for Security Pricing." *Journal of Economic Dynamics and Control* 21: 1267–1321.

Boyle, P., J. Evnine, and S. Gibbs. (1989). "Numerical Evaluation of Multivariate Contingent Claims." *Review of Financial Studies* 2: 241–250.

Boyle, P., and T. Vorst. (1992). "Options Replication in Discrete Time with Transaction Costs." *Journal of Finance* 47: 271–293.

Boyle, P., and T. Wang. (1999). "Valuation of New Securities in an Incomplete Market: The Catch of Derivative Pricing." Working Paper, School of Accountancy, University of Waterloo.

Brace, A. (1996). "Non-Bushy Trees for Gaussian HJM and Lognormal Forward Models." Working Paper, School of Mathematics, University of New South Wales, Australia.

Brace, A., and M. Musiela. (1994a). "A Multifactor Gauss Markov Implementation of Heath, Jarrow, and Morton." *Mathematical Finance* 4: 259–284.

Brace, A., and M. Musiela. (1994b). "Swap Derivatives in a Gaussian HJM Framework." Working Paper, Treasury Group, Citibank, Sydney, Australia.

Brace, A., and M. Musiela. (1995a). "Duration, Convexity and Wiener Chaos." Working Paper, Treasury Group, Citibank, Sydney, Australia.

Brace, A., and M. Musiela. (1995b). "Hedging, Duration, Bucketing and Convexity in a Gaussian Heath Jarrow Morton Framework." Working Paper, Treasury Group, Citibank, Sydney, Australia.

Brace, A., and M. Musiela. (1995c). "The Market Model of Interest Rate Dynamics." *Mathematical Finance* 7: 127–155.

Bray, M. (1994a). "The Arbitrage Pricing Theory is Not Robust 1: Variance Matrices and Portfolio Theory in Pictures." Working Paper, London School of Economics.

Bray, M. (1994b). "The Arbitrage Pricing Theory is Not Robust 2: Factor Structure and Factor Pricing." Working Paper, London School of Economics.

Breeden, D. (1979). "An Intertemporal Asset Pricing Model with Stochastic Consumption and Investment Opportunities." *Journal of Financial Economics* 7: 265–296.

Breeden, D. (1986). "Consumption, Production, Inflation and Interest Rates." *Journal of Financial Economics* 16: 3–39.

Breeden, D., M. Gibbons, and R. Litzenberger. (1989). "Empirical Tests of the Consumption Oriented CAPM." *Journal of Finance* 44: 231–262.

Breeden, D., and R. Litzenberger. (1978). "Prices of State-Contingent Claims Implicit in Option Prices." *Journal of Business* 51: 621–651.

Brémaud, P. (1981). *Point Processes and Queues: Martingale Dynamics*. New York: Springer.

Brennan, M., and E. Schwartz. (1977). "The Valuation of American Put Options." *Journal of Finance* 32: 449–462.

Brennan, M., and E. Schwartz. (1979). "A Continuous Time Approach to the Pricing of Bonds." *Journal of Banking and Finance* 3: 133–155.

Brennan, M., and E. Schwartz. (1980a). "Analysing Convertible Bonds." *Journal of Financial and Quantitative Analysis* 15: 907–929.

Brennan, M., and E. Schwartz. (1980c). "Conditional Predictions of Bond Prices and Returns." *Journal of Finance* 35: 405–419.

Brennan, M., and E. Schwartz. (1982). "An Equilibrium Model of Bond Pricing and a Test of Market Efficiency." *Journal of Financial and Quantitative Analysis* 17: 301–329.

Brennan, M., E. Schwartz, and R. Lagnado. (1997). "Strategic Asset Allocation." *Journal of Economic Dynamics and Control* 21: 1377–1403.

Broadie, M., J. Cvitanić, and M. Soner. (1998). "Optimal Replication of Contingent Claims Under Portfolio Constraints." *Review of Financial Studies* 11: 59–79.

Broadie, M., and J. Detemple. (1995). "American Capped Call Options on Dividend-Paying Assets." *Review of Financial Studies* 8: 161–191.

Broadie, M., and J. Detemple. (1996). "American Option Valuation: New Bounds, Approximations and a Comparison of Existing Methods." *Review of Financial Studies* 9: 1211–1250.

Broadie, M., and J. Detemple. (1997). "The Valuation of American Options on Multiple Assets." *Mathematical Finance* 7: 241–285.

Broadie, M., and P. Glasserman. (1996). "Estimating Security Price Derivatives Using Simulation." *Management Science* 42: 269–285.

Broadie, M., and P. Glasserman. (1997). "Pricing American Style Securities Using Simulation." *Journal of Economic Dynamics and Control* 21: 1323–1353.

Broadie, M., and P. Glasserman. (1998). "A Stochastic Mesh Method for Pricing High Dimensional American Options." Working Paper, Graduate School of Business, Columbia University, New York, NY.

Broadie, M., P. Glasserman, and S. Kou. (1997). "A Continuity Correction for Discrete Barrier Options." *Mathematical Finance* 7: 325–349.

Broadie, M., P. Glasserman, and S. Kou. (1999). "Connecting Discrete and Continuous Path-Dependent Options." *Finance and Stochastics* 3: 55–82.

Brock, W. (1979). "An Integration of Stochastic Growth Theory and the Theory of Finance, Part I: The Growth Model." In J. Green and J. Scheinkman (Eds.), *General Equilibrium, Growth, and Trade*, pp. 165–192. New York: Academic Press.

Brock, W. (1982). "Asset Prices in a Production Economy." In J. McCall (Ed.), *The Economics of Information and Uncertainty*, pp. 1–46. Chicago: University of Chicago Press.

Brown, D., P. DeMarzo, and C. Eaves. (1996a). "Computing Equilibria when Asset Markets are Incomplete." *Econometrica* 64: 1–27.

Brown, D., P. DeMarzo, and C. Eaves. (1996b). "Computing Zeros of Sections Vector Bundles Using Homotopies and Relocalization." *Mathematics of Operations Research* 21: 26–43.

Brown, D., and M. Gibbons. (1985). "A Simple Econometric Approach for Utility-Based Asset Pricing Models." *Journal of Finance* 40: 359–381.

Brown, R., and S. Schaefer. (1994a). "Interest Rate Volatility and the Shape of the Term Structure." *Philosophical Transactions of the Royal Society: Physical Sciences and Engineering* 347: 449–598.

Brown, R., and S. Schaefer. (1994b). "The Term Structure of Real Interest Rates and the Cox, Ingersoll, and Ross Model." *Journal of Financial Economics* 35: 3–42.

Brown, R., and S. Schaefer. (1996). "Ten Years of the Real Term Structure: 1984–1994." *Journal of Fixed Income* 6 (March): 6–22.

Broze, L., O. Scaillet, and J.-M. Zakoïan. (1993). "Testing for Continuous-Time Models of the Short-Term Interest Rate." Working Paper, CORE, Louvain-la-Neuve, Belgium.

Buckdahn, R. (1995a). "Backward Stochastic Differential Equations Driven by a Martingale." Working Paper, FB Mathematik der Humboldt-Universität zu Berlin, Berlin.

Buckdahn, R. (1995b). "BSDE with Non-Square Integrable Terminal Value—FBSDE with Delay." Working Paper, Faculté des Sciences, Département de Mathématiques, Université de Bretagne Occidentale, Brest, France.

Buckdahn, R., and Y. Hu. (1995). "Pricing of American Contingent Claims with Jump Stock Price and Constrained Portfolios." Working Paper, Département de Mathématiques, Université de Bretagne Occidentale.

Bühler, W., M. Uhrig-Homburg, U. Walter, and T. Weber. (1995). "An Empirical Comparison of Alternative Models for Valuing Interest Rate Options." Working Paper, Lehrstuehle für Finanzwirtschaft, Universität Mannheim.

Bühlmann, H., F. Delbaen, P. Embrechts, and A. Shiryaev. (1998). "On Esscher Transforms in Discrete Finance Models." *ASTIN Bulletin* 28: 171–186.

Bunch, D., and H. Johnson. (1993). "A Simple and Numerically Efficient Valuation Method for American Puts Using a Modified Geske-Johnson Approach." *Journal of Finance* 47: 809–816.

Buono, M., R. Gregory-Allen, and U. Yaari. (1992). "The Efficacy of Term Structure Estimation Techniques: A Monte Carlo Study." *Journal of Fixed Income* 2: 52–63.

Büttler, H. (1995). "Evaluation of Callable Bonds: Finite Difference Methods, Stability and Accuracy." *Economic Journal* 105: 374–384.

Büttler, H., and J. Waldvogel. (1996). "Pricing Callable Bonds by Means of Green's Function." *Mathematical Finance* 6: 53–88.

Cadenillas, A., and S. Pliska. (1999). "Optimal Trading of a Security when there are Taxes and Transaction Costs." *Finance and Stochastics* 3: 137–165.

Caflisch, R., and W. Morokoff. (1995). "Quasi-Monte Carlo Computation of a Finance Problem." Working Paper, Department of Mathematics, University of California, Los Angeles.

Caflisch, R., and W. Morokoff. (1996). "Valuation of Mortgage Backed Securities using the Quasi-Monte Carlo Method." Working Paper, Department of Mathematics, University of California, Los Angeles.

Caflisch, R., W. Morokoff, and A. Owen. (1997). "Valuation of Mortgage Backed Securities Using Brownian Bridges to Reduce Effective Dimension." *Journal of Computational Finance* 1 (Fall).

Calvet, L. (1999). "Incomplete Markets and Volatility." Working Paper, Department of Economics, Littauer Center, Cambridge, MA.

Campbell, J. (1986a). "Bond and Stock Returns in a Simple Exchange Model." *Quarterly Journal of Economics* 101: 785–803.

Campbell, J. (1986b). "A Defense of Traditional Hypotheses about the Term Structure of Interest Rates." *Journal of Finance* 41: 183–193.

Campbell, J. (1993). "Intertemporal Asset Pricing without Consumption." *American Economic Review* 83: 487–512.

Campbell, J. (1995). "Some Lessons from the Yield Curve." *Journal of Economic Perspectives* 9: 129–152.

Campbell, J., A. Lo, and C. MacKinlay. (1997). *The Econometrics of Financial Markets.* Princeton University Press.

Carassus, L., and E. Jouini. (1998). "Investment and Arbitrage Opportunities with Shortsale Constraints." *Mathematical Finance* 8: 169–178.

Carr, P. (1989). "European Option Valuation when Carrying Costs are Unknown." Working Paper, Johnson Graduate School of Management, Cornell University.

Carr, P. (1991). "Deriving Derivatives of Derivative Securities." Working Paper, Johnson Graduate School of Management, Cornell University. Forthcoming in *Journal of Computational Finance.*

Carr, P. (1993a). "European Put Call Symmetry." Working Paper, Johnson Graduate School of Management, Cornell University.

Carr, P. (1993b). "Valuing Bond Futures and the Quality Option." Working Paper, Johnson Graduate School of Management, Cornell University.

Carr, P. (1994). "On Approximations for the Values of American Options." Working Paper, Johnson Graduate School of Management, Cornell University.

Carr, P. (1995). "Two Extensions to Barrier Option Valuation." *Applied Mathematical Finance* 2: 173–209.

Carr, P. (1998). "Randomization and the American Put." *Review of Financial Studies* 11: 598–626.

Carr, P., and R.-R. Chen. (1993). "Valuing Bond Futures and the Quality Option." Working Paper, Johnson Graduate School of Management, Cornell University.

Carr, P., and K. Ellis. (1994). "Non-Standard Valuation of Barrier Options." Working Paper, Johnson Graduate School of Management, Cornell University.

Carr, P., and D. Faguet. (1994). "Fast Accurate Valuation of American Options." Working Paper, Johnson Graduate School of Management, Cornell University.

Carr, P., and D. Faguet. (1996). "Valuing Finite-Lived Options as Perpetual." Working Paper, Johnson School of Management, Cornell University.

Carr, P., and R. Jarrow. (1990). "The Stop-Loss Start-Gain Paradox and Option Valuation: A New Decomposition into Intrinsic and Time Value." *Review of Financial Studies* 3: 469–492.

Carr, P., R. Jarrow, and R. Myneni. (1992). "Alternative Characterizations of American Put Options." *Mathematical Finance* 2: 87–106.

Carr, P., and D. Madan. (1998). "Option Valuation Using the Fast Fourier Transform." *Journal of Computational Finance* 2 (Summer).

Carr, P., and D. Madan. (1999). "Option Valuation using the Fast Fourier Transform." *Journal of Computational Finance* 2: 61–74.

Carverhill, A. (1988). "The Ho and Lee Term Structure Theory: A Continuous Time Version." Working Paper, Financial Options Research Centre, University of Warwick.

Carverhill, A. (1990). "A Survey of Elementary Techniques for Pricing Options on Bonds and Interest Rates." Working Paper, Financial Options Research Centre, University of Warwick.

Carverhill, A. (1991). "The Term Structure of Interest Rates and Associated Options: Equilibrium versus Evolutionary Models." Working Paper, Financial Options Research Centre, University of Warwick.

Carverhill, A. (1995). "A Simplified Exposition of the Heath, Jarrow, and Morton Model." *Stochastics* 53: 227–240.

Carverhill, A. (1996). "Arbitrage, the Term Structure of Volatility, and the Long Forward Rate." Working Paper, Department of Finance, University of Science and Technology, Hong Kong.

Carverhill, A., and K. Pang. (1995). "Efficient and Flexible Bond Option Valuation in the Heath, Jarrow, and Morton Framework." *Journal of Fixed Income* 5 (September): 70–77.

Cass, D. (1984). "Competitive Equilibria in Incomplete Financial Markets." Working Paper, Center for Analytic Research in Economics and the Social Sciences, University of Pennsylvania.

Cass, D. (1989). "Sunspots and Incomplete Financial Markets: The Leading Example." In G. Feiwel (Ed.), *The Economics of Imperfect Competition and Employment: Joan Robinson and Beyond*, pp. 677–693. London: Macmillan.

Cass, D. (1991). "Incomplete Financial Markets and Indeterminacy of Financial Equilibrium." In J.-J. Laffont (Ed.), *Advances in Economic Theory*, pp. 263–288. Cambridge: Cambridge University Press.

Cassese, G. (1996). "An Elementary Remark on Martingale Equivalence and the Fundamental Theorem of Asset Pricing." Working Paper, Istituto di Economia Politica, Università Commerciale "Luigi Bocconi," Milan.

Chacko, G., and S. Das. (1998). "Pricing Average Interest Rate Options: A General Approach." Working Paper, Harvard Business School.

Chae, S. (1988). "Existence of Equilibria in Incomplete Markets." *Journal of Economic Theory* 44: 9–18.

Chalasani, P., S. Jha, and A. Varikooty. (1998). "Accurate Approximations for European Asian Options." *Journal of Computational Finance* 1 (Summer).

Chamberlain, G. (1988). "Asset Pricing in Multiperiod Securities Markets." *Econometrica* 56: 1283–1300.

Chan, K.-C., A. Karolyi, F. Longstaff, and A. Saunders. (1992). "An Empirical Comparison of Alternative Models of the Short-Term Interest Rate." *Journal of Finance* 47: 1209–1227.

Chan, Y.-K. (1992). "Term Structure as a Second Order Dynamical System, and Pricing of Derivative Securities." Working Paper, Bear Stearns and Company, New York.

Chang, F.-R. (1993). "Adjustment Costs, Optimal Investment and Uncertainty." Working Paper, Department of Economics, Indiana University.

Chapman, D. (1998). "Habit Formation, Consumption, and State-Prices." *Econometrica* 66: 1223–1230.

Charretour, F., R. Elliott, R. Myneni, and R. Viswanathan. (1992). "American Option Valuation Notes." Working Paper, Oberwohlfach Institute, Oberwohlfach, Germany.

Chen, L. (1996). *Stochastic Mean and Stochastic Volatility: A Three-Factor Model of the Term Structure of Interest Rates and Its Application to the Pricing of Interest Rate Derivatives: Part I.* Oxford: Blackwell Publishers.

Chen, R.-R., and L. Scott. (1992a). "Maximum Likelihood Estimation for a Multi-Factor Equilibrium Model of the Term Structure of Interest Rates." Working Paper, Department of Finance, Rutgers University.

Chen, R.-R., and L. Scott. (1992b). "Pricing Interest Rate Options in a Two-Factor Cox-Ingersoll-Ross Model of the Term Structure." *Review of Financial Studies* 5: 613–636.

Chen, R.-R., and L. Scott. (1993a). "Multi-Factor Cox-Ingersoll-Ross Models of the Term Structure: Estimates and Tests from a State-Space Model using a Kalman Filter." Working Paper, Department of Finance, Rutgers University.

Chen, R.-R., and L. Scott. (1993b). "Pricing Interest Rate Futures Options with Futures-Style Margining." *Journal of Futures Markets* 13: 15–22.

Chen, R.-R., and L. Scott. (1995). "Interest Rate Options in Multifactor Cox-Ingersoll-Ross Models of the Term Structure." *Journal of Derivatives* 3: 53–72.

Chen, R.-R., and B. Sopranzetti. (1999). "The Valuation of Default-Triggered Credit Derivatives." Working Paper, Rutgers Business School, Department of Finance and Economics.

Chen, Z., and L. Epstein. (1999). "Ambiguity, Risk and Asset Returns in Continuous Time." Working Paper, Department of Mathematics, Shandong University.

Chen, Z.-W. (1994). "Viable Costs and Equilibrium Prices in Frictional Securities Markets." Working Paper, Graduate School of Business, University of Wisconsin.

Cheng, S. (1991). "On the Feasibility of Arbitrage-Based Option Pricing when Stochastic Bond Price Processes are Involved." *Journal of Economic Theory* 53: 185–198.

Cherian, J., and R. Jarrow. (1998). "Options Markets, Self-Fulfilling Prophecies, and Implied Volatilities." *Review of Derivatives Research* 2: 5–37.

Cherif, T., N. El Karoui, R. Myneni, and R. Viswnathan. (1995). "Arbitrage Pricing and Hedging of Quanto Options and Interest Rate Claims with Quadratic Gaussian State Variables." Working Paper, Laboratoire de Probabilités, Université de Paris, VI.

Chernoff, H., and A. Petkau. (1984). "Numerical Methods for Bayes Sequential Decisions Problems." Working Paper, Technical Report 34, Statistics Center, Massachusetts Institute of Technology.

Chernov, M., and E. Ghysels. (2000). "A Study towards a Unified Approach to the Joint Estimation of Objective and Risk Neutral Measures for the Purpose of Options Valuation." *Journal of Financial Economics* 56: 407–458.

Cherubini, U. (1993). "The Orthogonal Polynomial Approach to Contingent Claim Pricing." Working Paper, Banco Commerciale Italiana, Ufficio Studi, Milan.

Cherubini, U., and M. Esposito. (1992). "Using Pearson's System to Characterize Diffusion Processes: A Note." Working Paper, Banco Commerciale Italiana, Ufficio Studi, Milan.

Cherubini, U., and M. Esposito. (1995). "Options in and on Interest Rate Futures Contracts: Results from Martingale Pricing Theory." *Applied Mathematical Finance* 2: 1–15.

Chesney, M., R. Elliott, and R. Gibson. (1993). "Analytical Solution for the Pricing of American Bond and Yield Options." *Mathematical Finance* 3: 277–294.

Chesney, M., M. Jeanblanc, and M. Yor. (1997). "Brownian Excursions and Barrier Options." *Advances in Applied Probability* 29: 165–184.

Chevance, D. (1995). "Discrétisation des Équations Différentielles Stochastiques Rétrogrades." Working Paper, I.N.R.I.A.

Chevance, D. (1996). "Discretization of Pardoux-Peng's Backward Stochastic Differential Equations." Working Paper, Université de Provence.

Chew, S.-H. (1983). "A Generalization of the Quasilinear Mean with Applications to the Measurement of Income Inequality and Decision Theory Resolving the Allais Paradox." *Econometrica* 51: 1065–1092.

Chew, S.-H. (1989). "Axiomatic Utility Theories with the Betweenness Property." *Annals of Operations Research* 19: 273–298.

Chew, S.-H., and L. Epstein. (1991). "Recursive Utility under Uncertainty." In A. Khan and N. Yannelis (Eds.), *Equilibrium Theory with an Infinite Number of Commodities*, pp. 353–369. New York: Springer-Verlag.

Cheyette, O. (1995). "Markov Representation of the Heath-Jarrow- Morton Model." Working Paper, BARRA Inc., Berkeley, California.

Cheyette, O. (1996). "Implied Prepayments." Working Paper, BARRA Inc., Berkeley, California.

Chiarella, C., and N. E. Hassan. (1997). "Evaluation of Derivative Security Prices in the Heath-Jarrow-Morton Framework as Path Integrals." *Journal of Financial Engineering* 6: 121–147.

Chidambaran, N., and S. Figlewski. (1995). "Streamlining Monte-Carlo Simulation with the Quasi-Analytic Method: An Analysis of a Path-Dependent Option Strategy." *Journal of Derivatives* 3: 29–51.

Choulli, T., L. Krawczyk, and C. Stricker. (1998). "ℰ-Martingales and Their Applications in Mathematical Finance." *Annals of Probability* 26: 853–876.

Chow, Y., and H. Teicher. (1978). *Probability Theory: Independence Interchangeability Martingales.* New York: Springer-Verlag.

Christensen, B. J. (1991). "Statistics for Arbitrage-Free Asset Pricing." Working Paper, Department of Finance, New York University.

Christensen, P. (1987). "An Intuitive Approach to the Harrison and Kreps Concept of Arbitrage Pricing for Continuous Time Diffusions." Working Paper, Department of Management, Odense University, Denmark.

Christensen, P., S. Graversen, and K. Miltersen. (1996). "Dynamic Spanning in the Consumption-Based Capital Asset Pricing Model." Working Paper, Department of Management, Odense University, Denmark.

Chuang, C. (1994). "Joint Distribution of Brownian Motion and Its Maximum, with a Generalization to Correlated BM and Applications to Barrier Options." Working Paper, Department of Statistics, Stanford University.

Chung, K. (1982). *Lectures from Markov Processes to Brownian Motion.* New York: Springer-Verlag.

Chung, K.-L. (1974). *A Course in Probability Theory* (2d ed.). New York: Academic Press.

Chung, K.-L., and R. Williams. (1990). *An Introduction to Stochastic Integration* (2d ed.). Boston: Birkhäuser.

Citanna, A., A. Kajii, and A. Villanacci. (1994). "Constrained Suboptimality in Incomplete Markets: A General Approach and Two Applications." *Economic Theory* 11: 495–521.

Citanna, A., and A. Villanacci. (1993). "On Generic Pareto Improvement in Competitive Economies with Incomplete Asset Structure." Working Paper, Center for Analytic Research in Economics and the Social Sciences, University of Pennsylvania.

Clark, P. (1973). "A Subordinated Stochastic Process with Finite Variance for Speculative Prices." *Econometrica* 41: 135–155.

Clark, S. (1993). "The Valuation Problem in Arbitrage Price Theory." *Journal of Mathematical Economics* 22: 463–478.

Clarke, N., and K. Parrott. (1996). "The Multigrid Solution of Two-Factor American Put Options." Working Paper, Oxford University Computing Laboratory.

Clewlow, L. (1990). "Finite Difference Techniques for One and Two Dimensional Option Valuation Problems." Working Paper, Financial Options Research Center, University of Warwick.

Clewlow, L., and A. Carverhill. (1992). "Efficient Monte Carlo Valuation and Hedging of Contingent Claims." Working Paper, Financial Options Research Centre, University of Warwick.

Clewlow, L., and A. Carverhill. (1995). "A Note on the Efficiency of the Binomial Option Pricing Model." Working Paper, Financial Options Research Center, University of Warwick.

Clewlow, L., and S. Hodges. (1996). "Optimal Delta-Hedging under Transactions Costs." Working Paper, Financial Options Research Center, University of Warwick.

Clewlow, L., K. Pang, and C. Strickland. (1997). "Efficient Pricing of Caps and Swaptions in a Multi-Factor Gaussian Interest Rate Model." Working Paper, University of Warwick.

Clewlow, L., and C. Strickland. (1996). "Monte Carlo Valuation of Interest Rate Derivatives under Stochastic Volatility." *Journal of Fixed Income* 7(3): 35–45.

Cohen, H. (1995). "Isolating the Wild Card Option." *Mathematical Finance* 2: 155–166.

Coleman, T., L. Fisher, and R. Ibbotson. (1992). "Estimating the Term Structure of Interest Rates from Data that include the Prices of Coupon Bonds." *Journal of Fixed Income* 2 (September): 85–116.

Collin-Dufresne, P., and R. Goldstein. (1999). "Do Credit Spreads Reflect Stationary Leverage Ratios? Reconciling Structural and Reduced Form Frameworks." Working Paper, GSIA, Carnegie Mellon.

Constantinides, G. (1982). "Intertemporal Asset Pricing with Heterogeneous Consumers and without Demand Aggregation." *Journal of Business* 55: 253–267.

Constantinides, G. (1986). "Capital Market Equilibrium with Transactions Costs." *Journal of Political Economy* 94: 842–862.

Constantinides, G. (1990). "Habit Formation: A Resolution of the Equity Premium Puzzle." *Journal of Political Economy* 98: 519–543.

Constantinides, G. (1992). "A Theory of the Nominal Term Structure of Interest Rates." *Review of Financial Studies* 5: 531–552.

Constantinides, G. (1993). "Option Pricing Bounds with Transactions Costs." Working Paper, Graduate School of Business, University of Chicago.

Constantinides, G., and D. Duffie. (1996). "Asset Pricing with Heterogeneous Consumers." *Journal of Political Economy* 104: 219–240.

Constantinides, G., and T. Zariphopoulou. (1999). "Bounds on Prices of Contingent Claims in an Intertemporal Economy with Proportional Transaction Costs and General Preferences." *Finance and Stochastics* 3: 345–369.

Cont, R. (1998). "Modeling Term Structure Dynamics: An Infinite Dimensional Approach." Working Paper, Centre de Mathématiques Appliquées, Ecole Polytechnique, Palaiseau, France.

Conze, A., and R. Viswanathan. (1991a). "Path Dependent Options: The Case of Lookback Options." *Journal of Finance* 5: 1893–1907.

Conze, A., and R. Viswanathan. (1991b). "Probability Measures and Numeraires." Working Paper, CEREMADE, Université de Paris.

Cooper, I., and M. Martin. (1996). "Default Risk and Derivative Products." *Applied Mathematical Finance* 3: 53–74.

Cooper, I., and A. Mello. (1991). "The Default Risk of Swaps." *Journal of Finance* XLVI: 597–620.

Cooper, I., and A. Mello. (1992). "Pricing and Optimal Use of Forward Contracts with Default Risk." Working Paper, Department of Finance, London Business School, University of London.

Cornell, B. (1981). "The Consumption Based Asset Pricing Model." *Journal of Financial Economics* 9: 103–108.

Corradi, V. (2000). "Degenerate Continuous Time Limits of GARCH and GARCH-type Processes." *Journal of Econometrics* 96: 145–153.

Courtadon, G. (1982). "The Pricing of Options on Default-Free Bonds." *Journal of Financial and Quantitative Analysis* 17: 75–100.

Cover, T., and E. Ordentlich. (1996). "Universal Portfolios with Side Information." *IEEE Transactions on Information Theory* 42: 348–363.

Cox, J. (1983). "Optimal Consumption and Portfolio Rules when Assets Follow a Diffusion Process." Working Paper, Graduate School of Business, Stanford University.

Cox, J., and C.-F. Huang. (1989). "Optimal Consumption and Portfolio Policies when Asset Prices Follow a Diffusion Process." *Journal of Economic Theory* 49: 33–83.

Cox, J., and C.-F. Huang. (1991). "A Variational Problem Arising in Financial Economics with an Application to a Portfolio Turnpike Theorem." *Journal of Mathematical Economics* 20: 465–488.

Cox, J., and C.-F. Huang. (1992). "A Continuous-Time Portfolio Turnpike Theorem." *Journal of Economic Dynamics and Control* 16: 491–508.

Cox, J., J. Ingersoll, and S. Ross. (1981a). "A Re-examination of Traditional Hypotheses about the Term Structure of Interest Rates." *Journal of Finance* 36: 769–799.

Cox, J., J. Ingersoll, and S. Ross. (1981b). "The Relation between Forward Prices and Futures Prices." *Journal of Financial Economics* 9: 321–346.

Cox, J., J. Ingersoll, and S. Ross. (1985a). "An Intertemporal General Equilibrium Model of Asset Prices." *Econometrica* 53: 363–384.

Cox, J., J. Ingersoll, and S. Ross. (1985b). "A Theory of the Term Structure of Interest Rates." *Econometrica* 53: 385–408.

Cox, J., and S. Ross. (1976). "The Valuation of Options for Alternative Stochastic Processes." *Journal of Financial Economics* 3: 145–166.

Cox, J., S. Ross, and M. Rubinstein. (1979). "Option Pricing: A Simplified Approach." *Journal of Financial Economics* 7: 229–263.

Cox, J., and M. Rubinstein. (1985). *Options Markets*. Englewood Cliffs, NJ: Prentice-Hall.

Cuoco, D. (1997). "Optimal Consumption and Equilibrium Prices with Portfolio Constraints and Stochastic Income." *Journal of Economic Theory* 72: 33–73.

Cuoco, D., and J. Cvitanić. (1998). "Optimal Consumption Choices for a 'Large' Investor." *Journal of Economic Dynamics and Control* 22: 401–436.

Cuoco, D., and H. He. (1992a). "Dynamic Aggregation and Computation of Equilibria in Finite-Dimensional Economies with Incomplete Financial Markets." Working Paper, Haas School of Business, University of California, Berkeley.

Cuoco, D., and H. He. (1992b). "Dynamic Equilibrium in Infinite-Dimensional Economies with Incomplete Financial Markets." Working Paper, Wharton School, University of Pennsylvania.

Cuoco, D., and H. Liu. (2000). "Optimal Consumption of a Divisible Durable Good." *Journal of Economic Dynamics and Control* 24: 561–613.

Cuoco, D., and F. Zapatero. (2000). "On the Recoverability of Preferences and Beliefs in Financial Models." *Review of Financial Studies* 13: 417–431.

Curran, M. (1996). "Adaptive Importance Sampling for Pricing Path Dependent Options." Working Paper, Banque Paribas, London.

Cutland, N., P. Kopp, and W. Willinger. (1991). "A Nonstandard Approach to Option Pricing." *Mathematical Finance* 1: 1–38.

Cutland, N., P. Kopp, and W. Willinger. (1993a). "From Discrete to Continuous Financial Models: New Convergence Results for Options Pricing." *Mathematical Finance* 3: 101–124.

Cutland, N., P. Kopp, and W. Willinger. (1993b). "Stock Price Returns and the Joseph Effect: Fractional Version of the Black-Scholes Model." Working Paper, School of Mathematics, University of Hull, England.

Cvitanić, J. (1995). "Nonlinear Financial Markets: Hedging and Portfolio Optimization." In *Mathematics of Derivative Securities*, pp. 227–254. Cambridge: Cambridge University Press.

Cvitanić, J. (1997). *Optimal Trading under Constraints*. Lecture Notes in Mathematics 1656. New York: Springer-Verlag.

Cvitanić, J. (1999). "Methods of Partial Hedging." *Asia-Pacific Financial Markets* 6: 7–35.

Cvitanić, J., and I. Karatzas. (1992). "Convex Duality in Constrained Portfolio Optimization." *Annals of Applied Probability* 2: 767–818.

Cvitanić, J., and I. Karatzas. (1993). "Hedging Contingent Claims with Constrained Portfolios." *Annals of Applied Probability* 3: 652–681.

Cvitanić, J., and I. Karatzas. (1995). "On Portfolio Optimization under 'Drawdown' Constraints." *IMA Volumes in Mathematics and its Applications* 65: 35–46.

Cvitanić, J., and I. Karatzas. (1996a). "Backward Stochastic Differential Equations with Reflection and Dynkin Games." *Annals of Probability* 24: 2024–2056.

Cvitanić, J., and I. Karatzas. (1996b). "Hedging and Portfolio Optimization under Transaction Costs: A Martingale Approach." *Mathematical Finance* 6: 133–165.

Cvitanić, J., I. Karatzas, and M. Soner. (1998). "Backward Stochastic Differential Equations with Constraints on the Gains-Process." *Annals of Probability* 26: 1522–1551.

Cvitanić, J., and J. Ma. (1996). "Hedging Options for a Large Investor and Forward-Backward SDEs." *Annals of Applied Probability* 6: 370–398.

Cvitanić, J., W. Schachermayer, and H. Wang. (1999). "Utility Maximization in Incomplete Markets with Random Endowment." Working Paper, Department of Mathematics, University of Southern California. Forthcoming in *Finance and Stochastics*.

Daher, C., M. Romano, and G. Zacklad. (1992). "Determination du Prix de Produits Optionnels Obligatoires à Partir d'un Modèle Multi-Facteurs de la Courbe des Taux." Working Paper, Caisse Autonome de Refinancement, Paris.

Dai, Q. (1994). "Implied Green's Function in a No-Arbitrage Markov Model of the Instantaneous Short Rate." Working Paper, Graduate School of Business, Stanford University.

Dai, Q. (1995). "Understanding the Interest Rate Yield Curve Dynamics with the Correlated Three-Factor Vasicek Model." Working Paper, Graduate School of Business, Stanford University.

Dai, Q. (1996). "Technical Notes on CIR Model." Working Paper, Graduate School of Business, Stanford University.

Dai, Q. (2000). "From Equity Premium Puzzle to Expectations Puzzle: A General Equilibrium Production Economy with Stochastic Habit Formation." Working Paper, Stern School, New York University.

Dai, Q., and K. Singleton. (2000). "Specification Analysis of Affine Term Structure Models." *Journal of Finance* 55: 1943–1978.

Daigler, R. (1993). *Financial Futures Markets.* New York: Harper Collins.

Dalang, R., A. Morton, and W. Willinger. (1990)." Equivalent Martingale Measures and No-Arbitrage in Stochastic Securities Market Models." *Stochastics and Stochastic Reports* 29: 185–201.

Daley, D., and D. Vere-Jones. (1988). *An Introduction to the Theory of Point Processes.* New York: Springer-Verlag.

Dana, R., and M. Jeanblanc. (1998). *Marchés Financiers en Temps Continu* (2d ed.). Paris: Economica.

Dana, R.-A. (1993a). "Existence and Uniqueness of Equilibria when Preferences are Additively Separable." *Econometrica* 61: 953–958.

Dana, R.-A. (1993b). "Existence, Uniqueness and Determinacy of Arrow-Debreu Equilibria in Finance Models." *Journal of Mathematical Economics* 22: 563–580.

Dana, R.-A., and C. Le Van. (1996). "Asset Equilibria in L^p Spaces with Complete Markets: A Duality Approach." *Journal of Mathematical Economics* 25: 263–280.

Dana, R.-A., and M. Pontier. (1990). "On the Existence of a Stochastic Equilibrium." Working Paper, Université de Paris VI, Paris.

Danesi, V., J.-P. Garcia, V. Genon-Catalot, and J.-P. Laurent. (1993). "Parameter Estimation for Yield Curve Models using Contrast Methods." Working Paper, Université Marne-La-Valeé, Noisy-Le-Grand, France.

Darling, R. (1995). "Constructing Gamma-Martingales with Prescribed Limit, Using Backward SDE." *Annals of Probability* 3: 431–454.

Das, S. (1993a). "Jump-Diffusion Processes and the Bond Markets." Working Paper, Department of Finance, Harvard Business School.

Das, S. (1993b). "Jump-Hunting Interest Rates." Working Paper, Department of Finance, New York University.

Das, S. (1993c). "Mean Rate Shifts and Alternative Models of the Interest Rate: Theory and Evidence." Working Paper, Department of Finance, New York University.

Das, S. (1995). "Pricing Interest Rate Derivatives with Arbitrary Skewness and Kurtosis: A Simple Approach to Jump-Diffusion Bond Option Pricing." Working Paper, Division of Research, Harvard Business School.

Das, S. (1997). "Discrete-Time Bond and Option Pricing for Jump-Diffusion Processes." *Review of Derivatives Research* 1: 211–243.

Das, S. (1998). "Poisson-Gaussian Processes and the Bond Markets." Working Paper, Department of Finance, Harvard Business School.

Das, S., and S. Foresi. (1996). "Exact Solutions for Bond and Option Prices with Systematic Jump Risk." *Review of Derivatives Research* 1: 7–24.

Das, S., and R. K. Sundaram. (2000). "A Discrete-Time Approach to Arbitrage-Free Pricing of Credit Derivatives." *Management Science* 46: 46–62.

Das, S., and P. Tufano. (1995). "Pricing Credit Sensitive Debt when Interest Rates, Credit Ratings and Credit Spreads are Stochastic." *Journal of Financial Engineering* 5(2): 161–198.

Dash, J. (1989). "Path Integrals and Options—I." Working Paper, Financial Strategies Group, Merrill Lynch Capital Markets, New York.

Dassios, A. (1994). "The Distribution of the Quantiles of a Brownian Motion with Drift and the Pricing of Related Path-Dependent Options." Working Paper, Department of Statistics, London School of Economics.

Davis, M. (1998). "A Note on the Forward Measure." *Finance and Stochastics* 2: 19–28.

Davis, M., and M. Clark. (1993). "Analysis of Financial Models including Transactions Costs." Working Paper, Imperial College, University of London.

Davis, M., and F. Lischka. (1999). "Convertible Bonds with Market Risk and Credit Risk." Working Paper, Tokyo-Mitsubishi International plc.

Davis, M., and V. Lo. (1999). "Infectious Defaults." Working Paper, Tokyo-Mitsubishi International plc.

Davis, M., and V. Lo. (2000). "Modelling Default Correlation in Bond Portfolios." Working Paper, Tokyo-Mitsubishi International plc.

Davis, M., and T. Mavroidis. (1997). "Valuation and Potential Exposure of Default Swaps." Working Paper, Research and Product Development, Tokyo-Mitsubishi International plc.

Davis, M., and A. Norman. (1990). "Portfolio Selection with Transaction Costs." *Mathematics of Operations Research* 15: 676–713.

Davis, M., and V. Panas. (1991). "European Option Pricing with Transaction Costs." Proceedings of the Thirtieth IEEE Conference on Decision and Control, Brighton, December, pp. 1299–1304.

Davis, M., A. Panas, and T. Zariphopoulou. (1993). "European Option Pricing with Transaction Costs." *SIAM Journal of Control and Optimization* 31: 470–493.

Davydov, D., and V. Linetsky. (1998). "Double Step Options." Working Paper, University of Michigan. Forthcoming in *Journal of Computational Finance.*

Davydov, D., and V. Linetsky. (1999a). "Pricing Options on One-Dimensional Diffusions: A Sturm-Liouville Approach." Working Paper, University of Michigan.

Davydov, D., and V. Linetsky. (1999b). "The Valuation and Hedging of Barrier and Lookback Options for Alternative Stochastic Processes." Working Paper, University of Michigan.

Davydov, D., V. Linetsky, and C. Lotz. (1999). "The Hazard-Rate Approach to Pricing Risky Debt: Two Analytically Tractable Examples." Working Paper, Department of Economics, University of Michigan.

Debreu, G. (1953). "Une Economie de l'Incertain." Working Paper, Electricité de France.

Debreu, G. (1954). "Valuation Equilibrium and Pareto Optimum." *Proceedings of the National Academy of Sciences* 40: 588–592.

Debreu, G. (1959). *Theory of Value.* Cowles Foundation Monograph 17. New Haven, CT: Yale University Press.

Debreu, G. (1972). "Smooth Preferences." *Econometrica* 40: 603–615; Corrigendum 44 (1976): 831–832.

Debreu, G. (1982). "Existence of Competitive Equilibrium." In K. Arrow and M. Intriligator (Eds.), *Handbook of Mathematical Economics, Volume II,* pp. 697–743. Amsterdam: North-Holland.

Décamps, J.-P., and A. Faure-Grimaud. (1998). "Pricing the Gamble for Resurrection and the Consequences of Renegotiation and Debt Design." Working Paper, University of Toulouse.

Décamps, J.-P., and A. Faure-Grimaud. (1999). "Should I Stay or Should I Go? Excessive Continuation and Dynamic Agency Costs of Debt." Working Paper, University of Toulouse.

Décamps, J.-P., and P. Koehl. (1994). "Pricing and Hedging Asian Options: A PDE Approach." Working Paper, GREMAQ, Universite des Sciences Sociales.

Décamps, J.-P., and J.-C. Rochet. (1997). "A Variational Approach for Pricing Options and Corporate Bonds." *Economic Theory* 9: 557–569.

Deelstra, G., and F. Delbaen. (1994). "Existence of Solutions of Stochastic Differential Equations Related to the Bessel Process." Working Paper, Department of Mathematics, Vrije Universiteit Brussel.

Deelstra, G., and F. Delbaen. (1995). "Long-Term Returns in Stochastic Interest Rate Models." *Insurance: Mathematics and Economics* 17: 163–169.

Dekel, E. (1989). "Asset Demands without the Independence Axiom." *Econometrica* 57: 163–169.

Delbaen, F. (1992). "Representing Martingale Measures when Asset Prices are Continuous and Bounded." *Mathematical Finance* 2: 107–130.

Delbaen, F. (1993). "Consols in the CIR Model." *Mathematical Finance* 3: 125–134.

Delbaen, F., P. Monat, W. Schachermayer, M. Schweizer, and C. Stricker. (1994). "Inégalités de Normes avec Poids et Fermeture d'un Espace d'Intégrales Stochastiques." *Comtes Rendus de l'Academie de Science de Paris* 319I: 1079–1081.

Delbaen, F., and W. Schachermayer. (1994a). "Arbitrage and Free Lunch with Bounded Risk for Unbounded Continuous Processes." *Mathematical Finance* 4: 343–348.

Delbaen, F., and W. Schachermayer. (1994b). "A General Version of the Fundamental Theorem of Asset Pricing." *Mathematische Annalen* 300: 463–520.

Delbaen, F., and W. Schachermayer. (1995a). "Arbitrage Possibilities in Bessel Processes and Their Relations to Local Martingales." *Probability Theory and Related Fields* 102: 357–366.

Delbaen, F., and W. Schachermayer. (1995b). "The Existence of Absolutely Continuous Local Martingale Measures." *Annals of Applied Probability* 5: 926–945.

Delbaen, F., and W. Schachermayer. (1995c). "The No-Arbitrage Property under a Choice of Numéraire." *Stochastics* 53: 213–226.

Delbaen, F., and W. Schachermayer. (1996a). "Attainable Claims with p'th Moments." *Annales de l' Institut Henri Poincaré* 33: 113–144.

Delbaen, F., and W. Schachermayer. (1996b). "A Compactness Principle for Bounded Sequences of Martingales with Applications." Working Paper, Departement für Mathematik, Eidgenössische Technische Hochschule Zürich.

Delbaen, F., and W. Schachermayer. (1998). "The Fundamental Theorem of Asset Pricing for Unbounded Stochastic Processes." *Mathematische Annalen* 312: 215–250.

Delbaen, F., and W. Schachermayer. (1999). "A General Version of the Fundamental Theorem of Asset Pricing." *Mathematische Annalen* 300: 463–520.

Delbaen, F., and H. Shirakawa. (1996). "A Note on the No Arbitrage Condition for International Financial Markets." *Financial Engineering and the Japanese Markets* 3: 239–251.

Delbaen, F., and M. Yor. (1999). "Passport Options." Working Paper, Presentation at Strobl, Austria.

Delgado, F., and B. Dumas. (1993). "How Far Apart Can Two Riskless Interest Rates Be?" Working Paper, Fuqua School of Business, Duke University.

Demange, G., and J.-C. Rochet. (1992). *Methodes Mathematique de la Finance.* Paris: Economica.

DeMarzo, P. (1988). "An Extension of the Modigliani-Miller Therorem to Stochastic Economics with Incomplete Markets." *Journal of Economic Theory* 45: 353–369.

DeMarzo, P., and B. Eaves. (1996). "A Homotopy, Grassmann Manifold, and Relocalization for Computing Equilibria of GEI." *Journal of Mathematical Economics* 26: 479–497.

de Matos, J. A. (1993). "MSM Estimators of American Option Pricing Models." Working Paper, INSEAD, Fontainebleau, France.

Dempster, M. (1994). "Fast Numerical Valuation of American, Exotic and Complex Options." Working Paper, Finance Research Group, Department of Mathematics and Institute for Studies in Finance, University of Essex.

Dempster, M., and J. Hutton. (1997). "Fast Numerical Valuation of American, Exotic and Complex Options." *Applied Mathematical Finance* 4: 1–20.

DeMunnik, J. (1992). *The Valuation of Interest Rate Derivative Securities.* Amsterdam: Tinbergen Institute.

Dengler, H., and R. Jarrow. (1996). "Option Pricing using a Binomial Model with Random Time Steps." *Review of Derivatives Research* 1: 107–138.

Derman, E., and I. Kani. (1994). "Riding on the Smile." *Risk* 7 (February): 32–39.

Derviz, A. (1996). "Adjoint Equations in Stochastic Optimal Control and Application to Portfolio Optimization with Borrowing Constraints." Working Paper, Institute of Information Theory and Automation, Academy of Sciences of the Czech Republic, Prague.

Detemple, J. (1986). "Asset Pricing in a Production Economy with Incomplete Information." *Journal of Finance* 41: 383–391.

Detemple, J. (1991). "Further Results on Asset Pricing with Incomplete Information." *Journal of Economic Dynamics and Control* 15: 425–454.

Detemple, J. (1995). "Asset Pricing in an Intertemporal Noisy Rational Expectations Equilibrium." Working Paper, Sloan School of Management, Massachusetts Institution of Technology. Forthcoming in *Journal of Mathematical Economics.*

Detemple, J., and S. Murthy. (1994b). "Intertemporal Asset Pricing with Heterogeneous Beliefs." *Journal of Economic Theory* 62: 294–320.

Detemple, J., and S. Murthy. (1997a). "Equilibrium Asset Prices and No-Arbitrage with Portfolio Constraints." *Review of Financial Studies* 10: 1133–1174.

Detemple, J., and S. Murthy. (1997b). "Pricing and Trade of Index Options under Heterogeneous Beliefs." Working Paper, Faculty of Management, McGill University and CIRANO.

Detemple, J., and L. Selden. (1991). "A General Equilibrium Analysis of Option and Stock Market Interactions." *International Economic Review* 32: 279–303.

Detemple, J., and A. Serrat. (1999). Dynamic Equilibrium with Liquidity Constraints." Working Paper, Faculty of Management, McGill University and CIRANO.

Detemple, J., and F. Zapatero. (1991). "Asset Prices in an Exchange Economy with Habit Formation." *Econometrica* 59: 1633–1658.

Detemple, J., and F. Zapatero. (1992). "Optimal Consumption-Portfolio Policies with Habit Formation." *Mathematical Finance* 2: 251–274.

Dewynne, J., and P. Wilmott. (1994). "Exotic Options: Mathematical Models and Computation." Working Paper, Department of Mathematics, Southampton University.

Dezhbakhsh, H. (1994). "Foreign Exchange Forward and Futures Prices: Are They Equal?" *Journal of Financial and Quantitative Analysis* 1: 75–87.

Diament, P. (1993). "Semi-Empirical Smooth Fit to the Treasury Yield Curve." Working Paper, Graduate School of Business, Columbia University.

Diener, F., and M. Diener. (1999). "Asymptotics of the Binomial Formula for Option Pricing." Working Paper, Université de Nice Sophia-Antipolis.

Dijkstra, T. (1996). "On Numeraires and Growth-Optimum Portfolios." Working Paper, Faculty of Economics, University of Groningen.

Dixit, A. (1989). "Entry and Exit Decisions Under Uncertainty." *Journal of Political Economy* 97: 620–638.

Dixit, A., and R. Pindyck. (1994). *Investment Under Uncertainty*. Princeton: Princeton University Press.

Donaldson, J., T. Johnson, and R. Mehra. (1990). "On the Term Structure of Interest Rates." *Journal of Economic Dynamics and Control* 14: 571–596.

Donaldson, J., and R. Mehra. (1984). "Comparative Dynamics of an Equilibrium Intertemporal Asset Pricing Model." *Review of Economic Studies* 51: 491–508.

Dothan, M. (1978). "On the Term Structure of Interest Rates." *Journal of Financial Economics* 7: 229–264.

Dothan, M. (1990). *Prices in Financial Markets*. New York: Oxford University Press.

Dothan, M., and D. Feldman. (1986). "Equilibrium Interest Rates and Multiperiod Bonds in a Partially Observable Economy." *Journal of Finance* 41: 369–382.

Douglas, J., J. Ma, and P. Protter. (1996). "Numerical Methods for Forward-Backward Stochastic Differential Equations." *Annals of Applied Probability* 6: 940–968.

Drèze, J. (1971). "Market Allocation under Uncertainty." *European Economic Review* 15 (Winter): 133–165.

Dritschel, M., and P. Protter. (1998). "Complete Markets with Discontinuous Security Price." Working Paper, Department of Statistics, Purdue University, West Lafayette.

Druskin, V., L. Knizhnerman, T. Tamarchenko, and S. Kostek. (1997). "Krylov Subspace Reduction and Its Extensions for Option Pricing." *Journal of Computational Finance* 1 (Fall).

Duan, J.-C. (1995). "The Garch Option Pricing Model." *Mathematical Finance* 5: 13–32.

Duan, J.-C., and J.-G. Simonato. (1993). "Estimating Exponential-Affine Term Structure Models." Working Paper, Department of Finance, McGill University and CIRANO.

Duffee, G. (1999a). "Estimating the Price of Default Risk." *Review of Financial Studies* 12: 197–226.

Duffee, G. (1999b). "Forecasting Future Interest Rates: Are Affine Models Failures?" Working Paper, Federal Reserve Board.

Duffie, D. (1985). "Predictable Representation of Martingale Spaces and Changes of Probability Measure." In J. Azéma and M. Yor (Eds.), *Séminaire de Probabilités XIX*. Lecture Notes in Mathematics Number 1123, pp. 278–284. Berlin: Springer-Verlag.

Duffie, D. (1986). "Stochastic Equilibria: Existence, Spanning Number, and the 'No Expected Financial Gain from Trade' Hypothesis." *Econometrica* 54: 1161–1184.

Duffie, D. (1987). "Stochastic Equilibria with Incomplete Financial Markets." *Journal of Economic Theory* 41, 405–416; Corrigendum 49 (1989): 384.

Duffie, D. (1988a). "An Extension of the Black-Scholes Model of Security Valuation." *Journal of Economic Theory* 46: 194–204.

Duffie, D. (1988b). *Security Markets: Stochastic Models*. New York: Academic Press.

Duffie, D. (1989). *Futures Markets*. Englewood Cliffs, N.J.: Prentice-Hall.

Duffie, D. (1992). *The Nature of Incomplete Markets*, pp. 214–262. Cambridge: Cambridge University Press.

Duffie, D. (1996). "Special Repo Rates." *Journal of Finance* 51: 493–526.

Duffie, D. (1998a). "Defaultable Term Structures with Fractional Recovery of Par." Working Paper, Graduate School of Business, Stanford University.

Duffie, D. (1998b). "First to Default Valuation." Working Paper, Graduate School of Business, Stanford University.

Duffie, D., and L. Epstein. (1992a). "Asset Pricing with Stochastic Differential Utility." *Review of Financial Studies* 5: 411–436.

Duffie, D., and L. Epstein. (1992b). "Stochastic Differential Utility." *Econometrica* 60: 353–394; Appendix with C. Skiadas.

Duffie, D., W. Fleming, M. Soner, and T. Zariphopoulou. (1997). "Hedging in Incomplete Markets with HARA Utility." *Journal of Economic Dynamics and Control* 21: 753–782.

Duffie, D., and N. Gârleanu. (2001). "Risk and Valuation of Collateralized Debt Valuation." *Financial Analysts Journal*, 57: 41–62.

Duffie, D., and M. Garman. (1991). "Intertemporal Arbitrage and the Markov Valuation of Securities." *Cuadernos economicos de ICE* 49: 37–60.

Duffie, D., J. Geanakoplos, A. Mas-Colell, and A. McLennan. (1994). "Stationary Markov Equilibria." *Econometrica* 62: 745–781.

Duffie, D., P.-Y. Geoffard, and C. Skiadas. (1994). "Efficient and Equilibrium Allocations with Stochastic Differential Utility." *Journal of Mathematical Economics* 23: 133–146.

Duffie, D., and P. Glynn. (1995). "Efficient Monte Carlo Estimation of Security Prices." *Annals of Applied Probability* 5: 897–905.

Duffie, D., and M. Harrison. (1993). "Arbitrage Pricing of Russian Options and Perpetual Lookback Options." *Annals of Applied Probability* 3: 641–651.

Duffie, D., and C.-F. Huang. (1985). "Implementing Arrow-Debreu Equilibria by Continuous Trading of Few Long-Lived Securities." *Econometrica* 53: 1337–1356.

Duffie, D., and C.-F. Huang. (1986). "Multiperiod Security Markets with Differential Information: Martingales and Resolution Times." *Journal of Mathematical Economics* 15: 283–303.

Duffie, D., and M. Huang. (1996). "Swap Rates and Credit Quality." *Journal of Finance* 51: 921–949.

Duffie, D., and M. Jackson. (1990). "Optimal Hedging and Equilibrium in a Dynamic Futures Market." *Journal of Economic Dynamics and Control* 14: 21–33.

Duffie, D., and R. Kan. (1996). "A Yield-Factor Model of Interest Rates." *Mathematical Finance* 6: 379–406; reprinted in *Options Markets*, edited by G. Constantinides and A. Malliaris, London: Edward Elgar, 2000.

Duffie, D., and D. Lando. (1998). "Term Structures of Credit Spreads with Incomplete Accounting Information." Working Paper, Graduate School of Business, Stanford University. Forthcoming in *Econometrica*.

Duffie, D., and P.-L. Lions. (1990). "PDE Solutions of Stochastic Differential Utility." *Journal of Mathematical Economics* 21: 577–606.

Duffie, D., J. Ma, and J. Yong. (1995). "Black's Consol Rate Conjecture." *Annals of Applied Probability* 5: 356–382.

Duffie, D., J. Pan, and K. Singleton. (2000). "Transform Analysis and Asset Pricing for Affine Jump-Diffusions." *Econometrica* 68: 1343–1376.

Duffie, D., L. Pedersen, and K. Singleton. (2000). "Modeling Sovereign Yield Spreads: A Case Study of Russian Debt." Working Paper, Graduate School of Business, Stanford University.

Duffie, D., and P. Protter. (1988). "From Discrete to Continuous Time Finance: Weak Convergence of the Financial Gain Process." *Mathematical Finance* 2: 1–16.

Duffie, D., and H. Richardson. (1991). "Mean-Variance Hedging in Continuous Time." *Annals of Applied Probability* 1: 1–15.

Duffie, D., M. Schroder, and C. Skiadas. (1996). "Recursive Valuation of Defaultable Securities and the Timing of the Resolution of Uncertainty." *Annals of Applied Probability* 6: 1075–1090.

Duffie, D., M. Schroder, and C. Skiadas. (1997). "A Term Structure Model with Preferences for the Timing of Resolution of Uncertainty." *Economic Theory* 9: 3–22.

Duffie, D., and W. Shafer. (1985). "Equilibrium in Incomplete Markets I: A Basic Model of Generic Existence." *Journal of Mathematical Economics* 14: 285–300.

Duffie, D., and W. Shafer. (1986a). "Equilibrium and the Role of the Firm in Incomplete Markets." Working Paper, Graduate School of Business, Stanford University.

Duffie, D., and W. Shafer. (1986b). "Equilibrium in Incomplete Markets II: Generic Existence in Stochastic Economies." *Journal of Mathematical Economics* 15: 199–216.

Duffie, D., and K. Singleton. (1993). "Simulated Moments Estimation of Markov Models of Asset Prices." *Econometrica* 61: 929–952.

Duffie, D., and K. Singleton. (1997). "An Econometric Model of the Term Structure of Interest Rate Swap Yields." *Journal of Finance* 52: 1287–1321; reprinted in *Options Markets*, edited by G. Constantinides and A. Malliaris, London: Edward Elgar, 2001.

Duffie, D., and K. Singleton. (1999). "Modeling Term Structures of Defaultable Bonds." *Review of Financial Studies* 12: 687–720.

Duffie, D., and C. Skiadas. (1994). "Continuous-Time Security Pricing: A Utility Gradient Approach." *Journal of Mathematical Economics* 23: 107–132.

Duffie, D., and R. Stanton. (1988). "Pricing Continuously Resettled Contingent Claims." *Journal of Economic Dynamics and Control* 16: 561–574.

Duffie, D., and T.-S. Sun. (1990). "Transactions Costs and Portfolio Choice in a Discrete-Continuous Time Setting." *Journal of Economic Dynamics and Control* 14: 35–51.

Duffie, D., and W. Zame. (1989)." The Consumption-Based Capital Asset Pricing Model." *Econometrica* 57: 1279–1297.

Duffie, D., and T. Zariphopoulou. (1993). "Optimal Investment with Undiversifiable Income Risk." *Mathematical Finance* 3: 135–148.

Dumas, B. (1989). "Two-Person Dynamic Equilibrium in the Capital Market." *Review of Financial Studies* 2: 157–188.

Dumas, B., and E. Luciano. (1989). "An Exact Solution to a Dynamic Portfolio Choice Problem under Transactions Costs." *Journal of Finance* 46: 577–595.

Dumas, B., R. Uppal, and T. Wang. (2000). "Efficient Intertemporal Allocations with Recursive Utility." *Journal of Economic Theory* 93: 240–259.

Dunn, K., and K. Singleton. (1986). "Modeling the Term Structure of Interest Rates under Nonseparable Utility and Durability of Goods." *Journal of Financial Economics* 17: 27–55.

Dupire, B. (1994b). "Pricing with a Smile." *Risk* January: 18–20.

Durrett, R. (1991). *Probability: Theory and Examples*. Belmont, CA: Wadsworth Publishing Co.

Dybvig, P. (1988). "Bond and Bond Option Pricing Based on the Current Term Structure." Working Paper, School of Business, Washington University, St. Louis.

Dybvig, P. (1989). "Hedging Nontraded Wealth." Working Paper, School of Business, Washington University, St. Louis.

Dybvig, P. (1995). "Duesenberry's Ratcheting of Consumption: Optimal Dynamic Consumption and Investment Given Intolerance for Any Decline in Standard of Living." *Review of Economic Studies* 62: 287–313.

Dybvig, P., and C.-F. Huang. (1988). "Nonnegative Wealth, Absence of Arbitrage, and Feasible Consumption Plans." *Review of Financial Studies* 1: 377–401.

Dybvig, P., J. Ingersoll, and S. Ross. (1996). "Long Forward and Zero-Coupon Rates Can Never Fall." *Journal of Business* 69: 1–25.

Dybvig, P., C. Rogers, and K. Back. (1999). "Portfolio Turnpikes." *Review of Financial Studies* 12: 165–195.

Dynkin, E., and A. Yushkevich. (1979). *Controlled Markov Processes.* Berlin, New York: Springer-Verlag.

Eberlein, E. (1991). "On Modelling Questions in Security Valuation." Working Paper, Institut für Mathematische Stochastik, Universität Freiburg.

Eberlein, E., and J. Jacod. (1997). "On the Range of Option Prices." *Finance and Stochastics* 1: 131–140.

Eberlein, E., and U. Keller. (1995). "Hyperbolic Distributions in Finance." *Bernoulli* 1: 281–299.

Eberlein, E., U. Keller, and K. Prause. (1998). "New Insights into Smile, Mispricing, and Value at Risk: The Hyperbolic Model." *Journal of Business* 71: 371–405.

Eberlein, E., and S. Raible. (1999). "Term Structure Models Driven by General Lévy Processes." *Mathematical Finance* 9: 31–53.

Ederington, L., G. Caton, and C. Campbell. (1997). "To Call or Not to Call Convertible Debt." *Financial Management* 26: 22–31.

Edirisinghe, C., V. Naik, and R. Uppal. (1993). "Optimal Replication of Options with Transactions Costs." *Journal of Financial and Quantitative Analysis* 28: 117–138.

Ekern, S. (1993). "Entry and Exit Decisions with Restricted Reversibility." Working Paper, Norwegian School of Economics, Bergen.

El Karoui, N. (1997). "Backward Stochastic Differential Equations: A General Introduction." In N. El Karoui and L. Mazliak (Eds.), *Backward Stochastic Differential Equations,* pp. 7–26. Essex: Addison Wesley Longman Ltd.

El Karoui, N., A. Frachot, and H. Geman. (1997). "On the Behavior of Long Zero Coupon Rates in a No Arbitrage Framework." *Review of Derivatives Research* 1: 351–369.

El Karoui, N., and H. Geman. (1994). "A Probabilistic Approach to the Valuation of General Floating-Rate Notes with an Application to Interest Rate Swaps." *Advances in Futures and Options Research* 7: 47–63.

El Karoui, N., and S.-J. Huang. (1997). "A General Result of Existence and Uniqueness of Backward Stochastic Differential Equations." In N. El Karoui and L. Mazliak (Eds.), *Backward Stochastic Differential Equations,* pp. 27–36. Essex: Addison Wesley Longman Ltd.

El Karoui, N., and M. Jeanblanc. (1998). "Optimization of Consumption with Labor Income." *Finance and Stochastics* 2: 409–440.

El Karoui, N., M. Jeanblanc, and S. Shreve. (1998). "Robustness of the Black-Scholes Formula." *Mathematical Finance* 8: 93–126.

El Karoui, N., C. Kapoudjian, E. Pardoux, S. Peng, and M. Quenez. (1997). "Reflected Solutions of Backward SDE's, and Related Obstacle Problems for PDE's." *Annals of Probability* 2: 702–737.

El Karoui, N., and V. Lacoste. (1992). "Multifactor Models of the Term Structure of Interest Rates." Working Paper, Laboratoire de Probabilités, Université de Paris VI.

El Karoui, N., C. Lepage, R. Myneni, N. Roseau, and R. Viswanathan. (1991a). "The Pricing and Hedging of Interest Rate Claims: Applications." Working Paper, Laboratoire de Probabilités, Université de Paris VI.

El Karoui, N., C. Lepage, R. Myneni, N. Roseau, and R. Viswanathan. (1991b). "The Valuation and Hedging of Contingent Claims with Gaussian Markov Interest Rates." Working Paper, Laboratoire de Probabilités, Université de Paris VI.

El Karoui, N., R. Myneni, and R. Viswanathan. (1992). "Arbitrage Pricing and Hedging of Interest Rate Claims with State Variables I: Theory." Working Paper, Laboratoire de Probabilités, Université de Paris VI.

El Karoui, N., S. Peng, and M. Quenez. (1997). "Backward Stochastic Differential Equations in Finance." *Mathematical Finance* 1: 1–71.

El Karoui, N., and M. Quenez. (1991). "Programmation Dynamique et Evaluation des Actifs Contingents en Marché Incomplet." *Comtes Rendus de l'Academie de Science de Paris* 313I: 851–854.

El Karoui, N., and M. Quenez. (1995). "Dynamic Programming and Pricing of Contingent Claims in an Incomplete Market." *SIAM Journal of Control and Optimzation* 33: 29–66.

El Karoui, N., and J.-C. Rochet. (1989). "A Pricing Formula for Options on Coupon Bonds." Working Paper, October, Laboratoire de Probabilités, Université de Paris VI.

Elliot, R., and J. Van der Hoek. (1999). "Stochastic Flows and the Forward Measure." Working Paper, Department of Mathematical Sciences, University of Alberta, Canada. Forthcoming, in *Finance and Stochastics.*

Elliott, R., M. Jeanblanc, and M. Yor. (1999). "Some Models on Default Risk." Working Paper, Department of Mathematics, University of Alberta. Forthcoming in *Mathematical Finance.*

Engle, R.(1982). "Autoregressive Conditional Heteroskedasticity with Estimates of the Variance of United Kingdom Inflation." *Econometrica* 50: 987–1008.

Epstein, L. (1988). "Risk Aversion and Asset Prices." *Journal of Monetary Economics* 22: 179–192.

Epstein, L. (1992). "Behavior under Risk: Recent Developments in Theory and Application." In J. Laffont (Ed.), *Advances in Economic Theory*, pp. 1–63. Cambridge: Cambridge University Press.

Epstein, L., and A. Melino. (1995). "A Revealed Preference Analysis of Asset Pricing under Recursive Utility." *Review of Economic Studies* 62: 597–618.

Epstein, L., and T. Wang. (1994). "Intertemporal Asset Pricing under Knightian Uncertainty." *Econometrica* 62: 283–322.

Epstein, L., and S. Zin. (1989). "Substitution, Risk Aversion and the Temporal Behavior of Consumption and Asset Returns I: A Theoretical Framework." *Econometrica* 57: 937–969.

Epstein, L., and S. Zin. (1999). "Substitution, Risk Aversion and the Temporal Behavior of Consumption and Asset Returns: An Empirical Analysis." *Journal of Political Economy* 99: 263–286.

Eraker, B., M. Johannes, and N. Polson. (1999). "Asset Return Dynamics with Jumps, Stochastic Volatility and Jumps to Volatility." Working Paper, Norwegian School of Economics and University of Chicago.

Ericsson, J., and O. Renault. (1999). "Credit and Liquidity Risk." Working Paper, Faculty of Management, McGill University.

Ethier, S., and T. Kurtz. (1986). *Markov Processes: Characterization and Convergence.* New York: Wiley.

Eydeland, A. (1994a). "A Fast Algorithm for Computing Integrals in Function Spaces: Financial Applications." Working Paper, Fuji Capital Markets Corporation, New York.

Eydeland, A. (1994b). "A Spectral Algorithm for Pricing Interest Rate Options." Working Paper, Department of Mathematics, University of Massachusetts.

Fan, H., and S. Sundaresan. (1997). "Debt Valuation, Strategic Debt Service and Optimal Dividend Policy." Working Paper, Columbia University.

Feller, W. (1951). "Two Singular Diffusion Problems." *Annals of Mathematics* 54: 173–182.

Filipović, D. (1999a). "A General Characterization of Affine Term Structure Models." Working Paper, ETH, Zurich. Forthcoming in *Finance and Stochastics.*

Filipović, D. (1999b). "A Note on the Nelson-Siegel Family." *Mathematical Finance* 9: 349–359.

Finger, C. (2000). "A Comparison of Stochastic Default Rate Models." Working Paper, The Risk Metrics Group.

Fisher, E., R. Heinkel, and J. Zechner. (1989). "Dynamic Capital Structure Choice: Theory and Tests." *Journal of Finance* 44: 19–40.

Fisher, M., and C. Gilles. (1996). "The Term Structure of Repo Spreads." Working Paper, Research and Statistics, Board of Governors of the Federal Reserve System.

Fisher, M., and C. Gilles. (1997). "The Equity Premium and the Term Structure of Interest Rates with Recursive Preferences." Working Paper, Research and Statistics, Board of Governors of the Federal Reserve System.

Fisher, M., and C. Gilles. (1998a). "Around and Around: The Expectations Hypothesis." *Journal of Finance* 53: 365–383.

Fisher, M., and C. Gilles. (1998b). "Consumption and Asset Prices with Recursive Preferences." Working Paper, Board of Governors of the Federal Reserve System.

Fisher, M., D. Nychka, and D. Zervos. (1994). "Fitting the Term Structure of Interest Rates with Smoothing Splines." Working Paper, Board of Governors of the Federal Reserve Board, Washington D.C.

Fitzpatrick, B., and W. Fleming. (1991). "Numerical Methods for Optimal Investment— Consumption Models." *Mathematics of Operations Research* 16: 823–841.

Fleming, J., and R. Whaley. (1994). "The Value of Wildcard Options." *Journal of Finance* 1: 215–236.

Fleming, W., S. Grossman, J.-L. Vila, and T. Zariphopoulou. (1989). "Optimal Portfolio Rebalancing with Transaction Costs." Working Paper, Department of Applied Mathematics, Brown University.

Fleming, W., and R. Rishel. (1975). *Deterministic and Stochastic Optimal Control.* Berlin: Springer-Verlag.

Fleming, W., and M. Soner. (1993). *Controlled Markov Processes and Viscosity Solutions.* New York: Springer-Verlag.

Fleming, W., and T. Zariphopoulou. (1991). "An Optimal Investment/Consumption Model with Borrowing Constraints." *Mathematics of Operations Research* 16: 802–822.

Flesaker, B. (1991). "Valuing European Options when the Terminal Value of the Underlying Asset is Unobservable." Working Paper, Department of Finance, University of Illinois at Urbana-Champaign.

Flesaker, B. (1993). "Testing the Heath-Jarrow-Morton/Ho-Lee Model of Interest Rate Contingent Claims Pricing." *Journal of Financial and Quantitative Analysis* 28: 483–495.

Florenzano, M., and P. Gourdel. (1993). "Incomplete Markets in Infinite Horizon: Debt Constraints versus Node Prices." *Mathematical Finance* 6: 167–196.

Florenzano, M., and P. Gourdel. (1994). "T-Period Economies with Incomplete Markets." *Economics Letters* 44: 91–97.

Foldes, L. (1978a). "Martingale Conditions for Optimal Saving—Discrete Time." *Journal of Mathematical Economics* 5: 83–96.

Foldes, L. (1978b). "Optimal Saving and Risk in Continuous Time." *Review of Economic Studies* 45: 39–65.

Foldes, L. (1990). "Conditions for Optimality in the Infinite-Horizon Portfolio-Cum-Saving Problem with Semimartingale Investments." *Stochastics and Stochastics Reports* 29: 133–170.

Foldes, L. (1991a). "Certainty Equivalence in the Continuous-Time Portfolio-Cum-Saving Model." In *Applied Stochastic Analysis*. London: Gordon and Breach.

Foldes, L. (1991b). "Optimal Sure Portfolio Plans." *Mathematical Finance* 1: 15–55.

Foldes, L. (1992). "Existence and Uniqueness of an Optimum in the Infinite-Horizon Portfolio-Cum-Saving Model with Semimartingale Investments." *Stochastic and Stochastic Reports* 41: 241–267.

Foldes, L. (1996). "The Optimal Consumption Function in a Brownian Model of Accumulation, Part A: The Consumption Function as Solution of a Boundary Value Problem." Working Paper, London School of Economics and Political Science.

Föllmer, H. (1981). "Calcul d'Ito Sans Probabilities." In J. Azéma and M. Yor (Eds.), *Séminaire de Probabilités XV*. Lecture Notes in Mathematics, pp. 143–150. Berlin: Springer-Verlag.

Föllmer, H. (1993). "A Microeconomic Approach to Diffusion Models for Stock Prices." *Mathematical Finance* 3: 1–23.

Föllmer, H., and M. Schweizer. (1990). "Hedging of Contingent Claims under Incomplete Information." In M. Davis and R. Elliott (Eds.), *Applied Stochastic Analysis*, pp. 389–414. London: Gordon and Breach.

Föllmer, H., and D. Sondermann. (1986). "Hedging of Non-Redundant Contingent Claims." In W. Hildenbrand and A. Mas-Colell (Eds.), *Contributions to Mathematical Economics*, pp. 205–224. Amsterdam: North-Holland.

Fournié, E. (1993). "Statistiques des Diffusions Ergodiques avec Applications en Finance." Working Paper, Université de Nice-Sophia Antipolis.

Fournié, E., and J.-M. Lasry. (1996). "Some Nonlinear Methods to Study Far-from-the-Money Contingent Claims." Working Paper, Caisse Autonome de Refinancement, Paris.

Fournié, E., J.-M. Lasry., J. Lebuchoux, P.-L. Lions, and N. Touzi. (1999). "Applications of Malliavin Calculus to Monte Carlo Methods in Finance." *Finance and Stochastics* 3: 391–412.

Fournié, E., J.-M. Lasry, and N. Touzi. (1996). "Méthode de Monte Carlo pour les Modéles á Volatilité Stochastique." Working Paper, Caisse Autonome de Refinancement, Paris.

Fournié, E., and D. Talay. (1991). "Application de la Statistique des Diffusions à un Modéle de Taux d'Interet." *Finances* 12: 79–111.

Frachot, A. (1995). "Factor Models of Domestic and Foreign Interest Rates with Stochastic Volatilities." *Mathematical Finance* 5: 167–185.

Frachot, A. (1996). "A Reexamination of the Uncovered Interest Rate Parity Hypothesis." *Journal of International Money and Finance* 15: 419–437.

Frachot, A., D. Janci, and V. Lacoste. (1993). "Factor Analysis of the Term Structure: A Probabilistic Approach." Working Paper, Banque de France, Paris.

Frachot, A., and J.-P. Lesne. (1993a). "Econometrics of Linear Factor Models of Interest Rates." Working Paper, Banque de France, Paris.

Frachot, A., and J.-P. Lesne. (1993b). "Expectations Hypotheses and Stochastic Volatilities." Working Paper, Banque de France, Paris.

Frachot, A., and J.-P. Lesne. (1993c). "Factor Models of Interest Rates with Stochastic Volatilities." Working Paper, Banque de France, Paris.

Freedman, D. (1983). *Markov Chains.* New York: Springer-Verlag.

Freidlin, M. (1985). *Functional Integration and Partial Differential Equations.* Princeton, N.J.: Princeton University Press.

Frey, R. (1996). "The Pricing and Hedging of Options in Finitely Elastic Markets." Working Paper, Department of Statistics, Faculty of Economics, University of Bonn.

Frey, R., and C. Sin. (1997). "Bounds on European Option Prices under Stochastic Volatility." Working Paper, Department Mathematik, ETH Zentrum, Zürich.

Frey, R., and A. Stremme. (1997). "Market Volatility and Feedback Effects from Dynamic Hedging." *Mathematical Finance* 7: 351–374.

Friedman, A. (1964). *Partial Differential Equations of the Parabolic Type.* Englewood Cliffs, N.J.: Prentice-Hall.

Friedman, A. (1975). *Stochastic Differential Equations and Applications, Vol. I.* New York: Academic Press.

Frittelli, M., and P. Lakner. (1995). "Arbitrage and Free Lunch in a General Financial Market Model; The Fundamental Theorem of Asset Pricing." *Mathematical Finance* 5: 237–261.

Fu, M., D. Madan, and T. Wang. (1999). "Pricing Continuous-Time Asian Options: A Comparison of Monte Carlo and Laplace Transform Methods." *Journal of Computational Finance* 2 (Winter): 49–74.

Gabay, D. (1982). "Stochastic Processes in Models of Financial Markets." Proceedings of the IFIP Conference on Control of Distributed Systems, Toulouse. Toulouse, France: Pergamon Press.

Gagnon, J., and J. Taylor. (1990). "Solving Stochastic Equilibrium Models with the Extended Path Method." *Economic Modelling* 7: 251–257.

Galai, D., and M. Schneller. (1978). "Pricing of Warrants and the Value of the Firm." *Journal of Finance* 33: 1333–1342.

Gale, D. (1960). *The Theory of Linear Economic Models.* New York: McGraw-Hill.

Gallant, R., and H. White. (1988). *A Unified Theory of Estimation and Inference for Nonlinear Dynamic Models.* New York: Basil Blackwell.

Gandhi, S., A. Kooros, and G. Salkin. (1993). "An Improved Analytic Approximation for American Option Pricing." Working Paper, Imperial College, University of London.

Gao, B., J.-Z. Huang, and M. Subrahmanyam. (1996). "An Analytical Approach to the Valuation of American Path-Dependent Options." Working Paper, Kenan-Flagler Business School, University of North Carolina. Forthcoming in *Journal of Economic Dynamics and Control.*

Garbade, K. (1996). *Fixed Income Analytics.* Cambridge, MA: MIT Press.

Garman, M. (1985). "Towards a Semigroup Pricing Theory." *Journal of Finance* 40: 847–861.

Gatarek, D., and M. Musiela. (1995). "Pricing of American Receiver Swaptions as Optimal Stopping of an Ornstein-Uhlenbeck Process." Working Paper, School of Mathematics, University of New South Wales, Sydney.

Geanakoplos, J. (1990). "An Introduction to General Equilibrium with Incomplete Asset Markets." *Journal of Mathematical Economics* 19: 1–38.

Geanakoplos, J., and A. Mas-Colell. (1989). "Real Indeterminacy with Financial Assets." *Journal of Economic Theory* 47: 22–38.

Geanakoplos, J., and H. Polemarchakis. (1986). "Existence, Regularity, and Constrained Suboptimality of Competitive Allocations when the Asset Market is Incomplete." In W. Heller and D. Starrett (Eds.), *Essays in Honor of Kenneth J. Arrow*, Volume III, pp. 65–96. Cambridge: Cambridge University Press.

Geanakoplos, J., and W. Shafer. (1990). "Solving Systems of Simultaneous Equations in Economics." *Journal of Mathematical Economics* 19: 69–94.

Geanakoplos, J., and W. Zame. (1999). "Collateral, Default, and Market Crashes." Working Paper, Cowles Foundation Working Paper, Yale University.

Gegout-Petit, A., and E. Pardoux. (1996). "Equations Différentielles Stochastiques Rétrogrades Réfléchies dans un Convexe." *Stochastics and Stochastics Reports* 57: 111–128.

Geman, H., N. El Karoui, and J. Rochet. (1995). "Changes of Numéraire, Changes of Probability Measure and Option Pricing." *Journal of Applied Probability* 32: 443–458.

Geman, H., D. Madan, and M. Yor. (1999). "Time Changes for Lévy Processes. Working Paper, Université Paris IX Dauphine and ESSEC.

Geman, H., and M. Yor. (1993). "Bessel Processes, Asian Options and Perpetuities." *Mathematical Finance* 3: 349–375.

Gennotte, G. (1986). "Continuous-Time Production Economies under Incomplete Information I: A Separation Theorem." *Journal of Finance* 41: 733–746.

Gerber, H., and E. Shiu. (1994). "Option Pricing by Esscher Transforms." *Transactions of the Society of Actuaries* 46: 51–92.

Geske, R. (1977). "The Valuation of Corporate Liabilities as Compound Options." *Journal of Financial Economics* 7: 63–81.

Geske, R. (1979). "The Valuation of Compound Options." *Journal of Financial Economics* 7: 63–81.

Geske, R., and H. Johnson. (1984). "The American Put Option Valued Analytically." *Journal of Finance* 39: 1511–1524.

Ghysels, E. (1986). "Asset Prices in an Economy with Latent Technological Shocks—Econometric Implications of a Discrete Time General Equilibrium Model." Working Paper, Department of Economics and Centre de Recherche et Développement en Économique, Université de Montréal.

Ghysels, E., C. Gourieroux, and J. Jasiak. (1995). "Market Time and Asset Price Movements Theory and Estimation." Working Paper, C.R.D.E., Université de Montreal.

Gibbons, M., and K. Ramaswamy. (1993). "A Test of the Cox-Ingersoll-Ross Model of the Term Structure of Interest Rates." *Review of Financial Studies* 6: 619–658.

Gibbons, M., and T. Sun. (1986). "The Term Structure of Interest Rates: A Simple Exposition of the Cox, Ingersoll, and Ross Model." Working Paper, Graduate School of Business, Stanford University.

Gibson, R., and S. Sundaresan. (1999). "A Model of Sovereign Borrowing and Sovereign Yield Spreads." Working Paper, School of HEC, University of Lausanne.

Gihman, I., and A. Skorohod. (1972). *Stochastic Differential Equations.* Berlin: Springer-Verlag.

Gilles, C., and S. LeRoy. (1991). "On the Arbitrage Pricing Theory." *Economic Theory* 1: 213–230.

Gilles, C., and S. LeRoy. (1992a). "Bubbles and Charges." *International Economic Review* 33: 323–339.

Gilles, C., and S. LeRoy. (1992b). "Stochastic Bubbles in Markov Economies." Working Paper, Board of Governors of The Federal Reserve System, Washington, D.C.

Gilles, C., and S. LeRoy. (1998). "Arbitrage, Martingales, and Bubbles." *Economics Letters* 60: 357–362.

Giovannini, A., and P. Weil. (1989). "Risk Aversion and Intertemporal Substitution in the Capital Asset Pricing Model." Working Paper, National Bureau of Economic Research, Cambridge, Massachusetts.

Girotto, B., and F. Ortu. (1994). "Consumption and Portfolio Policies with Incomplete Markets and Short-Sale Contraints in the Finite-Dimensional Case: Some Remarks." *Mathematical Finance* 4: 69–73.

Girotto, B., and F. Ortu. (1996). "Existence of Equivalent Martingale Measures in Finite Dimensional Securities Markets." *Journal of Economic Theory* 69: 262–277.

Girotto, B., and F. Ortu. (1997a). "Generic Existence and Robust Non-Existence of Numeraires in Finite Dimensional Securities Markets." Working Paper, Dipartimento di Matematica Applicata "B. de Finetti," Universitá di Trieste, Trieste.

Girotto, B., and F. Ortu. (1997b). "Numeraires, Equivalent Martingale Measures and Completeness in Finite Dimensional Securities Markets." *Journal of Mathematical Economics* 27: 283–294.

Glasserman, P., P. Heidelberger, and P. Shahabuddin. (1999). "Asymptotically Optimal Importance Sampling and Stratification for Pricing Path-Dependent Options." *Mathematical Finance* 9: 117–152.

Glasserman, P., and Y. Jin. (1999). "Comparing Stochastic Discount Factors through their Implied Measures." Working Paper, Columbia University.

Glasserman, P., and S. Kou. (1999). "The Term Structure of Simple Forward Rates with Jump Risk." Working Paper, Columbia University.

Glasserman, P., and X. Zhao. (1999). "Fast Greeks by Simulation in Forward LIBOR Models." *Journal of Computational Finance* 3 (Fall): 5–40.

Goldberg, L. (1998). "Volatility of the Short Rate in the Rational Lognormal Model." *Finance and Stochastics* 2: 199–211.

Goldman, B., H. Sosin, and M. Gatto. (1979). "Path Dependent Options: 'Buy at the Low, Sell at the High'." *Journal of Finance* 34: 1111–1127.

Goldstein, R. (1995). "On the Term Structure of Interest Rates in the Presence of Reflecting and Absorbing Boundaries." Working Paper, Walter A. Haas School of Business, University of California at Berkeley.

Goldstein, R. (1997). "Beyond HJM: Fitting the Current Term Structure While Maintaining a Markovian System." Working Paper, Fisher College of Business, The Ohio State University.

Goldstein, R. (2000). "The Term Structure of Interest Rates as a Random Field." *Review of Financial Studies* 13: 365–384.

Goldstein, R., and F. Zapatero. (1996). "General Equilibrium with Constant Relative Risk Aversion and Vasicek Interest Rates." *Mathematical Finance* 6: 331–340.

Goldys, B., and M. Musiela. (1996). "On Partial Differential Equations Related to Term Structure Models." Working Paper, School of Mathematics, University of New South Wales, Sydney.

Goldys, B., M. Musiela, and D. Sondermann. (1994). "Lognormality of Rates and Term Structure Models." Working Paper, School of Mathematics, University of New South Wales.

Goll, T., and J. Kallsen. (1999). "Optimal Portfolios for Logarithmic Utility." Working Paper, University of Freiburg.

Gorman, W. (1953). "Community Preference Fields." *Econometrica* 21: 63–80.

Gottardi, P. (1995). "An Analysis of the Conditions for the Validity of the Modigliani-Miller Theorem with Incomplete Markets." *Economic Theory* 5: 191–208.

Gottardi, P., and T. Hens. (1996). "The Survival Assumption and Existence of Competitive Equilibria when Asset Markets are Incomplete." *Journal of Economic Theory* 71: 313–323.

Gottardi, P., and A. Kajii. (1999). "The Structure of Sunspot Equilibria: The Role of Multiplicity." *Review of Economic Studies* 66: 713–732.

Gourieroux, C., and J. Jasiak. (2000). *Financial Econometrics*. Princeton, N.J.: Princeton University Press.

Gourieroux, C., and J.-P. Laurent. (1994). "Estimation of a Dynamic Hedging." Working Paper, CREST and CEPREMAP, Paris.

Gourieroux, C., J.-P. Laurent, and H. Pham. (1998). "Mean-Variance Hedging and Numeraire." *Mathematical Finance* 3: 179–200.

Gourieroux, C., and O. Scaillet. (1994). "Estimation of the Term Structure from Bond Data." Working Paper, CREST and CEPREMAP, Paris.

Grabbe, J. (1983). "The Pricing of Call and Put Options on Foreign Exchange." *Journal of International Money and Finance* 2: 239–253.

Grandell, J. (1976). *Doubly Stochastic Poisson Processes*. Lecture Notes in Mathematics, Number 529. New York: Springer-Verlag.

Grannan, E., and G. Swindle. (1996). "Minimizing Transaction Costs of Option Hedging Strategies." *Mathematical Finance* 6: 341–364.

Grant, S., A. Kajii, and B. Polak. (2000). "Temporal Resolution of Uncertainty and Recursive Non-Expected Utility Models." *Econometrica* 68: 425–434.

Grauer, F., and R. Litzenberger. (1979). "The Pricing of Commodity Futures Contracts, Nominal Bonds, and Other Risky Assets under Commodity Price Uncertainty." *Journal of Finance* 44: 69–84.

Grinblatt, M. (1994). "An Analytic Solution for Interest Rate Swap Spreads." Working Paper, Anderson Graduate School of Management, University of California, Los Angeles.

Grinblatt, M., and N. Jegadeesh. (1996). "The Relative Pricing of Eurodollar Futures and Forward Contracts." *Journal of Finance* 51: 1499–1522.

Grodal, B., and K. Vind. (1988). "Equilibrium with Arbitrary Market Structure." Working Paper, Department of Economics, University of Copenhagen.

Grosen, A., and P. Jorgensen. (1995). "The Valuation of Interest Rate Guarantees: An Application of American Option Pricing Theory." Working Paper, Department of Banking and Finance, Aarhus School of Business.

Grossman, S., and G. Laroque. (1990). "Asset Pricing and Optimal Portfolio Choice in the Presence of Illiquid Durable Consumption Goods." *Econometrica* 58: 25–51.

Grossman, S., and R. Shiller. (1982). "Consumption Correlatedness and Risk Measurement in Economies with Non-Traded Assets and Heterogeneous Information." *Journal of Financial Economics* 10: 195–210.

Grossman, S., and Z. Zhou. (1996). "Equilibrium Analysis of Portfolio Insurance." *Journal of Finance* 51: 1379–1403.

Gukhal, C. (1995a). "American Call Options on Stocks with Discrete Dividends." Working Paper, Graduate School of Business, Columbia University, New York.

Gukhal, C. (1995b). "The Analytic Valuation of American Options on Jump-Diffusion Processes." Working Paper, Graduate School of Business, Columbia University, New York.

Gul, F., and O. Lantto. (1990). "Betweenness Satisfying Preferences and Dynamic Choice." *Journal of Economic Theory* 52: 162–177.

Guo, D. (1998). "The Risk Premium of Volatility Implicit in Currency Options." *Journal of Business and Economics Statistics* 16: 498–507.

Haan, W. D. (1996). "Heterogeneity, Aggregate Uncertainty, and the Short-Term Interest Rate." *Journal of Business and Economic Statistics* 14: 399–411.

Hahn, F. (1994). "On Economies with Arrow Securities." Working Paper, Department of Economics, Cambridge University.

Hahn, F. (1999). "A Remark on Incomplete Markets Equilibrium." In G. Chichilnisky (Ed.), *Markets, Information and Uncertainty*, pp. 67–71. New York: Cambridge University Press.

Hakansson, N. (1970). "Optimal Investment and Consumption Strategies under Risk for a Class of Utility Functions." *Econometrica* 38: 587–607.

Hakansson, N. (1974). "Convergence to Isoelastic Utility and Policy in Multiperiod Portfolio Choice." *Journal of Financial Economics* 1: 201–224.

Hamza, K., and F. Klebaner. (1995). "A Stochastic Partial Differential Equation for Term Structure of Interest Rates." Working Paper, Department of Statistics, University of Melbourne.

Hansen, A., and P. Jorgensen. (1998). "Exact Analytical Valuation of Bonds when Spot Interest Rates are Log-Normal." Working Paper, Centre for Analytical Finance, University of Aarhus, Aarhus School of Business.

Hansen, L. (1982). "Large Sample Properties of Generalized Method of Moments Estimators." *Econometrica* 50: 1029–1054.

Hansen, L., and R. Jaganathan. (1990). "Implications of Security Market Data for Models of Dynamic Economies." *Journal of Political Economy* 99: 225–262.

Hansen, L., and S. Richard. (1987). "The Role of Conditioning Information in Deducing Testable Restrictions Implied by Dynamic Asset Pricing Models." *Econometrica* 55: 587–614.

Hansen, L., and T. Sargent. (1990). "Recursive Linear Models of Dynamic Economies." Working Paper, Department of Economics, University of Chicago.

Hansen, L., and K. Singleton. (1982). "Generalized Instrumental Variables Estimation of Nonlinear Rational Expectations Models." *Econometrica* 50: 1269–1286.

Hansen, L., and K. Singleton. (1983). "Stochastic Consumption, Risk Aversion, and the Temporal Behavior of Asset Returns." *Journal of Political Economy* 91: 249–265.

Hansen, L., and K. Singleton. (1996). "Efficient Estimation of Linear Asset-Pricing Models with Moving Average Errors." *Journal of Business and Economic Statistics* 14: 53–68.

Hara, C. (1993). "A Role of Redundant Assets in the Presence of Transaction Costs." Working Paper, Sloan School of Management, Massachusetts Institute of Technology.

Hara, C. (1994). "Marginal Rates of Substitution for Uninsurable Risks with Constraint-Efficient Asset Structures." Working Paper, Center for Operations Research and Econometrics, Université Catholique de Louvain.

Harris, M. (1987). *Dynamic Economic Analysis.* New York: Oxford University Press.

Harrison, M. (1985). *Brownian Motion and Stochastic Flow Systems.* New York: Wiley.

Harrison, M., and D. Kreps. (1979). "Martingales and Arbitrage in Multiperiod Securities Markets." *Journal of Economic Theory* 20: 381–408.

Harrison, M., and S. Pliska. (1981). "Martingales and Stochastic Integrals in the Theory of Continuous Trading." *Stochastic Processes and Their Applications* 11: 215–260.

Hart, O. (1975). "On the Optimality of Equilibrium when the Market Structure is Incomplete." *Journal of Economic Theory* 11: 418–430.

Harvey, A., E. Ruiz, and N. Shephard. (1994). "Multivariate Stochastic Variance Models." *Review of Economic Studies* 61: 247–264.

Harvey, A., and N. Shephard. (1993). "The Econometrics of Stochastic Volatility." Working Paper, Department of Statistical and Mathematical Sciences, London School of Economics.

Haug, E. (1999). "Closed Form Valuation of American Barrier Options." Working Paper, Derivatives Research, Tempus Financial Engineering, Norway.

He, H. (1990). "Convergence from Discrete- to Continuous-Time Contingent Claims Prices." *Review of Financial Studies* 3: 523–546.

He, H. (1991). "Optimal Consumption-Portfolio Policies: A Convergence from Discrete to Continuous Time Models." *Journal of Economic Theory* 55: 340–363.

He, H., and C. Huang. (1994). "Consumption-Portfolio Policies: An Inverse Optimal Problem." *Journal of Economic Theory* 62: 294–320.

He, H., and H. Leland. (1993). "On Equilibrium Asset Price Processes." *Review of Financial Studies* 6: 593–617.

He, H., and D. Modest. (1995). "Market Frictions and Consumption-Based Asset Pricing." *Journal of Political Economy* 103: 94–117.

He, H., and H. Pagès. (1993). "Labor Income, Borrowing Constraints, and Equilibrium Asset Prices." *Economic Theory* 3: 663–696.

He, H., and N. Pearson. (1991a). "Consumption and Portfolio Policies with Incomplete Markets: The Finite-Dimensional Case." *Mathematical Finance* 1: 1–10.

He, H., and N. Pearson. (1991b). "Consumption and Portfolio Policies with Incomplete Markets: The Infinite-Dimensional Case." *Journal of Economic Theory* 54: 259–305.

He, H., and A. Takahashi. (1995). "A Variable Separation Technique for Pricing Average-Rate Options." Working Paper, Salomon Brothers Asia Limited, Derivatives Analysis.

Heath, D. (1998). "Some New Term Structure Models." Working Paper, Department of Mathematical Sciences, Carnegie Mellon University.

Heath, D., R. Jarrow, and A. Morton. (1990). "Bond Pricing and the Term Structure of Interest Rates: A Discrete Time Approximation." *Journal of Financial and Quantitative Analysis* 25: 419–440.

Heath, D., R. Jarrow, and A. Morton. (1992a). "Bond Pricing and the Term Structure of Interest Rates: A New Methodology for Contingent Claims Valuation." *Econometrica* 60: 77–106.

Heath, D., R. Jarrow, and A. Morton. (1992b). "Contingent Claim Valuation with a Random Evolution of Interest Rates." Working Paper, Operations Research Department, Cornell University.

Heaton, J. (1993). "The Interaction between Time-Nonseparable Preferences and Time Aggregation." *Econometrica* 61: 353–386.

Heaton, J., and D. Lucas. (1996). "Evaluating the Effects of Incomplete Markets on Risk Sharing and Asset Pricing." *Journal of Political Economy* 104: 668–712.

Hellwig, M. (1996). "Rational Expectations Equilibria in Sequence Economies with Symmetric Information: The Two Period Case." *Journal of Mathematical Economics* 26: 9–49.

Hemler, M. (1990). "The Quality Delivery Option in Treasury Bond Futures Contracts." *Journal of Finance* 45: 1565–1586.

Henrotte, P. (1991). "Transactions Costs and Duplication Strategies." Working Paper, Graduate School of Business, Stanford University.

Henrotte, P. (1994). "Multiperiod Equilibrium with Endogenous Price Uncertainty." Working Paper, Groupe HEC, Département de Finance et Economie, Jouy en Josas, France.

Hens, T. (1991). "Structure of General Equilibrium Models with Incomplete Markets." Working Paper, Department of Economics, University of Bonn.

Hernandez, A., and M. Santos. (1996). "Competitive Equilibria for Infinite-Horizon Economies with Incomplete Markets." *Journal of Economic Theory* 71: 102–130.

Heston, S. (1988a). "Generalized Interest Rate Processes for the Goldman, Sachs, and Company Mortgage Valuation Model." Working Paper, Graduate School of Industrial Administration, Carnegie-Mellon University.

Heston, S. (1988b). "Testing Continuous Time Models of the Term Structure of Interest Rates." Working Paper, Graduate School of Industrial Administration, Carnegie-Mellon University.

Heston, S. (1989). "Discrete Time Versions of Continuous Time Interest Rate Models." Working Paper, Graduate School of Industrial Administration, Carnegie-Mellon University.

Heston, S. (1990). "Sticky Consumption, Optimal Investment, and Equilibrium Asset Prices." Working Paper, School of Organization and Management, Yale University.

Heston, S. (1993). "A Closed-Form Solution for Options with Stochastic Volatility with Applications to Bond and Currency Options." *Review of Financial Studies* 6: 327–344.

Heston, S. (1997). "Option Pricing with Infinitely Divisible Distributions." Working Paper, John M. Olin School of Business, Washington University, St. Louis.

Heston, S., and S. Nandi. (1997). "A Closed-Form GARCH Option Pricing Model." Working Paper, Federal Reserve Bank of Atlanta.

Heston, S., and G. Zhou. (1997). "On Rate of Convergence of Discrete Time Contingent Claims." Working Paper, Washington University, St. Louis.

Heynen, R., and H. Kat. (1993). "Volatility Prediction: A Comparison of the Stochastic Volatility, GARCH(1,1) and EGARCH(1,1) Models." Working Paper, Department of Operations Research, Erasmus University, Rotterdam.

Heynen, R., A. Kemna, and T. Vorst. (1994). "Analysis of the Term Structure of Implied Volatilities." *Journal of Financial and Quantitative Analysis* 1: 31–57.

Hildenbrand, W., and P. Kirman. (1989). *Introduction to Equilibrium Analysis* (2nd ed.). Amsterdam: North-Holland Elsevier.

Hindy, A., (1995). "Viable Prices in Financial Markets with Solvency Constraints." *Journal of Mathematical Economics* 24: 105–136.

Hindy, A., and C.-F. Huang. (1992). "Intertemporal Preferences for Uncertain Consumption: A Continuous Time Approach." *Econometrica* 60: 781–802.

Hindy, A., and C.-F. Huang. (1993). "Optimal Consumption and Portfolio Rules with Local Substitution." *Econometrica* 61: 85–122.

Hindy, A., C.-F. Huang, and D. Kreps. (1992). "On Intertemporal Preferences in Continuous Time: The Case of Certainty." *Journal of Mathematical Economics* 21: 401–440.

Hindy, A., C.-F. Huang, and H. Zhu. (1993). "Numerical Analysis of a Free Boundary Singular Control Problem in Financial Economics." Working Paper, Graduate School of Business, Stanford University.

Hindy, A., C.-F. Huang, and H. Zhu. (1997). "Optimal Consumption and Portfolio Rules with Durability and Habit Formation." *Journal of Economic Dynamics and Control* 21: 525–550.

Hindy, A., and M. Huang. (1993b). "Asset Pricing with Linear Collateral Constraints." Working Paper, Graduate School of Business, Stanford University.

Hirsch, M., M. Magill, and A. Mas-Colell. (1990). "A Geometric Approach to a Class of Equilibrium Existence Theorems." *Journal of Mathematical Economics* 19: 95–106.

Ho, T., and S. Lee. (1986). "Term Structure Movements and Pricing Interest Rate Contingent Claims." *Journal of Finance* 41: 1011–1029.

Hobson, D. (1998). "Bounds on the Lookback." *Finance and Stochastics* 98: 250–263.

Hobson, D., and C. Rogers. (1993). "Models of Endogenous Stochastic Volatility." Working Paper, Judge Institute of Management Studies, Cambridge University.

Hobson, D., and L. Rogers. (1998). "Complete Models with Stochastic Volatility." *Mathematical Finance* 8: 27–48.

Hodges, S., and A. Carverhill. (1992). "The Characterization of Economic Equilibria which Support Black-Scholes Options Pricing." Working Paper, Financial Options Research Centre, University of Warwick.

Hodges, S., and M. Selby. (1996). "The Risk Premium in Trading Equilibria Which Support Black-Scholes Option Pricing." In M. A. H. Dempster and S. R. Pliska (Eds.), *Mathematics of Derivative Securities*, pp. 41–52. Cambridge: Cambridge University Press.

Hofmann, N., E. Platen, and M. Schweizer. (1992). "Option Pricing Under Incompleteness and Stochastic Volatility." *Mathematical Finance* 2: 153–187.

Hogan, M. (1993a). "The Lognormal Interest Rate Model and Eurodollar Futures." Working Paper, Citibank, New York.

Hogan, M. (1993b). "Problems in Certain Two-Factor Term Structure Models." *Annals of Applied Probability* 3: 576–581.

Honda, T. (1992). "Equilibrium in Incomplete Real Asset Markets with Dispersed Forecast Functions." Working Paper, Engineering-Economic Systems Department, Stanford University.

Honda, T. (1996). "On the Consumption/Investment Problem with Stochastic 'Regime Switching' Parameters." Working Paper, Engineering-Economic Systems Department, Stanford University.

Honda, T. (1997a). "Equilibrium Asset Pricing with Unobservable Regime-Switching Mean Earnings Growth." Working Paper, Department of Engineering-Economic Systems and Operations Research, Stanford University.

Honda, T. (1997b). "Optimal Portfolio Choice and Equilibrium Valuation with Regime-Switching Mean Returns." Working Paper, Department of Engineering-Economic Systems and Operations Research, Stanford University.

Honda, T. (1997c). "Optimal Portfolio Choice for Unobservable and Regime-Switching Mean Returns." Working Paper, Department of Engineering-Economic Systems and Operations Research, Stanford University.

Hong, C., and L. Epstein. (1989). "Non-Expected Utility Preferences in a Temporal Framework with an Application to Consumption-Savings Behavior." *Journal of Economic Theory* 50: 54–81.

Howe, M., and B. Rustem. (1994a). "Minimax Hedging Strategy." Working Paper, Financial Options Research Centre, University of Warwick.

Howe, M., and B. Rustem. (1994b). "Multi-Period Minimax Hedging Strategies." Working Paper, Financial Options Research Centre, University of Warwick.

Huang, C.-F. (1985a). "Discussion on 'Towards a Semigroup Pricing Theory'." *Proceedings of the Journal of Finance* 40: 861–862.

Huang, C.-F. (1985b). "Information Structures and Equilibrium Asset Prices." *Journal of Economic Theory* 31: 33–71.

Huang, C.-F. (1985c). "Information Structures and Viable Price Systems." *Journal of Mathematical Economics* 14: 215–240.

Huang, C.-F. (1987). "An Intertemporal General Equilibrium Asset Pricing Model: The Case of Diffusion Information." *Econometrica* 55: 117–142.

Huang, C.-F., and R. Litzenberger. (1988). *Foundations for Financial Economics.* Amsterdam: North-Holland.

Huang, C.-F., and H. Pagès. (1992). "Optimal Consumption and Portfolio Policies with an Infinite Horizon: Existence and Convergence." *Annals of Applied Probability* 2: 36–64.

Huang, C.-F., and T. Zariphopoulou. (1999). "Turnpike Behavior of Long-Term Investments." *Finance and Stochastics* 3: 15–34.

Huang, J., M. Subrahmanyam, and R. Sundaram. (1999). "Costly Financing, Optimal Payout Policies and the Valuation of Corporate Debt." Working Paper, Department of Finance, Smeal School of Business, Penn State University.

Huang, J., M. Subrahmanyam, and G. Yu. (1996). "Pricing and Hedging American Options: A Recursive Integration Method." *Review of Financial Studies* 9: 277–300.

Huang, M. (1999). "Liquidity Shocks and Equilibrium Liquidity Premia." Working Paper, Graduate School of Business, Stanford University.

Huang, P., and H. Wu. (1994). "Competitive Equilibrium of Incomplete Markets for Securities with Smooth Payoffs." *Journal of Mathematical Economics* 23: 219–234.

Hubalek, F., and W. Schachermayer. (1998). "When Does Convergence of Asset Price Processes Imply Convergence of Option Prices?" *Mathematical Finance* 8: 215–233.

Huge, B., and D. Lando. (1999). "Swap Pricing with Two-Sided Default Risk in a Rating-Based Model." *European Finance Review* 3: 239–268.

Hull, J., (2000). *Options, Futures, and Other Derivative Securities* (4th ed.). Englewood Cliffs, NJ: Prentice-Hall.

Hull, J., and A. White. (1987). "The Pricing of Options on Assets with Stochastic Volatilities." *Journal of Finance* 2: 281–300.

Hull, J., and A. White. (1990a). "Pricing Interest Rate Derivative Securities." *Review of Financial Studies* 3: 573–592.

Hull, J., and A. White. (1990b). "Valuing Derivative Securities using the Explicit Finite Difference Method." *Journal of Financial and Quantitative Analysis* 25: 87–100.

Hull, J., and A. White. (1992). "The Price of Default." *Risk* 5: 101–103.

Hull, J., and A. White. (1993). "One-Factor Interest-Rate Models and the Valuation of Interest-Rate Derivative Securities." *Journal of Financial and Quantitative Analysis* 28: 235–254.

Hull, J., and A. White. (1994). "Numerical Procedures for Implementing Term Structure Models." *Journal of Derivatives* 7 (Fall): 7–16; (Winter): 37–48.

Hull, J., and A. White. (1995). "The Impact of Default Risk on the Prices of Options and Other Derivative Securities." *Journal of Banking and Finance* 19: 299–322.

Husseini, S., J.-M. Lasry, and M. Magill. (1990). "Existence of Equilibrium with Incomplete Markets." *Journal of Mathematical Economics* 19: 39–68.

Ibanez, A., and F. Zapatero. (1999). "Monte Carlo Valuation of American Options through Computation of the Optimal Exercise Frontier." Working Paper, Departamento de Administracion, ITAM, Mexico.

Ikeda, N., and S. Watanabe. (1981). *Stochastic Differential Equations and Diffusion Processes.* Amsterdam: North-Holland.

Imkeller, P., M. Pontier, and F. Weisz. (1999). "Free Lunch and Arbitrage Possibilities in a Financial Market Model with an Insider." Working Paper, Institute for Mathematics, Humboldt-University of Berlin.

Ingersoll, J. (1977). "An Examination of Corporate Call Policies on Convertible Securities." *Journal of Finance* 32: 463–478.

Ingersoll, J. (1987). *Theory of Financial Decision Making.* Totowa, N.J.: Rowman and Littlefield.

Ingersoll, J. (1992). "Optimal Consumption and Portfolio Rules with Intertemporally Dependent Utility of Consumption." *Journal of Economic Dynamics and Control* 16: 681–712.

Iyengar, G., and T. Cover. (1997). "Analysis of Growth-Rate in the Presence of Transaction Costs." Working Paper, Information Systems Laboratory, Stanford University.

Jacka, S. (1984). "Optimal Consumption of an Investment." *Stochastics* 13: 45–60.

Jacka, S. (1991). "Optimal Stopping and the American Put." *Mathematical Finance* 1: 1–14.

Jackwerth, J. (1997). "Generalized Binomial Trees." *Journal of Derivatives* 5 (2): 7–17.

Jackwerth, J., and M. Rubinstei. (1996a). "Implied Binomial Trees: Generalizations and Empirical Tests." Working Paper, Haas School of Business, University of California, Berkeley.

Jackwerth, J., and M. Rubinstein. (1996b). "Recovering Probability Distributions from Options Prices." *Journal of Finance* 51: 1611–1631.

Jackwerth, J., and M. Rubinstein. (1996c). "Recovering Stochastic Processes from Option Prices." Working Paper, Haas School of Business, University of California, Berkeley.

Jackwerth, J. C. (2000). "Recovering Risk Aversion from Options Prices and Realized Returns." *Review of Financial Studies* 13: 433–452.

Jacod, J., and P. Protter. (2000). *Probability Essentials.* New York: Springer-Verlag.

Jacod, J., and A. Shiryaev. (1987). *Limit Theorems for Stochastic Processes.* New York: Springer-Verlag.

Jacod, J., and A. Shiryaev. (1998). "Local Martingales and the Fundamental Asset Pricing Theorems in the Discrete-Time Case." *Finance and Stochastics* 2: 259–274.

Jaillet, P., D. Lamberton, and B. Lapeyre. (1988). "Inéquations Variationelles et Théorie des Options." *Comtes Rendus de l'Academie de Sciences de Paris* 307I: 961–965.

Jaillet, P., D. Lamberton, and B. Lapeyre. (1990). "Variational Inequalities and the Pricing of American Options." Working Paper, CERMA-ENPC, La Courtine, France.

Jakobsen, S. (1992). "Prepayment and the Valuation of Danish Mortgage-Backed Bonds." Working Paper, Ph.D. dissertation, Aarhaus School of Business, Denmark.

Jamshidian, F. (1989a). "Closed-Form Solution for American Options on Coupon Bonds in the General Gaussian Interest Rate Model." Working Paper, Financial Strategies Group, Merrill Lynch Capital Markets, New York.

Jamshidian, F. (1989b). "An Exact Bond Option Formula." *Journal of Finance* 44: 205–209.

Jamshidian, F. (1989c). "Free Boundary Formulas for American Options." Working Paper, Financial Strategies Group, Merrill Lynch Capital Markets, New York.

Jamshidian, F. (1989d). "The Multifactor Gaussian Interest Rate Model and Implementation." Working Paper, Financial Strategies Group, Merrill Lynch Capital Markets, New York.

Jamshidian, F. (1991a). "Bond and Option Evaluation in the Gaussian Interest Rate Model." *Research in Finance* 9: 131–170.

Jamshidian, F. (1991b). "Commodity Option Evaluation in the Gaussian Futures Term Structure Model." *Review of Futures Markets* 10: 324–346.

Jamshidian, F. (1991c). "Forward Induction and Construction of Yield Curve Diffusion Models." *Journal of Fixed Income* June: 62–74.

Jamshidian, F. (1993a). "Hedging and Evaluating Diff Swaps." Working Paper, Fuji International Finance PLC, London.

Jamshidian, F. (1993b). "Options and Futures Evaluation with Deterministic Volatilities." *Mathematical Finance* 3: 149–159.

Jamshidian, F. (1994). "Hedging Quantos, Differential Swaps and Ratios." *Applied Mathematical Finance* 1: 1–20.

Jamshidian, F. (1995). "A Simple Class of Square-Root Interest Rate Models." *Applied Mathematical Finance* 2: 61–72.

Jamshidian, F. (1996a). "Bond, Futures and Option Evaluation in the Quadratic Interest Rate Model." *Applied Mathematical Finance* 3: 93–115.

Jamshidian, F. (1996b). "Libor and Swap Market Models and Measures II." Working Paper, Sakura Global Capital, London.

Jamshidian, F. (1997a). "A Note on Analytical Valuation of Double Barrier Options." Working Paper, Sakura Global Capital.

Jamshidian, F. (1997b). "Pricing and Hedging European Swaptions with Deterministic (Lognormal) Forward Swap Volatility." *Finance and Stochastics* 1: 293–330.

Jamshidian, F. (1999). "Libor Market Model with Semimartingales." Working Paper, NetAnalytic Limited.

Jamshidian, F., and M. Fein. (1990). "Closed Form Solutions for Oil Futures and European Options in the Gibson-Schwartz Model: A Comment." Working Paper, Financial Strategies Group, Merrill Lynch Capital Markets, New York.

Jarrow, R. (1988). *Finance Theory*. Englewood Cliffs, N.J.: Prentice-Hall.

Jarrow, R., D. Lando, and S. Turnbull. (1997). "A Markov Model for the Term Structure of Credit Risk Spreads." *Review of Financial Studies* 10: 481–523.

Jarrow, R., D. Lando, and F. Yu. (1999). "Diversification and Default Risk: An Equivalence Theorem for Martingale and Empirical Default Intensities." Working Paper, Cornell University.

Jarrow, R., and D. Madan. (1991). "A Characterization of Complete Security Markets on a Brownian Filtration." *Mathematical Finance* 1: 31–44.

Jarrow, R. and D. Madan. (1999). "Hedging Contingent Claims on Semimartingales." *Finance and Stochastics* 3: 111–134.

Jarrow, R., and A. Rudd. (1983). *Option Pricing*. Homewood, Ill.: Richard D. Irwin.

Jarrow, R. and S. Turnbull. (1994). "Delta, Gamma and Bucket Hedging of Interest Rate Derivatives." *Applied Mathematical Finance* 1: 21–48.

Jarrow, R. and S. Turnbull. (1995). "Pricing Derivatives on Financial Securities Subject to Credit Risk." *Journal of Finance* 50: 53–85.

Jarrow, R. and S. Turnbull. (1997a). "An Integrated Approach to the Hedging and Pricing of Eurodollar Derivatives." *Journal of Risk and Insurance* 64: 271–299.

Jarrow, R., and S. Turnbull. (1997b). "When Swaps are Dropped." *Risk* 10 (May): 70–75.

Jarrow, R., and S. Turnbull (1999). *Derivative Securities* (2d ed.). Cincinnati: South-Western.

Jarrow, R., and F. Yu. (1999). "Counterparty Risk and the Pricing of Defaultable Securities." Working Paper, Cornell University.

Jaschke, S. (1996). "Arbitrage Bounds for the Term Structure of Interest Rates." *Finance and Stochastics* 2: 29–40.

Jaschke, S. (1997). "Super-Hedging and Arbitrage Pricing of Bonds and Interest Rate Derivatives." Working Paper, Institut für Mathematik, Humboldt-Universitat zu Berlin.

Jeanblanc, M., and M. Pontier. (1990). "Optimal Portfolio for a Small Investor in a Market Model with Discontinuous Prices." *Applied Mathematics and Optimization* 22: 287–310.

Jeanblanc, M., and M. Rutkowski. (1999). "Modelling of Default Risk: An Overview." Working Paper, University of Evry Val of Essonne and Technical University of Warsaw.

Jeffrey, A. (1995a). "A Class of Non-Markovian Single Factor Heath-Jarrow-Morton Term Structure Models." Working Paper, School of Banking and Finance, University of New South Wales, Sydney.

Jeffrey, A. (1995b). "An Empirical Test of Single Factor Heath-Jarrow-Morton Term Structure Models." Working Paper, School of Banking and Finance, University of New South Wales, Sydney.

Jeffrey, A. (1995c). "Single Factor Heath-Jarrow-Morton Term Structure Models Based on Markov Spot Interest Rate." *Journal of Financial and Quantitative Analysis* 30: 619–643.

Jegadeesh, N. (1993). "An Empirical Analysis of the Pricing of Interest Rate Caps." Working Paper, College of Commerce and Business Administration, University of Illinois at Urbana-Champaign.

Jin, Y., and P. Glasserman. (1998). "Equilibrium Positive Interest Rates: A Unified View." Working Paper, Columbia Business School, New York.

Johnson, B. (1994). "Dynamic Asset Pricing Theory: The Search for Implementable Results." Working Paper, Engineering-Economic Systems Department, Stanford University.

Johnson, H. (1987). "Options on the Maximum or the Minimum of Several Assets." *Journal of Financial and Quantitative Analysis* 22: 277–283.

Johnson, H., and D. Shanno. (1987). "The Pricing of Options when the Variance is Changing." *Journal of Financial and Quantitative Analysis* 22: 143–151.

Jones, R., and R. Jacobs. (1986). "History Dependent Financial Claims: Monte Carlo Valuation." Working Paper, Department of Finance, Simon Fraser University, Vancouver, Canada.

Jong, F.D. and P. Santa-Clara.(1999). "The Dynamics of the Forward Interest Rate Curve: A Formulation with State Variables." *Journal of Financial and Quantitative Analysis* 34: 131–157.

Jordan, B. (1995). "On the Relative Yields of Taxable and Municipal Bonds: A Theory of the Tax Structure of Interest Rates." Working Paper, Department of Finance, College of Business and Public Administration, University of Missouri-Columbia.

Jorgensen, P. (1994). "American Option Pricing." Working Paper, School of Business, Institute of Management, University of Aarhaus, Denmark.

Jorgensen, P. (1996). "American Bond Option Pricing in One-Factor Spot Interest Rate Models." *Review of Derivatives Research* 1: 245–267.

Jorion, P. (1988). "On Jump Processes in the Foreign Exchange and Stock Markets." *Review of Financial Studies* 1: 427–445.

Jouini, E., and H. Kallal. (1993a). "Efficient Trading Strategies in the Presence of Market Frictions." Working Paper, CREST-ENSAE, Paris.

Jouini, E., and H. Kallal. (1993b). "Portfolio Choice and Market Frictions." Working Paper, ENSAE, and Laboratoire d'Econométrie de l'Ecole Polytechnique, Paris, France.

Jouini, E., and H. Kallal. (1995). "Martingales, Arbitrage, and Equilibrium in Security Markets with Transactions Costs." *Journal of Economic Theory* 66: 178–197.

Jouini, E., P. Koehl, and N. Touzi. (1995). "Incomplete Markets, Transaction Costs and Liquidity Effects." Working Paper, Crest-Ensae, Université de Paris I.

Joy, C., P. Boyle, and K. Tan. (1996). "Quasi-Monte Carlo Methods in Numerical Finance." *Management Science* 42: 926–938.

Ju, N. (1997a). "Fourier Transformation, Martingale, and the Pricing of Average-Rate Derivatives." Working Paper, Haas School of Business, University of California at Berkeley.

Ju, N. (1997b). "Pricing American Perpetual Lookback Options." Working Paper, Haas School of Business, University of California at Berkeley.

Judd, K. (1989). "Minimum Weighted Residual Methods for Solving Dynamic Economic Models." Working Paper, Hoover Institution, Stanford University.

Judd, K. (1997). "Incomplete Asset Markets with Heterogenous Tastes and Idiosyncratic Income." Working Paper, Hoover Institution, Stanford University.

Judd, K., F. Kubler, and K. Schmedders. (1997). "Computing Equilibria in Infinite Horizon Finance Economies—The Case of One Asset." Working Paper, Hoover Institution, Stanford University.

Kabanov, Y. (1996). "On the FTAP of Kreps-Delbaen-Schachermayer." Working Paper, Laboratoire de Mathématiques, Université de Franche-Comté.

Kabanov, Y., and D. Kramkov. (1994). "Non-Arbitrage and Equivalent Martingale Measures: A New Proof of the Harrison-Pliska Theorem." *Theory of Probability and its Applications* 39: 523–527.

Kabanov, Y., and D. Kramkov. (1995). "Large Financial Markets: Asymptotic Arbitrage and Contiguity." *Theory of Probability and its Applications* 39: 182–187.

Kabanov, Y., and C. Stricker. (2000). "A Teacher's Note in No-Arbitrage Criteria." Working Paper, Laboratoire de Mathématiques, Université de Franche-Comté.

Kajii, A. (1994). "Anonymity and Optimality of Competitive Equilibrium when Markets are Incomplete." *Journal of Economic Theory* 64: 115–129.

Kakutani, S. (1941). "A Generalization of Brouwer's Fixed-Point Theorem." *Duke Mathematical Journal* 8: 451–459.

Kan, R. (1993). "Gradient of the Representative Agent Utility When Agents Have Stochastic Recursive Preferences." Working Paper, Graduate School of Business, Stanford University.

Kan, R. (1995). "Structure of Pareto Optima when Agents Have Stochastic Recursive Preferences." *Journal of Economic Theory* 66: 626–631.

Kandori, M. (1988). "Equivalent Equilibria." *International Economic Review* 29: 401–417.

Karatzas, I. (1988). "On the Pricing of American Options." *Applied Mathematics and Optimization* 17: 37–60.

Karatzas, I. (1989). "Optimization Problems in the Theory of Continuous Trading." *SIAM Journal of Control and Optimization* 27: 1221–1259.

Karatzas, I. (1991). "A Note on Utility Maximization under Partial Observations." *Mathematical Finance* 1: 57–70.

Karatzas, I. (1993). "IMA Tutorial Lectures 1–3: Minneapolis." Working Paper, Department of Statistics, Columbia University.

Karatzas, I. (1997). *Lectures on the Mathematics of Finance*. Providence: American Mathematical Society.

Karatzas, I., and S.-G. Kou. (1998). "Hedging American Contingent Claims with Constrained Portfolios." *Finance and Stochastics* 2: 215–258.

Karatzas, I., P. Lakner, J. Lehoczky, and S. Shreve. (1991). "Equilibrium in a Simplified Dynamic, Stochastic Economy with Heterogeneous Agents." In E. Meyer-Wolf, A. Schwartz, and O. Zeitouni (Eds.), *Stochastic Analysis: Liber Amicorum for Moshe Zakai*, pp. 245–272. New York: Academic Press.

Karatzas, I., J. Lehoczky, S. Sethi, and S. Shreve. (1986). "Explicit Solution of a General Consumption/Investment Problem." *Mathematics of Operations Research* 11: 261–294.

Karatzas, I., J. Lehoczky, and S. Shreve. (1987). "Optimal Portfolio and Consumption Decisions for a 'Small Investor' on a Finite Horizon." *SIAM Journal of Control and Optimization* 25: 1157–1186.

Karatzas, I., J. Lehoczky, and S. Shreve. (1990). "Existence and Uniqueness of Multi-Agent Equilibrium in a Stochastic Dynamic Consumption/Investment Model." *Mathematics of Operations Research* 15: 80–128.

Karatzas, I., J. Lehoczky, and S. Shreve. (1991). "Equilibrium Models with Singular Asset Prices." *Mathematical Finance* 1: 11–30.

Karatzas, I., J. Lehoczky, S. Shreve, and G.-L. Xu. (1991). "Martingale and Duality Methods for Utility Maximization in Incomplete Markets." *SIAM Journal of Control and Optimization* 29: 702–730.

Karatzas, I., and S. Shreve. (1988). *Brownian Motion and Stochastic Calculus.* New York: Springer-Verlag.

Karatzas, I., and S. Shreve. (1998). *Methods of Mathematical Finance.* New York: Springer-Verlag.

Karatzas, I., and X.-X. Xue. (1990). "Utility Maximization in a Financial Market with Partial Observations." Working Paper, Department of Mathematics, Rutgers University.

Karr, A. (1991). *Point Processes and Their Statistical Inference,* (2d ed.). New York: Marcel Dekker, Inc.

Kat, H. (1993). "Hedging Lookback and Asian Options." Working Paper, Derivatives Department, MeesPierson N.V., Amsterdam.

Kawazu, K., and S. Watanabe. (1971). "Branching Processes with Immigration and Related Limit Theorems." *Theory of Probability and its Applications* 16: 36–54.

Kehoe, T., and D. K. Levine. (1993). "Debt-Constrained Asset Markets." *Review of Economic Studies* 60: 865–888.

Kennedy, D. (1994). "The Term Structure of Interest Rates as a Gaussian Random Field." *Mathematical Finance* 4: 247–258.

Kifer, Y. (2000). "Game Options." *Finance and Stochastics* 4: 443–463.

Kijima, M. (1998). "Monotonicities in a Markov Chain Model for Valuing Corporate Bonds Subject to Credit Risk." *Mathematical Finance* 8: 229–247.

Kijima, M., and K. Komoribayashi. (1998). "A Markov Chain Model for Valuing Credit Risk Derivatives." *Journal of Derivatives* 6 (Fall): 97–108.

Kim, I. (1990). "The Analytic Valuation of American Options." *Review of Financial Studies* 3: 547–572.

Kim, J. (1992). "A Martingale Analysis of the Term Structure of Interest Rates." Working Paper, Graduate School of Industrial Administration, Carnegie-Mellon University.

Kim, J. (1993). "A Discrete-Time Approximation of a One-Factor Markov Model of the Term Structure of Interest Rates." Working Paper, Graduate School of Industrial Administration, Carnegie-Mellon University.

Kim, J. (1994). "A Model of the Term Structure of Interest Rates with the Time-Variant Market Price of Risk." Working Paper, Graduate School of Industrial Administration, Carnegie-Mellon University.

Kind, P., R. Liptser, and W. Runggaldier. (1991). "Diffusion Approximation in Past Dependent Models and Applications to Option Pricing." *Annals of Applied Probability* 1: 379–405.

Kishimoto, N. (1989). "A Simplified Approach to Pricing Path Dependent Securities." Working Paper, Fuqua School of Business, Duke University.

Kocherlakota, N. (1990). "On the Discount Factor in 'Growth' Economies." *Journal of Monetary Economics* 25: 43–47.

Koedijk, K., F. Nissen, R. Schotman, and C. Wolff. (1994). "The Dynamics of Short-Term Interest Rate Volatility Reconsidered." Working Paper, Limburg Institute of Financial Economics, University of Limburg.

Konno, H., and T. Takase. (1995). "A Constrained Least Square Approach to the Estimation of the Term Structure of Interest Rates." *Financial Engineering and the Japanese Markets* 2: 169–179.

Konno, H., and T. Takase. (1996). "On the De-Facto Convex Structure of a Least Square Problem for Estimating the Term Structure of Interest Rates." *Financial Engineering and the Japanese Market* 3: 77–85.

Koo, H.-K. (1998). "Consumption and Portfolio Selection with Labor Income: A Continuous-Time Approach." *Mathematical Finance* 8: 49–65.

Koo, H.-K. (1999). "Consumption and Portfolio Selection with Labor Income: A Discrete-Time Approach." *Mathematical Methods of Operations Research* 50: 219–243.

Koopmans, T. (1960). "Stationary Utility and Impatience." *Econometrica* 28: 287–309.

Korn, R. (1995). "Contingent Claim Valuation in a Market with Different Interest Rates." *Mathematical Methods of Operations Research* 42: 255–274.

Kou, S. (1999). "A Jump Diffusion Model for Option Pricing with Three Properties: Leptokurtic Feature, Volatility Smile, and Analytical Tractability." Working Paper, Department of IEOR, Columbia University.

Krasa, S., and J. Werner. (1991). "Equilibria with Options: Existence and Indeterminacy." *Journal of Economic Theory* 54: 305–320.

Kraus, A., and R. Litzenberger. (1975). "Market Equilibrium in a Multiperiod State Preference Model with Logarithmic Utility." *Journal of Finance* 30: 1213–1227.

Kraus, A., and M. Smith. (1993). "A Simple Multifactor Term Structure Model." *Journal of Fixed Income* 3: 19–23.

Kreps, D. (1979). "Three Essays on Capital Markets." Working Paper, Institute for Mathematical Studies in the Social Sciences, Stanford University.

Kreps, D. (1981). "Arbitrage and Equilibrium in Economies with Infinitely Many Commodities." *Journal of Mathematical Economics* 8: 15–35.

Kreps, D. (1982). "Multiperiod Securities and the Efficient Allocation of Risk: A Comment on the Black-Scholes Option Pricing Model." In J. McCall (Ed.), *The Economics of Uncertainty and Information*, pp. 203–232. Chicago: University of Chicago Press.

Kreps, D. (1988). *Notes on the Theory of Choice.* Boulder, CO, and London: Westview Press.

Kreps, D., (1990). *A Course in Microeconomics.* Princeton, NJ: Princeton University Press.

Kreps, D., and E. Porteus. (1978). "Temporal Resolution of Uncertainty and Dynamic Choice." *Econometrica* 46: 185–200.

Krylov, N. (1980). *Controlled Diffusion Processes.* New York: Springer-Verlag.

Kubler, F., and K. Schmedders. (1997). "Computing Equilibria in Stochastic Finance Economies." Working Paper, Department of Economics, Yale University. Forthcoming in *Computational Economics.*

Kunitomo, N. (1993). "Long-Term Memory and Fractional Brownian Motion in Financial Markets." Working Paper, Faculty of Economics, University of Tokyo.

Kunitomo, N., and A. Takahashi. (1996). "The Asymptotic Expansion Approach to the Valuation of Interest Rates Contingent Claims." Working Paper, Faculty of Economics, University of Tokyo.

Kurz, M. (1993). "General Equilibrium with Endogenous Uncertainty." Working Paper, Department of Economics, Stanford University.

Kurz, M. (1997). "Asset Prices with Rational Beliefs." In M. Kurz (Ed.), *Endogenous Economic Fluctuations: Studies in the Theory of Rational Beliefs.* New York: Springer Verlag.

Kurz, M. (1998). "Social States of Belief and the Determinants of the Equity Risk Premium in a Rational Belief Equilibrium." In E. A. Y. A. Abramovich and N. Yannelis (Eds.), *Functional Analysis and Economic Theory*, pp. 171–220. New York: Springer Verlag.

Kurz, M., and A. Beltratti. (1996). "The Equity Premium is No Puzzle." Working Paper, Department of Economics, Stanford University.

Kurz, M., and M. Motolese. (1999). "Endogenous Uncertainty and Market Volatility." Working Paper, Stanford University.

Kusuoka, S. (1992a). "Arbitrage and Martingale Measure." Working Paper, Research Institute for Mathematical Sciences, Kyoto University.

Kusuoka, S. (1992b). "Consistent Price System when Transaction Costs Exist." Working Paper, Research Institute for Mathematical Sciences, Kyoto University.

Kusuoka, S. (1993). "Limit Theorem on Option Replication Cost with Transaction Costs." Working Paper, Department of Mathematics, University of Tokyo.

Kusuoka, S. (1996). "A Remark on American Securities." Working Paper, Graduate School of Mathematical Sciences, University of Tokyo.

Kusuoka, S. (1999a). "Approximation of Expectation of Diffusion Process and Mathematical Finance." Working Paper, Graduate School of Mathematical Sciences, University of Tokyo. Forthcoming in *Advanced Studies in Pure Mathematics, Proceedings of Final Taniguchi Symposium, Nara 1998*, ed. T. Sunada.

Kusuoka, S. (1999b). "A Remark on Default Risk Models." *Advances in Mathematical Economics* 1: 69–82.

Kusuoka, S. (2000). "Term Structure and SPDE." *Advances in Mathematical Economics* 2: 67–85.

Kuwana, Y. (1994). Ph.D. Dissertation, Statistics Department, Stanford University.

Kuwana, Y. (1995). "Certainty Equivalence and Logarithmic Utilities in Consumption/Investment Problems." *Mathematical Finance* 5: 297–309.

Kydland, F. E., and E. Prescott. (1991). "Indeterminacy in Incomplete Market Economies." *Economic Theory* 1: 45–62.

Lacoste, V. (1995). "Wiener Chaos: A New Approach to Option Hedging." Working Paper, Department Finance, ESSEC.

Lagnado, R., and S. Osher. (1996). "A Technique for Calibrating Derivative Security Pricing Models: Numerical Solution of an Inverse Problem." Working Paper, C-ATS, Palo Alto.

Lakner, P. (1993a). "Equivalent Local Martingale Measures and Free Lunch in a Stochastic Model of Finance with Continuous Trading." Working Paper, Statistics and Operation Research Department, New York University.

Lakner, P. (1993b). "Martingale Measures for a Class of Right-Continuous Processes." *Mathematical Finance* 3: 43–54.

Lakner, P. (1994a). "Minimization of the Expected Squared Difference of a Random Variable and Stochastic Integrals with a Given Integrator." Working Paper, Statistics and Operation Research Department, New York University.

Lakner, P. (1994b). "Optimal Investment Processes for Utility Maximization Problems with Restricted Information." Working Paper, Statistics and Operation Research Department, New York University.

Lakner, P. (1995). "Utility Maximization with Partial Information." *Stochastic Processes and Their Applications* 56: 247–273.

Lakner, P., and E. Slud. (1991). "Optimal Consumption by a Bond Investor: The Case of Random Interest Rate Adapted to a Point Process." *SIAM Journal of Control and Optimization* 29: 638–655.

Lamberton, D. (1993). "Convergence of the Critical Price in the Approximation of American Options." *Mathematical Finance* 3: 179–190.

Lamberton, D. (1997). "Error Estimates for the Binomial Approximation of American Put Options." Working Paper, Equipe d'Analyse et de Mathématiques Appliquées, Université De Marne-La-Vallée. Forthcoming in *The Annals of Applied Probability*.

Lamberton, D., and B. Lapeyre. (1997). *Introduction au Calcul Stochastique Appliqué à la Finance*. Paris: Ellipses.

Lamberton, D., and G. Pagès. (1990). "Sur l'Approximation des Réduites." *Annales de l'Institut Henri Poincaré* 26: 331–355.

Lamoureux, C., and W. Lastrapes. (1993). "Forecasting Stock-Return Variance: Toward an Understanding of Stochastic Implied Volatilities." *Review of Financial Studies* 6: 293–327.

Lando, D. (1994). "Three Essays on Contingent Claims Pricing." Working Paper, Ph.D. dissertation, Statistics Center, Cornell University.

Lando, D. (1995). "On Jump-Diffusion Option Pricing from the Viewpoint of Semimartingale Characteristics." *Surveys in Applied and Industrial Mathematics* 2: 605–625.

Lando, D. (1998). "On Cox Processes and Credit Risky Securities." *Review of Derivatives Research* 2: 99–120.

Lang, L., R. Litzenberger, and A. Liu. (1996). "Interest Rate Swaps: A Synthesis." Working Paper, Faculty of Business Administration, The Chinese University of Hong Kong.

Langetieg, T. (1980). "A Multivariate Model of the Term Structure." *Journal of Finance* 35: 71–97.

Lawson, J., and J. Morris. (1978). "The Extrapolation of First Order Methods for Parabolic Partial Differential Equations I." *SIAM Journal of Numerical Analysis* 15: 1212–1224.

Lazrak, A., and M. Quenez. (1999). "A Generalized Stochastic Differential Utility." Working Paper, Department of Analysis and Probability, University of Evry.

Leblanc, B., and O. Scaillet. (1998). "Path Dependent Options on Yields in the Affine Term Structure Model." *Finance and Stochastics* 2: 349–367.

Lee, B., and B. Ingram. (1991). "Simulation Estimation of Time-Series Models." *Journal of Econometrics* 47: 197–205.

Lee, J.-J. (1990). "The Valuation of American Calls." Working Paper, Graduate School of Business, Stanford University.

Lee, J.-J. (1991). "A Note on Binomial Approximation for Contingent Securities." Working Paper, Graduate School of Business, Stanford University.

Lehoczky, J., S. Sethi, and S. Shreve. (1983). "Optimal Consumption and Investment Policies Allowing Consumption Constraints and Bankruptcy." *Mathematics of Operations Research* 8: 613–636.

Lehoczky, J., S. Sethi, and S. Shreve. (1985). "A Martingale Formulation for Optimal Consumption/ Investment Decision Making." In *Optimal Control and Economic Analysis 2*, pp. 135–153. Amsterdam: North-Holland.

Leland, H. (1985). "Option Pricing and Replication with Transactions Costs." *Journal of Finance* 40: 1283–1301.

Leland, H. (1994). "Corporate Debt Value, Bond Covenants, and Optimal Capital Structure." *Journal of Finance* 49: 1213–1252.

Leland, H. (1998). "Agency Costs, Risk Management, and Capital Structure." *Journal of Finance* 53: 1213–1242.

Leland, H., and K. Toft. (1996). "Optimal Capital Structure, Endogenous Bankruptcy, and the Term Structure of Credit Spreads." *Journal of Finance* 51: 987–1019.

LeRoy, S. (1973). "Risk Aversion and the Martingale Property of Asset Prices." *International Economic Review* 14: 436–446.

Lesne, J.-F. (1995). "Indirect Inference Estimation of Yield Curve Factor Models." Working Paper, Universite de Cergy-Pontoise, THEMA.

Lesne, J.-P., J.-L. Prigent, and O. Scaillet. (2000). "Convergence of Discrete Time Option Pricing Models Under Stochastic Interest Rates." *Finance and Stochastics* 4: 81–93.

Levental, S., and A. Skorohod. (1995). "A Necessary and Sufficient Condition for Absence of Arbitrage with Tame Portfolios." *Annals of Applied Probability* 5: 906–925.

Levental, S., and A. Skorohod. (1997). "On the Possibility of Hedging Options in the Presence of Transactions Costs." *Annals of Applied Probability* 7: 410–443.

Levhari, D., and T. Srinivasan. (1969). "Optimal Savings under Uncertainty." *Review of Economic Studies* 59: 153–165.

Levine, D. (1989). "Infinite Horizon Equilibria with Incomplete Markets." *Journal of Mathematical Economics* 18: 357–376.

Levine, D., and W. Zame. (1996). "Debt Constraints and Equilibrium in Infinite Horizon Economies with Incomplete Markets." *Journal of Mathematical Economics* 26: 103–131.

Levine, D., and W. Zame. (1999). "Does Market Incompleteness Matter?" Working Paper, Department of Economics, University of California, Los Angeles. Forthcoming in *Econometrica*.

Levy, A., M. Avellaneda, and A. Parás. (1994). "A New Approach for Pricing Derivative Securities in Markets with Uncertain Volatilities: A 'Case Study' on the Trinomial Tree." Working Paper, Courant Institute of Mathematical Sciences, New York University.

Li, A., P. Ritchken, and L. Sankarasubramanian. (1995). "Lattice Models for Pricing American Interest Rate Claims." *Journal of Finance* 50: 719–737.

Li, T. (1995). "Pricing of Swaps with Default Risk." Working Paper, Yale School of Management.

Linetsky, V. (1999). "Step Options." *Mathematical Finance* 9: 55–96.

Lintner, J. (1965). "The Valuation of Risky Assets and the Selection of Risky Investment in Stock Portfolios and Capital Budgets." *Review of Economics and Statistics* 47: 13–37.

Lions, P.-L. (1981). "Control of Diffusion Processes in R^N." *Communications in Pure and Applied Mathematics* 34: 121–147.

Lions, P.-L. (1983). "Optimal Control of Diffusion Processes." Working Paper, Université de Paris IX, Dauphine.

Lioui, A. (1995). "On Mean-Variance Hedging in Continuous Time with Imperfect Correlation." Working Paper, Department of Economics, Bar Ilan University.

Lipster, R., and A. Shiryaev. (1977). *Statistics of Random Processes, I.* New York: Springer-Verlag.

Litterman, R., and T. Iben. (1991). "Corporate Bond Valuation and the Term Structure of Credit Spreads." *Journal of Portfolio Management* Spring: 52–64.

Litterman, R., and J. Scheinkman. (1988). "Common Factors Affecting Bond Returns." Working Paper, Goldman Sachs, Financial Strategies Group, New York.

Litzenberger, R., (1992). "Swaps: Plain and Fanciful." *Journal of Finance* 47: 831–850.

Liu, J. (1999). "Portfolio Selection in Stochastic Environments." Working Paper, Stanford University.

Liu, J., J. Pan, and L. Pedersen. (1999). "Density-Based Inference in Affine Jump-Diffusions." Working Paper, Graduate School of Business, Stanford University.

Lobo, M., M. Fazel, and S. Boyd. (1999). "Portfolio Optimization with Linear and Fixed Transaction Costs and Bounds on Risk." Working Paper, Information Systems Laboratory, Stanford University.

Loewenstein, M., and G. Willard. (1998). "Rational Equilibrium Asset-Pricing Bubbles in Continuous Trading Models." Working Paper, Olin School of Business, Washington University in St. Louis.

Loewenstein, M., and G. Willard. (1999). "Local Martingales, Arbitrage, and Viability: Free Snacks and Cheap Thrills." Working Paper, Olin School of Business, Washington University in St. Louis.

Löffler, A. (1996). "Variance Aversion Implies μ-σ^2-Criterion." *Journal of Economic Theory* 69: 532–539.

Long, J. (1990). "The Numeraire Portfolio." *Journal of Financial Economics* 26: 29–69.

Longstaff, F. (1990). "The Valuation of Options on Yields." *Journal of Financial Economics* 26: 97–121.

Longstaff, F., and E. Schwartz. (1992). "Interest Rate Volatility and the Term Structure: A Two-Factor General Equilibrium Model." *Journal of Finance* 47: 1259–1282.

Longstaff, F., and E. Schwartz. (1993). "Implementing of the Longstaff-Schwartz Interest Rate Model." Working Paper, Anderson Graduate School of Management, University of California, Los Angeles.

Longstaff, F., and E. Schwartz, (1995a). "A Simple Approach to Valuing Risky Fixed and Floating Rate Debt." *Journal of Finance* 50: 789–819.

Longstaff, F., and E. Schwartz. (1995b). "Valuing Credit Derivatives." *Journal of Fixed Income* 5 (June): 6–12.

Longstaff, F., and E. Schwartz. (1998). "Valuing American Options By Simulation: A Simple Least-Squares Approach." Working Paper, Anderson Graduate School of Management, University of California, Los Angeles.

Loshak, B. (1996). "The Valuation of Defaultable Convertible Bonds under Stochastic Interest Rate." Working Paper, Krannert Graduate School of Management, Purdue University, West Lafayette.

Lu, S., and G. Yu. (1993). "Valuation of Options under Stochastic Volatility: The Garch Diffusion Approach." Working Paper, Department of Mathematics, University of Michigan.

Lucas, D. (1994). "Asset Pricing with Undiversifiable Income Risk and Short Sales Constraints: Deepening the Equity Premium Puzzle." *Journal of Monetary Economics* 34: 325–341.

Lucas, D. (1995). "Market Fractions, Savings Behavior and Portfolio Choice." Working Paper, Kellogg School of Management, Northwestern University.

Lucas, R. (1978). "Asset Prices in an Exchange Economy." *Econometrica* 46: 1429–1445.

Luenberger, D. (1969). *Optimization by Vector Space Methods*. New York: Wiley.

Luenberger, D. (1984). *Introduction to Linear and Nonlinear Programming* (2d ed.). Reading, MA: Addison-Wesley.

Luenberger, D. (1995). *Microeconomic Theory*. New York: McGraw-Hill.

Lund, J. (1999). "A Model for Studying the Effect of EMU on European Yield Curves." *European Finance Review, Journal of the European Finance Association* 2: 321–363.

Luttmer, E. (1996). "Asset Pricing in Economies with Frictions." *Econometrica* 64: 1439–1467.

Lynch, A., and P. Balduzzi. (1998). "Predictability and Transaction Costs: The Impact on Rebalancing Rules and Behavior." Working Paper, New York University.

Ma, C.-H. (1991). "Valuation of Derivative Securities with Mixed Poisson-Brownian Information and with Recursive Utility." Working Paper, Department of Economics, University of Toronto.

Ma, C.-H. (1993a). "Intertemporal Recursive Utility in the Presence of Mixed Poisson-Brownian Uncertainty." Working Paper, Department of Economics, McGill University.

Ma, C.-H. (1993b). "Market Equilibrium with Heterogeneous Recursive-Utility-Maximizing Agents." *Economic Theory* 3: 243–266; Corrigendum 6 (1995): 567–570.

Ma, C.-H. (1994). "Discrete-Time Model of Asset Pricing in Incomplete Market: GE Approach with Recursive Utility." Working Paper, Department of Economics, McGill University.

Ma, C.-H. (1996). "Attitudes Toward the Timing of Resolution of Uncertainty and the Existence of Recursive Utility." Working Paper, Department of Economics, McGill University, Montreal.

Ma, J., and J. Cvitanić. (1996). "Hedging Options for a Large Investor and Forward Backward SDEs." *Annals of Applied Probability* 6: 370–398.

Ma, J., P. Protter, and J. Yong. (1994). "Solving Forward-Backward Stochastic Differential Equations Explicitly—A Four Step Scheme." *Probability Theory and Related Fields* 98: 339–359.

Ma, J., and J. Yong. (1995). "Solvability of Forward-Backward SDEs and the Nodal Set of Hamilton-Jacobi-Bellman Equations." *Chinese Annals of Mathematics. Series B* 16: 279–298.

Ma, J., and J. Yong. (1999). *Forward-Backward Stochastic Differential Equations and their Applications.* New York: Springer-Verlag.

Machina, M. (1982). " 'Expected Utility' Analysis without the Independence Axiom." *Econometrica* 50: 277–323.

Madan, D. (1988). "Risk Measurement in Semimartingale Models with Multiple Consumption Goods." *Journal of Economic Theory* 44: 398–412.

Madan, D., and E. Chang. (1996). "Volatility Smiles, Skewness Premia and Risk Metrics: Applications of a Four Parameter Closed Form Generalization of Geometric Brownian Motion to the Pricing of Options." Working Paper, University of Maryland.

Madan, D., and F. Milne. (1991). "Option Pricing with V.G. Martingale Components." *Mathematical Finance* 1: 39–55.

Madan, D., F. Milne, and H. Shefrin. (1989). "The Multinomial Option Pricing Model and Its Brownian and Poisson Limits." *Review of Financial Studies* 2: 251–266.

Madan, D., and H. Unal. (1998). "Pricing the Risks of Default." *Review of Derivatives Research* 2: 121–160.

Maghsoodi, Y. (1996a). "Market's Change in Time, Time Change and Time Structured Term Structures." Working Paper, SCINANCE, UK, Southhampton and University of Southampton.

Maghsoodi, Y. (1996b). "Solution of the Extended CIR Term Structure and Bond Option Valuation." *Mathematical Finance* 6: 89–109.

Maghsoodi, Y. (1997a). "Term Structure, Solutions and Option Valuation Under Marked Point Process Square-Root Interest Rates." Working Paper, Department of Mathematics, University of Southampton, U.K.

Maghsoodi, Y. (1997b). "Two-Country Term Structure under Marked Point Process Diffusion Interest and Exchange Rates." Working Paper, Department of Mathematics, University of Southampton, U.K.

Maghsoodi, Y. (1998). "A Closed-Form Analytical Formula for Options with a Non-Linear Stochastic Volatility." Working Paper, University of Southampton, UK.

Magill, M., and M. Quinzii. (1994). "Infinite Horizon Incomplete Markets." *Econometrica* 62: 853–880.

Magill, M., and M. Quinzii. (1996a). "Incomplete Markets over an Infinite Horizon: Long-Lived Securities and Speculative Bubbles." *Journal of Mathematical Economics* 26: 133–170.

Magill, M., and M. Quinzii. (1996b). *Theory of Incomplete Markets.* Cambridge, MA: MIT Press.

Magill, M., and W. Shafer. (1990). "Characterization of Generically Complete Real Asset Structures." *Journal of Mathematical Economics* 19: 167–194.

Magill, M., and W. Shafer. (1991). "Incomplete Markets." In *Handbook of Mathematical Economics, Volume 4*, pp. 1523–1614. Amsterdam: North-Holland.

Mankiw, G. (1986). "The Equity Premium and the Concentration of Aggregate Shocks." *Journal of Financial Economics* 17: 211–219.

Marcet, A. (1993). "Simulation Analysis of Dynamic Stochastic Models: Applications to Theory and Estimation." Working Paper, Department of Economics, Universitat Pompeu Fabra, Barcelona.

Marcet, A., and D. Marshall. (1994). "Solving Nonlinear Rational Expectations Models by Parameterized Expectations: Convergence to Stationary Solutions." Working Paper, Universitat Pompeu Fabra, Department of Economics, Barcelona.

Marcet, A., and K. Singleton. (1999). "Equilibrium Asset Prices and Savings of Heterogeneous Agents in the Presence of Portfolio Constraints." *Macroeconomic Dynamics* 3: 243–277.

Marcozzi, M. (2000). "On the Approximation of Optimal Stopping Problems with Application to Financial Mathematics." Working Paper, Department of Mathematical Sciences, University of Nevada, Las Vegas.

Margrabe, W. (1978). "The Value of an Option to Exchange One Asset for Another." *Journal of Finance* 33: 177–186.

Marsh, T. (1994). "Term Structure of Interest Rates and the Pricing of Fixed Income Claims and Bonds." Working Paper, Haas School of Business, University of California, Berkeley.

Marshall, D. (1999). "Can Cost of Consumption Adjustment Explain Asset Pricing Puzzles?" *Journal of Finance* 54: 623–654.

Martin, M. (1997). "Credit Risk in Derivative Products." Working Paper, University of London, London Business School.

Mas-Colell, A. (1985). *The Theory of General Economic Equilibrium—A Differentiable Approach.* Cambridge: Cambridge University Press.

Mas-Colell, A. (1986a). "The Price Equilibrium Existence Problem in Topological Vector Lattices." *Econometrica* 54: 1039–1054.

Mas-Colell, A. (1986b). "Valuation Equilibrium and Pareto Optimum Revisited." In W. Hildenbrand and A. Mas-Colell (Eds.), *Contributions to Mathematical Economics*, pp. 317–332. Amsterdam: North-Holland.

Mas-Colell, A. (1987). "An Observation on Geanakoplos and Polemarchakis." Working Paper, Department of Economics, Harvard University.

Mas-Colell, A. (1991). "Indeterminacy in Incomplete Market Economies." *Economic Theory* 1: 45–62.

Mas-Colell, A., and P. Monteiro. (1996). "Self-Fulfilling Equilibria: An Existence Theorem for a General State Space." *Journal of Mathematical Economics* 26: 51–62.

Mas-Colell, A., and W. Zame. (1992). "Equilibrium Theory in Infinite Dimensional Spaces." In W. Hildenbrand and H. Sonnenschein (Eds.), *Handbook of Mathematical Econonomics, Volume 4*, pp. 1835–1898. Amsterdam: North-Holland.

McConnell, J., and E. Schwartz. (1986). "LYON Taming." *Journal of Finance* 41: 561–576.

McFadden, D. (1989). "A Method of Simulated Moments for Estimation of Discrete Response Models without Numerical Integration." *Econometrica* 57: 995–1026.

McKean, H. (1965). "Appendix: Free Boundary Problem for the Heat Equation Arising from a Problem in Mathematical Economics." *Industrial Management Review* 6: 32–39.

McKenzie, L. (1954). "On Equilibrium in Graham's Model of World Trade and Other Competitive Systems." *Econometrica* 22: 147–161.

McManus, D. (1984). "Incomplete Markets: Generic Existence of Equilibrium and Optimality Properties in an Economy with Futures Markets." Working Paper, Department of Economics, University of Pennsylvania.

Mehra, R. (1988). "On the Existence and Representation of Equilibrium in an Economy with Growth and Nonstationary Consumption." *International Economic Review* 29: 131–135.

Mehra, R., and E. Prescott. (1985). "The Equity Premium: A Puzzle." *Journal of Monetary Economics* 15: 145–161.

Mehrling, P. (1990). "Heterogeneity, Incomplete Markets, and the Equity Premium." Working Paper, Department of Economics, Barnard College and Columbia University.

Mehrling, P. (1998). "Idiosyncratic Risk, Borrowing Constraints and Asset Prices." *Metroeconomica* 49: 261–283.

Melino, A., and S. Turnbull. (1990). "Pricing Foreign Currency Options with Stochastic Volatility." *Journal of Econometrics* 45: 239–265.

Mella-Barral, P. (1999). "Dynamics of Default and Debt Reorganization." *Review of Financial Studies* 12: 535–578.

Mella-Barral, P., and W. Perraudin. (1997). "Strategic Debt Service." *Journal of Finance* 52: 531–556.

Merrick, J. (1999). "Crisis Dynamics of Russian Eurobond Implied Default Recovery Ratios." Working Paper, Stern School of Business, New York University.

Merton, R. (1969). "Lifetime Portfolio Selection under Uncertainty: The Continuous Time Case." *Review of Economics and Statistics* 51: 247–257.

Merton, R. (1970). "A Dynamic General Equilibrium Model of the Asset Market and its Application to the Pricing of the Capital Structure of the Firm." Working Paper, Sloan School of Management, Massachusetts Institute of Technology.

Merton, R. (1971). "Optimum Consumption and Portfolio Rules in a Continuous Time Model." *Journal of Economic Theory* 3: 373–413; Erratum 6 (1973): 213–214.

Merton, R. (1973a). "An Intertemporal Capital Asset Pricing Model." *Econometrica* 41: 867–888.

Merton, R. (1973b). "The Theory of Rational Option Pricing." *Bell Journal of Economics and Management Science* 4: 141–183.

Merton, R. (1974). "On the Pricing of Corporate Debt: The Risk Structure of Interest Rates." *Journal of Finance* 29: 449–470.

Merton, R. (1976). "Option Pricing when the Underlying Stock Returns are Discontinuous." *Journal of Financial Economics* 5: 125–144.

Merton, R. (1977). "On the Pricing of Contingent Claims and the Modigliani-Miller Theorem." *Journal of Financial Economics* 5: 241–250.

Merton, R. (1990). *Continuous-Time Finance.* Oxford: Basil Blackwell.

Meyer, P.-A. (1966). *Probability and Potentials.* Waltham, MA: Blaisdell Publishing Company.

Milshtein, G. (1974). "Approximate Integration of Stochastic Differential Equations." *Theory of Probability and Its Applications* 3: 557–562.

Milshtein, G. (1978). "A Method of Second-Order Accuracy Integration of Stochastic Differential Equations." *Theory of Probability and Its Applications* 23: 396–401.

Miltersen, K. (1993). "Pricing of Interest Rate Contingent Claims: Implementing the Simulation Approach." Working Paper, Department of Management, Odense University.

Miltersen, K. (1994). "An Arbitrage Theory of the Term Structure of Interest Rates." *Annals of Applied Probability* 4: 953–967.

Miltersen, K., and S.-A. Persson. (1997). "Pricing Rate of Return Guarantees in a Heath-Jarrow-Morton Framework." *Insurance: Mathematics and Economics* 25: 307–325.

Miltersen, K., K. Sandmann, and D. Sondermann. (1997). "Closed Form Solutions for Term Structure Derivatives with Log-Normal Interest Rates." *Journal of Finance* 52: 409–430.

Miltersen, K., and E. Schwartz. (1998). "Pricing of Options on Commodity Futures with Stochastic Term Structures of Convenience Yields and Interest Rates." *Journal of Financial and Quantitative Analysis* 33: 33–59.

Mirrlees, J. (1974). "Optimal Accumulation under Uncertainty: The Case of Stationary Returns to Investment." In J. Drèze (Ed.), *Allocation under Uncertainty: Equilibrium and Optimality,* pp. 36–50. New York: Wiley.

Mitchell, A., and D. Griffiths. (1980). *The Finite Difference Method in Partial Differential Equations.* New York: John Wiley.

Modigliani, F., and M. Miller. (1958). "The Cost of Capital, Corporation Finance, and the Theory of Investment." *American Economic Review* 48: 261–297.

Monat, P., and C. Stricker. (1994). "Décomposition de Föllmer-Schweizer et Fermeture de $G_T(\Theta)$." *Comtes Rendus de l'Academie de Science Paris* 318I: 573–576.

Monat, P., and C. Stricker. (1995). "Follmer-Schweizer Decomposition and Closedness of $G_T(\Theta)$." *Annals of Probability* 23: 605–628.

Monteiro, P. (1994). "Inada's Condition Imply Equilibrium Existence is Rare." *Economics Letters* 44: 99–102.

Monteiro, P. (1996). "A New Proof of the Existence of Equilibrium in Incomplete Markets Economies." *Journal of Mathematical Economics* 26: 85–101.

Moreleda, J. (1997). *On The Pricing of Interest Rate Options.* Tinbergen Institute Research Series., Rotterdam, The Netherlands: Erasmus University.

Morokoff, W., and R. Caflisch. (1993). "A Quasi-Monte Carlo Approach to Particle Simulation of the Heat Equation." *SIAM Journal of Numerical Analysis* 30: 1558–1573.

Morokoff, W., and R. Caflisch. (1994). "Quasi-Random Sequences and Their Discrepancies." *SIAM Journal of Scientific Computing* 15: 1251–1279.

Morokoff, W., and R. Caflisch. (1995). "Quasi-Monte Carlo Integration." *Journal of Computational Physics* 122: 218–230.

Moskowitz, B., and R. Caflisch. (1994). "Smoothness and Dimension Reduction in Quasi-Monte Carlo Methods." Working Paper, Department of Mathematics, University of California, Los Angeles.

Müller, S. (1985). *Arbitrage Pricing of Contingent Claims.* Lecture Notes in Economics and Mathematical Systems, vol. 254. New York: Springer-Verlag.

Munk, C. (1997). "No-Arbitrage Bounds on Contingent Claims Prices with Convex Constraints on the Dollar Investments of the Hedge Portfolio." Working Paper, Department of Management, Odense University, Denmark.

Munk, C. (2000b). "Optimal Consumption/Portfolio Policies with Undiversifiable Income Risk and Liquidity Constraints." *Journal of Economic Dynamics and Control* 24: 1315–1343.

Musiela, M. (1994a). "Nominal Annual Rates and Lognormal Volatility Structure." Working Paper, Department of Mathematics, University of New South Wales, Sydney.

Musiela, M. (1994b). "Stochastic PDEs and Term Structure Models." Working Paper, Department of Mathematics, University of New South Wales, Sydney.

Musiela, M., and M. Rutkowski. (1997). *Martingale Methods in Financial Modeling.* New York: Springer.

Musiela, M., and D. Sondermann. (1994). "Different Dynamical Specifications of the Term Structure of Interest Rates and their Implications." Working Paper, Department of Mathematics, University of New South Wales, Sydney.

Myneni, R. (1992a). "Continuous-Time Relationships between Futures and Forward Prices." Working Paper, Graduate School of Business, Stanford University.

Myneni, R. (1992b). "The Pricing of the American Option." *Annals of Applied Probability* 2: 1–23.

Nahum, E. (1998). "The Pricing of Options Depending on a Discrete Maximum." Working Paper, Department of Statistics, University of California, Berkeley.

Naik, V. (1994). "Asset Prices in Dynamic Production Economies with Time Varying Risk." *Review of Financial Studies* 7: 781–801.

Naik, V., and M. Lee. (1994). "The Yield Curve and Bond Option Prices with Discrete Shifts in Economic Regimes." Working Paper, University of British Columbia.

Naik, V., and R. Uppal. (1994). "Leverage Constraints and the Optimal Hedging of Stock and Bond Options." *Journal of Financial and Quantitative Analysis* 29: 199–222.

Nakagawa, H. (1999). "A Remark on Spot Rate Models Induced by an Equilibrium Model." *University of Tokyo Journal of Mathematical Sciences* 6: 453–475.

Neftci, S. (2000). *An Introduction to the Mathematics of Financial Derivatives.* New York: Academic Press.

Negishi, T. (1960). "Welfare Economics and Existence of an Equilibrium for a Competitive Economy." *Metroeconometrica* 12: 92–97.

Nelson, D. (1990). "ARCH Models as Diffusion Appoximations." *Journal of Econometrics* 45: 7–38.

Nelson, D. (1991). "Conditional Heteroskedasticity in Asset Returns: A New Approach." *Econometrica* 59: 347–370.

Nelson, D., (1992). "Filtering and Forecasting with Misspecified ARCH Models I." *Journal of Econometrics* 52: 61–90.

Nelson, D., and K. Ramaswamy. (1989). "Simple Binomial Processes as Diffusion Approximations in Financial Models." *Review of Financial Studies* 3: 393–430.

Nelson, J., and S. Schaefer. (1983). "Innovations in Bond Portfolio Management: Duration Analysis and Immunization." In *The Dynamic of the Term Structure and Alternative Portfolio Immunization Strategies*. Greenwich: JAI Press.

Newton, N. (1990). "Asymptotically Efficient Runge-Kutta Methods for a Class of Ito and Stratonovich Equations." Working Paper, Department of Electrical Engineering, University of Essex.

Nielsen, J., and K. Sandmann. (1996). "The Pricing of Asian Options Under Stochastic Interest Rates." *Applied Mathematical Finance* 3: 209–236.

Nielsen, L. (1990a). "Equilibrium in CAPM without a Riskless Asset." *Review of Economic Studies* 57: 315–324.

Nielsen, L. (1990b). "Existence of Equilibrium in CAPM." *Journal of Economic Theory* 52: 223–231.

Nielsen, L. (1993a). "Robustness of the Market Model." *Economic Theory* 3: 365–370.

Nielsen, L. (1993b). "Two-Fund Separation and Equilibrium." Working Paper, INSEAD, Fontainebleau, France.

Nielsen, L. T., and J. Saá-Requejo. (1992). "Exchange Rate and Term Structure Dynamics and the Pricing of Derivative Securities." Working Paper, INSEAD, Fontainebleau, France.

Nielsen, L. T., J. Saá-Requejo, and P. Santa-Clara. (1993). "Default Risk and Interest Rate Risk: The Term Structure of Credit Spreads." Working Paper, INSEAD, Fontainebleau, France.

Nielsen, S., and E. Ronn. (1995). "The Valuation of Default Risk in Corporate Bonds and Interest Rate Swaps." Working Paper, Department of Management Science and Information Systems, University of Texas at Austin.

Nunes, J., L. Clewlow, and S. Hodges. (1999). "Interest Rate Derivatives in a Duffie and Kan Model with Stochastic Volatility: An Arrow-Debreu Pricing Approach." *Review of Derivatives Research* 3: 5–66.

Nyborg, K. (1996). "The Use and Pricing of Convertible Bonds." *Applied Mathematical Finance* 3: 167–190.

Ocone, D., and I. Karatzas. (1991). "A Generalized Clark Representation Formula, with Application to Optimal Portfolios." *Stochastics and Stochastics Reports* 34: 187–220.

Ōhashi, K. (1991). "A Note on the Terminal Date Security Prices in a Continuous Time Trading Model with Dividends." *Journal of Mathematical Economics* 20: 219–224.

Oliveira, D. (1994). "Arbitrage Pricing of Integral Options." Working Paper, Instituto de Matemática Pura e Applicada, Rio de Janeiro.

Ordentlich, E. (1996). Ph.D. Dissertation, Department of Electrical Engineering, Stanford University.

Owen, A. (1996). "Monte Carlo Variance of Scrambled Net Quadrature." Working Paper, Department of Statistics, Stanford University. Forthcoming in *SIAM Journal*.

Owen, A. (1997). "Scrambled Net Variance for Integrals of Smooth Functions." *Annals of Statistics* 25: 1541–1562.

Owen, A., and D. Tavella. (1996). "Scrambled Nets for Value at Risk Calculations." Working Paper, Statistics Department, Stanford University.

Pagès, H. (1987). "Optimal Consumption and Portfolio Policies when Markets are Incomplete." Working Paper, Department of Economics, Massachusetts Institute of Technology.

Pagès, H. (2000). "Estimating Brazilian Sovereign Risk from Brady Bond Prices." Working Paper, Bank of France.

Pakes, A., and D. Pollard. (1989). "Simulation and the Asymptotics of Optimization Estimators." *Econometrica* 57: 1027–1057.

Pan, J. (1999). "Integrated Time-Series Analysis of Spot and Options Prices." Working Paper, Graduate School of Business, Stanford University.

Pan, W.-H. (1993). "Constrained Efficient Allocations in Incomplete Markets: Characterization and Implementation." Working Paper, Department of Economics, University of Rochester.

Pan, W.-H. (1995). "A Second Welfare Theorem for Constrained Efficient Allocations in Incomplete Markets." *Journal of Mathematical Economics* 24: 577–599.

Pang, K. (1996). "Multi-Factor Gaussian HJM Approximation to Kennedy and Calibration to Caps and Swaptions Prices." Working Paper, Financial Options Research Center, Warwick Business School, University of Warwick.

Pang, K., and S. Hodges. (1995). "Non-Negative Affine Yield Models of the Term Structure." Working Paper, Financial Options Research Center, Warwick Business School, University of Warwick.

Pappalardo, L. (1996). "Option Pricing and Smile Effect when Underlying Stock Prices are Driven by a Jump Process." Working Paper, Financial Options Research Centre, University of Warwick.

Pardoux, E. (1997). "Generalized Discontinuous Backward Stochastic Differential Equations." In N. El Karoui and L. Mazliak (Eds.), *Backward Stochastic Differential Equations*, pp. 207–220. Essex: Addison Wesley Longman Ltd.

Pardoux, E., and S. Peng. (1990). "Adapted Solution of a Backward Stochastic Differential Equation." *Systems and Control Letters* 14: 55–61.

Pardoux, E., and S. Peng. (1994). "Some Backward Stochastic Differential Equations with Non-Lipschitz Coefficients." Working Paper, Department of Mathematics, Université de Provence.

Pearson, N., and T.-S. Sun. (1994). "An Empirical Examination of the Cox, Ingersoll, and Ross Model of the Term Structure of Interest Rates using the Method of Maximum Likelihood." *Journal of Finance* 54: 929–959.

Pedersen, H., and E. Shiu. (1993). "Pricing of Options on Bonds by Binomial Lattices and by Diffusion Processes." Working Paper, Investment Policy Department, Great-West Life Assurance Company.

Pedersen, H., E. Shiu, and A. Thorlacius. (1989). "Arbitrage-Free Pricing of Interest Rate Contingent Claims." *Transactions of the Society of Actuaries* 41: 231–265.

Pedersen, L. (1997). "Affine Multifactor Term Structure Models—Theory and Inference." Working Paper, University of Copenhagen.

Pedersen, M. (1999). "Bermudan Swaptions in the LIBOR Market Model." Working Paper, Financial Research Department, SimCorp A/S.

Peng, S. (1993a). "Adapted Solution of Backward Stochastic Equations and Related Partial Differential Equations." Working Paper, Department of Mathematics, Shandong University.

Peng, S. (1993b). "Backward Stochastic Differential Equations and Applications to Optimal Control." *Applied Mathematics and Optimization* 27: 125–144.

Pennacchi, G. (1991). "Identifying the Dynamics of Real Interest Rates and Inflation: Evidence Using Survey Data." *Review of Financial Studies* 4: 53–86.

Pham, H. (1995). "Optimal Stopping, Free Boundary and American Option in a Jump Diffusion Model." Working Paper, CEREMADE Université de Paris IX Dauphine. Forthcoming in *Applied Mathematics and Optimization*.

Pham, H., and N. Touzi. (1993). "Intertemporal Equilibrium Risk Premia in a Stochastic Volatility Model." Working Paper, CREST, Paris.

Piazzesi, M. (1997). "An Affine Model of the Term Structure of Interest Rates with Macroeconomic Factors." Working Paper, Stanford University.

Piazzesi, M. (1999). "A Linear-Quadratic Jump-Diffusion Model with Scheduled and Unscheduled Announcements." Working Paper, Stanford University.

Pierides, Y. (1997). "The Pricing of Credit Risk Derivatives." *Journal of Economic Dynamics and Control* 21: 1579–1611.

Pietra, T. (1992). "Indeterminacy in General Equilibrium Economies with Incomplete Financial Markets—Mixed Asset Returns." *Journal of Mathematical Economics* 21: 155–172.

Pikovsky, I., and I. Karatzas. (1996). "Anticipative Portfolio Optimization." *Advances in Applied Probability* 28: 1095–1122.

Pikovsky, I., and I. Karatzas. (1998). "Stochastic Equilibrium with Differential Information." Working Paper, Department of Mathematics, Columbia University.

Pikovsky, I., and S. Shreve. (1996a). "Callable Convertible Bonds." Working Paper, Department of Mathematics, Courant Institute, New York.

Pikovsky, I., and S. Shreve. (1996b). "Perpetual Convertible Debt." Working Paper, Department of Mathematics, Courant Institute, New York.

Pitts, C., and M. Selby. (1983). "The Pricing of Corporate Debt: A Further Note." *Journal of Finance* 38: 1311–1313.

Platen, E., and M. Schweizer. (1994). "On Smile and Skewness." Working Paper, School of Mathematical Sciences Centre for Mathematics and Its Applications, The Australian National University, Canberra.

Platten, I. (1994). "Non-linear General Equilibrium Models of the Term Structure: Comments and Two-Factor Generalization." *Finance* 15: 63–78.

Pliska, S. (1986). "A Stochastic Calculus Model of Continuous Trading: Optimal Portfolios." *Mathematics of Operations Research* 11: 371–382.

Pliska, S., and M. Selby. (1994). "On a Free Boundary Problem that Arises in Portfolio Management." *Philosophical Transactions of the Royal Society of London. Series A.* 347: 555–561.

Polemarchakis, H., and B. Ku. (1990). "Options and Equilibrium." *Journal of Mathematical Economics* 19: 107–112.

Polemarchakis, H., and P. Siconolfi. (1993). "Competitive Equilibria without Free Disposal or Nonsatiation." *Journal of Mathematical Economics* 22: 85–99.

Pollard, D. (1984). *Convergence of Stochastic Processes*. New York: Springer-Verlag.

Pontier, M. (1997). "Solutions of Forward-Backward Stochastic Differential Equations." In N. El Karoui and L. Mazliak (Eds.), *Backward Stochastic Differential Equations*, pp. 39–46. Essex: Addison Wesley Longman Ltd.

Poteshman, A. M. (1998). "Estimating a General Stochastic Variance Model from Options Prices." Working Paper, Graduate School of Business, University of Chicago.

Pouque, J., G. Papanicolaou, and K. Sircar. (1999a). "Financial Modeling in a Fast Mean-Reverting Stochastic Volatility Environment." *Asia-Pacific Financial Markets* 6: 37–48.

Pouque, J., G. Papanicolaou, and K. Sircar. (1999b). "Mean-Reverting Stochastic Volatility." Working Paper, Department of Mathematics, North Carolina State University.

Pouque, J., G. Papanicolaou, and K. Sircar. (1999c). "Stochastic Volatility Correction to Black-Scholes." Working Paper, Department of Mathematics, North Carolina State University.

Prescott, E., and R. Mehra. (1980). "Recursive Competitive Equilibrium: The Case of Homogeneous Households." *Econometrica* 48: 1365–1379.

Press, W., B. Flannery, S. Teukolsky, and W. Vetterling. (1993). *Numerical Recipes in C: The Art of Scientific Computing* (2d ed.). Cambridge: Cambridge University Press.

Prigent, J.-L. (1994). "From Discrete to Continuous Time Finance: Weak Convergence of the Optimal Financial Trading Strategies." Working Paper, Institute of Mathematical Research of Rennes, University of Rennes.

Prigent, J.-L. (1995). "Incomplete Markets: Convergence of Options Values under the Minimal Martingale Measure." Working Paper, THEMA, Université de Cergy-Pontoise, Cergy-Pontoise.

Prisman, E. (1985). "Valuation of Risky Assets in Arbitrage Free Economies with Frictions." Working Paper, Department of Finance, University of Arizona.

Prisman, E. (2000). *Pricing Derivative Securities.* San Diego: Academic Press.

Protter, P. (1990). *Stochastic Integration and Differential Equations.* New York: Springer-Verlag.

Protter, P. (1999). "A Partial Introduction to Finance." Working Paper, Purdue University. Forthcoming in *Stochastic Processes and Their Applications.*

Pye, G. (1966). "A Markov Model of the Term Structure." *Quarterly Journal of Economics* 81: 61–72.

Pye, G. (1974). "Gauging the Default Premium." *Financial Analysts Journal* (January-February): 49–52.

Quenez, M.-C. (1992). "Méthodes de Controle Stochastique en Finance." Working Paper, Ph.D. diss., Laboratoires de Probabilités, Université de Paris VI.

Quenez, M.-C. (1997). "Stochastic Control and BSDEs." In N. El Karoui and L. Mazliak (Eds.), *Backward Stochastic Differential Equations,* pp. 83–100. Essex: Addison Wesley Longman Ltd.

Radner, R. (1967). "Equilibre des Marchés a Terme et au Comptant en Cas d'Incertitude." *Cahiers d'Econométrie* 4: 35–52.

Radner, R. (1972). "Existence of Equilibrium of Plans, Prices, and Price Expectations in a Sequence of Markets." *Econometrica* 40: 289–303.

Rady, S. (1993). "State Prices Implicit in Valuation Formula for Derivative Securities: A Martingale Approach." Working Paper, London School of Economics.

Rady, S. (1995). "Option Pricing with a Quadratic Diffusion Term." Working Paper, Financial Markets Group, London School of Economics.

Rebonato, R., and I. Cooper. (1996). "Coupling Backward Induction with Monte Carlo Simulations: A Fast Fourier Transform (FFT) Approach." Working Paper, Institute of Finance and Accounting, London Business School.

Redekop, J. (1995). "Extreme-value Distributions for Generalizations of Brownian Motion." Working Paper, Departments of Economics and Statistics and Actuarial Science.

Redekop, J., and R. Fisher. (1995). "Extreme-Value Diagnostic Statistics for Some Stochastic Volatility Models." Working Paper, Department of Economics, University of Waterloo.

Reisman, H. (1986). "Option Pricing for Stocks with a Generalized Log-Normal Price Distribution." Working Paper, Department of Finance, University of Minnesota.

Renault, E., S. Pastorello, and N. Touzi. (2000). "Statistical Inference for Random Variance Option Pricing." *Journal of Business and Economic Statistics* 18: 358–317.

Renault, E., and N. Touzi. (1992). "Stochastic Volatility Models: Statistical Inference from Implied Volatilities." Working Paper, GREMAQ IDEI, Toulouse, and CREST, Paris, France.

Repullo, R. (1986). "On the Generic Existence of Radner Equilibria when there are as Many Securities as States of Nature." *Economics Letters* 21: 101–105.

Revuz, D. (1975). *Markov Chains.* Amsterdam: North-Holland.

Revuz, D., and M. Yor. (1991). *Continuous Martingales and Brownian Motion.* New York: Springer.

Ricciardi, L., and S. Sato. (1988). "First-Passage-Time Density and Moments of the Ornstein-Uhlenbeck Process." *Journal of Applied Probability* 25: 43–57.

Rich, D. (1993). "The Valuation of Black-Scholes Options Subject to Intertemporal Default Risk." Working Paper, Department of Finance, Virginia Polytechnic Institute.

Richard, S. (1975). "Optimal Consumption, Portfolio, and Life Insurance Rules for an Uncertain Lived Individual in a Continuous Time Model." *Journal of Financial Economics* 2: 187–203.

Richard, S. (1978). "An Arbitrage Model of the Term Structure of Interest Rates." *Journal of Financial Economics* 6: 33–57.

Richardson, H. (1989). "A Minimum Variance Result in Continuous Trading Portfolio Optimization." *Management Science* 35: 1045–1055.

Ritchken, P., and L. Sankarasubramaniam. (1992). "Valuing Claims when Interest Rates have Stochastic Volatility." Working Paper, Department of Finance, University of Southern California.

Ritchken, P., and R. Trevor. (1993). "On Finite State Markovian Representations of the Term Structure." Working Paper, Department of Finance, University of Southern California.

Ritchken, P., and R. Trevor. (1999). "Option Pricing Options under GARCH and Stochastic Volatility." *Journal of Finance* 54: 377–402.

Rockafeller, T. (1973). *Convex Analysis.* Princeton, NJ: Princeton University Press.

Rogers, C. (1993). "Which Model for Term-Structure of Interest Rates Should One Use?" Working Paper, Department of Mathematics, Queen Mary and Westfield College, University of London.

Rogers, C. (1994). "Equivalent Martingale Measures and No-Arbitrage." *Stochastics and Stochastic Reports* 51: 1–9.

Rogers, C. (1998). "Arbitrage with Fractional Brownian Motion." Working Paper, University of Bath.

Rogers, C., and Z. Shi. (1995). "The Value of an Asian Option." *Journal of Applied Probability* 32: 1077–1088.

Rogers, C., and W. Stummer. (1994). "How Well Do One-Factor Models Fit Bond Prices?" Working Paper, School of Mathematical Sciences, University of Bath.

Rogers, L., and E. Stapleton. (1998). "Fast Accurate Binomial Pricing." *Finance and Stochastics* 2: 3–17.

Romano, M., and N. Touzi. (1997). "Contingent Claims and Market Completeness in a Stochastic Volatility Model." *Mathematical Finance* 7: 399–412.

Rosenberg, J., and R. Engle. (1999). "Empirical Pricing Kernels." Working Paper, Stern School of Business, New York University.

Ross, S. (1976). "The Arbitrage Theory of Capital Asset Pricing." *Journal of Economic Theory* 13: 341–360.

Ross, S. (1978). "A Simple Approach to the Valuation of Risky Streams." *Journal of Business* 51: 453–475.

Ross, S. (1987). "Arbitrage and Martingales with Taxation." *Journal of Political Economy* 95: 371–393.

Ross, S. (1989). "Information and Volatility: The Non-Arbitrage Martingale Approach to Timing and Resolution Irrelevancy." *Journal of Finance* 64: 1–17.

Royden, H. (1968). *Real Analysis* (2d ed.). New York: Macmillan.

Rubinstein, M. (1974a). "An Aggregation Theorem for Securities Markets." *Journal of Financial Economics* 1: 225–244.

Rubinstein, M. (1974b). "A Discrete-Time Synthesis of Financial Theory." Working Paper, Haas School of Business, University of California, Berkeley.

Rubinstein, M. (1976). "The Valuation of Uncertain Income Streams and the Pricing of Options." *Bell Journal of Economics* 7: 407–425.

Rubinstein, M. (1987). "Derivative Assets Analysis." *Economics Perspectives* 1: 73–93.

Rubinstein, M. (1994). "Implied Binomial Trees." *Journal of Finance* 49: 771–818.

Rubinstein, M. (1995). "As Simple as One, Two, Three." *Risk* 8 (January): 44–47.

Rubinstein, M. (1999). *Derivatives: A Power-Plus Picture Book.* Corte Madera, CA: In-The-Money.

Ruegg, M. (1996). "Optimal Consumption and Portfolio Choice with Borrowing Constraints." Working Paper, Department of Mathematics, ETH Zurich.

Rumsey, J. (1996). "Comparison of Tax Rates Inferred from Zero-Coupon Yield Curves." *Journal of Fixed Income* 6 (March): 75–81.

Rutkowski, M. (1995). "Pricing and Hedging of Contingent Claims in the HJM Model with Deterministic Volatilities." Working Paper, Institute of Mathematics, Politechnika Warszawska, Warszawa.

Rutkowski, M. (1996). "Valuation and Hedging of Contingent Claims in the HJM Model with Deterministic Volatilities." *Applied Mathematical Finance* 3: 237–267.

Rutkowski, M. (1998). "Dynamics of Spot, Forward, and Futures Libor Rates." *International Journal of Theoretical and Applied Finance* 1: 425–445.

Rydberg, T. (1997). "Existence of Unique Equivalent Martingale Measures in a Markovian Setting." *Finance and Stochastics* 1: 251–257.

Ryder, H., and G. Heal. (1973). "Optimal Growth with Intertemporally Dependent Preferences." *Review of Economic Studies* 40: 1–31.

Saà-Requejo, J. (1993). "The Dynamics of the Term Structure of Risk Premia in Foreign Exchange Markets." Working Paper, INSEAD, Fontainebleau, France.

Sabarwal, T. (1999). "Default and Bankruptcy in General Equilibrium." Working Paper, Department of Economics, University of California, Berkeley.

Saito, M. (1998). "Incomplete Insurance and Non-expected Utility." *Japanese Economic Review* 49: 271–83.

Samuelson, P. (1969). "Lifetime Portfolio Selection by Dynamic Stochastic Programming." *Review of Economics and Statistics* 51: 239–246.

Sandmann, K., and D. Sondermann. (1997). "On the Stability of Lognormal Interest Rate Models." *Mathematical Finance* 7: 119–125.

Sandroni, A. (1995). "The Risk Premium and the Interest Rate Puzzles: The Role of Heterogeneous Agents." Working Paper, University of Pennsylvania.

Santa-Clara, P., and D. Sornette. (1997). "The Dynamics of the Forward Interest Rate Curve with Stochastic String Shocks." Working Paper, University of California, Los Angeles.

Santos, M. (1991). "Smoothness of the Policy Function in Discrete Time Economic Models." *Econometrica* 59: 1365–1382.

Santos, M. (1994). "Smooth Dynamics and Computation in Models of Economic Growth." *Journal of Economic Dynamics and Control* 18: 879–895.

Santos, M., and J. Vigo. (1998). "Numerical Dynamic Programming Algorithm Applied to Economic Models." *Econometrica* 66: 409–426.

Santos, M., and M. Woodford. (1995). "Rational Asset Pricing Bubbles." *Econometrica* 65: 19–58.

Sbuelz, A. (1998). "A General Treatment of Barrier Options." Working Paper, London Business School.

Scaillet, O. (1996). "Compound and Exchange Options in the Affine Term Structure Model." *Applied Mathematical Finance* 3: 75–92.

Schachermayer, W. (1992). "A Hilbert-Space Proof of the Fundamental Theorem of Asset Pricing." *Insurance Mathematics and Economics* 11: 249–257.

Schachermayer, W. (1993). "A Counterexample to Several Problems in the Theory of Asset Pricing." *Mathematical Finance* 3: 217–230.

Schachermayer, W. (1994). "Martingale Measures for Discrete-Time Processes with Infinite Horizon." *Mathematical Finance* 4: 25–56.

Schachermayer, W. (1998). "Some Remarks on a Paper of David Kreps." Working Paper, Institut für Statistik der Universität Wien.

Schaefer, S., and E. Schwartz. (1984). "A Two-Factor Model of the Term Structure: An Approximate Analytical Solution." *Journal of Financial and Quantitative Analysis* 19: 413–423.

Scheinkman, J. (1989). "Market Incompleteness and the Equilibrium Valuation of Assets." In S. Bhattacharya and G. Constantinides (Eds.), *Theory of Valuation*, pp. 45–51. Totowa, NJ: Rowman and Littlefield.

Scheinkman, J., and L. Weiss. (1986). "Borrowing Constraints and Aggregate Economic Activity." *Econometrica* 54: 23–45.

Schoenmakers, J., and A. Heemink. (1996). "Fast Valuation of Financial Derivatives." Working Paper, Delft University of Technology, The Netherlands.

Schönbucher, P. (1998). "Term Structure Modelling of Defaultable Bonds." *Review of Derivatives Research* 2: 161–192.

Schroder, M. (1993). "Optimal Portfolio Selection with Transactions Costs." Working Paper, Finance Department, Northwestern University.

Schroder, M. (1999). "Changes of Numeraire of Pricing Futures, Forwards and Options." *Review of Financial Studies* 12: 143–164.

Schröder, M. (1999a). "On the Valuation of Arithmetic-Average Asian Options: Explicit Formulas." Working Paper, Fakultät für Mathematik und Informatik der Universität Mannheim.

Schröder, M. (1999b). "On the Valuation of Double-Barrier Options." Working Paper, Fakultät für Mathematik und Informatik der Universität Mannheim.

Schröder, M. (1999c). "On the Valuation of Paris Options: Foundational Results." Working Paper, Lehrstuhl Mathematik III Universität Mannheim.

Schröder, M. (1999d). "On the Valuation of Paris Options: The First Standard Case." Working Paper, Lehrstuhl Mathematik III Universität Mannheim.

Schroder, M. and C. Skiadas. (1997). "Optimal Consumption and Portfolio Selection with Temporally Dependent Preferences." Working Paper, School of Management, SUNY at Buffalo, NY.

Schroder, M., and C. Skiadas. (1999). "Optimal Consumption and Portfolio Selection with Stochastic Differential Utility." *Journal of Economic Theory* 89: 68–126.

Schroder, M., and C. Skiadas. (2000). "An Isomorphism between Asset Pricing Models with and without Linear Habit Formation." Working Paper, Eli Broad Graduate School of Management, Michigan State University.

Schwartz, E. (1977). "The Valuation of Warrants: Implementing a New Approach." *Journal of Financial Economics* 4: 79–94.

Schwartz, E. (1997). "Presidential Address: The Stochastic Behavior of Commodity Prices: Implications for Valuation and Hedging." *Journal of Finance* 52: 923–973.

Schweizer, M. (1992)."Martingale Densities for General Asset Prices." *Journal of Mathematical Economics* 21: 363–378.

Schweizer, M. (1994a). "Approximating Random Variables by Stochastic Integrals." *Annals of Probability* 22: 1536–1575.

Schweizer, M. (1994b). "Hedging and the CAPM." Working Paper, Department of Mathematics, University of Bonn.

Schweizer, M. (1994c). "A Projection Result for Semimartingales." *Stochastics and Stochastics Reports* 50: 175–183.

Schweizer, M. (1994d). "Risk-Minimizing Hedging Strategies under Restricted Information." *Mathematical Finance* 4: 327–342.

Scott, L. (1987). "Option Pricing when the Variance Changes Randomly: Theory, Estimation, and Application." *Journal of Financial and Quantitative Analysis* 4: 419–438.

Scott, L. (1992). "Stock Market Volatility and the Pricing of Index Options: An Analysis of Implied Volatilities and the Volatility Risk Premium in a Model with Stochastic Interest Rates and Volatility." Working Paper, Department of Finance, University of Georgia.

Scott, L. (1996a). "Simulating a Multi-Factor Term Structure Model over Relatively Long Discrete Time Periods." Working Paper, Department of Banking and Finance, University of Georgia, Athens.

Scott, L. (1996b). "The Valuation of Interest Rate Derivatives in a Multi-Factor Cox-Ingersoll-Ross Model that Matches the Initial Term Structure." Working Paper, Department of Banking and Finance, University of Georgia, Athens.

Scott, L. (1997). "Pricing Stock Options in a Jump-Diffusion Model with Stochastic Volatility and Interest Rates: Applications of Fourier Inversion Methods." *Mathematical Finance* 7: 413–426.

Sekine, J. (1998). "Mean-Variance Hedging in Continuous-Time with Stochastic Interest Rate." Working Paper, MTP Investment Technology Institute, Tokyo.

Selby, M., and S. Hodges. (1987). "On the Evaluation of Compound Options." *Management Science* 33: 347–355.

Selby, M., and C. Strickland. (1993). "Computing the Fong and Vasicek Pure Discount Bond Price Formula." Working Paper, FORC Preprint 93/42, October 1993, University of Warwick.

Selden, L. (1978). "A New Representation of Preference over 'Certain × Uncertain' Consumption Pairs: The 'Ordinal Certainty Equivalent' Hypothesis." *Econometrica* 46: 1045–1060.

Serrat, A. (1995). "An Equilibrium Analysis of Liquidity Constraints." Working Paper, Sloan School of Management, Massachusetts Institute of Technology.

Serrat, A. (2000). "Exchange Rate Dynamics in a Multilateral Target Zone." *Review of Economic Studies* 67: 193–211.

Sethi, S., and M. Taksar. (1988). "A Note on Merton's 'Optimum Consumption and Portfolio Rules in a Continuous-Time Model'." *Journal of Economic Theory* 46: 395–401.

Sethi, S., and M. Taksar. (1992). "Infinite-Horizon Investment Consumption Model with a Nonterminal Bankruptcy." *Journal of Optimization Theory and Applications* 74: 333–346.

Sethi, S., M. Taksar, and E. Prisman. (1992). "Explicit Solution of a General Consumption/Portfolio Problem with Subsistence Consumption and Bankruptcy." *Journal of Economic Dynamics and Control* 16: 747–768.

Shannon, C. (1996). "Determinacy of Competitive Equilibria in Economies with Many Commodities." Working Paper, Department of Economics, University of California, Berkeley. Forthcoming in *Economic Theory*.

Sharpe, W. (1964). "Capital Asset Prices: A Theory of Market Equilibrium under Conditions of Risk." *Journal of Finance* 19: 425–442.

Sharpe, W. (1985). *Investments* (3d ed.). Englewood Cliffs, NJ: Prentice-Hall.

Shepp, L., and A. N. Shiryaev. (1993). "The Russian Option: Reduced Regret." *Annals of Applied Probability* 3: 631–640.

Shimko, D., N. Tejima, and D. van Deventer. (1993). "The Pricing of Risky Debt when Interest Rates are Stochastic." *Journal of Fixed Income* 3 (September): 58–65.

Shirakawa, H. (1994). "Optimal Consumption and Portfolio Selection with Incomplete Markets and Upper and Lower Bound Constraints." *Mathematical Finance* 4: 1–24.

Shreve, S., and M. Soner. (1994). "Optimal Investment and Consumption with Transaction Costs." *Annals of Applied Probability* 4: 609–692.

Shreve, S., M. Soner, and G.-L. Xu. (1991). "Optimal Investment and Consumption with Two Bonds and Transaction Costs." *Mathematical Finance* 1: 53–84.

Shrikhande, M. (1995). "Nonaddictive Habit-Formation and the Equity Premium Puzzle." Working Paper, School of Management, Georgia Institute of Technology, Atlanta.

Siegel, D., and D. Siegel. (1990). *Futures Markets*. Orlando: The Dryden Press.

Singh, M. (1995). "Estimation of Multifactor Cox, Ingersoll, and Ross Term Structure Model: Evidence on Volatility Structure and Parameter Stability." *Journal of Fixed Income* 5 (September): 8–28.

Singleton, K. (1999). "Estimation of Affine Asset Pricing Models using the Empirical Characteristic Function." Working Paper, Stanford University and NBER. Forthcoming in *Journal of Econometrics*.

Sircar, R. (1996). "Feedback Effects in Option Pricing." Working Paper, SC-CM Program, Stanford University.

Skiadas, C. (1995). "On the (Super) Differentiability of the Utility of a Representative Agent at a Pareto Optimal Allocation." Working Paper, Private Written Communication, Kellogg School of Management, Northwestern University.

Skiadas, C. (1997). "Conditioning and Aggregation of Preferences." *Econometrica* 65: 347–367.

Skiadas, C. (1998). "Recursive Utility and Preferences for Information." *Economic Theory* 12: 293–312.

Smith, G. (1985). *Numerical Solution of Partial Differential Equations: Finite Difference Methods* (3d ed.). Oxford: Clarendon Press.

Soner, M., S. Shreve, and J. Cvitanić. (1994). "There is No Nontrivial Hedging Portfolio for Option Pricing with Transaction Costs." *Annals of Applied Probability* 5: 327–355.

Song, S. (1998). "A Remark on a Result of Duffie and Lando." Working Paper, Department of Mathematics, Université d'Evry, France.

Sorenson, E., and T. Bollier. (1995). "Pricing Default Risk: The Interest-Rate Swap Example." In *Derivative Credit Risk*. London: Risk Publications.

Sornette, D. (1998). "String Formulation of the Dynamics of the Forward Interest Rate Curve." Working Paper, Université des Sciences, Parc Valrose, France, and Institute of Geophysics and Planetary Physics, University of California, Los Angeles.

Stambaugh, R. (1988). "The Information in Forward Rates: Implications for Models of the Term Structure." *Journal of Financial Economics* 21: 41–70.

Stanton, R. (1995a). "A Nonparametric Model of Term Structure Dynamics and the Market Price of Interest Rate Risk." *Journal of Finance* 52: 1973–2002.

Stanton, R. (1995b). "Rational Prepayment and the Valuation of Mortgage-Backed Securities." *Review of Financial Studies* 8: 677–708.

Stanton, R., and N. Wallace. (1995). "ARM Wrestling: Valuing Adjustable Rate Mortgages Indexed to the Eleventh District Cost of Funds." *Real Estate Economics* 23: 311–345.

Stanton, R., and N. Wallace. (1998). "Mortgage Choice: What's the Point?" *Real Estate Economics* 26: 173–205.

Stapleton, R., and M. Subrahmanyam. (1978). "A Multiperiod Equilibrium Asset Pricing Model." *Econometrica* 46: 1077–1093.

Steenkiste, R. V., and S. Foresi. (1999). "Arrow-Debreu Prices for Affine Models." Working Paper, Salomon Smith Barney, Inc., Goldman Sachs Asset Management.

Stein, E., and J. Stein. (1991). "Stock Price Distributions with Stochastic Volatility: An Analytic Approach." *Review of Financial Studies* 4: 725–752.

Stokey, N., and R. Lucas. (1989). *Recursive Methods in Economic Dynamics (with Ed Prescott)*. Cambridge, MA: Harvard University Press.

Stoll, H., and R. Whaley. (1993). *Futures and Options: Theory and Applications*. Cincinnati: Southwestern.

Streufert, P. (1991a). "Existence and Characterization Results for Stochastic Dynamic Programming." Working Paper, Department of Economics, University of California, San Diego.

Streufert, P. (1991b). "Ordinal Dynamic Programming." Working Paper, Department of Economics, University of Wisconsin, Madison.

Streufert, P. (1996). "Biconvergent Stochastic Dynamic Programming, Asymptotic Impatience, and 'Average' Growth." *Journal of Economic Dynamics and Control* 20: 385–413.

Stricker, C. (1984). "Integral Representation in the Theory of Continuous Trading." *Stochastics and Stochastic Reports* 13: 249–265.

Stricker, C. (1990). "Arbitrage et Lois de Martingale." *Annales de l'Institut Henri Poincaré* 26: 451–460.

Strikwerda, J. (1989). *Finite Difference Schemes and Partial Differential Equations*. Belmont, CA: Wadsworth.

Stulz, R. (1982). "Options on the Minimum or the Maximum of Two Risky Assets: Analysis and Applications." *Journal of Financial Economics* 10: 161–185.

Subramanian, A. (1997). "European Option Pricing with General Transaction Costs." Working Paper, Center for Applied Mathematics, Cornell University.

Sun, T.-S. (1992). "Real and Nominal Interest Rates: A Discrete-Time Model and its Continuous-Time Limit." *Review of Financial Studies* 5: 581–612.

Sundaresan, S. (1989). "Intertemporally Dependent Preferences in the Theories of Consumption, Portfolio Choice and Equilibrium Asset Pricing." *Review of Financial Studies* 2: 73–89.

Sundaresan, S. (1997). *Fixed Income Markets and Their Derivatives.* Cincinnati: South-Western.

Svensson, L. E. O. (1989). "Portfolio Choice with Non-Expected Utility in Continuous Time." *Economic Letters* 30: 313–317.

Svensson, L. E. O. and M. Dahlquist. (1993). "Estimating the Term Structure of Interest Rates with Simple and Complex Functional Forms: Nelson and Siegel vs. Longstaff and Schwartz." Working Paper, Institute for International Economic Studies, Stockholm University.

Svensson, L. E. O. and I. Werner. (1993). "Non-Traded Assets in Incomplete Markets." *European Economic Review* 37: 1149–1168.

Taksar, M., M. Klass, and D. Assaf. (1988). "A Diffusion Model for Optimal Portfolio Selection in the Presence of Brokerage Fees." *Mathematics of Operations Research* 13: 277–294.

Talay, D. (1984). "Efficient Numerical Schemes for the Approximation of Expectations of Functionals of S.D.E." In *Filtering and Control of Random Processes.* Lecture Notes in Control and Information Sciences 61, pp. 294–313. New York: Springer-Verlag.

Talay, D. (1986). "Discrétiation d'une Equation Différentielle Stochastique et Calcul Approché d'Espérances de Fonctionelles de la Solution." *Mathematical Modeling and Numerical Analysis* 20: 141–179.

Talay, D. (1990). "Second Order Discretization Schemes of Stochastic Differential Systems for the Computation of the Invariant Law." *Stochastics and Stochastics Reports* 29: 13–36.

Talay, D., and L. Tubaro. (1990). "Expansion of the Global Error for Numerical Schemes Solving Stochastic Differential Equations." *Stochastic Analysis and Applications* 8: 94–120.

Taleb, N. (1997). "Transaction Costs: Much Smaller than We Thought." Working Paper, Paribas, Inc. and Universite Paris Dauphine.

Tanudjaja, S. (1995). "American Swaption Early Exercise Premium Approximation." Working Paper, Global Derivatives, Citibank, London.

Tauchen, G., and R. Hussey. (1991). "Quadrature-Based Methods for Obtaining Approximate Solutions to the Integral Equations of Nonlinear Rational Expectations Models." *Econometrica* 59: 371–396.

Tavella, D., and C. Randall. (2000). *Pricing Financial Instruments: The Finite Difference Method.* New York: Wiley.

Taylor, S. (1994). "Modeling Stochastic Volatility: A Review and Comparative Study." *Mathematical Finance* 4: 183–204.

Telmer, C. (1993). "Asset-Pricing Puzzles and Incomplete Markets." *Journal of Finance* 48: 1803–1832.

Tepla, L. (1996). "Revisiting Optimal Consumption and Portfolio Policies when Asset Prices Follow a Diffusion Process." Working Paper, Department of Engineering-Economic Systems, Stanford University.

Tepla, L. (2000). "A Characterization of Optimal Portfolio Policies with Borrowing and Short-sale Constraints." *Journal of Economic Dynamics and Control* 24: 1623–1639.

Tice, J., and N. Webber. (1997). "A Non-Linear Model of the Term Structure of Interest Rates." *Mathematical Finance* 7: 177–209.

Toft, K., and G. Brown. (1996). "Constructing Binomial Trees from Multiple Implied Probability Distributions." Working Paper, Department of Finance, University of Texas, Austin.

Topper, J. (1997). "Solving Term Structure Models with Finite Elements." Working Paper, Fachbereich Wirtschaftwissenschaften der Universität Hannover.

Török, C. (1993). "Numerical Solution of Linear Stochastic Differential Equations." Working Paper, Department of Mathematics, Technical University of Kosice.

Touzi, N. (1993). "Modèles de Volatilité Stochastique." Working Paper, Ph.D. Dissertation, CEREMADE, Université de Paris IX, Dauphine.

Touzi, N. (1995). "American Options Exercise Boundary when the Volatility Changes Randomly." Working Paper, CEREMADE, Université de Paris IX, Dauphine.

Tsiveriotis, K., and C. Fernandes. (1998). "Valuing Convertible Bonds With Credit Risk." *Journal of Fixed Income* 8: 95–102.

Turnbull, S. (1993). "Pricing and Hedging Diff Swaps." Working Paper, School of Business, Queen's University.

Turnbull, S. (1994). "Interest Rate Digital Options and Range Notes." Working Paper, School of Business, Queen's University.

Uhrig-Homburg, M. (1998). "Endogenous Bankruptcy when Issuance is Costly." Working Paper, Department of Finance, University of Mannheim.

Uzawa, H. (1968). "Time Preference, The Consumption Function and Optimal Asset Holdings." In J. Wolfe (Ed.), *Value, Capital, and Growth. Papers in Honour of Sir John Hicks*, pp. 485–504. Chicago: Aldine.

Van Horne, J. (1993). *Financial Market Rates and Flows* (4th ed.). Englewood Cliffs, NJ: Prentice-Hall.

Van Moerbeke, P. (1976). "On Optimal Stopping and Free Boundary Problems." *Archive for Rational Mechanics and Analysis* 60: 101–148.

Vargiolu, T. (1999). "Invariant Measures for the Musiela Equation with Deterministic Diffusion Term." *Finance and Stochastics* 3: 483–492.

Vasicek, O. (1977). "An Equilibrium Characterization of the Term Structure." *Journal of Financial Economics* 5: 177–188.

Vasicek, O. (1995). "The Finite Factor Model of Bond Prices." Working Paper, KMV Corporation, San Francisco.

Vayanos, D. (1998). "Transaction Costs and Asset Prices: A Dynamic Equilibrium Model." *Review of Financial Studies* 11: 1–58.

Vayanos, D., and J.-L. Vila. (1999). "Equilibrium Interest Rate and Liquidity Premium with Transaction Costs." *Economic Theory* 13: 509–539.

Vila, J.-L., and T. Zariphopoulou. (1997). "Optimal Consumption and Portfolio Choice with Borrowing Constraints." *Journal of Economic Theory* 77: 402–431.

Walras, L. (1874–1877). *Eléments d'Économie Politique Pure* (4th ed.). Lausanne: L. Corbaz, English translation of the definitive edition by W. Jaffé, *Elements of Pure Economics*. London: Allen and Unwin, (1954).

Wang, J. (1993a). "A Model of Intertemporal Asset Prices under Asymmetric Information." *Review of Economic Studies* 60: 249–282.

Wang, J. (1996). "The Term Structure of Interest Rates in a Pure Exchange Economy with Heterogeneous Investors." *Journal of Financial Economics* 41: 75–110.

Wang, S. (1993b). "The Integrability Problem of Asset Prices." *Journal of Economic Theory* 59: 199–213.

Wang, S. (1993c). "Is Kreps-Porteus Utility Distinguishable from Intertemporal Expected Utility?" *Economic Theory* 3: 119–127.

Wang, S. (1993d). "The Local Recoverability of Risk Aversion and Intertemporal Substitution." *Journal of Economic Theory* 59: 333–363.

Webber, N. (1990). "The Term Structure of Spot Rate Volatility and the Behavior of Interest Rate Processes." Working Paper, Financial Options Research Centre, University of Warwick.

Webber, N. (1992). "The Consistency of Term Structure Models: The Short Rate, the Long Rate, and Volatility." Working Paper, Financial Options Research Centre, University of Warwick.

Weerasinghe, A. (1998). "Singular Optimal Strategies for Investment with Transaction Costs." *Annals of Applied Probability* 8: 1312–1330.

Weil, P. (1992). "Equilibrium Asset Prices with Undiversifiable Labor Income Risk." *Journal of Economic Dynamics and Control* 16: 769–790.

Werner, J. (1985). "Equilibrium in Economies with Incomplete Financial Markets." *Journal of Economic Theory* 36: 110–119.

Werner, J. (1991). "On Constrained Optimal Allocations with Incomplete Markets." *Economic Theory* 1: 205–209.

Whalley, A. E., and P. Wilmott. (1997). "An Asymptotic Analysis of an Optimal Hedging Model for Options with Transaction Costs." *Mathematical Finance* 7: 307–324.

Wiggins, J. (1987). "Option Values under Stochastic Volatility: Theory and Empirical Estimates." *Journal of Financial Economics* 19: 351–372.

Willard, G. (1996). "Calculating Prices and Sensitivities for Path-Independent Derivative Securities in Multifactor Models." Working Paper, Washington University in St. Louis.

Willinger, W., and M. Tacqu. (1989). "Pathwise Stochastic Integration and Application to the Theory of Continuous Trading." *Stochastic Processes and Their Applications* 32: 253–280.

Willinger, W., and M. Tacqu. (1991). "Toward a Convergence Theory for Continuous Stochastic Securities Market Models." *Mathematical Finance* 1: 55–100.

Wilmott, P., J. Dewynne, and S. Howison. (1993). *Option Pricing: Mathematical Models and Computation.* Oxford: Oxford Financial Press.

Wilmott, P., S. Howison, and J. Dewynne. (1995). *The Mathematics of Financial Derivatives.* Cambridge: Cambridge University Press.

Won, D. (1996a). "Generic Existence of Equilibrium in Incomplete Markets: The Case of Differential Participation." Working Paper, Korea Economic Research Institute, Seoul.

Won, D. (1996b). "A New Approach to Equilibrium in Incomplete Markets." Working Paper, Korea Economic Research Institute, Seoul.

Wu, L. (1996). "The Front-Fixing Finite Difference Method for the Valuation of American Options." Working Paper, Department of Mathematics, University of Science and Technology, Hong Kong.

Xu, G.-L., and S. Shreve. (1992a). "A Duality Method for Optimal Consumption and Investment under Short-Selling Prohibition. I. General Market Coefficients." *Annals of Applied Probability* 2: 87–112.

Xu, G.-L., and S. Shreve. (1992b). "A Duality Method for Optimal Consumption and Investment under Short-Selling Prohibition. II. Constant Market Coefficients." *Annals of Applied Probability* 2: 314–328.

Yamada, T., and S. Watanabe. (1971). "On the Uniqueness of Solutions of Stochastic Differential Equations." *Journal of Mathematics of Kyoto University* 11: 155–167.

Yamazaki, A. (1991). "Equilibrium in Economies with Incomplete Markets and Outside Money: Transactions Costs and Existence." Working Paper, Department of Economics, Hitotsubashi University.

Yor, M. (1991). "On Some Exponential Functionals of Brownian Motion." Working Paper, Laboratoires de Probabilités, Université de Paris VI.

Yor, M. (1993). "The Distribution of Brownian Quantiles." Working Paper, Laboratoires de Probabilités, Université de Paris VI.

Yu, D. (1999). "Pricing of New Assets in an Infinite-Horizon Frictional Economy." *Pacific Economic Review* 4: 293–304.

Yu, G. (1993). "Essays on the Valuation of American Options." Working Paper, Stern School of Business, New York University.

Zapatero, F. (1993). "Interest Rates with Converging Heterogeneous Reliefs." Working Paper, Haas School of Business, University of California at Berkeley.

Zapatero, F. (1995). "Equilibrium Asset Prices and Exchange Rates." *Journal of Economic Dynamics and Control* 19: 787–811.

Zapatero, F. (1998). "Effects of Financial Innovations on Market Volatility when Beliefs are Heterogeneous." *Journal of Economic Dynamics and Control* 22: 597–626.

Zariphopoulou, T. (1992). "Investment-Consumption Models with Transactions Costs and Markov-Chain Parameters." *SIAM Journal on Control and Optimization* 30: 613–636.

Zariphopoulou, T. (1994). "Consumption-Investment Models with Constraints." *SIAM Journal on Control and Optimization* 32: 59–84.

Zhang, X. (1993). "Options Américaines et Modèles de Diffusion avec Sauts." *Comtes Rendus de l'Academie de Science de Paris* 317: 857–862.

Zhang, X. (1994). "Numerical Analysis of American Option Pricing in a Jump-Diffusion Model." Working Paper, CERMA, URA-CNRS 1502, E.N.P.C, Paris, France.

Zheng, C.-C. (1994). "Pricing Interest Rates Contingent Claims by a Pricing Kernel." Working Paper, NationsBank, New York.

Zhou, C. (1997a). "Path-Dependent Option Valuation when the Underlying Path is Discontinuous." Working Paper, Divisions of Research and Statistics and Monetary Affairs, Federal Reserve Board, Washington, D.C.

Zhou, C.-S. (2000). "A Jump-Diffusion Approach to Modeling Credit Risk and Valuing Defaultable Securities." Working Paper, Federal Reserve Board, Washington, D.C.

Zhou, Y.-Q. (1997b). "The Global Structure of Equilibrium Manifold in Incomplete Markets." *Journal of Mathematical Economics* 27: 91–111.

Zhu, Y.-I., and Y. Sun. (1999). "The Singularity-Separating Method for Two-Factor Convertible Bonds." *Journal of Computational Finance* 3 (Fall): 91–110.

Zou, J., and E. Derman. (1996). "Monte Carlo Valuation of Path-Dependent Options on Indexes with a Volatility Smile." Working Paper, Goldman, Sachs and Co., New York.

Zuasti, J. (1999). "Insurance with Frequent Trading." Working Paper, Pompeu Favra University, Barcelona.

Zvan, R., P. Forsyth, and K. Vetzal. (1998). "Robust Numerical Methods for PDE Models of Asian Options." *Journal of Computational Finance* 1 (Winter): 39–78.

Symbol Glossary

$(\cdot \mid \cdot)$, 16

$(x - K)^+$, 37

$B(D)$, 67

C^k, 13

E^Q, 324

H^2, 102

L^*-smooth, 71

L^2-closedness of the marketed space, 131

L^2-reducible, 114

$L^2(P)$, 117

T-period arbitrage, 70

T-period state-price deflator, 70

W^θ, 106

X^Y, 102

Φ, 89

δ^θ, 22

$\varnothing$, 323

$\frac{dQ}{dP} = Y$, 324

$\frac{dQ}{dP}$, 332

$\int \theta \, dB$, 84, 335

$\int \theta \, dS$, 87

$\int \theta \, dX$, 95

$\mathrm{corr}(\cdot)$, 12

$\mathrm{tr}(A)$, 95

$\max(x, y)$, 57

$\nabla U(x)$, 328

$\nabla U(x^*; y) \le 0$, 328

$\nabla U(c^*)$, 222

$\nabla U(c^*; c)$, 25

$\partial U(c^*)$, 5

$\partial^2 U(c^i)$, 13

σ-algebra, 21, 329

σ-field, 21, 329

$\sigma(Z)$, 324

$d(F, G) = 0$, 67

$\mathscr{D}$, 95

$\mathscr{H}^1$, 86, 94

$\mathscr{H}^2(S)$, 87

$\mathscr{H}^2(X)$, 95

$\mathscr{L}(S)$, 87

$\mathscr{L}(X)$, 95

$\mathscr{L}^1$, 86, 94

$\mathscr{L}^2$, 84, 94

Author Index

Aase, 232, 257
Abel, 79
Abken, 290
Acharya, 80, 289
Adams, 166
Adler, 233
Ahn, 133, 233
Aït-Sahalia, 165, 197
Aït-Sahlia, 199, 319
Aiyagari, 80
Akahari, 200
Akian, 234
Aliprantis, 255
Allegretto, 199
Allingham, 18
Alvarez, 233, 234
Amaro de Matos, 199
Amendinger, 132, 234
Amin, 165, 197, 198, 317, 319
Andersen, 162, 165, 197, 198, 200, 201, 318
Anderson, 289
Andreasen, 100, 162, 165, 198, 200, 318, 319
Ansel, 132, 233
Antonelli, 234
Apelfeld, 162
Araujo, 19, 79, 255
Arntzen, 234
Arrow, 17, 18
Artzner, 131, 133, 162, 166, 290
Arvantis, 290
Assaf, 234
Au, 164
Avellaneda, 133, 196, 234, 317, 318

Babbs, 133, 164, 166
Back, 132, 133, 166, 232, 233, 234, 256, 257
Backus, 165, 166

Bajeux-Besnainou, 47, 162, 233, 257
Bakshi, 198, 200
Balasko, 18
Balduzzi, 163, 166, 234
Ball, 165, 197, 199
Bally, 233, 318
Bank, 233
Banz, 132
Barberis, 80
Barles, 197, 199, 200, 233, 319
Barndorff-Nielsen, 199
Barone, 166
Barone-Adesi, 199
Barraquand, 318, 319
Basak, 257
Bates, 198, 199
Baxter, 164
Baz, 165
Beaglehole, 163, 319
Becker, 78
Beckers, 197
Beibel, 199
Bellman, 63
Beltratti, 79
Bensoussan, 46, 199, 232, 291
Benth, 232
Benveniste, 63, 78
Benzoni, 198
Berardi, 163
Bergman, 133, 198, 200, 233
Berk, 18, 19, 47
Bernard, 318
Bertola, 166
Bertsekas, 63, 78
Bertsimas, 317
Bewley, 79, 255
Bhar, 164

447

Bick, 100, 133, 196, 197, 234, 257, 336
Bielecki, 290
Billingsley, 317
Bjerksund, 319
Björk, 165, 166
Black, 17, 18, 64, 100, 161, 164, 197, 256, 288, 289, 319
Blackwell, 78
Blume, 79
Bodurtha, 165
Bollerslev, 198
Bonomo, 257
Bossaerts, 64, 166, 233
Bottazzi, 18, 47
Boudoukh, 165
Bouleau, 233, 320
Boyarchenko, 289
Boyd, 19, 78
Boyle, 19, 133, 318
Brace, 162, 164, 165, 166, 320
Bray, 18
Breeden, 132, 256
Bremaud, 289
Brennan, 164, 200, 233, 289, 319
Broadie, 199, 232, 317, 318, 319
Brock, 78
Brotherton-Ratcliffe, 197, 200
Brown, 47, 79, 162, 163, 197
Broze, 165
Buckdahn, 199, 233
Buff, 318
Bühler, 165
Bühlmann, 133
Bunch, 319
Buono, 165
Burdeau, 199
Burkinshaw, 255
Büttler, 162, 163, 319

Cadenillas, 234
Caflisch, 318
Calvet, 80
Campbell, 79, 165, 166, 257, 289
Cao, 198, 257
Carassus, 133
Carpenter, 289
Carr, 133, 162, 197, 198, 199, 200, 319, 320
Carverhill, 161, 162, 164, 165, 166, 234, 257, 317, 318
Cass, 18, 47
Cassese, 132
Caton, 289

Chacko, 162
Chae, 19, 47
Chalasani, 317
Chamberlain, 257
Chan, 163, 164, 165
Chang, 197, 234
Chapman, 46, 233, 256, 353
Charretour, 199
Chen, 133, 162, 163, 197, 198, 256, 289
Cheng, 165
Cherian, 197
Cherif, 163
Chernoff, 319
Chernov, 198
Cherubini, 161, 162
Chesney, 162, 200
Chevance, 318
Chew, 46
Cheyette, 164, 165
Chiarella, 164, 320
Chidambaran, 318
Chou, 198
Choulli, 131
Chow, 317
Christensen, 133, 166, 256
Chuang, 200
Chung, 317, 334
Citanna, 47
Clark, 132, 133, 198
Clarke, 319
Clewlow, 133, 162, 163, 234, 317, 318, 319
Cohen, 162
Colell, 255
Coleman, 166
Constantinides, 46, 80, 133, 163, 233, 234, 256
Cont, 164
Conze, 133, 162, 199
Cooper, 289, 290
Cornell, 256
Courtadon, 161, 318
Cover, 80, 234
Cox, 100, 161, 162, 163, 165, 196, 232, 234, 256, 257, 289, 317
Crouhy, 291
Cuoco, 46, 232, 233, 234, 257
Curran, 317
Cutland, 100, 317
Cvitanić, 133, 200, 232, 233, 234, 289

Daher, 162, 319
Dahlquist, 166
Dai, 163
Daigler, 196
Daley, 289
Dana, 255
Danesi, 165
Darling, 233
Das, 162, 163, 165, 290
Dash, 163, 319
Dassios, 200
Davis, 133, 161, 234, 289, 291
Davydov, 200, 201, 290
Dayal, 133
Debreu, 18, 45
Décamps, 162, 200, 289, 291
Deelstra, 161
Dekel, 46
Delbaen, 131, 132, 133, 161, 166, 290
Delgado, 256
DeMarzo, 47, 48
Dempster, 319
DeMunnik, 161, 162, 163, 164, 165, 166
Dengler, 319
der Hoek, 161
Derman, 64, 161, 164, 197, 200, 319
Derviz, 232
Detemple, 47, 199, 233, 234, 256, 257, 319, 353
Dewynne, 196, 318
Dezhbakhsh, 196
Diament, 166
Diener, 317
Dijkstra, 133
DiMasi, 165
Dixit, 196, 233, 289
Donaldson, 79
Dothan, 45, 133, 162, 163, 165, 234, 257
Douglas, 318
Dritschel, 132
Druskin, 318
Dreze, 17
Duan, 163, 197
Duffee, 163, 165
Duffie, 46, 47, 48, 63, 78, 79, 80, 100, 132, 162, 163, 164, 166, 196, 197, 198, 200, 233, 234, 255, 256, 257, 290, 291, 317, 318
Dumas, 79, 80, 234, 255, 256, 257
Dunn, 46
Dupire, 64, 197

Durrett, 317, 318
Dybvig, 131, 162, 165, 233, 234, 319
Dynkin, 78

Easley, 79
Eaves, 47
Eberlein, 165, 199, 317
Ederington, 289
Edirisinghe, 133, 234
Ekern, 233
El Karoui, 100, 131, 132, 133, 161, 162, 163, 164, 165, 198, 232, 233, 234
Elliot, 161
Elliott, 162, 199, 290
Ellis, 200
Embrechts, 133
Engle, 198
Epstein, 46, 64, 78, 80, 233, 256, 257, 353
Eraker, 199
Ericsson, 291
Esposito, 161, 162, 163
Evnine, 318
Eydeland, 320

Faguet, 199, 319
Fan, 289
Faure-Grimaud, 289
Fazel, 19
Fein, 197
Feldman, 162, 234, 257
Feller, 161
Fernandes, 289
Figlewski, 318
Filipović, 162, 163
Fisher, 166, 198, 233, 256, 288
Fitzpatrick, 232, 320
Flannery, 163, 318, 319
Fleming, 162, 197, 232, 233, 234, 320
Flesaker, 165, 201
Florenzano, 47, 79
Foldes, 233
Föllmer, 100, 233, 234, 257
Foresi, 163, 165, 166
Forsyth, 317
Fouque, 198
Fournié, 165, 317, 318, 320
Frachot, 162, 164, 165
Freedman, 63, 78
Freidlin, 346
Frey, 198, 200, 201, 257

Friedman, 318, 345
Frittelli, 132
Fu, 317

Gabay, 100
Gagnon, 320
Galai, 291
Gale, 18
Gallant, 79
Gandhi, 319
Gao, 319
Garbade, 161
Garcia, 165, 257
Garleanu, 291
Garman, 63, 319
Gatarek, 162
Gatto, 199
Geanakoplos, 18, 19, 46, 47, 79
Gegout-Petit, 234
Geman, 131, 162, 165, 198, 200
Gennotte, 234, 257
Genon-Catalot, 165
Geoffard, 234, 255
Gerber, 200, 317
Gertler, 80
Geske, 197, 199, 288
Ghysels, 64, 198, 257
Gibbons, 79, 161, 163, 256
Gibbs, 318
Gibson, 162, 290
Gihman, 161
Gilles, 18, 79, 166, 233, 256
Giovannini, 46
Girotto, 45, 47
Glasserman, 78, 165, 166, 317, 318, 319
Glynn, 318
Goldberg, 165
Goldman, 199
Goldstein, 164, 166, 256
Goldys, 164, 165
Goll, 234
Gombani, 166
Gorman, 18
Gottardi, 19, 47, 48
Gourdel, 47, 79
Gouriéroux, 64, 165, 198, 233
Grabbe, 200
Grandchamp, 318
Grannan, 133
Grant, 46
Grauer, 200
Graversen, 256

Gregory, 290
Gregory-Allen, 165
Griffiths, 318
Grinblatt, 162, 165, 166, 197
Grodal, 19
Grosen, 162
Grossman, 234, 256
Gruenewald, 319
Grundy, 100, 198
Gukhal, 199
Gul, 46
Guo, 198

Haan, 80
Hahn, 47
Hakansson, 79
Hamza, 164
Hansen, 47, 79, 80, 165, 257
Hara, 18, 47, 48
Harrison, 45, 100, 131, 132, 199, 200,
     233
Hart, 19, 47
Harvey, 198
Haug, 199, 200
He, 46, 47, 200, 232, 233, 234, 255, 256,
     317
Heal, 46, 233, 353
Heath, 131, 164, 165, 320
Heaton, 80, 257
Heemink, 318
Heidelberger, 317
Heinkel, 288
Hellwig, 19
Hemler, 197
Henrotte, 47, 133
Hens, 18, 47
Hernandez, 79
Heston, 163, 166, 197, 198, 200, 256, 257,
     317
Heynen, 197, 198
Hildenbrand, 18
Hillion, 233
Hindy, 47, 131, 233, 320, 354
Hirsch, 47
Ho, 64, 161, 319
Hobson, 198, 200
Hodges, 133, 163, 197, 234, 257
Hofmann, 197
Hogan, 163, 164, 165
Honda, 47, 234, 257
Hong, 78

Howe, 200
Howison, 196
Hu, 199
Huang, 46, 47, 80, 131, 132, 162, 199, 232,
    233, 234, 256, 257, 289, 290, 319, 320,
    354
Hubalek, 317
Hull, 100, 161, 164, 166, 196, 197, 290, 318,
    319
Husseini, 47
Hussey, 320
Hutton, 319

Ibanez, 319
Ibbotson, 166
Iben, 290
Ikeda, 342
Imkeller, 132, 234
Ingersoll, 161, 162, 163, 165, 196, 233, 234,
    256, 257
Ingram, 79
Iyengar, 234

Jacka, 199, 232
Jackson, 233
Jackwerth, 197
Jacobs, 318
Jacod, 132, 199
Jaganathan, 80
Jaillet, 199, 319
Jakobsen, 165
Jamshidian, 64, 161, 162, 163, 164, 197,
    199, 200, 318
Janci, 164, 165
Jarrow, 131, 133, 162, 164, 165, 196, 197,
    199, 290, 319, 320
Jaschke, 162, 166
Jasiak, 198
Jeanblanc, 100, 198, 200, 232, 233, 290
Jeffrey, 164
Jegadeesh, 162, 165, 197
Jensen, 100
Jha, 317
Jin, 78, 166
Johannes, 199
Johnson, 79, 100, 197, 199, 200, 257, 319
Jones, 318
Jong, 164
Jordan, 166
Jorgensen, 162, 165, 199
Jorion, 199
Jouini, 64, 133, 234

Joy, 318
Ju, 200
Judd, 80, 320

Kabanov, 132, 165
Kajii, 18, 19, 46, 47
Kakutani, 19
Kallal, 133, 234
Kallsen, 234
Kan, 46, 64, 78, 163, 165
Kandori, 79
Kani, 64, 164, 197
Kapoudjian, 233
Karasinski, 161
Karatzas, 46, 131, 133, 163, 198, 199, 232,
    233, 234, 255, 256, 257, 289, 334, 340
Karlsen, 232
Karolyi, 163, 165
Karr, 289
Kat, 197, 200
Kawazu, 162
Kehoe, 79
Keller, 199
Kemna, 198
Kennedy, 164
Khanna, 319
Kifer, 199, 289
Kijima, 290
Kim, 166, 199
Kind, 200
Kirman, 18
Kishimoto, 319
Klapper, 166
Klass, 234
Klebaner, 164
Knizhnerman, 318
Kocherlakota, 78
Koedijk, 165
Koehl, 64, 200
Kogan, 317
Komoribayashi, 290
Konno, 166
Koo, 233
Koopmans, 46
Kooros, 319
Kopp, 100, 317
Korn, 133
Kostek, 318
Kou, 133, 165, 199, 317
Kramkov, 132
Krasa, 47

Kraus, 47, 164
Krawczyk, 131
Kreps, 18, 45, 46, 47, 100, 131, 132, 199,
    233, 354
Kroner, 198
Kruk, 318
Krylov, 232, 345
Ku, 47
Kubler, 80, 320
Kunitomo, 100
Kurz, 79
Kusuoka, 132, 133, 164, 199, 290, 318
Kuwana, 234, 345
Kydland, 47

Lacoste, 100, 164, 165
Lagnado, 197, 233
Lai, 199, 319
Lakner, 132, 232, 233, 234, 255
Lamberton, 196, 199, 233, 317, 319
Lamoureux, 198
Lando, 199, 290
Lang, 162
Langetieg, 163
Lantto, 46
Lapeyre, 196, 199, 319
Laroque, 256
Lasry, 47, 317, 320
Lastrapes, 198
Laurence, 196
Laurent, 165, 233, 290
Lawson, 318
Lazrak, 233
Le Van, 255
Leblanc, 163
Lebuchoux, 320
Lee, 64, 79, 161, 165, 317, 319
Lehoczky, 232, 255, 256
Leland, 133, 234, 288, 289
Lepage, 162, 164
Lépingle, 320
Lerche, 199
LeRoy, 18, 78, 79
Lesigne, 233
Lesne, 163, 164, 165, 317
Levendorskii, 289
Levental, 132, 133
Levhari, 79
Levine, 79, 80
Levy, 317
Li, 290, 319
Linetsky, 200, 201, 290

Lintner, 18
Lions, 232, 233, 320
Lioui, 233
Lipschitz, 340
Lipster, 200, 234
Lischka, 289
Litterman, 165, 290
Litzenberger, 47, 132, 162, 200, 256, 290
Liu, 162, 163, 234
Lo, 197, 291, 317
Lobo, 19
Loewenstein, 131, 257
Löffler, 18
Longstaff, 162, 163, 165, 289, 319
Loshak, 289
Lotz, 290
Lu, 197
Lucas, 63, 78, 79, 80
Luciano, 79, 80, 234
Luenberger, 319, 326
Lund, 166
Luttmer, 133
Lynch, 234

Ma, 64, 78, 164, 200, 233, 234, 257, 318
Machina, 46
Madan, 80, 131, 133, 197, 198, 199, 200,
    256, 290, 317, 320
Maghsoodi, 162, 198
Magill, 19, 45, 46, 47, 79
Mankiw, 80
Marcet, 80, 320
Marcozzi, 289
Margrabe, 197
Marsh, 166
Marshall, 256, 320
Martin, 289, 290
Martineau, 319
Mas-Colell, 18, 19, 47, 79, 255
Mavroidis, 289
McFadden, 79
McKean, 199
McKenzie, 18
McLennan, 79
McManus, 46
Mehra, 79
Mehrling, 80
Melino, 197, 256
Mella-Barral, 289
Mello, 290
Menaldi, 234

Merrick, 290
Merton, 46, 100, 161, 198, 199, 200, 232, 255, 256, 288
Meyer, 289
Miller, 132
Milne, 199, 317
Milshtein, 318
Miltersen, 164, 165, 200, 256
Mirrlees, 232
Mitchell, 318
Modest, 256
Monat, 131
Monteiro, 19, 79, 255
Moreleda, 161
Morokoff, 318
Morris, 318
Morton, 164, 165, 197, 320
Moskowitz, 318
Motolese, 79
Mueller, 131, 133
Munk, 133, 233, 320
Murthy, 234, 257
Musiela, 161, 162, 164, 165, 166, 196
Myneni, 162, 163, 164, 197, 199

Nahum, 200
Naik, 48, 133, 165, 200, 234
Nakagawa, 257
Nandi, 198
Negishi, 18
Nelson, 161, 164, 198, 317, 319
Newman, 318
Newton, 318
Ng, 197
Nielsen, 18, 165, 200, 257, 289, 290, 319
Nissen, 165
Norman, 234
Nunes, 163
Nyborg, 289
Nychka, 166

Ocone, 232, 234
O'Hara, 79
Ōhashi, 132
Oliveira, 200
Ordentlich, 80, 200
Ortu, 45, 47
Osher, 197
Owen, 318

Pagès, 131, 232, 233, 290, 317
Pakes, 79

Pan, 47, 163, 198, 199, 289
Panas, 133, 234
Pang, 162, 163, 164, 319
Papanicolaou, 198
Pappalardo, 199
Parás, 133, 317
Pardoux, 233, 234
Parrott, 319
Páscoa, 79
Pearson, 47, 162, 232, 256
Pedersen, 162, 163, 166
Peng, 233, 234
Pennacchi, 163, 166
Perraudin, 289
Persson, 164
Petkau, 319
Pham, 199, 233, 257
Piazzesi, 166
Pierides, 289
Pikovsky, 199, 234, 257, 320
Pindyck, 196, 233, 289
Pitts, 288
Platen, 197
Platten, 164
Pliska, 131, 132, 133, 232, 133, 234
Polak, 46
Polemarchakis, 18, 19, 47
Pollard, 79
Polson, 199
Pontier, 232, 234, 255
Portait, 47, 162, 233, 257
Porteus, 46
Poteshman, 198
Poulsen, 100
Prause, 199
Prescott, 47, 79
Press, 163, 318, 319
Prigent, 317, 320
Prisman, 48, 196, 234
Protter, 131, 132, 133, 234, 317, 318, 334
Pudet, 319
Pye, 64, 161, 290

Quenez, 132, 133, 232, 233, 234
Quinzii, 45, 47, 79

Radner, 45
Rady, 133, 197
Raible, 165
Ramaswamy, 161, 163, 256, 317, 319
Rebonato, 320

Redekop, 198
Reikvam, 232
Reisman, 100, 197
Renault, 197, 198, 291
Repullo, 46
Revuz, 78, 334
Ricciardi, 200
Rich, 200
Richard, 47, 161, 164, 232
Richardson, 165, 232, 233
Riedel, 233
Risa, 166
Rishel, 232
Ritchken, 164, 319, 320
Rochet, 131, 161, 162, 164, 291
Rockafeller, 326
Rogers, 100, 132, 161, 163, 164, 166, 198, 200, 234, 317
Roma, 197
Romano, 162, 197, 198, 199, 319
Ronn, 290
Roseau, 162, 164
Ross, 17, 18, 46, 48, 100, 161, 162, 163, 165, 196, 234, 256, 257, 317
Royden, 132
Rubinstein, 48, 64, 100, 196, 197, 256, 317
Rudd, 196
Ruegg, 232
Ruiz, 198
Rumsey, 166
Runggaldier, 165, 200
Rustem, 200
Rutkowski, 161, 162, 164, 196, 290
Ryder, 46, 233, 353

Saá-Requejo, 165, 200, 257, 289
Sabarwal, 19
Saito, 257
Salkin, 319
Samsoen, 199
Samuelson, 79
Sandmann, 165, 319
Sandroni, 80
Sankarasubramanian, 164, 319
Santa-Clara, 164, 289
Santos, 78, 79, 80
Sargent, 79
Sato, 200
Saunders, 163, 165
Sbuelz, 200
Scaillet, 163, 165, 317
Schachermayer, 78, 131, 132, 233, 317

Schaefer, 162, 163, 164, 166
Scheinkman, 63, 78, 80, 165, 233
Schmedders, 80, 320
Schoenmakers, 318
Scholes, 100, 288
Schotman, 165
Schroder, 46, 161, 200, 201, 233, 234, 256, 290, 351
Schwartz, 162, 163, 164, 200, 233, 289, 291, 318, 319
Schweizer, 131, 132, 197, 233, 234
Scott, 162, 163, 197, 198, 199, 256, 319
Sekine, 233
Selby, 133, 162, 163, 197, 234, 257, 288
Selden, 46, 47
Serrat, 257
Sethi, 232, 234
Shafer, 19, 46, 47, 48
Shahabuddin, 317
Shanno, 100, 200
Shannon, 79
Sharpe, 18, 19
Shefrin, 317
Shephard, 198
Shepp, 200
Shi, 200
Shiller, 256
Shimko, 291
Shirakawa, 133, 233
Shiryaev, 132, 133, 200, 234
Shiu, 166, 200, 317
Shreve, 63, 78, 100, 133, 163, 198, 199, 232, 233, 234, 255, 256, 320, 334, 340
Shrikhande, 256
Siconolfi, 18
Siegel, 196
Simonato, 163
Sin, 198
Sinconolfi, 18
Singh, 163
Singleton, 46, 79, 80, 163, 198, 257, 290
Sircar, 198, 234
Skiadas, 19, 46, 233, 234, 255, 256, 290, 351
Skorohod, 132, 133, 161
Slud, 232
Smale, 318
Smith, 164, 318
Sondermann, 165, 233
Soner, 133, 200, 232, 233, 234, 320
Song, 290
Sopranzetti, 289

Sornette, 164
Sosin, 199
Srinivasan, 79
Stambaugh, 163
Stanton, 162, 165, 197, 318, 319
Stapleton, 47, 317
Stein, 198
Stensland, 319
Stokey, 63, 78, 79
Stoll, 196
Stremme, 201, 257
Streufert, 64, 78
Stricker, 131, 132, 233
Strickland, 162, 163, 319
Strikwerda, 318
Stulz, 197
Stummer, 163
Subrahmanyam, 47, 199, 289, 319
Subramanian, 200
Sulem, 234
Sun, 161, 162, 234, 256, 320
Sundaram, 163, 289, 290
Sundaresan, 161, 162, 233, 256, 289, 290
Svensson, 80, 166, 233
Swindle, 133

Tacqu, 100, 317
Takahashi, 200
Takase, 166
Taksar, 232, 234
Talay, 165, 318
Taleb, 133
Tamarchenko, 318
Tanudjaja, 162
Tauchen, 320
Tavella, 318
Taylor, 198, 320
Teicher, 317
Tejima, 291
Telmer, 80
Tenney, 163
Tepla, 232, 234
Teukolsky, 163, 318, 319
Thorlacius, 166
Thurston, 164
Tice, 166
Toft, 197, 289
Topper, 320
Török, 318
Torous, 165, 199
Tourin, 233

Touzi, 64, 197, 198, 257, 317, 320
Toy, 64, 161, 319
Trevor, 164, 320
Tsiveriotis, 289
Tubaro, 318
Tufano, 290
Turnbull, 162, 196, 197, 290

Uhlig, 47
Uhrig-Homburg, 165, 289
Unal, 290
Uppal, 133, 200, 234, 255, 256
Uzawa, 233

Van Deventer, 166, 291
Van Horne, 161
Van Moerbeke, 199
Vargiolu, 165
Varikooty, 317
Vasicek, 162, 163
Vayanos, 234, 256
Vere-Jones, 289
Vetterling, 163, 318, 319
Vetzal, 317
Vigo, 80
Vila, 233, 234
Villanacci, 47
Vind, 19
Viswanathan, 133, 162, 163, 164, 199
Vorst, 133, 198

Waldvogel, 162, 163, 319
Wallace, 165, 319
Walras, 17
Walter, 165
Wang, 19, 78, 80, 233, 234, 255, 256, 257, 317
Watanabe, 161, 162, 342
Webber, 166
Weber, 165
Weerasinghe, 234
Weil, 19, 46, 80
Weiss, 80, 233
Weisz, 132
Werner, 18, 47, 80, 233
Whaley, 162, 196, 197
Whalley, 133
White, 79, 161, 166, 197, 290, 318, 319
Whitelaw, 165
Wiener, 100, 198

Wiggins, 197
Willard, 131, 257, 319
Williams, 334
Willinger, 100, 317, 336
Wilmott, 133, 196, 318
Wolff, 165
Won, 47
Woodford, 78, 79
Wu, 47, 319

Xu, 232, 233, 234
Xue, 234

Yaari, 165
Yamada, 161
Yamazaki, 19
Yao, 161
Yong, 164, 234
Yor, 200, 290, 334

Yu, 78, 197, 199, 200, 290
Yushkevich, 78

Zacklad, 162
Zakoïan, 165
Zame, 19, 79, 80, 255, 256, 257
Zapatero, 233, 234, 256, 257, 319, 353
Zariphopoulou, 133, 232, 233, 234
Zechner, 288
Zervos, 166
Zhang, 199, 319
Zhao, 318
Zheng, 166
Zhou, 47, 200, 234, 317
Zhu, 233, 320
Zin, 46, 64, 78, 80, 165, 166
Zou, 200
Zuasti, 257
Zvan, 317

Subject Index

absence of arbitrage, 108
absolute priority, 263
actions, 203
adapted, 332
adapted process, 21
additive utility, 25, 60
admissible controls, 204
affine, 142, 179, 180
affine diffusion, 149
affine, intensity, 279
affine model, empirical estimation, 163
affine term-structure model, 142, 149, 162
affine volatility process, 179
after-tax, 268
agent, 5
aggregate endowment, 8
aggregation, 15, 18, 41
algebra, 323
allocation, 8
almost everywhere, 87
almost surely, 329
ambiguity aversion, 257
American barrier options, 199
American call, 36
American call, with dividends, 36
American option, early exercise premium, 199
American option, free boundary problem, 199
American option price, 46, 199
American option price, numerical solution, 309
American option, Stefan problem, 199
American options with jumps, 199
American put, 32, 36, 188, 309
American securities, using the semi-group approach to, 314
American security, 32, 46, 57, 182

analytic, 355
antithetic sampling, 299
approximate arbitrage, 121, 132
arbitrage, 1, 22, 70, 89, 102, 123, 126
arbitrage pricing theory, 18
ARCH, 198
arrears, 145
Arrow-Debreu equilibria in infinite-dimensional settings, 255
Arrow-Debreu equilibrium, 15, 40, 237
Arrow-Pratt measure, 245
Asian option, 190, 200, 317
asset pricing formula, 10
asset pricing, nonadditive utility, 256
asset substitution, 261, 271
assets, 260
asymmetric information, 257
asymptotic distribution, 76
at market, 145
augmented filtration of a process, 359
average-rate options, 200
Azema's martingale, 132

Bachelier, 84
backward difference equation, 305
backward Kolmogorov equation, 346
backward SDEs, 318
backward stochastic differential equations, 233
Banach lattice, 255
bankruptcy, 234
barrier option, 38, 200, 317
basic HJM drift restriction, 164
Bellman condition, 187
Bellman equation, 50, 53, 57, 68, 204
Bellman's principle of optimality, 63
Bermudan swaption, 146

Bernoulli trials, 295
Bessel function, 147
beta, 15, 107
betweenness certainty equivalent, 46
binary options, 201
Binomial Approximation of the
    Black-Derman-Toy, 316
Binomial Option Pricing, 14, 21, 37
binomial option pricing, limit, 293
binomial stock returns, 295
binomial term-structure models, 61, 64
bivariate binary options, 201
Black-Derman-Toy model, 64, 138, 147, 155,
    161
Black-Karasinski model, 138
Black-Scholes, 100, 133, 174, 294
Black-Scholes, convergence to, 294
Black-Scholes formula, 48, 90, 294
Black-Scholes implied volatilities, 174
Black-Scholes option pricing formula, in
    equilibrium, 257
Black-Scholes-Merton model, 259
Blackwell's Theorem, 78
bond, 88
bond options, American, 162
bond-option pricing in a Gaussian setting,
    164
Borel, 329
boundary condition, 91
bounded, 85
bounded adapted processes, 66
Brownian motion, geometric, 88
Brownian motion, martingale, 97
budget-feasible consumption set, 5, 24
buy-at-the-min, 190

calibration, 161, 165, 175, 197, 295
call option, 14
callable bonds, 281
callable convertible debt, 199
cancellable call option, 58
cap pricing, 145, 160, 162
Capital Asset Pricing Model, 12, 18, 257
capital structure, 261
capital-stock process, 246
caplet, 145, 161
CAPM, 12, 14, 15, 18
CAPM, two factor, 257
carrying costs, 197
cash settlement, 171
Cauchy problem, 302, 342
CBI processes, 162

CCAPM, 249
Central Limit Theorem, 293, 294, 296, 317,
    331
changes of numeraire, 201
cheapest-to-deliver option, 197
CIR, density function, 161
CIR, discrete-time model, 161, 256
CIR, empirical estimation, 162
CIR, empirical results, 256
CIR, Laplace transform, 161
CIR model, 141, 142, 161, 248, 254, 315,
    342
CIR model, calibration, 315
CIR, nonnegativity of interest rate, 161
closed, 118
collateral, 274
collateral constraints, 47, 257, 274
collateralized debt obligations, 291
commodity prices, 166
commodity, term-structure models, 200
compact metric space, 78
compensated counting process, 275
complement, 323, 329
complementary slackness condition, 327
complete, 8, 26, 117
complete markets, 8, 27, 117
completed, 330
completion, 84, 330
complex options, 291
compound options, 291
computation of equilibrium, 47
concave program, 327
conditional expectation, 324, 332
conditional expected rate of return, 106
cone, 4
consistency of GMM estimators, 76
consistent, 75
consol, 252, 263
consol rate, 164
constrained participation, 18
constraints, 200
consumption, 207
consumption process, 24, 39, 48, 66, 256
consumption-based CAPM, 108, 246, 256
consumption-based CAPM, incomplete
    markets, 249
consumption CAPM, transaction costs, 256
continually compounding interest rate, 88
continuation region, 187
continuous, 25
Continuous Mapping Theorem, 297, 317

continuous-branching processes, 162
continuously compounding yield, 137
control problem, 67
controlled diffusion function, 204
controlled drift function, 203
controls, 203
convergence, 171
convergence of the binomial model, 294, 317
converges in distribution, 293, 330
converges in probability, 330
convertible bond, 200, 274, 281, 289, 320
convexity, 198
corporate debt, 259
correlation, 12
cost-of-carry formula, 170
counting process, 357
covariance, 11
Cox-Ingersoll-Ross, 141, 147, 177, 197, 246, 341, 363
Cox-Ingersoll-Ross, fundamental solution, 147
Crank-Nicholson approach, 303, 311, 318
credit derivatives, 281
credit-constrained, 131
cum-dividend, 22, 23, 102, 126, 127, 308
cum-dividend value, 57
cumulative dividend, 123
cumulative dividend process, 97, 235
cumulative-return process, 106
currency convergence, 166
currency options, 158, 200
curve-fitting, 166

debt overhang, 272
decentralized production decisions, 254
default correlation, 291
default risk premium, 287
defaultable swaps, 290
default-adjusted short rate, 288
deflated cumulative-dividend process, 124
deflated gain process, 24, 124
deflator, 23, 102
delivery arbitrage, 43, 171
delivery date, 42
density process, 29, 110
derivative asset pricing, 48
derivative security, 92
derivatives, credit risk, 290
determinacy, 79
diff swaps, 162
differential approach, 18

diffusion, 87, 340
Diffusion Invariance Principle, 339
Dirac measure, 147
directional, 328
disappointment aversion, 257
discount, 5, 28
discount function, 137, 168
discount rate, 213
discretization errors, 317
dispersed expectations, 47
distance, 67
dividend process, 22
dividend yield, 98
dividend-price pair, 5, 22, 123
dividend-rate process, 123, 235
Dominated Convergence Theorem, 331
double-barrier, 200
double-step, 201
double-step options, 201
doubling strategies, 184
doubling strategy, 131
doubly stochastic, 276, 290, 359
doubly stochastic, counter-example, 288
down-and-outs, 200
drift, 87
driven by some filtration, 276
duality and optimality, 47
duality techniques, 232
Dudley's Theorem, 336
dynamic programming, 50, 63, 78, 320
dynamic programming, recursive-utility, 64
dynamic spanning condition, 256

early exercise, 36, 309
econometric estimation of term-structure models, 165
econometrics, 73
economy, 8
efficient allocation, 237
EGARCH, 198
elliptic, 344
empirical average, 74
empirical distribution vector, 73
endowment, 5, 24, 235
enlargement of filtrations, 132, 234
equilibrium, 1, 8, 26, 237
equilibrium, indeterminacy, 47
equilibrium, recursive utility, 256
equity, 259
equity-premium puzzle, 79
equivalent, 28, 108

equivalent martingale measure, 28, 41, 43, 45, 100, 108, 132, 167

equivalent martingale measure, constraints, 133

equivalent martingale measure, counterexample, 132

equivalent martingale measure, infinite-horizon case, 131

equivalent martingale measure, transactions costs, 133

equivalent measures, 324

error coefficient, 298

Escher transform, 200

essential supremum, 184

essentially bounded, 118

Euclidean norm, 340

Euler approximation, 298

European call option, 37, 89

European put option, 294

events, 21, 323

ex dividend, 22, 126, 236, 308

exercise, American calls, 36

exercise boundary, 199

exercise policy, 31, 182

exercise price, 14, 32, 37

exercise region, 186

existence with recursive utility, 255

exotic options, 191, 319

expectation, 324, 330

expectations hypothesis, 166

expected utility, 7

expiration time, 31, 32, 37

explicit methods, 318

exponential-affine, 179

fair price, 199

Farkas's Lemma, 12, 18

fast Fourier transform, 198

FBSDE, 234

feasible, 8, 237

feasible allocation, 8

feasible directions, 328

feedback, 54, 69, 205

Feynman-Kac solution, 94, 253, 343

field, 323

filtering, 162, 234, 257

filtration, 21, 324

filtration, right-continuous, 347

filtration, usual conditions, 347

finances a consumption process, 98, 236

finite-difference, 197, 302, 318

finite-difference, binomial method, 319

finite-variation process, 347

first to default, 288

first-order risk aversion, 80

first-order scheme, 298

fixed point, 68

Fixed Point Theorem, 19

fixed-income securities, 135

fixed-point, 78

floating-rate note, 286

floating-rate notes, 285

floor, 145

Fokker-Planck equation, 146, 311, 346

Fokker-Planck equation., 163

foreign bond options, 158

foreign exchange rates, 257

foreign term-structure models, 165

foreign-currency, 158

foreign-exchange option, 200

forward contract, 42

forward curves, commodities, 166

forward difference equation, 311

forward Kolmogorov equation, 146, 311, 346

forward measure, 201

forward price, 42, 151

forward-backward stochastic differential equations, 234

forward-measure approach, 161

forward-rate model, 164

forwards and futures, 196

Fourier transform, 180, 198

Fourier transform methods, 320

fractional Brownian motion, 100

free boundary problem, 319

free lunch, 132

free lunch with vanishing risk, 132

free-boundary problem, 199, 320

Frobenius-Perron Theorem, 73

Fubini's Theorem, 333

Fubini's Theorem for stochastic integrals, 339

fundamental solution, 146, 163, 310, 319, 345

fundamental solution, CIR model, 147

futures and forwards, 162

futures contract, 42

futures, hedging, 225

futures, interest rate, 162

futures position process, 172

futures price, 42

Futures-Forward Price Equivalence, 42

futures-price process, 171

gain process, 24, 87, 97, 123, 236
GARCH, 175, 198
GARCH, option pricing, 198
Gateaux, 328
Gaussian, 342
Gaussian forward-rate model, 156
Gaussian short-rate model, 161
general equilibrium, 45
generalized autoregressive conditional
    heteroscedastic, 175
generalized method of moments, 75, 79
generated, 22, 124
generic, 78
generic existence of equilibrium, 47
geometric Brownian motion, 88
Girsanov's Theorem, 111, 117, 337
gradient, 39, 328, 351
gradient, utility, 233
Green's function, 146, 163, 319, 345
Green's function, numerical solution, 310
grid, 303, 307
growth, 340
growth condition, 341
growth-optimal policies, 133, 234

habit-formation, 26, 40, 46, 80, 223, 233,
    256, 353
Hahn-Banach Theorem, 122
Hamilton-Jacobi-Bellman (HJB), 205, 232
HARA, 210
hazard function, 361
hazard rate, 361
Heath-Jarrow-Morton, 151, 155, 197
Heath-Jarrow-Morton model, 339
hedging under leverage constraints, 200
Hessian matrix, 13
Heston, 182, 193, 194
Heston model, 177, 179
heterogeneous agents and incomplete
    markets, 79
heterogeneous beliefs, 257
high-order-contact, 266
Hilbert space, 16, 255
HJM drift restriction, 164
HJM, estimation, 165
HJM model, 164, 320
HJM, model Markov variation, 164
HJM, numerical methods, 220
Hölder continuous, 344
Ho-Lee, 62, 64, 138, 140, 147
hyperbolic absolute risk averse (HARA),
    210

hyperbolic SPDEs, 155

illiquidity, 291
imperfect information, 162
implicit, 318
Implicit Function Theorem, 13, 244
implied volatility, 64, 197
irreversible investment, 233
Ito process, 86
Ito's Formula, 87
Ito's Lemma, 87

jointly measurable, 332
jump, 125, 347
jump-diffusion, 198

Kakutani's Fixed Point Theorem, 13
Knightian uncertainty, 80, 257
knock-ins, 190, 200
knock-outs, 31, 190, 200
Kreps-Porteus, 40
Kreps-Yan Theorem, 122

Lévy Inversion Formula, 180
Lévy's characterization of Brownian motion,
    337
Lagrange multiplier, 9, 327
Lagrangian, 327
Large Deviations Theorem, 318
large investor, 234
latent, 148
law of iterated expectations, 324, 332
law of large numbers, 73, 299, 317
law of large numbers for Markov chains, 73
left limits, 347
left-continuous, 347
leverage constraints, 200
LIBOR, 161, 162
limit in probability, 84
limited liability, 263
limited-rationality, 80
limited-risk options, 200
Lindeberg-Feller Central Limit Theorem,
    294, 331
linear equations of the tridiagonal form,
    306
linear regression, 11
linear stochastic differential equation, 342
linear subspace, 4, 121
linearity of stochastic integrals, 123
Lipschitz, 340

local martingale, 212
local martingale measure, 130
local substitution for consumption, 233
local time, 133
local-expected-utility, 46
locally, 344
locally Lipschitz, 341
lock-in options, 200
logarithmic additive utility, 234
log-normal, 88
log-optimal, 80
long-term interest rates, 165
lookback options, 189, 190, 200, 318
Lucas model, 1
lump-sum dividend, 125

Malliavin calculus, 221, 232, 320
marginal rates of substitution, 103
marginal utility, 5
marginal utility of a representative agent, 244
marginal-rate-of-substitution process, 23
market completeness under a change of measure, 132
market imperfections, 133, 261
market model, 165
market model, cap pricing, 160
market return, 15
market risk aversion, 250
market time, 198
marketed space, 22, 117
marketed space, L^2-closedness, 131
market-price-of-risk process, 112
market-value process, 106
marking to market, 42
Markov, 51, 52, 78, 96
Markov chain, 63, 65, 78
Markov chain, continuous-time, 349
Markov dynamic programming, 52
Markov equilibrium, 69
Markov single-agent asset pricing model, 252
Markovian versions of the HJM model, 164
martingale, 22, 24, 85, 97, 325, 332
martingale approach to optimal investment, 232
martingale generator, 238
martingale representation property, 117, 338, 339, 359
martingale representation theorem, 336, 359
maturity goes to infinity, 165

Mean Value Theorem, 351
mean-reversion, 138, 248
mean-summable, 71
mean-variance criteria in a continuous-time setting, 233
measurable, 323
median-price options, 200
Merton, 140
Merton model, 138
mesh sizes, 303
method-of-moments estimation, 79
Milshtein approximation, 298
minimax hedging, 200
Modigliani-Miller Theorem, 48, 261, 263
monetary integration, 166
money, 140, 141
Monte Carlo simulation, 299, 318
Monte Carlo simulation of the jump times, 359
mortgage-backed securities, 165, 319
multifactor term-structure model, 148

negative interest rates, 141
negative semi-definite, 13
Newton-Raphson, 315
Newton-Raphson search, 319
no free lunch with vanishing risk, 132
nominal consumption-price process, 244
nominal dividends, 47
nominal price process, 240
nonadditive recursive utility, 78
non-Brownian information, 132
non-bushy trees, 320
nonexplosive counting process, 357, 359
nonlinear least squares, 166
nonnegative wealth constraint, 77, 131
nonseparable preferences, 257
nonstandard analysis, 100
norm on matrices, 340
Novikov's condition, 337
null, 243
null set, 84, 243, 330
numeraire, 24
numeraire, changes, 201
numeraire deflator, 112, 257
numeraire portfolio, 133
Numerical Recipes in C, 363
numerical solution, 315, 363

oil, term-structure models, 200
one-factor term-structure models, 137

optimal control, 204
optimal exercise boundary, 188, 199
optimal exercise policy, 186
optimal feedback control, 68
optimal stopping, 32, 33, 57, 183, 199
optimal stopping problem, 32, 183
optimality, 1, 19
option, 47, 89
option, econometric estimation, 198
option price, convexity, 198
option pricing, with jumps, 198
option, unobservable underlying, 201
options, average-rate, 200
options, binary, 201
options, bonds, American, 162
options, double-step, 201
options, general equilibrium, 47
options, interest rate, 162
options, median-price, 200
options, on multiple assets, 199
options, on yields, 162
options, spanning, 47
options, step, 201
order of convergence, 298

par, 145
par coupon rate, 145, 264
par floating-rate note, 286
parabolic, 344
Pareto inefficiency of incomplete-markets, 47
Pareto optimal, 8, 42, 79, 237, 243
Pareto optimality in infinite-dimensional economies, 255
Parisian, 200
partial derivatives, 328
partial differential inequality, 188
partition, 41
passport options, 200
path dependent, 146, 189, 317, 319
path integrals, 319
pathwise integral, 100
perpetual options, 199
point process, 357
Poisson distribution, 276, 358
Poisson process, 358
Poisson random variable, 276
policy function, 69, 78
polynomial growth condition, 297, 344
portfolio constraints, 133, 233, 257
portfolio insurance, 234, 257
positive linear functionals, 132

pre-default price, 278
predictable, 357
price function, 237
price impact, 234
price, state, 3
pricing kernel, 23, 103
pricing semi-groups, 319
probabilistic solution, 343
probability, 4, 323
probability measure, 21, 323, 329
probability space, 21, 323
process, 83, 332
product measurable, 332
production under uncertainty, 233
proportional transactions costs, 234
protective covenant, 263
pseudo-price process, 93
pseudo-random, 299
put option, 182
put-call parity, 42, 99, 197, 296
puttable, 274

quadratic utilities, 39, 79
quadratic utility, 39
quality option, 197

Radon-Nikodym derivative, 324, 332
random field, 164
random variable, 323, 329
rational exercise policy, 32, 183
rational-beliefs, 79
rationality, 79
real options, 196, 272, 283, 289
real price process, 240
real short, 245
recursive, 26
recursive utility, 40, 46, 60, 64, 78, 223, 256
recursive utility in continuous-time settings, 233, 256
recursive utility, dynamic programming, 60
reduced-form models of debt, 81
redundant, 30, 31, 120, 124
regime switching, 234
regression coefficient, 11
regular preferences, 13, 18
relative risk aversion, 210
replicates, 30
repo rates, 166
representative agent, 10, 18, 27, 46, 79
resettlement, 42, 171
resolution of uncertainty, 46

return, 11, 15
Riccati equation, 143, 150, 181
Riesz representation, 11, 16, 23, 39, 237
Riesz Representation Theorem for $L^2(P)$, 122
Riesz-Frechet Theorem, 19
right continuous, 125, 347
risk-neutral intensity process, 277
risk-neutral probabilities, 5, 17
risk-neutral valuation, 93, 100
riskless, 5, 11
rolled over, 28
rolling spot futures contract, 191
Runge-Kutta method, 163
running reward function, 204

Saddle Point Theorem, 9, 217, 327
sample path, 83
scrambled-net, 318
SDE, 340
SDE existence, 342
second-order discretization schemes, 318
securities, 3, 22
security prices, 3
security-price process, 22
security-spot market equilibrium, 236
self-financing, 89, 102, 123, 126
sell-at-the-max option, 189
semi-group, 63, 313
semimartingale, 348
Separating Hyperplane Theorem, 4, 9, 23, 326
separation of cones, 326
separation-of-variables, 150, 181
sharp-brackets process, 337
short position, 171
short rate, 28, 88, 102, 245, 247
short-sales constraints, 233
short-term riskless borrowing, 28
simple, 330, 334
simple process, 335
simple random variables, 330
simulated-method-of-moments estimation, 199
single-agent equilibrium, 55
singular price, 256
skew, 177, 178, 197
Slater condition, 9, 327
smile curve, 64, 174, 197
smirk, 197
smooth-additive, 241
smoothness, 78

smooth-pasting condition, 265
Snell envelope, 33, 184
sovereign debt, 290
span, 8
spanning, 238
spanning number, 41, 46
SPDE, 155, 164
special repo rates, 166
spline, 166, 315
square root" diffusions, 341
square-integrable, 351
standard Brownian motion, 83
standard filtration, 84, 94
standard normal, 293
state-price, 3, 4
state-price beta, 12, 16, 40, 47, 108, 130
state-price deflator, 11, 23, 25, 71, 78, 103, 241, 245
state-price density, 11, 23, 103
state-price kernel, 11
state-price, uniqueness, 16, 43
state-price vector, 4
states, 3, 203
stationarity, 79
steady-state distribution, 73
Stefan problem, 199
Stieltjes integrals, 125
Stiemke's Lemma, 12, 18
stochastic control, 203
stochastic differential, 94
stochastic differential equation, 91, 340
stochastic differential utility, 233, 256, 353
stochastic Euler equation, 26, 52, 69
stochastic exponential, 113
stochastic flows, 198
stochastic game, 269
stochastic integral, 84, 335
stochastic integration, linearity, 85
stochastic return distributions, 234
stochastic volatility, 64, 197, 257
stochastic volatility, affine model, 179
stochastic volatility, econometric estimation, 198
stock, 88
stock-market equilibrium, 254
stopping game, 269
stopping time, 324, 332
stopping time, non-trivial, 275
strict priority, 263
strictly variance-averse, 15
string, 164

strong law of large numbers, 74, 78
strong law of large numbers, uniform, 75
strong Markov, 341
strong solution, 340
structural models of debt, 81, 340
submartingale, 325
subtribe, 324
sunspot, 19
superdifferential, 14
supermartingale, 325
super-replicating trading strategy, 33, 183
survival function, 361
swaps, 162
swaps, defaultable, 290
swap-spread model, 166
swaption, 146

tax, interest expense deduction, 268
taxable and nontaxable bonds, 166
temporary-equilibrium, 47
tenor, 160
term structure, 126, 246
term structure, binomial, 61
term structure, Black-Derman-Toy, 62
term structure, calibration, 314
term structure, econometrics, 165
term structure, Ho-Lee, 62
term structure of credit spreads, 288
term structure of interest rates, 137
terminal arbitrage issue, 132
terminal ex-dividend prices, 132
terminal reward function, 204
term-structure derivatives, 162
term-structure model, 64, 168
term-structure models, foreign exchange, 165
term-structure, numerical methods, 165
test moment function, 74
Theorem of the Alternative, 12, 18
theory of choice, 18
time aggregation, 257
time-homogeneous Markov chain, 51
timing of information, 47
totally inaccessible stopping times, 275, 289
tower property, 324
trace, 95
trading strategy, 22, 84, 123
transactions costs, 19, 64, 133, 234, 256
transform, 180, 198
transition matrix, 51
translated CIR model, 162
transversality condition, 213

triangular array, 294, 331
tribe, 21, 323, 329
tribe generated, 324, 329
tridiagonal matrix, 305, 306, 311, 318
turnpike, 79, 234
two-fund separation, 18

uniform strong law of large numbers, 79
uniformly in t, 341
uniformly integrable, 297, 316, 331
uniformly parabolic, 345
unique decomposition property of Ito processes, 87, 90
uniqueness of equilibria, 255
uniqueness of equivalent martingale measures, 114
unit zero-coupon riskless bond, 126
up-and-ins, 200
usual conditions, 347
utility function, 5
utility gradients, 233, 351
utility process, 40
utility representations, 18

value, 67, 204
value function, 50, 78
value function, differentiability, 59, 63
value iteration, 67
variance reduction techniques, 299
Vasicek term-structure model, 140, 160, 256
viscosity solutions, 232
volatility, 88
volatility, CIR process, 177
volatility, GARCH limit, 176
volatility, Heston model, 177
volatility process, 175
volatility, stochastic, 177
von Neumann-Morgenstern, 46

weak solution, 340
weakly arbitrage-free, 12
wealth process, 49
weighting matrices, 76
Wiener-Chaos, 100
wildcard option, 197

yield, 142
yield options, 162
yield-spread option, 159

zero-beta return, 15
zero-coupon bond, 136, 166, 238